D0050121

Guatemala

Lucas Vidgen
Daniel C Schechter

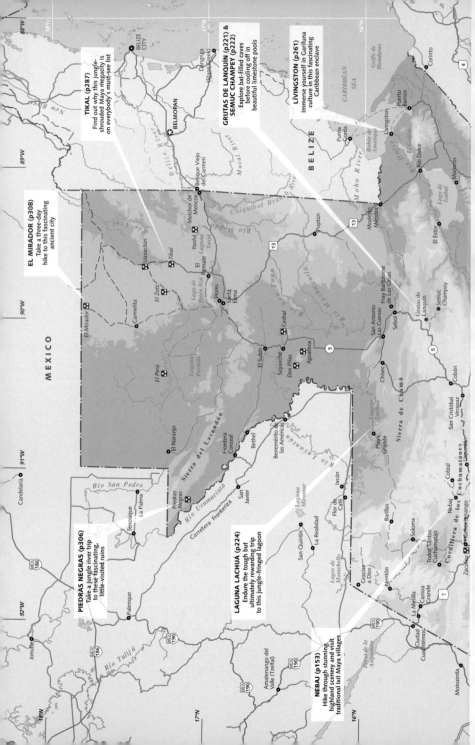

TIKAL (p287)
Find out why this jungle-shrouded Maya megacity is on everybody's must-see list

GRUTAS DE LANQUÍN (p221) & SEMUC CHAMPEY (p222)
Explore bat-filled caves before cooling off in beautiful limestone pools

LIVINGSTON (p261)
Immerse yourself in Garífuna culture in this fascinating Caribbean enclave

EL MIRADOR (p308)
Take a three-day hike to this fascinating ancient city

PIEDRAS NEGRAS (p306)
Take a jungle river trip to these fascinating, little-visited ruins

LAGUNA LACHUÁ (p224)
Endure the tough but ultimately rewarding trip to this jungle-fringed lagoon

NEBAJ (p153)
Hike through stunning highland scenery and visit traditional Ixil Maya villages

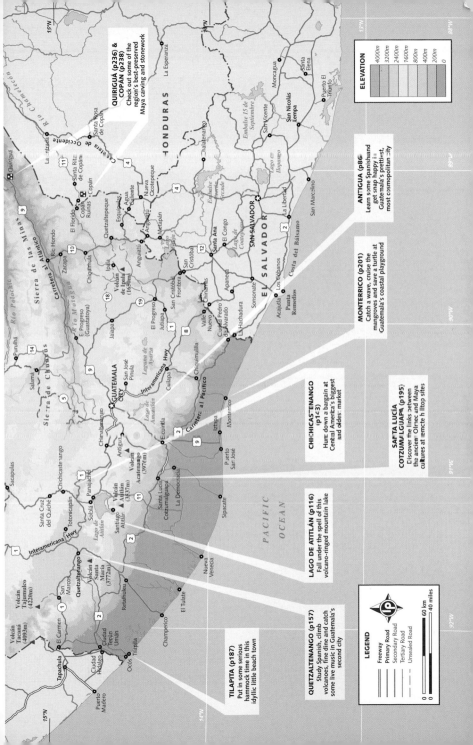

QUIRIGUÁ (p236) & COPÁN (p238)
Check out some of the region's best-preserved Maya carving and stonework

ANTIGUA (p86)
Learn some Spanish and get snap happy in Guatemala's prettiest, most cosmopolitan city

MONTERRICO (p201)
Catch a wave, cruise the mangroves and save a turtle at Guatemala's coastal playground

CHICHICASTENANGO (p143)
Hunt down a bargain at Central America's biggest and oldest market

SANTA LUCÍA COTZUMALGUAPA (p195)
Discover the links between the ancient Olmec and Maya cultures at remote hilltop sites

LAGO DE ATITLÁN (p116)
Fall under the spell of this volcano-ringed mountain lake

QUETZALTENANGO (p157)
Study Spanish, climb volcanoes, fine dine and catch some live music in Guatemala's second city

TILAPITA (p187)
Put in some serious hammock time in this idyllic little beach town

ELEVATION
- 4000m
- 3200m
- 2400m
- 1600m
- 800m
- 400m
- 200m
- 0

LEGEND
- Freeway
- Primary Road
- Secondary Road
- Tertiary Road
- Unsealed Road

0   60 km
0   40 miles

PACIFIC OCEAN

HONDURAS

EL SALVADOR

SAN SALVADOR

GUATEMALA CITY

On the Road

LUCAS VIDGEN Coordinating Author

The area around Río Dulce (p252) and Lívingston (p261) is fast becoming one of my favorites. I live in the mountains, so the lush countryside, mild climate and fresh sea breezes make for a welcome change. I especially love the boat ride down the river – the area teems with birdlife, and the section where the river narrows and flows through a steep-walled, jungle-covered canyon is one of Guatemala's truly unforgettable spots. There are some great places to stay along the river, and a host of colorful characters to meet. I'd definitely come here more often, if it weren't so far from home...

DANIEL C SCHECHTER Here I'm admiring the interior of the church of San Antonio Palopó (p129). Outside, a funeral procession had just taken place and the villagers – the women in royal blue *huipiles* (tunics), the men sporting woolen half-length skirts – were still praying over the deceased. I'm not a religious person but had no difficulty feeling the spirit that prevails in this remote, strongly traditional village on Lago de Atitlán's eastern shore.

For full author biographies see p348.

Guatemala Highlights

Better pack some extra camera batteries, people – and throw in some more memory while you're there. You're about to touch down in a land that was made to be photographed, and that you'll be struggling to do justice to with mere words once you return. As you'll see on the following pages, Guatemala's rugged mountains, technicolor markets, thick jungles and sleepy waterways are just the entrée to the visual feast that awaits. ¡Buen provecho!

RICHARD CUMMINS

1 ANTIGUA

Mammoth volcanic peaks and coffee-covered slopes make an appealing backdrop for a plethora of monastic complexes, the scattered remnants of Spanish occupation, now being repopulated by a unique confluence of foreign-language learners, *ladino* trendsetters and indigenous traders passing their time in Antigua (p86).

RICHARD I'ANSON

MARKET DAY

Get up early to beat the tour buses to one of Central America's most impressive street markets in Chichicastenango (p143). Don't be afraid to bargain hard (in fact, you're expected to), especially on Chichi's signature souvenir piece – wooden masks used in traditional Maya ceremonies.

3

2

TIKAL

Approaching Tikal's Gran Plaza (p291) early in the morning before the tour buses have arrived, witnessing the two stepped pyramids towering above the surrounding jungle canopy, you still get the sensation you've stumbled upon some long-buried secret. The radiant centerpiece of this ancient Maya capital, it's an amazing testament to the cultural and artistic heights scaled by this jungle civilization, occupied for some 16 centuries.

AARON MCCOY

4

VOLCANOES: A NATURAL HIGH

'We love the volcanoes here – we're trying to climb as many as we can. It's become like a game for us. We come from such a flat place, so we were excited about even seeing a volcano, but to be able to climb one, to see them erupt and the lava flowing… I'm just happy I have my camera. If I didn't have photos my friends wouldn't believe some of the things we've seen.'

Daantje, Traveler, the Netherlands

THOR VAZ DE LEON

SWEET RIVER

Connecting the country's largest lake to the Caribbean Sea and with a mild, inviting climate, the area around Río Dulce is one of those places where you come for a day and stay for a week. You can cruise it in a couple of hours (p264), taking in bird sanctuaries and hot springs, or kick back a while and stay in the yachtie enclave of Río Dulce town (p252), at secluded little lodges along the river (p253), or at the seaside Garífuna community of Lívingston (p261).

6
ALFREDO MAIQUEZ

5

FABRIC OF SOCIETY

Traditional Maya textiles (p47) aren't just pretty souvenir items – you'll see them in everyday use throughout the country, making the clothing, streets, markets and buses a wild explosion of vibrant colors.

RICHARD I'ANSON

7

HANDICRAFTS

The small mountain town of Totonicapán (p172) is absolutely unremarkable, but for the dozens of traditional tinsmiths, potters, weavers and woodworkers who live here, and whose workshops you can freely visit to watch them ply their trade.

CAPITAL IDEA

Love it or hate it, it's almost impossible to avoid the country's capital, Guatemala City (p63). With the best selection of museums, restaurants and nightlife in the country, it's a vibrant and fascinating place that many travelers end up enjoying a whole lot more than they thought they would.

8

DIEGO LEZAMA

A DAY AT THE POOL

Guatemala doesn't have that many freshwater swimming holes that you'd really want to dive into, but the jungle-shrouded oasis of Semuc Champey (p222) is definitely an exception. Turquoise-colored water cascades down a series of limestone pools, creating an idyllic setting that many call the most beautiful place in the country.

9

ALFREDO MAIQUEZ

CARVED IN STONE

The Maya were master stonemasons. Some of their best carvings are preserved in museums in Guatemala City (p69) and Santa Lucía Cotzumalguapa (p195), but others you can see where they stood at archaeological sites like Quiriguá (p236) and Copán (p239).

10

ERIC WHEATER

Contents

Regional Map Contents

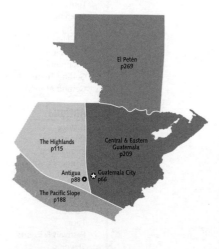

Destination Guatemala

There are things you'll experience in Guatemala that will stay with you forever: the smell of a freshly grilled tortilla; the assault-on-all-senses of the everyday street market; the bliss of swimming in a waterfall after a sweaty jungle trek; the people you bump into on the road who become lifelong friends.

Most stirring of all, perhaps, is experiencing Guatemala's thriving Maya heritage. This amazing culture has left some of the most impressive ruins in the region, many of which are still used for sacred rituals. The awe-inspiring temples of Tikal are easily visited from the charming island town of Flores, while deeper in the jungles of El Petén, getting to remote sites such as El Mirador is as much about the journey as the destination. Lesser-known sites like Quiriguá and Takalik Abaj are easily reached and some say more satisfying – the atmosphere amplified, as you'll most likely be the only visitor there.

The Maya legacy looms large in modern-day Guatemala, a complex panorama of urban bustle and back-country splendor. Shunned by many, the workaday capital is Guatemala at its liveliest, and home to some of the best museums, restaurants and cultural centers in the country. If that gets a little overwhelming, the colonial grandeur of Antigua is just down the road, where around every corner you'll find another picture-postcard scene. If you're looking for something in between, head to the mountains – many travelers find Guatemala's second city, Quetzaltenango, to be the perfect compromise between authentic grit and travelers' amenities.

And then there's the glory of Guatemala's countryside – volcanoes and lakes separated by wild forest, jungle, corn fields and small farms, and the charm of simple village life. A ride from the mountains to the coast takes you through 32 microclimates. In the west, a volcano looms on nearly every horizon, almost begging to be climbed. Up north, the steamy jungles of El Petén surround expansive Maya ruins, and teem with exotic wildlife. The center of the country is covered with lush hillsides, carpeted with cloud forest that the elusive quetzal bird calls home, and pocked by cave systems you can explore in a couple of hours on innertube or on all out two-day expeditions. To the east, the combined waterways of Río Dulce and the Lago de Izabal provide a safe haven, both for yachts in hurricane season and for wildlife in extensive wetlands reserves. And any discussion of the country's landscape would be incomplete without a mention of its crowning glory, the volcano-ringed Lago de Atitlán, which has been mesmerizing travelers for centuries.

Guatemalans are a friendly, welcoming bunch for the most part, and you won't feel like an outsider for long. There are a couple of ways to really get beneath the surface, though. The hundreds of cheap, reputable language schools around the country can not only give you the skills to get around and make some new friends on that next bus ride – they can also provide a much richer understanding of Guatemalan culture, history and customs. And once you've got your Spanish mojo working, you can take it a step further by volunteering in any of the countless worthwhile projects dotted around the country, gaining insight into the day-to-day realities of the place and maybe making a difference as well.

An adventure awaits, and while travel in Guatemala was once characterized by hardship and uncertainty, these days your biggest challenge is likely to be finding time to fit everything in.

FAST FACTS

Population: 15 million

Area: 108,894 sq km

Number of seats in Guatemalan Congress: 158

President: Álvaro Colom (Unidad Nacional de la Esperanza)

GDP (per head): US$5200 (2009)

Inflation: 2.3% (2007)

Unemployment: 3.2% (2005)

Main exports: coffee, sugar, petroleum, clothing, bananas, fruits and vegetables, cardamom

Ratio of cell phones to landlines: 10:1

Number of times Guatemala has qualified for the football World Cup: 0

Getting Started

Traveling in Guatemala requires little detailed planning. Local transportation is plentiful – for many trips all you need do is show up and hop on the next bus. Accommodations are equally easy: unless you have your heart set on one hotel, booking ahead isn't usually necessary. The major exception is Semana Santa (Easter) and around Christmas/New Year, when it seems the whole country takes a holiday – during these times you'll need to book rooms, and often transportation, in advance.

Guatemala is a country for any budget. It's popular with backpackers because you can survive on a few dollars a day, but also has many midrange lodgings and restaurants offering comfort and quality at good prices.

See the Directory (p311) for more details on climate, festivals and events.

WHEN TO GO

There's no bad time to visit Guatemala, although the rain can definitely alter your traveling patterns. Guatemala's weather can generally be broken down into two basic seasons. *Invierno* (winter, or the rainy season) runs from mid-May to mid-October, and into November and December in the north and east, and can make unpaved roads more difficult to traverse. In the lowland jungles of El Petén, the mud at this time will slow you down, guaranteed. Humidity – never low on the coasts or in El Petén – increases during the rainy season too. It doesn't rain all day at this time, but you can expect daily showers (downpours in the north) at the very least, usually in the afternoon. *Verano* (summer, or the dry season) runs from about November to April, and this sees more comfortable temperatures in El Petén and along the coasts, along with some chilly nights in the highlands (where temperatures regularly drop below zero around Christmastime). In the eastern parts of the country, rain is possible at any time.

The height of the foreign tourist season is from Christmas to Easter, and coincides with when Guatemalans tend to take their holidays. Another busy time is June to August, when throngs of North American college students descend on Guatemala to study Spanish and travel.

See p318 for a list of the major festivals and events around the country.

COSTS & MONEY

Prices in Guatemala are among the best in Central America. Beds in *hospedajes* (guesthouses) normally cost Q60 to Q80 per person. Markets sell fruit and snacks for pennies, cheap eateries called *comedores* offer one- or two-course meals for Q20 to Q30, and bus trips cost around Q10 per hour. It's completely realistic to spend Q200 a day in Guatemala without too much hardship. If you want more comfort – nice rooms with private hot-water bathrooms and well-prepared food in pleasant surroundings, you'll still only pay around Q300 per person for a room and two – or even three – meals. Add in transportation, admission fees, some shopping and a few beers and you're looking at a total of around Q450 a day.

PRICES IN THIS GUIDE

We give admission prices for sights (museums, parks etc) listed in this guide where they exist – if there is no entry price given, you can assume entry is free. Hotel prices are listed with private bathroom – if the bathroom is shared, it will be specifically noted, except in the case of dorm rooms, where this is, of course, the norm.

DON'T LEAVE HOME WITHOUT...

- Checking the visa situation (p322).
- Checking travel advisories (p316).
- Warm clothes for chilly highland nights – at least a sweater and a pair of warm pants.
- Photocopies of important documents (passport, plane tickets etc). For extra security, scan these and email them to yourself.
- Broken-in walking shoes or hiking boots.
- Ziplock bags – great for waterproofing your gadgets.
- Earplugs if you're a light sleeper and planning on sleeping in dorms.
- A flashlight (torch) for exploring caves, ruins and your room when the electricity fails (as has been known to happen).
- A mosquito net, if you're planning on hitting the jungle or sleeping in cheap rooms without screens.
- A basic understanding of Spanish, or a plan to learn some.
- Insect repellent containing DEET, for wet-season travels. You may also want to take medication against malaria, too.
- A small towel, for rooms without one.
- Telling your mother not to worry.

There are few bargains for solo travelers, as there often isn't much price difference between a single and double room. If it's practical, hook up with some other folks to defray room costs. Many places have rooms for three or four people, where the per-person price drops dramatically. In restaurants you can save money by opting for set two- or three-course meals (the *menú del día*). On the road, public buses are far cheaper than the more comfortable tourist shuttle buses.

While day to-day items are affordable, imported products (particularly electronics) are expensive in Guatemala – if there's something even slightly exotic that you can't live without you're better off buying it at home.

TRAVELING RESPONSIBLY

Responsible travel in Guatemala often comes down to using your common sense. By spending money in small, local businesses, staying for extended periods, volunteering and interacting with 'everyday' people, you have the chance to have a positive effect here.

Littering, disrespecting local customs and supporting unsustainable or harmful industries (drugs, souvenirs and menu items made from endangered species) are the main culprits here) are obvious no-nos.

In lowland areas try to use air-con sparingly – it's expensive and places a huge strain on local energy reserves. Instead, move more slowly than usual, keep out of the midday heat or (as a last resort) hang out in the lobby of a fancy hotel for some respite.

Small actions have big consequences here. Please be aware that industry professionals and community leaders are watching your habits and preferences closely. If you can, make the effort to visit a national park or reserve (see p58), try some community-based tourism (where proceeds go direct to the community, not to middlemen or tour operators – see our GreenDex, p358, for some ideas), or do some volunteer work (see p323). Be aware that tourist operators are well aware that Guatemala attracts altruistic types who

HOW MUCH?

Three-hour, 2nd-class bus ride Q30

A week of Spanish classes with homestay Q980-1600

Admission to Tikal Q150

Taxi from Guatemala City airport to city center Q80

Comfortable lakeside double with bathroom in Lago de Atitlán Q200-400

TOP 10

GUATEMALA

Honduras

Guatemala City •

BEST MAYA READS

The Maya, past and present, are the theme of whole libraries of writing. Here are our 10 favorite books on them:

1 *The Maya*, Michael D Coe

2 *The Blood of Kings: Dynasty & Ritual in Maya Art*, Linda Schele and Mary Ellen Miller

3 *Scandals in the House of Birds: Shamans and Priests on Lake Atitlán*, Nathaniel Tarn

4 *I, Rigoberta Menchú: An Indian Woman in Guatemala*, Rigoberta Menchú

5 *Maya of Guatemala – Life and Dress*, Carmen L Pettersen

6 *Chronicle of the Maya Kings and Queens*, Simon Martin and Nikolai Grube

7 *Unfinished Conquest: The Guatemalan Tragedy*, Víctor Perera

8 *The Maya Textile Tradition*, Margot Blum Schevill (ed)

9 *Breaking the Maya Code*, Michael D Coe

10 *The Ancient Maya*, Robert J Sharer

CELESTIAL EVENTS

The stars, moon and sun were important to the Maya, so while you're here, you might find yourself looking to the heavens for inspiration. Here are some good places to start:

1 Sunrise from Tajumulco volcano (p161)

2 Sunset with a daiquiri in hand from a hammock in Monterrico (p201)

3 Full moon parties in San Pedro La Laguna (p133)

4 Stargazing from El Mirador, deep in the Petén jungle (p305)

5 Watching the sun set over Lago de Petén Itzá in Flores (p272)

6 Hiking the Santa María volcano (p161) by the light of the full moon

7 Aligning your chakras by starlight in a pyramid in San Marcos La Laguna (p139)

8 Bathing by the light of the moon in Quetzaltenango (p157)

9 Catching the sunrise from Temple IV in Tikal (p287)

10 Listening to jazz in the Sunset Café (p126) in Panajachel as the sun disappears behind the volcanoes

FESTIVALS

If there's one thing that Guatemalans know how to do, it's throw a party. Here are 10 of the best:

1 Cristo de Esquipulas (Jan 15) Pilgrims flock to the small town of Esquipulas (p232)

2 Quetzaltenango Music Festival (late Mar; see p163) Live music fans shouldn't miss this one

3 Desfile de Bufos (The Parade of Fools; Friday before Good Friday) Guatemala City university students take to the streets

4 Semana Santa (Easter; dates vary) Easter is celebrated all over the country; check out Antigua (p100) and Guatemala City

5 Cubulco (Jul 25) Keeping the Palo Volador (flying pole, see p211) tradition alive

6 San José Petén (Oct 31) This town (p283) hosts a unique festival, which sees human skulls paraded around town

7 Día de Todos los Santos (Nov 1) Celebrated with panache in Santiago Sacatepéquez and Sumpango (p112)

8 Todos Santos Cuchumatán (Nov 1) This tiny highlands town (p180) has drunken horse races through the main street

9 Garífuna Day (Nov 26) Lívingston (p261) hosts the biggest Garífuna party

10 Quema del Diablo (Dec 7) People haul trash out into the street and make huge bonfires

are interested in supporting socially minded businesses. It's up to you, but if a business claims to support the community, it's always worth investigating a little before taking them at face value.

TRAVEL LITERATURE

Ronald Wright's *Time among the Maya* is a story of travels through the whole Maya region – Guatemala, Mexico, Belize and Honduras – delving into the glorious past and unlimited present of the Maya and their obsession with time. Wright visits many of the places you'll visit, and his book is a fascinating read, despite being written during the troubled 1980s as the civil war raged in the background.

Peter Canby's *The Heart of the Sky* also takes you on a journey through the '*mundo* Maya,' introducing you to a much wider cross-section of Guatemalan society.

Guatemalan Journey, by Stephen Connely Benz, casts an honest and funny modern traveler's eye on the country, as does Anthony Daniels' *Sweet Waist of America,* also published as *South of the Border: Guatemalan Days,* where the medic author pinpoints some of the country's contradictions.

Probably the most quoted travelogue on Guatemala is Aldous Huxley's *Beyond the Mexique Bay.* Written in the 1930s, many of Huxley's descriptions hold true today, particularly of Maya sites and natural wonders, such as Lago de Atitlán.

In *Sacred Monkey River,* Christopher Shaw explores by canoe the jungle-clad basin of the Río Usumacinta, a cradle of ancient Maya civilization along the Mexico–Guatemala border.

The 19th-century classic *Incidents of Travel in Central America, Chiapas and Yucatan,* by John L Stephens (illustrated by Frederick Catherwood), was the first serious look at many Maya archaeological sites. It's a laborious but interesting read.

The Full Montezuma, by Peter Moore, doesn't even approach literature, but it is a vaguely readable account of a young Australian backpacker's travels through the region.

INTERNET RESOURCES

Guatemala (www.visitguatemala.com) Moderately interesting official site of Inguat, the national tourism institute.

Guatemala Times (www.guatemala-times.com) The best English-language news source focusing on Guatemala.

Lanic Guatemala (http://lanic.utexas.edu/la/ca/guatemala) The University of Texas' magnificent collection of Guatemala links.

Lonely Planet (www.lonelyplanet.com) Succinct summaries on Guatemala travel, along with the popular Thorn Tree forum and links to the most useful travel resources elsewhere on the web.

Mostly Maya (www.mostlymaya.com) Extensive, practical information on visiting remote Maya sites, plus plenty more.

Xela Pages (www.xelapages.com) Good information on the highlands and coast and an excellent forum where you can get answers to even the most obscure questions.

Itineraries
CLASSIC ROUTES

HIGHLAND FLING   10 Days / Guatemala City to Todos Santos Cuchumatán

Guatemala's most spectacular scenery and strongest Maya traditions await you along this well-traveled route.

From **Guatemala City** (p63) head to gorgeous **Antigua** (p86) to enjoy the country's finest colonial architecture, great restaurants and the lively traveler and language-student scene. Several volcanoes wait to be climbed here. From Antigua move on to **Panajachel** (p118), on volcano-ringed **Lago de Atitlán** (p116). Hop in a boat to check out some traditional Maya villages such as **Santiago Atitlán** (p130), **San Pedro La Laguna** (p133), **San Marcos La Laguna** (p139) or **Santa Cruz La Laguna** (p141). Head north to **Chichicastenango** (p143) for its huge Thursday and Sunday market. If you have extra time, detour to **Nebaj** (p153), where you'll find great walking amid a strong Maya way of life amid stunning scenery.

From Chichicastenango follow the Interamericana Hwy west along the mountain ridges to **Quetzaltenango** (p157), Guatemala's clean, orderly, second city, with a host of intriguing villages, markets and natural wonders only short bus rides away. From Quetzaltenango you can head south, or on to Mexico – perhaps via **Todos Santos Cuchumatán** (p180), a fascinating Maya mountain town with great walking possibilities.

This 320km jaunt could take a few months if you stop off to learn some Spanish in Antigua, Panajachel, San Pedro La Laguna or Quetzaltenango, and you could more than double the distance with detours to Nebaj and Todos Santos Cuchumatán.

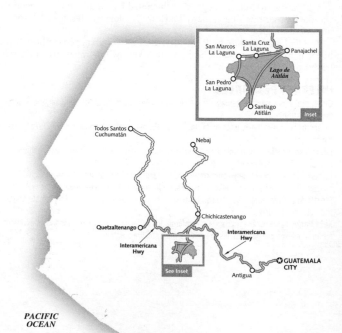

THE BIG LOOP   Three Weeks / Copán to Cobán

This trip takes you to the best of Guatemala's Maya ruins, into its dense jungles and to some of its spectacular natural marvels.

Start out heading northeast from Guatemala City and detour south into Honduras to see the great Maya site of **Copán** (p239). Return to Guatemala and continue northeastward to another fine Maya site, **Quiriguá** (p236) and on to the curious Garífuna enclave of **Lívingston** (p261) on the sweaty Caribbean coast. Take a boat up the jungle-lined Río Dulce to **Río Dulce town** (p252), then turn north up Hwy 13 to stay and chill out at **Finca Ixobel** (p271), just outside **Poptún** (p270) before continuing to **Flores** (p272), a quaint small town on an island in the Lago de Petén Itzá. From Flores, head for **Tikal** (p287), the most majestic of all Maya sites. Spend a night at Tikal itself or nearby **El Remate** (p284). While in the Flores-Tikal area, you should have time to take in further impressive Maya sites such as **Yaxhá** (p298) and **Uaxactún** (p295).

From Flores head southwest to the relaxed riverside town of **Sayaxché** (p301), which is at the center of another group of intriguing Maya sites – **Ceibal** (p302), **Aguateca** (p304) and **Dos Pilas** (p305). The road south from Sayaxché is now paved all the way to **Chisec** (p223) and **Cobán** (p213), jumping-off points for a whole series of pristine natural wonders such as jungle-ringed **Laguna Lachuá** (p224), the **Grutas de Lanquín** (p221) and the turquoise lagoons and waterfalls of **Semuc Champey** (p222).

This 1900km round trip takes you to all the top destinations in the center, east and north of the country. Really pushing, you might do it in two weeks, but if you have four, you'll enjoy it more.

HAMMOCK FRENZY
One week / Tilapita to Las Lisas

The beaches in Guatemala take some getting used to. Black volcanic sand makes them look dirty (and some are), but there are plenty of small, laid-back towns that are great for splashing around, surfing, cruising the mangroves and just generally chilling out. There's no coast road as such, so you'll find yourself popping in and out from the main highway all the way down the coast.

Starting way up near the Mexican border, make your way to **Tilapita** (p187), not to be confused with Tilapa – the former is far prettier, with exactly one hotel at the time of writing.

From there it's back out onto the highway, east to Mazatenango and on another bus for **Tulate** (p194), the best beach along here for swimming and bodysurfing. From Tulate, there's no need to go back to the main highway – just catch a bus back to La Máquina, then another on to **Chiquistepeque** (p195), a lovely, untouched stretch of beach where some visitors like to volunteer with the French-Guatemalan NGO, Proyecto Hamaca y Pescado, who work with the local community.

Moving on, it's back out to the highway, heading east with a bus change in Siquinala for the surfers' haven of **Sipacate** (p198).

The road could end at your next stop, **Monterrico** (p201), favorite of Guatemalan weekenders and Antigua language students alike. If you haven't had enough yet, make your way to **Las Lisas** (p204), where a gorgeous, exclusive island getaway near the Salvadoran border awaits.

It's only 220km as the turtle swims from the Mexican to the Salvadoran border – you could do it in a week, but what's the rush?

ROADS LESS TRAVELED

ACROSS THE IXCÁN   Two Days / Huehuetenango to Laguna Lachuá

Now that the road from Huehuetenango to Cobán is questionable due to landslides, adventure junkies and chicken-bus lovers have been turning northwards to make the trip across country without backtracking to the capital.

The route from Huehue to Laguna Lachuá pushes all the right buttons for these folks – bad roads, stunning scenery, fascinating villages and very, very few tourists.

Buses run, but less frequently than elsewhere. If you're thinking about going this route, you should have some spare time and be prepared to rumble around in the back of a pickup truck now and then.

Starting from **Huehuetenango** (p175) it's an easy, scenic ride up into the Cuchumatanes on a good road to **Soloma** (p183). Say goodbye to the asphalt here. From Soloma the road undulates over hills before reaching **Santa Eulalia** (p183), a pretty and interesting town where you may want to pause for a couple of hours.

Then it's up again, through pastures and pine forests to the town of **San Mateo Ixtatán** (p183), a good place to break for the night because transport drops off in the late afternoon and there are a few interesting sights around town.

Next day, it's a slow cruise downhill to **Barillas** (p184), from where you should be able to grab a bus or at least a pickup for the terrible-roads-but-great-scenery ride across to **Playa Grande** (p224) and **Laguna Lachuá** (p224).

There are serious plans to put in a highway along this 150km stretch between Huehue and Playa Grande – get in while the adventure's still alive!

TAILORED TRIPS

THE MAYA THEN & NOW

While in **Guatemala City** (p63), don't miss the museums dedicated to Maya archaeology and textiles. This is also a good jumping-off point for visits to Maya ruins at **Quiriguá** (p236) and, just over the Honduras border, **Copán** (p239).

West of Guatemala City are the ruins at **Iximché** (p117), and **Lago de Atitlán** (p116), surrounded by traditional villages such as **Santiago Atitlán** (p130). Don't miss the big Maya market at **Chichicastenango** (p143), also the scene of unique religious practices. To the north is the old K'iche' Maya capital **K'umarcaaj** (p149), still an important center for Maya rites. **Quetzaltenango** (p157) is a base for visiting many traditional villages and the sacred **Laguna Chicabal** (p175). Further north is the old Mam Maya capital, **Zaculeu** (p176), en route to **Todos Santos Cuchumatán** (p180), a mountain village with strong traditions and uniquely striking costumes.

Along the mountain roads of the Cuchutamanes ranges you'll find **Nebaj** (p153), a center of the colorful Ixil Maya, and **San Cristóbal Verapaz** (p220). **Sayaxché** (p301), in the north of Guatemala, is a good base for exploring several nearby Maya sites. From here you can visit the mother of all Maya cities, **Tikal** (p287), and in the Petén jungles there are plenty of opportunities for exploring more remote archaeological sites.

NATURAL WONDERS

Tone up your muscles by climbing a couple of the volcanoes that surround **Antigua** (p96). Nearby, **Lago de Atitlán** (p116) is certainly one of the most beautiful lakes in the world. There are more volcanoes around Quetzaltenango – check out **Santa María** (p161) and **Tajumulco** (p161), the highest peak in Central America. To the north you can experience the beauty of the Cuchumatanes mountains around **Todos Santos Cuchumatán** (p180) and **Nebaj** (p153). Nearby **Cobán** (p213) is a great stepping stone for visiting the lovely lagoons and waterfalls of **Semuc Champey** (p222), along with cave exploration and wildlife-watching galore. If you've got some time, don't miss the jungle-surrounded **Laguna Lachuá** (p224). To the north, in the thick jungles of El Petén, is the magnificent ancient Maya city of **Tikal** (p287), along with the ruins around **El Perú** (p306) – both are also fine spots for observing tropical wildlife. In the western part of the country, pause for cave exploration at **Finca Ixobel** (p271), take a boat ride along the beautiful, jungle-shrouded **Río Dulce** (p264) or enjoy a side trip to the **Refugio Bocas del Polochic** (p256), which supports more than 300 bird species.

History

ARCHAIC PERIOD (UP TO 2000 BC)

It's accepted that, barring a few Vikings in the north and conceivable direct transpacific contact with Southeast Asia, the pre-Hispanic inhabitants of the Americas arrived from Siberia. They came in several migrations between perhaps 60,000 and 8000 BC, during the last ice age, crossing land that is now submerged beneath the Bering Strait, then gradually moving southward.

These early inhabitants hunted mammoths, fished and gathered wild foods. The ice age was followed by a hot, dry period in which the mammoths' natural pastureland disappeared and the wild nuts and berries became scarce. The primitive inhabitants had to find some other way to survive, so they sought out favorable microclimates and invented agriculture, in which maize (corn) became king. The inhabitants of what are now Guatemala and Mexico successfully hybridized this native grass and planted it alongside beans, tomatoes, chili peppers and squash (marrow). They wove baskets to carry in the harvest, and they domesticated turkeys and dogs for food. These early homebodies used crude stone tools and primitive pottery, and shaped simple clay fertility figurines.

PRECLASSIC PERIOD (2000 BC–AD 250)

The improvement in the food supply led to an increase in population, a higher standard of living and developments in agricultural and artistic techniques. Decorative pots and healthier, fatter corn strains were produced. Even at the beginning of the Preclassic period, people in Guatemala spoke an early form of the Maya language. The early Maya also invented the *na* (thatched hut), still used today throughout much of the country. Where spring floods were a problem, a family would build its *na* on a mound of earth. When a family member died, burial took place right there in the living room, after which the deceased attained the rank of honored ancestor.

By the middle Preclassic period (800–300 BC) there were rich villages in the Copán Valley, and villages had been founded at what would become the majestic city of Tikal, amid the jungles of El Petén. Trade routes developed, with coastal peoples exchanging salt and seashells for highland tribes' tool-grade obsidian.

As the Maya honed their agricultural techniques, including the use of fertilizer and elevated fields, a noble class emerged, constructing temples which consisted of raised platforms of earth topped by thatch-roofed shelters. The local potentate was buried beneath the shelter, increasing the site's sacred power. Such temples have been found at Uaxactún, Tikal and El Mirador, another Petén site that flourished during the late Preclassic period (300 BC–AD 250). Kaminaljuyú, in Guatemala City, reached its peak from about

The Ancient Maya, by Robert J Sharer, is a 1990s update of Sylvanus G Morley's classic 1940s tome of the same name, and is admirably clear and uncomplicated.

Maya priests used a variety of drugs during divination rituals – ranging from fermented maize and wild tobacco to hallucinogenic mushrooms.

The Maya, by Michael D Coe, is probably the best single-volume, not-too-long telling of the ancient Maya story. Coe's *Breaking the Maya Code* recounts the modern decipherment of ancient Maya writing, and his *Reading the Maya Glyphs* will help you read ancient inscriptions.

TIMELINE

C 11,000 BC	Aug 13, 3114 BC	2000–250 BC
Large scale migration across the Bering Strait from Siberia to Alaska leads to the first human occupation of Guatemala. Tools and other objects found in the highlands date from 9000 BC.	The Maya creation story says that the world was created on this date, which corresponds to the first date on the Maya Long Count Calendar.	Known as the Preclassic period, this time saw a boom in salt, jade and cacao trade between Guatemalan Maya villages and also the formation of Nakbé and El Mirador, the first great cities.

IN THE BEGINNING...

The date of creation that appears in inscriptions throughout the Maya world is 13.0.0.0.0, 4 Ahaw, 8 Kumk'u, or August 13, 3114 BC on our calendar.

On that day the creator gods set three stones in the dark waters that covered the primordial world. These formed a cosmic hearth at the center of the universe. They then struck divine fire by means of lightning, charging the world with life.

This account of creation is echoed in the first chapters of the *Popol Vuh*, a book compiled by members of the Maya nobility soon after the Spanish Conquest.

This is the account of when all is still silent and placid. All is silent and calm. Hushed and empty is the womb of the sky. These then are the first words, the first speech. There is not yet one person, one animal, bird, fish, crab, tree, rock, hollow, canyon, meadow, or forest...

All alone are the Framer and the Shaper, Sovereign and Quetzal Serpent, They Who Have Borne Children and They Who Have Begotten Sons... There is also Heart of Sky [a lightning god], which is said to be the name of the god...

Then they called forth the mountains from the water. Straightaway the great mountains came to be. It was merely their spirit essence, their miraculous power, that brought about the conception of the mountains.

The Creation of Humankind

The gods made three attempts at creating people before getting it right. First they made deer and other animals, but not being able to speak properly to honor the gods, the animals were condemned to be eaten.

Next was a person made from mud. At first, the mud person spoke, 'but without knowledge and understanding,' and he soon dissolved back into the mud.

The gods' third attempt was people carved from wood. These too were imperfect and also destroyed. The *Popol Vuh* says that the survivors of these wooden people are the monkeys that inhabit the forests.

The gods finally got it right when they discovered maize, and made mankind:

Thus their frame and shape were given expression by our first Mother and our first Father. Their flesh was merely yellow ears of maize and white ears of maize...

400 BC to AD 100, with thousands of inhabitants and scores of temples built on earth mounds.

In El Petén, where limestone was abundant, the Maya began to build platform temples from stone. As each succeeding local potentate demanded a bigger temple, larger and larger platforms were built over existing platforms, eventually forming huge pyramids with a *na*-style shelter on top. The potentate was buried deep within the stack of platforms. El Tigre pyramid at El Mirador, 18 stories high, is believed to be the largest ever built by the Maya. More and more pyramids were built around large plazas, in the same way that everyday people clustered their thatched houses in compounds facing a communal open space. The stage was set for the flowering of Classic Maya civilization.

1100 BC	C 250 BC–AD 100	AD 230
Proto-Maya settlements begin to appear in the Copán Valley. By 1000 BC settlements on the Guatemalan Pacific coast show early signs of developing a hierarchical society.	Early Maya cities El Mirador and Kaminaljuyú flourish due to tactical and commercial advantages. Agricultural techniques are refined as the trade in obsidian and jade booms.	El Mirador begins to decline in importance. King Yax Moch Xoc of Tikal establishes the dynasty that will make Tikal the dominant city of the southern Maya world.

CLASSIC PERIOD (AD 250–900)

During the Classic period the Maya produced pre-Hispanic America's most brilliant civilization in an area stretching from Copán, in modern Honduras, through Guatemala and Belize to Mexico's Yucatán Peninsula. The great ceremonial and cultural centers included Copán; Quiriguá; Kaminaljuyú; Tikal, Uaxactún, Río Azul, El Perú, Yaxhá, Dos Pilas and Piedras Negras, all in El Petén; Caracol in Belize; Yaxchilán and Palenque in Chiapas, Mexico; and Calakmul, Uxmal and Chichén Itzá on the Yucatán Peninsula. All these sites can be visited today. Around the beginning of the Classic period, Maya astronomers began using the elaborate Long Count calendar (see p26).

While Tikal began to assume a primary role around AD 250, El Mirador had been mysteriously abandoned about a century earlier. Some scholars believe a severe drought hastened this great city's demise.

The Classic Maya were organized into numerous city-states. Each city-state had its noble house, headed by a priestly king who placated the gods by shedding his blood by piercing his tongue, penis or ears with sharp objects. (For more on these rites and other Maya beliefs, see p41.) As sacred head of his community, the king also had to lead his soldiers into battle against rival cities, capturing prisoners for use in human sacrifices.

A typical Maya city functioned as the religious, political and market hub for the surrounding farming hamlets. Its ceremonial center focused on plazas surrounded by tall temple pyramids and lower buildings with warrens of small rooms. Stelae and altars were carved with dates, histories and elaborate human and divine figures.

In the first part of the Classic period, most of the city-states were probably grouped into two loose military alliances centered on Calakmul, in Mexico's Campeche state, and Tikal. Like Kaminaljuyú and Copán, Tikal had strong connections with the powerful city of Teotihuacán, near modern Mexico City. When Teotihuacán declined, Tikal's rival Calakmul allied with Caracol to defeat a weakened Tikal in 562. However, Tikal returned to prominence under a militarily successful king named Moon Double Comb, also known as Ah Cacau (Lord Chocolate), who ruled from 682 to 734. Tikal conquered Calakmul in 695.

Archaeologists estimate that only 10% of Tikal – one of the country's biggest and most famous Maya sites – has been uncovered.

The Blood of Kings: Dynasty & Ritual in Maya Art, by Linda Schele and Mary Ellen Miller, is a heavily and fascinatingly illustrated guide to the art and culture of the ancient Maya.

PLAYTIME WITH THE MAYA

The recreation most favored by the Maya was *juego de pelota* (a ball game), courts for which can still be seen at many archaeological sites. It's thought that the players had to try to keep a hard rubber ball airborne using any part of their body other than their hands, head or feet. A wooden bat may also have been used. In some regions, a team was victorious if one of its players hit the ball through stone rings with holes little larger than the ball itself.

The ball game was taken very seriously and was often used to settle disputes between rival communities. On occasion, it is thought, the captain of the losing team was punished by execution.

250–900	562	682
The Classic period encompasses a time when the Maya first began to employ elaborate carvings on stelae, temples and elsewhere, and construction throughout the Maya world reaches its peak.	Tikal's major ally, Teotihuacán, declines in power. Calakmul forms regional alliances with surrounding settlements and Caracol in present-day Belize, eventually defeating – but not destroying – Tikal.	King Moon Double Comb, or Lord Chocolate, ascends Tikal's throne and begins remodeling and reconstructing Tikal's grand plazas and temples that had been destroyed by Caracol and Calakmul.

In the late 8th century, trade between Maya states waned and conflict grew. By the early 10th century the cities of Tikal, Yaxchilán, Copán, Quiriguá and Piedras Negras had reverted to minor towns or even villages, and much of El Petén was abandoned. Many explanations, including population pressure, drought and ecological damage, have been offered for the collapse of the Classic Maya period.

POSTCLASSIC PERIOD (900–1524)

Some of the Maya who abandoned El Petén must have moved southwest into the highlands of Guatemala. In the 13th and 14th centuries they were joined by Maya-Toltecs (a militaristic culture from central Mexico with powerful, wide-ranging influence) from the Tabasco or Yucatán areas of Mexico. Groups of these newcomers set up a series of rival states in the Guatemalan highlands: the most prominent were the K'iche' (or Quiché; capital, K'umarcaaj, near modern Santa Cruz del Quiché) the Kaqchiquels (capital, Iximché, near Tecpán); the Mam (capital, Zaculeu, near Huehuetenango); the Tz'utujil (capital, Chuitinamit, near Santiago Atitlán); and the Poqomam (capital, Mixco Viejo, north of Guatemala City). Another group from the Yucatán, the Itzáes, wound up at Lago Petén Itzá in El Petén, settling in part on the island that is today called Flores.

To translate a date using the Maya calendar, visit the Maya Date Calculator at www.mayan-calendar.com/calc.html.

SPANISH CONQUEST

Spaniards under Hernán Cortés defeated the Aztec Empire based at Tenochtitlán (modern Mexico City) in 1521. It only took a couple of years for the conquistadors to turn to Guatemala in their search for wealth. Pedro de Alvarado, one of Cortés' most brutal lieutenants, entered Guatemala in 1524 with about 600 Spanish and Mexican soldiers and the unanswerable advantages of firearms and horses. Alvarado defeated a small K'iche' force on the Pacific Slope and then the much larger main K'iche' army near Xelajú

MAYA COUNTING SYSTEM

The Maya counting system's most important use – and the one you will encounter during your travels – was in writing dates. It's an elegantly simple system: dots are used to count from one to four; a horizontal bar signifies five; a bar with one dot above it is six, a bar with two dots is seven, and so forth. Two bars signifies 10, three bars 15. Nineteen, the highest common number, is three bars stacked up and topped by four dots.

To signify larger numbers the Maya stack numbers from zero to 19 on top of each other. Thus the lowest number in the stack shows values from one to 19, the next position up signifies 20 times its face value, the third position up signifies 20 times 20 times its face value. The three positions together can signify numbers up to 7999. By adding more positions one can count as high as needed. Zero is represented by a stylized picture of a shell or some other object.

The Maya likely used the counting system from day to day by writing on the ground, the tip of the finger creating a dot, and using the edge of the hand to make a bar.

695	900	C 13th century
The Caracol-Calakmul alliance is weakened as Tikal captures two successive kings of Calakmul in two years. Tikal soon regains its position as regional superpower.	The collapse of Classic Maya civilization begins, and the Postclassic era starts. A century-long exodus from Tikal commences, after which the city will never be inhabited again.	Ruthlessly organized Toltec-Maya migrants from southeast Mexico establish kingdoms in Guatemala. Highlands Maya organize into competing kingdoms, establishing language and cultural groupings that survive today.

(modern Quetzaltenango) soon afterwards – killing the K'iche' leader Tecún Umán in hand-to-hand combat, or so legend has it. Alvarado then sacked the K'iche' capital, K'umarcaaj. The K'iche' had failed to persuade their traditional local enemies, the Kaqchiquels, to join forces against the invaders. Instead, the Kaqchiquels allied with the Spanish against the K'iche' and Tz'utujils, and so the Spanish set up their first Guatemalan headquarters next door to the Kaqchiquel capital, Iximché.

The romance between the Spanish and the Kaqchiquels soon soured and Alvarado burnt Iximché to the ground. And so it went throughout Guatemala as Alvarado sought fortune and renown by murdering and subjugating the Maya population. The one notable exception was the Rabinal of present-day Baja Verapaz, who survived with their preconquest identity intact and remain one of Guatemala's most traditional groups to this day.

Alvarado moved his base from Tecpán to Santiago de los Caballeros (now called Ciudad Vieja) in 1527, but shortly after his death in 1541, Ciudad Vieja was destroyed by a flood. The Spanish capital was relocated under the same name to a new site nearby, known today as Antigua.

COLONIAL PERIOD (1524–1821)

The Spanish effectively enslaved Guatemala's indigenous people to work what had been their own land for the benefit of the invaders, just as they did throughout the hemisphere. Refusal to work meant death. The colonists believed themselves omnipotent and behaved accordingly. That is to say, badly.

Enter the Catholic Church and Dominican friar Bartolomé de Las Casas. Las Casas had been in the Caribbean and Latin America since 1502 and had witnessed firsthand the near complete genocide of the indigenous populations of Cuba and Hispaniola. He described the fatal treatment of the population in his influential tract *A Very Brief Account of the Destruction of the Indies*. Horrified by what he had seen, Las Casas appealed to Carlos V of Spain to stop the violence. The king agreed that the indigenous people should no longer be regarded as chattels and should be considered vassals of the king (in this way they could also pay taxes). Carlos V immediately enacted the New Laws of 1542, which technically ended the system of forced labor. In reality, forced labor continued, but wanton waste of Maya lives ceased. Las Casas and other friars went about converting the Maya to Christianity – a Christianity that became imbued with many aspects of animism and ceremony from the indigenous belief system.

A large portion of the church's conversion 'success' can be attributed to its peaceful approach, the relative respect extended to traditional beliefs, and the education provided in indigenous languages. The Catholic Church became extremely powerful in Guatemala quite quickly – no clearer evidence existed of this than the 38 houses of worship (including a cathedral) built in Antigua, which became the colonial capital of all Central America from

Mundo Maya online (www.mayadiscovery.com) features a very accessible collection of Maya-related articles, plus a good little selection of Maya legends and other information on the region.

For detailed discussions in everyday language on everything Maya-related from past to present, have a look at www.mayainfo.org.

Mesoweb (www.mesoweb.com) is a great resource on the Maya, past and present.

1523	1527	1541
Spaniard Pedro de Alvarado begins the conquest of Guatemala. Alvarado quickly conquers much of the country, although parts of the highlands hold out for years and El Petén is not subdued for another 170 years.	Alvarado establishes his capital at Santiago de los Caballeros (modern Ciudad Vieja, near Antigua). When he dies in Mexico, 14 years later, his wife decrees the entire city be painted black.	An earthquake ruptures the walls of Volcán Agua and Santiago de los Caballeros is buried under a flood of water and mud. A new capital (now Antigua) is founded.

THE MAYA CALENDAR

The ancient Maya's astronomical observations and calculations were uncannily accurate. They could pinpoint eclipses and their Venus cycle erred by only two hours for periods covering 500 years.

Time was, in fact, the basis of the Maya religion. They believed the current world to be just one of a succession of worlds, each destined to end in cataclysm and be succeeded by another. This cyclicity enabled the future to be predicted by looking at the past. Most Maya cities were constructed in strict accordance with celestial movements, and observatories were not uncommon.

Perhaps the best analog to the Maya calendar is the gears of a mechanical watch, where small wheels mesh with larger wheels, which in turn mesh with other sets of wheels to record the passage of time.

Tzolkin or Cholq'ij or Tonalamatl

The two smallest wheels were two cycles of 13 days and 20 days. Each of the 13 days bore a number from one to 13; each of the 20 days bore a name such as Imix, Ik, Akbal or Xan. As these two 'wheels' meshed, the passing days received unique names. For example, when day one of the 13-day cycle fell on the day named Imix in the 20-day cycle, the day was called 1 Imix. Next came 2 Ik, then 3 Akbal etc. After 13 days, the first cycle began again at one, even though the 20-day name cycle still had seven days to run, so the 14th day was 1 Ix, followed by 2 Men, 3 Cib etc. When the 20-day name cycle was finished, it began again with 8 Imix, 9 Ik, 10 Akbal etc. The permutations continued for a total of 260 days, ending on 13 Ahau, before beginning again on 1 Imix.

The two small 'wheels' of 13 and 20 days thus created a larger 'wheel' of 260 days, called a *tzolkin*, *cholq'ij* or *tonalamatl*.

Visitors interested in Maya culture might want to head to one of the towns still observing the *tzolkin* calendar (such as Momostenango or Todos Santos Cuchumatán) for Wajshakib Batz, the start of the *tzolkin* year. It falls on December 19, 2007; September 4, 2008; May 22, 2009; February 6, 2010; October 24, 2010; and July 11, 2011. Outsiders are not necessarily invited to join in the ceremonies, as they tend to be sacred affairs, but it's still a good time to be in one of these traditional towns.

Vague Year (Haab)

Another set of wheels in the Maya calendar watch comprised 18 'months' of 20 days each, which formed the basis of the solar year or *haab* (or *ab'*). Each month had a name – Pop, Uo, Zip, Zotz, Tzec etc – and each day had a number from zero (the first day, or 'seating', of the month) to 19. So the month Pop ran from 0 Pop (the 'seating' of the month Pop), 1 Pop, 2 Pop and so forth to 19 Pop, and was followed by 0 Uo, 1 Uo and so on.

Chiapas to Costa Rica. But Antigua was razed by an earthquake in 1773 and the capital moved 25km east to present-day Guatemala City.

INDEPENDENCE

By the time thoughts of independence from Spain began stirring among Guatemalans, society was already rigidly stratified. Topping the colonial

1542	1609–1821	1697
Thanks in part to heavy lobbying from Fray Bartolomé de Las Casas, Spain enacts the New Laws, officially banning forced labor in its colonies. Catholic influence becomes more institutionalized and traditional Maya social structures transformed.	The Captaincy General of Guatemala (or Kingdom of Guatemala) comprises what are now Costa Rica, Nicaragua, Honduras, El Salvador, Guatemala and the Mexican state of Chiapas, with its capital at Antigua, then Guatemala City.	The Spanish conquest of Guatemala is completed as the island of Tayasal (present-day Flores) – home of the Itza, the last remaining unconquered tribe – is defeated.

Eighteen months, each of 20 days, equals 360 days, a period known as a *tun;* the Maya added a special omen-filled five-day period called the *uayeb* at the end of this cycle in order to produce a solar calendar of 365 days. Anthropologists today call this the Vague Year, its vagueness coming from the fact that the solar year is actually 365.24 days long (the reason for the extra day in leap years of our Gregorian calendar).

Calendar Round

The huge wheels of the *tzolkin* and the *haab* also meshed, so that each day actually had a *tzolkin* name-and-number and a *haab* name-and-number used together: 1 Imix 5 Pop, 2 Ik 6 Pop, 3 Akbal 7 Pop and so on – a total of 18,980 day-name permutations. These repeated every 52 solar years, a period called the Calendar Round. The Calendar Round was the dating system used not only by the Maya but also by the Olmecs, Aztecs and Zapotecs of ancient Mexico. It's still in use in some traditional Guatemalan villages, and you can see why a special Maya elder has to be designated to keep track of it and alert his community to important days in this complex system.

Long Count

For a people as obsessed with counting time as the Maya, the Calendar Round has one serious limitation: it only lasts 52 years. After that, it starts again, and there is no way to distinguish a day named 1 Imix 5 Pop in one 52-year Calendar Round cycle from the identically named day in the next cycle.

Hence the Long Count, which the Maya developed around the start of the Classic period (about AD 250). The Long Count uses the *tun*, the year of 18 20-day months, but ignores the *uayeb*, the final five-day period that follows the *tun* in the Vague Year. In Long Count terminology, a day was a *kin* (meaning 'sun'). A 20-*kin* 'month' is called a *uinal*, and 18 *uinals* make a *tun*. Twenty *tuns* make a *katun* (7200 days, nearly 20 of our Gregorian solar years), and 20 *katuns* make a *baktun* (144,000 days, about 394 years). Further gigantic units above *baktun* were only used for grandiose effect, as when a very self-important king wanted to note exactly when his extremely important reign took place in the awesome expanse of time. Curiously for us today, 13 *baktuns* (1,872,000 days, or 5125 Gregorian solar years) form something called a Great Cycle, and the first Great Cycle began on August 11, 3114 BC (some authorities say August 13) – which means it will end on December 23 (or 25), AD 2012. The end of a Great Cycle was a time fraught with great significance – usually fearsome. Stay tuned around Christmas 2012.

hierarchy were the European-born Spaniards; next were the *criollos*, people born in Guatemala of Spanish blood; below them were the *ladinos* or *mestizos*, people of mixed Spanish and Maya blood; and at the bottom were the Maya and black slaves. Only the European-born Spaniards had any real power, but the *criollos* lorded it over the *ladinos*, who in turn exploited the indigenous population who still remain on the bottom rung of the socioeconomic ladder.

1773	Sep 15, 1821	1823–40
Antigua, by now a jewel in the colonial crown, complete with a university, printing press, schools, hospitals and dozens of churches, is destroyed by an earthquake. The new capital is founded at present-day Guatemala City.	Guatemala (and the rest of the Captaincy General) declares independence from Spain, joining the short-lived Mexican Empire. The Mexican state of Chiapas is the only member that does not secede soon afterwards.	Guatemala, El Salvador, Honduras, Nicaragua and Costa Rica form the United Provinces of Central America. Liberal reforms are enacted, and vehemently opposed by conservative groups and the Catholic church.

Angered at being repeatedly passed over for advancement, Guatemalan *criollos* took advantage of Spanish weakness following a Napoleonic invasion in 1808, and in 1821 successfully rose in revolt. Independence changed little for Guatemala's indigenous communities, who remained under the control of the church and the landowning elite. Despite cuddly-sounding democratic institutions and constitutions, Guatemalan politics continues to this day to benefit the commercial, military, landowning and bureaucratic ruling classes.

Mexico, which had recently become independent, quickly annexed Guatemala, but in 1823 Guatemala reasserted its independence and led the formation of the United Provinces of Central America (July 1, 1823), along with El Salvador, Nicaragua, Honduras and Costa Rica. Their union lasted only until 1840 before breaking up into its constituent states. This era brought prosperity to the *criollos* but worsened the lot of the Guatemalan Maya. The end of Spanish rule meant that the crown's few liberal safeguards, which had afforded the Maya a minimal protection, were abandoned. Maya claims to ancestral lands were largely ignored and huge tobacco, sugarcane and henequen (agave rope fiber) plantations were set up. The Maya, though technically and legally free, were enslaved by debt peonage to the big landowners.

> Returning from the Americas, Christopher Columbus introduced Europeans to a whole range of foods they'd never seen before – including tomatoes, sweet potatoes, squash, potatoes, avocados, corn and cocoa.

THE LIBERALS & CARRERA

The ruling classes split into two camps: the elite conservatives, including the Catholic church and the large landowners, and the liberals, who had been the first to advocate independence and who opposed the vested interests of the conservatives.

During the short existence of the United Provinces of Central America, liberal president Francisco Morazán (1830–39) from Honduras instituted reforms aimed at ending the overwhelming power of the church, the division of society into a *criollo* upper class and an indigenous lower class, and the region's impotence in world markets. This liberal program was echoed by Guatemalan chief of state Mariano Gálvez (1831–38).

But unpopular economic policies, heavy taxes and a cholera epidemic led to an indigenous uprising that brought its leader, a conservative *ladino* pig farmer, Rafael Carrera, to power. Carrera held power from 1844 to 1865, undoing many of Morazán and Gálvez's achievements. He also ceded control

---

MAYA BEAUTY

The ancient Maya considered flat foreheads and crossed eyes beautiful. To achieve these effects, children would have boards bound tight to their heads and wax beads tied to dangle before their eyes. Both men and women made cuts in their skin to gain much-desired scar markings, and women sharpened their teeth to points, another mark of beauty – which may also have helped them to keep their men in line!

Feb 2, 1838	1840	1870s
Much of southwestern Guatemala declares independence, becoming the sixth member of the United Provinces. The new state, called Los Altos, has its capital at Quetzaltenango. It will secede, briefly, in 1844, 1848 and 1849.	Rafael Carrera, buoyed by a large indigenous following, seizes power and declares Guatemala fully independent and reincorporates Los Altos into Guatemala. He sets about dismantling many of the liberal reforms of the United Provinces.	Liberal governments modernize Guatemala but turn indigenous lands over to coffee plantations. European immigration increases and newcomers are given preferential treatment, forming another elite and further disenfranchising the Maya.

of Belize to Britain in exchange for construction of a road between Guatemala City and Belize City. The road was never built, and Guatemala's claims for compensation never resolved, leading to a quarrel that festers to this day.

LIBERAL REFORMS OF BARRIOS

The liberals returned to power in the 1870s, first under Miguel García Granados, next under Justo Rufino Barrios, a rich young coffee plantation owner who held the title of president, but ruled as a dictator (1873–79). Barrios modernized Guatemala's roads, railways, schools and banking system. Everything possible was done to stimulate coffee production. Peasants in good coffee-growing areas were forced off their land to make way for new coffee *fincas* (plantations), while those living at higher altitudes were forced to work on the *fincas*. Under Barrios' successors a small group of landowning and commercial families came to control the economy, foreign companies were given generous concessions, and political opponents were censored, imprisoned or exiled.

Guatemala takes its name from Quauhtlemallan which means 'place of many trees' in Nahuatl.

ESTRADA CABRERA & MINERVA

Manuel Estrada Cabrera ruled from 1898 to 1920, bringing progress in technical matters but placing a heavy burden on all but the ruling oligarchy. He fancied himself a bringer of light and culture to a backward land, styling himself the 'Teacher and Protector of Guatemalan Youth.'

He sponsored *Fiestas de Minerva* (Festivals of Minerva), inspired by the Roman goddess of wisdom, invention and technology, and ordered construction of temples to Minerva, some of which still stand (as in Quetzaltenango). Guatemala was to become a 'tropical Athens.' At the same time, however, Estrada Cabrera looted the treasury, ignored the schools and drastically increased military spending.

Around this time the *Huelga de Dolores* (Strike of Sorrows) began. Students from Guatemala City's San Carlos University took to the streets during Lent – wearing hoods to avoid reprisals – to protest against injustice and corruption. The tradition caught on in university towns across the country, culminating with a parade through the main streets on the Friday before Good Friday. The tradition continues today.

In *Silence on the Mountain*, Daniel Wilkinson uncovers in microcosm the social background to the civil war as he delves into the reasons for the burning of a coffee estate by guerrillas.

JORGE UBICO

Estrada Cabrera was overthrown in 1920 and Guatemala entered a period of instability, ending in 1931 with the election of General Jorge Ubico as president. Ubico insisted on honesty in government, and modernized the country's health and social welfare infrastructure. Debt peonage was outlawed, but a new bondage of compulsory labor contributions to the government road-building program was established in its place. His reign ended when he was forced into exile in 1944.

1901	1940s	1945–54
President Manuel Estrada Cabrera courts the US-owned United Fruit Company, a business of hegemonic proportions, to set up shop in Guatemala. United Fruit soon takes on a dominant role in national politics.	Bowing to pressure from the US (buyers of 90% of Guatemala's exports at the time), President Jorge Ubico expels German landowners from the country. Their lands are redistributed to political and military allies.	Juan José Arévalo, elected with 85% of the popular vote, comes to power, ushering in an era of enlightened, progressive government that is continued by his successor Jacobo Arbenz.

ARÉVALO & ARBENZ

Just when it appeared that Guatemala was doomed to a succession of harsh dictators, the elections of 1945 brought a philosopher – Juan José Arévalo – to the presidency. Arévalo, in power from 1945 to 1951, established the nation's social security system, a bureau of indigenous affairs, a modern public health system and liberal labor laws. He also survived 25 coup attempts by conservative military forces.

Arévalo was succeeded by Colonel Jacobo Arbenz, who continued Arévalo's policies, instituting agrarian reforms designed to break up the large estates and foster productivity on small, individually owned farms. He also expropriated vast, unused lands conceded to the United Fruit Company during the Estrada Cabrera and Ubico years. Compensation was paid at the value declared for tax purposes (far below its real value), and Arbenz announced that the lands were to be redistributed to peasants and put into cultivation for food. The announcement set off alarms in Washington, which supported United Fruit. In 1954 the US, in one of the first documented covert operations by the CIA, orchestrated an invasion from Honduras led by two exiled Guatemalan military officers. Arbenz stepped down, and the land reform never took place.

Arbenz was succeeded by a series of military presidents elected with the support of the officer corps, business leaders, compliant political parties and the Catholic Church. More covert (but well documented) support came from the US government, in the form of money and counterinsurgency training. Violence became a staple of political life. Opponents of the government regularly turned up dead or not at all. Land reforms were reversed, voting was made dependent on literacy (disenfranchising around 75% of the population), the secret police force was revived and military repression was common.

In 1960, left-wing guerrilla groups began to form.

THE CIVIL WAR BEGINS

Guatemalan industry developed fast, but the social fabric became increasingly stressed as most profits from the boom flowed upwards. Labor unions organized, and migration to the cities, especially the capital, produced urban sprawl and slums. A cycle of violent repression and protest took hold, leading to the total politicization of society. Everyone took sides; usually it was the rural poor against the urban elite. By 1979 Amnesty International estimated that 50,000 to 60,000 people had been killed during the political violence of the 1970s alone.

A severe earthquake in 1976 killed about 22,000 people and left around a million homeless. Most of the aid sent for those in need never reached them.

1980S

In the early 1980s four disparate guerilla groups united to form the URNG (the Guatemalan National Revolutionary Unity) and military suppression

For dates, themes and discussions about past and upcoming Huelgas, log on to the official Huelga de Dolores website at www.huelgade dolores.com.

Searching for Everardo, by US attorney Jennifer K Harbury, tells how she fell in love with and married a URNG guerrilla leader who then disappeared in combat, and of her dedicated and internationally publicized struggles with the US and Guatemalan governments – including a hunger strike outside the White House – to discover his fate.

1954	Mid-1950s–1960s	1967
Effecting the country's first serious attempt at land reform, Arbenz appropriates Guatemalan lands of the US-owned United Fruit Company. He is soon deposed in a US-orchestrated coup.	Military dictators rule the country, reversing liberal reforms of previous governments. Crackdowns and state-sponsored executions of opposition forces lead to the formation of left-wing guerrilla groups. The civil war begins.	Guatemalan writer and diplomat Miguel Ángel Asturias, credited as a pioneer of modernist Latin American literature, is awarded the Nobel Prize for Literature for his political novel El señor presidente.

of antigovernment elements in the countryside peaked, especially under the presidency of General Efraín Ríos Montt, an evangelical Christian who came to power by coup in March 1982. Huge numbers of people, mostly indigenous men, were murdered in the name of anti-insurgency, stabilization and anticommunism. Guatemalans refer to this scorched-earth strategy as *la escoba*, the broom, because of the way the reign of terror swept over the country. While officials did not know the identities of the rebels, they did know which areas were bases of rebel activity – chiefly poor, rural, indigenous areas – so the government terrorized the populations of those areas to kill off support for the rebels. Over 400 villages were razed, and most of their inhabitants massacred (often tortured as well).

It was later estimated that 15,000 civilian deaths occurred as a result of counterinsurgency operations during Ríos Montt's term of office alone, not to mention the estimated 100,000 refugees (again, mostly Maya) who fled to Mexico. The government forced villagers to form Patrullas de Autodefensa Civil (PACs; Civil Defense Patrols) to do much of the army's dirty work: the PACs were responsible for some of the worst human-rights abuses during Ríos Montt's rule.

As the civil war dragged on and both sides committed atrocities, more and more rural people came to feel caught in the crossfire.

In August 1983 Ríos Montt was deposed by General Oscar Humberto Mejía Victores, but the abuses continued. It was estimated that over 100 political assassinations and 40 abductions occurred each month under his rule. Survivors of *la escoba* were herded into remote 'model villages' known as *polos de desarrollo* (poles of development) surrounded by army encampments. The bloodbath led the US to cut off military assistance to Guatemala, which in turn resulted in the 1986 election of a civilian president, Marco Vinicio Cerezo Arévalo of the Christian Democratic Party.

Before turning over power to the civilians, the military established formal mechanisms for its continued control of the countryside. There was hope that Cerezo Arévalo's administration would temper the excesses of the power elite and the military and establish a basis for true democracy. But armed conflict festered in remote areas and when Cerezo Arévalo's term ended in 1990, many people wondered whether any real progress had been made.

The Foundation for the Advancement of Mesoamerica Studies website (www.famsi.org) is incredibly detailed, with information ranging from current and past research to studies on writing, educational resources, linguistic maps and more.

EARLY 1990S

President Jorge Serrano (1990–93) from the conservative Movimiento de Acción Solidaria (Solidarity Action Movement) reopened a dialogue with the URNG, hoping to bring the decades-long civil war to an end. When the talks collapsed, the mediator from the Catholic church blamed both sides for intransigence.

Massacres and other human-rights abuses continued during this period despite the country's return to democratic rule. In one dramatic case in 1990, Guatemalan anthropologist Myrna Mack, who had documented army

1976	Mid-1970s	Feb 1982
Earthquake kills 22,000 in Guatemala. Reconstruction efforts help to consolidate leftist opposition groups, who are met with fierce military reprisals. The Carter administration, citing human-rights abuses, bans military aid to Guatemala.	In the face of military massacres and the use of death squads, the Catholic church begins campaigning on human rights issues. Priests become targets of military reprisal and are routinely kidnapped, tortured and murdered.	Four powerful guerrilla organizations unite to form the URNG (Guatemalan National Revolutionary Unity). Perhaps half a million people, mostly peasants in the western and central highlands and El Petén, actively support the guerrilla movement.

RIGOBERTA MENCHÚ TUM

Of all the unlikely candidates for the Nobel Prize throughout history, a rural indigenous Guatemalan woman would have to be near the top of the list.

Rigoberta Menchú was born in 1959 near Uspantán in the highlands of Quiché department and lived the life of a typical young Maya woman until the late 1970s, when the country's civil war affected her tragically and drove her into the left-wing guerrilla camp. Her father, mother and brother were killed in the slaughter carried out by the Guatemalan military in the name of 'pacification' of the countryside and repression of communism.

Menchú fled to exile in Mexico, where her story *I, Rigoberta Menchú: An Indian Woman in Guatemala,* based on a series of interviews, was published and translated throughout the world, bringing the plight of Guatemala's indigenous population to international attention. In 1992 Rigoberta Menchú was awarded the Nobel Prize for peace, which provided her and her cause with international stature and support. The **Rigoberta Menchú Tum Foundation** (www.frmt.org), which she founded with the US$1.2 million Nobel Prize money, works for conflict resolution, plurality, and human, indigenous and women's rights in Guatemala and internationally.

Guatemalans, especially the Maya, were proud that one of their own had been recognized by the Nobel committee. In the circles of power, however, Menchú's renown was unwelcome, as she was seen as a troublemaker.

Anthropologist David Stoll's book *Rigoberta Menchú and the Story of All Poor Guatemalans* (1999) contested the truth of many aspects of Menchú's book, including some central facts. The *New York Times* claimed that Menchú had received a Nobel Prize for lying, and of course her detractors had a field day.

Menchú took the controversy in her stride, not addressing the specific allegations, and the Nobel Institute made it clear that the prize was given for Menchú's work on behalf of the indigenous, not the content of her book. More than anything, the scandal solidified support for Menchú and her cause while calling Stoll's motives into question.

In 1999, before a Spanish court, the Rigoberta Menchú Tum Foundation formally accused former dictators Efraín Ríos Montt (1982–83) and General Oscar Humberto Mejía Victores (1983–86) of genocide. Menchú pressed for extradition proceedings, but the Guatemalan Constitutional Court denied extradition in 2007.

In 1994 Menchú returned to Guatemala from exile. Since then her work with the Foundation has continued, alongside efforts to promote greater access to low-cost, generic pharmaceuticals and a stint as a UN goodwill ambassador for the Peace Accords. In 2007 she decided to run for president. The problematic, often fragmented nature of indigenous politics was highlighted when the World Indigenous Summit of that year chose not to support her. Menchú's party won a little over 3% of the popular vote in the presidential elections.

violence against the rural Maya, was fatally wounded after being stabbed dozens of times.

Serrano's presidency came to depend more on the army for support. In 1993 he tried to seize absolute power, but after a tense few days was forced to

1982–83	1990	1992
State terror against rural indigenous communities peaks during the rule of General Efraín Ríos Montt. Peasants, particularly in the highlands, begin an exodus to Mexico to escape violence from both sides.	The army massacres 13 Tz'utujil Maya (including three children) in Santiago Atitlán. Outraged, the people of Santiago fight back, becoming the first town to succeed in expelling the army by popular demand.	Indigenous rights and peace activist Rigoberta Menchú is awarded the Nobel Prize for peace. Menchú receives the award while living in exile in Mexico, returning to Guatemala two years later.

flee into exile. Congress elected Ramiro de León Carpio, an outspoken critic of the army's strong-arm tactics, as president to complete Serrano's term.

PEACE ACCORDS

President de León's elected successor, Álvaro Arzú of the center-right Partido de Avanzada Nacional (PAN; National Advancement Party), took office in 1996. Arzú continued negotiations with the URNG and, finally, on December 29, 1996, 'A Firm and Lasting Peace Agreement' was signed. During the 36 years of civil war, an estimated 200,000 Guatemalans had been killed, a million made homeless, and untold thousands had disappeared. The Peace Accords contained provisions for accountability for the human-rights violations perpetrated by the armed forces during the war and the resettlement of Guatemala's one million displaced people. They also addressed the rights of indigenous peoples and women, health care, education and other basic social services, and the abolition of obligatory military service.

Guatemala finally recognized Belizean independence in 1992, but the exact border remains in dispute. An agreement to take the matter to the International Court of Justice was signed in 2008.

GUATEMALA SINCE THE PEACE ACCORDS

Any hopes for a truly just and democratic society have looked increasingly frayed as the years have passed since 1996. While international organizations, from the European Parliament to the Inter-American Commission on Human Rights, regularly criticize the state of human rights in the country, Guatemalan Human Rights campaigners are threatened or simply disappear on a frighteningly regular basis. The major problems – poverty, illiteracy, lack of education and poor medical facilities (all much more common in rural areas, where the Maya population is concentrated) – remain a long way from being solved.

The 1999 presidential elections were won by Alfonso Portillo of the conservative Frente Republicano Guatemalteco (FRG). Portillo was seen as a front man for FRG leader, ex-president General Efraín Ríos Montt. The national anticorruption prosecutor, Karen Fischer, fled the country in 2003 in the face of threats received when she investigated Panamanian bank accounts allegedly opened for President Portillo. Portillo himself later fled the country, at the end of his presidency, in the face of allegations that he had diverted US$500 million from the treasury to personal and family bank accounts.

El Periódico newspaper printed an article in 2003 arguing that a 'parallel power structure' involving Efraín Ríos Montt had effectively run Guatemala ever since he had been ousted as president 20 years previously. Within days, the paper's publisher and his family were attacked in their home by an armed gang of 12. Days later, Ríos Montt himself was granted permission by Guatemala's constitutional court to stand in the 2003 elections, despite the fact that the constitution banned presidents who had taken power by coup in the past, as Ríos Montt had in 1982.

In the end Guatemala's voters dealt Ríos Montt a resounding defeat, electing Oscar Berger of the moderately conservative Gran Alianza Nacional

La Hija del Puma (The Daughter of the Puma), directed by Ulf Hultberg, is a powerful 1995 film, based on a true story, about a K'iche' Maya girl who survives the army massacre of her fellow villagers and sees her brother captured. She escapes to Mexico but then returns to Guatemala in search of her brother.

1996	1998	2000–04
After nearly a decade of talks, the Peace Accords are signed, bringing to an end the 36-year civil war in which an estimated 200,000 Guatemalans died.	The true nature of peace is questioned as Bishop Gerardi, author of a paper blaming the army for the overwhelming amount of civil war deaths, is found bludgeoned to death in his home.	Presidency of **Alfonso Portillo** of the FRG party, led by Efraín Ríos Montt. Portillo **begins** by finally prosecuting those responsible for **the death of** Bishop Gerardi, **but is soon** mired in corruption allegations.

as president. Berger managed to stay relatively untouched by political scandal, critics saying this was because he didn't really do *anything*, let alone anything bad.

Hurricane Stan hit the country in October 2005, causing massive devastation and loss of life. The country's infrastructure, never wonderful, was torn apart as roads and villages were buried under landslides, and bridges, electricity, power and phone lines went down.

The Central America Free Trade Agreement (CAFTA; TLC or Tratado de Libre Comercio, in Spanish) was ratified by Guatemala in 2006. Supporters claim it frees the country up for greater participation in foreign markets, while detractors state that the agreement is a bad deal for the already disenfranchised rural poor.

Guatemala: Nunca Mas (1998), published by ODHAG and REMHI, details many of the human-rights abuses committed during Guatemala's civil war, and includes moving testimonials.

GUATEMALA TODAY

Another round of elections was held in late 2007, bringing to power Álvaro Colom of the center-leftist Unidad Nacional de la Esperanza. Colom has followed on from Berger's example of steady, minimalist governance. The country's infrastructure has improved significantly over the last few years, but allegations of back room deals and political favoritism have dogged Colom throughout his term. One case in point is the 'Mi Familia Progresa' program, which uses cash incentives to encourage families to send their children to school and medical clinics. The program's lack of transparency was highlighted in 2010 when the Minister of Education preferred to be fired by the Supreme Court rather than produce a list naming recipients of funding. The suspicion is that Colom is using the program to pay back political favors, and that there are people collecting multiple payments.

See www.amnesty.org for Amnesty International reports on Guatemala.

Colom has also attracted criticism for green-lighting construction of a gas plant in the Punta de Manabique protected area in the country's southeast. Critics claim that construction began without the required environmental-impact study, and that the company building it contributed substantially to Colom's election campaign and loaned him an airplane on various occasions.

For reasonably up-to-date, objective reporting on Guatemalan elections (in Spanish) check out www.eleccionesguate mala.com.

But the major political scandal of Colom's term happened in 2009, with what came to be known as the Rosenberg Case. In May of that year, Guatemala City lawyer Rodrigo Rosenberg was shot and killed while riding his bicycle. Two days later a video surfaced showing Rosenberg himself stating that if he was found dead it would be because he had evidence incriminating President Colom and his government in a corruption scandal.

Cable news channels could hardly have hoped for better footage, which soon screened worldwide. Opposition parties were quick to act, too, staging massive demonstrations calling for Colom's resignation or impeachment. The case went from strange to weird as it was found that the assassination was masterminded by Rosenberg's friends and cousins. It quickly moved to the downright bizarre as investigators claimed that Rosenberg himself,

2002	2005	2006
US drops Guatemala as an ally in the war on drugs. Amnesty International reports that criminals, police and military are colluding with affiliates of multinational corporations to flout human rights.	Hurricane Stan hits southwest Guatemala. Landslides and flooding leave a death toll in the hundreds and leave thousands homeless. President Oscar Berger seeks massive foreign aid.	Guatemala ratifies CAFTA, a free-trade agreement between the US and Central America. Massive street protests and seemingly endless media discussion have little effect on the final document.

depressed and distraught after the death of his mother and other loved ones, ordered the assassination. While many seeking to make political mileage out of the event mistrust the investigation's findings, the incident has all but faded into the background.

The major concern for all Guatemalans is that of security. An estimated 5% of murders in the country are prosecuted and daily newspapers regularly feature body counts of 10 and upwards for Guatemala City alone. The *Prensa Libre* reports that in the last decade the number of kidnappings per year has quintupled, while annual murder rates have gone from 2001 to 6409. The police, understaffed and under-resourced (it's not unheard of for car chases to end when police car runs out of gas) struggle in the face of rising crime, unaided by the fact that over the same period they've had 14 directors, one of whom has been accused of stealing US$300,000 seized in a cocaine raid.

Gang violence continues to haunt Guatemala City, with city bus drivers who fail to pay extortionists being the most common targets. Rarely a day goes by without the papers reporting another murdered driver.

Violence against women has long been a concern in Guatemala and while Congress passed tough new penalties in 2008 for the murder of women, critics label them useless in a country where so many murders go unsolved and, according to the Myrna Mack Foundation, autopsies are only performed on 12% of female murder victims.

Contrary to the growing trend of lawlessness, human-rights campaigners have recently secured victories in bringing civil war criminals to justice – ex-colonel Marco Antonio Sánchez Samayoa was sentenced to 53 years in prison for his part in the murder of eight farmers in 1981.

At the time of writing it looks like former president Alfonso Portillo will be brought to justice, too – having evaded prosecution for years, he was finally charged by the United States for laundering money using US banks, and looks set to be extradited and put on trial there.

For the latest on the progress (or otherwise) of human rights in Guatemala, visit the Guatemala Human Rights Commission/USA website (www.ghrc-usa.org) or click on 'Human Rights' on the website of the US embassy in Guatemala City (http://guatemala.usembassy.gov).

You can watch the famous Rosenberg video (with subtitles) at www.youtube.com/watch?v=FzkMMtCOgw4.

December 2006	2007	2009
Mel Gibson's *Apocolypto* brings the Maya story to Hollywood audiences for the first time. Historians, archaeologists and Maya leaders condemn the movie for its many historical inaccuracies and portrayal of the Maya as bloodthirsty savages.	US President George W Bush visits Guatemala to discuss CAFTA, the war on drugs and immigration. Massive street protests ensue. Maya priests perform cleaning rituals after his departure.	The 'Rosenberg video' – in which the Guatemala city lawyer accuses President Portillo of murder from beyond the grave – airs globally. Thousands of pro- and anti-government protesters take to the streets of the capital.

The Culture

THE NATIONAL PSYCHE

You will be amazed when you first reach Guatemala by just how helpful, polite and unhurried Guatemalans are. Everyone has time to stop and chat and explain what you want to know. This is apparent even if you've just crossed the border from Mexico, where things aren't exactly rushed either. Most Guatemalans like to get to know other people without haste, feeling for common ground and things to agree on, rather than making blunt assertions and engaging in adversarial dialectic. Some observers explain this mild manner as a reaction to centuries of repression and violence by the ruling class, but whatever the truth of that, it makes most Guatemalans a pleasure to deal with.

What goes on behind this outward politeness is harder to encapsulate. Few Guatemalans exhibit the stress, worry and hurry of the 'developed' nations, but this obviously isn't because they don't have to worry about money or employment. They're a long-suffering people who don't expect wealth or good government but make the best of what comes their way – friendship, their family, a good meal, a bit of good company.

Guatemalans are a religious bunch – atheists and agnostics are very thin on the ground. People will often ask what religion you are quite early in a conversation. Unless you really want to get into it, saying 'Christian' generally satisfies.

Orthodox Catholicism is gradually giving way to evangelical Protestantism among the *ladinos*, with the animist-Catholic syncretism of the traditional Maya always present. People's faiths give them hope, not only of better things in the afterlife but also of improvements in the here and now – whether through answered prayers or, in the evangelicals' case, of a more sober, more gainful and happier existence without alcohol, gambling or domestic violence.

The tales of violence – domestic violence, civil-war violence, criminal violence – that one inevitably hears in Guatemala sit strangely with the mild-mannered approach you will encounter from nearly everybody. Whatever the explanation, it helps to show why a little caution is in order when strangers meet.

It has been said that Guatemala has no middle class, that it just has a ruling class and an exploited class. It's true that Guatemala has a small, rich, *ladino* ruling elite whose main goal seems to be to maintain wealth and power at almost any cost. It also has an indigenous Maya population, comprising more than half the people in the country, that tends to be poor, poorly educated and poorly provided for and has always been kept in a secondary role by the ruling elite. The Maya villagers' strengths lie in their strong family and community ties, and their traditions. Those who do break out of the poverty cycle, through business or education, do not turn their backs on their communities. But as well as these two groups at

While many rural houses now have running water, the village *pila* (communal laundry trough) remains a place to get together and exchange gossip.

Guatemala has the highest private ownership per capita of helicopters in the world – a fact many ascribe to the poor state of the highways and the healthy state of drug dealers' bank accounts.

GUATEMALANS ABROAD

More than one in every 10 Guatemalans – over 1.6 million people – lives in the US, an estimated 60% of them without documentation. There has been a steady northward flow of Guatemalans since the 1980s, growing each year since the early '90s and with a small dip in 2001. In 2010 it's expected that legal and illegal immigrants to the US will top the 200,000-per-year mark, although the global economic crisis has slowed immigration and even inspired some Guatemalans to return home.

Money sent home by US-based Guatemalans amounts to US$4.1 billion a year – that's US$4100 million – roughly equivalent to two-thirds of the country's total earnings from exports. More than 50% of Guatemalans in the US live either in Los Angeles, New York or Miami.

the extremes, there is also a large group of working-class and middle-class
ladinos, typically Catholic and family-oriented but with aspirations influenced by education, TV, international popular music and North America
(of which many Guatemalans have direct experience as migrant workers) –
and maybe by liberal ideas of equality and social tolerance. This segment of
society has its bohemian/student/artist circles whose overlap with educated,
forward-looking Maya may hold the greatest hope for progress toward an
equitable society.

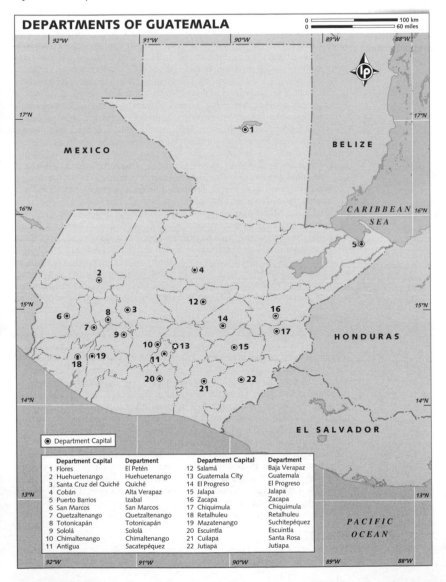

DEPARTMENTS OF GUATEMALA

	Department Capital	Department		Department Capital	Department
1	Flores	El Petén	12	Salamá	Baja Verapaz
2	Huehuetenango	Huehuetenango	13	Guatemala City	Guatemala
3	Santa Cruz del Quiché	Quiché	14	El Progreso	El Progreso
4	Cobán	Alta Verapaz	15	Jalapa	Jalapa
5	Puerto Barrios	Izabal	16	Zacapa	Zacapa
6	San Marcos	San Marcos	17	Chiquimula	Chiquimula
7	Quetzaltenango	Quetzaltenango	18	Retalhuleu	Retalhuleu
8	Totonicapán	Totonicapán	19	Mazatenango	Suchitepéquez
9	Sololá	Sololá	20	Escuintla	Escuintla
10	Chimaltenango	Chimaltenango	21	Cuilapa	Santa Rosa
11	Antigua	Sacatepéquez	22	Jutiapa	Jutiapa

LIFESTYLE

The majority of Guatemalans live in one-room houses of brick, concrete blocks or traditional *bajareque* (a construction of stones, wooden poles and mud), with roofs of tin, tiles or thatch. They have earth floors, a fireplace (but usually no chimney) and minimal possessions – often just a couple of bare beds and a few pots. These small homes are often grouped in compounds with several others, all housing members of one extended family. Thus live most of Guatemala's great Maya majority, in the countryside, in villages and in towns.

The few wealthier Maya and most *ladino* families have larger houses in towns and the bigger villages, but their homes may still not be much more than one or two bedrooms and a kitchen that also serves as a living area. Possessions, adornments and decorations may be sparse. Of course, some families have bigger, more comfortable and impressive homes. Middle-class families in the wealthier suburbs of Guatemala City live in good-sized one- or two-story houses with gardens. The most select residences will have their gardens walled for security and privacy. The elite few possess rural as well as urban properties – for example, a coffee *finca* (ranch) on the Pacific Slope with a comfortable farmhouse, or a seaside villa on the Pacific or Caribbean coast.

Despite modernizing influences – education, cable TV, contact with foreign travelers in Guatemala, international popular music, time spent as migrant workers in the USA – traditional family ties remain strong at all levels of society. Large extended-family groups gather for weekend meals and holidays. Old-fashioned gender roles are strong too: many women have jobs to increase the family income but relatively few have positions of much responsibility.

Traveling in Guatemala you will encounter a much wider cross-section of Guatemalans than many Guatemalans ever do, as they tend to live their lives within relatively narrow worlds. The Guatemalans you'll meet will also most likely be among the most worldly and open-minded, as a result of their contact with tourists and travelers from around the globe. Guatemala has a broad web of people, often young, who are interested in many things – things such as learning, other cultures, human rights, music and the arts, improving the position of women, the indigenous and the poor, and helping others. You only need to peel away one or two layers of the onion to uncover them.

ECONOMY

With a young population and an abundance of natural resources, you'd expect the Guatemalan economy to be at least vaguely healthy, but almost all the indicators point in the other direction. The CIA World Factbook states that 7.5 million Guatemalans – more than half the population – live in poverty. The official national minimum wage is only Q56 per day – and not everyone is entitled even to this. An established school teacher can earn around Q1800 per month. Poverty is most prevalent in rural, indigenous areas, especially the highlands. Wealth, industry and commerce are concentrated overwhelmingly in sprawling, polluted Guatemala City, the country's only large city. About 25% of the population live in Guatemala City and its surrounds.

What little industry that does exist is mostly foreign-owned, or is on such a small scale that it provides limited employment opportunities. A large stumbling block for foreign investors is Guatemala's relative insecurity – even the smallest stores are obliged to hire security guards (you'll see them out on the sidewalk toting heavy weaponry), making the cost of doing business in Guatemala relatively high.

POPULATION

The great majority of Guatemala's 15 million people live in the highland strip from Guatemala City to Quetzaltenango, the country's two biggest

Gregory Nava's tragic film *El Norte* (The North) brings home not only the tragedy of Guatemala's civil war but also the illusory nature of many Guatemalans' seeking the 'American dream.'

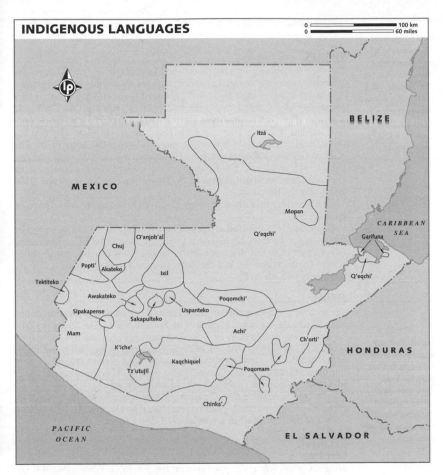

cities. Many towns and large villages are dotted around this region. Some 49% of the population lives in towns and cities, and 40% are aged under 15.

The Maya are spread throughout the country but are most densely concentrated in the highlands, which are home to the four biggest Maya groups, the K'iche' (Quiché), Mam, Q'eqchi' (Kekchí) and Kaqchiquel (Cakchiquel).

Some 41% of Guatemalans are indigenous, but this line is blurred as many people have indigenous blood, but some choose not to describe themselves as such. Nearly all of the indigenous population is Maya, although there is a very small population of non-Maya indigenous people called the Chinka' (Xinca) in the southeastern corner of the country. The rest of Guatemala's population are nearly all *ladinos* – descended from both the Maya and from European (mostly Spanish) settlers. There are also a few thousand Garífuna (descended from Caribbean islanders and shipwrecked African slaves) around the Caribbean town of Lívingston.

Maya languages are still how most Maya communicate, with 23 separate (and often mutually unintelligible) Maya languages spoken in different regions of the country. It's language that primarily defines which Maya people

For an online Spanish-Maya dictionary, log on to http://aulex.org/es-myn/.

someone belongs to. Though many Maya speak some Spanish, it's always a second language to them – and there are many who don't speak any Spanish.

SPORTS

The sport that most ignites the passion and enthusiasm of most Guatemalans is football (soccer). Though Guatemalan teams always flop in international competition, the 10-club Liga Mayor (Major League) is keenly followed by reasonably large crowds. Two seasons are played each year: the Torneo de Apertura (Opening Tournament) from July to November, and the Torneo de Clausura (Closing Tournament) from January to May. The two big clubs are Municipal and Comunicaciones, both from Guatemala City. The 'Clásico Gringo' is when teams from Quetzaltenango and Antigua (the two big tourist towns) play. The national press always has details on upcoming games. Admission to games runs from Q20 for the cheapest areas and Q100 and up for the best seats.

Road cycling, marathon running and weightlifting are other popular local sports.

Guatemala is recognized as a prime sportfishing destination, as shown by the hosting of the annual Presidential Challenge Sport Fishing Championships out of Puerto Quetzal. It's not a sport that has really caught on with mainstream Guatemalans yet, but the Zona 10 crowd from Guatemala City are starting to pick up on it.

MEDIA

Theoretically, the Guatemalan media enjoys freedom of expression and is not subject to government control or undue censorship. The reality is a little harder to pinpoint. In early 2009 the International Federation of Journalists spoke out against the murders of three Guatemalan journalists within as many months. Guatemala's appalling record when it comes to prosecuting murderers means that many investigative journalists are very careful about what they say and who they may offend while saying it.

As a counterbalance to this rather gloomy scenario of self-censorship, Freedom of Information legislation was passed by Congress in 2008 (after a decade of debate), albeit in a very watered-down form.

RELIGION
Christian

Roman Catholicism is the predominant religion in Guatemala, but it is not the only religion by any stretch of the imagination. Since the 1980s Evangelical

---

Sidebar (left margin):

Izabal in the east and El Petén in the north are the most sparsely populated of Guatemala's 22 departments, with 42 and 16 people per square kilometer respectively. The national average density is 137 people per square kilometer.

Football club Municipal, nicknamed Los Rojos (the Reds), tends to nurture young Guatemalan talent, while Comunicaciones (Las Cremas, the Creams) tends to import players from other countries.

WHO'S YOUR DADDY?

You might have noticed by now that Guatemalans have no problem with long names. Four is the norm – five is not out of the ordinary. As well as being tradition, it's also a form of social control – you can always tell who somebody's parents were, and thus which level of society they come from.

It may not sound like a big deal, but in status-conscious Guatemala, it certainly is. There have been cases of doctors and lawyers denied membership to country clubs here just because they have the wrong (ie indigenous) surname.

Here's how it works: when you're born, you get two first names, much like in many countries in the West. Next comes your father's family name, then your mother's family name, both these names being from the father's side of the family.

When a woman marries, she often changes the mother's family part of her surname to that of her husband's family, with a 'de' in front of it.

For everyday use, Guatemalans often use their first name, followed by their father's family name.

THE BIGGEST PARTY IN TOWN

It's Friday night in any small town in Guatemala. The music's pumping, there's singing and hands are clapping. Have you just stumbled onto a local jam session? Sorry to disappoint, but what you're most likely listening to is an evangelical church service.

The Evangelicals are the fastest-growing religion in Latin America – one estimate puts the number of new Latino converts at a staggering 8000 per day.

The Catholic church is worried – this is their heartland, after all, and the reasons that they're losing their grip aren't all that easy to identify.

Some say it's the Evangelicals' use of radio and TV that brings them wider audiences; for some it's their rejection of rituals and gestures and customs in favor of real human contact. Others say it's the way the newcomers go to the roughest barrios and accept anybody – including 'the drunks and the hookers,' as one priest put it.

For some, they're just more fun – they fall into trances and speak in tongues, heal and prophesy. And then there's the singing – not stale old hymns, but often racy pop numbers with the lyrics changed to more spiritual themes.

One thing's for sure – an Evangelical makes a better husband: drinking, smoking, gambling and domestic violence are all severely frowned upon. Maybe, once again in Guatemala, it's the wives who are really calling the shots.

Protestant sects, around 58% of them Pentecostal, have surged in popularity, and it is estimated that 30% to 40% of Guatemalans are now Evangelicals. These numbers continue to grow as evangelical churches compete for further souls.

Catholicism's fall can also be attributed in part to the civil war. On occasion, Catholic priests were (and still are) outspoken defenders of human rights, attracting persecution (and worse) from dictators at the time, especially the evangelical Ríos Montt.

The number of new evangelical churches (see above), especially in indigenous Maya villages, is astonishing. Catholicism is fighting back with messages about economic and racial justice, papal visits and new saints – Guatemala's most venerated local Christian figure, the 17th-century Antigua-hospital-founder Hermano Pedro de San José de Bethancourt, was canonized in 2002 when Pope John Paul II visited Guatemala.

Catholicism in the Maya areas has never been exactly orthodox. The missionaries who brought Catholicism to the Maya in the 16th century wisely permitted aspects of the existing animistic, shamanistic Maya religion to continue alongside Christian rites and beliefs. Syncretism was aided by the identification of certain Maya deities with certain Christian saints, and survives to this day. A notable example is the deity known as Maximón in Santiago Atitlán, San Simón in Zunil and Rilaj Maam in San Andrés Itzapa near Antigua, who seems to be a combination of Maya gods, the Spanish conquistador Pedro de Alvarado and Judas Iscariot (see boxed text, p146).

Maya
ANCIENT MAYA BELIEFS

For the ancient Maya, the world, the heavens and the mysterious underworld called Xibalbá were one great, unified structure that operated according to the laws of astrology, cyclical time and ancestor worship. (For more on astrology and the calendar, see boxed text, p24.) The towering, sacred ceiba tree symbolized the world-tree, which united the heavens (represented by the tree's branches and foliage), the earth (the trunk) and the nine levels of Xibalbá (the roots). The heavens, the earth and the underworld were also all aspects of the single supreme creator, called Itzamná or Hunab Ku or Lizard House. The world-tree had a sort of cruciform shape and was associated with

For up-to-the-minute news on the football scene in Guatemala, log on to www.guatefutbol.com.

For some of the best and boldest investigative journalism about Guatemala, try to track down a copy of *Revista …Y Qué?* It's available at some gas stations and pharmacies, and online at www.revistayque.com.

the color green. In the 16th century, when the Franciscan friars came bearing a cross and required the Maya to venerate it, the symbolism meshed easily with the established Maya belief in the ceiba or world-tree.

Each point of the compass had a color and a special religious significance. East, where the sun was reborn each day, was most important; its color was red. West, where the sun disappeared, was black. North, where the all-important rains came from, was white. South, the 'sunniest' point of the compass, was yellow. Everything in the Maya world was seen in relation to these cardinal points, with the world-tree at the center.

Just as the great cosmic dragon shed its blood, which fell as rain to the earth, so humans had to shed blood to link themselves with Xibalbá. Bloodletting ceremonies were the most important religious ceremonies, and the blood of kings was seen as the most acceptable for these rituals. Maya kings often initiated bloodletting rites to heighten the responsiveness of the gods. Thus, when the Christian friars said that the blood of Jesus, the King of the Jews, had been spilled for the common people, the Maya could easily understand and embrace the symbolism.

Maya ceremonies were performed in natural sacred places as well as their human-made equivalents. Mountains, caves, lakes, cenotes (natural limestone cavern pools), rivers and fields were – and still are – sacred. Pyramids and temples were thought of as stylized mountains. A cave was the mouth of the creature that represented Xibalbá, and to enter it was to enter the spirit of the secret world. This is why some Maya temples have doorways surrounded by huge masks: as you enter the door of this 'cave' you are entering the mouth of Xibalbá.

Ancestor worship was very important to the ancient Maya, and when they buried a king beneath a pyramid or a commoner beneath the floor or courtyard of a *na* (thatched Maya hut), the sacredness of the location was increased.

Mayan Folktales, edited by James D Sexton, brings together the myths and legends of the Lago de Atitlán area, translated into English.

To get a handle on Maximón and shamanism around Lago de Atitlán, check out *Scandals in the House of Birds: Shamans and Priests on Lake Atitlán*, by anthropologist and poet Nathaniel Tarn.

MODERN MAYA RITUALS

Many sites of ancient Maya ruins – among them Tikal, Kaminaljuyú and K'umarcaaj – still have altars where prayers, offerings and ceremonies continue to take place today. Fertility rites, healing ceremonies and sacred observances to ring in the various Maya new years are still practiced with gusto. These types of ceremony are directed or overseen by a Maya priest known as a *tzahorín* and usually involve burning candles and copal (a natural incense from the bark of various tropical trees), making offerings to the gods

EDUCATION IN GUATEMALA

Education is free and in theory compulsory between the ages of seven and 14. Primary education lasts for six years, but the average school-leaving age is 11 years, according to UN statistics. Secondary school begins at age 13 and comprises two cycles of three years each, called *básico* and *magisterio*. Not all secondary education is free – a major deterrent for many. Some people continue studying for their *magisterio* well into adulthood. Completing *magisterio* qualifies you to become a school teacher yourself. It's estimated that only about 34% of children of the 13-to-18 age group are in secondary school. Guatemala has five universities. The Universidad de San Carlos, founded in 1676 in Antigua (later moved to Guatemala City), was the first university in Central America.

Overall, adult literacy is around 73% in Guatemala, but it's lower among women (68%) and rural people. Maya children who do seasonal migrant work with their families are least likely to get an education, as the time the families go away to work falls during the school year. A limited amount of school teaching is done in Maya languages – chiefly the big four, K'iche', Mam, Kaqchiquel and Q'eqchi' – but this rarely goes beyond the first couple of years of primary school. Spanish remains the necessary tongue for anyone who wants to get ahead in life.

THE MAYA BURY THEIR DEAD

It is the night before the funeral, and the shaman is in the house of the deceased, washing candles in holy water. If he misses one, a family member could go blind or deaf. He has counted off the days, and divined that tomorrow will be propitious for the burial.

He prays to the ancestral spirits, asking for the health of the family and the absence of disaster. The list is long and detailed. Personal objects are placed in the coffin; if they're not, the man's spirit might return home looking for them.

Members of the cofradía (fraternity) bear the coffin to the cemetery; a trail of mourners following. Four stops are made on leaving the house: at the doorway, in the yard, on entering the street, and at the first street corner. At each stop, mourners place coins on the coffin – in reality to buy candles, symbolically so that the spirit can buy its way out of purgatory and into heaven.

As the coffin is lowered into the ground, mourners kiss handfuls of dirt before throwing them on top. Once the coffin is buried, women sprinkle water on top, packing down the soil and protecting the corpse from werewolves and other dark spirits.

Every All Soul's Day (November 2) the family will come to the cemetery to honor their dead. Sometimes this will stretch over three days (beginning on the first). They will come to clean and decorate the grave, and set out food such as roasted corn, sweet potatoes, vegetable pears (*chayote* or chokos), and other fresh-picked fruit of the field. The church bells will ring at midday to summon the spirits, who feast on the smells of the food.

---

and praying for whatever the desired outcome may be – a good harvest, a healthy child or a prosperous new year, for example. Some ceremonies involve chicken sacrifices as well. Each place has its own set of gods – or at least different names for similar gods.

Visitors may also be able to observe traditional Maya ceremonies in places such as the Pascual Abaj shrine at Chichicastenango (p146), the altars on the shore of Laguna Chicabal outside Quetzaltenango (p175), or El Baúl near Santa Lucía Cotzumalguapa (p196), but a lot of traditional rites are off-limits to foreigners.

WOMEN IN GUATEMALA

One of the goals of the 1996 Peace Accords was to improve women's rights in Guatemala. By 2003 the Inter-American Commission on Human Rights had to report that laws discriminating against women had yet to be repealed. Women got the vote and the right to stand for election in 1946, but in 2010 only 8% of congressional deputies were women. Women's leaders repeatedly criticize Guatemala's *machista* culture, which believes a woman's place is in the home (unless she's out washing the clothes or at the market or collecting firewood). The situation is, if anything, worse for indigenous women in rural areas, who also have to live with most of the country's direst poverty.

The international organization Human Rights Watch reported in 2002 that women working in private households were persistently discriminated against. Domestic workers, many of whom are from Maya communities, lack certain basic rights, including the rights to be paid the minimum wage and to work an eight-hour day and a 48-hour week. Many domestic workers begin working as young adolescents, but Guatemalan labor laws do not provide adequate protection for domestic workers under the age of 18.

Probably of greatest concern are the reports of escalating violence against women, accompanied by a steadily rising murder rate. These victims were once brushed off as being 'just' gang members or prostitutes, but it is now clear that murder, rape and kidnapping of women is a serious issue. The international community has begun to put pressure on Guatemala to act,

Maya Cosmos – Three Thousand Years of the Shaman's Path, by David Freidel, Linda Schele and Joy Parker, traces Maya creation myths from the past to the present with a dose of lively personal experience.

but the realities of *machista* society mean that crimes against women are seldom investigated and rarely solved.

ARTS
Literature

Despite men taking the lead in Guatemala's *machista* culture, women live longer, averaging 72 years against 68 for men.

A great source of national pride is the Nobel Prize for Literature that was bestowed on Guatemalan Miguel Ángel Asturias (1899–1974) in 1967. Best known for *Men of Maize,* his magical-realist epic on the theme of European conquest and the Maya, and for his thinly veiled vilification of Latin American dictators in *The President,* Asturias also wrote poetry (collected in the early volume *Sien de Alondra,* published in English as *Temple of the Lark*). He also served in various diplomatic capacities for the Guatemalan government. Other celebrated Guatemalan authors include short-story master Augusto Monterroso (1921–2003), who is credited as having written the shortest story in published literature. Look also for his published work *The Black Sheep and Other Fables.* Luis Cardoza y Aragón (1901–92) is principally known for his poetry and for fighting in the revolutionary movement that deposed dictator Jorge Ubico in 1944. Gaspar Pedro Gonzáles' *A Mayan Life* is claimed to be the first novel written by a Maya author.

For information on Guatemalan women's organizations (and much, much more) visit EntreMundos (www. entremundos.org).

One of Central America's largest literary competitions, the Juegos Florales Hispanoamericanos, is held in Quetzaltenango in September to coincide with Independence Day celebrations.

GETTING ALONG WITH GUATEMALANS

While Guatemalans tend to give foreigners a fair amount of leeway, at least trying to adapt to local ways is bound to make your travels run more smoothly.

- Even in such routine situations as entering a store or taking a bus seat, a simple greeting is often exchanged: *buenos días* or *buenas tardes* and a smile is all that's needed.

- When entering a room – including public places such as a restaurant or waiting room – make a general greeting to everyone – again, *buenos días* or *buenas tardes* will do.

- When leaving a restaurant, it is common to wish other diners *buen provecho* (bon appétit).

- Many Maya are *very* touchy about being photographed. Always ask permission before taking pictures.

- Many Maya women avoid contact with foreign men, as virtuous Maya women don't talk with strange men. Male travelers in need of information should ask another man.

- In general, the Maya are a fairly private people and some communities are still recovering from the nightmare of the civil war. People may be willing to share their war stories, but don't dig for information – let your hosts offer it.

- Referring to a Maya person as *indio* (Indian) is considered racist. The preferred term is *indígena.*

- Pay attention to your appearance. Even poor Guatemalans do their best to look neat, and you should do the same.

- When dealing with officialdom (police, border officials, immigration officers), try to appear as conservative and respectable as possible.

- General standards of modesty in dress have relaxed somewhat. Coastal dwellers tend to show a lot more skin than highland types, but not all locals appreciate this type of attire.

- Dress modestly when entering churches.

- Shorts are usually worn, by men or women, only at the beach and in coastal towns.

MAYA WRITING

During the Classic period, the Maya lowlands were divided into two major linguistic groups. In the Yucatán Peninsula and Belize people spoke Yucatec, and in the eastern highlands and Motagua Valley of Guatemala they spoke a language related to Chol. People in El Petén likely spoke both languages. Scholars have suggested that the written language throughout the Maya world was a form of Chol.

Long before the Spanish conquest, the Maya developed a sophisticated hieroglyphic script which is partly phonetic (glyphs representing sounds), and partly logographic (glyphs representing words).

Music

The marimba is considered the national instrument, although scholars cannot agree whether this xylophone-type instrument already existed in Africa long before and was brought to Guatemala early on by slaves. Marimbas can be heard throughout the country, often in restaurants or in plazas in the cool of an evening. The earliest marimbas used a succession of increasingly large gourds as the resonator pipes, but modern marimbas are more commonly fitted with wooden pipes, though you may see the former type in more traditional settings. The instrument is usually played by three men and there is a carnival-like quality to its sound and traditional compositions.

Guatemalan festivals provide great opportunities to hear traditional music featuring instruments such as cane flutes, square drums and the *chirimía*, a reed instrument of Moorish roots related to the oboe.

Guatemalan tastes in pop music are greatly influenced by the products of other Latin American countries. Reggaetón is huge – current favorites being Pitbull, Wisin & Yandel and Calle 13.

The only record label seriously promoting new Guatemalan artists (mostly in the urban/hip hop vein) is Guatemala City–based **UnOrthodox Productions** (www.uoproductions.com).

Guatemalan rock went through its golden age in the '80s and early '90s. Bands from this era like Razones de Cambio, Bohemia Suburbana and Viernes Verde still have their diehard fans. The most famous Guatemalan-born musician is Ricardo Arjona, who has lived in Mexico since the '90s.

Architecture

Modern Guatemalan architecture, apart from a few flashy bank and office buildings along Av La Reforma in Guatemala City, is chiefly characterized by expanses of drab concrete. Some humbler rural dwellings still use a traditional wall construction known as *bajareque*, where a core of stones is held in place by poles of bamboo or other wood, which is faced with stucco or mud. Village houses are increasingly roofed with sheets of tin instead of tiles or thatch – less aesthetically pleasing but also less expensive.

MAYA ARCHITECTURE

Ancient Maya architecture is a mixed bag of incredible accomplishments and severe limitations. The Maya's great buildings are both awesome and beautiful, with their aesthetic attention to intricately patterned facades, delicate 'combs' on temple roofs, and sinuous carvings. These magnificent structures, such as the ones found in the sophisticated urban centers of Tikal, El Mirador and Copán, were created without beasts of burden (except for humans) or the luxury of the wheel. Nor did Maya builders ever devise the arch: instead, they used what is known as a corbeled arch, consisting of two walls leaning toward one another, nearly meeting at the top and surmounted by a capstone. This created a triangular rather than rounded arch and did not allow any great width or make for much strength. Instead, the building's

The marimba became hip in the 1940s when jazz greats such as Glenn Miller started to include it in their compositions.

La Casa de Enfrente, an award-winning film directed by Tonatiúh Martinez, dealing with such gritty subjects as corruption and prostitution, is part of the new wave of Guatemalan film making.

To find out about up-and-coming Guatemalan rock bands, the best place to go is www.rockrepublik.net.

Looking for Palladin, written and directed by Andrzej Krakowski is shot on location in Antigua and features some great street and crowd shots and quite a few local actors.

foundations and substructure needed to be very strong. Once structures were completed, experts hypothesize, they were covered with stucco and painted red with a mixture of hematite and most probably water.

Although formal studies and excavations of Maya sites in Guatemala have been ongoing for more than a century, much of their architectural how and why remains a mystery. For example, the purpose of *chultunes,* underground chambers carved from bedrock and filled with offerings, continues to baffle scholars. And while we know that the Maya habitually built one temple on top of another to bury successive leaders, we have little idea how they actually erected these symbols of power. All the limestone used to erect the great Maya cities had to be moved and set in place by hand – an engineering feat that must have demanded astronomical amounts of human labor. Try to imagine mining, shaping, transporting and hefting two million cubic meters of limestone blocks: this is the amount of rock scholars estimate was used in the construction of the Danta complex at El Mirador.

COLONIAL ARCHITECTURE

Mary Ellen Miller's well-illustrated *Maya Art and Architecture* paints the full picture from gigantic temples to intricately painted ceramics.

During the colonial period (the early 16th to early 19th centuries) churches, convents, mansions and palaces were all built in the Spanish styles of the day, chiefly Renaissance, baroque and neoclassical. But while the architectural concepts were European-inspired, the labor used to realize them was strictly indigenous. Thus, Maya embellishments – such as the lily blossoms and vegetable motifs that adorn Antigua's La Merced – can be found on many colonial buildings, serving as testament to the countless laborers forced to make the architectural dreams of Guatemala's newcomers a reality. Churches were built high and strong to protect the elite from lower classes in revolt.

Guatemala does not have the great colonial architectural heritage of neighboring Mexico, partly because earthquakes destroyed many of its finest buildings. But the architecture of Antigua is particularly striking, as new styles and engineering techniques developed following each successive earthquake. Columns became lower and thicker to provide more stability.

For a 3D representation of the Tikal archaeological site, check out www.tikalpark.com/map.htm.

Some Antigua buildings, including the Palacio de los Capitanes and Palacio del Ayuntamiento on the central plaza, were given a double-arch construction to strengthen them. With so many colonial buildings in different states of grandeur and decay, from nearly crumbled to completely restored, Antigua was designated a World Heritage Site by Unesco in 1979.

After the 1776 earthquake, which prompted the relocation of the capital from Antigua to Guatemala City, the neoclassical architecture of the day came to emphasize durability. Decorative flourishes were saved for the interiors of buildings, with elaborate altars and furniture adorning churches and homes. By this time Guatemalan architects were hell-bent on seeing their buildings stay upright, no matter how powerful the next earthquake. Even though several serious quakes have hit Guatemala City since then, many colonial buildings (such as the city's cathedral) have survived. The same cannot be

---

MAYA CITIES AS THE CENTER OF CREATION

The ancient Maya built their communities to reflect sacred geography, often choosing a lakeside site overlooked by three volcanoes.

The lowland Maya didn't have mountains so they built them in the form of plaza-temple complexes. In hieroglyphic inscriptions the central plazas of Maya cities were called *nab'* (sea) or *lakam ja'* (great water). Rising above were massive pyramid-temples, often in groups of three, representing the first mountains to emerge out of the 'waters' of the plaza.

WHAT ARE ALL THESE PEOPLE DOING HERE?

There's no doubt that tourism has an impact. Lago de Atitlán, for example, is straining under the pressure of its own popularity – the drains for one, just aren't holding up, and every year as more visitors arrive and more hotels are built, more sewerage flows into the lake. Tourists, it seems, kill the thing that they love.

We've all seen tourism at its worst – temples eroded by too many people climbing over them, forests cut down to make way for ecolodges. Village kids in Nikes leaving their traditional family life to tout hotels or sell drugs.

But there's another side to all this – what looks to the outsider like a culture disappearing often feels to the person living in that culture like progress. And who are we to say that people should stay in their mud huts without electricity while we go home to our plasma screen TVs and microwave dinners?

There are plenty of reasons for the erosion of traditional lifestyles – consumer culture, the lure of big cities, TV and Hollywood to name just a few. Tourism does some terrible stuff, there's no doubt, but managed properly, it can keep cultures alive.

Take backstrap weaving for example. Just about every tourist who comes to Guatemala wants to take a typical fabric home with them. This demand (and the income it generates) means that young people learn to weave, as it offers viable employment. Without the tourists, who knows what they'd be doing for work, or who would be keeping the craft alive.

---

said for the humble abodes of the city's residents, who suffered terribly when the devastating quake of 1976 reduced their homes to rubble.

Weaving

Guatemalans make many traditional handicrafts, both for everyday use and to sell to tourists and collectors. Crafts include basketry, ceramics and wood carving, but the most prominent are weaving, embroidery and other textile arts practiced by Maya women. The beautiful *traje* (traditional clothing) made and worn by local women is one of the most awe-inspiring expressions of Maya culture.

The most arresting feature of these costumes is their highly colorful weaving and embroidery, which makes many garments true works of art. It's the woman's *huipil*, a long, sleeveless tunic, that receives the most painstaking loving care in its creation. Often entire *huipiles* are covered in a multicolored web of stylized animal, human, plant and mythological shapes, which can take months to complete. Each garment identifies the village from which its wearer hails (the Spanish colonists allotted each village a different design in order to distinguish their inhabitants from each other) and within the village style there can be variations according to social status, as well as the creative individual touches that make each garment unique.

Maya men now generally wear dull Western clothing, except in places such as Sololá and Todos Santos Cuchumatán where they still sport colorful *trajes*. For more on the various types of traditional garments, see p138. Materials and techniques are changing, but the pre-Hispanic backstrap loom is still widely used. The warp (long) threads are stretched between two horizontal bars, one of which is fixed to a post or tree, while the other is attached to a strap that goes round the weaver's lower back. The weft (cross) threads are then woven in. Throughout the highlands you can see women weaving in this manner outside the entrance to their homes. Nowadays, some *huipiles* and *fajas* are machine made, as this method is faster and easier than weaving by hand.

Yarn is still hand-spun in many villages. For the well-to-do, silk threads are used to embroider bridal *huipiles* and other important garments. Vegetable dyes are not yet totally out of use, and red dye from cochineal insects and

For an extensive, searchable database of photographs of pre-Columbian ceramics, have a look at www.mayavase.com.

Well-illustrated books on Maya textiles will help you to start identifying the wearers' villages. Two fine works are *Maya of Guatemala – Life and Dress*, by Carmen L Pettersen, and *The Maya Textile Tradition*, edited by Margot Blum Schevill.

natural indigo are employed in several areas. Modern luminescent dyes go down very well with the Maya, who are happily addicted to bright colors, as you will see.

The colorful traditional dress is still generally most in evidence in the highlands, which are heavily populated by Maya, though you will see it in all parts of the country. The variety of techniques, materials, styles and designs is bewildering to the newcomer, but you'll see some of the most colorful, intricate, eye-catching and widely worn designs in Sololá and Santiago Atitlán, near the Lago de Atitlán, Nebaj in the Ixil Triangle, Zunil near Quetzaltenango, and Todos Santos and San Mateo Ixtatán in the Cuchumatanes mountains.

You can learn the art of backstrap weaving at weaving schools in Quetzaltenango, San Pedro La Laguna and other towns – see p315 for details. To see large collections of fine weaving, don't miss the Museo Ixchel in Guatemala City (p71) or the shop Nim Po't in Antigua (p109). If you're interested in buying fabrics straight from the weavers, see the list on p150.

For a wonderful collection of photos of *huipiles* and other Maya textiles, see the website of Nim Po't (www.nimpot.com).

Food & Drink

What you eat in Guatemala will be a mixture of Guatemalan food, which is nutritious and filling without sending your taste buds into ecstasy, and inter-national traveler-and-tourist food, which is available wherever travelers and tourists hang out. Your most satisfying meals in both cases will probably be in smaller eateries where the boss is also the one in the kitchen. Guatemalan cuisine reflects both the old foodstuffs of the Maya (such as corn/maize, beans, squashes, potatoes, avocados, chilies and turkey), and the influence of the Spanish (bread, greater amounts of meat, rice and European vegetables). Modern international cuisine comes in considerable variety in places such as Antigua, Guatemala City, Quetzaltenango and around Lago de Atitlán. In vil-lages and ordinary towns off the tourist trail, food will be strictly Guatemalan.

A woman feeding a fam-ily of eight (not unusual in Guatemala) makes around 170 tortillas a day.

STAPLES & SPECIALTIES
Travelers attempting an Atkins diet may have to put it on hold for the duration. Guatemala is carbohydrate heaven – don't be surprised if your plate comes with rice, potatoes and corn and is served up with a healthy stack of tortillas.

The fundamental staple is indeed the tortilla – a thin round patty of corn dough cooked on a griddle called a *comal*. Tortillas can accompany any meal; if you know Mexican tortillas, you'll find that Guatemalan ones are smaller and a little plumper – except if they appear on a menu under the heading 'Tortillas' (with chicken or meat or eggs etc), when they'll be bigger and perform a function vaguely like a pizza base. Fresh handmade tortillas can be delicious. Fresh machine-made ones are sold at a *tortillería*. The tortillas sold in restaurants are fairly fresh and kept warm in a hot, moist cloth. These are all right, but will eventually become rubbery. Tortillas accompanying meals are unlimited; if you run out, just ask for more.

The second staple is *frijoles* (fri-*hoh*-les), or black beans. These can be eaten boiled, fried, refried, in soups, spread on tortillas or with eggs. *Frijoles* may be served in their own dark sauce, as a runny mass on a plate, or as a thick and almost black paste. No matter how they come, they can be delicious and are always nutritious. The third Maya staple is the squash.

Guatemalans celebrate All Saints' Day (Día de Todos los Santos, Novem-ber 1) by eating *fiambre*, a large salad-type dish made from meats and/or seafood and a huge range of vegetables and herbs, all prepared in a vinegar base.

Bread (*pan*; sold in *panaderías*) replaces tortillas in some tourist restau-rants and for some Guatemalans who prefer not to eat *a la indígena*.

The above staples accompany all sorts of things at meal times. There's always a hot sauce on hand, either bottled or homemade: the extra kick it provides can make the difference between a so-so meal and a tasty one.

On the coast, seafood is the go. Generally, your fish or shrimp will come fried in oil, but for a little more flavor you can always specify *con ajo* (with garlic). These plates come with salad, fries and tortillas. Also good is *caldo de mariscos*, a seafood stew that generally contains fish, shrimp and mussels.

THE PEOPLE OF MAIZE
The Maya refer to themselves as 'true people' and consider themselves literally of a different flesh from those who do not eat maize. Traditionalist mothers in the highlands place an ear of maize into the palm of newborns, and eat only dishes made from maize while breastfeeding to ensure that the child grows 'true flesh.'

No Maya raised in the traditional way would eat a meal that didn't include maize. Women do not let grains of maize fall on the ground or into an open fire. If it happens accidentally, the woman will gently pick up the grains and apologize to them.

Be careful with salads and fruit: if they have been washed in dodgy water or cut with a dirty knife, they can cause you problems. Salads are so common that it can be hard *not* to eat them. If the establishment you're eating in impresses with its cleanliness, the salad is likely to be safe.

Breakfast

Desayuno chapín (Guatemalan breakfast) is a large affair involving (at least) eggs, beans, fried plantains, tortillas and coffee. This will be on offer in any *comedor* (basic eatery). It may be augmented with rice, cheese or *mosh,* an oatmeal/porridge concoction. Scrambled eggs are often made with chopped tomatoes and onions.

Anywhere tourists go, you'll also find a range of other breakfasts on offer, from light continental-style affairs to US-style bacon, eggs, *panqueques* (pancakes), cereals, fruit juice and coffee. Breakfast is usually eaten between 6am and 10am.

Food Culture in Central America is much more than a simple cookbook. Written by anthropologist Michael R McDonald, it examines almost every conceivable aspect of food in Central America.

Lunch

This is the biggest meal of the day and is eaten between noon and 2pm. Eateries usually offer a fixed-price meal of several courses called an *almuerzo* or *menú del día,* which may include from one to four courses and is usually great value. A simple *almuerzo* may consist of soup and a main course featuring meat with rice or potatoes and a little salad or vegetables, or just a *plato típico:* meat or chicken, rice, beans, cheese, salad and tortillas. More expensive versions may have a fancy soup or *ceviche* (seafood marinated in lemon juice), a choice of main course such as steak or fish, salad, dessert and coffee. You can also order à la carte from the restaurant's menu, but it will be more expensive.

For classic Guatemalan recipes collected by a French-trained chef, try tracking down a copy of Favorite Recipes from Guatemala by Laura Lynn Woodward.

Dinner & Supper

La cena is, for Guatemalans, a lighter version of lunch, usually eaten between 7pm and 9pm. Even in cities, few restaurants will serve you after 10pm. In rural areas, sit down no later than 8pm to avoid disappointment. In local and village eateries supper may be the same as breakfast: eggs, beans and plantains. In restaurants catering to tourists, dinner might be anything from pepper steak to vegetarian Thai curry.

DRINKS
Coffee, Tea & Chocolate

While Guatemala grows some of the world's richest coffee, a good cup is only generally available in top-end and (some) tourist restaurants and cafes,

---

TRAVEL YOUR TASTE BUDS

Guatemala's most sensational flavors can be sampled on the Caribbean coast where the specialty is *tapado,* a mouthwatering casserole of seafood, plantain, coconut milk, spices and a few vegetables. Yummmmm!

Less tongue-tingling but filling and warming on chilly mountain mornings is *mosh,* a breakfast dish that sounds just like what it is, an oatmeal/porridge that ranges from sloppy to glutinous.

More flavorsome, and found widely around the country, is *pepián* – chicken or turkey in a spicy sesame-seed-and-tomato sauce. Keep your fingers crossed that the bird under the sauce has some flesh on it. *Jocón* is a green stew of chicken or pork with green vegetables and herbs.

In Cobán and the Alta Verapaz department, try *kac-cik* (kak-ik or sack'ik), a turkey soup/stew with ingredients such as pepper (capsicum), garlic, tomato and chili.

In the Ixil Triangle around Nebaj the local favorite is *boxbol* – maize dough and chopped meat or chicken, wrapped tightly in leaves of the *güisquil* squash and boiled. It's served with salsa.

ONES TO AVOID

Guatemalans, particularly in El Petén, eat a lot of wild game, much of which ends up on the menu at restaurants. You may come across armadillo, *venado* (venison), *paca* or *tepescuintle* (agouti), *tortuga* or *caguama* (turtle), and iguana (lizard). Don't order them: they may well be endangered species.

Down on the coast, a local favorite is *sopa de tortuga* (turtle soup). The same applies here – no matter how tasty people say it is, you're eating something into extinction.

---

because most of the quality beans are exported. Guatemalans tend to drink weak percolated or instant coffee with plenty of sugar. Sometimes sugar is added before it reaches the table, so make sure you specify in advance if you want it 'without sugar' *(sin azúcar)*. Black tea *(té negro)*, usually made from bags, can be disappointing. Herbal teas are much better. Chamomile tea *(té de manzanilla)*, common on restaurant and cafe menus, is a good remedy for a queasy gut.

Hot chocolate or cocoa was the royal stimulant during the Classic period of Maya civilization, being drunk on ceremonial occasions by the kings and nobility. Their version was unsweetened and dreadfully bitter. Today it's sweetened and, if less authentic, at least more palatable. Hot chocolate can be ordered *simple* (with water) or *con leche* (with milk).

Juices & Shakes

Fresh fruit and vegetable juices *(jugos)*, shakes *(licuados)* and long, cool, fruit-flavored water drinks *(aguas de frutas)* are wildly popular. Many cafes and eateries offer them and almost every village market and bus station has a stand with a battalion of blenders. The basic *licuado* is a blend of fruit or juice with water and sugar. A *licuado con leche* uses milk instead of water.

Limonada is a delicious thirst-quencher made with lime juice, water and sugar. Try a *limonada con soda*, which adds a fizzy dimension, and you may have a new drink of choice. *Naranjada* is the same thing made with orange juice.

On the coast, the most refreshing nonalcoholic option is a green coconut – you'll see them piled up on the roadside. The vendor simply slices the top off with a machete and sticks a straw in. If you've never drunk green coconut juice, you *have* to give it a go – it's delicious!

Alcoholic Drinks

Breweries were established in Guatemala by German immigrants in the late 19th century, but they didn't bring a heap of flavor with them. The two most widely distributed beers are Gallo (rooster; pronounced 'gah-yoh') and Cabro. The distribution prize goes to Gallo – you'll find it everywhere – but Cabro is darker and more flavorful. Moza is the darkest local beer, but its distribution is limited. Brahva, the Guatemalan-produced version of the Brazilian Brahma beer, is preferred by many foreigners (and some locals) and is becoming more widely available, as are 'boutique' imported beers such as Heineken and Quilmes. Up north, Mexican beers, especially Tecate, are more readily available and sometimes cheaper than domestic brands.

Rum *(ron)* is one of Guatemala's favorite strong drinks, and though most is cheap in price and taste, some local products are exceptionally fine. Zacapa Centenario is a smooth, aged Guatemalan rum made in Zacapa. It should be sipped slowly and neat, like fine cognac. Ron Botrán Añejo, another dark rum, is also good. Cheaper rums such as Venado are often mixed with soft drinks to make potent but cooling drinks such as the *Cuba libre*, a combination of rum and Coke.

Hibiscus *(jamaica;* pronounced 'hah-*my*-cah') flowers are the basis of two refreshing drinks. *Agua de jamaica* is a long, cool thirst-quencher. *Té de rosa de jamaica* is a tasty herbal tea.

The History of Coffee in Guatemala by Regina Wagner is a thorough investigation of one of the country's most important crops. Text, tables and graphs are accompanied by some wonderful old photographs.

Aguardiente is a sugarcane firewater that flows in cantinas and on the streets. Look for the signs advertising Quetzalteca Especial. This is the *aguardiente* of choice.

Ponche is a potent potable made from pineapple (or coconut) juice and rum and served hot.

Water & Soft Drinks

Purified water *(agua pura)* is widely available in hotels, shops and restaurants (see p338). Salvavidas is a universally trusted brand. You can order safe-to-drink carbonated water by saying *'soda.'*

Soft drinks are known as *aguas* (waters). If you want straight unflavored water, ask for *'agua pura.'*

WHERE TO EAT & DRINK

A *comedor* is a basic, no-fuss eatery serving straightforward local food in plain surroundings for low prices. If the place looks clean and busy, it will likely be hygienic and good value; the best *comedor* food is equivalent to good home cooking. There is unlikely to be a printed or written menu or even much choice: the staple fare is set breakfasts, set lunches and set suppers, each for around Q20 to Q40. The cheapest *comedores* of all are tables and benches set up in markets, with the cooking done on the spot.

A *restaurante* is at least a little fancier than a *comedor*. It will have pretensions (at least) to decor, staff might wear some kind of uniform, and there'll be a menu. A typical set meal in a decent restaurant costs Q30 to Q60, à la carte a little more. In Guatemala City, Antigua, Quetzaltenango and around Lago de Atitlán you can eat at specialist and ethnic restaurants and some quite classy, moderately expensive establishments. But even in the capital's most exclusive spots you'll find it hard to leave more than Q200 lighter.

Comedores and *restaurantes* typically open from 7am to 9pm, but the hours can vary by up to a couple of hours either way. Places close earlier in small towns and villages, later in cities and tourist destinations. A few fancier city places may not open until 11am or noon and close from 3pm to 6pm. If a restaurant has a closing day, it is usually Sunday, with Antigua restaurants being the exception – if they close it will usually be Monday or Tuesday.

A *café* or *cafetería* will offer coffee and usually food of some kind. This might be light snacks or it might be a wider range akin to a restaurant. A

Guatemala claims two rather dubious contributions to the culinary world: both instant coffee and the McDonald's Happy Meal were invented here.

Guatemala's first winery, Chateau de Fay, started bottling in 2007. It's open for visits and tastings – see www.chateaudefay vineyards.com for more details.

Always tip, around 10%: the wages of the people who cook and serve your food are often pitifully low.

THE BIG NIGHT OUT

Guatemalans love going out and you shouldn't have any trouble finding a place to grab a beer anywhere you go in the country. The only question remains where. Generally speaking, you can go anywhere without too much trouble, but you should be aware that there are a couple of significant differences in the way that nightspots get named here.

Cantinas, for example, are generally the roughest of the drinking establishments – this is where you go to get falling down drunk, and listen to *ranchera* (Mexican cowboy) music. It's an all-male atmosphere, and while women are most certainly welcome, they won't feel comfortable.

Bars are a tricky one. In big cities, a bar can be exactly what we understand it to be – a place with music, mixed drinks and a mixed crowd. In smaller towns, however, a bar generally has the same atmosphere as a cantina, except it doubles as a brothel.

Nightclubs (or, as most of these places would have it, '*Nigthclubs*') are not at all the same here as they are back home. These places are basically strip joints, with prostitutes working.

Discotecas are more what we think of when we say nightclub. They have big dance floors, dress codes and sometimes charge an entry fee.

A CHICKEN'S TALE

No matter where you go or what you do in Guatemala, there's one thing that you're pretty much guaranteed to see: a Pollo Campero outlet. Campero (as it's known) is one of the few great Guatemalan success stories. What started out as a simple fried chicken restaurant back in 1971 had become a chain of Central American outlets by the mid '70s and has grown today to be a chain of over 300 restaurants worldwide, with an estimated 80 million customers chomping down in 13 countries, including such unlikely places as China, Indonesia, India, Andorra and Bahrain.

Even so, US-bound Central Americans like to take the stuff from the source. If you're flying that way, no doubt you'll see at least some of your fellow passengers with a good-sized stash of Campero in their hand luggage. It's got to the point where more than one airline has requested that Campero outlets in Central American airports provide smell free packaging to stop the odor from permeating its planes.

The obvious parallel to Campero would be US-based KFC, but Campero's chicken is spicier and a tad less greasy. Its Guatemalan restaurants also feature table service, along with real cutlery and plates. Still – the Colonel's got Guatemala in his sights. After a failed opening back in the '70s, KFC recently opened an outlet in Guatemala City's Zona 9. Queues were reminiscent of (but nowhere near equal to) Campero's first opening on US soil, in Los Angeles in 2002, where the 90-seat restaurant served 300,000 people in its first week of operation.

Let the juicy, tender, crispy marketing war commence.

pastelería is a cake shop, and often it will provide tables and chairs where you can sit down and enjoy its baked goods with a drink.

Guatemala has plenty of fast-food restaurants, but most ubiquitous is the local chicken franchise, Pollo Campero (see boxed text, above).

Bars are open long hours, typically from 10am or 11am to 10pm or 11pm. If they have a closing day, it's usually Sunday. Officially, no alcohol may be served in Guatemala after 1am, but the smaller the town (and the lower the police presence), the less likely this rule is adhered to.

Quick Eats

Bus snacks can become an important part of your Guatemalan diet, as long bus rides with early departures are not uncommon. Women and girls board the bus proclaiming '¡Hay comida!' ('I've got food!'). This is usually a small meal of tortillas smeared with beans, accompanied by a piece of chicken or a hard-boiled egg. Other snacks include fried plantains, ice cream, peanuts, *chocobananos* (chocolate-covered bananas), *hocotes* (a tropical fruit eaten with salt, lime and nutmeg) and *chuchitos* (small parcels of corn dough filled with meat or beans and steamed inside a corn husk). *Elotes* are grilled ears of corn on the cob eaten with salt and lime.

Much the same cheap fare is doled out at street stalls around bus stations, markets, street corners and so on. It's rare for any of these items to cost as much as Q10, and if you're on a tight budget, you may do quite a lot of your eating at street stalls. On buses and streets alike, take a good look at the cleanliness of the vendor and stall: this is a good indication of how hygienic the food will be.

VEGETARIANS & VEGANS

Given that meat is a bit of a luxury for many Guatemalans, it's not too hard to get by without it. The basic Maya combination of tortillas, beans and vegetables is fairly nutritious. If you request a set lunch *(plato típico)* without meat *(sin carne)* at a *comedor* you'll still get soup, rice, beans, cheese, salad and tortillas. Indeed some restaurants offer just this combination of items under the name *plato vegetariano*. If you eat eggs, dairy products or fish, you can eat more or less the same breakfast as anyone else, and your options for other

For culinary events, a few recipes and other gastronomical details, have a look at www.chefsdeguatemala.com

The biggest internet collection of Guatemalan recipes is good for those with some Spanish language skills – see www.quetzalnet.com/recetas.

meals increase greatly. In most places that travelers go, many restaurants – especially ethnic ones – have items without meat on the menu. There are even a few dedicated vegetarian restaurants in cities and tourist haunts. Chinese restaurants are also a good bet for vegetarian food. Plenty of fruit, vegetables and nuts are always available in markets.

EAT YOUR WORDS

Communicating successfully with restaurant staff is halfway to eating well. For further guidance on pronouncing Spanish words, see p339.

Food Glossary

a la parrilla	a la pa·*ree*·ya	grilled, perhaps over charcoal
a la plancha	a la *plan*·cha	grilled on a hotplate
aguacate	a·gwa·*ka*·te	avocado
ajo	*a*·kho	garlic
almuerzo	al·*mwer*·so	lunch
antojitos	an·to·*khee*·tos	snacks (literally 'little whims')
arroz	*a*·ros	rice
atole	a·*to*·le	a hot gruel made with maize, milk, cinnamon and sugar
aves	*a*·ves	poultry
azúcar	a·*soo*·kar	sugar
banano	ba·*na*·no	banana
bebida	be·*bee*·da	drink
bistec or *bistec de res*	*bees*·tek/*bees*·tek de res	beefsteak
café (negro/con leche)	ka·*fe* (*ne*·gro/kon *le*·che)	coffee (black/with milk)
calabaza	ka·la·*ba*·sa	squash, marrow or pumpkin
caldo	*kal*·do	broth, often meat-based
camarones	ka·ma·*ro*·nes	shrimps
camarones gigantes	ka·ma·*ro*·nes khee·*gan*·tes	jumbo shrimp
carne	*kar*·ne	meat
carne asada	*kar*·ne a·*sa*·da	grilled beef
cebolla	se·*bo*·ya	onion
cerveza	ser·*ve*·sa	beer
ceviche	se·*vee*·che	raw seafood marinated in lime juice and mixed with onions, chilies, garlic, tomatoes and cilantro (coriander)
coco	*ko*·ko	coconut
chicharrón	chee·cha·*ron*	pork crackling
chile relleno	*chee*·le re·*ye*·no	bell pepper stuffed with cheese, meat, rice or other foods, dipped in egg whites, fried and baked in sauce
chuchito	choo·*chee*·to	small *tamal*
chuletas (de puerco)	choo·*le*·tas (de *pwer*·ko)	(pork) chops
churrasco	choo·*ras*·ko	slab of thin grilled meat
cuchara	koo·*cha*·ra	spoon
cuchillo	koo·*chee*·yo	knife
ensalada	en·sa·*la*·da	salad
filete de pescado	fee·*le*·te de pes·*ka*·do	fish fillet
flan	flan	custard, crème caramel
fresas	*fre*·sas	strawberries
frijoles	free·*kho*·les	black beans
frutas	*froo*·tas	fruits
güisquil	gwees·*keel*	type of squash
hamburguesa	am·boor·*ge*·sa	hamburger
helado	e·*la*·do	ice cream
huevos fritos/revueltos	*we*·vos *free*·tos/re·*vwel*·tos	fried/scrambled eggs
jamón	kha·*mon*	ham

jícama	khee·ka·ma	a popular root vegetable resembling a potato crossed with an apple
jocón	kho·kon	green stew of chicken or pork with green vegetables and herbs
leche	le·che	milk
lechuga	le·choo·ga	lettuce
legumbres	le·goom·bres	root vegetables
licuado	lee·kwa·do	milkshake made with fresh fruit, sugar and milk or water
limón	lee·mon	lemon
limonada	lee·mo·na·da	drink made from lemon juice
mantequilla	man·te·kee·yah	butter
margarina	mar·ga·ree·na	margarine
mariscos	ma·rees·kos	seafood
mesa	me·sa	table
melocotón	me·lo·ko·ton	peach
miel	myel	honey
mosh	mosh	oatmeal/porridge
naranja	na·ran·kha	orange
naranjada	na·ran·kha·da	like a limonada but made with oranges
pacaya	pa·ka·ya	a squashlike staple
papa	pa·pa	potato
papaya	pa·pa·ya	pawpaw
pastel	pas·tel	cake
pato	pa·to	duck
pavo	pa·vo	turkey
pepián	pe·pee·an	chicken and vegetables in a piquant sesame and pumpkin seed sauce
pescado (al mojo de ajo)	pes·ka·do (al mo·kho de a·kho)	fish (fried in butter and garlic)
piña	pee·nya	pineapple
pimienta	pee·myen·ta	pepper (black)
plátano	pla·ta·no	plantain (green banana), edible when cooked (usually fried)
plato	pla·to	plate
plato típico	pla·to tee·pee·ko	set meal
pollo (asado/frito)	po·yo (a·sa·do/free·to)	(grilled/fried) chicken
postre	pos·tre	dessert
propina	pro·pee·na	tip
puerco	pwer·ko	pork
puyaso	poo·ya·so	a choice cut of steak
queso	ke·so	cheese
sal	sal	salt
salchicha	sal·chee·cha	sausage
sopa	so·pa	soup
tamal	ta·mal	corn dough stuffed with meat, beans, chilies or nothing at all, wrapped in banana leaf or corn husks and steamed
tapado	ta·pa·do	a seafood, coconut milk and plantain casserole
tarta	tar·ta	cake
taza	ta·sa	cup
tenedor	te·ne·dor	fork
tocino	to·see·no	bacon
tomate	to·ma·te	tomato
vaso	va·so	glass
verduras	ver·doo·ras	green vegetables
zanahoria	sa·na·o·rya	carrot

Environment

THE LAND

Guatemala covers an area of 109,000 sq km – a little less than the US state of Louisiana, a little more than England. Geologically, most of the country lies atop the North American tectonic plate, but this abuts the Cocos plate along Guatemala's Pacific coast and the Caribbean plate in the far south of the country. When any of these plates gets frisky, earthquakes and volcanic eruptions ensue. Hence the major quakes of 1773, 1917 and 1976 and the spectacular chain of 30 volcanoes – some of them active – running parallel to the Pacific coast from the Mexican border to the Salvadoran border. North of the volcanic chain rises the Cuchumatanes range.

North of Guatemala City, the highlands of Alta Verapaz gradually decline to the lowland of El Petén, occupying northern Guatemala. El Petén is hot and humid or hot and dry, depending on the season. Central America's largest tracts of virgin rainforest straddle El Petén's borders with Mexico and Belize, although this may cease to be true if conservation efforts are not successful.

Northeast of Guatemala City, the valley of the Río Motagua (dry in some areas, moist in others) runs down to Guatemala's short, very hot Caribbean coast. Bananas and sugarcane thrive in the Motagua valley.

Between the volcanic chain and the Pacific Ocean is the Pacific Slope, with rich coffee, cotton, rubber, fruit and sugar plantations, cattle ranches, beaches of black volcanic sand and a sweltering climate.

Guatemala's unique geology also includes tremendous systems of caves. Water coursing for eons over a limestone base created aquifers and conduits that eventually gave way to subterranean caves, rivers and sinkholes when the surface water drained into underground caverns and streams. This type of terrain (known as karst) is found throughout the Verapaces region and makes Guatemala a killer spelunking destination.

WILDLIFE

Guatemala's natural beauty, from volcanoes and lakes to jungles and wetlands, is one of its great attractions. With its 19 different ecosystems, the variety of fauna and flora is great – and if you know where to go, opportunities for seeing exciting species are plentiful.

Animals

Estimates point to 250 species of mammals, 600 species of birds, 200 species of reptiles and amphibians and many species of butterflies and other insects.

The national bird, the resplendent quetzal (for which the national currency is named) is small but exceptionally beautiful. The male sports a bright-red breast, brilliant blue-green neck, head, back and wings, and a blue-green tail several times as long as the body, which stands only around 15cm tall. The female has far duller plumage. The quetzal's main habitat is the cloud forests of Alta Verapaz. For more on the quetzal, see p212.

Exotic birds of the lowland jungles include toucans, macaws and parrots. If you visit Tikal, you can't miss the ocellated turkey, also called the Petén turkey, a large, multicolored bird reminiscent of a peacock. Tikal is an all-round wildlife hot spot: you stand a good chance of spotting howler and spider monkeys, coatis (locally called *pisotes*) and other mammals, plus toucans, parrots and many other birds. Some 300 endemic and migratory bird species have been recorded at Tikal, among them nine hummingbirds and

Tajumulco (4220m), west of Quetzaltenango, is the highest peak in Central America. La Torre (3837m), north of Huehuetenango, is the highest nonvolcanic peak in Central America.

Guatemala sits at the confluence of three tectonic plates – hence its 30 volcanoes and frequent earthquakes.

Timber, Tourists, and Temples, edited by Richard Primack and others, brings together experts on the forests of Guatemala, Mexico and Belize for an in-depth look at the problems of balancing conservation with local people's aspirations.

four trogons. Good areas for sighting waterfowl – including the jabiru stork, the biggest flying bird in the western hemisphere – are Laguna Petexbatún and the lakes near Yaxhá ruins, both in El Petén, and the Río Dulce between the Lago de Izabal and Lívingston.

Guatemala's forests still host many mammal and reptile species. Petén residents include jaguars, ocelots, pumas, two species of peccary, opossums, tapirs, kinkajous, agoutis (*tepescuintles;* rodents 60cm to 70cm long), white-tailed and red brocket deer, and armadillos. Guatemala is home to at least five species of sea turtle (the loggerhead, hawksbill and green ridley on the Caribbean coast, and the leatherback and olive ridley on the Pacific) and at least two species of crocodile (one found in El Petén, the other in the Río Dulce). Manatees (see p257) exist in the Río Dulce, though they're notoriously hard to spot.

ENDANGERED SPECIES

Guatemala's wildlife faces two major threats. The first is the loss of habitat, as more land is turned over to farming. The second threat is hunting, which is mostly done for food, but also takes place for collection of skins and other products, as is the case for deer, turtles and some reptiles. Endangered mammals include jaguars, howler monkeys, manatees, several species of mice and bats, and the Guatemalan vole.

More than 25 bird species native to the region are listed as endangered, including the Atitlán grebe (found only in Guatemala) and the national bird, the resplendent quetzal. Of the reptiles, almost all of those listed above are disappearing, as well as Morelet's crocodile.

Plants

Guatemala has more than 8000 species of plants in 19 different ecosystems ranging from mangrove forests and wetlands on both coasts to the tropical rainforest of El Petén and the pine forests, open grasslands and cloud forests of the mountains. The cloud forests, with their epiphytes, bromeliads and dangling old-man's-beard, are most abundant in Alta Verapaz department. Trees of El Petén include the sapodilla, wild rubber trees, mahogany, several useful palms and the ceiba (Guatemala's national tree for its manifold symbolism to the Maya, also called the kapok or silk-cotton tree in English).

The national flower, the *monja blanca* (white nun orchid), is said to have been picked so much that it's now rarely seen in the wild; nevertheless, with 550 species of orchid (one third of them endemic to Guatemala), you shouldn't have any trouble spotting some. If you're interested in orchids, be sure to visit the Vivero Verapaz orchid nursery (p215) at Cobán and try to land in town for their annual orchid festival, held every December.

Domesticated plants, of course, contribute at least as much to the landscape as wild ones. The *milpa* (maize field) is the backbone of agricultural subsistence everywhere. *Milpas* are, however, usually cleared by the slash-and-burn method, which is a major factor in the diminution of Guatemala's forests. Cities such as Antigua become glorious with the lilac blooms of jacaranda trees in the early months of the year.

Les D Beletsky's *Belize & Northern Guatemala: The Ecotravellers' Wildlife Guide* is a comprehensive, all-in-one guide to flora and fauna in the region. The book features hundreds of illustrations and photos and some welcome splashes of humor.

Bird lovers must get hold of either *The Birds of Tikal: An Annotated Checklist*, by Randell A Beavers, or *The Birds of Tikal*, by Frank B Smythe. If you can't find them elsewhere, at least one should be on sale at Tikal itself, and both are useful much further afield.

SNAKE IN THE GRASS

The Central American or common lancehead, also called the fer-de-lance (locally known as *barba amarilla*, 'yellow beard') is a highly poisonous viper with a diamond-patterned back and an arrow-shaped head. The *cascabel* (tropical rattlesnake) is the most poisonous of all rattlers. Both inhabit jungles and savanna.

PARKS & PROTECTED AREAS

Guatemala has more than 90 protected areas, including *reservas de biosfera* (biosphere reserves), *parques nacionales* (national parks), *biotopos protegidos* (protected biotopes), *refugios de vida silvestre* (wildlife refuges) and *reservas naturales privadas* (private nature reserves). Even though some areas are contained within other, larger ones, they amount to 28% of the national territory. Tikal National Park is the only such area on the Unesco World Heritage list in Guatemala, and owes half its listing to the archaeological site found within.

Many of the protected areas are remote and hard to access for the independent traveler; the table (p60) shows those that are easiest to reach and/or most interesting to visitors (but excludes volcanoes, nearly all of which are protected, and areas of mainly archaeological interest).

ENVIRONMENTAL ISSUES

Environmental consciousness is not enormously developed in Guatemala, as the vast amounts of garbage strewn across the country and the choking clouds of diesel gas pumped out by its buses and trucks will quickly tell you. Despite the impressive list of parks and protected areas, genuine protection for those areas is harder to achieve, partly because of official collusion to ignore the regulations and partly because of pressure from poor Guatemalans in need of land.

Guatemala's popularity as a tourist destination leads to a few environmental problems – the question of sewerage and trash disposal around Lago de Atitlán being a major one (see p133 for more on Atitlán's environmental challenges), and some inappropriate development in the rainforests of El Petén being another. Infrastructure development in Guatemala is moving at such a pace, though, that these problems seem minor compared to some of the other challenges that environmentalists face.

Deforestation is a problem in many areas, especially El Petén, where jungle is being felled at an alarming rate not just for timber but also to make way for cattle ranches, oil pipelines, clandestine airstrips, new settlements and new maize fields cleared using the slash-and-burn method.

In 2009 a drought associated with the climactic phenomenon known as El Niño hit most of Central America, demonstrating just how precarious the existence of subsistence farmers here is. The huge majority of small farms don't use irrigation – instead they plant their crops according to the seasons, timed so that young plants will be nourished by the intense, regular downpours of the wet season.

When the rains didn't come, many crops failed and a food crisis loomed as families ate into their reserves without having any certainty they'd be able to replenish them.

Oil exploration is a concern all over the country – the Guatemalans are scrambling to start drilling in El Petén, as the Mexicans have been doing for years, tapping into a vast subterranean reserve that runs across the border. In his short stint in office, then-president Alfonso Portillo came up with the crazy idea of drilling for oil in the middle of Lago de Izabal. The plan was only shelved after massive outcry from international and local environmental agencies and some not too subtle pressure from Guatemala's trading partners. It's a project that's gone but unfortunately not forgotten.

Large-scale infrastructure projects are being announced with frightening regularity, often in environmentally sensitive areas. The most controversial of these is called the Northern Transversal, a strip of highway consolidating existing roads that will stretch from the Mexican border at Gracias a Dios, pass Playa Grande and eventually connect up to Modesto Méndez, where a new border crossing for Belize is planned. Concerns with the project are

To see rare scarlet macaws in the wild, the place to head is La Ruta Guacamaya (the Scarlet Macaw Trail) of El Perú ruins in El Petén (p306).

Jonathon Maslow's *Bird of Life, Bird of Death* begins as a story about a naturalist's search for the quetzal, but quickly develops into a terrifying portrait of Guatemala during the civil war.

For a good introduction to the many community-based tourism initiatives around the country, click on the Guatemala link at www.redturs.org.

many, as the road passes through sites of archaeological, environmental and cultural significance. Local environmental groups fear that the real reason for its construction is to facilitate oil exploration in the Ixcán. One component of the plan is the construction of the Xalalá dam, a hydroelectric project. The construction will displace local communities, affect water quality downstream and alter the ecology of the area through habitat loss.

At the time of writing, the project was stalled, due to problems with the tendering process and a constitutional challenge by environmental groups

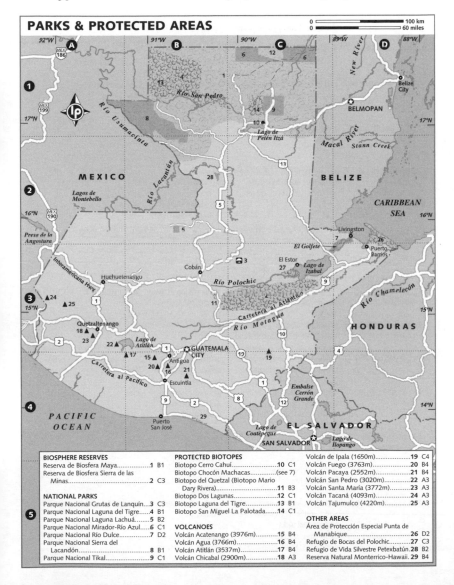

PARKS & PROTECTED AREAS

BIOSPHERE RESERVES
Reserva de Biosfera Maya.................1 B1
Reserva de Biosfera Sierra de las
  Minas..2 C3

NATIONAL PARKS
Parque Nacional Grutas de Lanquín...3 C3
Parque Nacional Laguna del Tigre......4 B1
Parque Nacional Laguna Lachuá.........5 B2
Parque Nacional Mirador-Río Azul.....6 C1
Parque Nacional Río Dulce...............7 D2
Parque Nacional Sierra del
  Lacandón......................................8 B1
Parque Nacional Tikal......................9 C1

PROTECTED BIOTOPES
Biotopo Cerro Cahuí.......................10 C1
Biotopo Chocón Machacas..............(see 7)
Biotopo del Quetzal (Biotopo Mario
  Dary Rivera)................................11 B3
Biotopo Dos Lagunas.....................12 C1
Biotopo Laguna del Tigre................13 B1
Biotopo San Miguel La Palotada......14 C1

VOLCANOES
Volcán Acatenango (3976m)...........15 B4
Volcán Agua (3766m)....................16 B4
Volcán Atitlán (3537m)..................17 B4
Volcán Chicabal (2900m)................18 A3

Volcán de Ipala (1650m)................19 C4
Volcán Fuego (3763m)...................20 B4
Volcán Pacaya (2552m)..................21 B4
Volcán San Pedro (3020m).............22 A3
Volcán Santa María (3772m)...........23 A3
Volcán Tacaná (4093m)..................24 A3
Volcán Tajumulco (4220m).............25 A3

OTHER AREAS
Área de Protección Especial Punta de
  Manabique...................................26 D2
Refugio de Bocas del Polochic.........27 C3
Refugio de Vida Silvestre Petexbatún.28 B2
Reserva Natural Monterrico-Hawaii..29 B4

PARKS & PROTECTED AREAS

Protected Area	Features	Activities	Best Time to Visit	Page
Área de Protección Especial Punta de Manabique	large Caribbean wetland reserve; beaches, mangroves, lagoons, birds, crocodiles, possible manatee sightings	boat trips, wildlife observation, fishing, beach	any	p260
Biotopo Cerro Cahuí	forest reserve beside Lago de Petén Itzá; Petén wildlife including monkeys	walking trails	any	p284
Biotopo del Quetzal (Biotopo Mario Dary Rivera)	easy-access cloud forest reserve; howler monkeys, birds	nature trails, bird-watching, possible quetzal sightings	any	p211
Biotopo San Miguel La Palotada	within Reserva de Biosfera Maya, adjoins Parque Nacional Tikal; dense Petén forest with millions of bats	jungle walks, visits to El Zotz archaeological site and bat caves	any, drier November-May	p307
Parque Nacional Grutas de Lanquín	large cave system 61km from Cobán	seeing bats; don't miss the nearby Semuc Champey lagoons and waterfalls	any	p221
Parque Nacional Laguna del Tigre	remote, large park within Reserva de Biosfera Maya; freshwater wetlands, Petén flora and fauna	spotting wildlife including scarlet macaws, monkeys, crocodiles; visiting El Perú archaeological site; volunteer opportunities at Las Guacamayas biological station	any, drier November-May	p306
Parque Nacional Laguna Lachuá	circular, jungle-surrounded, turquoise lake, 220m deep; many fish, occasional jaguars and tapir	camping, swimming	any	p224
Parque Nacional Mirador–Río Azul	national park within Reserva de Biosfera Maya; Petén flora and fauna	jungle treks to El Mirador archaeological site	any, drier November-May	p308
Parque Nacional Río Dulce	beautiful jungle-lined lower Río Dulce between Lago de Izabal and the Caribbean; manatee refuge	boat trips	any	p264
Parque Nacional Tikal	diverse jungle wildlife among Guatemala's most magnificent Maya ruins	wildlife spotting, seeing spectacular Maya city	any, drier November-May	p289
Refugio de Bocas del Polochic	delta of Río Polochic at western end of Lago de Izabal; Guatemala's second-largest freshwater wetlands	bird-watching (more than 300 species), howler monkey observation	any	p256
Refugio de Vida Silvestre Petexbatún	lake near Sayaxché; water birds	boat trips, fishing, visiting several archaeological sites	any	p304
Reserva Natural Monterrico-Hawaii	Pacific beaches and wetlands; birdlife, turtles	boat tours, bird-watching and turtle watching	June-November (turtle nesting)	p201
Reserva de Biosfera Maya	vast 21,000 sq km area stretching across northern Petén; includes four national parks	jungle treks, wildlife spotting	any, drier November-May	p307
Reserva de Biosfera Sierra de las Minas	cloud-forest reserve of great biodiversity; key quetzal habitat	hiking, wildlife spotting	any	p256

SAVING THE RAINFOREST

The Reserva de Biosfera Maya, in northern Guatemala, along with the adjoining Calakmul reserve in southern Mexico, comprises 3.9 million acres of tropical forest – the second-largest such area in the Americas, after the Amazon.

The forest is shrinking daily, under the strain of human immigration from other parts of Guatemala, illegal logging, oil exploration and the spread of the agricultural frontier.

Wildlife here is particularly vulnerable, too – a victim of habitat loss, unsustainable hunting, and capture for the illegal pet trade. Species that were once abundant, such as scarlet macaws, Baird's tapirs, jaguars, giant anteaters and the harpy eagle, are becoming rare. Some are presumed extinct.

Some well-established organizations in El Petén accept volunteers to help out with conservation efforts:

Arcas (www.arcasguatemala.com) This animal rescue center has a cooperative agreement with the Guatemalan government and is recognized as the official destination for all confiscated wildlife taken from smugglers in the Reserva de Biosfera Maya.

Rainforest Alliance (www.rainforest-alliance.org) An organization that works to promote the sustainable use of the forest and green products.

The Equilibrium Fund (www.theequilibriumfund.org) An alliance of US, Guatemalan and Nicaraguan professionals who work with indigenous and marginalized women to produce food, earn income and raise healthy families without destroying their environment. They focus on the uses and processing techniques for the Maya nut *(Brosimum alicastrum)*, a nutritious and easy-to-harvest rainforest tree food that was once abundant and is now threatened with extinction by logging and land conversion for pasture and agriculture.

on the grounds that the new highway will pass through the Parque Nacional Laguna Lachuá.

Transnational mining companies are moving in, most notably in San Marcos in the western highlands and the Sierra de las Minas in the southeast. Without the proper community consultation called for by law, the government has granted these companies license to operate open-cut mines in search of silver and gold. Chemical runoff, deforestation, eviction of local communities and water pollution are the main issues here. Police have been used to forcibly evict residents and quash community groups' peaceful protests. Environmentalists saw some joy in 2010 when the Canadian Supreme Court ordered that mining companies operating in Guatemala conduct thorough environmental impact studies.

On the Pacific side of the country, where most of the population of Guatemala lives, the land is mostly agricultural or given over to industrial interests. The remaining forests in the Pacific coastal and highland areas are not long for this world, as local communities cut down the remaining trees for heating and cooking.

Nevertheless, a number of Guatemalan organizations are doing valiant work to protect their country's environment and biodiversity. The following are good sources of information for finding out more about Guatemala's natural and protected areas:

Alianza Verde (www.alianzaverde.org, in Spanish; Parque Central, Flores, Petén) Association of organizations, businesses and people involved in conservation and tourism in El Petén; provides information services such as *Destination Petén* magazine, and Cincap, the Centro de Información Sobre la Naturaleza, Cultura y Artesanía de Petén, in Flores.

Arcas (Asociación de Rescate y Conservación de Vida Silvestre; ☎ 7830-1374; www.arcasguatemala. com; Km 30, Calle Hillary, Lote 6, Casa Villa Conchita, San Lucas Sacatepéquez, Guatemala) NGO working with volunteers in sea turtle conservation and rehabilitation of Petén wildlife (see also p202 and p282).

Asociación Ak' Tenamit (www.aktenamit.org) Guatemala City (off Map p66; ☎ 2254-1560; 11a Av A 9-39, Zona 2); Río Dulce (☎ 5908-3392) Maya-run NGO working to reduce poverty and promote conservation and ecotourism in the rainforests of eastern Guatemala.

Ecotravels in Guatemala (www.planeta.com/guatemala.html) has arresting articles, good reference material and numerous links.

Find out about the Yaxhá Private Reserve and what you can do to protect it at www.yaxhanatural.org.

DON'T LET YOUR MOM READ THIS

We don't want to worry you, but Guatemala, along with being Land of the Eternal Spring, the Land of Smiles, and Land of the Trees also seems to be the Land of the Natural Disaster. Don't panic – there are really only three biggies you have to worry about:

- **Earthquakes** – Sitting on top of three tectonic plates hasn't really worked out that well for Guatemala. The present-day capital was founded after Antigua got flattened, but Guatemala City still got pummeled in 1917, 1918 and 1976. This last one left 23,000 people dead.

- **Hurricanes** – Nobody likes a hurricane. They're windy and noisy and get mud and water everywhere. Guatemala has two coastlines, so theoretically the hit could come from either angle, although it's statistically more likely to come from the Pacific side. Hurricane Stan was the worst the country's seen, killing more than 1500 and affecting nearly half a million people. Hurricane season runs June to November – for the latest news, you can check with the **National Hurricane Center & Tropical Prediction Center** (www.nhc.noaa.gov).

- **Volcanoes** – Great to look at, fun to climb, scary when they erupt. Guatemala has four active volcanoes: Pacaya, Volcán de Fuego, Santiaguito and Tacaná. The nastiest event to date was back in 1902, when Santa María erupted, taking 6000 lives. Since late 2006, Pacaya (in between Guatemala City and Escuintla) has been acting up, with increased lava flow and ash. If you feel you need to keep an eye on it, log on to the Humanitarian Early Warning website (www.hewsweb.org/volcanoes).

For information about the spectacular Chelemhá cloud forest, check out www.chelemha.org.

Cecon (Centro de Estudios Conservacionistas de la Universidad de San Carlos; Map p66; ☎ 2331-0904; www.usac.edu.gt/cecon, in Spanish; Av La Reforma 0-63, Zona 10, Guatemala City) Manages six public *biotopos* and one *reserva natural*.

Conap (Consejo Nacional de Áreas Protegidas; Map p66; ☎ 2238-0000; http://conap.online.fr; Edificio IPM, 5a Av 6-06, Zona 1, Guatemala City) The government arm in charge of protected areas.

Fundación Defensores de la Naturaleza (off Map p66; ☎ 2310-2900; www.defensores.org.gt; 2a Av 14-08, Zona 14, Guatemala City) NGO that owns and administers several protected areas.

Green Deal Certifies and promotes ecologically friendly and low-impact businesses, mostly in El Petén.

Planeta (www.planeta.com/guatemala.html) Focuses on sustainable tourism in Guatemala.

ProPetén (☎ 7867-5296; www.propeten.org; Calle Central, Flores, Petén) NGO that works in conservation and natural resources management in Parque Nacional Laguna del Tigre.

Proyecto Ecoquetzal (☎ 7952-1047; www.ecoquetzal.org; 2a Calle 14-36, Zona 1, Cobán, Alta Verapaz) Works in forest conservation and ecotourism.

Trópico Verde (Map p66; ☎ 2339-4225; Edificio Castañeda, Oficina 41, Vía 6 4-25 Zona 4, Guatemala City) Monitors developments in the country's protected areas, mangroves and wetlands.

Guatemala City

Guatemala's capital city, the largest urban agglomeration in Central America, spreads across a flattened mountain range run through by deep ravines.

Depending on who you talk to, Guate (as it's known) is either big, dirty, dangerous and utterly forgettable or big, dirty, dangerous and fascinating. Either way, there's no doubt that there's an energy here unlike that found in the rest of Guatemala.

It's a place where dilapidated buses belch fumes next to Beamers and Hummers, where skyscrapers drop shadows on shantytowns and immigrants from the countryside and the rest of Central America eke out a meager existence, barely noticed by the country's elite.

This is the real cultural capital of Guatemala – the writers, the thinkers, the artists mostly live and work here. All the best museum pieces go to the capital, and while nearly every city dweller dreams of getting away to Antigua or Monterrico for the weekend, this is where they spend most of their time, a fact reflected in the growing sophistication of the restaurant and bar scene.

Guate is busy reinventing itself as a people-friendly city. Public transport is being over-hauled, plazas and parks constructed and family-oriented events are offered on weekends. It's got a long way to go, but it's headed in the right direction.

Many travelers skip the city altogether, preferring to make Antigua their base. Still, you may want, or need, to get acquainted with the capital because this is the hub of the country, where all transportation lines meet and all services are available.

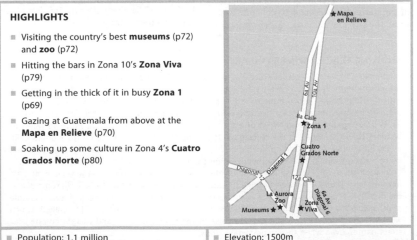

HIGHLIGHTS

- Visiting the country's best **museums** (p72) and **zoo** (p72)
- Hitting the bars in Zona 10's **Zona Viva** (p79)
- Getting in the thick of it in busy **Zona 1** (p69)
- Gazing at Guatemala from above at the **Mapa en Relieve** (p70)
- Soaking up some culture in Zona 4's **Cuatro Grados Norte** (p80)

- Population: 1.1 million
- Elevation: 1500m

HISTORY

Kaminaljuyú, one of the first important cities in the Maya region, flourished two millennia ago in what's now the western part of Guatemala City. By the time Spanish conquistadors arrived in the 16th century, only overgrown mounds were left. The site remained insignificant until the earthquake of July 29, 1773, razed much of the then Spanish colonial capital, Antigua. The authorities decided to move their headquarters to La Ermita valley, hoping to escape further destruction, and on September 27, 1775, King Carlos III of Spain signed a royal charter for the founding of La Nueva Guatemala de la Asunción. Guatemala City was officially born.

Unfortunately, the colonial powers didn't quite move the capital far enough, for earthquakes in 1917, 1918 and 1976 rocked the capital and beyond, reducing buildings to rubble. The 1976 quake killed nearly 23,000, injured another 75,000 and left an estimated one million homeless.

ORIENTATION

The formal and ceremonial center of Guatemala City is the Parque Central at the heart of Zona 1, which is home to most of the city's better budget and midrange hotels, many of its bus stations and a lot of commerce. South down 6a or 7a Av from Zona 1 is Zona 4. Straddling the border of the two zones is the Centro Cívico (Civic Center), with several large, modern government and institutional buildings, including the main tourist information office. Zona 4 is a chaotic area where the city's local market district and the biggest 2nd-class bus station, the Terminal de Autobuses, fuse into one overcrowded mess.

South from the southeast corner of Zona 4 runs Av La Reforma, a broad boulevard forming the boundary between Zonas 9 and 10. These zones are among the city's poshest residential and office areas, especially Zona 10 with its Zona Viva (Lively Zone) where deluxe hotels, fancy restaurants and nightclubs, and glitzy malls are all congregated.

The city's airport, Aeropuerto La Aurora, is in Zona 13, just south of Zona 9 and a 6km drive or bus ride from the heart of Zona 1. Zona 13 has several museums and the parklike La Aurora Zoo.

Maps

Intelimapas' *Mapa Turístico Guatemala*, Inguat's *Mapa Vial Turístico* and International Travel Maps' *Guatemala* all contain useful maps of Guatemala City (see p319). **Sophos** (below) is one of the most reliable places to get maps. The **Instituto Geográfico Nacional** (IGN; ☎ 2248-8100; www.ign.gob.gt; Av Las Américas 5-76, Zona 13; ⊙ 9am-5pm Mon-Fri) sells 1:50,000 and 1:250,000 topographical sheets of all parts of Guatemala, costing Q60 each.

INFORMATION

Bookstores

Sophos (☎ 2419-7070; Plaza Fontabella, 4a Av 12-59, Zona 10) Relaxed place to read while in the Zona Viva, with a good selection of books in English on Guatemala and the Maya, including Lonely Planet guides, and maps.

Vista Hermosa Book Shop (☎ 2369-1003; 2a Calle 18-50, Zona 15) Good range of books in English, but rather far from the center of things.

KNOWING EXACTLY WHERE YOU ARE

Guatemala City, like (almost) all Guatemalan towns, is laid out on a logical street grid. Avenidas run north–south; calles run east–west. Each avenida and calle has a number, with the numbers usually rising as you move from west to east and north to south. Addresses enable you to pinpoint exactly which block a building is in, and which side of the street it's on. The address 9a Av 15-24 means building No 24 on 9a Av in the block after 15a Calle; 9a Av 16-19 refers to building No 19 on 9a Av in the block after 16a Calle; 4a Calle 7-3 is building No 3 on 4a Calle in the block after 7a Av. Odd-numbered buildings are on the left-hand side as you move in the rising-numbers direction; even numbers are on the right.

In addition, most cities and towns are divided into a number of zonas – 21 in Guatemala City, fewer in other places. You need to know the zona as well as the street address, for in some places the numbers of avenidas and calles are repeated in more than one zona. Beware, too, a couple of other minor wrinkles in the system. Short streets may be suffixed 'A,' as in 14a Calle A, which will be found between 14a Calle and 15a Calle. In some smaller towns and villages no one uses street names, even when they're posted on signs.

Internet Access

Zona 1 throngs with inexpensive internet cafes. Elsewhere, rates tend to be higher.

Café Internet Navigator (14a Calle, Zona 1; per hr Q6; ⏰ 8am-8pm) East of 6a Av.

Carambolo Café Internet (14a Calle, Zona 1; per hr Q6; ⏰ 8:30am-8:30pm) East of 7a Av.

Internet (local 3, 6a Av 9-27, Zona 1; por hr Q6; ⏰ 8am-7pm)

Web Station (2a Av 14-63, Zona 10; per hr Q5; ⏰ 10am-midnight Mon-Sat, noon-midnight Sun) One of the cheapest in the Zona Viva.

Laundry

Lavandería El Siglo (12a Calle 3-42, Zona 1; ⏰ 8am-6pm Mon-Sat) Charges Q40 per load to wash, dry and fold.

Medical Services

Guatemala City has many private hospitals and clinics. Public hospitals and clinics provide free consultations but can be busy; to reduce waiting time, get there before 7am.

Clínica Cruz Roja (Red Cross Clinic; ☎ 2381-6565; 3a Calle 8-40, Zona 1; ⏰ 8am-5:30pm Mon-Fri, 8am-noon Sat) This public clinic charges for consultations but is inexpensive.

Farmacia del Ejecutivo (☎ 2423-7111; 7a Av 15-13, Zona 1) Public pharmacy. Open 24 hours and accepts Visa and MasterCard.

Hospital Centro Médico (☎ 2361-1649, 2361-1650; 6a Av 3-47, Zona 10) Recommended. This private hospital has some English-speaking doctors.

Hospital General San Juan de Dios (☎ 2256-1486; 1a Av 10-50, Zona 1) One of the city's best public hospitals.

Hospital Herrera Llerandi (☎ 2384-5959, emergencies 2334-5955; 6a Av 8-71, Zona 10) Another recommended private hospital with some English-speaking doctors.

Money

Take normal precautions when using ATMs.

ABM (☎ 2361-5602; Plazuela España, Zona 9) Changes euros into quetzals.

American Express (☎ 2331-7422; Centro Comercial Montufar, 12a Calle 0-93, Zona 9; ⏰ 8am-5pm Mon-Fri, 8am-noon Sat) In an office of Clark Tours.

Banco Agromercantil (7a Av 9-11, Zona 1; ⏰ 9am-7pm Mon-Fri, 9am-1pm Sat) Changes US-dollar cash (not traveler's checks).

Banco de la República (Aeropurto Internacional La Aurora; ⏰ 6am-8pm Mon-Fri, 6am-6pm Sat & Sun) Currency-exchange services and a MasterCard ATM. On the airport departures level.

Banco Uno (☎ 2366-1861; Edificio Unicentro, 18a Calle 5-56, Zona 10) Changes cash euros into quetzals.

Credomatic (Edificio Testa, cnr 5a Av & 11a Calle, Zona 1; ⏰ 8am-7pm Mon-Fri, 9am-1pm Sat) Gives cash advances on Visa and MasterCard – take your passport.

Edificio Testa (cnr 5a Av & 11a Calle, Zona 1) Visa, MasterCard and American Express ATMs.

Lloyds TSB (Edificio Europlaza, 5a Av 5-55, Zona 14) Changes euro traveler's checks.

MasterCard ATM (Hotel Stofella, 2a Av 12-28, Zona 10)

Visa ATMs Zona 1 (cnr 5a Av & 6a Calle) Opposite Parque Centenario; Zona 10 (2a Av) South of 13a Calle; Zona 10 (Edificio Unicentro, 18a Calle 5-56); Zona 9 (Guatemala Barceló Guatemala, 7a Av 15-45).

Post

DHL (☎ 2379-1111; www.dhl.com; 12a Calle 5-12, Zona 10) Courier service.

Main post office (Palacio de Correos; 7a Av 11-67, Zona 1; ⏰ 8:30am-5pm Mon-Fri, 8:30am-1pm Sat) In a huge yellow building at the Palacio de Correos. There's also a small post office at the airport.

UPS (☎ 2421-6000; www.ups.com; 12a Calle 5-53, Zona 10) Courier service.

Telephone

Telgua public phones are plentiful on the street, and take Telgua phone cards.

Telefónica office (2a Av, Zona 10) Between 13a and 14a Calles. Telefónica phones are fairly common too, and use Telefónica phone cards; cards can be bought at the Telefónica office.

Tourist Information

Disetur (Tourist Police; ☎ 2251-4897; cnr 17 Calle & 11 Av, Zona 1) Travelers are advised to contact their liaison, Asistur (☎ 1500 toll free, in English).

Inguat (Centro Cívico (☎ 2421-2854, 2421-2800; info@inguat.gob.gt; 7a Av 1-17, Zona 4; ⏰ 8am-4pm Mon-Fri) Located in the lobby of the Inguat (Guatemalan Tourism Institute) headquarters in the Centro Cívico, this main office has limited handout material, but staff are extremely helpful; Aeropuerto La Aurora (☎ 2260-6320; ⏰ 6am-9pm) In the arrivals hall; Mercado de Artesanías (☎ 2475-5915; 6a Calle 10-95, Zona 13).

Travel Agencies

Servisa (☎ 2361-4417; agservisa@gmail.com; Av La Reforma 8-33, Zona 10) An efficient agency.

Viajes Tivoli (☎ 2285-1050; www.viajestivoli.com; Edificio Herrera, 12a Calle 4-55, Zona 1) Housed in a building with several other travel agencies; take your pick.

DANGERS & ANNOYANCES

Street crime, including armed robbery, has increased in recent years. Use normal urban caution (behaving as you would in, say,

GUATEMALA CITY

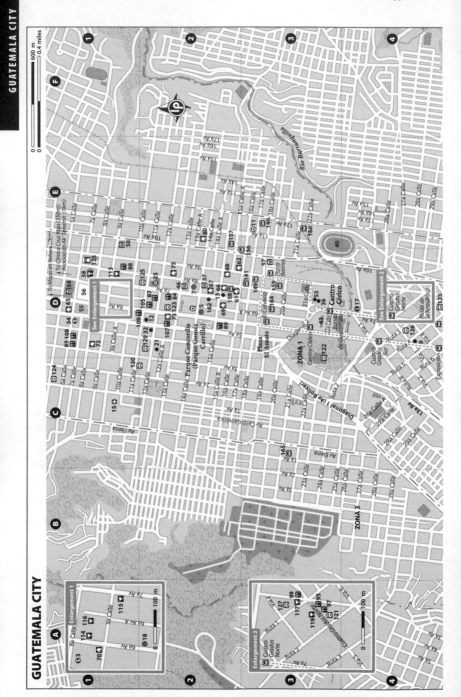

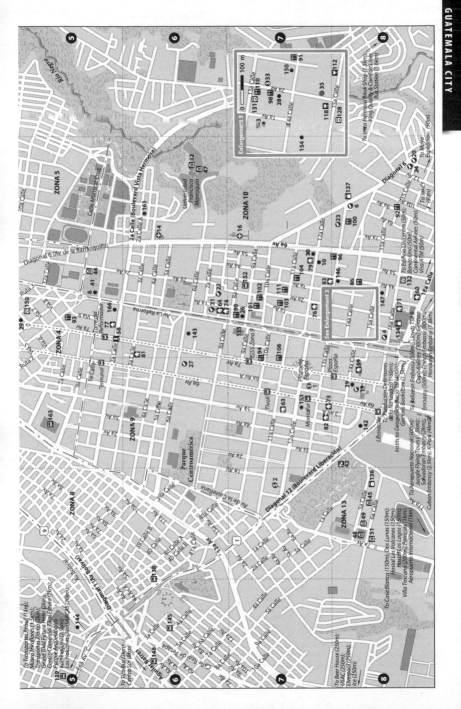

Manhattan or Rome): don't walk down the street with your wallet bulging out of your back pocket, and avoid walking alone downtown late at night. Work out your route before you start so that you're not standing on corners looking lost or peering at a map. It's safe to walk downtown in the early evening, as long as you stick to streets with plenty of lighting and people. Stay alert and leave your valuables in your hotel. Don't flaunt anything of value, and be aware that women and children swell the ranks of thieves here. The incidence of robbery increases around the 15th and the end of each month, when workers get paid.

The area around 18a Calle in Zona 1 has many bus stations, and hosts the lowlife and hustlers who tend to lurk around them. Nearly half of Zona 1 robberies happen here, the worst black spots being the intersections with 4a, 6a and 9a Avs. This part of town (also a red-light district) is notoriously dangerous at night; if you are arriving by bus at night or must go someplace on 18a Calle at night, take a taxi.

The more affluent sections of the city – Zonas 9, 10 and 14, for example – are safer but crimes against tourists and street crime in general is on the rise in these areas, too. The Zona Viva, in Zona 10, has police patrols at night. But even here, going in pairs is better than going alone. Never try to resist if you are confronted by a robber.

The red city buses are temptingly cheap, particularly if you have to cross town, but there are so many stories of robberies, pickpockets and even shootouts that it is not advisable to catch them. An exception are the new green TransMetro buses, which have a policeman on board at all times – for more information on this service, see boxed text, p85.

For a warning on solo female travelers traveling on intercity buses, see boxed text, p329.

SIGHTS

The major sights are in Zona 1 (the historic center) and Zonas 10 and 13, where the museums are grouped. If you're in town on a Sunday, consider taking the TransMetro's **SubiBaja** (free; ⏱ 9am-2pm) self-guided tour. Modern, air-conditioned TransMetro buses run a circuit passing every 20 minutes, with 10 stops including the Parque Central, Centro Cívico, Zoo (and museums), the Zona Viva, Pasos y Pedales, Cuatro Grados Norte and Mapa en Relieve. Volunteer guides give an on-board commentary and each bus is staffed by a member of the Transit Police. It's an excellent way to see many of these sights without worrying about public transport or taxis.

Zona 1

The main sights here are grouped around the **Parque Central** (officially the Plaza de la Constitución). The standard colonial urban-planning scheme required every town in the New World to have a large plaza for military exercises and ceremonies. On the north side of the plaza was usually the *palacio de gobierno* (colonial government headquarters). On another side, preferably the east, would be a church (or cathedral). On the other sides of the square there could be additional civic buildings or the imposing mansions of wealthy citizens. Guatemala City's Parque Central is a classic example of the plan.

The Parque Central and adjoining Parque Centenario are never empty during daylight hours, with shoeshine boys, ice-cream vendors and sometimes open-air political meetings and concerts adding to the general bustle.

On the north side of the Parque Central is the imposing **Palacio Nacional de la Cultura** (☎ 2253-0748; cnr 6a Av & 6a Calle; admission Q30; ⏱ 9-11:45am & 2-4:45pm Mon-Sat), built as a presidential palace between 1936 and 1943 during the dictatorial rule of General Jorge Ubico at enormous cost to the lives of the prisoners who were forced to labor here. It's the third palace to stand on the site. Despite its tragic background, architecturally the palace is one of the country's most interesting constructions, a mélange of multiple earlier styles from Spanish Renaissance to neoclassical. Today, most government offices have been removed from here and it's open as a museum and for a few ceremonial events.

Visits are by guided tour (available in English). You pass through a labyrinth of gleaming brass, polished wood, carved stone and frescoed arches. Features include an optimistic mural of Guatemalan history by Alberto Gálvez Suárez above the main stairway, and a two-ton gold, bronze and Bohemian-crystal chandelier in the reception hall. The banqueting hall sports stained-glass panels depicting – with delicious irony – the virtues of good government. From here your guide will probably take you out onto the presidential balcony, where you can imagine yourself a banana-republic dictator reviewing your troops. In the western courtyard, the Patio de la Paz, a monument depicting two hands stands where Guatemala's Peace Accords were signed in 1996; each day at 11am the rose held by the hands is changed by a military guard and that of the previous day tossed to a woman among the spectators.

On the first floor of the Palacio de Correos you'll find the **Centro Cultural Metropolitano** (7a Av 11-67; 🕑 9am-5pm Mon-Fri), a surprisingly avant-garde cultural center, hosting art exhibitions, book launches, handicraft workshops and film nights.

The **Casa MIMA** (8a Av 14-12; 🕑 9am-12:30pm & 2-6pm Mon-Fri, 9am-5pm Sat) is a wonderfully presented museum and cultural center set in a house dating from the late 1800s. The owners of the house were collectors with eclectic tastes ranging from French neo-rococo, Chinese, and art deco to indigenous artifacts. The place is set up like a functioning house, filled with curios and furniture spanning the centuries.

One of the odder museums you're ever likely to visit is the **Museo de Músicos Invisibles** (13a Calle 7-30; admission Q20; 🕑 9am-6pm Mon-Sat), featuring an astounding collection of automated instruments, from early Victorolas to grinder organs and complete, air-powered orchestras. Many of the pieces – dating from 1840 to 1950 – are still in working condition and the guide will crank them up for you, free.

Demonstrations of the more elaborate models cost Q10 per song.

The **Railway Museum** (Museo de Ferrocarril; www.museodelferrocarrilguatemala.com; 9a Av 18-03; 🕑 9am-12:30pm & 2-4pm) is one of the city's more intriguing museums. Documented here are the glory days of the troubled Guatemalan rail system, along with some quirky artifacts, such as hand-drawn diagrams of derailments and a kitchen set up with items used in dining cars. You can go climbing around the passenger carriages, but not the locomotives.

The **Catedral Metropolitana** (7a Av; 🕑 6am-noon & 2-7pm), facing Parque Central, was constructed between 1782 and 1815 (the towers were finished in 1867). It has survived earthquake and fire well, though the quake of 1917 did substantial damage and the one in 1976 did even more. Its heavy proportions and sparse ornamentation don't make for a particularly beautiful building, but it does have a certain stateliness, and the altars are worth a look.

The **Mercado Central**, behind the cathedral, was one of the city's major markets for food and other daily necessities until the building was destroyed by the 1976 earthquake. Reconstructed in the late 1970s, it now specializes in tourist-oriented handicrafts. The food market thrives on the lowest floor.

The **Museo Nacional de Historia** (☎ 2253-6149; 9a Calle 9-70; admission Q50; 🕑 9am-5:30pm Mon-Fri) is a jumble of historical relics with an emphasis on photography and portraits. Check the carefully coiffed hairstyles of the 19th-century generals and politicos.

Zona 2

North of Zona 1, Zona 2 is mostly a middle-class residential district, but it's worth venturing along to Parque Minerva to see the **Mapa en Relieve** (Relief Map; www.mapaenrelieve.org; Av Simeón Cañas Final; admission Q25; 🕑 9am-5pm), a huge open-air map of Guatemala showing the country at a scale of 1:10,000. The vertical scale is exaggerated to 1:2000 to make the volcanoes and mountains appear dramatically higher and steeper than they really are. Constructed in 1905 under the direction of Francisco Vela, it was fully restored and repainted in 1999. Viewing towers afford a panoramic view. This is an odd but fun place, and it's curious to observe that Belize is still represented as part of Guatemala. To get there take bus V-21 northbound on 7a Av just north or south of the Parque Central.

Zona 4

Pride of Zona 4 (actually straddling its borders with Zonas 1 and 5) is the **Centro Cívico**, a set of large government and institutional buildings constructed during the 1950s and '60s. One is the headquarters of **Inguat** (Guatemalan Tourist Institute; see p65), housing the city's main tourist office. Nearby are the **Palacio de Justicia** (High Court; cnr 7a Av & 21a Calle, Zona 1), the **Banco de Guatemala** (7a Av, Zona 1) and the **Municipalidad de Guatemala** (City Hall; 22a Calle, Zona 1). The bank building bears relief sculptures by Dagoberto Vásquez depicting his country's history; the city hall contains a huge mosaic by Carlos Mérida, completed in 1959.

Behind Inguat is the national stadium, **Estadio Nacional Mateo Flores** (10a Av, Zona 5).

If you're looking for a stress-free stroll, check out the pedestrianized **Cuatro Grados Norte** (Vía 5 btw Rutas 1 & 3, Zona 4) area – a few traffic-free blocks filled with restaurants, bars and cultural centers.

Zona 7

The **Parque Arqueológico Kaminaljuyú** (cnr 11a Calle & 24a Av, Zona 7; admission Q50; ☯ 8am-4:30pm), with remnants of one of the first important cities in the Maya region, is just west of 23a Av and is some 4km west of the city center. At its peak, from about 400 BC to AD 100, ancient Kaminaljuyú (kah-mih-nahl huh-*yuh*) had thousands of inhabitants and scores of temples built on earth mounds, and probably dominated much of highland Guatemala. Large-scale carvings found here were the forerunners of Classic Maya carving, and

Kaminaljuyú had a literate elite before anywhere else in the Maya world. The city fell into ruin before being reoccupied around AD 400 by invaders from Teotihuacán in central Mexico, who rebuilt it in Teotihuacán's *talud-tablero* style, with buildings stepped in alternating vertical *(tablero)* and sloping *(talud)* sections. Unfortunately, most of Kaminaljuyú has been covered by urban sprawl: the archaeological park is but a small portion of the ancient city and even here the remnants consist chiefly of grassy mounds. To the left from the entrance is La Acrópolis, where you can inspect excavations of a ball court and *talud-tablero* buildings from AD 450 to 550.

A couple of hundred meters south of the entrance and across the road are two burial statues from the late Preclassic era. They're badly deteriorated, but the only examples of carving left at the site – the best examples have been moved to the new Museo Nacional de Arqueología y Etnología (p72).

You can get here by bus No 35 from 4a Av, Zona 1, but check that the bus is going to the *ruinas de Kaminaljuyú* – not all do. A taxi from Zona 1 costs around Q50.

Zona 10

Two of the country's best museums are housed in large, modern buildings at the Universidad Francisco Marroquín, 1km east of Av La Reforma.

The **Museo Ixchel** (☎ 2331-3739; www.museoixchel. org; 6a Calle Final; admission Q20; ☯ 8am-6pm Mon-Fri, 9am-1pm Sat) is named for the Maya goddess of the moon, women, reproduction and, of

---

GUAT THE...?

In many ways, Guatemala City is a very straightforward place – streets are laid out on a (mostly) regular grid, architecture is functional and unexotic and people move from point A to point B with a quiet determination.

But there are a couple of unexpected little pockets in the city, and if you're looking for something out of the ordinary while you're here, check out these places:

- **Torre del Reformador** (cnr 7a Av & 2a Calle, Zona 9) It's been a long time since anybody called Guatemala City the Paris of anywhere, which makes it all the more remarkable to find a replica of the Eiffel Tower straddling a busy downtown intersection. The tower (originally named the 'Torre Conmemorativa del 19 del Julio') was completed in 1935, to celebrate the 100th anniversary of the birth of former president and reformer Justo Rufino Barrios.

- **Museo de Músicos Invisibles** (see p70) An entire museum dedicated to automated instruments which were extremely popular among Guatemala City's elite, back in the pre-MP3 era.

- **Mapa en Relieve** (see p70) A product of happier, more hopeful times, this 3D model of the country's peaks and rivers recently celebrated its 100th birthday.

course, textiles. Photographs and exhibits of indigenous costumes and other crafts show the incredible richness of traditional arts in Guatemala's highland towns. If you enjoy Guatemalan textiles at all, you must visit this museum. It has disabled access, a section for children, a cafe, a shop and a library, and guided tours are available in English or Spanish.

Behind it is **Museo Popol Vuh** (☎ 2361-2301; www.popolvuh.ufm.edu; 6a Calle Final; adult/child Q20/6; ⏰ 9am-5pm Mon-Fri, 9am-1pm Sat), where well-displayed pre-Hispanic figurines, incense burners and burial urns, plus carved wooden masks and traditional textiles, fill several rooms. Other rooms hold colonial paintings and gilded wood and silver artifacts. A faithful copy of the Dresden Codex, one of the precious 'painted books' of the Maya, is among the most interesting pieces, and there's a colorful display of animals in Maya art.

The Universidad de San Carlos has a large, lush **Jardín Botánico** (Botanical Garden; Calle Mariscal Cruz 1-56; admission Q10; ⏰ 8am-3:30pm Mon-Fri, 8am-noon Sat) on the northern edge of Zona 10. The admission includes the university's **Museo de Historia Natural** (Natural History Museum; ⏰ 8am-3:30pm Mon-Fri, 8am-noon Sat) at the site.

If you're here on a Sunday, check out **Pasos y Pedales** (⏰ 10am-3pm Sun), a wonderful municipal initiative that sees the Av de las Americas (Zona 10) and its continuation, Av la Reforma in Zona 13, blocked off to traffic for three kilometres and taken over by jugglers, clowns, in-line skaters, dogwalkers, food vendors, t'ai chi classes, skate parks and playgrounds for kids. It's great place to go for a walk (or you can hire bikes or in-line skates on the street) and check out a very relaxed, sociable side of the city that is rarely otherwise seen.

Zona 11

Museo Miraflores (☎ 2470-3415; www.museomiraflores. org; 7a Calle 21-55, Zona 11; admission Q40; ⏰ 9am-7pm Tue-Sun) is an excellent, modern museum inauspiciously jammed between two shopping malls a few kilometers out of town. Downstairs focuses on objects found at Kaminaljuyú (see p71), with fascinating trade route maps showing the site's importance.

Upstairs there are displays on textiles and indigenous clothing, separated by region, from around the country. Signs are in Spanish and (for the most part) English. Out back is a pleasant grassy area with paths and seating – a

good place to take a breather. To get there, catch any bus from the center going to Centro Comercial Tikal Futura and get off there. The museum is 250m down the road between it and the Miraflores shopping center.

Zona 13

The attractions here in the city's southern reaches are all ranged along 5a Calle in the Finca Aurora area, northwest of the airport. While here you can also drop into the **Mercado de Artesanías** (Crafts Market; ☎ 2472-0208; cnr 5a Calle & 11a Av; ⏰ 9:30am-6pm).

La Aurora Zoo (☎ 2472-0894; www.aurorazoo.org.gt; 5a Calle; adult/child Q20/10; ⏰ 9am-5pm Tue-Sun) is not badly kept as zoos go, and the lovely, parklike grounds alone are worth the admission fee.

Almost opposite the zoo entrance is the **Museo de los Niños** (Children's Museum; ☎ 2475-5076; www.museodelosninos.com.gt; 5a Calle 10-00; admission Q35; ⏰ 8am-noon & 1-4:30pm Tue-Fri, 9:30am-1:30pm & 2:30-6pm Sat & Sun), a hands-on affair that is a sure success if you have kids to keep happy. The fun ranges from a giant jigsaw-map of Guatemala to an earthquake simulator and, most popular of all, a room of original and entertaining ball games.

The **Museo Nacional de Arqueología y Etnología** (☎ 2475-4399; www.munae.gob.gt; Sala 5, Finca La Aurora; admission Q60; ⏰ 9am-4pm Tue-Fri, 9am-noon & 1:30-4pm Sat & Sun) has the country's biggest collection of ancient Maya artifacts, but explanatory information is very sparse. There's a great wealth of monumental stone sculpture, including Classic-period stelae from Tikal, Uaxactún and Piedras Negras, a superb throne from Piedras Negras and animal representations from Preclassic Kaminaljuyú. Also here are rare wooden lintels from temples at Tikal and El Zotz, and a room of beautiful jade necklaces and masks. Don't miss the large-scale model of Tikal. The ethnology section has displays on the languages, costumes, dances, masks and homes of Guatemala's indigenous peoples.

Next door is the **Museo Nacional de Arte Moderno** (☎ 2472-0467; Sala 6, Finca La Aurora; admission Q50; ⏰ 9am-4pm Tue-Fri, 9am-noon & 1:30-4pm Sat & Sun), with a collection of 20th-century Guatemalan art including works by well-known Guatemalan artists such as Carlos Mérida, Carlos Valente and Humberto Gavarito. Behind the archaeology museum is the **Museo Nacional de Historia Natural Jorge Ibarra** (☎ 2472-0468; 6a Calle 7-30; admission Q50; ⏰ 9am-4pm Tue-Fri, 9am-noon & 2-4pm Sat & Sun), whose claim to fame is its large collection of dissected animals.

About 10 minutes' drive south of the airport is **X-Park** (2380 2080; www.xpark.net; Av Hincapié Km 11.5; admission Q15; 11am-7pm Tue-Fri, 10am-9pm Sat, 10am-7pm Sun), a very well-constructed 'adventure sports' park. Attractions (they prefer to call them 'challenges') cost between Q15 and Q45 each and include bouldering and climbing walls, reverse bungees, mechanical bulls, a rope course, zip lines and an excellent adventure playground for kids. A fairly limited range of fast food is available at the cafeteria. A taxi here from Zona 10 should cost you around Q30.

GUATEMALA CITY FOR CHILDREN

Guatemala City has enough children's attractions to make it worth considering as an outing from Antigua if you have kids to please. The Museo de los Niños (see left) and La Aurora Zoo (see left), conveniently over the road from each other in Zona 13, top the list. Kids might also relish the dead animals in various states of preservation at the nearby Museo Nacional de Historia Natural Jorge Ibarra (see left). It shouldn't be too hard to

find some food that the littl'uns are willing to eat at the food courts in the malls **Centro Comercial Los Próceres** (www.proceres.com; 16a Calle, Zona 10) or **Oakland Mall** (www.oaklandmall.com.gt; Diagonal 6 13-01, Zona 10), where everyone can also enjoy a little air-con and shopping (window or otherwise). At Oakland Mall you'll find the restaurant **Nais** (mains Q40-120; breakfast, lunch & dinner), which is a winner with the kids for the huge aquarium (a scuba diver swims through periodically, cleaning the tank and feeding the fish) filled with tropical fish.

On Sundays, kids and adults will enjoy the relaxed atmosphere and abundant free entertainment on offer at Pasos y Pedales (see left). The Mapa en Relieve (p70), too, amuses most ages, and there are a few swings and climbing frames in the adjacent park.

TOURS

Clark Tours (2412-4700; www.clarktours.com.gt; 7a Av 14-76, Zona 9; morning tour per person Q237, private day tour per person from Q1140) Guatemala's longest-established tour operator offers morning and full-day city tours. The morning tour (available Mon-Wed, Sat and Sun) visits the Palacio Nacional de la Cultura, cathedral and Centro Cívico. The day tour adds the Ixchel and Popul

Vuh museums. Clark Tours also has branches in **Zona 10** (☎ 2363-3920; cnr 14a Calle & Av La Reforma) at the Westin Camino Real, and in **Zona 9** (☎ 2362-9716) inside the Barceló Guatemala.

Maya Expeditions (☎ 2363-4955; www.mayaexpeditions.com; 15a Calle A 14-07, Zona 10) Guatemala's most respected adventure-tourism company specializes in white-water rafting and trekking, but also offers archaeological trips, wildlife-watching expeditions and a whole lot more, mostly in the Alta Verapaz and Petén regions.

SLEEPING

For budget and many midrange hotels, make a beeline for Zona 1. If you have just flown in or are about to fly out, a few guesthouses near the airport are as convenient as you could get. Top-end hotels are mostly around Zona 10.

Zona 1

BUDGET

Many of the city's cheaper lodgings are clustered in the area between 6a and 9a Avs and 14a and 17a Calles, 10 to 15 minutes' walk south from the Parque Central. Keep street noise in mind as you look for a room.

Hotel Fenix (☎ 2251-6625; 15a Calle 6-56; s/d Q70/100) Zona 1's classic budget hotel has found a new home, just around the corner from where it used to be. The building's actually more atmospheric than the last and rooms here are still a very good deal.

Hotel Ajau (☎ 2232-0488; hotelajau@hotmail.com; 8a Av 15-62; s/d Q150/190, without bathroom Q70/110; P 💻) If you're coming or going to Cobán, the Ajau's the obvious choice, being right next door to the Monja Blanca bus station. It's still a pretty good deal, anyway, with lovely polished floor tiles and cool, clean rooms.

Hotel Capri (☎ 2232-8191; 9a Av 15-63; s/d Q120/170, without bathroom Q80/120; P) This modern four-story number is in a decent location and rooms are set back from the street, so they're quiet. Big windows looking onto patios and light wells keep the place sunny and airy.

Chalet Suizo (☎ 2251-3786; chaletsuizo@gmail.com; 7a Av 14-34; s/d Q150/200, without bathroom Q100/150; P) One of the better deals in this price range, the Suiza offers spacious, simple rooms in a modern building. Get one at the back to avoid street noise.

Hotel Spring (☎ 2230-2858; www.hotelspring.com; 8a Av 12-65; s/d from Q180/260, without bathroom Q110/140; P 💻) With a beautiful courtyard setting, the Spring has a lot more style than other Zona 1 joints. It has central but quiet sunny patios.

The 43 rooms vary greatly, but most are spacious and clean with high ceilings. Have a look around if you can. All rooms have cable TV; some of the more expensive ones are wheelchair accessible. It's worth booking ahead. A *cafetería* serves meals from 6:30am to 1:30pm.

MIDRANGE

Hotel Clariss (☎ 2232-1113; 8a Av 15-14; s/d Q170/220, without bathroom Q130/175; P 💻) This friendly place next to the Cobán bus terminal is in a modern building. There are some good-sized rooms (and other, smaller ones). Those at the front get more air and light, but also the bulk of the street noise.

Hotel Colonial (☎ 2232-6722; www.hotelcolonial.net; 7a Av 14-19; s/d Q170/250, without bathroom Q130/190; P 💻) This is a large old house converted to a hotel with spacious communal areas and heavy, dark, colonial decor. It's a very well-run establishment whose 42 rooms are clean, good-sized and adequately furnished. Nearly all have a private bathroom and TV.

Hotel Centenario (☎ 2338-0381; centenario@itelgua.com; 6a Calle 5-33; s/d Q165/225) Although it's looking a bit worn around the edges (and not that flash in the middle, either), the Centenario offers a pretty good deal, right on the park. Rooms are basic and unrenovated, with TV and hot showers.

Hotel Excel (☎ 2253-0140; hotelexcel@hotmail.com; 9a Av 15-12; s/d Q170/210; P 💻) The Excel's bright, modern motel-style may be a bit bland for some, but the rooms are spotless and the showers blast hot water.

Hotel Quality Service (☎ 2251-8005; www.qualityguate.com; 8a Calle 3-18; s/d Q170/230; P 💻 📶) There's a pleasing, old-timey feel about this place, which is balanced perfectly by the modern-but-not-overly-so rooms. Prices include breakfast. The best pick near the park.

ourpick Posada Belen (☎ 2232-9226; www.posadabelen.com; 13a Calle A 10-20; s/d Q360/400; 💻 📶) One of Zona 1's most stylish options, this boutique hotel has just 10 rooms, arranged around a couple of lush patios. Rooms are well decorated with *típico* (traditional) furnishings and there's a good restaurant onsite.

TOP END

Hotel Royal Palace (☎ 2416-4400; www.hotelroyalpalace.com; 6a Av 12-66; s/d Q330/520; P 🅿 💻 🕭) A little island of glamor amid the rough and tumble of 6a Av, this place offers most comforts. The style is modern-reconstruction, with plenty of dark woods and fancy tiling around the place. Rooms are large, sparkling clean and wheelchair-accessible. Those at the front have balconies overlooking the street – a fascinating, if noisy, spectacle. Facilities include a restaurant, bar, gym, sauna and free airport transfers.

Hotel Pan American (☎ 2232-6807; www.hotel panamerican.com.gt; 9a Calle 5-63, s/d Q300/420, (P) (🖳)) Guatemala City's luxury hotel before WWII, the Pan American is one of the few hotels in the city with any air of history. There's a fine, art-deco lobby that's filled with plants and a not-too-shabby restaurant. Rooms are spacious and simple, often with three or more beds. The bathrooms are stylish and modern, with good-sized tubs. Avoid rooms facing the noisy street.

Zona 9

BUDGET

Hotel Carrillon (☎ 2332-4267; hcarrillon@guate.net.gt; 5a Av 11-25; s/d Q190/230; (P)) In a fairly ordinary section of Zona 9 (but within walking distance of all the Zona 10 action), this hotel offers a reasonable deal. Rooms are smallish, wood-paneled affairs. Some lack decent ventilation – ask to see a few.

MIDRANGE

Tivoli Travel Lodge (☎ 5510-0032; 5a Av A 13-42; s/d Q290/375) Across the street from Mi Casa, the Tivoli offers plainer rooms at slightly better prices.

Hotel Villa Española (☎ 2339-0190; www.hotelvilla espanola.com; 2a Calle 7-51; s/d Q370/410; (P) (🄭) (🛜)) One of the very few options with colonial stylings in this part of town, the Villa Española has some beautiful touches. It's on a busy road, but rooms are set well back, so there's little noise. There's a good restaurant on the premises.

Mi Casa (☎ 2332-1364; www.hotelmicasa.com; 5a Av A 13-51; s/d Q375/460; (P) (🖳)) Set in a family house on a quiet street, rooms here are big and sunny, with private bathrooms, lino floors, standard acrylic paintings, fans and reading lamps. Price includes breakfast, which is served in a leafy little patio out back. You can call ahead for airport pickup.

Residencia del Sol (☎ 2360-4823; www.residenciadel sol.com; 3a Calle 6-42; s/d Q380/420; (P) (🄭) (🖳)) The spacious, good-looking rooms here make up for the slightly out-of-the-way location. There's no wi-fi, but you can hook your computer up via network cables in your room. Pay an extra Q80 for wooden floorboards and a balcony.

TOP END

Barceló Guatemala (☎ 2378-4031; www.barceloguate malacity.com; 7a Av 15-45; s/d from Q700/770; (P) (🄭) (🖳) (🛜) (🄬)) For that big, corporate I'd-rather-not-be-here hotel experience, it's hard to go past the local outlet of the Spanish Barceló hotel chain.

Zona 10

BUDGET

Xamanek Inn (☎ 2360-8345; www.mayaworld.net; 13a Calle 3-57; dm/d Q120/280; (🖳) (🛜)) This comfy place is a welcome addition to the frequently over-priced Zona Viva area. Dorms are spacious and airy, separated into male and female and there are a couple of very good value doubles. Rates include a light breakfast and free internet. It offers a book exchange, kitchen use and a delightful little garden out the back. There are a couple of discos in this area, meaning noise at night (particularly on weekends) can be a problem.

MIDRANGE

Eco Hotel los Próceres (☎ 2337-3250; www.posadadelos proceres.com; 18a Calle 3-03; s/d Q320/400; (P) (🄬)) The spotless, brightly painted rooms here are a pretty good deal. They're a bit cramped, but tasteful decoration and modern bathrooms (with tub!) make up for that. Price includes free airport pickup.

Hotel Posada de los Próceres (☎ 2385-4302; www. posadadelosproceres.com; 16a Calle 2-40; s/d Q320/400; (P) (🄬) (🖳) (🛜)) Twenty brightly decorated, if slightly tatty, rooms right on the edge of the Zona Viva. They're surprisingly large, with attractive tiled bathrooms, phone, clock, cable TV, wooden furniture and minifridge. Price includes free airport pickup.

TOP END

Hotel Casa Grande (☎ 2332-0914; www.casagrande -gua.com; Av La Reforma 7-67; s/d Q540/625; (P) (🄬) (🖳)) Located within spitting distance of the US embassy (not that we're trying to give you any ideas), this is a refined option that mostly caters to the business crowd. Several patio areas and a log fire in the lounge area crank up the comfort factor.

Hotel San Carlos (☎ 2332-6055; www.hsancarlos. com; Av La Reforma 7-89; s/d Q660/750, apt from Q1250; (P) (🖳) (🛜) (🄬)) OK, so it goes a little heavy on the baroque furnishings, but this place is still a good deal. Set well back from the busy street, it's quiet, and the well-appointed rooms and apartments are spacious and comfortable. Rates include breakfast and airport pickup.

Hotel Stofella (☎ 2410-8600; www.stofella.com; 2a Av 12-28; s/d Q750/800; P X ⬚) This pleasant, medium-sized Zona Viva hotel is part of the international Best Western chain, and provides quality rooms – with air-con, safes and phones in bedroom – at reasonable prices. Rate includes breakfast.

our pick **Otelito** (☎ 2339-1811; www.otelito.com; 12a Calle 4-51; s/d Q900/1000; P X ⬚ �) Imbued with Zen tranquility, this place features bamboo, mood lighting and polished steel. Rooms are spacious and minimalist and bathrooms modern, with big glassed-in shower stalls. There's a garden restaurant/cafe out the front. Book ahead.

Zona 11

Grand Tikal Futura Hotel (☎ 2410-0800; www.grand tikalfutura.com.gt; Calzada Roosevelt 22-43; r from Q880; P X ⬚ ⬚ ⬚) The towering glass architecture here is a contemporary reinterpretation of the grandiose concepts of ancient Tikal. The 205 luxurious rooms and suites all enjoy spectacular views and have their own safes. Hook up with a Guatemalan and you can take advantage of hefty 'local discounts.' On the lower levels of the complex, you'll find one the city's biggest shopping malls, 10 cinemas and a bowling alley. It's to the west of the city on the road to Antigua, 3km from Zona 1, Zona 10 or the airport.

Zona 13

Four dependable guesthouses in a middle-class residential area in Zona 13 are very convenient for the airport. All their room rates include breakfast and airport transfers (call from the airport on arrival). There are no restaurants out here, but these places offer breakfast and have the complete lowdown on fast-food home delivery in the area.

BUDGET

Patricia's Guest House (☎ 2261-4251; www.patriciasho tel.com; 19 Calle 10-65; s/d Q130/260, without bathroom Q115/230; P ⬚ ⬚) The most relaxed and comfortable option is in this family house with a sweet little backyard where guests can hang out. It also offers private transport around the city and shuttles to bus stations.

Hostal Los Volcanes (☎ 2261-3040; www.hostallos volcanes.com; 16a Calle 8-00; dm Q125, s/d Q240/330, without bathroom Q160/240; P ⬚) A cozy place with big, clean, shared bathrooms and some decent

rooms with private bathroom. There's plenty of Nahual furniture and *típica* fabrics around, giving the place a good atmosphere.

MIDRANGE

Hostal Los Lagos (☎ 2261-2809; www.loslagoshostal.com; 8a Av 15-85; dm Q160, s/d Q250/500; P ⬚) This is the most hostel-like of the near-the-airport options. Rooms are mostly set aside for dorms, which are airy and spacious, but there are a couple of reasonable-value private rooms. The whole place is extremely comfortable, with big indoor and outdoor sitting areas.

Casa Blanca (☎ 2261-3116; www.hotelcasablanca inn.com; 15a Calle C 7-35; s/d Q300/400; P ⬚ ⬚) A stylishly modern, if somewhat stark, hotel. Rooms are spacious, beds are huge and the full bar and restaurant downstairs are welcome bonuses.

TOP END

Villa Toscana (☎ 2261-2854; www.hostalvillatoscana.com; 16a Calle 8-20; s/d Q350/460; P ⬚ ⬚) One of the 'new breed' of airport hotels, this one features big, comfortable rooms, a tranquil atmosphere, an onsite restaurant and a lovely backyard.

EATING

Cheap eats are easy to find in Zona 1. Fine dining is more prevalent in Zona 10.

Zona 1

BUDGET

Dozens of restaurants and fast-food shops are strung along, and just off, 6a Av between 8a and 15a Calles. American fast-food chains such as McDonald's and Burger King are sprinkled liberally throughout Zona 1 and the rest of the city. They're open long hours, often from 7am to 10pm. Pollo Campero is Guatemala's KFC clone: a serve of chicken, fries, Pepsi and bread costs around Q45.

Restaurante Rey Sol (11a Calle 5-51; mains Q20-30; ☽ 8am-5pm Mon-Sat; Ⓥ) Good, fresh ingredients and some innovative cooking keep this strictly vegetarian restaurant busy at lunchtime.

Café-Restaurante Hamburgo (15a Calle 5-34; set meal Q30-50; ☽ 7am-9:30pm) This bustling spot facing the south side of Parque Concordia serves good Guatemalan food, with chefs at work along one side and orange-aproned waitresses scurrying about. At weekends a marimba band adds atmosphere.

Restaurante Long Wah (6a Calle 3-70; mains Q40-60; ☽ 11am-10pm) With friendly service and decorative red-painted arches, the Long Wah is a good choice from Zona 1's other concentration of Chinese eateries, in the blocks west of Parque Centenario.

Bar-Restaurante Europa (Local 201, Edificio Testa, cnr 5a Av & 11a Calle; mains Q40-60; 8am-8:30pm Mon-Sat) The Europa is a comfortable, relaxed, 11-table restaurant, bar and gathering place for locals and foreigners alike (the bar stays open till midnight). It has international cable TV and good-value food – try chicken cordon bleu for dinner, or eggs, hash browns, bacon and toast for breakfast.

Picadilly (cnr 6 Av & 11a Calle; mains Q40-80; lunch & dinner) Right in the thick of the 6a Av action, this bustling restaurant does OK pizzas and pastas and good steak dishes. The place is clean and street views out of the big front windows are mesmerizing.

Coffee culture is just beginning to hit Zona 1, and there are a number of cool little cafes springing up where you can enjoy good coffee, sandwiches and snacks.

Café Leon (8a Av 9-15; 8am-6pm Mon-Sat) Hugely popular and atmospheric with some great old photos of the city on the walls. There's another branch at 12a Calle 6-23.

Bar Céntrico (7a Av 12-32; 8am-7pm Mon-Sat) A hip little bar/cafe with comfy sofas out on the passageway.

Café de Imeri (6a Calle 3-34; mains Q27-40; 8am-7pm Tue-Sat) Interesting breakfasts, soups and pastas. The list of sandwiches is impressive and there's a beautiful little courtyard area out the back.

GOURMET GUATE

'Fine Dining' is a relative concept in Guatemala. Many fancier restaurants simply take standard dishes and improve on them with better presentation and fresher ingredients. There is a small foodie scene in the capital, though, where some chefs are busy experimenting with gourmet and fusion styles. The restaurants listed below are world-class, but – and this is the best part – their prices are more-or-less Guatemalan.

Pecorino (2360-3035; 11a Calle 3-36, Zona 10; mains Q60-120; lunch & dinner Mon-Sat, lunch Sun) With a beautiful courtyard setting, this is widely regarded as the city's best Italian restaurant. The menu features a huge selection of antipasto, pizza, pasta, meat and seafood dishes. The wine list is equally impressive, offering hundreds of bottles from all over the world, starting from around Q160 per bottle.

Camille (2368-0048; 9a Av 15-27, Zona 10; mains Q100-150; dinner Mon-Fri) The simple, elegant dining room here is matched by the menu. Entrees are more imaginative than mains, where options go heavy on seafood. There's a very good almond-covered squid schnitzel in burnt-butter sauce and some simple but well-prepared beef dishes. Make sure you leave room for dessert, and if you're impressed, ask about its highly regarded cooking school.

Casa Yurrita (2360-1615; Ruta 6 8-52, Zona 4; mains Q120-200; lunch & dinner Tue-Sat) Set in a gorgeous, parquetry-floored house decked out in baroque stylings, this is one of the city's snootier restaurants. The small menu is almost exclusively French-inspired (garlic snails, champagne pâté etc). The only two 'regional' ingredients used are jamaica (hibiscus) and Zacapa rum (both used in sauces for duck dishes). The wine list is surprisingly minimal and the atmosphere hushed and formal.

Tamarindos (2360-2815; www.tamarindos.com.gt; 11a Calle 2-19; mains Q110-180; lunch & dinner Mon-Sat) A chic and delicious Asian/Italian restaurant with a Guatemalan twist. There's an inspiring range of salads on offer and some very good Japanese and Thai-inspired dishes. The fettuccine al Carciofi showcases rare (for Guatemala) ingredients such as artichokes and prosciutto and the shrimps with sticky rice and calamondin sauce display a subtle blend of flavors. The decor is stylish and service prompt but friendly.

Jake's (2368-0351; www.grupoculinario.com/jakes; 17 Calle 10-40, Zona 10; mains Q120-270; lunch & dinner Mon-Sat, lunch Sun) The most formal of the restaurants listed here, with an army of white-jacketed waiters buzzing around. There are a few dining rooms to choose from, but on a sunny day the shady courtyard can't be beat. The menu focuses heavily on steak – the imported US beef being the star here (Q250 to Q350) and the '$500 hamburger' (a snap at only Q160) – but there's also a decent range of pasta, chicken, shrimp and fish dishes. Flavors incorporate Mexican, Asian, Italian and 'International' influences. The wine list is small, but well-chosen, featuring a white merlot from Guatemala's only winemaker, Chateau de Fay (Q60 per glass).

MIDRANGE & TOP END

Hotel Pan American (☎ 2232-6807; 9a Calle 5-63; breakfast Q40-80, mains Q60-120; ✆ breakfast, lunch & dinner) The restaurant at this venerable hotel (see p75) is high on ambience. It has highly experienced and polished waiters sporting traditional Maya regalia. The food (Guatemalan, Italian and American) is fine, although it is a little on the expensive side.

Restaurante Altuna (☎ 2232-0669; 5a Av 12-31; mains Q80-150; ✆ lunch & dinner Tue-Sat, lunch Sun) This large and classy restaurant has the atmosphere of a private club. It has tables in several rooms that are off a skylit patio. The specialties are seafood and Spanish dishes; service is both professional and welcoming.

Zona 4

Cuatro Grados Norte, situated on Vía 5 between Rutas 1 and 3, is the name for a two-block pedestrianized strip of restaurants and cafes with sidewalk tables and relaxed cafe society. Inaugurated in 2002, and the only place of its kind in Guatemala City, it is conveniently close to the main Inguat tourist office. Unfortunately, skyrocketing rents have seen several businesses close here, but it still gets lively in the evening, particularly around weekends.

La Esquina Cubana (cnr Vía 5 & Ruta 1, Cuatro Grados Norte; mains Q30-60; ✆ lunch & dinner Tue-Sun) For authentic Cuban dishes, washed down with some very tasty mojitos, try this laid-back little spot out the back of the parking area.

Del Paseo (Vía 5 1-81, Cuatro Grados Norte; mains Q50-100; ✆ lunch & dinner Tue-Sun) This spacious, artsy, Mediterranean-style bistro is one of Cuatro Grados Norte's most popular spots. Relaxed jazz plays in the background unless there's a live band (try Thursday from 9pm). You might select roast chicken breast with tropical fruits and grated coconut – or spinach-and-ricotta filo pastry parcels? Wine goes for Q30 a glass.

Kabala (Vía 5, Cuatro Grados Norte; mains Q60-120; ✆ lunch & dinner Tue-Sun) The best Japanese restaurant for miles around is at this 'fusion' place (we're not quite sure what they're fusing with). It doubles as a cocktail bar later on.

Zona 9

Celeste Imperio (cnr 7a Av & 10a Calle; mains Q50-100; ✆ lunch & dinner) One of the city's many Chinese restaurants, this one gets the thumbs up from locals. All your favorites are here, plus some oddities such as baked pigeon (Q80).

Puerto Barrios (☎ 2334-1302; 7a Av 10-65; mains Q80-160; ✆ lunch & dinner) The Puerto Barrios specializes in tasty prawn and fish dishes and is awash in nautical themes – paintings of buccaneers, portholes for windows, a big compass by the door. If you're having trouble finding it, just look for the big pirate ship in which it's housed.

Zona 10

BUDGET

A couple of nameless *comedores* opposite the Los Próceres mall serve up the cheapest eats in Zona 10. There's nothing fancy going on here – just good, filling eats at rock bottom prices.

Cafetería Patsy (Av La Reforma 8-01; set lunch Q25; ✆ 7:30am-8pm) A bright, cheerful place popular with local office workers, offering subs, sandwiches and good-value set lunches.

San Martín & Company (13a Calle 1-62; light meals Q30-50; ✆ 6am-8pm Mon-Sat) Cool and clean, with ceiling fans inside and a small terrace outside, this Zona Viva cafe and bakery is great at any time of day. For breakfast try a scrumptious omelet and croissant (the former arrives inside the latter). Later there are tempting and original sandwiches, soups and salads. The entrance is on 2a Av.

Los Alpes (10a Calle 1-09; breakfast Q40-60; ✆ breakfast & lunch) A relaxing garden restaurant/bakery. It's set well back from the road, behind a wall of vegetation, giving it a feeling of deep seclusion. The freshly made sandwiches and cakes really hit the spot.

A cheap lunch in Zona 10? These places are nothing fancy, but are popular with local office workers:

Panes del Sol (1a Av 10-50; mains Q20-40; ✆ lunch & dinner) Down-home Guatemalan food served in the eatery at the side of a *kiosko* (small store).

Cafetería Solé (14a Calle btwn 3a & 4a Avs; set lunch Q30; ✆ lunch) Good value set meals.

Café Gourmet (cnr 4a Av & 14a Calle; set lunch Q22; ✆ lunch) 'Gourmet' may be stretching it, but these are good, cheap eats.

MIDRANGE

La Lancha (13a Calle 7-98; mains Q50-80; ✆ lunch & dinner) French/Guatemalan probably isn't a combination you were expecting, but this little place does it well, with some good French dishes (including garlic snails, Q45), imported wines and live music on Fridays.

our pick **Kakao** (2a Av 13-44; mains Q60-150; ✆ lunch & dinner Tue-Sun) Set under a thatched *palapa* roof with a soft marimba soundtrack, this is

Zona 10's best *comida típica* (regional food) restaurant. The atmosphere and food are both outstanding.

El Gran Pavo (cnr 6a Av & 13a Calle; mains Q70-120; ☺ lunch & dinner) It's not the cheapest Mexican food you're ever going to eat, but it is tasty and well-presented. The atmosphere livens up on Friday night with roaming mariachi musicians and two-for-one tequila shots.

TOP END

Marea Viva (10a Calle 1-89; mains Q80-180, buffet Q120; ☺ lunch & dinner) Specializing in imported seafood, this place has some good prices considering the location. The lunchtime buffet (Monday to Wednesday) is a winner, as is the surf 'n' turf platter for Q100.

DRINKING
Zona 1

Staggering from bar to bar about the darkened streets of Zona 1 is not recommended, but fortunately there's a clutch of good drinking places all within half a block of each other just south of the Parque Central.

Las Cien Puertas (Pasaje Aycinena 8-44, 9a Calle 6-45) This superhip (but not studiously so) little watering hole is a gathering place for all manner of local creative types (and a few travelers) who may be debating politics, strumming a guitar or refining the graffiti when you show up. Tasty snacks such as tacos and quesadillas are served. It's in a shabby colonial arcade that's said to have a hundred doors (hence the name) and is sometimes closed off for live bands. Little bars spring up all the time in this arcade and the surrounding streets – it's one of the few places in Zona 1 you can really go barhopping.

La Arcada (7a Av 9-10) Drop into this friendly little neighborhood bar for a few drinks – they'll let you pick the music, or spin some of their own – anything from Guat rock to ambient trance.

El Portal (Portal del Comercio, 6a Av; ☺ 10am-10pm Mon-Sat) This atmospheric old drinking den serves fine draft beer (around Q15 a mug) and free tapas. Che Guevara was once a patron. Sit at the long wooden bar or one of the wooden tables. Clients are mostly, but not exclusively, men. To find it, enter the Portal del Comercio arcade from 6a Av a few steps south of the Parque Central.

El Gran Hotel (www.elgranhotel.com.gt; 9a Calle 7-64) You can't actually stay here, but the downmarket renovated lobby of this classic hotel is one of downtown's better-looking bars. There's poetry, live music and film nights throughout the week – check the website for details.

Zona 4

Guate's restaurant/bar precinct, Cuatro Grados Norte, rivaled Zona 10's nightlife for a while, but seems to be declining. You can just have a drink at any of the restaurants along here, but there are a couple of good bars.

Suae (Vía 5, Cuatro Grados Norte) Hip, but not exclusive, this bar has a great, laid-back ambience in the day and heats up at night. Changing art exhibitions, a funky clothes boutique and guest DJs all add to the appeal.

Manacho's (9a Av 0-81, Cuatro Grados Norte) If Cuatro Grados Norte's polished sheen is getting to you, try dropping into this friendly little hole-in-the-wall bar. It's just grungy enough.

Zona 10

The best place to go bar-hopping is the **Zona Viva** around the corner of 2a Av and 15a Calle – there are plenty of places to choose from – check and see who's got the crowd tonight.

Mi Guajira (2a Av 14-42) This happening little disco/bar has a pretty good atmosphere and goes fairly light on the snob factor. Music varies depending on the night, but be prepared for anything from salsa to reggaetón to trance.

Bajo Fondo (15a Calle 2-55) One of the more atmospheric little bars in the area, this place has good music and the occasional spontaneous jam session.

Zona 12

For a seriously down-to-earth night out, you should go out partying with the students from USAC, Guatemala's public university. The strip of bars along 31a Calle at the corner of 11a Av, just near the main entrance to the university, all offer cheap beer, loud music and bar/junk food. Like student bars all over the world, they're busy any time of day, but nights and weekends are best. A taxi out here from the center should cost about Q50 if it's not too late.

Beer House (31a Calle 13-08) The most formal of the bunch (in that it has menus, vaguely comfortable seats and draft beer) has a dance floor out back.

Liverpool (31a Calle 11-53) Plenty of pool tables and cheap drinks keep this place swinging.

Ice (31a Calle 13-39) This one heats up later into the night, when the dance floor fills with students dancing salsa, merengue and reggaetón.

ENTERTAINMENT

Cinema

Various multiscreen cinema complexes show Hollywood blockbuster movies, often in English with Spanish subtitles. Unless they're kids' movies, in which case they'll most likely be dubbed into Spanish. Most convenient are **Cine Capitol Royal** (Centro Comercial Capitol; ☎ 2251-8733; 6a Av 12-51, Zona 1) or **Cinépolis Oakland Mall** (Oakland Mall; ☎ 2269-6990; www.cinepolis.com.gt; Diagonal 6 13-01, Zona 10). Tickets cost between Q18 and Q34. Movie listings can be found in the *Prensa Libre* newspaper.

Gay Venues

Don't get too excited about this heading: there are only a couple of places worthy of mention for men, and nothing much for women.

Genetic (Ruta 3 3-08, Zona 4; ☾ 9pm-1am Fri & Sat) This used to be called Pandora's Box, and has been hosting Guatemala's gay crowd since the '70s, although it gets a mixed crowd and is one of the best places in town to go for trance/dance music. It has two dance floors, a rooftop patio and a relaxed atmosphere. Friday is 'all you can drink.'

Black & White Lounge (www.blackandwhitebar.com; 11a Calle 2-54, Zona 1; ☾ 7pm-1am Wed-Sat) A well-established gay disco-bar in a former private house near the city center, often with strippers.

Club SO36 (www.clubso36.com; 5a Calle 1-24, Zona 1; ☾ 4-10pm) A combination bar/strip club/gay cinema.

Theater

Two very good cultural centers in Cuatro Grados Norte host regular theatrical performances and other artistic events. It's always worth dropping in or checking their websites to see what's on.

The English-language magazine *Revue* (www.revuemag.com) has events details, although it focuses more on Antigua. Your hotel should have a copy, or know where to get one. Free events mags in Spanish come and go. At the time of writing, *El Azar* (www.elazarcultural.blogspot.com) had the best info. Pick up a copy at any cultural center listed below.

IGA Cultural Center (☎ 2422-5555; www.iga.edu; Ruta 1, 4-05, Zona 4) The Instituto Guatemalteco Americano hosts art exhibitions and live theater.

Centro Cultural de España (☎ 2385-9066; www.centroculturalespana.com.gt; Via 5 1-23, Zona 4) The Spanish Cultural Center hosts an excellent range of events, including live music, film nights and art exhibitions, mostly with free admission.

Centro Cultural Miguel Ángel Asturias (☎ 2332-4041; www.teatronacional.com.gt; 24a Calle 3-81, Zona 1) Cultural events are also held here.

Live Music

La Bodeguita del Centro (12a Calle 3-55, Zona 1) There's a hopping, creative local scene in Guatemala City, and this large, bohemian hang-out is one of the best places to connect with it. Posters featuring the likes of Che, Marley, Lennon, Victor Jara, Van Gogh and Pablo Neruda cover the walls from floor to ceiling. There's live music of some kind almost every night from Tuesday to Saturday, usually starting at 9pm, plus occasional poetry readings, films or forums. Entry is usually free Tuesday to Thursday, with a charge of Q25 to Q60 on Friday and Saturday nights. Food and drinks are served. Pick up a monthly schedule of events.

Rattle & Hum (cnr 4a Av & 16 Calle, Zona 10) One of the last places in Zona 10 to still be hosting live music, this Australian-owned place has a warm and friendly atmosphere.

TrovaJazz (www.trovajazz.com; Via 6 No 3-55, Zona 4) Jazz, blues and folk fans should look into what's happening here.

Box Lounge (15a Calle 2-53, Zona 10) With live DJs Tuesday to Saturday, this is one of the best spots in town to connect with Guatemala's growing electronic music scene.

Dancing

La Estación Norte (Ruta 4 6-32, Zona 4) As far as megadiscos go, this one around the corner from Cuatro Grados Norte is kind of interesting. It's done out in a train theme, with carriages for bars and platforms for dance floors. Dress well, but not over the top.

El Círculo (7a Av 10-33, Zona 1; ☾ Wed-Sat 7pm-1am) One of the most reliable dance floors in the downtown area. The crowd is mostly young, and the music is mostly latina, along the lines of salsa, merengue and reggaetón. Occasional live music.

Zona 10 has a bunch of clubs attracting 20-something local crowds along 13a Calle and adjacent streets such as 1a Av. The area's exclusivity means that door staff are well versed in the old 'members only' and 'sorry, we're full' routines. If you want to try your luck, the universal rules apply: dress up, go before 11pm and make sure your group has more women than men in it. Check flyers around town for special nights. Here are a couple to get you started:

Kahlua (15a Calle & 1a Av, Zona 10) For electronica and bright young things.

Mr Jerry (13a Calle 1-26, Zona 10) For salsa and merengue.

SHOPPING

Mercado Central (9a Av btwn 6a & 8a Calles; ☻ 9am-6pm Mon-Sat, 9am-noon Sun) Until the quake of 1976, Mercado Central, behind the cathedral, was where locals shopped for food and other necessities. Reconstructed after the earthquake, it now deals in colorful Guatemalan handicrafts such as textiles, carved wood, metalwork, pottery, leather goods and basketry, and is a pretty good place to shop for these kinds of things, with reasonable prices.

Mercado de Artesanías (Crafts Market; ☎ 2472-0208; cnr 5a Calle & 11a Av, Zona 13; ☻ 9:30am-6pm) This sleepy official market near the museums and zoo sells similar goods in less-crowded conditions.

For fashion boutiques, electronic goods and other first-world paraphernalia, head for the large shopping malls such as **Centro Comercial Los Próceres** (www.proceres.com; 16a Calle, Zona 10) or **Oakland Mall** (www.oaklandmall.com.gt; Diagonal 6 13-01, Zona 10).

For a more everyday Guatemalan experience, take a walk along 6a Av between 8a and 16a Calles in Zona 1. Back in the '70s, before the big shopping malls started stealing all the customers away, there was a verb 'sexteando,' which meant going for a stroll along the 6a Av (La Sexta) to see what was on offer. The scene has quietened down a bit, but it's still ground central for cheap copied CDs, shoes, underwear, overalls and pretty much everything else under the sun. Various attempts have been made to move these unofficial vendors away from this area and the most serious one was under way at the time of writing, with the construction of **Plaza El Amate** (cnr 18a Calle & 4a Av, Zona 1). Once the plaza is opened, the plan is to move all these vendors here.

GETTING THERE & AWAY
Air

Guatemala City's **Aeropuerto La Aurora** (☎ 2321-5050) is the country's major airport. All international flights to Guatemala City land and take off here. Renovation work on the airport has dragged on for years and was still not complete at the time of research. One major improvement is a working ATM and a currency-exchange booth in the arrivals hall. Various readers have complained about the

rates given at the exchange booth inside the airport and instead recommend the Banrural bank on the 3rd floor of the parking garage.

At the time of writing, the country's only *scheduled* domestic flights are between Guatemala City and Flores. Grupo Taca makes two round-trip flights daily (one in the morning, one in the afternoon), plus an extra flight four mornings a week which continues from Flores to Cancún (Mexico) and flies back from there via Flores in the afternoon. TAG offers one flight daily, leaving Guatemala at 6:30am and returning from Flores at 4:30pm

Tickets to Flores cost around Q1330/2245 one-way/round-trip with Grupo Taca and Q1150/1980 with TAG, but some travel agents, especially in Antigua, offer large discounts on these prices.

AIRLINE OFFICES

International carriers that have offices in Guatemala City are listed here.

American Airlines (www.aa.com) airport (☎ 2260-6550; Aeropuerto Internacional La Aurora); city (☎ 2422-0000; Barceló Guatemala, 7a Av 15-45, Zona 9)

Continental Airlines (www.continental.com) airport (☎ 2260-6733; Aeropuerto Internacional La Aurora); city (☎ 2385-9610, Edificio Unicentro, 18a Calle 5-56, Zona 10)

Copa Airlines (www.copaair.com) airport (☎ 2385-1826; Aeropuerto Internacional La Aurora); city (☎ 2353-6555; Edificio Europlaza, 5a Av 5-55, Zona 14)

Cubana (www.cubana.cu) airport (☎ 2361-0857; Aeropuerto Internacional La Aurora); city (☎ 2367-2288/89/90; local 29, Edificio Atlantis, 13a Calle 3-40, Zona 10)

Delta Air Lines (www.delta.com) airport (☎ 2360-7956; Aeropuerto Internacional La Aurora); city (☎ 2263-0600; Edificio Centro Ejecutivo, 15a Calle 3-20, Zona 10)

Grupo Taca (☎ 2470-8222; www.taca.com; Hotel Intercontinental, 14a Calle 2-51, Zona 10)

Iberia (www.iberia.com) airport (☎ 2260-6291; Aeropuerto Internacional La Aurora); city (☎ 2332-0911; Oficina 507, Edificio Galerías Reforma, Av La Reforma 8-00, Zona 9)

Mexicana (www.mexicana.com) airport (☎ 2260-6335; Aeropuerto Internacional La Aurora); city (☎ 2333-6001; Local 104, Edificio Edyma Plaza, 13a Calle 8-44, Zona 10)

TAG (☎ 2380-9401; www.tag.com.gt; Aeropuerto Internacional La Aurora)

United Airlines (www.united.com) airport (☎ 2332-2764; Aeropuerto Internacional La Aurora); city (☎ 2336-9923; Oficina 201, Edificio El Reformador, Av La Reforma 1-50, Zona 9)

Bus

Buses from here run all over Guatemala and into Mexico, Belize, Honduras, El Salvador and beyond. Most bus companies have their own terminals, some of which are in Zona 1. The city council has been on a campaign to get long-distance bus companies out of the city center, so it may be wise to double check with Inguat or staff at your hotel about the office location before heading out there.

INTERNATIONAL BUS SERVICES
The following companies offer first-class bus services to international destinations.

For destinations in Honduras, try **Hedman Alas** (☎ 2362-5072/6; www.hedmanalas.com; 2a Av 8-73, Zona 10).

Copán, Honduras (Q291, five hours) Daily departures at 5am and 9am.

La Ceiba, Honduras (Q433, 12 hours) Daily departures at 5am and 9am.

San Pedro Sula, Honduras (Q374, eight hours) Daily departures at 5am and 9am.

Tegucigalpa, Honduras (Q433, 12 hours) Daily departures at 5am and 9am.

A number of Central American destinations are covered by **King Quality & Comfort Lines** (☎ 2369-7070; www.king-qualityca.com; 18a Av 1-96, Zona 15).

Managua, Nicaragua (Q460 to Q740, 14 hours) Daily departures at 4am & 7:30am. Involves changing buses in El Salvador.

San José, Costa Rica (Q625 to Q1200, 30 hours) Daily departures at 3:30pm. Involves an overnight stopover in El Salvador.

San Pedro Sula, Honduras (Q616 to Q933, 30 hours). Daily departures at 7am and 3:30pm. Involves an overnight stopover in El Salvador.

San Salvador, El Salvador (Q210, five hours) Daily departures at 8am, 2pm and 3:30pm.

Tegucigalpa, Honduras (Q516 to Q824, 36 hours) Daily departures at 7am and 3:30pm. Involves an overnight stopover in El Salvador.

For buses to various destinations from Mexico to Panama, see **Tica Bus** (☎ 2473-0633; www.ticabus.com; Calzada Aguilar Batres 22-55, Zona 12).

Managua, Nicaragua (Q430, 28-35 hours) Departures at 5:30am and 1pm daily, with an overnight stop in San Salvador.

Panama City, Panama (Q790, 76 hours) Departures at 1pm daily, with overnight stops in San Salvador and Managua.

San José, Costa Rica (Q566, 53-60 hours) Departures at 5:30am and 1pm daily, with overnight stops in San Salvador and Managua.

San Salvador, El Salvador (Q125, five hours) Departures at 1pm daily.

Tapachula, Mexico (Q125, five hours) Departures at noon daily.

Tegucigalpa, Honduras (Q250, 35 hours) Departures at 5:30am daily, with an overnight stop in San Salvador.

Línea Dorada (☎ 2415-8900; www.lineadorada.com.gt; cnr 10a Av & 16a Calle, Zona 1) has a service to Belize City, Belize (Q350, 15 hours), often a direct connection, or with a few hours' wait in Flores. Alternatively, take any bus to Flores/Santa Elena and an onward bus from there. It also serves Mexico, with destinations such as Chetumal (Q415, 23 hours, 9pm daily), and Tapachula (Q150, seven hours, 6am daily).

Pullmantur (☎ 2367-4746; www.pullmantur.com; Holiday Inn, 1a Av 13-22, Zona 10) has services to San Salvador, El Salvador (Q290, 4½ hours), with departures at 6:45am and 2:45pm Monday to Thursday and Saturday, 6:45am and 1:45pm Friday, and 8:30am and 1:30pm Sunday. It also has services to Tegucigalpa, Honduras (Q516, 10½ hours); buses depart at 6:45am Tuesday, Thursday and Friday, and at 8:30am Sunday. Change buses in San Salvador.

Rutas Orientales (☎ 2253-7282; 21a Calle 11-60, Zona 1) has services to San Pedro Sula, Honduras (Q200, nine hours). Daily departures are at 6am and 2:30pm.

Transportes Galgos Inter (☎ 2232-3661; www.transgalgosinter.com.gt; 7a Av 19-44, Zona 1) can book connections as far north as the US, including Tapachula, Mexico (Q205, five to seven hours), with departures at 7:30am, 1:30pm and 3:30pm daily.

NATIONAL PULLMAN BUS SERVICES
The following bus companies have Pullman services to Guatemalan destinations. See boxed text, right, for details. For a warning on solo female travelers traveling on intercity buses, see p329.

ADN (☎ 2251-0050; www.adnautobusesdelnorte.com; 8a Av 16-41, Zona 1) Flores.

Monja Blanca (☎ 2238-1409; www.tmb.com.gt; 8a Av 15-16, Zona 1) For Cobán and points in between.

Fortaleza del Sur (☎ 2230-3390; Calzada Raúl Aguilar Batres 4-15, Zona 12) Covers the Pacific coast.

Fuente del Norte (☎ 2238-3894; www.autobuses fuentedelnorte.com; 17a Calle 8-46, Zona 1) Covers the whole country.

Hedman Alas (☎ 2362-5072/6; www.hedmanalas.com; 2a Av 8-73, Zona 10) Antigua.

NATIONAL PULLMAN BUS DEPARTURES FROM GUATEMALA CITY

Destination	Cost	Duration (hr)	Departures	Frequency	Company
Antigua	Q40	1	2pm & 6pm	2	Litegua
	Q50	1	7pm	1	Hedman Alas
Biotopo del Quetzal	Q43	3½	4am-5pm	half hourly	Monja Blanca
Chiquimula	Q35	3	4:30am-6pm	hourly	Rutas Orientales
Cobán	Q50	4½	4am-5pm	half hourly	Monja Blanca
El Carmen	Q65	7	12:15am-6:30pm	half hourly	Fortaleza del Sur
Esquipulas	Q50	4½	4:30am-5:30pm	half hourly	Rutas Orientales
Flores/Santa Elena	Q110	10	nonstop	hourly	Fuente del Norte
	Q150-190	8	10am-9pm	3	Línea Dorada
	Q120	10	6am & 9pm	2	Rapidos del Sur
	Q150	8	9pm & 10pm	2	ADN
Huehuetenango	Q65	5	noon & 4pm	2	Los Halcones
	Q90	5	6:30am & 10:30pm	2	Línea Dorada
La Mesilla	Q130	7	6:30am & 10:30pm	2	Línea Dorada
Melchor de Mencos	Q125-170	11	9pm & 10pm	2	Fuente del Norte
Panajachel	Q40	3	5:15am	1	Transportes Rebuli
Poptún	Q115	8	11:30am, 10:30pm & 11pm	3	Línea Dorada
Puerto Barrios	Q60-90	5	3:45am-7pm	half hourly	Litegua
Quetzaltenango	Q65	4	8:30am-2:30pm	4	Transportes Galgos
	Q60	4	6:15am-5:30pm	4	Alamo
	Q70	4	4am & 2:30pm	2	Línea Dorada
	Q55	4	6:30am-5pm	hourly	Transportes Marquensita
Retalhuleu	Q70	3	9.30am-7:30pm	5	Fuente del Norte
Río Dulce	Q60	4	6am-4:30pm	half hourly	Litegua
Sayaxché	Q135	11	5:30pm & 7pm	2	Fuente del Norte
Tecún Umán	Q55	6	6am-6pm	hourly	Fortaleza del Sur

Línea Dorada (☎ 2415-8900; cnr 10a Av & 16a Calle, Zona 1) Luxury buses to El Petén, Quetzaltenango, Huehuetenango, Río Dulce etc.

Litegua (☎ 2220-8840; www.litegua.com; 15a Calle 10-40, Zona 1) Covers the east and Antigua.

Los Halcones (☎ 2432-5364; Calzada Roosevelt 37-47, Zona 11) For Huehuetenango.

Rapidos del Sur (☎ 2232-7025; 20a Calle 8-55, Zona1) For the Pacific coast and El Petén.

Rutas Orientales (☎ 2253-7282; www.rutasorientales. com; 21a Calle 11-60, Zona 1) Covers the east.

Transportes Álamo (☎ 2471-8646; 12a Av A 0-65, Zona 7) For Quetzaltenango.

Transportes Galgos (☎ 2253-4868; 7a Av 19-44, Zona 1) For Quetzaltenango.

Transportes Marquensita (☎ 2451-0763; 1a Av 21-31, Zona 1) For Quetzaltenango.

Transportes Rebuli (☎ 2230-2748; www.toursrebusa. com; 23a Av 1-39, Zona 7) For Panajachel.

2ND-CLASS BUS SERVICES

The services listed are all 2nd-class bus ('chicken bus') services; see boxed text, p84 for details of departures. Most Pacific coast services leave from Centra Sur, a large terminal on the southern outskirts of the city which is connected to the center by TransMetro buses (see boxed text, p85). Buses for the Western highlands leave from a series of roadside *paradas* (bus stops) on 41a Calle between 6a and 7a Avs in Zona 8.

Car

Most major rental companies have offices both at La Aurora airport (in the arrivals area) and in Zona 9 or 10. Companies include the following:

Ahorrent (www.ahorrent.com) Aeropuerto Internacional La Aurora (☎ 2385-8656); Zona 9 (☎ 2383-2800; Blvd Liberación 4-83)

Avis (www.avis.com) Aeropuerto Internacional La Aurora
(☎ 2385-8781); Zona 9 (☎ 2339-3249; 6a Calle 7-64)
Guatemala Rent a Car (www.guatemalarentacar.com)
Aeropuerto Internacional La Aurora (☎ 2329-9012); Zona
9 (☎ 2329-9020; Oficina 15, 12a Calle 5-54) Cheapest
rates in town.
Hertz (www.hertz.com.gt) Aeropuerto Internacional La Au-
rora (☎ 2470-3800); Barceló Guatemala (☎ 2470-3860);
Holiday Inn (☎ 2470-3870; 1a Av 13-22, Zona 10); Westin
Camino Real (☎ 2470-3810; Av La Reforma 0-20, Zona 10)
Tabarini (www.tabarini.com) Aeropuerto Internacional La
Aurora (☎ 2331-4755); Zona 10 (☎ 2331-2643; 2a Calle
A 7-30)
Tally Renta Autos (www.tallyrentaautos.com) Aero-
puerto Internacional La Aurora (☎ 2334-5925, 2277-9072);
Zona 1 (☎ 2251-4113, 2232-3327; 7a Av 14-60)
Thrifty (☎ 2379-8747; www.thrifty.com; Aeropuerto
Internacional La Aurora)

Shuttle Minibus

Door-to-door minibuses run from the airport
to any address in Antigua (usually Q80 per
person, one hour). Look for signs in the airport exit hall or people holding up 'Antigua
Shuttle' signs. The first shuttle leaves for
Antigua about 7am and the last around 8pm
or 9pm. Shuttle services from Guatemala City

to popular destinations such as Panajachel
and Chichicastenango (via Antigua – both
around Q180) are offered by travel agencies in
Antigua – see p92 for contact details.

GETTING AROUND
To/From the Airport

Aeropuerto La Aurora is in Zona 13, in the
southern part of the city, 10 to 15 minutes
from Zona 1 by taxi, or 30 minutes by bus.
See boxed text, right, for a warning on city
buses and details on getting to and from the
airport by bus.

Taxis wait outside the airport's arrivals exit.
'Official' fares are Q60 to Zona 9 or 10, Q85
to Zona 1, Q250 to Antigua, but in reality you
may have to pay a bit more. Be sure to establish the destination and price before getting
in. Prices for taxis *to* the airport, hailed on
the street, are likely to be lower – around Q50
from Zona 1. For Antigua, shuttle minibuses
are more economical than taxis if there's only
one or two of you.

Bus & Minibus

Due to an alarming increase in (often violent) crime on Guatemala City's red city

2ND-CLASS BUS SERVICES FROM GUATEMALA CITY

Destination	Cost	Duration (hr)	Departures	Frequency	Departs
Amatitlán	Q3	30 mins	7am-8:45pm	every 5 mins	Centra Sur
Antigua	Q5	1	7am-8pm	every 5 mins	Calz Roosevelt btwn 4a Av & 5a Av, Zona 7
Chichicastenango	Q12	3	5am-6pm	hourly	Parada, Zona 8
Ciudad Pedro de Alvarado	Q25	2½	5am-4pm	half hourly	Centra Sur
Escuintla	Q15	1	6am-4:30pm	half hourly	Centra Sur
Huehuetenango	Q50	5	7am-5pm	half hourly	Parada, Zona 8
La Democracia	Q20	2	6am-4:30pm	half hourly	Centra Sur
La Mesilla	Q75	8	noon	1	Parada, Zona 8
Monterrico	Q30	3	10:20am-2:20pm	hourly	Centra Sur
Panajachel	Q30	3	7am-5pm	half hourly	Parada, Zona 8
Puerto San José	Q20	1	4:30am-4:45pm	every 15 mins	Centra Sur
Salamá	Q30	3	5am-5pm	hourly	17a Calle 11-32, Zona 1
San Pedro La Laguna	Q35	4	2pm, 3pm & 4pm	3	Parada, Zona 8
Santa Cruz del Quiché	Q35	3½	5am to 5pm	hourly	Parada, Zona 8
Santiago Atitlán	Q25	4	4am-5pm	half hourly	Parada, Zona 8
Tecpán	Q7	2	5:30am-7pm	every 15 mins	Parada, Zona 8

lonelyplanet.com   GUATEMALA CITY •• Getting Around   85

GUATEMALA CITY

TRANSMETRO

In early 2007, in answer to growing concerns about traffic congestion and insecurity on urban buses, Guatemala City inaugurated the TransMetro system. TransMetro buses differ from regular old, red urban buses because they are prepaid (the driver carries no money, thus reducing risk of robberies), travel in their own lanes (not getting caught in traffic jams), only stop at designated stops and are new, comfortable and bright green.

The first route to be opened connects the Centro Cívico in Zona 4 to Centra Sur, a new bus terminal where the majority of buses for the Pacific coast now depart. At the time of writing the Central Corridor route, connecting Zona 1 with Zonas 9 and 10, was about to be inaugurated. This new route and its stops are marked on the Guatemala City map (p66).

Crime has got so bad on Guate's regular red buses that travelers are advised not to use them, but TransMetro buses are safe, fast and comfortable. All rides cost Q1, payable at the bus stop before boarding. If you'd like to try one out for free, consider catching a SubiBaja bus (see p69) on any Sunday.

buses, it is pretty much universally accepted that tourists should only use them in case of dire emergency. The major exception to this is the TransMetro system of green, articulated buses (see boxed text, above). This may all change as a new system of prepaid, security-camera monitored buses called Transurban comes into effect sometime in 2010, but critics of the system say that the new buses will be more of the same. Catch them or not, if you spend any time out and about in Guatemala City, especially Zona 1, its buses will become a major feature of your existence as they roar along in large numbers belching great clouds of black smoke. Jets flying low over the city center intermittently intensify the cacophony.

For the thrillseekers out there, listed below are the most useful routes. Buses will stop anywhere they see a passenger, but street corners and traffic lights are your best bet for hailing them – just hold out your hand. Buses cost

Q1.10 per ride in the daytime: you pay the driver or his helper as you get on. Don't catch them at night.

Zona 1 to Zona 10 (Bus No 82 or 101) Travels via 10a Av, Zona 1, then 6a Av and Ruta 6 in Zona 4 and Av La Reforma.
Zona 10 to Zona 1 (Bus No 82 or 101) Travels via Av La Reforma then 7a Av in Zona 4 and 9a Av, Zona 1.
Airport to Zona 1 (Bus No 82) Travels via Zonas 9 and 4.
Zona 1 to Airport (Bus No 82) Travels via 10a Av in Zona 1 then down 6a Av in Zonas 4 and 9.

Taxi

Plenty of taxis cruise most parts of the city. Fares are negotiable; always establish your destination and fare before getting in. Zona 1 to Zona 10, or vice-versa, costs around Q40 to Q60. If you want to phone for a taxi, **Taxi Amarillo Express** (☎ 2232-1515) has metered cabs that often work out cheaper than others, although true *capitaleños* (capital city residents) will tell you that taxi meters are all rigged and you get a better deal bargaining.

Antigua

Antigua remains far more than a tourist attraction – it's Guatemala's showpiece. A place of rare beauty, major historical significance and vibrant culture, it's a must-visit destination.

A former capital – the seat of government was relocated to Guatemala City following several major earthquakes during the colonial period – Antigua boasts an astonishing catalogue of colonial relics in a magnificent setting. Its streetscapes of pastel facades under terracotta roofs unfold amid three volcanoes: Agua (3766m), Fuego (3763m) and Acatenango (3976m). Designated a Unesco World Heritage Site and with an ideal climate, it's a splendid place for walking (though it can get chilly after sunset). While many old ecclesiastical and civic structures are beautifully renovated, others retain tumbledown charm, with fragments strewn about parklike grounds and sprays of bougainvillea sprouting from the crumbling ruins.

Thanks to the dozens of Spanish language schools that operate here, Antigua has become a global hot spot as well, but the foreign presence by no means dominates the atmosphere. Antigua remains a vibrant Guatemalan town, its churches, plazas and markets throbbing with activity.

Perhaps the real miracle of Antigua is its resilience. Despite the destructive forces that have conspired against it – earthquakes, volcanic eruptions and floods, followed by virtual abandonment and centuries of neglect – it's reemerged with a vengeance, buoyed by the pride of its inhabitants.

HIGHLIGHTS

- Peering down into the crater of active **Volcán Pacaya** (p96)
- Resurrecting your high-school Spanish at one of the highly regarded language schools, such as the **Proyecto Lingüístico Francisco Marroquín** (p99)
- Dining fine at **Caffé Mediterráneo** (p107), just one among the wide variety of international restaurants found in Guatemala
- Getting historical in Antigua's museums, monasteries, mansions, churches and convents, starting with the spectacular **Iglesia y Convento de Santo Domingo** (p95)
- Admiring and acquiring traditional textiles at **Nim Po't** (p109), a cavalcade of Maya crafts

- Population: 58,150
- Elevation: 1530m

HISTORY

Antigua wasn't the Spaniards' first choice for a capital city. That honor goes to Iximché, settled in 1524 in order to keep an eye on the Kaqchiquel, with whom they had an uneasy truce. Things got uneasier when the Kaqchiquel rebelled, so the city was moved in 1527 to present-day Ciudad Vieja (p111) on the flanks of Volcán Agua. That didn't work out, either – the town practically disappeared under a mudslide in 1541 and everybody packed up and moved again. And so it was that on March 10, 1543, La muy Noble y muy Leal Ciudad de Santiago de los Caballeros de Goathemala, the Spanish colonial capital of Guatemala, was founded. The long-winded title attests to the founders' reverence for Saint James, to whom their early military victories were attributed.

Antigua was once the epicenter of power throughout Central America, and during the 17th and 18th centuries little expense was spared on the city's architecture, despite the regular ominous rumbles from the ground below. Indigenous labor was marshaled to erect schools, hospitals, churches and monasteries, their grandeur only rivaled by the houses of the upper clergy and the politically connected.

At its peak Antigua had no fewer than 38 churches, as well as a university, printing presses, a newspaper and a lively cultural and political scene. Those rumblings never stopped, though, and for a year the city was shaken by earthquakes and tremors until the devastating earthquake of July 29, 1773. A year later, the capital was transferred again, this time to Guatemala City. Antigua was evacuated and plundered for building materials but, despite official mandates that its inhabitants relocate and that the city be systematically dismantled, it was never completely abandoned. Fueled by a coffee boom early in the next century, the town, by then known as La Antigua Guatemala (Old Guatemala), began to grow again. Ongoing renovation of battered buildings helped maintain the city's colonial character despite an official lack of interest. During the 20th century, modernization dealt further blows but lobbying by Antigua's citizens led to President Ubico's declaration of the city as a national monument, and restoration ensued in earnest. But just as serious efforts were being made to return the city to its former splendor, disaster struck again with another major quake in February 1976,

leaving thousands dead and undoing much of the restoration work.

Unesco's designation of Antigua as a World Heritage Site in 1979 added new impetus to the restoration campaign. Within this new climate, Spanish-language schools began popping up, pulling in droves of foreign students and leading to a genuine cultural renaissance.

ORIENTATION

Antigua's focal point is the broad Parque Central; few places in town are more than 15 minutes' walk from here. Compass points are added to the numbered Calles and Avs, indicating whether an address is *Norte* (north), *Sur* (south), *Poniente* (west) or *Oriente* (east) of the Parque Central, though signage is frustratingly sparse.

Three volcanoes provide easy reference points: Volcán Agua is south of the city and visible from most points within it; Volcán Fuego and Volcán Acatenango rise to the southwest (Acatenango is the more northerly of the two).

Another useful Antigua landmark is the Arco de Santa Catalina, an arch spanning 5a Av Norte, 2½ blocks north of the Parque Central, on the way to La Merced church.

Buses arrive at and depart from the streets around the large open-air market, about 400m west of the Parque Central.

INFORMATION

Bookstores

Dyslexia Books (1a Av Sur 11) Mostly used books, mainly in English.

El Cofre (6a Calle Poniente 26) Used books, including some regional travel guides.

Hamlin y White (☎ 7832-7075; 4a Calle Oriente 12A) English and Spanish titles, with several shelves of Lonely Planet guides.

Librería La Casa del Conde (Portal del Comercio 4) Excellent selection of Central American history and politics and nature guides in English, literature in Spanish, and Lonely Planet guides.

Rainbow Reading Room (7a Av Sur 8) Thousands of used books in English and Spanish for sale, rent or trade. Also one of the best notice boards in town.

Emergency

Asistur (☎ 5978-3586; asisturantiguaguatemala@gmail. com; 6a Calle Poniente Final; ⏰ 24hr). The helpful tourism assistance agency has its headquarters on the west side of town, three blocks south of the market. If you're the victim of a crime, they'll accompany you to the national police and

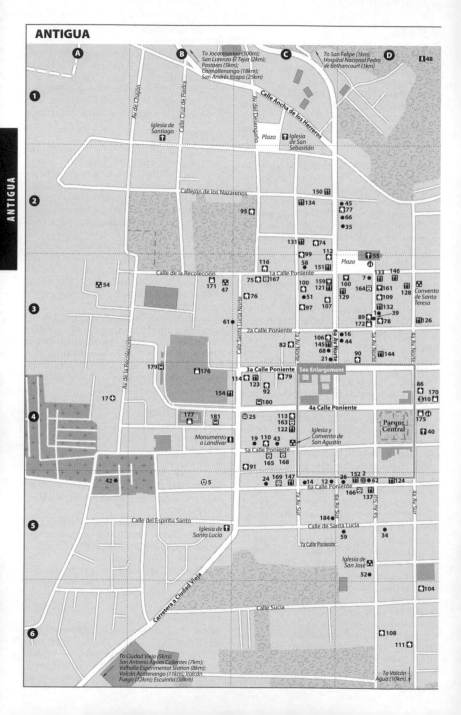

ANTIGUA

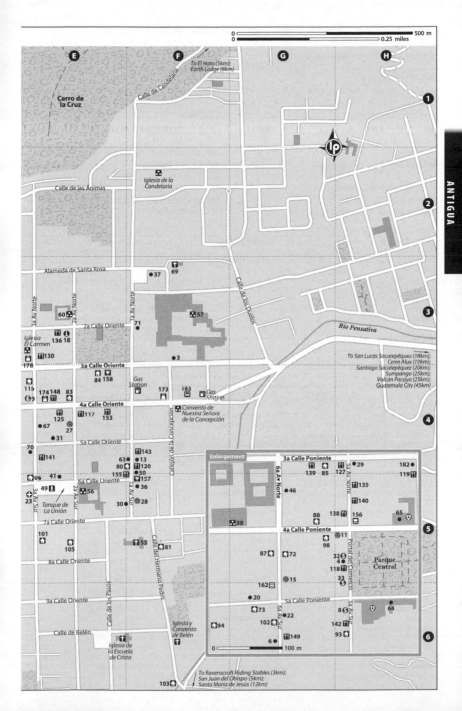

assist with the formalities, including any translating that's needed. Given advance notice, they can provide an escort for drivers heading out on potentially risky roads.

Internet Access

Aside from an abundance of affordable cybercafes, wi-fi is available in restaurants, cafes and elsewhere – even the Parque Central is a wireless hot spot.

Aló Internet (5a Calle Poniente 28; per hr Q5) Inside reception.

Antigua Net (6a Calle Poniente 8; per hr Q6)

Conher (☎ 5521-2823; 4a Calle Poniente 5; per hr Q10) All-purpose communications center, offering printing, scanning and CD burning.

El Cofre (6a Calle Poniente 26)

Enlaces (☎ 7832-5555; 6a Av Norte 1; per hr Q7)

Funky Monkey (5a Av Sur 6, Pasaje El Corregidor; per hr Q8; ✆ 8am-12:30am) Inside Monoloco; open latest of Antigua's cybercafes.

Roy.com (1a Av Sur 21; per hr Q8)

Roy.com (2a Av Norte 6B; per hr Q8)

Laundry

Laundromats are easy to find; most charge Q6 per pound to wash, dry and fold.

Laundry Gilda (5a Calle Poniente 12; ✆ 8am-6pm Mon-Fri, 8am-3pm Sat).

Quick Laundry (6a Calle Poniente 14; ✆ 9am-6pm Mon-Sat, 9am-2pm Sat)

Spring Laundry (1a Av Sur 20A; ✆ 7:30am-5pm Mon-Fri, 10am-4pm Sat)

Media

The Antigua-based *Revue Magazine* (www. revuemag.com) runs about 90-percent ads, but has reasonable information about cultural events. It's available everywhere.

La Cuadra (www.lacuadraonline.com), published by Café No Sé (see p108), presents the gringo-bohemian perspective, mixing politics with irreverent commentary. Pick up a copy at the cafe.

Medical Services

Casa de Salud Santa Lucía (☎ 7832-3122; Calz de Santa Lucía Sur 7) Comprises various private clinics, some specializing in gynecology, pediatrics etc. Emergency service available 7am to 7pm.

Farmacia Ivori Select (☎ 7832-1559; 6a Av Norte 19) Twenty-four-hour pharmacy.
Hospital Nacional Pedro de Bethancourt
(☎ 7831-1319) A public hospital in San Felipe, 2km north of the center, with emergency service.
Hospital Privado Hermano Pedro (☎ 7832-1197; Av de la Recolección 4) Private hospital that offers 24-hour emergency service and accepts foreign insurance.
Obras Sociales de Hermano Pedro (Hospital San Pedro; ☎ 7832-0883; 6a Calle Oriente 20) Primarily a refuge for the handicapped, elderly and abused, this public hospital offers low cost checkups Monday to Friday from 6am to 8am.

Money

Banco Industrial (5a Av Sur 4; ☏ 9am-7pm Mon-Fri, 9am-1pm Sat) Has a reliable ATM and changes US dollars (cash and traveler's checks). Another useful BI ATM is inside Café Barista, across the square.

Citibank (cnr 4a Calle Oriente & 4a Av Norte; ☏ 9am-4:30pm Mon-Fri, 9:30am-1pm Sat) Gives Visa (not MasterCard) cash advances. A second branch, one block east, changes US dollars and euros.

Visa & MasterCard ATM (5a Av Norte) Facing Parque Central.

Western Union (5a Av Norte) At Parque Central. Change cash dollars and euros here. There's a Visa/MasterCard ATM to the left of the entrance.

Post

DHL (☏ 7832-3718; 6a Calle Poniente 16) Offers door-to-door service.

Post office (cnr 4a Calle Poniente & Calz de Santa Lucía) Opposite the market.

Telephone & Fax

Most internet cafes offer cut-rate international calls, though Skype calls may be even cheaper. If you plan to be around a while, consider purchasing a local cell phone.

Conher (☏ 5521-2823; 4a Calle Poniente 5) Charges Q0.75 per minute to USA or Europe.

Funky Monkey (5a Av Sur 6, Pasaje El Corregidor) Inside Monoloco.

La Bodegona (5a Calle Poniente 32; ☏ 7am-8pm) This giant supermarket is a good place to get a cell phone.

Tourist Information

Inguat (☏ 7832-3782; 2a Calle Oriente 11; info-antigua@inguat.gob.gt; ☏ 8am-5pm Mon-Fri, 9am-5pm Sat & Sun) Inside a colonial mansion near the Capuchinas convent, the tourist office has free city maps, bus information and helpful, bilingual staff.

Travel Agencies

Numerous agencies offer international flights, shuttle minibuses, tours to interesting sites around Antigua and elsewhere in Guatemala, and more. Warning: although the agency gRuta Maya on the Parque Central claims to be 'operated by Lonely Planet,' there is absolutely no connection – in fact, we've received more complaints about this company than any other in town.

Adrenalina Tours (☏ 7832-1108; www.adrenalinatours.com; 5a Av Norte 31) Specialists in the western highlands; can arrange everything from tours and shuttles to domestic and international flights.

Adventure Travel Center (☏ /fax 7832-0162; viareal@hotmail.com; 5a Av Norte 25B)

Antigua Tours (☏ /fax 7832-5821; www.antiguatours.net; 3a Calle Oriente 22) Known for quality city tours (see

p99); additional branch inside Café El Portal on west side of Parque Central.

Atitrans (☏ 7832-3371; www.atitrans.com; 6a Av Sur 8)

Aviatur (☏ 7832-5989; aviaturfer@yahoo.com.mx; 5a Av Norte 34)

LAX Travel (☏ 7832-1621; laxantigua@intelnett.com; 3a Calle Poniente 12) International flight specialist.

Onvisa Travel Agency (☏ 5909-0160; onvisatravel@hotmail.com; 6a Calle Poniente 40) Operates shuttles to Copán and elsewhere.

National Travel (☏ 7832-8383; antigua@nationalgua.com; 6a Av Sur 1A) Offers one-way flights, including student and teacher fares.

Rainbow Travel Center (☏ /fax 7832-4202; www.rainbowtravelcenter.com; 7a Av Sur 8) Student and teacher air fares are its specialty.

Sinfronteras (☏ 7720-4400; www.sinfront.com; 5a Av Norte 15A) Arranges a variety of cultural and adventure tours, primarily designed for European groups. Also sells discount international air tickets, and issues student and youth cards.

Turansa (☏ 7832-2928; www.turansa.com; 5a Calle Oriente 10A)

DANGERS & ANNOYANCES

Antigua generally feels safe to walk around but muggings do occur, so don't let your guard down completely. This holds doubly true after the bars close at 1am, when muggers are on the lookout for inebriated visitors. After 10pm, consider taking a taxi back to your lodging, especially if you're female. Pickpockets work the busy market, doing overtime on paydays at the middle and end of the month. December (bonus time) brings a renewed wave of robberies.

Some of the more remote hiking trails have been the scene of muggings, though stepped-up police patrols have reduced the likelihood of such incidents in recent years. If you're planning on hiking independently to any of the volcanoes, check with Asistur (see p87) about the current situation.

SIGHTS
Parque Central

Surrounded by superb colonial structures, the broad, verdant plaza is the gathering place for *antigüeños* and visitors alike – a fine place to sit or stroll and observe the goings-on, from hawkers and shoeshines to school kids and tourists. The buxom mermaids in the fountain are a reconstruction of the original 1738 version, which was trashed early in the 20th century.

PALACIO DE LOS CAPITANES GENERALES

Dating from 1558, the Palacio de los Capitanes Generales (Captain-Generals' Palace) was the governmental center of all Central America from Chiapas to Costa Rica until 1773. The stately double-arcaded facade that anchors the southern side of the park was added later. At the time of writing, it was all that remained of the old palace, as major renovations were underway to restore the interior to its original splendor.

CATEDRAL DE SANTIAGO

On the east side of the park, the Catedral de Santiago was begun in 1542, wrecked by the quake of 1773, and only partially rebuilt over the next century. The present sliver of a church – the parish of San José – occupies only the entrance hall of the 17th-century edifice and contains a fraction of its original baroque art collection, much of which ended up in Guatemala City churches. The grand facade, recently repainted in 'Antigua white,' is studded with replicas of the original saints – handless because that part of their anatomy could not be faithfully reproduced. Behind this structure are the roofless **ruins** (admission Q3; 9am-5pm) of the main part of the cathedral, entered from 5a Calle Oriente. It's a haunting place, with massive chunks of pillars strewn beneath sweeping brick archways and vegetation sprouting from wall cracks. Reproductions of the intricate plasterwork figures and moldings between the arches seem all that more impressive against the ruined backdrop. Behind the main altar, steps lead down to a former crypt now serving as a chapel, with a smoke-blackened Christ.

PALACIO DEL AYUNTAMIENTO

The Palacio del Ayuntamiento (City Hall), the solid double-arcaded structure on the north side of the park, dates mostly from the 18th century. In addition to town offices, it houses the **Museo de Santiago** (7832-2868; admission Q30; 9am-4pm Mon-Fri, 9am-noon & 2-4pm Sat & Sun), in the former town jail – one of the original cells has been left intact with its torture devices. The mermaid statues that once graced the fountain in Parque Central are here (now headless), along with a hodgepodge of portraiture, weaponry, coins and colonial knickknacks. Far more worthwhile is the **Museo del Libro Antiguo** (Old Book Museum; 7832-5511; admission Q30; 9am-4pm Tue-Fri, 9am-noon & 2-4pm Sat & Sun) next door, showcasing the early days of Guatemalan printing, plus a replica of Guatemala's first printing press, which began work here in 1660. One of its earliest products is prominently displayed: a first edition of the second part of *Don Quixote de la Mancha*.

UNIVERSIDAD DE SAN CARLOS

The Universidad de San Carlos, now in Guatemala City, was founded in Antigua in 1676. What used to be the main building, half a block east of the park, features a magnificent cloister with a stunningly sculpted frieze. For the past eight decades, it's been the setting for the **Museo de Arte Colonial** (Museum of Colonial Art; 7832-0429; 5a Calle Oriente 5; admission Q50; 9am-4pm

---

ANTIGUA IN...

Two Days

Start with breakfast in colonial surroundings at **Café Condesa** (p105), then drop by a recommended agency (see left) to set up a volcano trip for the following day. Spend the day exploring some of Antigua's colonial buildings – the **Catedral de Santiago** (above), **Santo Domingo** (p95), **Las Capuchinas** (p94), **La Merced** (p94) – with a light lunch along the way. Eat a hearty traditional dinner at **La Cuevita de Los Urquizú** (p105) then stop into **Café No Sé** (p108) for a late-evening drink. The second morning starts early for your **volcano tour** (p96). Afterwards enjoy a well-earned dinner at **Mesón Panza Verde** (p107), or **Bistrot Cinq** (p107) if you're craving French cuisine, followed by drinks at **El Muro** (p108) or **Reilly's** (p108). Round things off, if you still can, with a shimmy at **La Casbah** (p108).

Four Days

Follow the two-day itinerary, then visit the **Centro Cultural La Azotea** (p110) at Jocotenango on day three. Head back to Antigua to catch a dinner show at **La Peña de Sol Latino** (p108), then stop off for a drink at **La Sala** (p108) on the way home. On day four reactivate with an out-of-town **guided hike** (p96), **bike ride** (p97) or **horseback ride** (p97). Watch the sun go down from **Café Sky** (p108) before enjoying food and lounging at **La Esquina** (p105). Then revisit your favorite bar...

Tue-Fri, 9am-noon & 2-4pm Sat & Sun), and it underwent a complete restoration in 2009. On display are paintings by leading Mexican artists of the colonial era, most notably *The Life of Saint Francis of Assisi* by Cristóbal del Villalpando, as well as a treasure trove of Guatemalan sacred statuary.

Churches & Monasteries

Once glorious in their gilded baroque finery, Antigua's churches have suffered indignities from both nature and humankind. Rebuilding after earthquakes gave the churches thicker walls, lower towers and belfries, and unembellished interiors. Furthermore, moving the capital to Guatemala City deprived Antigua of the population needed to maintain the churches in their traditional richness, though they remain impressive. In addition to those churches mentioned below, you'll find many others scattered around town in various states of decay.

IGLESIA Y CONVENTO DE NUESTRA SEÑORA DE LA MERCED

At the northern end of 5a Av is La Merced – a striking yellow structure trimmed with plaster filigree. Unveiled in the late 18th century, the squat, thick-walled building was built to withstand earthquakes, and over three centuries later it remains in pretty good shape. Inside the **monastery ruins** (admission Q5; 8:15am-5:45pm) is a fountain 27m in diameter, said to be the largest in Hispanic America. It's in the shape of a water lily (traditionally a symbol of power for Maya lords), and lily motifs also appear on the church's entrance arch. Go upstairs for a bird's-eye view of the fountain and the town. A candlelit procession, accompanied by bell ringing and firecrackers, starts and ends here on the last Thursday evening of each month.

IGLESIA DE SAN FRANCISCO

Little of the original 16th-century **Iglesia de San Francisco** (cnr 8a Calle Oriente & Calle do los Pasos) remains, but reconstruction and restoration over the centuries have left a handsome structure. The church is imbued with the spirit of Santo Hermano Pedro de San José de Bethancourt, a Franciscan monk who founded a hospital for the poor in Antigua and earned the gratitude of generations (see boxed text, right). His intercession is still sought by the ill, who pray fervently by his tomb, which was moved to an elaborate pavilion north of the church after he

was canonized in 2002; devotees may enter via a garden north of the church. On the south side are the **Museo del Hermano Pedro** and the ruins of the adjoining **monastery** (joint admission adult/child Q5/2; 8am-4:30pm Tue-Sun). The museum houses relics from the church and Santo Hermano's curiously well-preserved personal belongings, including some spectacularly uncomfortable-looking underwear. The *pasillo de los milagros* is a corridor jam-packed with testimonials, photos, plaques and crutches donated by people who claim to have been healed by the brother.

LAS CAPUCHINAS

Inaugurated in 1736 by nuns from Madrid, the convent of **Las Capuchinas** (Iglesia y Convento de Nuestra Señora del Pilar de Zaragoza; cnr 2a Av Norte & 2a Calle Oriente; adult/student Q30/15; 9am-5pm) was seriously damaged by the 1773 earthquake and thereafter abandoned. But thanks to meticulous renovations in recent decades, it's possible to get a sense of the life experienced by those cloistered nuns, who ran an orphanage and women's hospital. Wander round to admire the fine cloister with its stout columns and high arched passageways, remarkably restored wash basins and well-tended gardens. At the rear you'll find the convent's most unique feature, a towerlike structure of 18 nuns' cells built around a circular patio. The headquarters of the Antigua preservation commission is located here.

IGLESIA Y CONVENTO DE LA RECOLECCIÓN

A serene air pervades the remains of the massive monastery of **La Recolección** (Av de la Recolección; admission Q30; 9am-5pm), which stands well west of the center across a busy thoroughfare. It was erected in the early 1700s by the Récollets (a French branch of the Franciscan order) despite initial opposition from local authorities, who ultimately granted them space in the western suburb of San Jerónimo. The earthquake of 1773 toppled the structure; enormous chunks of masonry still lie jumbled around the ruined church, of which the great arched doorway remains intact. Despite its short life as a monastery, the complex was left alone, serving variously as a squatters' residence, fairground and art-restoration workshop. Clamber up to the 2nd floor for better views, but watch your step.

COLEGIO DE SAN JERÓNIMO

Built in 1757, the **Colegio de San Jerónimo** (Real Aduana; cnr Calz de Santa Lucía & Calle de la Recolección; adult/

student Q30; 9am-5pm) was used as a school by friars of the Merced order, but because it did not have royal authorization, it was taken over by Spain's Carlos III, and in 1765 designated for use as the Real Aduana (Royal Customs House). Today it's a tranquil, mostly open-air site. The handsome cloister centers around an octagonal fountain – it's an evocative setting for dance and other cultural performances. Upstairs you'll find excellent photo angles of Volcán Agua through stone archways.

IGLESIA Y CONVENTO DE SANTA CLARA

Established by sisters from Puebla, Mexico, **Santa Clara** (2a Av Sur 27; admission Q30; 9am-5pm) was inaugurated in 1734, destroyed four decades later by the great quake and abandoned. Fortunately some elements of the original structure remain intact, such as the church's stonework facade, the arched niches along the nave that served as confessionals, and an underground chamber where provisions were stored. Most captivating of all is the cloister, centering on a fountain bordered by gardens, though only one side of the upper-level arcade is still in place.

IGLESIA Y CONVENTO DE SANTO DOMINGO

Founded by Dominican friars in 1542, **Santo Domingo** (7820-1220; 3a Calle Oriente 28; archaeological area Q40; 9am-6pm Mon-Sat, 11am-6pm Sun) became the biggest and richest monastery in Antigua. Damaged by three 18th-century earthquakes, the buildings were later pillaged for construc-

tion material in the 20th century. The site was acquired as a private residence in 1970 by an American archaeologist, who performed extensive excavations before it was taken over by the Casa Santo Domingo Hotel (see p104). The archaeological zone has been innovatively restored as a 'cultural route' where visitors can wander freely. It includes the picturesque ruined monastery church, the adjacent cloister with a replica of the original fountain, workshops for candle and pottery makers and two underground crypts that were discovered during the church excavations. One of these, the Calvary Crypt, contains a well-preserved mural of the Crucifixion dating from 1683. Also part of the archaeological zone are five museums, known collectively as the **Paseo de Los Museos** (admission Q40; 9am-6pm Mon-Sat, 11am-6pm Sun), which can all be visited with one admission ticket. This museum route may be entered either through the hotel or the Universidad de San Carlos extension on 1a Av. Starting from the hotel side, they include the following:

Museo Colonial Canvases, silverwork and wood sculpture on religious themes from the 16th to 18th centuries.

Museo Arqueológico Ceramic and stone objects from the Maya Classic period.

Museo de Arte Precolombino y Vidrio Moderno Glass works by modern artists and the pre-Hispanic ceramic pieces that inspired them.

Museo de Artes y Artesanías Populares de Sacatepéquez Exhibits on traditional handicrafts from the Antigua region.

ANTIGUA

O BROTHER THOU ART HERE

The spirit of Hermano Pedro, Antigua's most venerated Christian, looms large more than three centuries after his death. The site of the recently canonized saint's tomb, inside the Iglesia de San Francisco (see left) overflows with devotional plaques, amulets and tokens from the faithful offering gratitude for his miraculous healing powers. Antigua's only public hospital (see p91), southeast of the Parque Central, was dubbed in his honor and carries on his mission of providing health services to those unable to afford them. (Inside the adjacent church a mural depicts Hermano Pedro's inspiration on contemporary medicine in Guatemala.)

Born on Tenerife in the Canary Islands in 1627, Pedro de Bethancourt labored as a shepherd until he hung up his staff at the age of 24 and made for Guatemala to help the poor, though the arduous journey left Pedro himself impoverished. Further hardship awaited when he flunked his studies at the Franciscan seminary in Antigua. Undaunted, he took to picking up dying Maya off the street and treating them during the plagues of the 1600s. He had found his true calling, and a few years later built a hospital devoted to healing the indigent, then built homeless shelters and schools for poor students. His efforts gave rise to a new religious order, the Bethlehemites, which took on his mantle after his death in 1667. To this day, flocks of devotees visit his tomb, a phenomenon the Vatican recognized when Pope John Paul II canonized the good brother in 2002, making him Guatemala's only officially authorized saint.

Museo de la Farmacia Restored version of a 19th-century apothecary's shop from Guatemala City.

ANTIGUO COLEGIO DE LA COMPAÑÍA DE JESÚS

With all the totally or partially ruined structures scattered around Antigua, here's one that's been completely restored. Established in 1626, the Jesuit monastery and college was a vital component of Antigua life until the order was expelled by the Spanish crown in 1767; just six years later, the great earthquake left it in ruins. Rescued from the rubble by the Spanish government over the past decade, the enormous educational and ecclesiastical complex has been reborn as a cultural center, the **Centro de Formación de la Cooperación Española** (☎ 7832-1276; www.aecid-cf.org.gt; 6a Av Norte; admission free), with the former offices, classrooms and refectories now containing lecture halls, exhibit spaces and an excellent library. The three cloisters have been made over with fine wood columns and balconies, a brilliant setting for photo exhibits, films, lectures, book presentations and workshops on the visual arts. One component remains respectfully unrestored, though: the Compañía de Jesús church, whose grand facade stands to the left of the main entrance of the complex.

Cementerio General

Antigua's **municipal cemetery** (☺ 7am-noon & 2-6pm), southwest of the market and bus terminal, is a conglomeration of tombs and mausoleums decked with wreaths, exotic flowers and other signs of mourning. Asistur (see p87) offers an escort to this out-of-the-way site on request.

ACTIVITIES

The following are professional, established outfits offering a range of activities. Drop by either one to chat about possibilities.

Old Town Outfitters (☎ 5399-0440; www.adventure guatemala.com; 5a Av Sur 12C) Works with guides from local communities.

Guatemala Ventures (☎ /fax 7832-3383; www. guatemalaventures.com; 1a Av Sur 15)

Volcano Ascents

All three volcanoes overlooking Antigua are tempting challenges but how close you can get to **Fuego** depends on recent levels of activity. In many ways the twin-peaked **Acatenango**, overlooking Fuego, is the most exhilarating summit. For an active-volcano experience many people take tours to **Pacaya** (2552m), 25km southeast of Antigua (a 1½-hour drive).

Get reliable advice about safety before you climb regarding the possible dangers from volcanic activity as well as from armed robbers preying on tourists along some trails; Inguat (see p92) is helpful for this information. In general the weather and the views on all the volcanoes are better in the morning. Take sensible precautions: wear adequate footwear (volcanic rock can be very rough on shoes), warm clothing and, in the rainy season (May to October), some sort of rain gear. Carry a flashlight in case the weather changes; it can get as dark as night when it rains on the mountain – though it's better not to go at all if rain is expected. Don't forget to bring food and water with you.

It's advisable to go with a reputable agency (see p92). **Volcán Agua** trips with Guatemala Ventures (Q810) provide transport to the end of the dirt road, well beyond the village of Santa María de Jesús. The summit is about two hours' walk from this point (compared to five hours from the village).

One-day Pacaya trips, with 1½ to two hours' walking uphill and one to 1½ hours down, cost around Q350, including lunch and an English-speaking guide. With luck you'll be able to look down into the active crater. Various travel agencies run bargain-basement, seven-hour Pacaya trips daily for Q80 (leaving Antigua at 6am and 2pm); food or drinks are not included, nor is the Q40 admission to the Pacaya protected area.

Other Hikes

Old Town Outfitters (see left) has a popular range of guided half-day walks (Q320 per person) in the hills around Antigua. It can also take you to any summit in the country or on a four- to five-day trek through eastern Guatemala's Sierra de las Minas, with its cloud forests and abundance of quetzal nesting areas. It rents out and sells camping gear too. Guatemala Ventures (see left) offers a range of hikes including some interesting cloud-forest, bird-watching and ridge-hiking options.

Volunteer Work

Many of Antigua's language schools can help you find volunteer work. See p98 for more details.

Niños de Guatemala (☎ 4379-1557; www.ninosde
guatemala.org; 6a Av Norte 45). This organization supports
a new elementary school in Ciudad Vieja (see p111), 5km
west of Antigua, where low-income kids receive quality
education. Volunteers assist Guatemalan teachers and create extracurricular activities. Make arrangements through
the Cima Del Mundo language school in Antigua whose
volunteer center can set up other opportunities as well.

Proyecto Mosaico Guatemala (☎/fax 7832-0955,
www.promosaico.org; 3a Av Norte 3; ⊙ 10am-4pm Mon-
Fri, except Wed to 2pm) This German nonprofit organization provides volunteers and resources to some 50 projects
in Guatemala. Its voluminous database matches volunteers
with projects. The greatest demand is for people with
medical experience but there's work for periods from one
week to one year for carpentry, teaching, environmental
protection, helping HIV-positive kids, and organic farming.
You need to be at least 18 and fit.

Cycling

Old Town Outfitters (see left) offers a range of
mountain-bike tours at all levels of difficulty,
including the two-day Pedal & Paddle Tour
(Q1750 to Q2500), which includes kayaking
and hiking at Lago de Atitlán.

Guatemala Ventures (see left) also offers
some bike tours, from intermediate to expert
levels. It does half- or full-day rides through
the Antigua valley (Q1075), two-day bike-
and-kayak trips to Lago de Atitlán (Q1550
per person) and weeklong jaunts encompassing volcanic slopes, highland forest and
Pacific mangroves, as well as Lago de Atitlán
(Q8600). Another, lazier, option is its trip up
Cerro Alto in a minibus with a coast back
down on mountain bike (Q250).

If you'd rather pedal off on your own, **Ox
Expeditions** (☎ 7832-0074; www.guatemalavolcano.com;
1 Av Sur 4B) rents out quality mountain bikes for
Q30 per hour.

Horseback Riding

Ravenscroft Riding Stables (☎ 7830-6669; 2a Av Sur 3,
San Juan del Obispo), 3km south of Antigua on the
road to Santa María de Jesús, offers English-
style riding, with scenic rides of three, four
or five hours in the valleys and hills around
Antigua, at Q205 per hour per person for
experienced riders, Q250 for beginners. You
need to be fairly fit. Reservations and information are available through the **Hotel San Jorge**
(☎ 7832-3132; 4a Av Sur 13). Reach the stables on
a bus bound for Santa María de Jesús (p109).

You can also ride at La Azotea in
Jocotenango (p110).

Spa & Massage

El Temascal Spa & Café (☎ 4146-4122; www.
saunamaya-eltemascal.com; 1 Av Sur 11A) The main
attraction here is the *temascal*, a pre-Hispanic style sauna
permeated with aromatic herbs (Q58 per hr), plus massages, pedicures, haircuts and tapas.

Mayan Spa (☎ 7832-3537; Calz Santa Lucía Norte 20)
Offers massage, facials, exfoliations, manicures, Pilates
and yoga.

WALKING TOUR

For the big picture, take a taxi up **Cerro de
La Cruz (1)**, north of town. Beyond the stone
cross that gives the hill its name, Antigua
spreads out, with the majestic Volcán Agua
as a backdrop. See if you can spot the Parque
Central, the 5a Av Arch and the Iglesia de San
Francisco. Descend the wooded slopes via the

> **WALK FACTS**
>
> **Start:** Cerro de la Cruz
> **End:** Café Sky
> **Distance:** 3.2km
> **Duration:** Four hours

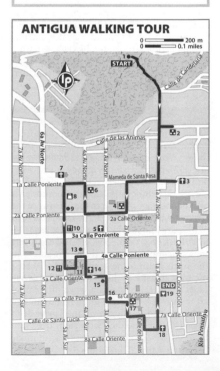

ANTIGUA WALKING TOUR

path to the left. (The park is patrolled during the day by tourist police, greatly reducing the risk of muggings.) At the bottom, turn right, down a cobblestoned street. You'll come to a basketball court backed by the ruins of **Iglesia de la Candelaria (2)**. Examine it closely – there's a lot going on between the swirly columns. Proceed one block south to a small plaza with a fountain. Go left alongside a high yellow wall to glimpse the **Templo de Santa Rosa de Lima (3)**, a small church with an elaborate facade that stands on a private estate. Turn around and head west along the jacaranda-lined Alameda de Santa Rosa. Take the first left, onto 2a Av, past an ironworks shop. At the next corner on the right are the ruins of the convent of **Las Capuchinas (4**; p94), with its unique tower. Go right on 2a Calle two blocks, past the Inguat office. Passing 3a Av, look down to your left to see the multicolumned facade of **Iglesia El Carmen (5)** and the adjacent handicrafts market. Continue another block west and turn right on 4a Av. Near the next corner on the right is the old **Convento de Santa Teresa (6)**, which until recently served as the men's prison. Go left on 1a Calle. You'll see the yellow bell tower of the **Iglesia de Nuestra Señora de la Merced (7**; p94). Turn left, down 5a Av, jam-packed with tourist-friendly locales, including the handicrafts center, **Nim Po't (8**; p109). Proceed beneath the **Arco de Santa Catalina (9)**. A remnant of the 17th-century convent that stood here (now occupied by a luxury hotel and B&B), the tunnel-like arch enabled nuns to cross the street unseen; the clock is a recent addition. The next block down, peek into the patios of the **Posada de Don Rodrigo (10**; p105), where marimba combos accompany classy dining. Continue down 5a Av to **Parque Central (11**; p92), perhaps stopping for a cappuccino and a wedge of fig cheesecake at **Café Condesa (12**; p105) before inspecting the monuments around the park. Ascend to the balcony of the **Palacio del Ayuntamiento (13**; p93) for photo ops of the park and nearby **Catedral de Santiago (14**; p93). Back on ground level, proceed east along the cathedral's right-hand side for access to the ruins behind the grand facade. Across the way, the site of the old **Universidad de San Carlos (15**; p93) contains a trove of colonial art treasures. Turn right on 3a Av Sur and go a block south to emerge on the **Tanque de La Unión (16)**, a plaza lined with palm trees and taco vendors. At its center stands a gift made to Antigua in 1998 by the city of Santiago

de Compostela in Galicia, Spain: a *cruceiro*, a Galician stone cross carved with biblical scenes. At the eastern end of the plaza are public basins, where some women still come to do their washing, spreading their laundry out on the ground to dry. Cross 2a Av to enter the serene cloister of **Iglesia y Convento de Santa Clara (17**; p95). Leaving the convent, circle around its south side, then take the next right to enter the busy compound of the **Iglesia y Convento de San Francisco (18)**, where you might light a candle at Hermano Pedro's tomb. Leave through the north portal and proceed up 1a Av, concluding the tour with cocktails atop **Café Sky (19**; p108), weather permitting.

COURSES
Language Courses
Antigua's Spanish-language schools attract students from around the world. There are dozens of schools to choose from. Price, teaching quality and student satisfaction vary greatly. Often the quality of instruction depends upon the particular teacher, and thus may vary even within a single school. Visit a few schools before you choose and, if possible, talk to people who have studied recently at schools you like the look of – you're bound to run into a few. The Inguat tourist office has a list of authorized schools. They include the following:

Academia Colonial (☎ 7882-4244; www.academia colonial.com; 7a Calle Poniente 11) American-run school with attractive study environment in colonial courtyard; cappuccinos on the house. Activities include trips to weaving cooperatives and cooking classes.

Academia de Español Probigua (☎ 7832-2998; www.probigua.org; 6a Av Norte 41B) Well-regarded, nonprofit school that donates the school's profits to establish and maintain libraries in rural villages. Offers special courses for healthcare workers.

Academia de Español Sevilla (☎ /fax 7832-5101; www.sevillantigua.com; 1a Av Sur 17C) Well-managed with a good program of free activities; can arrange volunteer work in local community projects. Beautiful installations with study carrels amid remnants of a colonial monastery. Offers shared student house as an accommodation option.

Academia de Profesores Privados de Español (☎ /fax 7882-4284; www.appeschool.com; 1a Calle Oriente 15) Founded and run by ex–Peace Corps volunteers. Besides standard Spanish instruction, it offers courses for tourism, educational and healthcare personnel, and an opportunity to study in the outlying village of San Juan del Obispo.

Centro Lingüístico Maya (☎ 7832-0656; www. clmaya.com; 5a Calle Poniente 20) Large, professionally managed, slightly pricier institute with 30 years' experience training diplomatic personnel and journalists.

Cima Del Mundo (☎ 7832-3327; www.cdmschool. com; 6a Av Norte 45) Small institute emphasizing student-centered learning. Donates profits to and offers volunteer opportunities with Niños de Guatemala school (see p97) for low income kids in nearby Ciudad Vieja.

Coined Spanish School (☎ 7832-4846; www.cdl.edu. gt; 6a Av Norte 9) New branch of Latin American chain that follows communicative methodology of Madrid's Cervantes Institute. Volunteer opportunities available through Nuestros Ahijados relief organization.

Escuela de Español San José el Viejo (☎ 7832-3028; www.sanjoseelviejo.com; 5a Av Sur 34) Long-standing school with parklike study environment, featuring tennis court and pool and its own tasteful accommodations. Students may switch teachers each week. Accredited by Guatemalan Ministry of Education.

Instituto Antigüeño de Español (☎ 7832-7241; www.spanishacademyantiguena.com; 1a Calle Poniente 10) Highly recommended school, authorized by Ministry of Education. They can arrange volunteer work at Hermano Pedro hospital for social workers and childcare specialists on request.

Proyecto Lingüístico Francisco Marroquín (☎ /fax 7832-1422; www.spanishschoolplfm.com; 6a Av Norte 43) Antigua's oldest Spanish school, founded in 1969; run by a nonprofit foundation to preserve indigenous languages and culture, with capacity to teach K'iche' and Kaqchiquel, among other Maya tongues.

Other recommended schools include the following:

Christian Spanish Academy (☎ 7832-3922; www. learncsa.com; 6a Av Norte 15)

Escuela de Español Cooperación (☎ 5812-2482; www.spanishschoolcooperacion.com; 7a Av Norte 15 B)

Ixchel Spanish School (☎ /fax 7832-0364; www. ixchelschool.com; 7a Calle Poniente 15)

Spanish Language Center (☎ 7832-6608; www. bestspanishlesson.com; 6a Av Norte 16A)

Classes start every Monday at most schools, though you can usually be placed with a teacher any day of the week. Most schools cater for all levels and allow you to stay as long as you like. Three or four weeks is typical, though it's perfectly OK to do just one week. The busiest seasons are during January and from April to August, and some schools request advance reservations for these times.

Instruction is nearly always one-on-one and costs Q750 to Q1515 per week for four

hours of classes daily, five days a week. You can enroll for up to 10 hours a day of instruction, although most people find that four to five hours is plenty. Most schools offer to arrange room and board with local families, usually with your own room, for around Q700 per week, a bit more with private bathroom, and three meals daily (except Sunday). Some schools may offer accommodations in guest houses or their own hostels.

Homestays are meant to promote the total immersion concept of language learning, but this becomes less viable where there are several foreigners staying with one family, or where there are separate mealtimes for students and the family. Indeed, there are so many foreigners about Antigua, it takes some real discipline to converse in Spanish rather than your native tongue. Many enjoy this social scene, but if you think it may deter you, consider studying in Quetzaltenango, El Petén or elsewhere, where there are fewer foreign students.

Cooking Courses

Antigua Cooking School (☎ 5944-8568; www.anti guacookingschool.com; 5a Av Norte 25B; 4hr class Q520) Offers classes in traditional Guatemalan cuisine, preparing classics such as corn tamales, subanik, pepián and chuchitos. Classes are available Monday to Saturday.

El Frijol Feliz (☎ 7882-4244; www.frijolfeliz.com; 7a Calle Poniente 11; 3hr class Q330) Hands-on instruction on preparing Guatemalan meals; students may choose their own menu.

TOURS

Inguat-authorized guides around the Parque Central offer city walking tours, with visits to convents, ruins and museums, for Q100 to Q160. Similar guided walks are offered daily by Antigua travel agencies, including Adrenalina Tours, Aviatur, Atitrans and Sinfronteras (see p92). Also on offer are trips to the surrounding villages and coffee plantations for around Q200.

Elizabeth Bell, a local scholar of Antigua history, or her knowledgeable associates lead three-hour cultural walking tours of the town (in English and/or Spanish) on Tuesday, Wednesday, Friday and Saturday at 9:30am, and on Monday and Thursday at 2pm. The cost is Q160. Reservations can be made through **Antigua Tours** (☎ /fax 7832-5821; www.antiguatours.net; 5a Av Norte 6), inside Café El Portal (Portal del Comercio 6) off the Parque

ANTIGUA

Central; groups congregate at the park's fountain at the appointed hour. Bell's book, *Antigua Guatemala: The City and Its Heritage*, is well worth picking up: it has extensive descriptions of all the monuments and neatly encapsulates the history and fiestas. Bell and company also do tours to the nearby villages of San Antonio Aguas Calientes and San Andrés Itzapa to investigate weaving workshops and Maya shrines, respectively.

Adrenalina, Sinfronteras, Turansa and other agencies also offer tours to more distant places, including Tikal, the Cobán area, Monterrico, Chichicastenango and Lago de Atitlán. Two-day trips to Tikal, flying from Guatemala City to Flores and back, start at around Q3600 per person. A hectic one-day Tikal round-trip costs Q2415. Two-day land tours to Copán (some including Quiriguá and Río Dulce) are between Q1300 and Q3420 per person, depending on the number of participants, standard of accommodations and guide availability.

CATours (☎ 7832-9638; www.catours.co.uk; 6a Calle Oriente 14) offers two-day motorbike tours to Lago de Atitlán or Monterrico from Q1385.

FESTIVALS & EVENTS

The most exciting time to be in Antigua is **Semana Santa** (Easter), when hundreds of devotees garbed in deep purple robes bear revered icons from their churches in daily street processions in remembrance of Christ's crucifixion and the events surrounding it. Dense clouds of incense envelop the parades and the streets are covered in elaborate *alfombras* (carpets) of colored sawdust and flower petals. These fragile works of art are destroyed as the processions shuffle over them but are re-created each morning for another day of parades.

The fervor and the crowds peak on Good Friday, when an early-morning procession departs from La Merced, and a late afternoon one leaves from the Escuela de Cristo. There may also be an enactment of the crucifixion in Parque Central. Have ironclad Antigua room reservations well in advance of Semana Santa, or plan to stay in Guatemala City or elsewhere and commute to the festivities.

Processions, *velaciones* (vigils) and other events actually go on every weekend through Lent, the 40-day period prior to Semana Santa. Antigua's tourist office has schedules of everything, and the booklet *Lent and Holy Week in Antigua* by Elizabeth Bell gives explanations.

SLEEPING

With 140 hotels, *posadas* and hostels, by Inguat's estimate, Antigua has a wide range of accommodations to suit any traveler's style or budget. Finding a room is generally a simple task, with the major exception of Semana Santa, for which you should book as far ahead as possible and be prepared to pay double normal rates. Some Antigua hotels have desks in the Guatemala City airport arrivals area, where you can book a room and/or obtain transportation (often free) to the hotel.

Budget

When checking budget establishments, look at several rooms, keeping an eye out for such variables as comfort, light and noise level. Where hot water is indicated, expect an electric unit taped to the shower head; feel especially blessed if there's actually a separate hot-water tap.

Asistur (☎ 5978-3586; asisturantiguaguatemala@gmail. com; 6a Calle Poniente Final; P 🛜) You can park an RV or pitch a tent on the grounds of Asistur, the tourism police. There's no charge, but it's appreciated if campers contribute items such as tools or bug spray. There are toilets, showers and electric hookups.

Hostal Umma Gumma (☎ 7832-4413; ummagumma@ itelgua.com; 7 Av Norte 15; s/d Q85/170, dm/s/d without bathroom Q40/60/120; 🖥) Though scruffy at the edges, this psychedelically decorated hostel boasts a sociable vibe – it's a great place to relax, meet people and hang out on the leafy rooftop terrace. A well-stocked kitchen is available for guest use and the owners run a good travel agency.

Dionisio Guest House (☎ 5644-9486; ciuisis@yahoo. com; 3a Calle Poniente Callejón; dm with/without bathroom Q45/40, d/tr Q150/200, without bathroom Q120/150; 🖥 🛜) This is the most relaxed of four guesthouses along a cul-de-sac between 7a Av and Calz Santa Lucía. It features spanking clean and nicely decorated rooms along a sunny terrace, plus a well-supplied kitchen (including an espresso maker!) and a cozy recreational nook where guests settle down to check their laptops or watch Bob Marley videos.

Kafka (6a Av Norte 40; dm incl breakfast Q50; 🛜) Though not its mainstay, Kafka has basic but clean dorms downstairs from its popular bar (see p107), with thick blankets and clean tiled bathrooms. The ones at the rear are quietest.

Jungle Party Hostal (☎ 7832-0463; www.jungle partyhostal.com; 6a Av Norte 20; dm Q50; 🛜) With bar service, hammock hangouts and the famous all-you-can-eat Saturday barbecue, the Jungle Party has a great atmosphere, and the smiling staff know exactly what's needed by travelers.

Black Cat Hostel (☎ 7832-1229; www.blackcathostels. net; 6 Av Norte 1A; dm Q60, d/tr Q150/225) Though the dorms are cramped and you can't use the kitchen, this place is always hopping, both as a hostel and at the bar out the front for the nightly happy hour (for guests only). Plenty of tours are on offer, plus free movies, good local advice and a huge breakfast, included in the price.

our pick **Yellow House** (☎ 7832-6646; yellowhouse antigua@hotmail.com; 1a Calle Poniente 24; s/d without bathroom Q75/130; 🖳) Simple but thoughtfully designed, ecologically conscious and damn friendly, this makes a superior budget choice. Rooms vary in style and size but comfy beds, recessed lighting, and mosquito-screened windows are the norm. If possible, get an upstairs unit, along a plant-filled terrace that's perfect for enjoying the huge, healthy breakfast. It can get crowded with just three bathrooms downstairs, but they're kept immaculate and use solar-heated water.

El Hostal (☎ 7832-0442; elhostal.antigua@gmail. com; 1a Av Sur 8; dm Q/5-90, s/d/tr without bathroom Q120/220/300; 🛜) This hostel is a popular new option within stumbling distance of Café No Sé. Set around a cheery little patio-cafe are half a dozen neatly kept private rooms and dorms with sturdy single beds or well-spaced bunks, a few sticks of furniture and freshly painted walls with patches of exposed brick.

Casa Jacaranda (☎ /fax 7832-7589; hyrcasajacaranda@ gmail.com; 1a Calle Poniente 37; dm Q82, s/d without bathroom Q165/287; 🖳 🛜) At this original new hostel (not a party center), the rooms are simple but display a bit of flair. So does the airy front lounge, with a mural after Klimt (except the female figure is garbed in a *huipil*). Four-bed dorms leave plenty of elbow room, and the shared bathrooms are thoughtfully designed. At the rear is a grassy patio under a jacaranda tree, a surprisingly tranquil retreat considering the hostel's busy location.

Hotel Burkhard (☎ 7832-4316; hotelburkhard@hot mail.com; 3a Calle Oriente 19A; r Q100) Usefully located next to the excellent bar El Muro (p108), this tiny establishment has a dozen compact, fancifully decorated rooms over two levels.

Posada Don Diego (☎ 7832-1401; posadadondiego@ gmail.com; 6a Av Norte 52; s/d Q160/285, without bath-room Q110/185; 🖳 🛜) Located behind a donut purveyor that's just across the way from La Merced, Don Diego's has a handful of comfortable, simply furnished rooms facing a patch of lawn with a stone fountain. The pricier units come with private bathrooms and flat-screen TVs.

Posada Juma Ocag (☎ 7832-3109; Calz de Santa Lucía Norte 13; s/d/tr Q120/140/200) The seven spotless, comfortable rooms here have quality mattresses and traditional appointments including wrought-iron bedsteads, decorative ceramic masks and mirrors crafted in-house. Despite the hectic location opposite the market, it remains peaceful – especially the upstairs rooms – with a rooftop patio and well-tended little garden. Reservations are accepted in person only.

Hotel la Casa de Don Ismael (☎ /fax 7832-1932; www.casadonismael.com; 3a Calle Poniente 6, Lotificación Cofiño 2a Callejón; s/d Q120/175, incl breakfast 160/225; 🛜) Expect to share the premises with the family at this homey, humble guesthouse, hidden down a small side street and overseen by its kind, cordial namesake. Seven rustic rooms share three hot-water bathrooms, and there's a pleasant roof terrace.

Casa Santa Lucía No 2 (☎ 7832-7418; Calz de Santa Lucía Norte 21; s/d Q120/180; 🅿) Accommodations at this securely gated locale across the way from the ruins of San Jerónimo are sparklingly clean, with terracotta floors waxed to perfection and plenty of colonial charm. The showers are rippers, too – just make sure you know what time they turn on the hot water.

Casa Santa Lucía No 3 (☎ 7832-1386; 6a Av Norte 43; r Q186) Step back in time, down arched hallways with heavy exposed beams, to reach the well-maintained paint-dappled rooms equipped with blasting hot showers. Though the staff could be a tad more communicative, the price is right and the location is convenient, just north of La Merced.

Midrange
Some of Antigua's midrange hotels allow you to wallow in colonial charm for a moderate outlay of cash.

Black Cat Inn (☎ 7832-4698; blackcathostels.net/anti gua/inn; 5a Calle Poniente 11A; dm Q60, s/d/tr Q150/250/375; 🛜) Opened in August '09, this upscale version of its nearby sister hostel, shares a maroon color scheme, hip global staff, laundry service and free breakfast. Rooms are larger, though (if just as haphazardly furnished), and set along a colonial corridor that opens onto a neat patio. A dozen people squeeze into the dorm.

Las Golondrinas (☎ 7832-3343; drrios@intel.net.gt; 6a Av Norte 34; s/d Q150/300, with kitchen Q170/340; 🛜) The apartment-like rooms at this tranquil complex are an excellent option for serious self-caterers. Units are set around a tree-studded garden, and all feature front terraces with tables suitable for al fresco dining. The place is run by an inveterate traveler who's climbed hundreds of volcanoes, and good weekly and monthly discounts are available.

Posada Asjemenou (☎ 7832-2670; www.hotel posadaasjemenou.com; 5a Av Norte 31; s/d Q215/290, without bathroom Q166/215; 🛜) Just north of the Arco de Santa Catalina, the Asjemenou is built around two patios once home to an esteemed Guatemalan poet. The front patio, where a complimentary breakfast is served, looks nicer, but the rooms around the rear one are in better shape.

Casa Cristina (☎ 7832-0623; www.casa-cristina.com; Callejón Camposeco 3A; s/d downstairs Q185/224, upstairs Q224/275; 🛜) There are just a dozen rooms at this comfy little two-story hotel on a pretty backstreet near La Merced. All are quaintly appointed with indigenous bedspreads, brushed-on pastels and wood-stained furniture, and the roof terrace (only open till 8pm) makes a nice retreat. *Muy tranquilo*.

Hotel La Tatuana (☎ 7832-1223; latatuana@hotmail. com; 7a Av Sur 3; s/d Q200/256) This cozy little hotel a few blocks from Parque Central features a cute patio and small roof terrace. Rooms get the rustic treatment, with sponged-on pastels, stained wood and painted panels over beds. The hotel's name refers to a figure of Antigua lore, which the friendly staff will gladly describe.

Hotel Posada San Vicente (☎ /fax 7832-3311; hotel_san_vicente@yahoo.com.mx; 6a Av Sur 6; s/d Q200/300; Ⓟ 🛜) This family-overrun establishment a block west of the Parque Central can get a little hectic after school lets out, but the central patio – a veritable botanical garden of ferns and bromeliads – has a calming effect. Clean, colorful rooms on two stories sport the usual colonial kitsch.

Posada Doña Luisa (☎ 7832-3414; posadadonaluisa@ hotmail.com; 7a Av Norte 4; s/d/tr Q230/293/341) A new contender in the small colonial guesthouse game, Doña Luisa keeps things simple: four rooms upstairs, four rooms down, all freshly painted and spacious, facing a rectangular lawn with fountain.

Hotel Posada San Pedro (☎ 7832-0718; www. posadasanpedro.net; 7a Av Norte 29; s/d/tr Q240/320/360) Somebody's restored this place with a whole lot of love and attention to detail. Rooms are spacious and well furnished and look out onto two lush patios surrounded by hanging plants.

Hotel Posada San Pedro (☎ 7832-3594; www.posada sanpedro.net; 3a Av Sur 15; s/d/tr Q240/320/360) The 10 rooms at the second San Pedro are extremely neat and inviting, with swabbed-on mustard or chocolate tones, *azulejo*-tiled bathrooms and cable TV. A guest kitchen, several spacious sitting rooms and two terraces with great views add to the comfortable, friendly atmosphere.

Hotel Las Campanas (☎ 7832-3396; losbucaros@intel nett.com; Av del Desengaño 24; s/d Q240/320) Though a bit of a hike from the center, this rustic/ modern lodging offers excellent value for the comfort level. The nine immaculate rooms surround a plant-filled fantasy of archways, balconies and wooden columns.

Hotel La Sin Ventura (☎ 7832-0581; www.lasinven tura.com; 5a Av Sur 8; s/d/tr incl breakfast Q249/390/564; Ⓟ) Just half a block south of the Parque Central, this faux colonial palace is above an entertainment center that includes a cinema, disco and the ever-popular Monoloco bar. The 35 pastel-tinted rooms line up along attractively tiled corridors on two levels. Excellent views can be enjoyed from the small roof terrace.

Hotel Posada La Merced (☎ 7832-3197; www.hotel merced.com; 7a Av Norte 43A; s/d Q374/498, without bathroom Q249/332; 🛜) Behind the big wooden doors, La Merced sports a modern interior. Rooms in the rear section surround a tranquil patio suitable for hammock lounging and have a bit more pizzazz, with *típico* (traditional) weavings and colonial furniture. Bonuses include a rooftop terrace, well-appointed guest kitchen, morning coffee and gracious staff.

our pick Hostal el Montañes (☎ 5308-6223; www. hostalelmontanesantigua.com Calle del Hermano Pedro 19B; d incl breakfast Q498, s/d/tr without bathroom Q250/332/415) There are just four rooms at this neat and cozy family home behind San Francisco church. All are spacious, bright and lovingly decorated; three share a big sparkling bathroom. Guests have the run of the TV lounge, dining area and delightful front garden.

our pick Hotel Casa Rústica (☎ 7832-3709; www. casarusticagt.com; 6a Av Norte 8; s/d Q357/440, without bathroom Q274/323; 🖳 🛜) Everything about the 'rustic house' feels right, from the octagonal fountain in the cobblestoned patio to the tiled tables on the sun-splashed top deck.

Designed by Tennessee-bred owner Darryl, it's also one of the few hotels in this price range to offer guests full kitchen access, not to mention a pool table and entertainment lounge. Attractively done up with regional textiles, the 14 rooms occupy two buildings on the upper level.

Hotel Santa Clara (☎ 7832-4291; www.hotelsanta claraantigua.com; 3a Av Sur 30; s/d/tr Q391/374/457) In a quiet area south of the center, the Santa Clara boasts brilliantly restored antique chambers alongside a small courtyard, with carved-wood bedsteads and skylights set into the roof beams. Toward the rear are two levels of newer, mostly brighter rooms, with glimpses of the San Francisco convent from the upper level.

Posada de Don Valentino (☎ 7832-0384; www.posadadonvalentino.com; 5a Calle Poniente 28; s/d/tr Q307/390/457) Beyond the busy cybercafe in the entry hall is a friendly little guesthouse with spacious, cheerfully decorated rooms of varying brightness. Best of all are the three suites around the upper-level terrace.

Hotel Plaza Mayor (☎ 7832-0055; juanchew@gmail. com; 4a Calle Poniente 9; s/d/tr Q307/407/506) This modern/rustic lodging has spacious rooms, all facing the tranquil interior. But the big plus here is the location, a few short steps from the park.

Hotel Centro Colonial Antigua (☎ 7832-1641; juanchew@gmail.com; 4a Calle Poniente; s/d/tr Q374/457/540) Half a block west of the Parque Central, this colonial confection goes heavy on the chintz, with bright rooms redolent of pine, decorated roof beams and furniture of recent purchase.

ourpick Posada San Sebastián (☎ 7832-2621; snse bast@hotmail.com; 3a Av Norte 4; s/d/tr Q374/498/580; ☎) As carpenter, antique restorer and occasional xylophone player, Luis Méndez Rodríguez is the auteur of this converted mansion. Each of the nine uniquely appointed rooms display his knack for finding and refurbishing art and furniture. Big bathrooms with tub are a bonus, as are the roof terrace, the pretty little courtyard garden, and use of a kitchen.

Hotel Palacio Chico (Casa 1940) (☎ 7832-3895; www.hotelpalaciochico.com; 7a Av Norte 15; s/d/tr incl breakfast Q374/580/664; ☎) Though on the small side, rooms at this stylish, well-managed place are nicely decked out, with classic tile work, crafted iron bed frames and sponged on paint. Get a pedicure at the ground-level spa or catch some rays on the top deck terrace.

Hotel Palacio Chico (Casa 1850) (☎ 7832-7137; www.hotelpalaciochico.com; 3a Av Sur 6; s/d/tr incl breakfast Q374/580/664; P 🖥 ☎) Close to the Tanque de

La Unión plaza, this small hotel occupies a handsome colonial mansion, and the central courtyard is bursting with plants and flowers. Rooms are spacious, with tiled ceilings and fine antique furniture, though the street-side windows are prone to traffic noise.

Hotel San Jorge (☎ 7832-3132; sanjorge@terra.com. gt; 4a Av Sur 13; s/d Q438/504; P ☎) A midpriced hotel in a tony neighborhood, the San Jorge strives for elegance while keeping things nice and cozy. Fourteen carpeted rooms face a broad lawn replete with gurgling fountain and parakeets, and sport fireplaces, paintings of colonial scenes and big bathrooms with tubs.

Hotel Casa Antigua (☎ 7832-9090; www.hotel casa-antigua.com; 3a Calle Poniente 5; s/d Q450/535; P 🖥 ☎ 🕭) Under the same gringo ownership as Hotel Casa Rústica, this is a similarly well-managed establishment in a refurbished old home that for generations belonged to an aristocratic Nicaraguan family. All rooms are decorated with weavings, antique furniture and a few chandeliers (one of which did time in the Antigua cathedral), though size and configuration vary greatly. A rooftop terrace, well-equipped guest kitchen and airport pickup (Q300 for up to three people) are among the bonus features.

Hotel Entre Volcanes (☎ 7832-9436; www.hotelentre volcanes.com; Calz Santa Lucía Sur 5; s/d/tr Q457/540/623; P 🖥 ☎) Yet another of Antigua's beautifully restored colonial hotels, Entre Volcanes stands out with its location right next to the market. The 15 rooms line up on two levels along corridors supported by rough-hewn beams and pillars.

Hotel Aurora (☎ 7832-0217; www.hotelauroraantigua. com; 4a Calle Oriente 16; s/d/tr Q540/580/640; P 🖥 ☎) The Aurora has a good, old-timey feel to it. The 17 large rooms are centered on a grassy patio replete with tinkling fountain and wicker lawn chairs. Breakfast (included in the price) is served on wide interior balconies.

Top End

Hotel Quinta de las Flores (☎ 7832-3721; www.quintade lasflores.com; Calle del Hermano Pedro 6; s/d from Q540/623, bungalow Q996; P 🖥 🐾) More a village than a hotel, this property on the southeastern edge of town is bursting with charms. Pebbly paths weave by stands of bird-of-paradise and African tulip trees, cobblestoned plazas with weathered colonial fountains, a good-sized swimming pool amid tropical foliage, and an open-air restaurant. There are eight large,

ANTIGUA

luxurious rooms in the main building, most with a fireplace and five more secluded 'garden rooms' with private terraces, plus five two-story *casitas*, each with two bedrooms, a kitchen and living room. Considerable discounts are offered for stays by the week.

Hotel Convento Santa Catalina (☎ 7832-3080; www.conventohotel.com; 5a Av Norte 28; s/d/tr Q664/763/863; P 🖳) Of all the dressed-up renovations in town, this is among the most impressive. Antigua's signature arch, right outside the front door, was built for the nuns of the convent the hotel now occupies. Both the front colonial section and the rear 'modern' part are beautiful, though the latter is quieter, with picture windows facing the old convent walls across a lawn; these have good kitchenettes.

Hotel El Mesón de María (☎ 7832-6068; www.hotel mesondemaria.com; 3a Calle Poniente 8; s/d incl breakfast from Q705/863; 🖳 🛜) Everything is as fabulous as it should be at this restored 20th-century mansion – firm beds with carved headboards, a couple of flower-filled breakfast areas and a roof terrace suitable for volcano gawking. You'll forgive the rooms for being a bit, ahem, tight on space when you see that the bathrooms feature real tubs. Note: rates are 15 percent higher on weekends.

Hotel Casa Azul (☎ 7832-0961; www.guate.com/ casaazul; 4a Av Norte 5; r from Q797; P 🛋) One of Antigua's original boutique hotels, this little place near the park is seriously stylish, combining a designer's eye with colonial charms. Each room has a unique layout but all are picture-perfect. The upstairs units are spectacular, with sweeping views, luxurious baths and minibars. Cheaper downstairs rooms lack views but give easier access to the pool, spa and sauna.

Mesón Panza Verde (☎ 7832-2925; www.panza verde.com; 5a Av Sur 19; r/ste Q830/1370; P 🖳 🛋) The Panza Verde is an elegant American-owned, Euro-style B&B with three rooms and nine suites. It's decked out with sumptuous furniture and fittings, some pieces ever so fashionably tatty due to being semi-outdoors. Upstairs is an art gallery, reached by a staircase with an iron balustrade. The atmosphere and restaurant here (see p107) are among the most appealing in Antigua.

Cloister (☎ 7832-0712; www.thecloister.com; 5a Av Norte 23; r incl breakfast Q1079; P) Occupying the former school of the 16th-century Santa Catalina convent, the lovingly renovated Cloister makes a romantic option. Each of the seven rooms

and suites has been uniquely appointed by the Boston-bred owner, with homey touches such as fireplaces, antique furniture, shelves of books and a loft for the kids. The garden courtyard is a horticultural triumph. Be aware that credit cards are not accepted.

Casa Santo Domingo Hotel (☎ 7820-1222; www. casasantodomingo.com.gt; 3a Calle Oriente 28A; r from Q1619; P 🖳 🛜 🛋) Innovatively resurrected from the remains of the sprawling Santo Domingo monastery, this is Antigua's premier lodging. The 128 rooms and suites are of an international five-star standard, while the grounds retain their colonial splendor, dotted with archaeological relics and featuring a large swimming pool, several fine restaurants, shops and five museums (see p95). The Dominican friars never had it so good. Prices go down from September to November and up during weekends.

Posada del Ángel (☎ 7832-5244; www.posadadel angel.com; 4a Av Sur 24A; r Q1670; P 🛋) The Posada became Antigua's most celebrated B&B when Bill Clinton bedded down here in 1999. It doesn't look like much from the outside, but behind the garage door the luxury just keeps unfolding. If you didn't think it was possible to fit a swimming pool into an Antigua patio, stop by. The five rooms and two suites all have fireplaces, fresh lilies, four-poster beds and highly polished tile floors.

EATING

Note that most formal restaurants in Antigua whack on a 10-percent tip before presenting the bill. It should be itemized, but if in doubt, ask.

Guatemalan

In the early evening, Doña María takes up her post in front of La Merced, at the top of 5a Av, and serves fine tamales and *chuchitos*, laced with hot sauce and pickled cabbage, along with bowls of *atol blanco* (corn-based hot beverage). Talk about comfort food!

our pick **Tienda La Canche** (6a Av Norte 42) A hole in the wall if there ever was one, the restaurant, behind a 'mom and pop' store, consists of two tables with floral tablecloths. From the rear table, there's a good view of the narrow kitchen, where five or six women in *huipiles* busily stir the contents of huge pots. They prepare a couple of traditional options daily, such as *pepián de pollo*, a hearty chicken stew containing chunks of potato and huizquil, a yucca-like tuber, accompanied by a tray of thick tortillas and half an avocado. *Frescos,* home-squeezed fruit beverages, are served alongside.

Doña María Gordillo Dulces Típicos (4a Calle Oriente 11) This shop opposite Hotel Aurora is filled with traditional Guatemalan sweets, and there's often a crowd of *antigüeños* lined up to buy them.

La Cenicienta (5a Av Norte 7; slice of pie Q20) This old-fashioned pastry shop near the Parque Central is an obligatory stop for a slice of cheesecake, pineapple upside-down cake, almond torte or macadamia-nut pie, and the attentive staff know how to use that espresso machine behind the counter.

Casa de las Mixtas (3a Callejón; mains Q20-30; ☺ breakfast, lunch & dinner) For down-home Guatemalan fare with a bit of style, try this family-run operation on a quiet backstreet across from the market. Aside from its namesake snack (*mixtas* are Guatemalan-style hot dogs, wrapped in tortillas) it also serves *paches* – like tamales, but made of mashed potatoes instead of corn dough – and offer a range of set breakfasts. Regulars make for the little terrace upstairs.

Restaurante Doña Luisa Xicotencatl (☎ 7832-2578; 4a Calle Oriente 12; sandwiches & breakfast dishes Q30-40) Probably Antigua's best-known restaurant, this is a place to enjoy the colonial patio ambience over breakfast or a light meal. The attached bakery sells all kinds of bread and rolls: banana bread comes hot-from-the-oven around 2pm daily.

Café Condesa (☎ 7832-0038; Portal del Comercio 4; breakfast & snacks from Q35; ☺ 7am-8pm Sun-Thu, 7am-9pm Fri & Sat) Go through the bookstore to reach this restaurant, set around the patio of a 16th-century mansion. Baked goods are the strong suit – pies, cakes, quiches, scones and house-baked whole-wheat sandwich bread. The Sunday buffet, from 9am to 1pm, a lavish spread for Q58, is an Antigua institution.

ourpick La Esquina (☎ 7882-4761; 6a Calle Poniente 7; soups & salads Q35, steak Q110; ☺ noon-10pm Tue-Sat, noon-3:30pm Sun; ☺ ☺) There aren't a lot of items on the menu at this cool restaurant-bar amid a tropically abundant patio, but it's a classy Guatemalan-international mix, from tortilla soup to Lebanese salad. Eduardo, the congenial force behind La Esquina, has great taste in music, too, and doubles as the house DJ on Friday night. The ingeniously designed chicken-bus bar is something to behold.

Café La Escudilla (4a Av Norte 4; pasta Q44, mains Q68-80; ☺ 8am-midnight Wed-Mon; ☺ ☺) Popular with the language-school crowd, La Escudilla is a patio restaurant with tinkling fountain, lush foliage and some tables under the open sky. The food is simple but well prepared with plenty of vegetarian options, as well as economical breakfasts and a one-course set lunch or dinner for under Q25.

La Cuevita de Los Urquizú (☎ 4593-5619; 2a Calle Oriente 9D; lunch combo Q60; ☺ lunch & dinner) Sumptuous *típico* food is the draw here, all kept warm in earthenware pots out front, making it almost impossible to go past. Choose from *pepián* (chicken and vegetables in a piquant sesame and pumpkin seed sauce), *kaq'ik* (spicy turkey stew), *jocón* (green stew of chicken or pork with green vegetables and herbs) or other such Guatemalan favorites, and you'll get two accompaniments (Q60).

La Fonda de la Calle Real (mains Q66-70) 3a Calle Poniente 7 (☎ 7832-0507; ☺ noon-10pm Tue-Sun); 5a Av Norte 5 (☎ 7832-2629; ☺ noon-10pm); 5a Av Norte 12 (☺ 8am-10pm Sun-Thu, 8am-11pm Fri & Sat) This restaurant with three spacious branches, all in appealing colonial style, has a good menu ranging from generous salads and sandwiches (Q37) to grilled meats (up to Q99). The specialty is *caldo real*, a hearty chicken soup that makes a good meal. The branch at 3a Calle Poniente 7 is the most attractive, with several rooms and patios.

Posada de Don Rodrigo (☎ 7832-0387; 5a Av Norte 17; mains Q120-180; ☺ breakfast, lunch & dinner) The food's up to scratch here – the seafood crêpes, steaks and sausages have a subtle Guatemalan accent. The real draw, though, is the setting, a gorgeous courtyard with plenty of wrought iron, blossoming flowers and tinkling fountains.

International

For global gourmands, Antigua is a banquet. Within 10 minutes' walk of Parque Central you can dine well and inexpensively on Italian, Belgian, French, Thai, Korean, Indian, Irish, Israeli, Japanese, German, American, Chinese, Mexican and Salvadoran cuisines.

BUDGET

Travel Menu (6a Calle Poniente 14; mains Q25-32; ☺ noon-7:30pm Tue-Sun; ☺) Not nearly as unimaginative as the name would imply, this little bar-restaurant serves up food that you may have been craving (chow mein, curry etc) in an intimate candlelit environment. Its motto: 'small place, big portions.'

Y Tu Piña También (1a Av Sur 10B; sandwiches & salads Q30-35; 7am-8pm Mon-Fri, 8am-7pm Sat & Sun;) This natural-foods cafe does healthy, sophisticated fare for foreign students on the go. There's a tempting array of sandwiches (served on whole wheat, pita or bagel), salads and crêpes. It opens early and makes for a good breakfast stop, with omelets, waffles and abundant fruit salads, plus excellent coffee.

Café No Sé (1 Av Sur 11C; snacks Q30-40; noon-1am Mon-Sat, 10am-1am Sun) Advertising uncomfortable seats, confused staff and battered books, this is a pleasantly downbeat option among all of Antigua's finery. There's a little bit of everything here – breakfast (Sunday is the big pancake brunch), nachos, fried chicken, salads, movies, a mescal bar and live music.

Weiner (Calz Santa Lucía Norte 8; mains Q35-60; lunch & dinner) Though not authentically German like Jardín Bavaria (see right), it does serve what's possibly the biggest wiener schnitzel you've ever seen, alongside some good-value set lunches. No German beer, either, but there's plenty of cold Gallo.

Sabe Rico (7832-0648; 6a Av Sur 7; sandwiches & salads Q40; 8am-7pm Mon & Wed, 11am-3pm Tue, 8am-8pm Thu-Sat, 9am-4pm Sun) This little deli whips up tasty salads and sandwiches, using ingredients from its herb garden, as well as offering fresh-baked breads and brownies. It also sells fine wines and imported foods. Eat in one of the various salons or have a picnic.

Casa de Corea (5550-0771; 7a Av Norte 2; mains Q40-50; 10am-9pm Mon & Wed-Fri, noon-9pm Sat & Sun) This Korean-owned eatery, with guest-generated graffiti covering the walls, has all the Seoul food you need. Wash down your kimchi or *sundubu jjigae* (chili-spiked stew of tofu and shellfish) with a Korean beer or some rice wine!

Rainbow Café (7832-1919; 7a Av Sur 8; breakfast Q40, mains Q40-60; 8am-midnight Mon-Sat, 7am-11pm Sun;) Fill up from an eclectic range of all-day breakfasts, curries, stir-fries, Cajun chicken, guacamole and more, and enjoy the relaxed patio atmosphere. Between meals, check out the bookstore, bulletin board and live music.

Pushkar (7979-7848; 6a Av Norte 18; curries Q45-79; lunch & dinner) Overseen by an English chef, Pushkar prepares curries, tandoori and thalis that measure up to anything on Brick Lane. Dine in the stylish lounge with Hindi calligraphy on the walls or at candlelit tables on the back lawn.

Café Rocío (7832-1871; 6a Av Norte 34; mains Q50-60; lunch & dinner) Ensconced in a pleasant little patio, the Rocío takes a good stab at Thai food, with curries, satays, gado gado and veggie stir-fries served in abundant portions.

Sunshine Grill (5964-7620; 6a Av Norte 68; pizza Q60-140; Wed-Mon) A friendly neighborhood joint with scribbling on the walls, a karaoke jukebox and a big screen for the game, the Grill makes amazing pizzas, just like the kind owner Edgar learned to make in New Jersey's pizzerias. It also does some fine French fries.

MIDRANGE

El Papaturro (7832-0445; 2a Calle Oriente 4; pupusas Q25, mains Q60-95; lunch & dinner) For *pupusas*, *rellenitos* and other Salvadoran staples, this homey spot run by natives of Guatemala's southern neighbor serves authentic dishes and good steak plates in a relaxed courtyard.

Jardín Bavaria (7832-5904; 7a Av Norte 49; breakfast Q32, sausages Q64; 8am-4pm Mon & Tue, 8am-8pm Wed-Sun) This bar-restaurant has a verdant patio and spacious roof terrace, and offers a mixed Guatemalan-German menu including suckling pig and various *wursts*. Among the extensive range of brews on offer are Bavarian lagers and *hefeweizens*.

Quesos y Vino (7832-7785; 1a Calle Poniente 1; mains Q40-60; lunch & dinner Wed-Mon) This Italian-owned establishment is comprised of three rustic buildings, with a lovely outdoor patio and adjoining deli. Like the 'cheese and wine' of the restaurant's name, the food is basic and satisfying: hearty soups, well-stuffed sandwiches on homemade bread, salads and wood-fired pizzas.

Monoloco (7832-4235; 5a Av Sur 6, Pasaje El Corregidor; burgers & burritos Q40-80; noon-midnight) A long-time tourist hangout, the 'wacky monkey' serves up a good blend of comfort foods and local dishes, as well as ice-cold beers, in a relaxed environment.

Epicure (sandwiches Q50-58, mains Q65-100) 3a Av Norte 11B (7832-5545; 10am-10pm); 6a Av Norte 11B (7832-1414; 10am-7pm) A good place to stock up on sandwiches for the volcano climb is this Euro-standard deli, with all kinds of gourmet items. The larger branch on 3a Av offers elegant open-air dining under the rear arbor; the smaller is just for take-out.

our pick El Sabor del Tiempo (7832-0516; cnr 5a Av Norte & 3a Calle Poniente; mains Q50-80; lunch & dinner) One of the town's more atmospheric eateries, done out in rich woods and antique fittings. The menu features good Italian-themed dishes like rabbit in white wine (Q60) and there's draft beer on tap.

Gaia (☎ 7832-3670; 5 Av Norte 35A; mains Q58-90; ⊗ lunch & dinner) This aggressively hip locale covers the Middle East, with curtained alcoves and cushioned sofas around the perimeter of the rear room. After the couscous and falafel, kick back with a *nargila* (water pipe, Q95).

Fridar (☎ 7832-1130; 5a Av Norte 30; mains Q80-100; ⊗ lunch & dinner) Dedicated to Ms Kahlo, this bright bar-restaurant serves tasty Mexican fare and is always busy.

TOP END

Nokiate (☎ 7821-2896; 1a Av Sur 7; sushi Q25-50, rolls Q40-80; ⊗ dinner Tue-Thu, lunch & dinner Fri-Sun) Antigua's most authentic Japanese restaurant has the lot – the tranquil, minimalist atmosphere, the sake and excellent, fresh sushi.

ourpick Caffé Mediterráneo (☎ 7882-7180; 6a Calle Poniente 6A; mains Q90-130; ⊗ lunch & dinner Wed-Mon) Here you'll find the finest, most authentic Italian food in Antigua – if not all Latin America – in a lovely candlelit setting with superb service. Hailing from Calabria, chef Francesco does a tantalizing array of salads and pasta, using seasonally available ingredients.

Como Como (☎ 7832-0478; 6a Calle Poniente 6; mains Q95-125; ⊗ lunch & dinner Tue-Sun) The Belgian chef here knows it's tough to choose, so he offers a sampler *(mise en bouche)* of the day's specials, which usually include some tantalizing variation on fresh fish and soups from seasonal vegetables. Dining is al fresco in the cobblestoned courtyard.

Las Antorchas (☎ 7832-0806; 3a Av Sur 1; steaks Q95-125; ⊗ lunch & dinner Mon-Sat, lunch Sun) The courtyard here makes a beautiful backdrop for sumptuous grilled steaks and seafood; the *pincho gigante* (giant shish kebab; Q125) should be enough for two. The French-run establishment also features an impressive wine list.

Bistrot Cinq (☎ 7832-5510; 4a Calle Oriente 7; mains Q100-130; ⊗ 6-11pm Mon-Thu, noon-11pm Fri-Sun) Popular among the mature expat crowd, the Cinq is a faithful replica of its Parisian counterparts, offering zesty salads and classic entrees such as trout amandine and filet mignon. Check the blackboard for exciting nightly specials. Be sure to make it down for Sunday brunch (served from noon to 3pm).

Mesón Panza Verde (☎ 7832-2925; 5a Av Sur 19; mains Q100-165; ⊗ lunch & dinner) The restaurant of the exclusive B&B dishes up divine continental cuisine in an appealing Antiguan atmosphere. There are just 10 items on the menu; the French-trained chef puts an emphasis on fresh seafood and local ingredients. The hotel's Café Terraza is a good option if you'd just like to bask in the ambience of the gorgeous patio, have a drink or snack. Live jazz or Cuban combos perform several nights a week.

Welten (☎ 7832-6967; 4a Calle Oriente 21; mains Q125; ⊗ lunch & dinner Wed-Mon) Started by a German architect in 1984 and named after her grandmother, this elaborately decorated restaurant serves up an imaginative hybrid of European and Central American cuisine.

El Sereno (☎ 7832-0501; 4a Av Norte 16; mains Q130-200; ⊗ lunch & dinner) Another of Antigua's beautiful courtyard restaurants, this one offers a careful blend of Asian, Italian and Guatemalan influences. There's a full bar inside, but outside is the place to be for lunch, under the shade of two big trees.

DRINKING
Cafes

Café Barista (4a Calle 12; ⊗ 7am-10pm; ☎) Though some may be dismayed to see this sleek, modern franchise on the Parque Central's northwest corner, true coffee aficionados should head here for Antigua's finest lattes and cappuccinos, made with Guatemalan coffee varieties.

Café Condesa Express (Portal del Comercio 4; ⊗ 6am-6:30pm) For a quick caffeine fix, hit this outlet on the west side of the Parque Central.

Bars

The bar scene jumps, especially on Friday and Saturday evenings when the hordes roll in from Guatemala City for some Antigua-style revelry. While the nationwide mandate that all bars close at 1am puts a damper on things, keep your eye out for flyers advertising 'after parties,' unauthorized events in people's homes. Besides the following watering holes, the restaurants La Esquina (p105), Nokiate (see left) and Bistrot Cinq (see left) are at least as popular for the cocktails as the cuisine. Start drinking early and save: *cuba libres* and mojitos are half price between 5pm and 8pm at many bars.

Kafka (6a Av Norte 40) This expat haven, named enigmatically after the Czech surrealist writer, has an intimate rooftop bar where bonfires blaze nightly. 'Happy Hour' goes till closing time.

Monoloco (5a Av Sur 6, Pasaje El Corregidor) The atmosphere can get pretty rowdy here after hours, with plenty of newcomers filing in. The two-level place (open-air upstairs, with benches and long tables) has scores of TVs tuned to the big game.

Reilly's (5a Av Norte 31) Just up from the Arco de Santa Catalina, Antigua's Irish pub packs them in from afternoon onwards during its extended happy hour. The music is loud, the pub grub tasty and the Guinness pricey, at Q60. The Sunday evening trivia quiz (6:30pm) is a pretty big deal.

El Muro (3a Calle Oriente 19D; ☻ closed Sun) 'The Wall' is a friendly neighborhood pub with a range of beers, an eclectic menu of snacks and plenty of sofas to lounge around on. Music, which tends toward '70s and '80s rock (think Pink Floyd), is kept low enough for conversation.

Café No Sé (1 Av Sur 11C) This downbeat little bar is a point of reference for Antigua's budding young Burroughses and Kerouacs. It's also the core of a lively music scene, with players wailing from a corner of the room most evenings. A semi-clandestine attached salon serves its own brand of mescal, 'smuggled' over from Oaxaca. After hours, just bang on the door.

Café Sky (☎ 7832-7300; 1a Av Sur 15) The rooftop is deservedly popular for sunset drinks and snacks, weather permitting. Below deck, there's a candlelit tiki bar with freaky warrior outfits covering the walls.

Reds (1a Calle Poniente 3) Across the way from La Merced, Reds is a low-key clubhouse that draws a refreshingly mixed crowd, often more Guatemalan than gringo. Come here to shoot pool (tournaments on Thursday night), drink cut-rate mojitos or watch sports TV.

JP's Rumbar (☎ 7882-4244; 7a Calle Poniente; ☻ Thu-Tue) Hailing from New Orleans, JP serves up great gumbo alongside the rum, plus a heaping helping of second-line jazz and blues. The cream of Antigua's music scene perform here nightly.

ENTERTAINMENT
Live Music

Apart from the following venues, La Esquina (p105), Café No Sé (p106), JP's Rumbar (see above), the Rainbow Café (p106), and the Mesón Panza Verde (p107) all host folk, rock or jazz performances.

Proyecto Cultural El Sitio (☎ 7832-3037; www.elsitio cultural.org; 5a Calle Poniente 15) This arts center has

lots going on, from concerts and plays (some in English) to photo exhibits and music workshops. Stop by to check the schedule.

La Sala (6a Calle Poniente 9; ☻ Tue-Sun) Crowds pour into this boisterous hall for live rock, blues or reggae – or maybe it's the cheap liquor. Bands hit the stage nightly around 9pm.

El Chamán (7a Av Norte 2; cover Q10) This roof terrace venue is attached to the ruins of the Convento de San Agustín, a suitably trippy backdrop for live reggae or rock.

La Peña de Sol Latino (☎ 7882-4468; 5a Calle Poniente 15C) This supper club is named after its headlining band, who play their distinctive brand of Andean progressive music Wednesday to Sunday night from 7:30pm.

Cinema & TV

Antigua's only proper cinema, **Cine Lounge La Sin Ventura** (☎ 7832-0581; 5a Av Sur 8; ☻ noon-8:30pm Tue-Sat) projects videos of recent Hollywood (not dubbed) and Spanish-language releases on a big screen all day long, with nightclub-style seating. The movies are free; pay just for the food and drink you consume (mains Q30 to Q40). To see what's playing, check the board outside.

Two cultural centers, the Centro de Formación de la Cooperación Española (see p96) and Proyecto Cultural El Sitio (see below left), run thematic series of documentaries or foreign arthouse films on Wednesday and Thursday night, respectively.

For North American and European sports on TV, check the programs at **Café 2000** (6a Av Norte 2), Reds (see left) and Monoloco (above left).

Dancing

La Casbah (☎ 7832-2640; 5a Av Norte 30; admission Q30; ☻ 8:30pm-1am Tue-Sat) This two-level disco near the Santa Catalina arch has a warm atmosphere, is reportedly gay-friendly and quite a party most nights.

Estudio 35 (5a Av Norte 35; ☻ 5pm-midnight Tue-Fri, noon-1am Sat, noon-9pm Sun) Popular with weekenders from Guatemala City who like the reasonably priced drinks, this 'resto-bar' really gets going later in the evening when Latin dance combos perform in the rear lounge.

La Sin Ventura (5a Av Sur 8; ☻ Tue-Sat) The liveliest dance floor in town is packed with Guatemalan youth toward the weekend. There's live salsa and merengue on Thursday night.

You can learn to move at several places around town. Both **Salsa Chapina Dance Company**

(☎ 5270-6453; 6a Calle Poniente 26) and **New Sensation Salsa Studio** (☎ 5033-0921; 1a Calle Poniente 27) offer one-on-one instruction in salsa, merengue, bachata and cha-cha.

SHOPPING

Antigua's **market** (Calz de Santa Lucía Sur) – chaotic, colorful and always busy – sprawls north of 1a Calle. The best days are the official market days – Monday, Thursday and Friday – when villagers from the vicinity roll in and spread their wares north and west of the main market building. Immediately south, the **Mercado de Artesanías** (4a Calle Poniente; ☼ 8am-8pm) displays masses of Guatemalan handicrafts. While not at the top end of quality, you'll find colorful masks, blankets, jewelry, purses and more. Don't be afraid to bargain. The **Mercado del Carmen**, next to the ruins of the Iglesia del Carmen, is a good place to browse for textiles, pottery and jade, particularly on weekends, when activity spills out onto 3a Av.

Nim Po't (☎ 7832-2681; www.nimpot.com; 5a Av Norte 29) This sprawling hall boasts a huge collection of Maya clothing, as well as hundreds of masks and wood carvings. The *huipiles, cortes, fajas* and other garments are arranged by region, so it makes for a fascinating visit whether you're buying or not.

Casa del Tejido Antiguo (☎ 7832-3169; Calle de la Recolección 51; admission Q5; ☼ 9am-5:30pm Mon-Sat) Claiming to be the only place in Antigua managed by indigenous people, this is another intriguing place for textiles; it's like a museum, market and workshop rolled into one, with exhibits on regional outfits and daily demonstrations of backstrap weaving techniques.

Centro de Arte Popular (4a Calle Oriente 10; ☼ 9:30am-6:30pm) Inside the Casa Antigua El Jaulón, a courtyard shopping arcade, this shop/museum displays Tz'utujil oil paintings (see boxed text, p134), cedar figurines, masks and other crafts in four galleries. The pieces are arranged thematically, with sections for music, markets, medicine and religious rituals.

GETTING THERE & AROUND

Bus

Buses from Guatemala City, Ciudad Vieja and San Miguel Dueñas arrive and depart from a street just south of the market, alongside the Mercado de Artesanías. Buses to Chimaltenango, Escuintla, San Antonio Aguas Calientes and Santa María de Jesús go from a lot behind the main market building. If you're heading out to local villages, go early in the morning and return by mid-afternoon, as bus services drop off dramatically as evening approaches.

To reach highland towns such as Chichicastenango, Quetzaltenango, Huehuetenango or Panajachel, take one of the frequent buses to Chimaltenango, on the Interamericana Hwy, then catch an onward bus. Making connections is easy, as many folks will jump to your aid as you alight from one bus looking for another. But stay alert and watch your pack; bag slashing isn't unheard of in Chimal.

Chimaltenango (Q5, 45 minutes, 19km, every 15 minutes from 6am to 6pm)

Ciudad Vieja (Q5, 20 minutes, 7km, every half hour from 7am to 8pm) Take a San Miguel Dueñas bus.

Escuintla (Q8, one hour, 39km, every half hour from 5am to 4pm)

Guatemala City (Q8, one hour, 45km, every few minutes from 5am to 6:30pm) Litegua (☎ 7832-9850;

TRUE JADE

Jade, beloved of the ancient Maya, isn't always green. It can be lilac, yellow, pink, white or even black. However, a lot of stones passed off as jade are not the real thing. There are two main forms of genuine jade: nephrite, found in Asia, and jadeite, found in Guatemala. Albite, serpentine, chrysoprase, diopside, chrysolite and aventurine – none of these are true jade. It seems that the ancient Maya themselves had a hard time telling the difference. Many items of Maya 'jade' in museums have been revealed, on testing, to be one of these inferior stones.

To discern quality jade, look for translucency, purity and intensity of color and absence of flaws – and ask if you can scratch the stone with a pocket knife: if it scratches, it's not true jadeite.

Several Antigua shops specialize in jade, including **La Casa del Jade** (www.lacasadeljade.com; 4a Calle Oriente 10), **Jades SA** (www.jadessa.com; 4a Calle Oriente 1, 4a Calle Oriente 12 & 4a Calle Oriente 34) and **El Reino del Jade** (5a Av Norte 28). At La Casa del Jade and Jades SA's 4a Calle Oriente 34 branch, you can visit the workshops behind the showrooms. Ask about prices at a few places before making any purchase.

ANTIGUA

www.litegua.com/litegua; 4a Calle Oriente 48) offers Pullman service (Q40) from their office at the east end of town at 10am and 4pm.

Panajachel (Q36, 2½ hours, 146km, one Pullman bus daily at 7am by Transportes Rebulli) Departs from Panadería Colombia on 4a Calle Poniente, half a block east of the market.

San Antonio Aguas Calientes (Q5, 30 minutes, 9km, every half hour from 7am to 8pm)

Santa María de Jesús (Q5, one hour, 12km, every hour from 5am to 8pm)

Shuttle Minibus

Numerous travel agencies (see p92) and tourist minibus operators offer frequent shuttle services to places tourists go, including Guatemala City and its airport, Panajachel and Chichicastenango. They cost more than buses, but they're comfortable and convenient, with door-to-door service at both ends. These are some typical one-way prices:

Chichicastenango Q90

Cobán Q250

Copán (Honduras) Q275

Guatemala City Q83

Monterrico Q115

Panajachel Q100

Quetzaltenango Q210

Pin down shuttle operators about departure times and whether they require a minimum number of passengers. Be careful of 'shuttles' to Flores or Tikal. This service may consist of taking you to Guatemala City and putting you on a public bus there.

Car & Motorcycle

To park in Antigua, you're supposed to have a *marbete* (label) hanging from your rearview mirror, or risk a fine. Purchase these from traffic cops for Q20.

If you're planning to drive out of town on a reportedly hijack-prone road (such as to Panajachel via Patzún), you may request an escort from Asistur (see p87) by emailing them at least 72 hours in advance. There's no fee other than the escort's expenses.

Rental companies include the following:

CATour (☎ 7832-9638; www.catours.co.uk; 6a Calle Oriente 14) Rents motorcycles from Q10/45 per hour/day and offers motorcycle tours from Q140.

Guatemala Renta Autos (☎ 2329-9030; www.guatemalarentacar.com; 4a Av Norte 6)

Tabarini (☎ 7832-8107; www.tabarini.com; 6a Av Sur 22)

Taxi

Taxis and tuk-tuks wait where the Guatemala City buses stop and on the east side of Parque Central. An in-town taxi ride costs around Q25; tuk-tuks are Q10. Note that tuk-tuks are not allowed in the center of town; you'll have to hike a few blocks out to find one.

AROUND ANTIGUA

JOCOTENANGO

This village just northwest of Antigua provides a window on a less self-conscious, less Unesco-authorized version of Guatemalan life than does downtown Antigua. Though Jocotenango is now plagued by traffic, the **church** stands proudly at the center as it has for centuries, with its peach facade graced by baroque columns and elaborate stuccowork, facing a garden aflame with African tulip trees. The town is known for its processions during Lent – or perhaps more so as the birthplace of Latin American pop star Ricardo Arjona.

Jocotenango's main attraction lies outside the village on a small coffee plantation: the **Centro Cultural La Azotea** (☎ 7831-1120; www.centroazotea.com; Calle del Cementerio Final; adult/child Q30/5; ☿ 8:30am-4pm Mon-Fri, 8:30am-2pm Sat) features a well-designed complex of three museums – on coffee, music and indigenous life. The coffee section includes a 19th-century waterwheel-powered processing plant. The tour ends with a complimentary cup of the plantation's own brew. Part two of the center is the Casa K'ojom, a superb collection of traditional Maya musical instruments, masks, paintings and other artifacts. The objects are displayed within the context of the ceremonies and customs in which they are used, with an interesting section on Maximón, the semipagan deity revered by many highland Maya (see p146). A good audiovisual show illustrating the musical instruments in action is included. The third exhibit is the Rincón de Sacatepéquez, displaying the multicolored outfits and crafts of the Antigua valley. The English translations throughout are of a high standard. Afterward, you can roam the coffee plantation itself, which is crisscrossed by nature trails.

A shop sells quality coffee, local crafts and Maya instruments, and a restaurant offers good, moderately priced Guatemalan food. There is also the **Establo La Ronda**, where you can take a one-hour morning horse ride round the grounds for Q108 (minimum two persons; ring the museum two days ahead).

Free minibuses to La Azotea leave from Antigua's Parque Central hourly from 9am to 2pm, returning from 9:40am to 4:40pm. You're free to explore the village before hopping back on the bus. From La Azotea's ticket office, walk 350m back along the driveway then 050m along the street ahead (1a Calle) to reach Jocotenango's main square.

EL HATO

An excellent excursion from Antigua is the **Earth Lodge** (☎ 5664-0713; www.earthlodgeguatemala. com; dm Q35, s/d/tr cabin Q90/140/165), high in the hills above Jocotenango. Overseen by an affable, young Canadian-American couple, the 40-acre spread is set on a working avocado farm, and the views of the Panchoy valley and volcanoes are truly mesmerizing. There's plenty to do out here – hiking trails, bird-watching, Spanish lessons, Bocce ball, a *chuj* (Maya sauna), as well as just hanging in a hammock and taking it all in. Lip-smacking, nutritious vegetarian food is served with a slew of avocado-based fare at harvest time (January and July). Accommodation is in comfortable A-frame cabins, an eight-bed dorm and a couple of fabulous tree houses. Another option is camping for Q20 per person. You can work on the farm for a reduction in room rates.

A portion of the profits buys supplies for the village school, where guests can do volunteer work.

To get there, your best bet is to call at least a day in advance to see if the lodge can pick you up from Antigua (Q50 for one to five passengers). Otherwise, a bus leaves infrequently from in front of the Iglesia de la Candelaria on 1a Av Norte in Antigua for Aldea El Hato (Q4). From there it's a 20-minute walk – any villager can give you directions – just ask for 'los gringos.'

CIUDAD VIEJA & AROUND

Seven kilometers southwest of Antigua along the Escuintla road is **Ciudad Vieja** (Old City), near the site of the first capital of the Captaincy General of Guatemala. Founded in 1527, it met its demise 14 years later when Volcán Agua loosed a flood of water that had been penned up in its crater. The water deluged the town with tons of rock and mud, leaving only the ruins of La Concepción church.

The actual site of the former capital is a bit to the east at San Miguel Escobar; Ciudad Vieja was populated by survivors of the flood. The pretty church on the main square has an impressive stuccowork facade, though it's about two centuries newer than the plaque by the door boasts it to be.

The NGO Niños de Guatemala (see p97), which runs a school for low-income kids above the town, leads alternative **tours** (adult/ child Q200/100; ⊗ Tue, Thu & Fri) of Ciudad Vieja that really get beneath the surface of the community. A half-day tour takes you through the poorer section of town, where many of the schoolchildren reside, then focuses on two of the town's principal industries: 'chicken bus' rebuilding and coffin-making. At the end of the tour, local chefs prepare you a traditional meal.

Your best bet for accommodation in Ciudad Vieja is **Hotel Santa Valentina** (☎ 7831-5044; 2a Av 0-01, Zona 3; s/d Q150/250; **P**), offering rooms with private bathroom and TV.

Java junkies in this neck of the woods should investigate the coffee plantation **Finca los Nietos** (☎ 7831-5438; www.fincalosnietos.com; ⊗ 8-11am Mon-Fri) for a tour and a taste. The 1½ hour tour (Q50 per person, minimum two people) answers all your nitty-gritty coffee questions, from how seedlings are propagated to how beans are roasted. Phone for an appointment and mention if you want to roast your own beans (minimum 2.5kg or 5lb). The *finca* is 7km from Antigua, just off the bus route to San Antonio Aguas Calientes: you go through Ciudad Vieja and San Lorenzo El Cubo, then get off at the crossroads known as 'El Guarda,' just before the road goes downhill to San Antonio. Walk two blocks to the right (toward Volcán Agua) until you come to a wall with a mosaic sign; ring the bell to enter.

A tranquil village surrounded by farmed volcanic slopes, **San Antonio Aguas Calientes** is noted for its textiles, and the Mercado de Artesanías (handicrafts market) stands prominently beside the town hall. Inside, women work on hip-strap looms and on the upper level there's an exhibit of traditional outfits, with examples from all over Guatemala. Ceremonial *huipiles*, embroidered on both sides, can go for as much as Q2800 here.

Between San Antonio and Ciudad Vieja, near the village of San Miguel Dueñas, is the **Valhalla Experimental Station** (☎ 7831-5799; www.exvalhalla.net; ⊗ 8am-4:30pm), a macadamia farm raising 300 species of the remarkable nut. You can tour this organic, sustainable agriculture project and sample nuts, oils and cosmetics made from the

ANTIGUA

ANTIGUA

EXPLORE MORE OF ANTIGUA

While Antigua itself is pretty much well-trodden territory from end to end, there are plenty of little villages just outside of town just begging to be explored:

- Santa María de Jesús, at the foot of Volcán Agua, holds a major market on Sundays.
- San Juan del Obispo has a wonderful colonial church and panoramic views of Antigua.
- San Felipe, an artisans' village, has some of the finest jade, silver and ceramic work in the area.
- San Lorenzo El Tejar is worth the 25-minute ride northwest to soak in its popular hot springs.
- Pastores is ground zero for leatherwork. This is the place to come for handmade cowboy boots and stock whips.
- Cerro Alux (www.cerroalux.com), near the village of San Lucas Sacatepéquez, is a hilltop ecopark with interpretive trails and good bird-watching opportunities.

---

harvest. Be sure to sample the macadamia-nut pancakes, served amid the lush tropical foliage.

A good way to tour these villages is by bicycle (see p97). Head out of Antigua along the Ciudad Vieja road south of the market. It's a 4km ride along a moderately busy road to Ciudad Vieja. Take 4a Calle west through the restored colonial part of town. Back at the main road, turn left. When you reach the cemetery, go right, following signs for San Miguel Dueñas. From there, it's about a 10-minute ride downhill to the Valhalla Experimental Station, on the left side. The road goes on to San Miguel Dueñas. Coming into that town, you'll go over a small bridge. Bear right, then turn right at the sign for San Antonio Aguas Calientes. This road, unpaved for much of the way, winds for the next 5km through coffee *fincas*, hamlets and vegetable fields. Arriving in San Antonio, turn right at the communal wash basins to reach the main plaza. Leaving town, go around the left side of the church, then head left up 2a Calle. From there, it's a steep climb but you're rewarded with breathtaking views of the village. Beyond the Finca Los Nietos coffee plantation (see p111), you'll reach the RN-14 Hwy. Turn left there and go 2km, taking the second right onto a dirt road. This will take you back to the Ciudad Vieja–Antigua road, where a left turn leads you back into town.

For information on buses to these villages, see p109.

SAN JUAN COMALAPA

Set on the side of a deep ravine, this artisans' village 16km north of Chimaltenango is best known for its tradition of primitive folk painting. It's a relatively modern town, founded by

the Spanish when they amalgamated several Kaqchiquel communities.

Comalapa gained its reputation during the 1950s when native son Andrés Curruchich (1891–1969) rose to fame for his primitive paintings of village life and his works ended up on display as far away as San Francisco, Dallas and Detroit. Considered the father of Guatemalan primitivist painting, he was awarded the prestigious Order of the Quetzal in the 1960s. Several pieces are displayed at the Museo Ixchel in Guatemala City (p71) – though sadly, the artist remains more seriously collected abroad than in his native land.

In Comalapa, you can visit the house Curruchich was born in, on the main street. His daughter and granddaughter will show you around and there is some information about the artist. His legacy lives on as some of his offspring and other villagers took up the brush and started working in a similar primitive style. Scenes of traditional festivals and ritual dances predominate in the paintings of Comalapa, though you'll also see some highland landscapes. Several galleries around the plaza show and sell their work.

Several *comedores* line the plaza, dishing out decent grub. If you want to stay the night, your best bet is **Hotel Pixcayá** (☎ 7849-8260; 0 Av 1-82; s/d Q80/140, without bathroom Q65/80; **P**).

Buses (Q8, 45 minutes, hourly) run from Chimaltenango; minibuses and pickups leave when full.

SANTIAGO SACATEPÉQUEZ & SUMPANGO

All Saints' Day (November 1) is best known in Guatemala as the time when families visit cemeteries to spruce up the tombstones of loved ones with poignant floral designs, but locals add another quirk to this seasonal ritual. It's also the time of the **Feria del Barrilete Gigante** (Festival of the Giant Kite). The biggest parties happen in Santiago Sacatepéquez and Sumpango, about 20km and 25km north of Antigua respectively. Fabricated weeks ahead of the event, these kites are giants. Made from tissue paper with wood and bamboo braces, and with guide ropes as thick as a human arm, most are more than 13m wide, with intricate, colorful designs that combine Maya cosmology and popular iconography. In Santiago they're flown over the cemetery, some say to communicate with the souls of the dead. Kids fly their own small kites right in the cemetery, running around the gravestones. Food and tchotchke vendors sell their wares right next to the graveyard. In Sumpango it's a somewhat more formal affair (and the crowds more manageable), with the kites lined up at one end of a football field and bleachers set up at the other. Judges rank the big flyers according to size, design, color, originality and elevation. Part of the fun is watching the crowd flee when a giant kite takes a nose dive!

Various travel agencies run day trips from Antigua to Santiago Sacatepéquez on November 1 (charging around Q200 per person including lunch and English-speaking guide), though you can easily get there on your own by taking any Guatemala City-bound bus and getting off with the throngs at the junction for Santiago. From here, take one of the scores of buses covering the last few kilometers. The fastest way to Sumpango is to take a bus to Chimaltenango and backtrack to Sumpango; this will bypass all of the Santiago-bound traffic, which is bumper to bumper on fair day.

ANTIGUA

114

The Highlands

Guatemala's most dramatic region – Los Altos – stretches from Antigua to the Mexican border northwest of Huehuetenango. Here the verdant hills sport emerald-green grass, cornfields and towering stands of pine, and every town and village has a story.

The traditional values and customs of Guatemala's indigenous peoples are strongest in the highlands. Maya dialects are the first language, Spanish a distant second. The age-old culture based on maize (from which the Maya believe that humans were created) is still alive; a sturdy cottage in the midst of a thriving *milpa* (maize field) is a common sight. And on every road you'll see men, women and children carrying burdens of *leña* (firewood), to be used for heating and cooking.

Most towns were already populated by the Maya when the Spanish arrived. History turned bloody with the beginning of the civil war in 1960, when the highlands were targeted heavily by guerrillas and the army alike.

The poster child for Guatemala's natural beauty, the volcano-ringed Lago de Atitlán has been attracting tourists for decades. Surrounded by small villages, each possessing a distinctive character, the lake generally deals with its popularity well, though a major bacteria outbreak in late 2009 alerted inhabitants to the perils of rapid growth. West of the lake stands Guatemala's second city, Quetzaltenango, a cultural haven with a significant contingent of foreign volunteers and language students. To the north spread the Cuchumatanes mountains, truly a world apart, where indigenous life follows its own rhythms amid fantastic mountain landscapes. For hikers, this is the promised land.

HIGHLIGHTS

- Soaring over, diving under or relaxing alongside sublime **Lago de Atitlán** (p116)
- Hunting for *huipiles* (long embroidered tunics) at vibrant indigenous markets in **Chichicastenango** (p143) and **San Francisco El Alto** (p173)
- Polishing your Spanish and hiking volcanoes in and around **Quetzaltenango** (p157)
- Taking in the stunning Cuchumatanes scenery and village life of the Ixil Triangle around **Nebaj** (p153)
- Mingling with the Maya in **Todos Santos Cuchumatán** (p180), **San Mateo Ixtatán** (p183) and other remote villages

CLIMATE

Abundant rains fall between May and October. During the rainy season, be prepared for some dreary, chilly, damp days. At high altitudes it gets cold at night at any time of year. But when the sun comes out, this land is stunning to behold.

GETTING AROUND

The meandering Interamericana (Hwy 1), running 345km along the mountain ridges between Guatemala City and the Mexican border at La Mesilla, passes close to all of the region's most important places, and countless buses roar up and down it all day, every day. Two key intersections act as major bus interchanges: Los Encuentros for Panajachel and changes: Los Encuentros for Panajachel and

Chichicastenango, and Cuatro Caminos for Quetzaltenango. If you can't find a bus going to your destination, simply get one to either of those points. Transfers are usually seamless, with not-too-frustrating waiting times and locals who are ready to help travelers find the right bus.

Travel is easiest in the morning and, for smaller places, on market days. By mid- or late afternoon, buses may be difficult to find; besides, it's not a good idea to be out on the roads after dark. Further off the beaten track you may be relying more on pickups than buses for transportation.

Microbuses – large vans that depart as soon as they fill with passengers – are increasingly becoming the dominant mode of transport along

THE HIGHLANDS

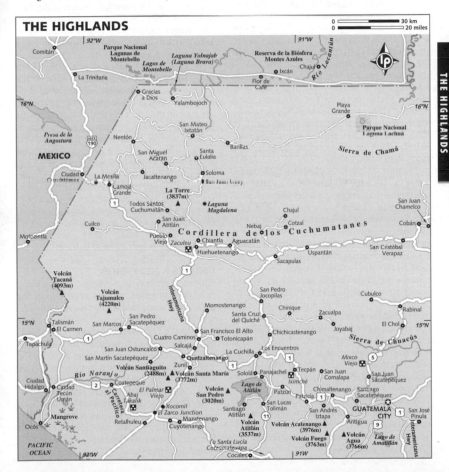

THE HIGHLANDS

highland routes such as Santa Cruz del Quiché–Nebaj and Chichicastenango–Los Encuentros. Though not as exotic as chicken buses (former US school buses now used for public transport), they're preferred by many locals for their convenience and are only slightly more expensive.

Otherwise, minibuses run by tour operators shuttle tourists between the major destinations of the region and beyond. They travel faster, more comfortably and more expensively than buses.

LAGO DE ATITLÁN

Nineteenth-century traveler/chronicler John L Stephens, writing in *Incidents of Travel in Central America,* called Lago de Atitlán 'the most magnificent spectacle we ever saw,' and he had been around a bit. Today even seasoned travelers marvel at this spectacular environment. Fishermen in rustic crafts ply the lake's aquamarine surface, while indigenous women in multicolored outfits do their washing by the banks where trees burst into bloom. Fertile hills dot the landscape, and over everything loom the volcanoes, permeating the entire area with a mysterious beauty. It never looks the same twice. No wonder many outsiders have fallen in love with the place and made their homes here.

Though volcanic explosions have been going on here for millions of years, today's landscape has its origins in the massive eruption of 85,000 years ago, termed Los Chocoyos, which blew volcanic ash as far as Florida and Panama. The quantity of magma expelled from below the earth's crust caused the surface terrain to collapse, forming a huge, roughly circular hollow that soon filled with water – the Lago de Atitlán. Smaller volcanoes rose out of the lake's southern waters thousands of years later: Volcán San Pedro (today 3020m above sea level) about 60,000 years ago, followed by Volcán Atitlán (3537m) and Volcán Tolimán (3158m). The lake today is 8km across from north to south, 18km from east to west, and averages around 300m deep, though the water level fluctuates curiously from year to year.

Around 900 AD, when the Maya highland civilization was in decline, the region was settled by two groups that had migrated from the Toltec capital of Tula in Mexico, the Kaqchiquel and Tz'utujil. The latter group settled at Chuitinamit, across the way from the present-day village of Santiago Atitlán, while the former occupied the lake's northern shores; this demographic composition persists to this day. By the time the Spanish showed up in 1524, the Tz'utujil had expanded their domain to occupy most of the lakeshore. Pedro de Alvarado exploited the situation by allying with the Kaqchiquels against their Tz'utujil rivals, whom they defeated in a bloody battle at Tzanajuyú. The Kaqchiquels subsequently rebelled against the Spanish and were themselves subjugated by 1531.

Today, the main lakeside town is Panajachel, or 'Gringotenango' as it is sometimes unkindly called, and most people initially head here to launch their Atitlán explorations. To the south, Santiago Atitlán, along the lake's southern spur, has the strongest indigenous identity of any of the major lake towns. Up the western shore, the town of San Pedro La Laguna has a reputation as a countercultural party center. On the north side, San Marcos La Laguna is a haven for contemporary new-agers, while Santa Cruz La Laguna and Jaibalito, nearer to Panajachel, are among the lake's most idyllic, picturesque locales.

The lake is a three-hour bus ride west from Guatemala City or Antigua. There is an ersatz town at the highway junction of Los Encuentros, based on throngs of people changing buses here. From La Cuchilla junction, 2km further west along the Interamericana, a road descends 12km southward to Sololá, and then there's a sinuous 8km descent to Panajachel. Sit on the right-hand side of the bus for views of the lake and its surrounding volcanoes.

Dangers & Annoyances

Although most visitors never experience any trouble, robberies have occurred along the paths that run around Lago de Atitlán. The security situation is forever changing – some months it's OK to walk between certain villages, then that route suddenly becomes dangerous. The more troublesome spots at the time of research are noted in their respective sections, but it's best to check with Asistur (see p119) about the current situation.

In late 2009 an outbreak of bacteria seriously marred the lake's natural beauty and discouraged swimming, though toxicity levels were subsequently deemed acceptable (see boxed text, p133).

IXIMCHÉ

K'icab the Great, leader of the Kaqchiquels, relocated his capital here in 1463 from its previous location near the K'iche' Maya stronghold of K'umarcaaj. At that time, the Kaqchiquel were at war with the K'iche', and the natural defenses of the new location, a flat promontory surrounded by ravines, served them well.

The Spanish, who arrived in 1524, set up their first Guatemalan headquarters here, forming an alliance with the resident Kaqchiquels against their K'iche' enemies. However, the European invaders' demands for gold and other loot soon put an end to their alliance with the Kaqchiquel, who were defeated in an ensuing guerrilla war.

Entering the **archaeological site** (admission Q50; 8am-4:30pm), visit the small museum (closed Monday) on the right, then continue to the four ceremonial plazas, which are surrounded by temple structures up to 10m high, and ball courts. Some structures have been uncovered: on a few the original plaster coating is still in place.

Today Iximché remains an important ceremonial site for indigenous pilgrims, who visit the area to perform magic rituals, burning liquor, paraffin or sticks of wood in front of the pyramids to ward off illness or bring down enemies. After George W Bush visited the site in 2007, local shamans got to work cleansing the zone of any lingering malevolence.

LAGO DE ATITLÁN

THE HIGHLANDS

Sleeping & Eating

The town of Tecpán, off the Interamericana, has the nearest lodging. Just off the plaza, the **Hotel Iximché** (☎ 7840-3495; 1a Av 1-38, Zona 2; s/d Q75/150, without bathroom Q35/70) features two facing buildings, one with private bathrooms, both offering decent-sized, clean rooms with tacky bedspreads. The adjacent eatery serves Chinese food.

Getting There & Away

'Ruinas' microbuses to the site (Q2.50, 10 minutes) leave from near Tecpán's main plaza, opposite the Iglesia Bautista Horeb, at least every hour till 4pm. The last bus back leaves the site no later than 4:30pm.

Buses traveling east from La Cuchilla junction can drop you at the turnoff for Tecpán; from there it's about a 1km walk (or, if you're lucky, a short ride on an urban bus) to the center of town.

SOLOLÁ

pop 41,100 / elev 1978m

There was a Kaqchiquel town (called Tzoloyá) here long before the Spanish showed up. Sololá's importance comes from its location on trade routes between the *tierra caliente* (hot lands of the Pacific Slope) and *tierra fría* (the chilly highlands). All the traders meet here, and Sololá's **market** (☺ Tue, Fri & Sun) is one of the most vivid in the highlands. On market mornings the plaza next to the cathedral is ablaze with the colorful costumes of people from surrounding villages and towns. Displays of meat, vegetables, fruit, house wares and clothing are neatly arranged in every available space, with tides of buyers ebbing and flowing around the vendors. Elaborate stands are stocked with brightly colored yarn for making the traditional costumes you see around you. Friday sees the most activity.

Sunday mornings the officers of the traditional *cofradías* (religious brotherhoods) parade ceremoniously to the cathedral.

Virtually everyone stays in Panajachel, but if you need a bed in Sololá, **Hotel Belén** (☎ 7762-3105; 10a Calle 4-36, Zona 1; s/d Q60/120) has eight basic but clean upstairs rooms with hot-water bathroom. It's a block uphill behind the clock tower that overlooks the main square.

All buses between Panajachel and Los Encuentros stop at Sololá. It's Q3 and 15 minutes to either place.

PANAJACHEL

pop 19,900 / elev 1595m

The busiest and most built-up lakeside settlement, Panajachel ('Pana' to pretty much the entire country) has developed haphazardly and, some say, in a less than beautiful way. Strolling the main street, Calle Santander, chock-a-block with cybercafes, travel agencies, handicraft hawkers and rowdy bars, dodging noisome tuk-tuks all the way, you may be forgiven for supposing this paradise lost.

A hike down to the lakeshore, though, will give you a better idea why Pana attracts so many visitors. Aside from the astounding volcano panorama, the town's excellent transportation connections, copious accommodations, varied restaurants and thumping nightlife make it a favorite destination for weekending Guatemalans.

Several different cultures mingle on Panajachel's dusty streets. *Ladinos* and gringos control the tourist industry. The Kaqchiquel and Tz'utujil Maya from surrounding villages come to sell their handicrafts to tourists. Tour groups arrive by bus for a few hours or overnight. This mix makes Pana a curiously cosmopolitan crossroads in an otherwise remote, rural vicinity. All of this makes for a convenient transition into the Atitlán universe – but to truly experience the beauty of the lake, most travelers venture onward soon after arrival.

Orientation

Calle Principal (also called Calle Real) is nominally Pana's main street, although with Calle Santander's plethora of tourist-related businesses, you'll probably find yourself spending much more time there. Calle Santander is 'officially' an 'Avenida,' but local usage sees it referred to as Calle Santander, or simply Santander; we've followed this usage here, but don't get confused if you hear it referred to as Avenida Santander. Many local establishments don't use street addresses.

Most buses stop at the intersection of Calle Principal and Calle Santander, the main road to the lake. Beyond the Calle Santander corner, Calle Principal continues 400m to 500m northeast to the town center, where you'll find the daily market (busiest on Sunday and Thursday), church, town hall and a further smattering of places to sleep and eat.

Calle Rancho Grande, parallel to Calle Santander, is the other main road to the beach. The pedestrian Calle del Lago runs along the lakeside to the Río San Francisco, making for a pretty stroll; near its south end an agglomeration of open-air thatched-roof restaurants crowds the lakefront.

Information

BOOKSTORES

Bus Stop Books (Centro Comercial El Dorado, Calle Principal; 9am-1:30pm Wed-Mon, 8am-6pm Tue) A good range of mainly used books to swap and buy, and a small selection of guidebooks.

Gallery Bookstore (Comercial El Pueblito, Av Los Árboles) Eclectic selection of used books for sale or exchange.

Libros del Lago (Calle Santander) Excellent stock of books in English and other tongues on Guatemala, the Maya and Mesoamerica, plus maps, English and Latin American literature in English, and Lonely Planet guidebooks.

EMERGENCY

Asistur (☎ 5874-9450; Edificio Las Manos, Av El Tzalá, Barrio Jucanyá; 9am-5pm)

Disetur (Tourist Police; ☎ 5531-3982; Playa Pública) The station is in a small building near the Santiago boat dock.

INTERNET ACCESS

Standard rates are Q5 to Q10 an hour; typical hours are 9am to 10pm daily, perhaps shorter on Sunday.

Get Guated Out (Comercial El Pueblito, Av Los Árboles)

MayaNet (Calle Santander 3-62)

Multiservicios J&M (Calle Rancho Grande)

LAUNDRY

Lavandería Il Bucato (Centro Comercial El Dorado, Calle Principal; 9am-6:30pm Mon-Sat) Q30 for up to 5lb.

Lavandería Santander (Calle Santander 1-83) Reliable place; charges Q5 per pound.

MEDICAL SERVICES

The nearest hospital is at Sololá.

Centro de Salud (Clinic; ☎ 7762-1158; Calle Principal; 8am-6pm Mon-Fri, 8am-1pm Sat)

MONEY

All of the following banks have Visa/MasterCard ATMs.

Banco Agromercantil (cnr Calles Principal & Santander; 9am-6pm Mon-Sat, 9am-1pm Sun) Changes traveler's checks.

Banco de América Central (Centro Comercial San Rafael, Calle Santander; 9am-5pm Mon-Fri, 9am-1pm Sat) Visa and MasterCard cash advances.

Banco Industrial (Comercial Los Pinos, Calle Santander; 9am-4pm Mon-Fri, 9am-1pm Sat) Offers Visa-card cash advances.

Banrural (Calle del Campanario; 9am-5pm Mon-Fri, 9am-1pm Sat) Changes traveler's checks.

Some of the travel agencies, shops and hotels along Calle Santander will change US dollars or euros cash, but not at the best rates. Try El Güipil, opposite Pana Pan, or Americo's Tours.

POST

DHL (Edificio Rincón Sai, Calle Santander)

Get Guated Out (☎ /fax 7762-0595; gguated@yahoo.com; Comercial El Pueblito, Av Los Árboles) English-speaking outfit that can ship your important letters and parcels by air freight or international courier.

Post Office (cnr Calles Santander & 15 de Febrero)

Realworld Export (☎ 5634-5699; Centro Comercial San Rafael, Calle Santander) Courier service that arranges bulk shipments from multiple handicrafts buyers to reduce charges, an economical solution for shipment of larger items.

TELEPHONE

Some cybercafes and travel agencies located on Calle Santander offer moderately cheap phone calls – around Q2/3.50 a minute to call a landline/cell phone in North America or Central America and Q3/4.50 a minute to Europe. Otherwise, just Skype your loved ones from any internet cafe. For local calls there are card phones outside **Telgua** (Calle Santander).

TOURIST INFORMATION

Inguat (☎ 7762-1106; info-panajachel@inguat.gob.gt; Centro Comercial San Rafael Local 11, Calle Santander; 9am-1pm & 2-5pm) This tourist office is in a little shopping center off the main street. A few brochures are available and staff can answer straightforward questions.

TRAVEL AGENCIES

Many of Panajachel's full-service travel agencies are scattered along Calle Santander. These establishments offer trips, tours and shuttle services to other destinations around Guatemala. The ones listed below have their own shuttle vehicles.

Atitrans (☎ 7762-2336; www.atitrans.com; Edificio Rincón Sai, 3a Av 1-30; 8am-8pm)

Eternal Spring (☎ 7762-6043; eternalspring_reservations@hotmail.com; Calle Santander) Shuttles to San Cristóbal de Las Casas, Mexico.

Servicios Turísticos Atitlán (☎ /fax 7762-2246; turisticosatitlan@yahoo.com; Calle 14 de Febrero 2-81)

Servicios Turísticos Los Volcanes (☎ 7762-1096; www.posadadevolcanes.com; Calle Santander 5-51) Inside Posada Los Volcanes.

THE HIGHLANDS

Sights

The **Museo Lacustre Atitlán** (Calle Santander; admission Q35; ☼ 8am-6pm Sun-Fri, 8am-7pm Sat), inside the Hotel Posada de Don Rodrigo, has displays on the history of the Atitlán region and the volcanic eruptions that created its landscape, plus a collection of ancient artifacts recovered from the lake. Overflowing with art by

Guatemalan painters and sculptors, **La Galería** (☎ 7762-2432; panagaleria@hotmail.com; Calle Rancho Grande; ☼ 9am-noon & 2-6pm Wed-Mon) functions as both an exhibit space and cultural center, hosting lectures, films and occasional concerts. Started in 1971 by Nan Cuz, an indigenous Guatemalan painter who grew up in Germany, the gallery has canvases by some

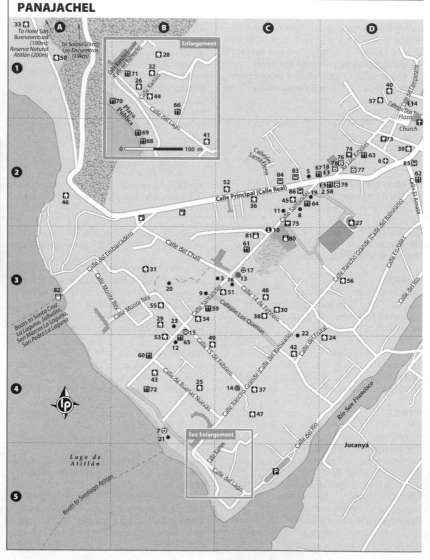

PANAJACHEL

500 painters. Among them are a number of the hallucinatory landscapes that garnered Cuz recognition in the European art world.

RESERVA NATURAL ATITLÁN
A former coffee plantation being retaken by natural vegetation, the **Reserva Natural Atitlán** (☎ 7762-2565; www.atitlanreserva.com; adult/child Q45/25;

8am-5pm) is 200m past the Hotel Atitlán on the northern outskirts of town. It makes a good outing on foot or bicycle. You can leisurely walk the main trail in an hour: it leads up over swing bridges to a waterfall, then down to a platform for viewing local spider monkeys. You should also see *pisotes* (coatis), relatives of the raccoon with long snouts and

THE HIGHLANDS

long, upright, furry tails. The reserve includes a butterfly enclosure and herb garden, an interpretive center, zip lines, a small shade coffee plantation and an aviary. For longer stays, there are some excellent rooms with private decks, and camping.

Activities
CYCLING, HIKING & KAYAKING
Lago de Atitlán is a cycling and hiking wonderland, spreading across hill and dale. **Roger's Tours** (☎ 7762-6060; www.rogerstours.com; Calle Santander) rents quality mountain bikes for Q40/250 per hour/day and leads a variety of cycling tours (Q415 to Q500 including helmet, guide and lunch). One tour travels by boat from Panajachel to the village of Tzununá, then proceeds by bike west via dirt trail to San Marcos La Laguna and paved road to San Pedro La Laguna, with a swimming stop at Playa Las Cristalinas, and finally returns to Pana by boat. Another tour hits the villages on the east side of the lake.

See Santiago Atitlán (p130) and following sections for information on walks around Lago de Atitlán.

Before setting out for any hike or ride, make enquiries about safety with Asistur (see p119) and keep asking as you go.

A one-day walking trip from Panajachel to the top of Volcán San Pedro and back should cost around Q540 per person, including boat transport, taxi to the trailhead, entry fees and guide.

Kayaks are available for rent (Q30 per hour) from the pier at the foot of Calle del Rancho Grande.

PARAGLIDING
'Too much of a good thing' is how Aldous Huxley described Lago de Atitlán in his 1934 travel work *Beyond the Mexique Bay*. That applies well to the experience of soaring over the Lago de Atitlán with parachute-like wings, enjoying a falcon's view of the lake's rippling expanse and the villages that tumble down from green hills to its shores. The lake has become a center for paragliding enthusiasts and several operators provide tandem flights, with passengers seated in a canvas chair attached to the flyer's harness so they're free to take photos or simply gaze in amazement at the panorama below.

Realworld Paragliding (☎ 5634-5699; realworld paragliding@gmail.com; Centro Comercial San Rafael, Calle Santander) is the most reliable outfit around. Christian is a patient, personable English-speaking guide who's made more than 500 tandem flights. Inquire at the office about suitable wind conditions. If winds are from the south, you'll take off in the afternoon from above Santa Catarina Palopó and land at Pana; if winds are from the north you'll fly from Santa Clara to San Juan La Laguna, usually in the morning. In the latter scenario, you'll travel by boat to San Pedro La Laguna (additional Q25 per person), then catch a pickup to Santa Clara. The charge is Q665 for the flight, which takes 20 minutes to an hour, depending on wind conditions and passenger preferences. In optimal conditions, you can fly as high as 700m above the lake (2300m above sea level). You might also do a few acrobatics, approaching the cliffs to pick up dynamic winds that lift you up like a wave.

Courses
Panajachel has a niche in the language-school scene. Two well-set-up schools are **Jardín de América** (☎ /fax 7762-2637; www.jardindeamerica.com; Calle del Chalí) and **Jabel Tinamit** (☎ 7762-6056; www. jabeltinamit.com; Callejón Las Armonías). Both have ample gardens and good atmospheres. Four hours of one-on-one study five days per week, including a homestay with a local family, will cost around Q1400 per week. The latter institute also offers courses in Kaqchiquel and Maya weaving.

Tours
If you're pressed for time, a boat tour of the lake, stopping at a few villages, is a fine idea. Boats leave the Playa Pública quay daily at 8:30am and 9:30am for tours to San Pedro La Laguna (where you stop for about 1½ hours), Santiago Atitlán (1½ hours) and San Antonio Palopó (one hour). Both return at 3:30pm. Cost is Q100 for either tour. Travel agencies (p119) offer more expensive tours (around Q540 per person), which may include weaving demonstrations, visits to the shrine of Maximón in Santiago, and so on.

Posada Los Encuentros (☎ 7762-2093; www.losen cuentros.com; Callejón Chotzar 0-41) offers educational tours to lakeside villages, focusing on such topics as Maya medicine, Tz'utujil oil painting and organic coffee cultivation. The per-person price is Q500/985 for a half-/full-day tour with two participants, less with a larger group. The guide, Richard Morgan, is a scholar of Maya history and culture and longtime lake resident. Hiking tours and volcano climbs are also offered.

Festivals & Events

The **festival of San Francisco de Asís**, October 4, is celebrated with massive drinking and fireworks in Panajachel. On September 14, the day before **Independence Day**, torch-bearing athletes run in marathons throughout the country, but the tradition is celebrated with special fervor in Panajachel, where it all started in 1957. Early that morning schoolchildren from different villages arrive in buses to visit the lake; around noon, each group of kids gets a torch and runs back home. The main event, though, is the marathon from Guatemala City to Panajachel. The runners arrive in Pana's main square around midnight, heralded by cheering crowds, marimbas and fireworks displays.

Sleeping

BUDGET

Budget travelers will rejoice at the profusion of family-run *hospedajes* (guesthouses). They're simple – perhaps two rough beds, a small table and a light bulb in a bare room – but cheap. The pricier ones offer generous discounts for longer stays.

Hospedaje Santo Domingo (off Calle Monte Rey; s/d Q50/70, without bathroom Q20/30) The cheapest rooms at this amicable establishment are very basic wood plank affairs painted by former guests, but there are also better shared-bathroom doubles in a newer, two-story block. What makes this place, though, is the grassy hang-out area.

Hotel Visión Azul (☎ 5759-7321; eugestra@yahoo.com; Finca San Buenaventura; campsite per person Q35; ☎ 🕮) This semi-secluded location just outside town is the best, most secure camping option around. Set amid well-tended, lakefront gardens, the campsites have sheltered grilling areas, and there are hot showers. The friendly English-speaking owners also provide kayaks. Rooms with private terraces are available, too.

Villa Lupita (☎ 5054-2447; Callejón Don Tino; s/d Q60/120, without bathroom Q40/70) Family-run Lupita is great value for staying in the town center. Facing a plaza below the church, it's removed from the tourist drag. Accommodations are basic but quite clean and a flower-filled patio softens the environment.

Casa Linda (☎ 7762-0386; Callejón El Capulin; s/d Q100/130, without bathroom Q49/98) Spotless little rooms surround a garden at this tranquil establishment down an alley off Calle Santander. Upstairs units get a nice breeze and the balconies are good for afternoon siestas.

Hotel El Sol (☎ 7762-6090; www.panamuraoka.com; Carretera a Santa Catarina Palopó; dm/s/d/tr Q50/150/200/250; P ☎) Along the road to Santa Catarina, about a 15-minute walk or lightning tuk-tuk ride outside Pana, this modern hostel is a slice of Japan. Hailing from Hiroshima, owner Kazuomi and family prepare sushi and offer a Japanese tub fed by natural hot springs. Accommodations include an eight-bed dorm and five private rooms.

Hospedaje García (☎ 7762-2187; Calle 14 de Febrero; s/d Q80/150, without bathroom Q50/80) The best of the rooms here are actually the cheaper ones – they're about twice the size of the bathroom-equipped units and have balconies looking out onto the patio.

Casa Loma (☎ 7762-1447; Calle Rancho Grande; s/d Q100/150, without bathroom Q50/100) Helpfully managed by a Kaqchiquel family, the Casa Loma has basic wood-plank units near the beach. Airy upstairs units with good, firm beds share a bathroom below. The grassy lawn out back makes a great hang-out.

Mario's Rooms (☎ 7762-2370; www.mariosrooms.com.gt; Calle Santander; s/d incl breakfast Q90/160, without bathroom Q60/110; 🕮) Among the best in the budget category, Mario's smallish rooms are arranged on two floors facing a plant-filled courtyard, and have blasting-hot showers.

Hospedaje El Viajero (☎ 7762-0128; www.sleeprentbuy.com/elviajero; s/d Q60/100) El Viajero is at the end of a short lane off lower Calle Santander, making it quiet and peaceful yet near everything. Nothing fancy here but the rooms are spacious and bright and there's plenty of balcony seating. You can use a cooker, microwave and fridge, and it has laundry service and free drinking water.

Hotel Tzutujil (☎ 7762-0102; www.panajachel.com/tzutujil.htm; Calle Rancho Grande; s/d with cable TV Q100/200, without bathroom Q60/120) Almost hidden down a narrow alley through cornfields, the Tzutujil is a budget marvel – a solitary structure with balconies, arched windows and a spiral staircase to a roof terrace. On the downside, the boxy rooms are of a low-budget standard, with lumpy beds and dodgy electric showers behind a partition.

Hotel Maya-Kanek (☎ 7762-1104; Calle Principal; s/d Q75/130; P) Don Arturo, owner of this old-fashioned, family-friendly establishment in the town center, claims it's Pana's first lodging. Bare-bones basic but comfortable rooms line a cobbled courtyard with flitting hummingbirds and fanciful skeleton-shaped benches.

Hotel Jere (☎ 7762-2781; www.hoteljere.com; Calle Rancho Grande; s/d Q80/100; P ⬚) The Jere's big, tasteful rooms are another class act in this part of town. Everything is enlivened with textiles, photos, maps and informative posters, and you can book shuttle buses and lake tours on the spot.

Hotel Posada Viñas del Lago (☎ 7762-0389; Playa Pública; s/d Q100/150; P) Steps from the lakefront, this garishly painted lodging is managed by indigenous locals. Rooms are quite basic but lake views make up for it; the best are units 21 to 23.

Posada Monte Rosa (☎ 7762-0055; Calle Monte Rey; s/d Q100/150) A short distance off Calle Santander, rooms here are sizable, with Maya fabric curtains, and fronted by patches of lawn. No phone reservations.

Hotel Larry's Place (☎ 7762-0767; Calle 14 de Febrero; s/d Q100/150; P) Set back from the road behind a wall of vegetation, Larry's Place offers good-sized, cool rooms in a sylvan setting. Furnishings are tasteful and the balconies welcome, though they lack views. No TV or internet, but who needs 'em anyway?

Apartamentos Sulita (☎ 4055-7939; Calle del Frutal 3-42; cabins per week Q1040) These cute little one- or two-person cabins are a great option if you're hanging around for a while – they come equipped with kitchen, lounge, bathroom and one bedroom. The garden here presents ample bird-watching opportunities.

MIDRANGE

Midrange lodgings are busiest on weekends. From Sunday to Thursday you may get a discount, likewise if you're planning on staying for longer than four days. Many establishments raise rates during July, August, Semana Santa and the Christmas–New Year holidays.

Hotel Fonda del Sol (☎ 7762-1162; h_fondadelsol@ yahoo.com; Calle Principal; s/d Q120/180; P ⬚ 🛜) Though located along the noisy stretch of road near the bus stop, this motel-like establishment remains solid value with friendly management. Large rooms with textured stone walls, some colonial furnishings and comfy terraces or balconies occupy a double-deck block facing a lawn.

Hotel Utz Rajil (☎ 7762-0303; gguated@yahoo.com; Calle 14 de Febrero; s/d Q125/200) A modern, three-story hotel with bigger rooms than most. Try to snag a front one with balcony views. Otherwise, enjoy captivating vistas from the roof terrace.

Hospedaje Sueño Real (☎ 7762-0608; hotelsueno real@hotmail.com; Calle Ramos; s/d/tr Q150/200/350; P ⬚ 🛜) Raising its head above the budget pack, the Sueño Real has cheerfully decorated, if cramped, rooms with TV and fan. The best are the upstairs triples, opening on a plant-festooned, lakeview terrace.

Mini Hotel Riva Bella (☎ 7762-1348; Calle Principal 2-21; s/d Q150/200; P) These neat two-room bungalows are attractively spread amid a piney, parklike setting. They're clean and modern with huge bathrooms.

Hotel Montana (☎ 7762-0326; Callejón Don Tino; s/d Q150/250; P) Down a narrow street near the church, the Montana has 23 clean, bright rooms. The curvy balconies and Maya fabrics thrown around the place give it a touch of style. It's in a quiet location with a green courtyard/parking lot full of birdsong.

Hotel Utz-Jay (☎ 7762-0217; www.hotelutzjay.com; Calle 15 de Febrero 2-50; s/d/tr incl breakfast Q195/280/366; P ⬚ 🛜) These eight adobe cottages are decorated with traditional fabrics and have cozy sitting areas out front. Good breakfasts and laundry service are available and there's a *chuj* (traditional Maya sauna). The multilingual owners have lots of information about the area, and run hiking and camping trips around the lake.

Hotel Playa Linda (☎ 7762-0097; www.hotelplay alinda.com; Calle del Lago, Playa Pública; r with/without lake view Q300/200; P 🐾) The rambling Playa Linda has 17 good-sized rooms, most with fireplaces, and welcoming owners and staff. Rooms 1 to 5 have the best lake views, with large balconies from which to enjoy them. The gardens out front are a fecund fantasy of blooming roses and squawking parrots.

Posada de los Volcanes (☎ 7762-0244; www.posada delosvolcanes.com; Calle Santander 5-51; s/d Q200/350) Sharing the property with its own travel agency, this chalet-style lodging has lovely wood-paneled rooms redolent of pine. On the 4th floor, you'll be rewarded with your own private terrace, suitable for kicking back with cocktails and surveying the lakescape.

Hotel Primavera (☎ 7762-2052; www.primaveratitlan. com; Calle Santander; s/d/tr Q249/332/415; 🛜) This stylish, German-owned hotel near Pana's main intersection just feels right. Ten large rooms with plant-filled window boxes, soft lighting and handsome fabrics face a wood-decked patio, making for a relaxing atmosphere.

Bungalows El Rosario (☎ 7762-1491; Playa Pública; www.atitlandonmoises.com; s/d Q250/400; P) Though not exactly 'bungalows,' these stone-walled rooms around a parking lot have the feel of a rural retreat, and they're literally stumbling distance from the lake. The larger rooms are designed for families, with one queen-sized bed and two singles.

Hotel Posada Chinimaya (☎ 7762-0142; www.hotelchinimaya.com; s/d Q290/374; Callejón Chinimaya; P 🖥 🛜) Big minimally furnished rooms with tile floors and ultra-modern bathrooms occupy two pink, arcaded wings at this just-unwrapped place by the river. Breakfast is served in the patio, which should be shady when the trees grow up.

our pick Posada Los Encuentros (☎ 7762-1603; www.losencuentros.com; Callejón Chotzar 0-41; s/d Q249/332, with kitchen Q415/498) Just across the river is this 'ecocultural B&B,' featuring seven cozy rooms in a relaxed home, plus a volcanically heated pool, medicinal plant garden, sunning terrace and fitness center. Owner Richard Morgan is happy to share his encyclopedic knowledge of the lake and offers cultural tours of the area.

Bungalows El Aguacatal (☎ 7762-1482; www.atitlandonmoises.com; Calle las Buenas Nuevas; 4-person bungalow with/without kitchen Q550/400; P) The decorations may seem a little drab, but these concrete bungalows are a good deal for groups, especially if you're planning on cooking. Each bungalow has two bedrooms (two beds each) and salon.

TOP END

Hotel Dos Mundos (☎ 7762-2078; www.hoteldosmundos.com; Calle Santander 4-72; s/d/tr incl breakfast Q415/457/748; P 🛝) Italian-owned Dos Mundos stands toward the lake end of busy Calle Santander but its installations are set well away from the street. The 22 rooms, all with terracotta floors and woven bedspreads, are set around tropical gardens with a tiny pool. It has a good Italian restaurant, an inhouse travel agency and a sleek continental-style bar fronting the street.

Hotel San Buenaventura (☎ 7762-2559; www.hotelsanbuenaventura.net; Finca San Buenaventura; s/d Q415/674, 4-/6-person cottage Q1347/2020; P 🛝) These beautifully designed brick cottages can be hired either in part or entirely, giving you a living room, kitchen and terrace with barbecue area. You can rent bicycles to explore the wooded grounds, sweat it out in the sauna or unwind at the private beach.

Hotel Tzanjuyú Bay (☎ 5305-2704; www.hoteltzanjuyubay.blogspot.com; Calle Principal 4-96; r Q440; P 🛝) Probably quite stylish a century ago, this sprawling hotel retains a cobwebbed grandeur, despite recent renovations. It's right on the lakeshore, and each room has volcano views from private balconies. Camping is an option. Boats will drop you off at the hotel's dock on request.

Rancho Grande Inn (☎ 7762-2255; www.ranchograndeinn.com; Calle Rancho Grande; r incl breakfast Q500; P 🛜 🛝) Founded in the 1940s, the Rancho Grande has a dozen rooms, suites and *cabañas* in German country-style villas amid manicured lawns dotted with fruit trees. Rates include a filling breakfast featuring original pancakes and homegrown honey and coffee. Best of all, there's bar service in the swimming pool until 9pm.

Hotel Posada de Don Rodrigo (☎ 7762-2326; www.posadadedonrodrigo.com; Calle Santander; s/d Q906/1014, with lake view 1014/1114; P 🛝) Down by the lakeside, the landscaped grounds here hold many delights – a couple of saunas, restaurants and bars, squash courts, a swimming pool with a water slide, and a fine museum. Large rooms are decorated in colonial style and open onto private grassy sitting areas.

Hotel Atitlán (☎ 7762-1441; www.hotelatitlan.com; Finca San Buenaventura; r incl breakfast Q1214; P 🖥 🛝) A coffee plantation for much of the 20th century, this estate was remade as Pana's loveliest hotel in the 1970s. Located on the lakeshore 1.5km northwest of the town center, it's a rambling, three-story, semi-colonial affair surrounded by tropical gardens. The 65 rooms all have lake-facing balconies; decorations go heavy on religious imagery, wood carvings and wrought iron. A restaurant, bar and a well-stocked gift shop ensure you'll never want to leave the premises.

Eating
BUDGET

Pana Pan (Calle Santander 1-61; pastries Q7; 🕓 breakfast & lunch) Cinnamon rolls, banana and chocolate muffins, and whole-wheat bread make a call here obligatory. Take away or sit down with a coffee.

Las Pitayas (Calle Santander) Head here for fresh-squeezed, seasonal fruit juices and *licuados* (fresh fruit drinks). When the heat overwhelms, have a refreshing *panatonic* – a cocktail of lemon juice, ginger and mint. For food, it's got panini and wraps.

Deli Jasmín (☎ 7762-2585; Calle Santander; items Q25-45; ☽ 7am-6pm Wed-Mon) This tranquil garden restaurant serves a range of healthy foods and drinks to the strains of soft classical music. Breakfast is served all day, and you can buy whole-wheat or pita bread, hummus or mango chutney to take away.

Deli Llama de Fuego (☎ 7762-2586; Calle Santander; items Q25-45; ☽ 7am-10pm Thu-Tue) With the same excellent menu as Deli Jasmín, this natural-foods haven revolves around a *llama de fuego* tree (African tulip).

La Rosticería (☎ 7762-2063; Av Los Árboles; mains Q25-40; ☽ 8am-10pm Mon-Sat) Run by a cheerful Canadian dude, 'the rotisserie' specializes in spit-roasted chicken, served at a street-side terrace. A quarter chicken, fries and slaw will set you back Q25.

El Patio (☎ 7762-2041; Plaza Los Patios, Calev Santander; mains Q35; ☽ breakfast, lunch & dinner) This is a locally popular joint for lunch; the front terrace makes an obvious meeting place. Try to make it for Monday lunch when everyone chows down on *caldo de res* (chunky broth), served with all the trimmings.

If you're looking for cheap with a view, check out the touristy restaurants crowding the east end of Calle del Lago, such as Restaurante Taly, Restaurante Catamarán or Restaurante Chichoy, all with decks overlooking the lake. Los Pumpos, up at street level, reportedly has the best quality and variety. All the beach restaurants serve seafood and *caldo de mariscos* (shellfish stew), though lake fish has not been served since an outbreak of bacteria in late 2009.

Another obvious choice for cheap meals are the myriad taco and fried chicken stalls that proliferate along Calle Santander every afternoon and evening. You might try the appropriately named Humo en Tus Ojos, last spotted near the intersection of Calles Principal and Santander; this is where the cops eat.

For food shopping, there's the Despensa Familiar, at the north end of Calle El Amate.

MIDRANGE & TOP END

Atlantis (☎ 7762-1015; Calle Principal; mains Q40-60; ☽ breakfast, lunch & dinner) This cafe-bar serves up excellent submarines (Q35) alongside more substantial meals. The back garden is the place to be on a balmy night.

Guajimbo's (Calle Santander; mains Q40-70; ☽ breakfast, lunch & dinner) This Uruguayan grill is one of Pana's best eateries, serving up generous meat and chicken dishes with vegetables, salad, garlic bread and rice or boiled potatoes. You won't leave hungry. There are vegetarian dishes too, good-value breakfasts, and bottomless cups of coffee.

Café Bombay (☎ 7762-0611; Calle Santander; mains Q45; ☽ 11am-9pm Wed-Mon; Ⓥ) This cozy joint plays up the international angle, with creative vegetarian dishes from 14 countries: everything from spinach lasagna to miso to curries, and there's even a veggie version of that Guatemalan classic *pepián* (hearty chicken stew with a piquant sesame-and-pumpkin-seed sauce) served with veggies, rice and *chuchito* (a small tamal).

Sunset Café (cnr Calles Santander & del Lago; mains Q50-65; ☽ lunch & dinner) This open-air eatery at the lake end of Calle Santander has great vistas and serves meat, fish and vegetarian dishes. With a bar and live music nightly, it's the place to enjoy those phantasmagoric volcano sundowns.

Ristorante La Lanterna (Hotel Dos Mundos, Calle Santander 4-72; mains Q50-85; ☽ 7am-3pm & 6-10pm) Part of the Hotel Dos Mundos, this Italian restaurant makes its own pasta and stocks an impressive range of wines from the motherland. The adjacent cafe makes a mean espresso from Guatemala's prized beans. Bonus: you're welcome to use the hotel swimming pool if you eat here.

Restaurante Casablanca (☎ 7762-1015; Calle Principal; mains Q55-96; ☽ 11am-11pm) Easily spotted at the top end of Calle Santander by its magical mystery mural, this restaurant run by the German honorary consul features fondues, steaks and pastas of a Euro standard. There are airy dining rooms both upstairs and down, plus an excellent bar.

La Terraza (☎ 7762-0041; Edificio Rincón Sai, Calle Santander; mains Q60-150; ☽ lunch & dinner; 🛜) One of Calle Santander's most atmospheric spots, this breezy upstairs restaurant has French, Mexican and Asian influences. It's a good idea to book on weekends.

Restaurante Tocoyal (Calle del Lago; mains Q95-115; ☽ 8:30am-5pm Sun-Fri, 8:30am-8pm Sat) The Tocoyal is a cut above the other Calle del Lago eateries. Grilled meat and seafood are its strong points.

Chez Alex (☎ 7762-2052; Hotel Primavera, Calle Santander; mains Q99-150; ☽ lunch & dinner) This is some of Pana's finest dining, with plenty of European influence. It serves fondue, stuffed trout and other delicacies, and has Habana cigars.

Drinking

Crossroads Café (☎ 5292-8439; www.crossroadscafepana.com; Calle del Campanario 0-27; 9am-1pm & 3-7pm Tue-Sat) Bay area native Mike Roberts has made Panajachel a major crossroads for coffee aficionados. When he's not roasting beans or working the Cimbali at his hole-in-the-wall cafe near the center of town, Mike spends his time combing the highlands for small estate coffees to add to his roster, now starring the smooth Huehue organic.

Pana Rock Café (☎ 7762-2194, Calle Santander) This is a good place to start, continue or finish your night's imbibing, with a seemingly endless happy hour. The classic rock may not be to your liking, but two mixed drinks for Q25 is hard to argue with.

Pana Lounge (Av Los Árboles) The action at this low-lit bar revolves around the pool table (Q40 per hour) and the beer (Q40 per *cubetazo,* ie bucket of five bottles).

Entertainment

Panajachel's miniature Zona Viva (party zone) focuses on Av Los Árboles. Things can be quiet from Sunday to Wednesday.

DANCING

If your rumba's rusty, drop by La Terraza (see opposite), a haven for salsaphiles, especially on Friday and Saturday nights when guest instructors conduct workshops. Classes are Q100 per hour (half that for long-termers).

Chapiteau (Av Los Árboles; minimum Q20) After the music stops at the Circus Bar, simply cross the street and check out this strobe-lit disco-bar.

El Aleph (Av Los Árboles) DJs keep the multitudes moving with a spirited mix of reggaetón, merengue, electronica and salsa. Beer is cheapest by the bucket (aka *cubetazo*).

Rumba (Calle Principal) Opposite the start of Av Los Árboles, Rumba is a large disco-bar playing thumping Latin pop, popular with the Guatemalan teens and 20-somethings who descend on Pana during weekends and holidays.

LIVE MUSIC

Apart from the following venues, also check out Pana Rock Café (see above) and the Sunset Café (see opposite).

Circus Bar (☎ 2333-7470; Av Los Árboles; noon-midnight) Behind the cowboy swinging doors, Circus Bar has a cabaret atmosphere, with live music nightly from 8:30pm to 11pm. Flamenco, folk, marimbas and other musical styles nicely complement the cozy atmosphere, as do the substantial list of imported liquors, Q10 cocktails and good pizza.

Rock On Café (Av Los Árboles; 9pm-1am Thu-Sat) This hole-in-the-wall next door to El Aleph is a sometime showcase for *rock en español* cover bands.

Solomon's Porch (☎ 7762-6032; Centro Comercial El Dorado, Calle Principal, noon-10pm Tue-Sat,) A coffee house inside a shopping center, Solomon's Porch hosts a variety of activities, from billiards to movies to live music, often by foreign visiting artists. And for something completely different, there's a 'worship gathering' every Sunday at 4pm (with free coffee).

Shopping

Some travelers prefer the Pana shopping scene to the well-known market at Chichicastenango because the atmosphere is lower key and you're not bumping into tour groups with video cameras at every turn. Calle Santander is lined with booths, stores and complexes that sell (among other things) traditional Maya clothing, jade, Rasta berets with built-in dreadlocks, colorful blankets, leather goods and wood carvings. Freelance vendors and artisans also set up tables or blankets, especially on weekends.

Comerciales de Artesanías Típicas Tinamit Maya (7am-7pm) Be sure to browse the many stalls of this extensive handicrafts market, which has an impressive variety. Booths also adorn the beach end of Calle Rancho Grande.

Pana Health Food Store (☎ 5720-5725; Plaza Los Patios, Calle Santander) Sells medicinal herbs and health foods, and can put you in touch with an acupuncturist or masseur.

La Señora de Cancuén (☎ 7762-2602; Calle Santander) Displays the innovative clothing of Guatemalan designer Ana Kayax, produced by a cooperative of indigenous weavers.

Getting There & Away

BOAT

Passenger boats for Santiago Atitlán (35 minutes) depart from the Playa Pública (public beach) at the foot of Calle Rancho Grande. All other departures leave from the Embarcadero Tzanjuyú, at the foot of Calle del Embarcadero. Frequent canopied *lanchas* (small motorboats) go counterclockwise around the lake, stopping in Santa Cruz La Laguna (15 minutes), Jaibalito, Tzununá, San Marcos La Laguna (30 minutes), San Juan La Laguna and San Pedro

La Laguna (45 minutes). The last boat departs around 7:30pm. To the villages along the lake's eastern shore, there are no public boat services; take a bus or pickup instead.

One-way passage anywhere on Lago de Atitlán costs Q20, though local inhabitants are charged much less. Some travelers get indignant about this two-tier system, but it's been institutionalized and complaints generally fall on deaf ears. Ignore all middlemen and negotiate the fare directly with the captain. *Lanchas* are also available for private hire from the Playa Pública or Embarcadero Tzanjuyú: expect to pay around Q350 to San Pedro La Laguna.

BUS

Panajachel's main bus stop is at the junction of Calles Santander and Principal, across from the Banco Agromercantil. The taxi and shuttle bus booth nearby on Calle Principal can usually give you the general picture on bus schedules, but this is not an exact science. Departures – approximately and subject to change – are as follows:

Antigua A direct Pullman bus (Q35, 2½ hours, 146km) by Transportes Rébuli departs at 11am Monday to Saturday. Or take a Guatemala City bus and change at Chimaltenango. Rébuli buses depart from the south side of Calle Principal, across from the main bus stop.

Chichicastenango About five buses (Q20, 1½ hours, 37km) depart 7am to 3pm daily. Or take any bus heading to Los Encuentros and change buses there.

Ciudad Tecún Umán (Mexican border) By the Pacific route (220km), take a bus to Cocales and change there; by the highland route (204km), transfer at Quetzaltenango.

Cocales (Carretera al Pacífico) Buses en route from Chichicastenango to Nueva Concepción stop at Cocales (Q15, 2½ hours, 65km), passing through Pana at approximately 6:30am, 10am, 3pm and 5pm daily.

Guatemala City Transportes Rébuli (3½ hours, 150km) departs at 5am, 6am, 7:30am, 11am, noon and 1pm daily; the 11am departure is a Pullman (Q35), the rest are chicken buses (Q25). Or take a bus to Los Encuentros and change there.

Huehuetenango Take a bus to Los Encuentros (3½ hours, 140km) then wait for a Huehue- or La Mesilla–bound bus. Or catch one heading to Quetzaltenango, alight at Cuatro Caminos and change buses there. There are buses at least hourly from these junctions.

Los Encuentros Take any bus heading towards Guatemala City, Chichicastenango, Quetzaltenango or the Interamericana (Q6, 35 minutes, 20km). Make sure it's going to one of those destinations and not just to Sololá, where you'll have to change for another bus.

Quetzaltenango Buses (Q30, 2½ hours, 90km) depart at 7am, 11am and 2pm daily. Or take a bus to Los Encuentros and change there.

San Lucas Tolimán There's one Transportes Rébuli bus at 5:30pm (Q10, one hour, 28km), or you can take any bus heading for Cocales, get off at Santa Alicia and walk or take a tuk-tuk 1km into town.

Santa Catarina Palopó. Get a pickup (Q3, 20 minutes, 4km) at the corner of Calles Principal and El Amate.

Sololá Frequent direct local buses (Q3, 15 minutes, 8km). Or take any bus heading to Guatemala City, Chichicastenango, Quetzaltenango or Los Encuentros.

SHUTTLE MINIBUS

Tourist shuttle buses take half the time of buses, for several times the price. You can book at a number of travel agencies on Calle Santander (p119). The **Microbuses y Taxis San Francisco booth** (☎ 7762-0556; www.mitasfa.com; Calle Principal) also sells shuttle-bus seats. Despite advertised lists of departures, real shuttle schedules depend on how many customers there are, so try to establish a firm departure time before parting with money. Typical fares: Antigua Q125; Chichicastenango Q58; Guatemala City Q183; San Cristóbal de Las Casas, Mexico Q332, Quetzaltenango Q166.

AROUND PANAJACHEL

Southeast of Pana, 5km and 10km respectively along a winding road, lie the lakeside hamlets of Santa Catarina Palopó and San Antonio Palopó. (The name 'Palopó is a Spanish-Kaqchiquel amalgam referring to a type of fig tree that grows here.) Compared with nearby Pana, the Palopós feel sublimely remote, with narrow streets paved in stone blocks and adobe houses with roofs of thatch or tin. Many villagers, both men and women, go about their daily activities clad in traditional outfits, and these are good places to look for the luminescent indigo weavings you see all around Lago de Atitlán. Also out here is a surprising little clutch of midrange and top-end places to stay.

Santa Catarina Palopó
pop 4200 / elev 1663m

On weekends and holidays, young textile vendors line the path to the lakeside at Santa Catarina Palopó with their wares, and any day you can step into wooden storefronts hung thick with bright cloth.

Hospedaje Santa Catarina (☎ 5715-7131; Calle Principal; s/d Q50/100), a cinderblock structure just above the church, has basic beds and plywood ceilings, with a little balcony for watching the goings-on in the plaza.

Villa Santa Catarina (☎ 7762-1291; www.villasde guatemala.com; s/d Q975/1125; P ⚡) is a treat for a drink or a meal. The dining room serves moderately priced *table d'hôte* meals and the hotel has a swimming pool and gardens almost on the lakeshore. The 36 neat rooms have wood beams, colorful weavings and lake views. Rooms 24, 25, 26 and 27 (partly) and the two suites face across the lake to Volcán San Pedro. Two children under 12 can share with two adults for free.

One of several lavish villas in the hills south of Santa Catarina, **Nimajay** (☎ 5756-8500; www.nimajayatitlan.com; Camino a Santa Catarina Km 7.5; r from Q1400; P ⚡ ⚡) covers a 2 hectare estate formerly owned by the country's wealthiest family. Its current American owners have renovated it as a boutique hotel, furnishing the rooms and villas with handcrafted mahogany cabinets, original artwork and Carrara marble bathrooms. There's a suitably fabulous terrace for munching on hors d'oeuvre while gazing at volcanoes.

The open-air **Restaurante Laguna Azul** (mains Q45), on the lakeshore below the Villa Santa Catarina, serves fried fish, grilled chicken and a few *típico* dishes like *pollo en pulike* (chicken in a toothsome red salsa).

San Antonio Palopó
pop 4040 / elev 1773m

San Antonio Palopó is a larger village. Entire families clean mountains of scallions by the lakeshore and tend their terraced fields in traditional outfits – women in indigo-striped *huipiles* (long embroidered tunics), dark blue *cortes* (long skirts) and sparkly headbands, some of the men in traditional wool skirts. Up the hillside, the gleaming white church forms the center of attention. **Cerámica Palopó Atitlán** (⚡ 8am-6pm), to the right as you descend toward the lake from the church, sells attractive blue stoneware pottery, a craft brought here by an American who taught the local people the techniques of Mexican kiln-fired ceramics. A bit further down, the **Tienda Candelaria** houses a weaving cooperative, where women produce shawls, *huipiles* and *tocoyales* (headdresses) on backstrap looms and get a fair price for them.

ourpick Hotel Terrazas del Lago (☎ 7762-0157; www.hotelterrazasdellago.com; s/d Q180/240; ⚡), almost on the lakeshore, has 15 attractive stone-walled rooms climbing the hillside, with small

terraces and hammocks, and serves good, inexpensive meals (Q45 to Q75) with views straight across to Volcán Tolimán.

GETTING THERE & AWAY
Pickups to both Santa Catarina and San Antonio leave about every half-hour from the corner of Calles Principal and El Amate in Panajachel. It takes 20 minutes to Santa Catarina (Q3) and 30 minutes to San Antonio (Q5). Frequency drops after noon, and the last pickup back to Pana leaves San Antonio about 5pm.

San Lucas Tolimán
pop 19,100 / elev 1962m

Further around the lake from San Antonio Palopó, but reached by a different, higher-level road, San Lucas Tolimán is busier and more commercial than most lakeside villages. Set at the foot of the dramatic Volcán Tolimán, it's a coffee-growing town and a transportation point on a route between the Interamericana and the Carretera al Pacífico. Market days are Sunday, Tuesday and Friday. Atypically not standing on the town's plaza but along the street to the lakefront, the 16th-century **Parroquia de San Lucas** parish church has a beautiful children's folk choir, which sings at 10:30am mass most Sundays. The parish, aided by Catholic missionaries from Minnesota and volunteers from North America and Europe, has been active in redistributing coffee-plantation land, setting up the Juan-Ana fair-trade coffee cooperative and founding schools, a clinic and a reforestation program. For visits to the cooperative and information on volunteering, contact the **parish office** (☎ 7722-0112; www.sanlucasmission.com/Home.htm).

There's a Cajero 5B next to the town hall on the central plaza.

From San Lucas, a paved road goes west around Volcán Tolimán to Santiago Atitlán.

Down by the waterfront, **Hotel Don Pedro** (☎ 7722-0028; Final de Calle Principal; s/d Q70/130; P) is made entirely of stone and rough-hewn timber beams. The unfinished construction feels like a medieval inn, and the relaxed restaurant/bar (meals Q40 to Q60) sports the same motif. Upstairs units have fine lake views.

Just above it, **Hotel Tolimán** (☎ 7722-0033; www. hoteltoliman.com; Calle Principal Final; s/d Q415/580; P ⚡) is a low-key resort on the site of a former coffee-processing plant, with 20 colonial-style rooms and suites in cottages around a spreading *amate* tree. A terrace restaurant overlooks a fountain-fed pool amid landscaped grounds leading down to the lakeshore.

For details on bus and boat transportation, see p133. On market days, there's public boat service between San Antonio Palopó and San Lucas, running roughly from 8am to 2pm.

Parque Ecológico Corazón del Bosque

A community-run ecological park a 45-minute drive (25km) northwest of Panajachel, **Corazón del Bosque** (☎ 7723-4140; www.corazondelbosque.com; Km 145 Carretera Interamericana; adult/child Q5/3; ☺ 8am-6pm) covers a 35 hectare encino oak forest at the highest point within the Lago de Atitlán protected area. From the log-cabin restaurant by the entrance, well-maintained hiking trails lead up through coniferous forests to the summit at 2640m, where there's a Maya ceremonial site and shrine to the Virgin of Guadalupe. At least 100 bird species have been spotted in the forest, including the endemic pink-headed warbler and brown-backed solitaire. The restaurant, open for breakfast and lunch, serves park-raised rabbit, as well as some vegetarian dishes. If you'd like to stick around, there are well-maintained **dorms** (Q80 per person, eight beds per room with two showers and toilets), and a few **cabins** (s/d/tr Q120/200/280) with kitchens up in the woods. Guests can use a *chuj* (Maya sauna, Q40 per person). Microbuses, every half-hour from Solalá to Novillero (Q6), can drop you at the entrance; or take any bus plying the Interamericana between Los Encuentros (Q5, 15 minutes) and Quetzaltenango.

SANTIAGO ATITLÁN

pop 32,000 / elev 1606m

Across the lake from Panajachel, on an inlet between the volcanoes of Tolimán and San Pedro, lies Santiago Atitlán, the largest of the lake communities, with a strong indigenous identity. Many *atitecos* (as its people are known) cling to a traditional Tz'utujil Maya lifestyle. Women wear purple-striped skirts and *huipiles* embroidered with colored birds and flowers, while a few older men still wear white-striped embroidered pants. The town's *cofradías* maintain the syncretic traditions and rituals of Maya Catholicism. There's a large art and crafts scene here, too. Boat-building is a local industry, and rows of rough-hewn *cayucos* are lined up along the shore. The best days to visit are Friday and Sunday, the main market days, but any day will do.

It's the most workaday of the lake villages, home to Maximón (mah-shee-*mohn;* see boxed text, p146), who is paraded around during Semana Santa – a good excuse to head this way during Easter. The rest of the year, Maximón resides with a caretaker, receiving offerings. He changes house every year, but he's easy enough to find by asking around.

The Tz'utujil had been in this area for generations when the Spanish arrived, with their ceremonial capital at Chuitinamit, across the inlet. Santiago was established by Franciscan friars in 1547, as part of the colonial strategy to consolidate the indigenous population. In the 1980s, left-wing guerrillas had a strong presence in the area, leading to the killings or disappearance of hundreds of villagers at the hands of the Guatemalan army.

Orientation & Information

From the dock, a path leads up through rows of craft stalls and cook shacks to reach the main shopping street, Calle Principal. Proceeding about 500m up from the dock, turn left past the Hotel Tzutujil to arrive at the central plaza and, behind it, the Catholic church.

There's a Cajero 5B at **Banrural** (☺ 8:30am-5pm Mon-Fri, 9am-1pm Sat), a block west of the plaza.

You'll find a lot of fascinating information about Santiago, in English, at www.santiago atitlan.com.

Dangers & Annoyances

The road between Santiago and San Pedro La Laguna has a certain notoriety for bandits, carjackers, kidnappers etc. Asistur, the security branch of the tourist board, warns that travelers run a 99% risk of getting held up at gunpoint along this route, and thus recommends taking a ferry between the towns instead.

Santiago children may greet you at the dock or in the central plaza, offering to act as guides. If you hire them, agree on the price beforehand.

Sights

The formidable parish church, the **Iglesia Parroquial Santiago Apóstol**, was built by the Franciscans between 1571 and 1582. A memorial plaque on your right just inside the entrance commemorates Father Stanley Francis Rother, a missionary priest from Oklahoma. Beloved by the local people, he was murdered by ultraright death squads in the parish rectory next door in 1981. Along the walls are wooden statues of the saints, each of whom has new clothes made by local women every year. On the carved wooden pulpit, note the figures of corn (from which humans were formed, according to Maya religion) and of the angel, quetzal bird, lion and horse (symbolo of the four evangelioto, with the quotaal replacing the more traditional eagle). At the far end of the church stand three colonial altarpieces that were renovated between 1976 and 1981 by brothers Diego Chávez Petzey and Nicolás Chávez Sojuel. The brothers subtly changed the central altarpiece from a traditional European vision of heaven to a more Maya vision representing a sacred mountain with two Santiago *cofradía* members climbing towards a sacred cave. The altarpieces symbolize the three volcanoes around Santiago, which are believed to protect the town.

In the **Parque Central**, a stone monument commemorates Concepción Ramírez, the woman on the back of the 25-centavo coin, (see boxed text, below), and a basin contains a relief version of the lake.

During the civil war, Santiago became the first village in the country to succeed in expelling the army, following a notorious massacre of 13 villagers on December 2, 1990. The site of this massacre, where troops were encamped, is now the **Parque de Paz** (Peace Park), about 500m beyond the Posada de Santiago.

The **Cojolya Association of Maya Women Weavers** (☎ 7721-7268; www.cojolya.org; ☻ 9am-4pm Mon-Fri, 9am-1pm Sat) has a small museum of backstrap loom weaving. The well-designed exhibit shows the history of the craft and the process from spinning the cotton fibers to the finished textile. There are also daily demonstrations of backstrap loom techniques, and a small shop. The entrance is just up from the dock on the left, tucked between some craft stalls.

Activities

There are several rewarding **day hikes** around Santiago. Most enticing of all are the three volcanoes in the vicinity: Tolimán, Atitlán and San Pedro. Before attempting a climb, enquire about the current security situation. It's best to go with a guide; the Posada de Santiago (p132) can set up a reliable one. Guided volcano climbs run about Q200 per person.

The **Cerro de Oro** (1892m) poses a less daunting challenge, but a climb up the hill still yields great views, and there's a pretty church in the nearby village of the same name. It's some 8km northeast, about halfway between Santiago and San Lucas Tolimán. You could travel at least one way by one of the pickups running between Santiago and San Lucas Tolimán.

Another worthy destination is the **Mirador de Tepepul**, about 4km south of Santiago (four to five hours round trip). The hike goes through cloud forest populated with many birds, including parakeets, currasows, swifts, boat-tailed grackles and tucanets, and on to a lookout point with views all the way to the coast. **Miguel Pablo** (☎ 4245-8019, 5450-2381) guides hikers to the *mirador* (lookout point) or Cerro de Oro for about Q200 each. **Fedepma**

A TALE OF TWO CHOCAS

Check your change, and if you've got any *chocas* (25-centavo coins), have a look at the tail side. The Tz'utujil woman portrayed there, sporting a *tocoyal* (headdress) on her head, is named Concepción Ramírez Mendoza, aka Doña Chonita, born in Santiago Atitlán in 1942. In 2009 she was paid homage when a large stone replica of the *choca* was unveiled on the lake village's main plaza, and during the unveiling ceremony she told of her struggles as a widowed mother, asking her indigenous sisters to summon the strength to carry on.

A nice story, but ask around and you may hear a more complicated version. Some say there are two Chonitas, and that the one who was feted at the ceremony is not in fact the one on the coin. The story goes that both women grew up in Santiago in the 1940s, and both had their portraits taken by photographer Julio Zadik as candidates for the *choca* image. One of them was chosen for her iconic indigenous features. Some locals say this Doña Chonita died childless in 2007 and was buried with little fanfare. The woman who was paid homage in 2009, also named Chonita and the daughter of a prominent politician, was by then widely considered the *choca* woman, something which has also been authorized by the government, which provides her a home in faraway Guatemala City from where she returns to the lake once in a while to visit her brother.

(Federación de Pueblos Mayas; info@fedepmasolola.org.gt) also organizes hikes to Cerro de Oro, where it has an office.

Aventura en Atitlán (☎ 5811-5516; wildwestgua@ yahoo.com) offers well-recommended **horseback rides** to the Mirador de Tepepul and elsewhere, for Q450 to Q620. Most rides include a gourmet meal. They do guided hikes, too.

The pre-Hispanic Tz'utujil capital of **Chuitinamit** is across the inlet from Santiago. This hilltop archaeological site features some carved petroglyphs and the ruins of the area's first church and Franciscan monastery, founded about 1540. From the dock, it's a 20-minute hike to the top, where there are good views of Santiago. Guided walks with the Posada de Santiago cost Q166 per person.

Walking to San Pedro La Laguna is not recommended due to the risk of robberies.

Tours

Dolores Ratzan Pablo (☎ 5730-4570; dolores_ratzan@ yahoo.com) is a knowledgeable, erudite, English-speaking guide specializing in Maya ceremonies. This Tz'utujil woman can introduce you to the wonders of Maya birthing and healing, point out examples of Maya-Catholic syncretism at the church and *cofradías*, and describe the incidents that led to the massacre at Peace Park in 1990. Tours typically last two hours and cost Q300 for up to four people.

The **Cojolya Association of Maya Women Weavers** (☎ 7721-7268; www.cojolya.org) leads 'Meet the Weavers' tours daily at 11am and 1pm (Q50, in Spanish). The tour takes you to three traditional homes where women demonstrate how to set up a backstrap loom, warp the threads and perform the *jaspe* technique, a form of Japanese tie-dye that reached Guatemala through indirect contact with Spain's Pacific trade routes.

Sleeping & Eating

Hotel Tzanjuyu (☎ 5590-7980; s/d Q55/100) Decent, plain rooms with a choice of volcano or lake views. It is prohibited, as signs point out, to spit on the walls here.

Hotel Lago de Atitlán (☎ 7721-7174; r Q75-85) An atypically modern five-story block, this nondescript hotel has bland but mostly bright rooms, many having large windows with decent views. Go up to the rooftop for great sunsets. From the dock, walk four blocks uphill to find the hotel on the left. Reception is in the hardware store next door.

Posada de Santiago (☎ 7721-7366; www.posadade santiago.com; s/d Q249/374, cottages d/tr Q540/623, ste from Q705; P 🖳 🛜) Striking a balance between rustic charm and luxury, the long-standing *posada* makes a nice retreat. Seven cottages and three suites, all with stone walls, fireplaces, porches, hammocks and folk art, are set around gardens stretching up from the lake. Some less expensive rooms are in a two-story building. The restaurant serves delicious, natural fare, as well as homegrown and roasted coffee. The *posada* can set up hikes and cycling trips. It's 1.5km from the dock. Catch a tuk-tuk (Q5) or hire a *lancha* over to the hotel dock (Q70).

Hotel Bambú (☎ 7721-7332; www.ecobambu.com; s/d incl breakfast Q498/623; P 🛋) Run by an amiable Spaniard, the Bambú is an ecologically harmonious hotel. Scattered around wild-yet-manicured grounds, the 10 spacious rooms are in grass- or bamboo-roofed buildings, with cypress fittings and earthy tile floors. A pebbly path leads to a swimming pool in a serene, jungle-like setting. The restaurant serves Spanish dishes (Q50 to Q90) and has views over the lake towards San Pedro volcano. It's 600m from the dock; you're best off taking a tuk-tuk over. If you're arriving by boat, ask to be dropped off at the hotel dock.

Hotel Tiosh Abaj (☎ 7721-7656; www.tioshabaj. com; s/d Q508/647; P 🛜 🛋) This former private residence near the center of town has landscaped grounds leading to a private beach at the lakefront. Thirty spacious rooms and suites feature balconies overlooking lush gardens where ripe guavas drop off trees and arbors brim with bougainvillea. From the Santiago dock walk up the hill; take a right as you enter the village continuing until you see the sign.

Restaurant El Gran Sol (☎ 7721-7157; mains Q35-40) Two blocks up from the dock on the left, this family-run establishment is a good bet for breakfast, lunch or snacks, with a spiffy kitchen and lovely thatched roof terrace. The Mexican-born proprietor, Thelma, loves to cook; ask her to make one of her specials.

El Pescador (☎ 7721-7147; Calle Principal; fish dishes Q60; 🕑 breakfast, lunch & dinner) Two blocks up the street from the dock, this is a busy restaurant with neatly laid tables. A typical *menú del día* (set lunch) might bring you fish, rice, salad, guacamole, tortillas and a drink.

You could also try the various *comedores* (basic eateries) down by the dock, serving cheap snacks and seafood dishes to the flocks of weekenders who arrive here.

Shopping

Craft stalls crowd the paths leading from the dock to the town center, selling leather belts and hats, carved wooden animals, colorful textiles, masks and paintings. For contemporary bags, clothing and accessories with Tz'utujil elements, check out the Cojolya Association of Maya Women Weavers (p130), whose shop displays woven items designed by the association's American founder, Candis E Krummel.

Getting There & Away

Subject to change, boats leave Santiago for San Pedro La Laguna (Q25, 45 minutes) at 7am, 9am, 10:30am, 11am, noon, 1pm, 2pm, 3:30pm and 5pm. Pickups to Cerro de Oro and San Lucas Tolimán depart from in front of the market. Buses to Guatemala City (Q40, 3½ hours) leave every half hour from 3am to 6am, then hourly until 3pm, from the main plaza. For transportation from Panajachel, see p127.

SAN PEDRO LA LAGUNA

pop 10,000 / elev 1610m

Standing at the base of the volcano of the same name, San Pedro remains among the most visited of the lakeside villages – due as much to its reasonably priced accommodations and global social scene as its beautiful setting. Travelers tend to dig in here for a spell, in pursuit of (in no particular order) drinking, fire-twirling, African drumming, Spanish classes, painting classes, volcano hiking, hot-tub soaking and hammock swinging.

While this scene unfolds at the lakefront, up the hill San Pedro follows more traditional rhythms. Clad in indigenous outfits, the predominantly indigenous *pedranos* (as the locals are called) congregate around the market zone. You'll see coffee being picked on the volcano's slopes and spread out to dry on wide platforms at the beginning of the dry season.

Orientation & Information

San Pedro has two docks, about 1km apart. The one on the southeast side of town serves boats going to and from Santiago Atitlán; the other, on the northwest side, serves Panajachel. From each dock, streets run ahead to meet outside the market in the town center, a few hundred meters uphill. Most of the tourism activity is in the lower part of town, between and on either side of the two docks. To work your way across this lower area from the Panajachel dock, turn left at the first intersection you come to. Follow this path about 200m

THE HIGHLANDS

EVIL BLOOM

In late 2009 during an unusually warm spell, a massive bloom of cyanobacteria covered the turquoise waters of Lago de Atitlán with malodorous sheets of brownish sludge. Also called blue-green algae, cyanobacteria occur naturally in oceans and lakes, but the ecological imbalance of Lago de Atitlán following decades of unchecked development created the conditions for their proliferation. The primary cause was increased nutrients, copiously provided by agrochemicals from surrounding communities, which thanks to widespread deforestation flow almost unobstructed with the rains. These chemicals are high in phosphorous, which the bacteria gobble up like Pac-Men. With the increase in temperatures, a trend seen since Hurricane Stan in 2005, the organisms proliferated, bloomed and died, leaving the thick mats of smelly crud. The news fell hard on an already anemic tourism climate, but more gravely threatened the surrounding communities, for whom the lake has been a source of water, food and jobs for thousands of years. Within a month, the blight had receded and the lake seemed to return to its usual pristine state, raising hopes that this was a nasty case of a cyclical phenomenon. Whether the cyanobacteria caused permanent damage to the lake's biology was uncertain. No dead fish were found, and initial tests by UC Davis found the bloom did not produce enough toxins to pose health risks, though they advised continuous monitoring of lake fish quality. People were back swimming and diving within a few months, which by all accounts is not dangerous. Still, the blight was viewed as a symptom of an ailing ecosystem. The federal government pledged funds to build proper sewage-treatment facilities, and some of the more progressive tourism providers have banded together to implement their own anti-phosphate campaign. For more information on their efforts, see www.savelakeatitlan.blogspot.com and www.lakeatitlanhealth.com.

until you reach a store called Las Estrellitas, then take the trail on the right where there's a large mural. Soon afterward, the path angles left and passes the Museo Tz'unun'Ya, then takes a sharp left into a busy bar and restaurant zone. From the Santiago dock, turn right immediately before the Hotel Villasol. Street names or numbers are seldom used in San Pedro, but there are plenty of painted signs pointing to various businesses.

There is no tourist information office in San Pedro, but the staff at the Alegre Pub near the Pana dock are well informed, and have a folder full of answers to most FAQs.

There's a Cajero 5B just up from the Panajachel dock on the left. You can change traveler's checks at **Banrural** (☺ 8:30am-5pm Mon-Fri, 9am-1pm Sat), in the town center 1½ blocks south of the market. For internet access, visit D'Noz or Casa Verde Tours, both just up the street from the Panajachel dock, or Idea Connection, along the path in between the docks; the typical rate is Q8 an hour. Call North America/Europe for Q2/4 at Casa Verde Tours, or use Skype at any of the above internet cafes.

Zuyuva (☺ noon-4pm Thu-Mon) is a secondhand bookstore with a decent selection of fiction and Guatemala titles. An alley opposite the Museo Tz'unun Ya' leads there.

Sights

Two worthwhile museums focusing on local Maya culture operate in San Pedro. They're both on the path between the docks.

Museo Maya Tz'utujil (admission Q10; ☺ 8am-noon Mon-Fri), opposite Buddha bar, humbly displays the various *trajes* (traditional costumes) worn around the lake and some great old photographs, and has a lending library/bookstore. Once a month or so, a Maya priest performs ceremonies here, and the public is welcome to attend – ask about the next one.

Museo Tz'unun 'Ya (7a Av; admission Q35; ☺ 8am-noon & 2-6pm Tue-Fri, 8am-noon Sat & Sun) is an excellent, modern museum focusing on the history and geology of the region. As it's located in a sacred spot, there's also a Maya altar.

Activities

ASCENDING VOLCÁN SAN PEDRO

Looming above the village, Volcán San Pedro almost asks to be climbed by anyone with an adventurous spirit. It is the most accessible of the three volcanoes in the zone and now that it's classified as a municipal ecological park

---

TZ'UTUJIL OIL PAINTING

Emanating primarily from the Lago de Atitlán towns of Santiago Atitlán, San Pedro La Laguna and San Juan La Laguna, Tz'utujil oil painting has a distinctive primitivist style, with depictions of rural life, local traditions and landscapes in vibrant colors.

This distinctly Maya mode is generally handed down through generations of the same family, and the leading artists share surnames. In San Pedro La Laguna the name of note is González. Legend has it that Tz'utujil art began when Rafael González y González noticed some dye that had dripped and mixed with the sap of a tree; he made a paintbrush from his hair and began creating the type of canvases still popular today. His grandson Pedro Rafael González Chavajay and Pedro's cousin Mariano González Chavajay are leading contemporary exponents of the Tz'utujil style. The artist Emilio González Morales pioneered the motif of depicting rural scenes from above – the *vista del pájaro*, or bird's-eye view – as well as from below, an ant's-eye view. In San Pedro, you can see and buy their work at the **Galería de Arte**, on the road leading uphill from the Santiago dock, or even learn to paint in this style (see Courses, opposite).

The granddaddy of Santiago painting was Juan Sisay; success at an international art exhibition in 1969 sparked an explosion of painters working in his style. His grandson, Juan Diego Chávez, carries his banner and manages the **Juan Sisay Gallery** in Santiago, about 200m up from the dock on the left side. Another well-regarded Santiago painter, Nicolás Reanda, has his gallery on the main street. Among the leading figures in San Juan are Antonio Coché Mendoza and Angelina Quic, one of the few women in the field; their paintings are exhibited at the **Galería Xocomil**, near the top of the street leading up from the dock.

If you've got more than a passing interest, consider taking the 'Maya Artists & Artisans' tour offered by Posada Los Encuentros in Panajachel (see p122) or visit the website **Arte Maya Tz'utuhil** (www.artemaya.com).

it's regularly patrolled by tourism police to reduce the incidence of assaults.

Excursion Big Foot (☎ 7721-8203; 7a Av, Zona 2), 50m to the left at the first crossroads up from the Panajachel dock, has a track record of responsibility and departs at 3am when there are at least six people (Q100 each). The ascent is through fields of maize, beans and squash, followed by primary cloud forest. It's a three-hour ascent; take water, snacks, a hat and sunblock.

Matthew Purvis (☎ 4091-7051; mattpurvis83@googlemail.com), an English geologist, leads volcano climbs, providing knowledgeable commentary on plants and minerals and the lake's formation. He charges Q250 per person, including transport to the park entrance, park entry fees and accompanying local guide. Matthew can usually be found at D'Noz (p137).

OTHER ACTIVITIES

Another popular hike goes up the hill to the west of the village that is referred to as **Indian Nose** – its skyline resembles the profile of an ancient Maya dignitary. **Asoantur** (☎ 4379 4545; 7:30am-7pm), an association made up of 25 Tz'utujil guides from the local community, will lead a minimum of two people up there for around Q150 per person. They also offer cultural tours of San Pedro and nearby coffee plantations, horseback riding tours, and kayak, bicycle and motorbike rentals. They operate from a hut on the lane up from the Pana dock.

Walking from San Pedro to other lakeside villages is potentially risky. In particular the trail between San Pedro La Laguna and Santiago Atitlán had been repeatedly targeted by bandits at time of research, and about four holdups a year have been reported along the path to San Marcos La Laguna. We don't recommend these walks except with a responsible guide or police escort, the latter available for groups by request from **Asistur** (☎ 2421-2800, ext 11305; nleon@inguat.gob.mx). **Casa Verde Tours** (☎ 7721-8349; www.casaverdetours.com), just up from the Pana dock, leads a six-hour hike to Santa Cruz La Laguna, returning by boat, charging Q166 per person.

Kayaks are available for hire (per hour Q15), turning right from the Pana dock. Ask for Walter.

After all that activity, one of the best places for a good soak is in the solar-heated tubs at **Los Termales** (8:30am-11:55pm; per person Q35), down a small path next to the Buddha bar.

Book ahead so that the pool is already hot when you arrive.

If you're wary of the lake water quality, have a swim at **La Piscina** (adult/child Q20/10; 11am-dusk Tue-Sun;), 50m up from the Santiago dock, a global gathering place that revolves around a pool. Weekends are busiest with barbecues and Bocce ball.

Hatha yoga sessions (Q30) are held Monday to Saturday at 9am in a circular garden along the path below the Buddha bar.

Courses

Pick up a brush at **Chi Ya'a** (☎ 5636-0176; chiyaa.weebly.com; per hr Q30), where local artist Gaspar shows how to create oil paintings in the Maya bird's-eye view and from-behind styles. The studio is at the waterfront just below Los Thermales.

Grupo Ecológico Teixchel (☎ 5932-0000; teixchel@gmail.com; 8:30am-noon & 2-6pm) is a Tz'utujil women's collective that sells fair-trade woven goods and offers weaving classes for Q25 per hour (not including materials).

LANGUAGE COURSES

San Pedro is making quite a name for itself in the language game, with ultra-economical rates at its many Spanish schools. Check out a couple of schools before deciding. Some of them are distinctly rustic, rather amateurish affairs; others are professional enterprises with good reputations. Optional extras range from volcano hikes and dance classes to Maya culture seminars and volunteer work opportunities. The standard price for four hours of one-on-one classes, five days a week, is Q550 to Q600. Accommodation with a local family, with three meals daily (except Sunday) typically costs Q500. Schools can also organize other accommodation options.

Casa Rosario (☎ 5613-6401; www.casarosario.com) Classes held in little huts amid gardens near the lake. Weaving classes and *huipil* appreciation (from the owner's voluminous collection) are among the extracurricular activities. In addition to homestays, accommodation is offered at the school. The office is along the first street to the left as you walk up from Santiago dock.

Cooperativa Spanish School (☎ 5398-6448; www.cooperativeschoolsanpedro.com) Run as a cooperative (therefore guaranteeing fair wages for teachers); a percentage of profits goes to needy families around the lake. After-school activities include videos, conferences, salsa classes, volunteer work, kayaking and hiking. Access is via a path off the street that ascends from the Santiago dock.

Corazón Maya (☎ 7721-8160; www.corazonmaya.com) Well-established, family-run school with lakeside setting, offering activities such as cooking classes, visits to local artists, and conferences about current political, social and cultural issues in Latin America. Take the first left up from Santiago dock.

Escuela Mayab (☎ 5098-1295; franciscopuac@yahoo. com) Professionally run institute holding classes under shelters in artistic gardens. They also teach Maya languages. Activities include videos, kayaking and horseback rides. It is associated with a medical clinic in Chirijox and can organize volunteer work for doctors, nurses and assistants. Located down a laneway coming off the street between the two docks.

San Pedro Spanish School (☎ 5715-4604; www. sanpedrospanishschool.org; 7a Av 2-20) Well-organized school on the street between the two docks, with consistently good reviews. Classes are held in an attractive garden setting. The school supports Niños del Lago, an organization that provides education, health care and nutrition for local Tz'utujil children.

Sleeping

In many places in San Pedro it's possible to negotiate deals for longer stays and during low season. For longer stays, it's also possible to rent a room or an entire house in town. Ask around.

NEAR THE PANA DOCK

Hospedaje Xocomil (☎ 5598-4546; s/d Q40/80, without bathroom Q25/50) Up the lane to the right about 50m past the Gran Sueño, this family-run place is in the basic backpacker category, but the staff is kind and there's a kitchen for guests.

Hotel Mansión del Lago (☎ 7721-8124; www. hotelmansiondellago.com; 3a Vía & 4a Av, Zona 2; s/d/tr Q75/150/225) Straight up from the Pana dock is this concrete monster. Large rooms are done up in a cloud motif, with wide balconies looking right at the Indian's Nose.

ourpick Hotel Gran Sueño (☎ 7721-8110; 8a Calle 4-40, Zona 2; s/d Q75/125) Beyond a plant-draped entryway and up a spiral staircase are bright rooms with colorful abstract designs and more style than elsewhere. Rooms 9 and 11 are fantastic lake-view perches. The hotel is up the street to the left of the Mansión del Lago.

Hotel Nahual Maya (☎ 7721-8158; 6 Av 8C-12; r Q100; P) The forest of rooftop rebar somewhat mars the Mediterranean villa motif, but the rooms are sparkling clean and homey and have little balconies with hammocks out front.

BETWEEN THE DOCKS

Zoola (☎ 5847-4857; zoolapeople.com; dm Q30, s/d 60/100, without bathroom Q40/70) 'Laid-back' is the operative phrase at this Israeli-run establishment, a place to crash after a Mideast feast at the adjoining restaurant. Reached down a long, jungly boardwalk opposite the Museo Tz'unun Ya', it features eight brightly colored rooms around a peaceful garden. There's a two-night minimum stay.

ourpick Hotelito El Amanecer Sak'cari (☎ 7721-8096; www.hotelsakcari.com; 7a Av 2-12, Zona 2; s/d Q160/260; P 🛜) On the left just after San Pedro Spanish School, the efficient Sak'cari has clean, tangerine-colored rooms with lots of shelves and wood paneling. Rooms at the rear are best, with big balconies overlooking a vast landscaped lawn.

Hotel Mikaso (☎ 5973-3129; www.mikasohotel.com; 4a Callejon A-88; d/tr/ste Q374/457/580) The only real upmarket hotel in San Pedro, this prominent tower stands proudly by the lakefront. Big, colonially furnished rooms cooled by ceiling fans ring a garden bursting with birds-of-paradise. The rooftop bar/Spanish restaurant boasts fantastic lake views.

NEAR THE SANTIAGO DOCK

Hotel Peneleu (☎ 5925-0583; 5a Av 2-20, Zona 2; s/d Q35/50, without bathroom Q15/30) Beyond an unassuming dirt yard, you'll find a concrete tower with well-maintained if modestly furnished rooms. Try to get No 1 or 2, which are up top with big windows overlooking the lake. Genial proprietor Don Alberto will gladly negotiate rates for longer stays. To find it, head 500m up from the dock and turn left; if you're laden with luggage, take a tuk-tuk up the steep approach.

Hotel Villa Cuba (☎ 7959-5044; www.hotelvillacuba. com; Camino a la Finca, Zona 4; s/d Q60/120) A large, modern hotel on grounds that sweep down to the lake, this former private residence sits amid cornfields on the road to Santiago. The seven rooms are furnished with quality blankets and towels, plus metal racks for storage. Swimming is good here, and it's only a tuk-tuk away from the bar and restaurant scene. To find it, take the first road to the left up from the dock and continue for 2km.

Eating

There are plenty of places to get your grub lakeside. Prices are low, but if you're hurting, there are a bunch of *comedores* up the hill in the main part of town.

Shanti Shanti (8a Calle 3-93; mains Q20-25; ☺ breakfast, lunch & dinner; Ⓥ) With terraced seating cascading down to the lakeside, this makes a pleasant perch for hippie staples like falafel, curried veggies and hearty soups.

our pick **Café La Puerta** (☎ 4050-0500; mains Q25-35; ☺ breakfast & lunch) It's not just the lakefront setting (just below Hotel Mikaso) that makes this such an appealing spot for breakfast and bird-watching, but also the abundant, natural fare. For lunch, they feature Mexican burritos, tacos and quesadillas.

Zoola (☎ 5847-4857; zoolapeople.com; mains Q25-40; ☺ 9am-9pm; ☎) Since its inception in 2003, this Israeli joint has become San Pedro's premier global chillage venue. Travelers kick back on cushions around low tables, munching scrumptious Mideast fare, grooving on Manu, playing board games and generally unwinding. Aside from the all-day breakfasts and falafel platters, there's more unusual Israeli fare like *ktzitzot* (meatballs in a special tomato sauce) and sauteed chicken livers.

Ventana Blue (mains Q35-46; ☺ dinner Wed-Sun) There are just four tables at this cozy bistro at a bend in the path between the docks. Created by Santa Cruz La Laguna native Santos Canel, the brief but exciting menu features an array of Asian and Guatemalan dishes, from Thai coconut curries to *jocóm* (chicken and vegetables in a cilantro sauce).

Buddha (☎ 4178-7979; 2a Av 2-24; mains Q35-40; ☺ lunch & dinner Wed-Mon) The Eastern-inspired Buddha can be enjoyed on various levels – downstairs there's a pool table and boisterous bar, upstairs a restaurant doing convincing versions of Thai, Indian and other Asian dishes, and up top a thatched roof lounge for hookah smoking.

D'Noz (☎ 5578-0201; 4a Av 8-18; mains Q36-45; ☺ breakfast, lunch & dinner) Another popular hangout, D'Noz, right up from the Pana dock, is San Pedro's closest thing to a cultural center, with free movies, a big bar and a lending library. The menu spans the globe from Asian fusion to French quiche to Tecpán sausage.

Mikaso (4a Callejon A 1-88; mains Q60-Q85; ☺ breakfast, lunch & dinner) This rooftop restaurant specializes in Iberian fare, with a nice range of Spanish *bocadillos* on fresh-baked baguettes. If you want the paella, they need 24 hours' notice.

Drinking & Entertainment

Café Las Cristalinas (☺ 7am-9pm; ☎) To savor a shot of the coffee grown on the surrounding slopes (and roasted here), head for this thatched-roof structure on the way up from the Pana dock to the center of town. You can take your laptop online upstairs.

El Barrio (7a Av 2-07, Zona 2; ☺ 5pm-1am) This cozy little bar on the path between the two docks has one of the most happening happy hours in town, food till midnight and drinks till 1am.

Alegre Pub (8a Calle 4-10) Near the Pana dock the Alegre is always, well, *alegre*, with a real British pub feel – drinks specials, a Sunday roast and trivia nights. There are free movies nightly in the way-laid-back rooftop garden, and loads of free, reliable tourist info.

En Vivo (☺ Thu-Tue) As the name suggests, live music is the focus at this stylish log-lined hall, with performances nightly in styles ranging from merengue to reggae. It's on your left coming up from the Pana dock.

Freedom Bar (☎ 5422-9930; 8a Calle 3-95, Zona 2; ☺ to 1am Mon-Sat) The hardest-partying bar in town, the Freedom features lounges, a pool table and a dance floor, and often hosts guest DJs on weekends. It's on the first street to your right coming up from the Pana dock.

Chile's (4a Av 8-12) Chile's lake-view deck is a perennially popular option, with free salsa lessons after dinner Tuesday and Friday nights and nightly happy hours from 6pm to 10pm.

While many *pedranos* spend their evenings shouting the lord's praises at evangelical congregations, visitors go to the movies. At the Panajachel dock, D'Noz and the Alegre Lounge show films most nights, as does Buddha between the docks, and Mikaso hosts its own little cinema paradiso Wednesday (English) and Sunday (Spanish) nights at 8pm.

Shopping

About 100m uphill from Hotel Mansión del Lago is Caza Sueños, a leather shop owned by brothers Fernando and Pedro González. They handcraft leather goods, including vests, boots and bags. Some of their paintings are exhibited and sold here. Yabalám, downstairs from D'Noz, is a good place to look for contemporary indigenous handicrafts, including jewelry, textiles and paper hot-air balloons.

Getting There & Away

Passenger boats arrive here from/depart for Panajachel (see p127) and Santiago Atitlán (see p133). Boats from San Pedro to Santiago (Q20, 45 minutes) run hourly from 6am to 4pm. Boats from San Pedro to San Marcos

THE HIGHLANDS

La Laguna, Jaibalito, Santa Cruz La Laguna and Panajachel run approximately every half hour or so from 6am to 5pm.

San Pedro is connected by paved roads to Santiago Atitlán (although this stretch is plagued by bandits) and to the Interamericana at Km 148 (about 20km west of Los Encuentros). A paved branch off the San Pedro–Interamericana road runs along the northwest side of the lake from Santa Clara to San Marcos La Laguna. Buses by Transportes Wendy, San Pedrano and Méndez leave for Quetzaltenango (Q35, three hours) from San Pedro's Catholic church, up in the town center, at 5am, 5:30am and 8am.

Casa Verde Tours (☎ 7721-8349; www.casaverdetours. com) offers daily shuttles to Antigua (Q83), Guatemala City (Q166), Monterrico (Q166) and San Cristóbal de Las Casas, Mexico (Q249), among other places.

SAN JUAN LA LAGUNA
pop 5600 / elev 1567m

Just 2km east of San Pedro, this mellow lakeside village has escaped many of the excesses of its neighbors, and some travelers find it a more tranquil setting in which to study Spanish or experience indigenous life. San

Juan is special: the Tz'utujil inhabitants take pride in their craft traditions – particularly painting and weaving – and have developed their own tourism infrastructure to highlight them to outsiders. There are trash cans, neatly cobblestoned streets, bus shelters and nicely painted facades.

The **Asociación de Guías de Ecoturismo Rupalaj K'istalin** (☎ 5964-0040; www.sanjuanlalaguna.org; ☽ 8am-noon & 2-5pm), around the corner from the market, offers a worthwhile cultural tour of the village's points of interest by indigenous guides (Q110 per person), in Spanish. It include visits to two weaving cooperatives, both of which use dyes from native plants; an art studio/gallery featuring the Tz'utujil primitivist painting style; a cooperative that produces herbal remedies and cosmetics from native plants; and a *cofradía* that looks after Saint Simón and his mischievous alter ego Maximón. The tour also takes in the murals around town depicting various aspects of San Juan life and legend, including the coffee harvest and the mudslide caused by Hurricane Stan in 2005. Other **tours** (each tour per person Q140) offered include trips with local fisherman in rustic *cayucos* to learn about traditional lake fishing techniques and a demonstration of the

---

TRADITIONAL MAYA CLOTHING

Anyone visiting the highlands can delight in the beautiful *traje indígena* (traditional Maya clothing). The styles, patterns and colors used by each village – originally devised by the Spanish colonists to distinguish one village from another – are unique, and each garment is the creation of its weaver, with subtle individual differences.

The basic elements of the traditional wardrobe are the *tocoyal* (head covering), *huipil* (blouse), *corte* or *refago* (skirt), *calzones* (trousers), *tzut* or *kaperraj* (cloth), *paz* (belt) or *faja* (sash) and *caïtes* or *xajáp* (sandals).

Women's head coverings are beautiful and elaborate bands of cloth up to several meters long, wound about the head and often decorated with tassels, pompoms and silver ornaments.

Women proudly wear *huipiles* every day. Though some machine-made fabrics are now being used, many *huipiles* are still made completely by hand. The white blouse is woven on a backstrap loom, then decorated with appliqué and embroidery designs and motifs common to the weaver's village. Many of the motifs are traditional symbols. No doubt all motifs originally had religious or historical significance, but today that meaning is often lost to memory.

Cortes (refagos) are pieces of cloth 7m to 10m long that are wrapped around the body. Traditionally, girls wear theirs above the knee, married women at the knee and old women below the knee, though the style can differ markedly from region to region.

Both men and women wear *fajas*, long strips of backstrap-loom-woven cloth wrapped around the midriff as belts. When they're wrapped with folds upward like a cummerbund, the folds serve as pockets.

Tzutes (for men) or *kaperraj* (for women) are the all-purpose cloths carried by local people and used as head coverings, baby slings, produce sacks, basket covers and shawls. There are also shawls for women called *perraj*.

harvesting of the lakeshore reeds, which are used as material for *petates,* the woven mats the town is known for.

The association can also set up guides for one-way walks to San Marcos La Laguna (Q120 per person), returning by *lancha;* and hikes up Rupalaj K'istalin (Q130 per person), the mountain that towers above San Juan and is the site of Maya religious rituals.

There's a sandy beach suitable for swimming about 2km west of town, **Las Cristalinas,** though its crystallinity varies from day to day.

The village has two language institutes: **San Juan Spanish School** (☎ 4257-7899), connected to the Hotel Pa Muelle; and the **Eco Spanish School** (☎ 4168-8806; www.ecolanguages.org), along a path that's 500m up from the dock on the right.

There are a number of fine accommodations for a village of this size. **Hotel Pa Muelle** (☎ 4141-0820; hotelpamuelle@turbonett.com; Camino al Muelle; s/d Q100/200) has small, blue rooms overlooking the lake. It's near the top of the hill coming up from the dock. The **Hotel Maya San Juan** (☎ 5294-3395; s/d Q100/200), near the center of town, is set around a virtual rainforest, and the rooms, though dim, show some creative flair, with blue-painted ceiling planks and angels as bathroom fixtures. Within the garden is a **restaurant/bar** (mains Q50), serving Guatemalan favorites like *patín de pescado,* along with strawberry daiquiris. Coming up from the dock, it's a block left from the market.

Uxlabil Eco Hotel (☎ 2366-9555; www.uxlabil.com; s/d Q435/595) is the classiest option in town, with hand-carved stone trimmings by local craftsmen. The hotel sits on a small coffee plantation and has a good swimming dock.

To get to San Juan, ask any boat coming from Pana to drop you off at the dock. Otherwise it's a 15-minute pickup or tuk-tuk ride (Q10) from San Pedro.

SAN MARCOS LA LAGUNA
pop 3800 / elev 1562m

Without doubt the prettiest of the lakeside villages, San Marcos La Laguna lives a double life. The mostly Maya community occupies the higher ground while expats and visitors cover a flat jungly patch toward the shoreline with paths snaking through banana, coffee and avocado trees. The two converge under the spreading ceiba trees of the delightful central plaza.

San Marcos has become a magnet for global seekers, who believe the place has a spiritual energy that's conducive to learning and practicing meditation, holistic therapies, massage, reiki and other spiritually oriented activities. Whatever you're into, it's a great spot to kick back and distance the everyday world for a spell. Lago de Atitlán is beautiful and clean here, and you can swim off the rocks. Boats put in at a central dock below Posada Schumann. The path leading from there to the village center and a parallel one about 100m west are the main axes for most visitors.

There's a community information board in front of the San Marcos Holistic Center with postings on events and housing options. You'll find plenty of useful information and web links at www.atitlanresource.com. Get online at **Prolink** (☽ 9am-7pm Mon-Sat, 10am-5pm Sun; per hr Q12), across from the Paco Real hotel.

The NGO **La Cambalacha** (☎ 5445-7521; www.lacambalacha.org) provides space, technical training and teachers for projects that involve local kids in theater and the arts. They're always looking for volunteers.

Mariposas (☽ 11am-5pm), next door to Paco Real, has a few shelves of fiction in English, French and Spanish, plus some Lonely Planet guides.

Sights & Activities

The village's claim to fame is **Las Pirámides Meditation Center** (☎ 5205-7151; www.laspiramidesdelka.com), which maintains its own dock just down from Posada Schumann. Most structures on the property are pyramidal in shape and oriented to the four cardinal points, including the two temples where sessions are held. A one-month personal development course begins every full moon. There's also a three-month solar course running from each equinox to the following solstice (the moon course is a prerequisite). Other experiences available here include yoga, aura work, Shaluha-Ka massage and tarot readings. Monday through Saturday, nonguests can come for the meditation (5pm to 6:15pm, Q40) or Hatha yoga (7pm to 8:15am, Q30) sessions. Accommodations are available, to course participants only, in pyramid-shaped houses for Q150 per day, slightly less by the week or month. This price includes the course, use of the sauna, and access to a fascinating library. It also has a vegetarian restaurant, and room to wander about in the medicinal herb garden.

Next door to Hotel El Unicornio, **San Marcos Holistic Centre** (www.sanmholisticcentre.com; ☽ 10am-

5pm Mon-Sat), run by various resident and visiting practitioners, provides a range of massages, holistic therapies and training courses in kinesiology, EFT, reiki, shiatsu, massage and reflexology. The approach is relaxed and you're welcome to discuss possibilities before committing to anything. Most massages and therapies cost around Q250 per 90-minute session.

Guy (☎ 5854-5365), at Restaurant Tul y Sol along the lakefront trail, offers paragliding rides (Q665) in the mornings from Santa Clara down to San Juan. It's an exhilarating ride offering some great photo opportunities.

The walks along the lake west to Santa Clara La Laguna and east to Santa Cruz La Laguna are breathtaking. Seek local advice before setting out, though: attacks and robberies do occur, most often along the stretch between Tzununá and Santa Cruz La Laguna. Your best bet is to go with **Jovenes Maya Kaqchikeles** (☎ 5527-2017; atitlanresource.com/jovenesmayas_eng.htm; ☻ 9am-5pm Mon-Sat), a group of bright, ecologically minded local lads who speak English. They offer guided hikes to San Pedro (2½ hours) and Santa Cruz La Laguna (four hours), each at Q100 per person, including the *lancha* back. They can also take you to Tzununá via the Palitz waterfalls; to Santa Lucía Utatlán along the old Maya trail; and around the barrios of San Marcos to visit families who weave bags with maguey fibers. The Jovenes rent kayaks, too. Stop by their clubhouse, just above the Posada del Bosque Encantado, to discuss the possibilities.

The best swimming is off the rocks west of the village. From Aaculaax (see right) follow the trail down to the rocky outcrop and make your way to the best dive perch. (Locals advise you to have someone watch your things while you're swimming.)

Sleeping

There aren't any street signs but most lodgings have posted their own fancifully painted versions to at least point you in the right direction.

Hospedaje Panabaj (☎ 5091-9227; s/d Q30/60) The only accommodation in the village center, the basic Panabaj stands behind the school that's immediately above the main plaza. Elevated rooms get plenty of light through stained-glass windows, and though the wooden beds are somewhat droopy, it's pretty quiet aside from the fluttering of butterfly wings in the garden. Clean toilets and showers are down the hall.

El Unicornio (hotelunicorniosm.8m.com; s/d incl breakfast Q50/100) Associated with the adjacent San Marcos Holistic Center, El Unicornio has 10 rooms in thatch-roofed A-frame bungalows amid gardens, sharing hot showers, nice hangout areas, a sauna and a kitchen. Mexican owner Chus is a musician who enjoys jamming with guests. It's a short distance from the lakefront along the western path.

Hotel La Paz (☎ 5702-9168; lapazcolection@homtail.com; r per person Q50-60) Near the west end of the upper path that links the two main paths, La Paz has rambling grounds holding four- or five-bed dormitory-style rooms and a couple of private rooms. All are in bungalows of traditional *bajareque* (a stone, bamboo and mud construction) with thatch roofs; some have loft beds. The organic gardens and vegetarian restaurant, traditional Maya sauna and morning yoga sessions (Q30) are additional attractions.

Hotel Paco Real (☎ 5891-7215; elpacoreal@hotmail.com; s Q80-150, d Q140-200) A two-minute walk down the path off San Marcos' central plaza, the Paco Real has simple but stylish rooms in thatched cottages, each uniquely designed. Also here is a restaurant with wood-fired pizzas (Q25 to Q65).

Aaculaax (☎ 5287-0521; www.aaculaax.com; r Q100-395, ste from Q700) The eco-conscious Aaculaax is built around the living rock of the hillside, with lots of recycled glass and plastic utilized as construction materials. Each of the 11 rooms is unique, with handcrafted furnishings, picture windows and lake-view terraces; some have kitchens. From the Posada Schumann dock, it's a six-minute walk to the left (west) along the lakeside path. A fabulous breakfast, with homemade bread and granola, is served at the terrace restaurant.

Posada del Bosque Encantado (☎ 5208-5334; www.hotelposadaencantado.com; s/d Q120/160) Set in jungly grounds that could well be an enchanted forest, these rooms strike a good balance between rustic and stylish. Each has a loft with a double bed and another bed downstairs. Walls are mud-brick, beds are big and firm and hammocks are strewn around the place.

Posada Schumann (☎ 5202-2216; s Q125-234, d Q250-468) Set in gardens that stretch right to the lakeside, Posada Schumann has neat rooms in stone or wooden cottages, some with kitchen, most with bathroom. Skip the overpriced restaurant but spend some time in the igloo-shaped sauna or lakefront gazebo. The boat dock is right outside the gate.

Eating

Almost all of the above hotels feature their own restaurants; Aaculaax and Paco Real are among the best of these. The latter hosts live music two or three nights a week.

Moonfish (mains Q25-40; 7am-6pm Wed-Mon; V) After a morning dive off the rocks, stroll up the path to Moonfish, which has a lakeside terrace. Hippie-friendly fare includes tempeh sandwiches, tofu scrambles, and fresh salads with ingredients from the adjacent garden.

Comedor Susy (Comedor Mi Marquensita; Parque Central; set lunch Q30; breakfast, lunch & dinner) This 'mom and pop' store on the central plaza is where many expats go for a cheap, home-cooked meal, which might explain why tofu dishes pop up among the chicken and pork chops.

Blind Lemon's (www.blindlemons.com; mains Q35; lunch & dinner;) Named after one of owner Carlos' blues heroes, this hangout brings the Mississippi Delta to Atitlán, with weekly blues jams by Carlos and special guests in a colonial-style mansion. The menu features chicken platters, Cajun-blackened fish, pizza, burgers and other gringo comfort food. It's at the top of the western path.

Restaurant Fe (mains Q80; breakfast, lunch & dinner) This recently inaugurated restaurant, a short walk toward the lake from the Paco Real, features a sophisticated Asian-influenced menu, with exotic items like banana-smoked chicken on creamed cabbage and Caesar salad garnished with eel. The thatched-roof bar makes a nice perch, especially to marimba accompaniment on Sundays.

Getting There & Away

The last dependable boat back to Jaibalito, Santa Cruz La Laguna and Panajachel usually goes about 5pm. For information on boats from Panajachel, see p127.

A paved road runs east from San Marcos to Tzununá and west to San Pablo and Santa Clara, where it meets the road running from the Interamericana to San Pedro. You can travel between San Marcos and San Pedro by pickup, with a transfer at San Pablo.

JAIBALITO

pop 600 / elev 1562m

This Kaqchiquel hamlet is only accessible by boat, or on foot via a ridgeline trail from Santa Cruz La Laguna, 4km to the east (45 minutes). The equally picturesque hike west, to San Marcos (6km), is best undertaken with local guides, such as Jovenes Maya Kaqchikeles (see p139). There are several marvelous places to stay.

Sleeping & Eating

Posada Jaibilito (5598-1957; www.posada-jaibalito. com; dm Q25, s Q30-50, d Q50-80) Jaibalito's budget choice is just up from the dock on the left. The German-owned operation is a remarkable value, with dorm and a few private rooms occupying a garden flanked by coffee plants. Some little houses are available for longer-term renters.

our pick **La Casa del Mundo Hotel & Café** (5218-5332; www.lacasadelmundo.com; r Q550, without bathroom Q288) On a secluded cliff facing the volcanoes is one of Guatemala's most spectacular hotels. It features sumptuous gardens, lake swimming from Mediterranean-style terraces, and a wood-fired hot tub overhanging the lake (Q275 for up to 10 people). Every room is outfitted with comfortable beds, Guatemalan fabrics and fresh flowers. The best rooms seem to float above the water, with no land visible beneath. The restaurant serves a toothsome four-course dinner (Q85). You can rent kayaks (Q25 to Q50 per hour) for exploring the lake. Reservations are advisable.

Vulcano Lodge (5410-2237; www.vulcanolodge. com; r from Q325) Towards the back of the village, this Norwegian-designed-and-operated retreat contains nine trim and spotless rooms scattered amid tropical gardens. There's also a restaurant, serving a lavish five-course dinner with fresh, local ingredients. The owners, Terje and Monica, are well versed in local walking routes. Coming up from the dock, take a right though the village and over a bridge to get here.

Club Ven Acá (5051-4520; pasta Q40, mains Q80) On the lakefront a bit east of La Casa del Mundo is this trendy restaurant with a fusion menu and a popular happy hour with Q20 purple-basil mojitos. Guests tend to unwind in the hot tub or infinity pool.

Getting There & Away

Jaibalito is a 20-minute *lancha* ride from Panajachel or San Pedro (Q20). As well as the public dock roughly in the center of the village, La Casa del Mundo has a pier.

SANTA CRUZ LA LAGUNA

pop 1700 / elev 1833m

With the typically dual nature of the Atitlán villages, Santa Cruz comprises both a waterfront

THE HIGHLANDS

A FLIGHTY WIND

Though Lago de Atitlán is usually placid early in the day, by noon the Xocomil may have risen to ruffle the water's surface. This legendary wind results when warm air from the Pacific coast clashes against cooler northern currents, forming waves up to 3m high, mainly in the middle of the lake. It can make for a chaotic crossing for small boats plying between the lakeside villages, particularly between Tzununá and Santa Cruz La Laguna where whirlpools may form. Experienced boatmen are capable of handling it, though fatal accidents have occurred, especially in cases where boats were overloaded with passengers. This occurred in 2008, when a boat full of tourists capsized near Santiago and six people died. Maximum capacity is 14 passengers, and in Xocomil season you must be particularly careful not to board a boat with more people on it, which at the very least will make for a hair-raising journey. The Xocomil is most intense between January and March, known as the windy season in these parts. It's best to do your traveling in the morning, when weather conditions are better and there is more traffic.

---

resort – home of the lake's scuba-diving outfit – and a rather ramshackle indigenous Kaqchiquel village, about 600m uphill from the dock. The cobblestoned road makes a nice if strenuous walk; it's a route villagers customarily take lugging sacks of avocados or firewood. The inaccessibility of the spot – it can only be reached by boat or on foot – may impede its development but also enhances its rugged beauty.

Amigos de Santa Cruz (www.amigosdesantacruz.org) is a grassroots program focusing on Santa Cruz's families in need. It's always looking for mid- to long-term volunteers for projects including fuel-efficient stoves, nutritional programs, technology training, school sponsorships and medical care.

Activities

British- and American-run **ATI Divers** (☎ 5706-4117; www.laiguanaperdida.com/ati_divers.php) leads dive trips from Santa Cruz. They offer a four-day PADI open-water diving certification course (Q1835), as well as a PADI high-altitude course and fun dives. It's based at La Iguana Perdida hotel. ATI also offers advanced certification, fun dives for certified divers (Q250/415 for one/two dives), and specialty courses including a two-dive altitude course (Q665). Lago de Atitlán is an interesting site because it's a collapsed volcanic cone with bizarre geological formations and places where hot water vents directly into the lake, though there's little aquatic flora or fauna. This is one of the rare places in the world where you can dive at altitude without using a dry suit. Diving at altitude brings its own challenges – you need better control over your buoyancy, and visibility is reduced. During

the rainy season the water clouds up, so the best time to dive is between October and May (in the morning).

Kayak rentals and multiday excursions around the lake are offered by **Los Elementos Adventure Center** (☎ 5359-8328; www.kayakguatemala.com/adventurecenter.html). Its two-day paddle-and-hike tour includes a visit to Santa Catarina Palopó, followed by kayaking along the lake's northern shore and hiking along the old Maya trail through Tzununá and Jaibalito. The cost of Q1335 per person (minimum four participants) includes meals and a night's lodging. Its base is a 10-minute walk west of La Iguana Perdida along the lakeside trail.

Sleeping & Eating

La Iguana Perdida (☎ 5706-4117; www.laiguanaperdida.com; dm Q25-35, r Q240-300, s/d without bathroom Q70/90; 🖥) The first place you see as you step off the dock, La Iguana Perdida makes a great hangout to enjoy the lake views and meet other travelers, go scuba diving or kayaking, learn Spanish or sweat it out in the sauna. Managed mainly by alternative-minded gringos (volunteers often needed), it features a range of rooms, from primitive (electricity-free dorm in an A-frame cabin) to luxurious (new adobe structure with stylish furnishings, lake-view windows and balconies). Meals are served family-style; a three-course dinner is Q50. Everything is on the honor system: your tab is totaled up when you leave. Don't miss the Saturday night cross-dressing, fire and music barbecues!

Arca de Noé (☎ 5515-3712; www.arcasantacruz.com; s/d Q200/240, without bathroom Q70/100) Spread out along the lakeside, the rooms and bungalows at Noah's Ark are simple but bright, clean and spacious. It's an ecofriendly operation: solar energy, lake-treated drinking water, locally grown produce and no cans or bottles. It has a welcoming, sociable atmosphere and great food: the candlelit six-course dinner, always with a vegetarian option, is Q75.

ourpick **Hotel Isla Verde** (☎ 5760-2648; www.isla verdeatitlan.com; s/d Q332/374, without bathroom Q249/291; 🔲) Designed by an artist from Bilbao, Spain, this stylish, environmentally friendly lodging makes the most of its spectacular setting. A mosaic stone path winds through exuberant vegetation to the nine hillside cabins (six with private bathroom); the higher you go, the more jaw-dropping the picture-window views. Simple rooms are tastefully done with the owner's paintings and *típica* fabrics and pillows. Bathrooms are jungle-chic affairs, and water and electricity are solar powered. A terrace restaurant serves slow-food cuisine, and there's a glass pavilion for meditation and dance. It's a 10-minute walk west of the dock along the lakefront trail.

Getting There & Away

For information about boats travelling to Santa Cruz, see Panajachel (p127) and San Pedro La Laguna (p137).

QUICHÉ

The road into Quiché department leaves the Interamericana at Los Encuentros, winding northward through pine forests and cornfields. Quiché is the homeland of the K'iche' people, though other groups form the fabric of this culturally diverse region, most notably the Ixil of the eastern Cuchumatanes mountains. Most visitors who come to this largely forgotten pocket of the country are on a jaunt to the famous market at Chichicastenango, though similarly captivating commerce is conducted in Santa Cruz del Quiché, the departmental capital to the north, and it's less trammeled territory. On its outskirts lie the mysterious ruins of K'umarcaaj, the last capital city of the K'iche'. Adventurous souls push further north for Nebaj, heart of the culturally vibrant Ixil Triangle, with myriad hiking opportunities.

CHICHICASTENANGO
pop 66,100 / elev 2172m

Surrounded by valleys, with mountains serrating the horizons, Chichicastenango can seem isolated in time and space from the rest of Guatemala. When its narrow cobbled streets and red-tiled roofs are enveloped in mist, it's downright magical. The crowds of crafts vendors and tour groups who flock in for the huge Thursday and Sunday markets lend it a much worldlier, more commercial atmosphere, but Chichi retains its mystery. *Maxeños* (citizens of Chichicastenango) are famous for their adherence to pre-Christian beliefs and ceremonies. *Cofradías* (Maya religious brotherhoods) hold processions in and around the church of Santo Tomás on Sunday.

Once called Chaviar, Chichi was an important Kaqchiquel trading town long before the Spanish conquest. In the 15th century the group clashed with the K'iche' (based at K'umarcaaj, 20km north) and were forced to move their headquarters to the more defensible Iximché. When the Spanish conquered K'umarcaaj in 1524, many of its residents fled to Chaviar, which they renamed Chugüilá (Above the Nettles) and Tziguan Tinamit (Surrounded by Canyons). These are the names still used by the K'iche' Maya, although everyone else calls the place Chichicastenango, a name given by the Spaniards' Mexican allies.

Today, Chichi has two religious and governmental establishments. On the one hand, the Catholic Church and the Republic of Guatemala appoint priests and town officials; on the other, the indigenous people elect their own religious and civil officers to manage local matters, with a separate council and mayor, and a court that decides cases involving only local indigenous people.

Orientation & Information

Buses approaching from the south go up 7a Av, dropping off passengers two blocks east of the central plaza, dominated on its southeast corner by the big Santo Tomás church. Most of the banks and businesses are in the grid north of here. As you leave Chichi heading north along 5a Av, you pass beneath the Arco Gucumatz, an elaborately painted arch named after the founder of the old K'iche' Maya capital.

Hotel Santo Tomás (p148) sells a good selection of books in its lobby.

INTERNET ACCESS
Cibernet Café (5a Av 6-44; per hr Q6) Upstairs from Tu Café.

CHICHICASTENANGO

INFORMATION
Banco Industrial	**1** D2
Banrural	**2** D2
Cibernet Café	(see 32)
Hospital El Buen Samaritano	**3** C2
Hotel Santo Tomás	(see 23)
Inguat	**4** D2
MG Internet	**5** C2
Post Office	**6** C2
Tecnología y Soluciones	**7** D3
Visa/MasterCard ATM	**8** C2

Buses to Los Encuentros, Interamericana & Guatemala City	**34** D2
Buses to Santa Cruz del Quiché	**35** D2
Chichi Turkaj Tours	(see 19)
Micros to Los Encuentros, Quetzaltenango	**36** D2
Micros to Santa Cruz del Quiché	**37** C2

SIGHTS & ACTIVITIES
Capilla del Calvario	**9** C2
Centro Comercial Santo Tomás	**10** C2
Galería Pop-Wuj	**11** B3
Iglesia de Santo Tomás	**12** C2
Morería	**13** B4
Morería	**14** B4
Municipalidad (Town Hall)	**15** C2
Museo Arqueológico Regional	**16** C2
Pascual Abaj	**17** B4

SLEEPING 🏠
Chalet House	**18** D1
Hotel Chugüilá	**19** D2
Hotel Mashito	**20** B2
Hotel Pop Wuj	**21** C3
Hotel San Jerónimo	**22** C3
Hotel Santo Tomás	**23** C3
Hotel Tuttos	**24** C3
Maya Lodge	**25** C2
Mayan Inn	**26** C2
Mini-Hotel Chichicasteca	**27** C1
Posada El Arco	**28** C1
Posada El Teléfono	**29** B2

EATING 🍴
Blintz Café	(see 19)
Casa de San Juan	**30** C2
Hotel Santo Tomás	(see 23)
Las Brasas	**31** C2
Mayan Inn	(see 26)
Tu Café	**32** C2

TRANSPORT
Agencia de Viajes Maya Chichi Van	**33** D2

MG Internet (5a Av 5-70; per hr Q5) Upstairs, next to Restaurant Los Cofrades.

Tecnología y Soluciones (10a Calle; per hr Q5; 🕑 9am-10pm)

MEDICAL SERVICES

Hospital El Buen Samaritano (☎ 7756-1163; 6a Calle 3-60) Maintains 24-hour emergency clinic.

MONEY

Chichi's many banks all stay open on Sunday.

Banco Industrial (🕑 10am-2pm Mon, 10am-5pm Wed & Fri, 9am-5pm Thu & Sun, 10am-3pm Sat) Visa/MasterCard ATM.

Banrural (5 Av & 5 Calle; 🕑 9am-5pm Sun-Fri, 8am-noon Sat) Changes traveler's checks; Cajero 5B.

Visa/MasterCard ATM (cnr 5a Av & 6a Calle)

POST

Post office (4a Av 6-58) Northwest of the main plaza.

TOURIST INFORMATION

Inguat (☎ 7756-2022; 7a Calle 5-43; 🕑 8am-noon daily plus 2-6pm Mon-Sat) Chichi's Inguat office, on the block east of the plaza, provides information and maps (Q5), plus internet access (Q5 per hour).

Dangers & Annoyances

Hola, amigo! is the refrain you'll hear from the myriad vendors and touts who depend on tourism for their livelihood; it can wear you down, but try to be polite. Ignore touts offering assistance in finding a hotel: showing up at a hotel with one means you'll be quoted a higher price, as the hotel has to give them a kickback. In fact, you'll have no difficulty finding lodgings on your own.

Crowded markets are the favorite haunts of pickpockets, so be alert while you wander in the labyrinth of stalls here.

Chichi is plagued by traffic and exhaust fumes. Keep an eye out for buses tearing around corners.

Sights

Take a close look at the mural running alongside the wall of the town hall on the east side of the plaza. It's dedicated to the victims of the civil war and tells the story using symbology from the *Popol Vuh*.

Inguat-authorized guides in beige vests charge Q50 for a village tour, Q100 for a walk to Pascual Abaj.

MARKET

In the past villagers would walk for hours carrying their wares to Chichi's market, one of Guatemala's largest. Some still do, and when they reach Chichi the night before, they lay down their loads in one of the arcades around the plaza, cook some supper, spread out blankets and go to sleep.

At dawn on Thursday and Sunday they spread out their vegetables, chunks of chalk (ground to a powder, mixed with water and used to soften dried maize), handmade harnesses and other merchandise and wait for customers. Tourist oriented handicraft stalls selling masks, textiles, pottery and so on now occupy much of the plaza and the streets to the north. Things villagers need – food, soap,

clothing, sewing notions, toys – cluster at the north end of the square, in the **Centro Comercial Santo Tomás**, off the north side, and in streets to the south.

The market starts winding down around 3pm. By then you'll notice quite a few drunks staggering around or lying comatose in the street.

IGLESIA DE SANTO TOMÁS

The church on the plaza's east side dates from 1540 and is often the scene of rituals that are more distinctly Maya than Catholic. The front steps serve much the same purpose as did the great flights of stairs leading up to Maya pyramids. For much of the day (especially Sunday), they smolder with incense of copal resin, while indigenous prayer leaders called *chuchkajaues* (mother-fathers) swing censers (usually tin cans poked with holes) and chant magic words marking the days of the ancient Maya calendar and in honor of ancestors.

Inside, the floor of the church may be spread with pine boughs and dotted with offerings of maize, flowers, bottles of liquor wrapped in corn husks, and candles. Many local families trace their lineage back centuries, even to the ancient K'iche' kings. The candles and offerings recall those ancestors, many of whom are buried beneath the floor just as Maya kings were buried beneath pyramids. Please note that photography is not permitted in this church.

On the west side of the plaza is another whitewashed church, the **Capilla del Calvario**,

---

THE MAYA 'BIBLE'

One of the most important Maya texts, the *Popol Vuh* was written down in the 16th century after the Spanish conquest, in K'iche' Maya, using Latin script. The K'iche' scribes showed their book to Francisco Ximénez, a Dominican friar in Chichicastenango, who copied the volume word for word, then translated it into Spanish. Both his copy and the Spanish translation survive, though the Maya original has been lost. The *Popol Vuh* – or 'Book of Council' – relates the odyssey of the K'iche''s forebears from Tula, the sacred city of the Toltecs in central Mexico, to the Guatemalan highlands. It further deals with the dawn of life and the glories of gods and kings. Its tale is somewhat cyclical and not always consistent, but its gist is as follows: the great god K'ucumatz created humankind first from earth (mud), but these earthlings were weak and dissolved in water. The god tried again, using wood. The wood people had no hearts or minds and could not praise their creator, so these too were destroyed, all except the monkeys of the forest, the descendants of the wood people. The creator tried once again, using material recommended by four animals – the gray fox, the coyote, the parrot and the crow – and this time he was successful. The substance was white and yellow corn, ground into meal to form flesh and stirred into water to make blood. Thus do Guatemalans think of themselves with pride as *hombres de maíz*, men of corn.

THAT'S ONE SMOKIN' GOD

The Spanish called him San Simón, the *ladinos* (persons of mixed indigenous and European race) named him Maximón and the Maya know him as Rilaj Maam (ree-lah-*mahm*). By any name, he's a deity revered throughout the Guatemalan highlands. Assumed to be a combination of Maya gods, Pedro de Alvarado (the Spanish conquistador of Guatemala) and the biblical Judas, San Simón is an effigy to which Guatemalans of every stripe go to make offerings and ask for blessings. The effigy is usually housed by a member of a *cofradía* (Maya Catholic brotherhood), moving from one place to another from year to year, a custom anthropologists believe was established to maintain the local balance of power. The name, shape and ceremonies associated with this deity vary from town to town, but a visit will be memorable no matter where you encounter him. For a small fee, photography is usually permitted, and offerings of cigarettes, liquor or candles are always appreciated.

In Santiago Atitlán, Maximón is a wooden figure draped in colorful silk scarves and smoking a fat cigar. Locals guard and worship him, singing and managing the offerings made to him (including your Q10 entry fee). His favorite gifts are Payaso cigarettes and Venado rum, but he often has to settle for the cheaper firewater Quetzalteca Especial. Fruits and gaudy, flashing electric lights decorate his chamber; effigies of Jesus Christ and Christian saints lie or stand either side of Maximón and his guardians. Fires may be burning in the courtyard outside as offerings are made to him.

In Nahualá, between Los Encuentros and Quetzaltenango, the Maximón effigy is à la Picasso: a simple wooden box with a cigarette protruding from it. Still, the same offerings are made and the same sort of blessings asked for. In Zunil, near Quetzaltenango, the deity is called San Simón but is similar to Santiago's Maximón in custom and form.

San Jorge La Laguna on Lago de Atitlán is a very spiritual place for the highland Maya; here they worship Rilaj Maam. It is possible that the first effigy was made near here, carved from the *palo de pito* tree that spoke to the ancient shamans and told them to preserve their culture, language and traditions by carving Rilaj Maam (*palo de pito* flowers can be smoked to induce hallucinations). The effigy in San Jorge looks like a joker, with an absurdly long tongue.

In San Andrés Itzapa near Antigua, Rilaj Maam has a permanent home, and is brought out on October 28 and paraded about in an unparalleled pagan festival. This is an all-night, hedonistic party where dancers grab the staff of Rilaj Maam to harness his power and receive magical visions. San Andrés is less than 10km south of Chimaltenango, so you can easily make the party from Antigua.

similar in form and function to Santo Tomás, but smaller.

MUSEO ARQUEOLÓGICO REGIONAL

Chichi's **archaeology museum** (5a Av 4-47; admission Q5; ☖ 8am-12:30pm & 2-4:30pm Tue-Sat, 8am-2pm Sun), entered from the south side of the square, holds the collection of Hugo Rossbach, a German who served as Chichi's Catholic priest until his death in 1944. (His portrait hangs above the arched entryway.) It includes some beautiful jade necklaces and figurines, along with ceremonial masks, obsidian spearheads, incense burners, figurines and *metates* (grindstones for maize).

PASCUAL ABAJ

On a hilltop south of town, **Pascual Abaj** (Sacrifice Stone) is a shrine to the Maya earth god Huyup Tak'ah (Mountain Plain). Standing amid a circle of squat stone crosses in a clearing, the stone-faced idol looks like something from Easter Island. Said to be hundreds – perhaps thousands – of years old, it has suffered numerous indignities at the hands of outsiders, but local people still revere it.

Chuchkajaues come regularly to offer incense, food, cigarettes, flowers, liquor, and perhaps even a sacrificial chicken, in thanks and hope for the earth's continuing fertility. The area is littered with past offerings. The worshippers won't mind if you watch the goings on, but be sure to request permission before taking any photos. You may be asked if you want to make an offering yourself.

Even if there are no ceremonies going on, you can still see the idol and enjoy the walk up the pine-clad hill. To get there from the plaza, walk downhill on 5a Av, turn right into 9a Calle and proceed downhill. At the bottom, bear left along a path and head up through either of the **morerías** (ceremonial mask workshops) that are signposted here. Exiting at the rear, follow the path uphill through the trees to the top of the hill. (To reduce the risk of muggings, join others for the hike up if possible.)

On the way back to town, you might stop into the **Galería Pop-Wuj** (☎ 7756-1324), a studio/gallery on the right-hand side. Developed as an art institute for local children with the backing of **Projectguggenheim** (www.projectguggenheim.org), it holds a small but *sui generis* collection of oil paintings by the artist Juan Andrés Cortéz and their pupils.

Festivals & Events

December 7 sees the **Quema del Diablo** (Burning of the Devil), when residents burn their garbage in the streets and usher a statue of the Virgin Mary to the steps of the Iglesia de Santo Tomás. There are lots of incense and candles, a marimba band and a fireworks display that has observers running for cover. The following day is the **Feast of the Immaculate Conception**; don't miss the early-morning dance of the giant, drunken cartoon characters in the plaza.

The **fiesta of Santo Tomás** starts on December 13 and culminates on December 21 when pairs of brave (some would say mad) men fly about at high speeds suspended from a tall, vertical pole (see boxed text, p211, for more about this festival). Traditional dances and parades also feature.

Sleeping

If you want to secure a room the night before the Thursday or Sunday market, it's a good idea to call or arrive fairly early on Wednesday or Saturday.

BUDGET

Posada El Teléfono (☎ 7756-1197; 8a Calle A 1-64; r Q30/60) The former phone call center, if you were wondering, has neat little orange rooms with TV. Stay on the tippy top for views of the town's technicolor cemetery.

Hotel Mashito (☎ 7756-1343; 8a Calle 1-72; s/d Q50/100, without bathroom Q40/80) Also on the road to the cemetery, the homey Mashito is built around a plant-filled patio where local geezers exchange views. Maintained by the kind matriarch of the establishment, the rooms have multicolored patchwork bedspreads. The shared-bath units get more light.

Mini-Hotel Chichicasteca (☎ 7756-2111; 5a Calle 4-42; s/d Q40/80) Despite the miniature scale and minimal facilities – just one bathroom to share – the brick-walled rooms here are kept very neat and the proprietress is super nice.

The only drawback is the racket from passing buses starting at 6:30am.

Hotel San Jerónimo (☎ 7756-1838; Final de 5a Av; r Q50/100) The neat brick colonial structure at the bottom end of 5a Av makes an outstanding budget option. Decorative touches are few but rooms sparkle, with neatly made, firm beds, fine window frames and, in some, lovely balconies.

Hotel Tuttor (☎ 7756-1640; hoteltuttor@yahoo.com; 12a Calle 6-29; dm Q50, s/d Q100/200) Nothing fancy, but this hotel on the south end of town is nice and quiet with comfortably designed rooms, and the staff is just swell. There are views across the valley from rooms 4, 5 and 6. Bonus: the restaurant makes great pizzas.

Hotel Pop Wuj (☎ 7756-2014; hotelpopwuj@yahoo.com; 6a Av 10-18; s/d Q100/200, without bathroom Q75/150) This family-run establishment sports 20 stylish rooms with tile floors and huge, comfy beds. Proprietor Pedro may be willing to negotiate rates if he's in the mood.

MIDRANGE

Hotel Chugüilá (☎ 7756-1134; hotelchuguila@yahoo.com; 5a Av 5-24; s/d Q100/200; P) This longstanding lodging feels like a colonial village with porches fronting on cobblestoned courtyards and decidedly rustic furnishings – though the decorative saddles and wagon wheels could use a dusting. Rooms are enormous, closets immense. Avoid the rear units, which get rumbled by morning buses.

Chalet House (☎ 7756-1360; www.chalethotelguatemala.com; 3a Calle C 7-44; s/d incl breakfast Q150/200; 🛜) In a quieter residential zone north of the center, this feels like an apartment building, though the rooftop terrace is an exotic extra. Simply furnished rooms have a few *típica* touches and real gas-fueled showers, and there's a guest kitchen.

Posada El Arco (☎ 7756-1255; 4a Calle 4-36; s/d Q150/200) Near the Arco Gucumatz, this homey spread is one of Chichi's more original accommodations. All eight rooms are idiosyncratically appointed, with Maya weavings, colonial bedsteads and sparkly bathrooms; room 8 is best. Lounge around in the garden and enjoy a northward view of the mountains. Reservations are a good idea.

Maya Lodge (☎ 7756-1167; 6a Calle A 4-08; s/d Q209/259; P) Right on the plaza, this has a colonial atmosphere, though it's a bit frayed at the edges. Adorned with woven rugs and Maya-style bedspreads, the 10 rooms are set alongside a patio dotted with rosebushes. The front restaurant is seldom occupied.

TOP END

Hotel Santo Tomás (☎ 7756-1061; hst@itelgua.com; 7a Av 5-32; s/d Q792/917; P 🏊) Chichi's loveliest hotel is big on plant-filled patios, tinkling fountains and decorations that include local handicrafts and religious relics. Each room has a tub and fireplace. It has a good bar and dining room (see opposite).

Mayan Inn (☎ 7756-1176; info@mayaninn.com.gt; 8a Calle A 1-91; s/d/tr Q922/1127/1229) Founded in 1932, the Inn today encompasses several restored colonial houses on either side of 8a Calle, their courtyards planted with tropical flora, their walls draped in indigenous textiles. Each of the 16 rooms is uniquely appointed, with carved armoires and fireplaces. Those on the south side have the best views. Proprietor Carlos Keller, whose German father came here for the banana trade, is a gracious host who'll show you around.

Eating

BUDGET

As may be expected, most restaurants here remain empty when not occupied by tour groups, with sullen underage waiters hovering in the background. The real action is in the central plaza, where attentive *abuelitas* (grandmas) ladle chicken soup, beef stew, tamales and *chiles rellenos* from huge pots as their beautiful daughters and granddaughters minister to the throngs of country folk sitting at long tables covered with oilcloth. At Vendedores de Arroz María by the central fountain, a *chuchito* – small tamal wrapped in a corn husk – and chocolate will get you change from Q10. What are called *tamales* here are made of rice and laced with sauce.

Sliced watermelon and papaya can be had at other stalls. As you eat, you can listen to the endless drone of vendors hawking gastritis cures.

Blintz Café (☎ 7755-1672; 5a Calle 5-26; ☺ 7:30am-9:30pm) Yes, you can find decent espresso in Chichi – plus smoothies and a variety of crepes – at this chic location inside a shopping center above the Hotel Chugüilá.

Tu Café (5a Av, main plaza; mains Q30-50; ☺ breakfast, lunch & dinner) The *plato vegetariano* here is soup, rice, beans, cheese, salad and tortillas, for a reasonable Q30. Add *lomito* (pork fillet) and it becomes a *plato típico*.

MIDRANGE

Las Brasas (6a Calle 4-52; mains Q45-60; ☺ breakfast, lunch & dinner) *Parrillas* (grilled meats) are the thing at this semi-formal upstairs hall. A gut-stuffing platter of char-grilled sausage, chicken or steak comes with halved potatoes, tortillas, rice, country cheese and black beans.

Casa de San Juan (☎ 7756-2086; 4a Av 5-58; mains Q60; ☺ breakfast, lunch & dinner) One of the more stylish eateries, the San Juan features art on the walls and the tables themselves, jugs of lilies, wrought-iron chairs and balconies overlooking the market. Offerings range from burgers and sandwiches to more traditional fare, including some pretty good *chiles rellenos* laced with zesty salsas.

Mayan Inn (☎ 7756-1176; 8a Calle A 1-91; 5-course lunch Q105; ☺ breakfast, lunch & dinner) The three dining rooms at Chichi's classiest hotel feature colonial-style furnishings and canvases by Guatemala's most renowned painter, Humberto Garabito. Waiters wear costumes evolved from the dress of Spanish colonial

---

COFRADÍAS

Chichicastenango's religious life is centered on traditional brotherhoods known as *cofradías*. Membership is an honorable civic duty, and election as leader is the greatest honor. Leaders must provide banquets and pay for festivities for the *cofradía* throughout their term. Though it is expensive, a *cofrade* (brotherhood member) happily accepts the burden, even going into debt if necessary.

Each of Chichi's 14 *cofradías* has a patron saint. Most notable is the *cofradía* of Santo Tomás, the town's patron saint. *Cofradías* march in procession to church every Sunday morning and during religious festivals, with the officers dressed in costumes showing their rank. Before them is carried a ceremonial staff topped by a silver crucifix or sun-badge that signifies the *cofradía's* patron saint. A drum, flute and perhaps a trumpet may accompany the procession, as do fireworks.

During major church festivals, effigies of the saints are carried in grand processions, and richly costumed dancers wearing wooden masks act out legends of the ancient Maya and of the Spanish conquest. For the rest of the year, these items are kept in storehouses-cum-workshops called *morerías*; two prominent ones are at the start of the trail leading up to the Maya shrine of Pascual Abaj (see p146).

farmers: colorful headdresses, sashes, black embroidered tunics, half-length trousers and squeaky leather sandals called *caïtes*. The food is less traditional – steak platters, roast chicken, mixed grills – though lavishly presented and abundantly served.

Hotel Santo Tomás (7a Av 5-32; 3-course dinner Q110; breakfast, lunch & dinner) Chichi's other top-end hotel has a sumptuous dining room with waiters in farmers' outfits, too. Try to get one of the courtyard tables to enjoy the sun and the marimba band that plays at market-day lunchtimes and the evenings before.

Getting There & Away

Buses heading south to Panajachel, Quetzaltenango and all other points reached from the Interamericana arrive and depart from 5a Calle near the corner of 5a Av, one block uphill from the Arco Gucumatz. Northbound buses leave from the opposite side of 5a Calle.

Antigua (3½ hours, 108km) Take any bus heading for Guatemala City and change at Chimaltenango.

Guatemala City (Q30, 2½ hours, 145km) Buses every 20 minutes from 3am to 5pm.

Los Encuentros (Q7, 30 minutes, 17km) Take any bus heading south for Guatemala City, Panajachel, Quetzaltenango and so on. Otherwise, frequent microbuses to Los Encuentros (Q5) leave from in front of the Telgua building on 7a Av.

Nebaj (103km) Take a bus to Santa Cruz del Quiché and change there.

Panajachel (Q10, 1½ hours, 37km) Buses at 9am, 11:30am, 12:30pm and 1pm; or take any southbound bus and change at Los Encuentros.

Quetzaltenango (Q20, three hours, 94km) Nine buses between 4:30am and 1pm; or take any southbound bus and change at Los Encuentros. Frequent microbuses (Q20) pass the Telgua building until 7:30am, then hourly till noon.

Santa Cruz del Quiché (Q7, 30 minutes,19km) Buses depart every 20 minutes, 5am to 7pm. Microbuses to Quiché leave from 5a Calle on the west side of 5a Av between 6am and 11pm.

Chichi Turkaj Tours (7742-1359; 5a Av 5-24), inside the Hotel Chugüilá, offers shuttles to Guatemala City (Q190), Antigua (Q125), Panajachel (Q140) and Quetzaltenango (Q125) on Monday and Friday at 9am and Sunday and Thursday at 5pm. **Agencia de Viaje Maya Chichi Van** (7756-2187; 6a Calle 6-45) goes to the same destinations on Sunday and Thursday, at similar fares. In most cases they

need at least five customers unless you're prepared to rent the whole vehicle (around Q750 to Antigua). These agencies also run tours to K'umarcaaj near Santa Cruz del Quiché, Nebaj and elsewhere.

SANTA CRUZ DEL QUICHÉ
pop 30,000 / elev 1979m

Without Chichicastenango's big market and attendant tourism, Santa Cruz – or just El Quiché – presents a less self-conscious slice of regional life and is refreshingly free of competition for tourist lucre. Just 19km north of Chichi, it's the capital of Quiché department, drawing a diverse populace on business and administrative affairs. The main market days are Thursday and Sunday, boosting the bustle considerably. Travelers who come here usually do so to visit K'umarcaaj, the ruins of the old K'iche' Maya capital, or to change buses en route further north.

The most exciting time to be here is mid-August during the **Fiestas Elenas** (www.fiestaselenas.com), a week of festivities and a proud display of indigenous traditions. It all leads up to the *convite feminino*, when El Quiché's women don masks and dance up a storm to marimba accompaniment.

Orientation & Information

Everything you need is within a few short blocks of the tripartite plaza. The top square is flanked on its east side by Gobernación (the departmental government palace), the middle one by the cathedral and *municipalidad* (town hall), and the bottom one by the big domed market building (though commerce actually takes place behind it). The main bus terminal is located four blocks south and two blocks east of the plaza. Note that each *zona* has its own street-avenue grid, so numbered *calles* and *avenidas* repeat themselves.

Quiché's **tourist office** (7755-1106; turismoenquiche@gmail.com; 8am-4:30pm Mon-Fri), inside the town hall, has all the answers and they'll give you a baroquely detailed map. **Banrural** (8am-5:30pm Mon-Fri, 8am-2pm Sat, 8am-noon Sun), at the plaza's north end, changes euros and has a Cajero 5B. Get online at **Bear Net** (0 Av 7-52; 8am-8:30pm), 1½ blocks south of the plaza.

Sights
K'UMARCAAJ

The ruins of the ancient K'iche' Maya capital of **K'umarcaaj** (aka Gumarkaaj or Utatlán; admission Q30;

WEAVING COOPERATIVES

Any traveler who's spent time in Chichicastenango, Antigua or Panajachel is familiar with the scene: an indigenous Guatemalan woman, weighed down by scarves, bags and blankets, approaches a group of tourists with a 'good price.' But the price isn't good enough for the tourists, who insist on bargaining it down to Wal-Mart levels. Never mind that the garment in question represents generations of accumulated artistic knowledge and takes weeks of painstaking labor plus a considerable investment in materials and dyes. In need of a quick sale, the vendor takes whatever price she can get.

Weaving cooperatives provide a viable alternative for Guatemalan women to carry on the traditional craft of backstrap loom weaving. Not only do the following associations of craftswomen pool the cost of materials, provide the artisans with a place to work and seek markets for their products, they also instill a sense of value among the weavers and help them get a fair price for their work. Most also give visitors a chance to observe the weaving process and a few offer instruction in the craft.

- Antigua: **Casa del Tejido Antiguo** (p109)
- Quetzaltenango: **Manos Creativas** (p163)
- San Antonio Palopó: **Tienda Candelaria** (p129)
- San Juan La Laguna: **Lema** (p138)
- San Pedro La Laguna: **Grupo Ecológico Teixchel** (p135)
- Santiago Atitlán: **Cojolya Association of Maya Women Weavers** (p130)
- Zunil: **Cooperativa Santa Ana** (p170)

8am-4:30pm) are 3km west of El Quiché. It is still a sacred site for the Maya, and contemporary rituals are customarily enacted there. Take a flashlight (torch).

The kingdom of K'iche' was established in late Postclassic times (about the 14th century) by a mixture of indigenous people and invaders from the Tabasco-Campeche border area in Mexico. Around 1400, King Ku'ucumatz founded K'umarcaaj and conquered many neighboring settlements. During the long reign of his successor Q'uik'ab (1425–75), the K'iche' kingdom extended its borders to Huehuetenango, Nebaj, Rabinal and the Pacific Slope. At the same time the Kaqchiquel, a vassal people who once fought alongside the K'iche', rebelled, establishing an independent capital at Iximché.

When Pedro de Alvarado and his Spanish conquistadors hit Guatemala in 1524, it was the K'iche', under their king Tecún Umán, who led the resistance to them. In the decisive battle fought near Quetzaltenango on February 12, 1524, Alvarado and Tecún locked in mortal combat. Alvarado prevailed. The defeated K'iche' invited him to visit K'umarcaaj. Smelling a rat, Alvarado enlisted the aid of his Mexican auxiliaries and the anti-K'iche' Kaqchiquel, and together they captured

the K'iche' leaders, burnt them alive in K'umarcaaj's main plaza and then destroyed the city.

The ruins have a fine setting, shaded by tall trees and surrounded by ravines. Archaeologists have identified 100 or so large structures here, but only limited restoration has been done. The **museum** at the entrance will help orientate you. The tallest of the structures round the central plaza, the Templo de Tohil (a sky god), is blackened by smoke and has a niche where contemporary prayer-men regularly make offerings to Maya gods.

Down the hillside to the right of the plaza is the entrance to a long tunnel known as the *cueva*. Legend has it that the K'iche' dug the tunnel as a refuge for their women and children in preparation for Alvarado's coming, and that a K'iche' princess was later buried in a deep shaft off this tunnel. Revered as the place where the K'iche' kingdom died, the *cueva* is sacred to highland Maya and is an important location for prayers, candle burning, offerings and chicken sacrifices.

If there's anyone around the entrance, ask permission before entering. Inside, the long tunnel (perhaps 100m long) is blackened with smoke and incense and littered with candles and flower petals. Use your flashlight and watch your footing: there are several side tunnels and at least one of them, on the right near the end, contains a deep, black shaft.

Gray 'Ruinas' microbuses depart for K'umarcaaj from in front of the cathedral in Santa Cruz every 20 minutes (Q1). The last one back is at 6:50pm.

Sleeping & Eating

The main hotel district is along 1a Av (Zona 5) north of the bus terminal, with at least five hotels within two blocks, and two more on either side along 9a Calle.

Posada Santa Cecilia (☎ 5332-8811; cnr 1a Av & 6a Calle; s/d Q75/170) Conveniently placed above an espresso vendor just south of the main plaza, this modern establishment offers a handful of bright, spiffy units with comfy beds and pretty quilts.

Hotel Rey K'iche (☎ 7755-0827; 8a Calle 0-39, Zona 5; s/d Q100/180; 🖳) Between the bus station and plaza, the Rey K'iche is generally excellent, with well-maintained, brick-walled rooms around a quiet interior and affable indigenous women running things. It has free drinking water and a decent cafe upstairs serving breakfast and dinner.

El Sitio Hotel (☎ 7755-3656; elsitiohotel@gmail.com; 9a Calle 0-41, Zona 5; s/d Q150/250; P 🛜) *Muy nice*, this recently built structure that resembles a modern evangelical church is two blocks north of the bus terminal. The efficiently run hotel offers business-class accommodations with a bit of *típica* decor and a stylish cafe.

For budget grub, there's plenty of grilling action going on around the market.

Café San Miguel (☎ 7755-1488; 2 Av 4-42; sandwiches Q12; ⏲ 8am-8pm) Opposite the cathedral, this little bakery-cafe is a popular gathering place, with good coffee and fresh baked goods on offer. Cookies are called *tostadas* here; *pan dormido* is bread that's been allowed to lie around for a few days.

Restaurant El Chalet (☎ 7755-0618; 2a Av 2-29, Zona 5; mains Q49-60; ⏲ breakfast, lunch & dinner) The specialty here is grilled meats, served with homemade salsas. You could make a light meal of the tortilla-sized portions. Dining is in pleasant gardens beneath an arbor. It's a few blocks east of the big clock tower.

Getting There & Away

El Quiché is the jumping-off point for the remote reaches of northern Quiché, which extend all the way to the Mexican border.

Departures from the bus station, a dusty lot at 1 Av and 10a Calle in Zona 5, include the following:

Chichicastenango (Q6, 30 minutes, 19km) Take any bus heading for Guatemala City. Otherwise, frequent microbuses depart from the southwest corner of the main plaza.

Guatemala City (Q30, three hours, 163km) Buses every 15 minutes, 3am to 5pm.

Huehuetenango (Q35, two hours, 173km) Microbuses every half hour from 6am to 5:30pm, via the new Río Negro road, 22km north.

Los Encuentros (Q15, one hour, 36km) Take any bus heading for Guatemala City.

Nebaj (Q25, two hours, 75km) Five buses via Sacapulas, 8:30am to 5pm. Microbuses run from 5:30am to 8pm.

Sacapulas (Q10, one hour, 45km) Take any bus or microbus bound for Nebaj or Uspantán.

Uspantán (Q25, 2¼ hours, 75km) Microbuses every 20 minutes from 6:30am to 8pm.

SACAPULAS

About 45km north of Santa Cruz del Quiché over a good paved road, Sacapulas sits at an isolated spot at the foot of the Cuchumatanes range, hugging the broad Río Negro. When the river is low, people bathe in a section near the bank that's heated by volcanic springs. Standing at the intersection of the El Quiché Nebaj and Huehuetenango–Cobán roads, the town makes a pleasant stopover, with a winning combination of busyness and riverside ease.

Traffic clatters over a metal bridge to and from the town center, up a rise on the south side. The main plaza is a gem, with two gigantic ceiba trees in front of a gleaming yellow arcade that contains the Banrural; the Cajero 5B is on the opposite side of the square.

On the southern bank, you'll find the friendly **Comedor & Hospedaje Tujaal** (☎ 4383-7657; s/d Q60/120). Rooms are on the grungy side but the location is brilliant, perched above the river, which you can hear flowing by from the open-air terrace. Go for rooms 1 or 11. There's a decent dining hall downstairs. Otherwise, head for **Comedor Berta** (mains Q20-30), amid the shops on the north side, where women in traditional garb slap out tortillas over a pile of glowing embers.

The spectacular mountain roads to Huehuetenango, Uspantán and Nebaj are all paved. Microbuses come and go continuously, from about 5:30am to 6pm, on the north side, with the occasional *camioneta* (pickup truck) rolling through. Destinations

THE HIGHLANDS

include Huehuetenango (Q20, 2½ hours), El Quiché (Q10, one hour) and Nebaj (Q15, 1½ hours). To get to Cobán, you'll have to change at Uspantán, but see the boxed text, below, before contemplating such a precarious journey.

USPANTÁN
pop 3500

Uspantán has customarily been used as a transfer point between Huehuetenango and Cobán along the 7W road. Now that the eastern stretch of that road has been destroyed by a landslide with no foreseeable plans for repair (see the boxed text, below), that is no longer the case. Nevertheless, Uspantán is a benevolent town, offering a few attractions of its own, and the sky-high journey through the Cuchumatanes is reason enough to travel there.

Founded by the Uspanteko Maya around the 6th century AD, it was originally dubbed Tz'unun Kaab' – place of hummingbirds. The severe repression it experienced during the armed conflict of the 1980s forged indigenous leader Rigoberta Menchú (see p32), who grew up a five-hour walk through the mountains in the village of Laj Chimel – though some locals wonder why she hasn't returned to her hometown. Cardamom is grown and pigs and sheep are raised in the surrounding slopes, and gravel mining is a key industry.

The helpful **tourist office** (☎ 7951-8125; visitasuspantan@gmail.com; ⊗ 8am-6pm Mon-Fri), on the central plaza, offers a range of interesting trips, including one to the cloud forest around Laj Chimel (Q140 per person, five-person minimum), with guides recounting the civil war atrocities that occurred here. Another tour visits the Maya ceremonial center at Cerro Xoqoneb' (Q50 per person), a half-hour hike from the center of town.

Sleeping & Eating

Hotel La Villa Maya (☎ 5423-4493; 6a Calle 2-17; s/d Q55/100, without bathroom Q25/50; P) Four blocks east of the plaza is this humble, motel-style guesthouse, with clean rooms behind a row of bright yellow pillars decorated with Maya motifs.

Hotel Posada Doña Leonor (☎ 7951-8041; 6a Calle 4-25; s/d/tr Q75/130/165; P ⊗) This well-maintained option a couple of blocks east of the plaza features 21 rooms around a courtyard with a cook shack in the middle for breakfast and supper. You'll find firm beds, fresh paint, and huge spotless bathrooms with blasting-hot showers.

Kape San José (7 Av 4-33, Zona 2; mains Q25-40; ⊗ breakfast, lunch & dinner) Meat is the go in this tropically decorated hut three blocks west of the plaza; the *parrillada* (mixed grill, Q60) is hard to beat. In the evenings, sports events are projected on a big screen.

Restaurant Al Ast (6a Av 7-50; mains Q30-40; ⊗ 7:30am-9pm) Catalonian cuisine in Uspantán? Go figure. Hailing from that Iberian region, the owner of this unpretentious eatery whips up things like *fidevada* (a paella variation) and *butifarra* sausage with green beans.

ROAD OUT

Renowned for its incredible views, highway 7W was until recently the most direct route from Huehuetenango to Cobán. But in late 2008, disaster struck when a mountain collapsed atop the road at Cerro de los Chorros, leaving its east end in shambles. Since then, federal authorities have made no attempt to rebuild the 2km stretch of the road between the village of Chicamán and San Cristóbal Veracruz, considering the volatility of this fault zone. Yet so essential is it to regional commerce that local communities chose to bridge the gap themselves, however makeshift their efforts. But the hastily constructed detour is considered unsafe, and the government has posted signs warning of the perils of attempting the journey.

Buses going from Uspantán to Cobán regularly plow through the debris anyway, despite the dangers. By all accounts, it's a hair-raising journey. After a section littered with boulders, the road seems to end at the brink of an abyss, then descends relentlessly into a valley along a rock-strewn track and up again over a similarly ravaged surface, as drivers boldly navigate hairpin turns and passengers pray their vehicle doesn't lose its grip over the muddy surface. Things get even worse when it rains and even the most intrepid drivers refuse to risk the gap, so passengers have to hike through the mud for 2km to continue the journey. A far saner alternative is to detour to Guatemala City, a loss of about four hours but an infinite gain in peace of mind.

Getting There & Away

Microbuses for Quiché (Q25, 2¼ hours), via Sacapulas, leave whenever full from in front of the plaza's bandshell, until 6:15pm; chicken buses depart at 3am and 7am. For Cobán (Q30, 3¼ hours), microbuses go twice an hour from 3:30am to 6am, then hourly till 3:30pm, but see the boxed text, opposite. For Nebaj, there's one direct microbus (coming from Cobán) at 4pm. Otherwise, get a Sacapulas microbus and change at the *entronque de Nebaj* (Nebaj turnoff), about 8km before Sacapulas.

NEBAJ

pop 35,900 / elev 2000m

Hidden in a remote fold of the Cuchumatanes mountains north of Sacapulas is the Triángulo Ixil (Ixil Triangle), a 2300-sq-km zone comprising the towns of Santa María Nebaj, San Juan Cotzal and San Gaspar Chajul, as well as dozens of outlying villages and hamlets. The local Ixil Maya people, though they suffered perhaps more than anybody in Guatemala's civil war, cling proudly to their traditions and speak the Ixil language. Nebaj women are celebrated for their beautiful purple, green and yellow pom-pommed hair braids, and for their *huipiles* and *rebozos* (shawls), with many bird and animal motifs.

Living in this beautiful mountain vastness has long been both a blessing and a curse. The invading Spaniards found it difficult to conquer, and they laid waste to the inhabitants when they did. During the civil war years, massacres and disappearances were rife, with more than two dozen villages destroyed. According to estimates by church groups and human-rights organizations, some 25,000 Ixil inhabitants (of a population of 85,000) were either killed or displaced by the army between 1978 and 1983 as part of the genocidal campaign to expunge guerrilla activity. You may hear some appalling personal experiences from locals while you're here.

The people of the Ixil Triangle are making a heroic effort to build a new future with the help of development organizations and NGOs, whose workers you're likely to encounter during your visit.

Orientation & Information

Nebaj sits neatly at the foot of a bowl ringed by green mountains. A block east of the Parque Principal is the market (busiest on Sunday), with the bus terminal just below it. Calz 15 de Septiembre runs northeast from the Parque to become the road to Cotzal and Chajul.

The **tourist office** (☎ 7755-8182; ✆ 8am-5pm Mon-Sat, 8am-noon Sun), inside the Mercado de Artesanías (see p156), can answer any question as long as it's posed in Spanish.

Banrural (✆ 8:30am-5pm Mon-Fri, 7am-1pm Sat), on the Parque Principal, changes traveler's checks; the Cajero 5B is in the Town Hall building, opposite the park. The **post office** (5a Av 4-37) is one block northwest of the park. **La Red**, inside Restaurante El Descanso, offers internet access. Otherwise, try **System-IC** (Calz 15 de Septiembre; ✆ 8am-8pm).

Sights

The formidable **Iglesia de Nebaj** dominates the south side of the park. Inside, to the left of the entrance is a memorial to Juan José Gerardi, the socially progressive priest who as bishop of Quiché witnessed widespread human rights abuses here. Soon after he released a report about these atrocities, Gerardi himself was assassinated. That incident is the subject of a book by Francisco Goldman, *The Art of Political Murder*. Several hundred crosses around the monument memorialize the Nebaj inhabitants who were murdered during a massacre in the early 1980s.

Activities

HIKING

Started as a Peace Corps project, **El Descanso** (☎ 5311-9100; 3a Calle, Zona 1) houses a useful info center and espresso provider. It offers a range of hikes, courses, projects and other activities. The hiking component of the organization, **Guías Ixil**, offers half-day walks to **Las Cataratas** (Q75 for one person plus Q25 for each extra person), a series of waterfalls north of town, or around town with visits to the **sacred sites** of the *costumbristas* (people who still practice non-Christian Maya rites). They also lead three-day treks over the Cuchumatanes to Todos Santos Cuchumatán (see p180).

Las Cataratas is easy enough to reach on your own. Walk 1.25km past the Hotel Ilebal Tenam along the Chajul road to a bridge over a small river. Immediately before the bridge, turn left (north) onto a gravel road and follow the river. Walking downriver for an hour (6km one way), you'll pass several small waterfalls before reaching a larger waterfall about 25m high.

THE HIGHLANDS

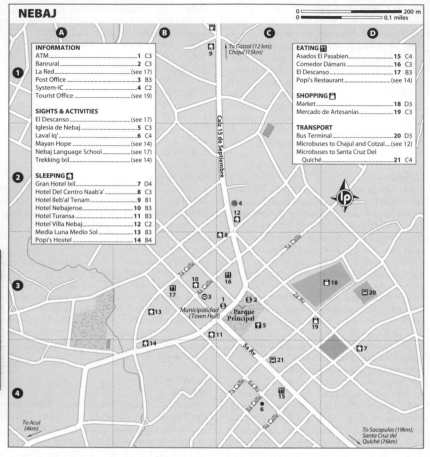

NEBAJ

0 — 200 m
0 — 0.1 miles

INFORMATION
ATM 1 C3
Banrural 2 C3
La Red .... (see 17)
Post Office 3 B3
System-IC 4 C2
Tourist Office .... (see 19)

SIGHTS & ACTIVITIES
El Descanso .... (see 17)
Iglesia de Nebaj 5 C3
Laval Iq' 6 C4
Mayan Hope .... (see 14)
Nebaj Language School .... (see 17)
Trekking Ixil .... (see 14)

SLEEPING
Gran Hotel Ixil 7 D4
Hotel Del Centro Naab'a' 8 C3
Hotel Ileb'al Tenam 9 B1
Hotel Nebajense 10 B3
Hotel Turansa 11 B3
Hotel Villa Nebaj 12 C2
Media Luna Medio Sol 13 B3
Popi's Hostel 14 B4

EATING
Asados El Pasabien 15 C4
Comedor Dámaris 16 C3
El Descanso 17 B3
Popi's Restaurant .... (see 14)

SHOPPING
Market 18 D3
Mercado de Artesanías 19 C3

TRANSPORT
Bus Terminal 20 D3
Microbuses to Chajul and Cotzal.... (see 12)
Microbuses to Santa Cruz Del
  Quiché 21 C4

To Cotzal (12 km);
Chajul (15km)

Calz 15 de Septiembre

Municipalidad (Town Hall)
Parque Principal

To Acul (4km)

To Sacapulas (19km);
Santa Cruz del Quiché (76km)

The group **Laval Iq'** (☎ 7755-8337; www.region ixil.com; cnr 6a Av & 8a Calle) is comprised of former civil war combatants from 19 Ixil communities. Not only do these guides know the trails better than anyone, they also have lots of tales to tell about the region's turbulent history. Laval Iq' has designed two- to four-day treks to seven different parts of the Ixil region, each taking long-trodden trails across mountain landscapes to indigenous communities. The Ruta Vi' Cruz visits Chajul, then continues east via former guerrilla camps near Tzitze and climbs the Cerro Vi' Cruz where a downed helicopter from the conflict remains. Another hike, the Ruta Wukup Noj, takes off from Nuevo Amak'txe'l, 54km north of Chajul, and explores the nearby

cloud forests where quetzals may be spotted. The two-day Ruta Markao visits Cocop, 4km east of Nebaj, one of the worst hit of all villages in the civil war. Treks of two/three/four days cost Q700/1130/1580 per person, including transport, meals and lodging at *posadas comunitarias* – community-run lodges with wooden-board beds, drinking water and toilets.

Trekking Ixil (☎ 7756-0159), based at Popi's Restaurant (see opposite), leads similar two- and three-day hikes to a number of villages in the region.

If you prefer to hike on your own, take a copy of the *Guía de Senderismo Región Ixil* (Q50), with detailed descriptions and maps (in Spanish) for 20 treks in the Ixil region, and organize lodging and food on arrival in villages. This guidebook is sold at the tourist office in the Mercado de Artesanías (see p156). There are *posadas comunitarias* at Xexocom, Chortiz and Parramos Grande, west of Nebaj, on a possible four-day hike route.

VOLUNTEER WORK

Mayan Hope (☎ 7756-0159; www.mayanhope.org), a US-based NGO that supports educational opportunities for students with disabilities, uses volunteers to work as teacher aides, eco-tour guides and agricultural consultants. It's associated with Popi's Hostel and Restaurant (see below and right).

Courses

Nebaj Language School (☎ 5311-9100; www.nebaj. com/nebajlanguageschool.html; El Descanso Bldg, 3a Calle, Zona 1) charges Q600 for 20 hours a week of one-to-one Spanish lessons, including some hiking and cultural activities. Home stays, with two meals a day, cost Q500 a week. You can also learn how to make regional dishes like *boxboles* (corn dough wrapped in squash leaves, served with a spicy peanut sauce) for Q50 per hour.

Festivals & Events

Nebaj's annual **festival**, coinciding with the Assumption of the Virgin Mary, runs for 10 days in mid-August.

Sleeping

Hotel Nebajense (cnr 5a Av & 4a Calle; r per person Q25) Though it's quite basic, you'll feel at home here. There are two to five lumpy beds per fluorescent-lit room on the upper level, but it's all kept clean and there's lots of family activity on the sun-splashed patio. Guests may share the kitchen.

Popi's Hostel (☎ 7756-0159; 5a Calle 6-74; dm Q30) This popular cafe-bakery has a couple of plain dorm rooms, each with six beds and bathroom. Choose your bed carefully – some sag dramatically. Profits go to support Mayan Hope (see above).

Media Luna Medio Sol (☎ 5749-7450; www.nebaj. com/hostel.htm; 3a Calle 6-15; dm Q35, r per person Q45; ☎) Entry to this hostel is via a passageway beside a store. Upstairs, three six-bed dorm rooms and one private room share toilets and showers. There are a ping-pong table, sauna and kitchen facilities to keep you busy.

our pick **Hotel Ileb'al Tenam** (☎ 7755-8039; Calz 15 de Septiembre; s/d Q55/95, without bathroom Q30/555; P) This cordially managed lodging at the north edge of town (only 500m from the park) features two sections: a long wooden house with simple rooms along a plank veranda; and at the rear, an 'annex' with more modern units around a tranquil patio.

Gran Hotel Ixil (☎ 7755-8036; cnr 8a Av & 9a Calle; s/d Q60/100; P) Rooms here are set around a leafy courtyard with good hammocking opportunities. The ones on the top level are more spacious, with wood-beamed ceilings. Warning: services at the evangelical church round the corner can reach thunderous volumes.

Hotel Del Centro Naab'a' (☎ 4145-6243; 3a Calle 3-18; s/d Q65/130; P) Neat and clean with friendly staff, this place won't win any awards for interior decoration, but the tile floors sparkle and the beds are nice and firm.

Hotel Turansa (☎ 4144-7609; cnr 5a Calle & 6a Av; s/d from Q67/134; P) This friendly, central establishment has decent-sized rooms along plant-draped balconies. Top-floor triples open on a sunny terrace.

Hotel Villa Nebaj (☎ 7756-0005; Calz 15 de Septiembre 2-37; s/d Q175/250, with bathroom Q85/150; P) Nebaj's fanciest hotel is a pretty good deal – slate-tiled courtyards with fountains and well-decorated, comfortable rooms in a three-story building.

Eating

Popi's Restaurant (☎ 7756-0159; 5a Calle 6-74; mains Q22-40; ☺ breakfast, lunch & dinner) This low-key bakery/hostel bakes bread and pies and whips up gringo comfort foods. The copious breakfast menu includes three-egg omelets, granola and burritos. Big Popi is a good resource for local info.

Comedor Dámaris (4a Calle; meals Q30; ☺ lunch & dinner) The set lunch here might be a tasty *caldo de res* (a broth with large chunks of meat and veggies), half an avocado, tortillas and a soft drink.

El Descanso (3a Calle, Zona 1; mains Q30-50; ☺ breakfast, lunch & dinner) Sharing a property with the Nebaj Language School, this cozy restaurant features a bar and lounge areas, good music and board games in Nebaj's most alternative ambience. A range of snacks, salads and soups is served.

Asados El Pasabien (cnr 5a Av & 9a Calle; mains Q30-40; ☺ lunch & dinner) Steaks, chicken and shrimp are

THE HIGHLANDS

skillfully grilled and served up with heaping portions of halved potatoes and salad at this locally popular dining hall.

Shopping

You can buy local textiles inside the **Mercado de Artesanías** (Handicrafts Market; cnr 7a Calle & 2a Av, Zona 1; 9am-5pm Mon-Sat, 9am-noon Sun). The numerous vendor stalls offer well-made *rebozos, cintas* (the pom-pommed braid woven into Ixil women's hair) and *huipiles*, which can cost anywhere from Q300 to Q5000, depending on quality.

Getting There & Away

Microbuses bound for Santa Cruz del Quiché, via Sacapulas, go every half hour from 4am until 5pm (Q25, two hours), departing from behind the church at the corner of 5a Av and 7a Calle. To head west to Huehuetenango or east to Cobán, change at Sacapulas (p151). Microbuses to Cobán depart at 5am and noon from the Quetzal gas station on 15 de Septiembre, but see the boxed text, p152. There's a midnight bus all the way to Guatemala City (Q55, 5½ hours) via Chichicastenango, leaving from the main terminal behind the market.

AROUND NEBAJ
Chajul
pop 15,3000

A good paved road winds northeast through piney slopes to Chajul, an impoverished but intensely traditional village, where hundreds-of-years-old customs are still widely practiced. Women stroll arm-in-arm, wearing maroon *cortes* (wraparound skirts), earrings made with silver coins, and bright blue or purple *huipiles* woven with geometric patterns. Along the dirt streets, adobe structures with tile roofs propped up by carved wooden pillars are interspersed with patches of maize and squash. Tuesday and Friday are market days.

The small **Museo Maya Ixil** (6:30am-5:30pm) displays local artifacts and jewelry, as well as evidence of Chajul's resistance during the armed conflict of the 1980s.

Limitless Horizons Ixil (5763-8030; www.limitlesshorizonsixil.org), an NGO based in Chajul working to expand educational opportunities for local children, offers home visits and meals with indigenous families, guided hikes to sacred Maya sites, classes in weaving and the Ixil language, and lots of other fun and fascinat-

ing activities. LHI also accepts volunteers for a variety of projects.

Among a handful of places to stay is the basic **Hotel San Gaspar** (5230-6468; s/d Q75/120), two blocks below the church. Run by friendly people, the **Posada Vetz K'aol** (5784-8802; posada@asociacionchajulense.org; r per person with/without bathroom Q80/66) has five rooms, one with private bathroom, and there's a sitting room with fireplace. Located a 10-minute stroll from the center of Chajul, down a little path off the road from Nebaj, it's owned by a local cooperative that offers half-day tours of the area for Q50 per person.

Microbuses to Chajul (Q7, 45 minutes) depart every 20 minutes or so until 7:30pm from in front of the Hotel Villa Nebaj, on Calz 15 de Septiembre in Nebaj.

Acul

Acul, 4km west of Nebaj, was founded as the first *polo de desarrollo* (pole of development) in 1983. Considered 'strategic hamlets,' these settlements were actually constructed to enable the army to keep inhabitants from having contact with the guerrillas. After the civil war, some people returned to their original homes but others stayed on since they'd received plots of land. Set astride the bucolic Río Acul Valley, it retains a functional appearance, with stores and evangelical prayer halls along either side of a broad dirt street. These days the main activities are weaving, cattle ranching and loom building.

Just north of Acul is a pair of farms devoted to the making of cheese. They were started by two immigrant brothers, the Azzaris, cheese makers in their native Italian Alps who moved to Guatemala in the 1930s, perhaps choosing the Acul valley because of its alpine appearance. Older brother José gained renown as a prize wrestler before being killed in the ring.

Both farms offer excellent accommodations. The first you come to, the **Hacienda Mil Amores** (5704-4817; r per person Q183), has four country cabins on a hillside, and they serve a superb lunch (Q55, by reservation). Just across the way, the humbler **Hacienda San Antonio** (5702-1907; r per person Q153) has half a dozen neat, wood-floored rooms, some with hot-water bathroom, and does meals (Q45). Microbuses ply the paved road between Nebaj and Acul every half hour, or consider hiking over with Guías Ixil (p153) or Trekking Ixil (p154) and taking the bus back.

WESTERN HIGHLANDS

The mountainous departments of Quetzaltenango, Totonicapán and Huehuetenango are generally less frequented by tourists than regions closer to Guatemala City. But with extraordinarily dramatic scenery and vibrant indigenous culture, this part of the country presents an invariably fascinating panorama. Highlights of any visit include Quetzaltenango, Guatemala's second-largest city, with an ever-growing language-school and volunteer-work scene; the pretty nearby town of Zunil, with its volcanically heated springs; ascents of the volcanoes around Quetzaltenango; and the remote mountain enclave of Todos Santos Cuchumatán, north of Huehuetenango, with a strong traditional culture and excellent walking possibilities.

CUATRO CAMINOS

Westward from Los Encuentros, the Interamericana twists and turns ever higher, bringing still more dramatic scenery and cooler temperatures. It reaches its highest point, 3670m, after the village of Nahualá, 42km from Los Encuentros. Seventeen kilometers beyond, you come to another important highway junction, Cuatro Caminos (Four Ways). You'll know the place by the many parked buses and people milling about as they change buses. The road southwest leads to Quetzaltenango (15km); to the east is Totonicapán (12km); northward, the Interamericana continues to Huehuetenango (77km) and La Mesilla on the Mexican border (154km).

QUETZALTENANGO

pop 159,700 / elev 2367m

Quetzaltenango may well be the perfect Guatemalan town – not too big, not too small, enough foreigners to support a good range of hotels and restaurants, but not so many that it loses its national flavor. The Guatemalan 'layering' effect is at work in the city center – once the Spanish moved out, the Germans moved in and their architecture gives the zone a somber, even Gothic, feel.

Quetzaltenango is big, like its name – which the locals kindly shorten to Xela (*shell*-ah), itself an abbreviation of the original Quiché Maya name, Xelajú – but by Guatemalan standards, it is an orderly, clean and safe city. It tends to attract a more serious type of traveler – people who really want to learn Spanish

and then stay around and get involved in the myriad volunteer projects on offer.

Xela also functions as a base for a range of spectacular hikes through the surrounding countryside – the ascent to the summit of Volcán Tajumulco (Central America's highest point) and the three-day trek to Lago de Atitlán, to name a few.

History

Quetzaltenango came under the sway of the K'iche' Maya of K'umarcaaj when they began their great expansion in the 14th century. Before that it had been a Mam Maya town. It was near here that the K'iche' leader Tecún Umán was defeated and killed by the Spanish conquistador Pedro de Alvarado in 1524.

The town prospered in the late-19th-century coffee boom, with brokers opening warehouses and *finca* (plantation) owners coming to town to buy supplies. This boom busted when a combined earthquake and eruption of Santa María in 1902 wreaked mass destruction. Still, the city's position at the intersection of roads to the Pacific Slope, Mexico and Guatemala City guaranteed it some degree of prosperity. Today it's again busy with commerce, of the indigenous, foreign and *ladino* varieties.

Orientation

The heart of Xela is the oblong Parque Centro América, graced with neoclassical monuments and surrounded by the city's important buildings. Most accommodations are within a few blocks of this plaza.

The main bus station is Terminal Minerva, on the western outskirts and next to one of the principal markets.

Information

BOOKSTORES

North & South (Map p160; 8a Calle & 15a Av 13-77, Zona 1) Broad selection of titles on Latin America, politics, poetry and history. Also plenty of new and used guidebooks and Spanish student resources.

Vrisa Books (Map p160; 15a Av 3-64) Excellent range of secondhand books in English and European languages, including Lonely Planet guides, plus a rental library (Q20 per book per week).

EMERGENCY

Asistur (tourist assistance; ☎ 4149-1104)
Bomberos (firefighters; ☎ 7761-2002)

Cruz Roja (Red Cross; ☎ 7761-2746)
Policía Municipal (☎ 7761-5805)
Policía Nacional (☎ 7765-4990)

INTERNET ACCESS

It only costs Q5 to Q6 per hour to get online
here. See the publication *XelaWho* for a wi-fi
hot-spot finder.

Café Digital (Map p159; Diagonal 9 19-77A, Zona 1)
Café El Guru (Map p160; 6a Calle 14-55, Zona 1)
Guate Linda (Map p160; 12a Calle 3-12, Zona 1)
Xela Pages (Map p159; 4 Calle 19-48, Zona 1)

INTERNET RESOURCES

Xela Pages (www.xelapages.com) Packed with information about Xela and nearby attractions, with a useful
discussion forum.

LAUNDRY

It costs around Q5 to wash and dry 1kg loads
at a laundry here.

Lavandería Mini-Max (Map p160; 14a Av C47;
☽ 7:30am-7:30pm Mon-Sat)
Rapi-Servicio Laundromat (Map p160; 7a Calle 13-
25A, Zona 1; ☽ 8am-6:30pm Mon-Sat)

MEDIA

These English-language publications are
available free in bars, restaurants and cafes
around town.

EntreMundos (www.entremundos.org) Published every
two months by the Xela-based organization of the same
name, this newspaper has plenty of information on political developments and volunteer projects in the region.
XelaWho (www.xelawho.com) Billing itself as 'Quetzaltenango's leading Culture & Nightlife Magazine,' this little
monthly lists cultural events in the city, with some fairly
irreverent takes on life in Guatemala in general.

MEDICAL SERVICES

Both of the following hospitals maintain a
24-hour emergency service.

Hospital Privado Quetzaltenango (Map p159;
☎ 7761-4381; Calle Rodolfo Robles 23-51) Usually has an
English-speaking doctor on staff.
Hospital San Rafael (Map p160; ☎ 7761-4414; 9a
Calle 10-41, Zona 1)

MONEY

Parque Centro América is the place to go for
banks. **Banco Industrial** (Map p160; ☽ 9am-6:30pm
Mon-Fri, 9am-1pm Sat) has branches on the north
and east sides of the plaza. Both change traveler's checks and give advances on Visa; the
latter, in the *municipalidad* building, has an

ATM on the Plus network. There's a Cajero 5B
in the Edificio Rivera just north of the Muni.

POST

Main post office (Map p160; Calz Sinforoso Aguilar
15-07, Zona 1)

TELEPHONE

Use your Skype account at any of the cybercafes listed under Internet Access. Otherwise,
there are four card phones outside **Telgua** (Map
p160; Calz Sinforoso Aguilar).

TOURIST INFORMATION

Inguat (Map p160; ☎ /fax 7761-4931; ☽ 9am-5pm Mon-
Fri, 9am-1pm Sat), at the southern end of Parque
Centro América, is hit or miss, with staff
attitudes ranging from helpful to clueless.

There's a plethora of tourist maps circulat-
ing; look for them at internet cafes, language
schools and hotels. Though they're essentially
advertising flyers, the better ones like *Xelamap*
include plenty of useful information, including an events calendar, hiking options and
current bus fares.

TRAVEL AGENCIES

Adrenalina Tours (Map p160; ☎ 7761-4509; www.
adrenalinatours.com; 13a Av, Zona 1, inside Pasaje
Enríquez) Flights and package deals to anywhere in the
country (and the world); it has its own fleet of shuttle
buses for intercity transport.
Altiplano's Tour Operator (Map p160; ☎ 7766-9614;
www.altiplanos.com.gt; 12a Av 3-35, Zona 1) Besides hikes
and tours, it offers luggage storage, bike rentals and hotel
bookings.
Diversity Tours (Map p160; ☎ /fax 7761-2545; www.
diversitytours.com.gt; 15a Av 3-86, Zona 1) Student
airfares and international flights, plus Inguat-authorized
guides for local tours.
Ícaro Tours (Map p160; ☎ 7765-8205; www.icarotours.
com; 15a Av 6-75, Zona 1)

Sights

PARQUE CENTRO AMÉRICA

Most of Xela's sights crowd in and around
the broad central plaza, known as the **Parque
Centro América**. The original version, designed by Italian architect Alberto Porta in
the 1800s, comprised two separate parks;
these were combined in a 1930s update
into its current oblong shape. Most notable of the monuments scattered along its
expanse is the **Templo Abesta**, a rotunda of
Ionic columns near the north end, and in the

THE HIGHLANDS

QUETZALTENANGO

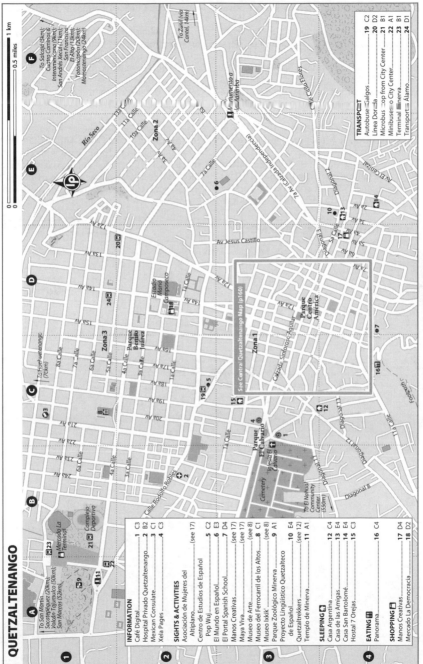

INFORMATION

Café Digital..	1 C3
Hospital Privado Quetzaltenango..........	2 B2
Mexican Consulate.................................	3 C1
Xela Pages...	4 C3

SIGHTS & ACTIVITIES

Asociación de Mujeres del Altiplano.....	(see 17)
Centro de Estudios de Español Pop Wuj..	5 C2
El Mundo en Español.............................	6 E3
El Portal Spanish School.........................	7 D4
Manos Creativas....................................	(see 17)
Maya Viva..	(see 17)
Museo de Arte.......................................	(see 8)
Museo del Ferrocarril de los Altos.........	8 C1
Museo Ixkik...	(see 8)
Parque Zoológico Minerva......................	9 A1
Proyecto Lingüístico Quetzalteco de Español..	10 E4
Quetzaltrekkers....................................	(see 12)
Templo de Minerva...............................	11 A1

SLEEPING ☐

Casa Argentina......................................	12 C4
Casa de las Amigas...............................	13 E4
Casa San Bartolomé.............................	14 E4
Hostal 7 Orejas....................................	15 C3

EATING ☐

Panorama..	16 C4

SHOPPING ☐

Manos Creativas....................................	17 D4
Mercado La Democracia........................	18 D2

To San Martín Sacatepéquez (20km); Volcán Tajumulco (50km); San Marcos (52km);

To San Martín Sacatepéquez (20km);

To Salcajá (5km); Cuatro Caminos & Interamericana (9km); San Andrés Xecul (17km); San Francisco El Alto (18km); Totonicapán (20km); Momostenango (24km)

To Zunil (via Cantel, 14km)

To Huehuetenango (70km)

To Huehuetenango

Río Seco

Zona 2

Zona 3

Zona 1

Av Jesús Castillo

Estadio Mario Camposeco

Parque Benito Juárez

Parque Centro América

Parque El Calvario

Calle Rodolfo Robles

Cementerio

Iglesia El Calvario

Hotel Nohual Community Center (550m)

Mercado La Terminal

Complejo Deportivo

Monumento a Marimba

Calle Cinta Flores

Calz. Sinforoso Aguilar

Calz. (Calzada Independencia)

See Central Quetzaltenango Map (p160)

1 km / 0.5 miles

center a pillar is dedicated to Justo Rufino Barrios, the 19th-century president whose 'reforms' transferred land ownership from Maya peasants to coffee-plantation owners. At the southern end, the Casa de Cultura houses the **Museo de Historia Natural** (Map p160; ☎ 7761-6427; 7a Calle; admission Q6; ☽ 8am-noon & 2-6pm Mon-Fri, 9am-5pm Sat & Sun). The museum holds a hodgepodge of Maya artifacts, vintage photos, dried leaves, old coins, marimbas, sports trophies, stuffed mammals and birds, all displayed in cases reminiscent of elementary school outings.

The gleaming white facade of the **Iglesia del Espíritu Santo** is the only bit that remains of the original 1535 construction, pulverized by the quakes of 1853 and 1902. The modern

Metropolitan Cathedral behind it was finished in the 1990s.

The **municipalidad** (town hall; Map p160), at the northeastern end of the park, was rebuilt after the 1902 earthquake in the grandiose neoclassical style. Step inside to see a flowery mosaic of the town seal. Another neoclassical structure just north, the **Edificio Rivera**, has been handsomely renovated (complete with fast-food franchise).

On the west side of the park between 4a and 5a Calles is the **Pasaje Enríquez**, an imposing arcade built to be lined with elegant shops – but as Quetzaltenango has few elegant shoppers, it instead houses an assortment of travel agencies, language institutes, cafes and one major bar.

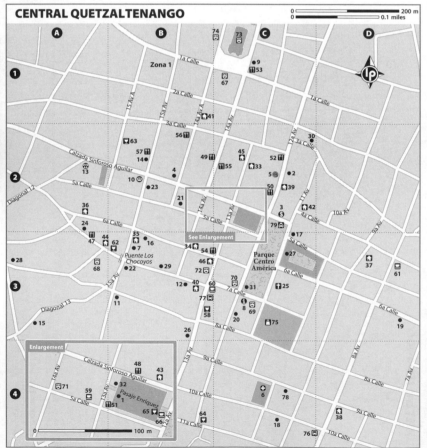

CENTRAL QUETZALTENANGO

OTHER SIGHTS

About 2km northwest of Parque Centro América, near the Terminal Minerva bus station, is the **Parque Zoológico Minerva** (Map p159; ☎ 7763-5637; Av Las Américas 0-50, Zona 3; ☺ 9am-5pm Tue-Sun), a zoo-park with monkeys, coyotes and Barbary sheep, plus a few rides for children. Outside the zoo on an island in the middle of 4a Calle stands the neoclassical **Templo de Minerva** (Map p159), built by dictator Estrada Cabrera to honor the Roman goddess of education and to inspire Guatemalans to new heights of learning.

Quetzaltenango's railroad station, 1km east of the Templo de Minerva along 4a Calle, lay dormant for years until the city converted it into the **Centro Intercultural de Quetzaltenango**, with schools of art and dance and three fine museums. The **Museo Ixkik'** (Map p159; ☎ 7761-6472; 4a Calle & 19 Av, Zona 3; admission Q25; ☺ 9am-1pm & 3-6pm) is devoted to Maya weaving and traditional outfits. The **Museo de Arte** (Map p159; 4a Calle & 19 Av, Zona 3; ☺ 8am-noon & 2-6pm) holds 200 paintings by Guatemala's leading modernists, including Efraín Recinos, Juan Antonio Franco and the landscape artist José Luis Álvarez. And the **Museo del Ferrocarril de los Altos** (Map p159; admission Q6; ☺ 8am-noon & 2-6pm) covers the ambitious rail project that connected Quetzaltenango to the Pacific coast but operated for just three years: 1930 to 1933.

Activities

VOLCANO ASCENTS & TREKS

There are many exciting walks and climbs to be done from Xela. **Volcán Tajumulco** (4220m), 50km northwest, is the highest point in Central America and is a challenging trip of one long day from the city or two days with a night camping on the mountain. This includes about five hours' walking up from the starting point, Tuhichan (2½ hours by bus from Xela).

With early starts, **Volcán Santa María** (3772m), towering to the south of the city, and the highly active **Santiaguito** (2488m), on Santa María's southwest flank, can both be

THE HIGHLANDS

done in long mornings from Xela, though the tough, slippery trail is recommended only for seasoned hikers. You start walking at the village of Llanos del Pinal, 5km south of Xela (Q5 by bus), from which it's four to five hours up to the summit of Santa María. Getting too close to Santiaguito is dangerous, so people usually just look at it from a point about 1½ hours' walk from Llanos del Pinal.

Kaqchikel Tours (Map p160; ☎ 5010-4465; www.kaqchikeltours.com/ENindex.htm; 7a Calle 15-36, Zona 1) is a locally owned outfit specializing in volcano ascents. Two-day Tajumulco trips cost around Q370 per person. Kaqchikel also offers full-moon ascents of Santa María (Q150) and challenging two-day Santiaguito trips (Q600), camping on a small hill as close as is safely possible to the crater. A three-day Quetzaltenango–Lago de Atitlán trek is Q650, and a five-day Nebaj–Todos Santos jaunt across the Cuchumatanes mountains is Q1350. Prices (all with a minimum of four participants) include transportation, food, equipment and a guide.

Monte Verde Tours (Map p160; ☎ 7761-6105; www.monte-verdetours.com; 13a Av 8-34, Zona 1) Does a variety of volcano hikes and offbeat tours around Xela.

Quetzaltrekkers (Map p159; ☎ 7765-5895; www.quetzaltrekkers.com; Diagonal 12 8-37, Zona 1) Most of the guides at this unique outfit are foreign volunteers (and experienced trekkers can join their ranks). Two-day hikes to Fuentes Georginas and Pico Zunil (Q380 per person), three-day trips to Lago de Atitlán (Q600) and six-day treks to Nebaj (Q1100) embark on a weekly basis; check the calendar to see when they go. Based at the Casa Argentina hotel, they provide both monetary and logistical support for various social projects.

CYCLING

Biking is a great way to explore the surrounding countryside or commute to Spanish class. Fuentes Georginas, San Andrés Xecul and the steam vents at Los Vahos (see p169) are all attainable day trips. **Vrisa Books** (Map p160; 15a Av 3-64, Zona 1) rents mountain and town bikes for Q40/100/200 per day/week/month; it also offers cycling tours to some of the above destinations.

Courses
LANGUAGE COURSES

Quetzaltenango's many language schools attract students from around the world. Unlike Antigua, it isn't overrun with foreigners, though there is a growing social scene revolv-

ing around language students and volunteer workers.

Most schools provide opportunities to get involved in social action programs working with the local K'iche' Maya. The standard price is Q920/1050 per week for four/five hours of instruction per day, Monday to Friday. Add around Q330 for room and board with a local family. Some places charge up to 20% more for tuition from June to August, and many require nonrefundable registration fees. Extras range from movies and free internet to dancing, cooking classes and lectures on Guatemalan politics and culture.

Reputable language schools (there are more!) include the following:

Casa Xelajú (Map p160; ☎ 7761-5954; www.casaxelaju.com; Callejón 15, Diagonal 13-02, Zona 1) One of the biggest, also offering classes in K'iche', and college credit.

Celas Maya (Map p160; ☎ 7761-4342; www.celasmaya.edu.gt; 6a Calle 14-55, Zona 1) Busy, professional outfit, set around a garden-courtyard. Also offers classes in K'iche'.

Centro de Estudios de Español Pop Wuj (Map p159; ☎ /fax 7761-8286; www.pop-wuj.org; 1a Calle 17-72, Zona 1) Pop Wuj's profits go to development projects in nearby villages, in which students can participate. The school also offers medical and social-work language programs.

El Mundo en Español (Map p159; ☎ 7761-3256; www.elmundoenespanol.org; 8 Av Calle B A-61, Zona 1) The extended family environment here is intended to promote natural language learning; most students reside on the premises. Located in a residential neighborhood east of the center.

El Nahual Community Center (off Map p159; ☎ 7765-2098; www.languageselnahual.com; 28 Av 9-54, Zona 1) Runs some excellent, grassroots community projects in which students can participate, such as teaching underprivileged kids and maintaining an organic community garden.

El Portal Spanish School (Map p159; ☎ 7761-5275; www.spanishschoolelportal.com; 9a Callejón A 11-49, Zona 1) Small outfit (15 students), with enthusiastic and supportive atmosphere. Earnings provide scholarships for children of single mothers.

El Quetzal Spanish School (Map p160; ☎ 7765-1085; www.elquetzalspanishschool.com; 10a Calle 10-29, Zona 1) One of the few indigenous-run businesses in town, offering plenty of activities and a reading room.

Escuela de Español Miguel de Cervantes (Map p160; ☎ 7765-5554; www.learn2speakspanish.com; 12a Av 8-31) Friendly owner, attractive learning environment in a historic building, onsite accommodation available.

Inepas (Instituto de Español y Participación en Ayuda

Social; Map p160; ☎ 7765-1308; www.inepas.org; 15a Av 4-59) Students can participate in a variety of worthy projects, including a Unesco-recognized rural school. Offers a selection of inexpensive accommodations besides home stays.

Madre Tierra (Map p160; ☎ 7761-6105; www.madre -tierra.org; 13 Av 8-34, Zona 1) Classes held in the courtyard of a classic colonial house. Activities include conferences with guest speakers from the community.

Proyecto Lingüístico Quetzalteco de Español (Map p159; ☎ /fax 7763-1061; www.plqe.org; 5a Calle 2-40, Zona 1) This collectively managed and politically minded institute also runs the Escuela de la Montaña, a limited-enrollment language-learning program on an organic coffee finca near Xela, where participation in local culture and volunteering are strongly encouraged.

Utatlán Spanish School (Map p160; ☎ 7763-0446; www.xelapages.com/utatlan; Pasaje Enríquez, 12a Av 4-32, Zona 1) Young and energetic, with plenty of parties and activities.

DANCE COURSES

The highly recommended **Salsa Rosa** (Map p160; Diagonal 11 7-79) gets top marks for its fun atmosphere and professionalism. Group and private salsa and merengue classes are offered. The more central **Sangre Latina** (Map p160; ☎ 7768-3270; Info@sangrelatinaguatemala.com; 7a Calle 14 27, Zona 1) is staffed by internationally prominent instructors. If you're just looking to make a night of it, the dance club La Parranda (see p167) offers free salsa classes Wednesday from 9pm.

WEAVING COURSES

Two women's cooperatives offer backstrap weaving classes and operate fair-trade fabric shops. Both places charge Q325 for 10 hours of instruction, in which learners produce a scarf, Q650 for 20 hours and the chance to make an embroidered table runner. For a simple demonstration of techniques they charge Q35.

Manos Creativas (Map p159; ☎ 7761-6408; claudi-alamam@yahoo.com; cnr 6a Calle & 5 Av 6-17)

Trama Textiles (Map p160; ☎ 7765-8564; trama. textiles@yahoo.com; 3a Calle 10-56, Zona 1)

Tours

A professional and amiable outfit, **Adrenalina Tours** (Map p160; ☎ 7761-4509; www.adrenalinatours.com; Pasaje Enríquez, Zona 1) provides a range of trips in the Xela area, including to Zunil, Fuentes Georginas and little-visited parts of the department of Huehuetenango. **Altiplano's Tour Operator** (Map p160; ☎ 7766-9614; www.altiplanos.

com.gt; 12a Av 3-35, Zona 1) offers some interesting half-day tours to indigenous villages and markets, colonial churches and coffee plantations around Xela.

The **Tranvía de los Altos** (Map p160; ☎ 7765-5342; www.tranviadelosaltos.com) is a pseudo-streetcar that does various circuits of the city, complete with knowledgeable commentary (in Spanish) and cheesy sound effects. Two-hour tours start at 11am and 3pm (Q70 per person), departing from the southwest corner of the park, opposite the Casa No'j. English-language tours (Q125) are available with two days' notice.

Maya Viva (Map p159; ☎ 7761-6408; www.amaguate. org; 5a Av & 6a Calle 6-17, Zona 1) is a community tourism program organized by the Asociación de Mujeres del Altiplano, a group that seeks to empower Maya women in the countryside. Visitors get to experience life in one of five rural communities near Quetzaltenango and learn about their customs, traditions and daily activities.

Festivals & Events

Xela Music Festival Organized by the French cultural institute, this performance event takes place in late March or early April, with local musicians playing on five or six stages around the city center.

Feria de la Virgen del Rosario (Feria Centroamericana de Independencia) Held in late September or early October, this is Xela's big annual party. Residents kick up their heels at a fairground on the city's perimeter and there's plenty of entertainment at selected venues around town, including a battle of the brass bands in the Parque Centro América. An international Spanish-language literary competition, hosted by the city, goes simultaneously.

Sleeping
BUDGET

All of the places listed here are in Zona 1.

Casa Argentina (Map p159; ☎ 7761-2470; casargentina. xela@gmail.com; Diagonal 12 8-37, Zona 1; dm Q20, s/d Q30/60) An institution with itinerant quetzal-pinchers, this sprawling guesthouse west of the center is making efforts to upgrade, but steer clear of the outrageously overcrowded dorms and opt for the marginally pricier private rooms with cinderblock decor. Señora Argentina and daughter Leonor are eager to please.

Casa de las Amigas (Map p159; ☎ 7763-0014; 5a Calle 2-59; r Q25-35) Opposite the Proyecto Lingüístico Quetzalteco Spanish school six blocks east of the park, this simple, women-run guesthouse is often occupied by Proyecto students.

Though rooms are bare, guests appreciate the homey atmosphere and kitchen facilities.

Guest House El Puente (Map p160; ☎ 7761-4342; 15a Av 6-75; s/d Q50/100, without bathroom Q40/80) The four rooms here surround a large garden; three share well-used bath facilities. Connected to the Celas Mayas Spanish school, it's often occupied by language learners who congregate in the kitchen.

Hostal Don Diego (Map p160; ☎ 5308-5106; www.hostaldondiegoxela.com; 6a Calle 15-12; dm Q45, s/d from Q55/100; ☎) A nifty little budget choice: sparely furnished rooms with parquetry floors and good firm beds flank a sunny courtyard. Reduced rates are offered for weekly or monthly stays, with optional fee for kitchen use.

Miguel de Cervantes Guesthouse (Map p160; ☎ 7765-5554; www.learn2speakspanish.com; 12 Av 8-31; r per person incl breakfast Q48; 🖳 ☎) The nine guest rooms at the MdC Spanish school are spiffy wood-and-concrete affairs, set around one of the cutest courtyards in Xela. When there's water pressure, the showers in the shared bathrooms rock. Even if you're not taking classes, you can join in the student activities.

ourpick Los Chocoyos (Map p160; ☎ 7761-6497; centroculturalloschocoyos.com; 7a Calle 15-20; r per person Q60; ☎) One component of a multi-use cultural center, this guesthouse is designed for longer stays, and rates drop for weekly or monthly guests (your laundry is done gratis). An old structure redesigned by its architect owner, it features eight split-level units along one side of the events hall; the bedroom is upstairs, a lounge with TV downstairs. It also has one of the nicest guest kitchens around, with hot and cold drinking water and various teas.

Black Cat Hostel (Map p160; ☎ 7756-8951; www.blackcathostels.net; 13a Av 3-33; dm incl breakfast Q60, r Q160; ☎) A great place to stay if you're looking to meet up with other travelers, this full-service hostel features a sunny courtyard, a bar-restaurant and lounge/TV area. Though sparsely furnished, the rooms are done up in soothing colors with nice wood floors.

Hostal 7 Orejas (Map p159; ☎ 7768-3218; www.7orejas.com; 2a Calle 16-92, Zona 1; dm incl breakfast Q95) This is a cordially managed and scrupulously maintained hostel on a quiet street northwest of the center. The pseudo-colonial structure features spacious, fresh-smelling rooms alongside a strip of garden. Each has three queen-size beds with carved-wood chests for storage. Music, movies and cocktails

keep guests occupied upstairs at the El Orejón lounge.

Hotel Casa Real del Viajero (Map p160; ☎ 7761-4594; www.hotelcasarealdelviajero.com; cnr 8a Av & 9a Calle 9017, Zona 1; s/d/tr Q100/150/180; ☎) This popular option stands at a high-traffic intersection, though things are considerably calmer beyond the reception area. A series of flourescent-lit, brick-walled rooms of varying size and shape open onto a quiet interior patio. Guests may use the large kitchen.

MIDRANGE

Casa Doña Mercedes (Map p160; ☎ 7765-4687; cnr 6a Calle & 14a Av 13-42; s/d Q170/280, without bathroom Q86/175) In the heart of downtown, this tranquil little guesthouse is quite luxurious for the price, with plenty of colonial style. The shared-bath accommodations are actually the better way to go here.

Los Olivos (Map p160; ☎ 7761-0215; hotel.losolivos13@hotmail.com; 13a Av 3-32; s/d Q130/200; 🅿) Up a side street from the park, this one offers neat, comfortable rooms with firm beds and wood slat ceilings, all opening on plant-filled interior balconies.

Hotel Kiktem-Ja (Map p160; ☎ 7761-4304; 13a Av 7-18, Zona 1; s/d Q135/160; 🅿) Set in a great old colonial building downtown, the Kiktem-Ja is all floorboards at weird angles, stone arches and squiggly wood columns along plant-draped corridors. Rooms are spacious with sturdy bedsteads, fireplaces and pretty tiled bathrooms.

Villa de Don Andrés (Map p160; ☎ 7761-2014; villadedonandres@gmail.com; 13a Av 6-16, Zona 1; s/d Q225/422, without bathroom Q150/300; 🅿 ☎) This recently opened B&B in the center of town is a welcoming sort of place. Done up with antique decor, the large carpeted rooms are pleasantly arranged along a broad patio where a complimentary breakfast is served.

Hotel Flora Inn (Map p160; ☎ 7761-2326; florainnhotel@gmail.com; 12a Av 3-61, Zona 1; s/d Q190/270; 🅿) The Euro-managed Flora Inn is a modern, smartly furnished option half a block up from the park. Spacious rooms with big, comfy beds and flatscreen TVs face a tranquil patio where breakfast is available.

Casa San Bartolomé (Map p159; ☎ 7761-9511; www.casasanbartolome.com; 2a Av 7-17, Zona 1; s/d/tr Q205/287/328; ☎) In the family for generations, this atmospheric old residence a 15-minute walk east of the park has been converted into a cozy B&B. There are six rooms, three apartments (with kitchens) and a cottage. All have beautiful furniture and modern art. Amiable owner Anabela maintains an excellent library, which you're welcome to browse. An elaborate breakfast featuring herbal tea from the garden is served on the lovely rear terrace. Long-termers get substantial discounts.

Hotel Villa Real Plaza (Map p160; ☎ 7761-4045; Calz Sinforoso Aguilar, Zona 1; s/d Q275/360; P) By far the grandest-looking hotel in town, the Real Plaza started life as a prison. Looking at the stone archways, high ceilings and spacious rooms, you'd never know. It has a courtyard restaurant, bar and sauna.

Hotel Modelo (Map p160; ☎ 7761-2529; www.hotel modelo1892.com; 14a Av A 2-31, Zona 1; s/d incl breakfast Q318/380; P ☎) Set in a beautiful old colonial house, the Modelo offers some atmospheric rooms with wooden floorboards, firm beds and spacious bathrooms. Some are along a pretty patio at one side but tend to be noisier because they front the street.

TOP END

Hotel Casa Mañen (Map p160; ☎ 7765-0786; www.come seeit.com; 9a Av 4-11; s/d incl breakfast from Q488/535) The town residence of coffee barons through the 19th century, this atmospheric guesthouse was thoughtfully renovated by an American couple in the 1980s to become one of Xela's top hotels, with traditionally outfitted rooms, tranquil gardens and a distinguishing style. Upstairs units have balconies and views, as does the roof terrace/bar.

Hotel Pensión Bonifaz (Map p160; ☎ 7765-1111; www.quetzalnet.com/bonifaz; 4a Calle 10-50, Zona 1; s/d Q525/630; P 🖥 🖳) The oldest and grandest hotel in Xela stands right next to the Parque Centro América. Rooms are on the top three floors; the 2nd-floor chambers surround a leafy colonial patio where breakfast is served. Though interior decor is not as fabulous as you might expect, the opulent front bar makes up for it.

Eating

Quetzaltenango has a good selection of places to eat in all price ranges. Cheapest are the food stalls on the lower level of the central market, where snacks and main-course plates are sold for Q10 or less. One very popular breakfast spot is Doña Cristy (Map p160), serving *atol de elote* (a hot maize beverage), empanadas and *chuchitos* (small tamales).

GUATEMALAN & LATIN AMERICAN CUISINE

Café Canela (Map p160; 7a Calle 15-24; lunch plates Q15; 🕑 breakfast, lunch & dinner Sun-Fri) This unassuming lunch joint has yummy home-cooked fare by gregarious Nicaraguan owner/chef Marta. There are three daily specials to choose from, with one veggie option.

Café Sagrado Corazón (Map p160; 14a Av 3-08, Zona 1; lunch plates Q25; 🕑 6:30am-7pm) This hole-in-the-wall eatery is a good place to try Guatemalan home cooking, with regional specialties like *pepián* and *jocón* (green stew of chicken or pork with green vegetables and herbs). Meals are truly filling, coming with soup, tamalitos, rice, potatoes, avocado and salad.

Casa Ut'z Hua (Map p160; ☎ 7768-3469; 12a Av 3-05; meals Q25-30; 🕑 breakfast, lunch & dinner) Delicious, authentic Guatemalan and Quetzalteco dishes are the draw at this kitschily decorated country hut.

Maya Café (Map p160; 13 Av 5-48; mains Q25-30; 🕑 7am-6pm) Plenty of *típica* Xela fare on offer at this locally popular dining hall – try the *quichom*, a spicy chicken concoction. Lunch comes with soup and some fresh-squeezed beverage.

La Taberna de Don Rodrigo (Map p160; 14a Av C-51, Zona 1; sandwiches Q32; 🕑 9am-9pm) This lively pub/cafe/snack bar is reportedly the first place to serve Xela's signature Cabro beer on tap, poured copiously into pitchers and mugs (three per customer) and served by waitresses in mustard-colored dresses. To go along, they grill up long bologna-and-cheese sandwiches, brought to the table with squeeze bottles of green sauce. Classic!

INTERNATIONAL CUISINE

Al-Natur (Map p160; 13a Av 8-34A; 🕑 9am-7:30pm Mon-Sat, 1-7pm Sun; 🛜) For politically correct snacks, head here: all sandwiches, milkshakes, cappuccinos and pastries are organically grown, fair-trade approved and/or produced by cooperatives.

Casa Antigua (Map p160; ☎ 5826-4520; 12a Av 3-26; sandwiches Q28; 🕑 noon-9pm Mon-Sat, 4-9pm Sun; 🛜) Sandwiches are big, chunky affairs at this casual eatery near the park, and there are plenty of steaks flame-grilling out front. Seating is at sturdy wooden tables along a pleasant patio.

Panorama (Map p159; ☎ 5319-3536; 13a Av A; meals Q40-80; 🕑 dinner Wed-Fri, lunch & dinner Sat & Sun) This Swiss-owned restaurant (a 10-minute slog up the hill at the south end of town) does good set meals and serves Swiss raclette cheese. The view is amazing and it's a romantic spot for that special night out.

Royal Paris (Map p160; ☎ 7761-1942; 14 Av A 3-06; salads Q45; ☻ lunch & dinner; ☎) Overseen by the French consul himself, this bistro ought to be authentic, and the escargots, baked camembert and filet mignon approach Parisian standards. Check the blackboard for nightly specials. The cozy ambience is augmented by a sweet terrace and live folk and jazz Wednesday, Friday and Saturday nights.

Casa Babylon (Map p160; ☎ 7761-2120; 5a Calle 12-54; mains Q50-85; ☻ breakfast, lunch & dinner Mon-Sat; ☎) With the widest menu in town, the Babylon is a travelers' favorite. Dishes run from big, tasty sandwiches to Guatemalan classics to more exotic fare such as fondue and Middle Eastern dishes.

Café El Árabe (Map p160; 4a Calle 12-22, Zona 1; mains Q55; ☻ noon-midnight; **V**) Fans of Middle Eastern food will be pleased to find this authentic place just off Parque Centro América. Pitas are made on the premises and the ingredients are lovely and fresh, with plenty of vegetarian choices. Bands perform weekends on the Arabesque stage.

Restaurante Cardinali (Map p160; ☎ 7761-0924; 14 Av 3-25; pastas Q60, mains Q125; ☻ lunch & dinner) With checkered tablecloths and hundreds of wine bottles hanging from the rafters, this feels like it was lifted from the Mediterranean, and indeed owner/chef Benito hails from Parma, Italy. The manicotti and ravioli are made inhouse.

our pick **Sabor de la India** (Map p160; 15 Av 3-64; mains Q60-70; ☻ noon-10pm Tue-Sun; **V**) What is surely the most authentic Indian fare in the country is whipped up here by a friendly fellow from Kerala. Servings are huge; the *thalis* – assortments of curried veggies – are highly recommended.

Drinking
CAFES
Coffee plays an important part in Xela's economy, and there are plenty of places to grab a cup.

Café Baviera (Map p160; ☎ 7761-5018; 5a Calle 13-14; ☻ 7am-8:30pm; ☎) This cozy European-style cafe has quality espresso, with coffee beans roasted on the premises, and it's a fine place for breakfast or snacks (crêpes, croissants, soups and salads Q30 to Q40). The wooden walls are hung with countless photos and clippings on Xela and international themes.

Time Coffee Shop (Map p160; ☎ 7768-3467; Pasaje Enríquez, 12 Av 4-52, Zona 1; ☻ 8am-8pm Tue-Sun; ☎) Squeezed into the facade of the Pasaje Enríquez, this stylish place has just a few tables on two levels, and the baristas know what they're doing.

our pick **Café La Luna** (Map p160; ☎ 5174-6769; 8a Av 4-11; ☻ 9:30am-9pm Mon-Fri, 4-9pm Sat; ☎) For chocolate aficionados, this is a shrine. Made from scratch on the premises, the chocolate is velvety smooth and served in a variety of beverages: the chocolate cappuccino, topped with fresh whipped cream, is mind-blowing. The place has a strong neighborhood character, with groups of friends gathering in the various salons, which are littered with vintage bric-a-brac.

Café El Balcón del Enríquez (Map p160; Pasaje Enríquez, 12 Av 4-40; ☻ breakfast, lunch & dinner) With specially designed viewing counters overlooking the Parque Centro América, this lively cafe on the upper level of the Pasaje Enríquez makes a nice perch for morning espresso or evening cocktails.

Café El Cuartito (Map p160; 13a Av 7-09; ☻ 11am-11pm Wed-Mon; ☎ **V**) This offbeat cafe is a point of reference for travelers and language students, with quirky decor made from found objects. It serves a good range of vegetarian snacks, herbal teas and coffee just about any way you want it, plus some creative cocktails – how about a raspberry mojito? On weekends there's DJ action.

El Infinito Lounge (Map p160; 7a Calle 15-18, Zona 1; ☻ 11am-11pm Mon-Sat; ☎) With a highly eclectic range of art on the walls and coffee tables, tofu-intensive snacks, bubble tea, board games and a few PCs to browse, El Infinito makes an ideal spot to while away an afternoon, and owner and part-time DJ Pedrín makes a mean espresso.

BARS
Xela's Zona Viva revolves around the Teatro Municipal, with discos and clubs popping up along 1a and 2a Calles and up 14 Av.

Salón Tecún (Map p160; Pasaje Enríquez; ☻ 8am-1am) On the plaza end of the elegant Pasaje Enríquez, alive day and night with a healthy mix of Guatemalans and foreigners quaffing Cabro by the liter, the Tecún claims to be the country's longest-running bar (since 1935). They also serve good bar food including the best burgers in town. Don't miss it.

Pool & Beer (Map p160; ☎ 4301-6560; 12a Av 10-21; ☻ 6pm-1am Tue-Sun) The pool tables are worn and the cues crooked, but this slackers' clubhouse remains a friendly and refreshingly non-trendy spot. If the tables are occupied, you can be the DJ, choosing from the PC's 30,000-odd tracks.

Ojalá (Map p160; ☎ 7763-0206; 15 Av A 3-33, Zona 1; ☻ 5pm-1am Tue-Sat; ☜) A fun clubhouse for a predominately global clientele, Ojalá has a series of comfy salons centering on a colonial patio where various events take place (trivia contests, live music). Local microbrews (Q40) are among the quaffs available at the lovely bar.

Arguile (Map p160; ☎ 7761-2228; 13a Av 7-31; ☻ noon-1am Mon-Sat; ☜) Nominally a Middle Eastern snack bar, after hours Arguile becomes a trendy lounge, where a mixed Guatemalan/*extranjero* crowd smoke hookahs (Q50) or dance to the DJs.

Entertainment

It gets chilly when the sun goes down, so you won't want to sit out in the Parque Centro América enjoying the balmy breezes – there aren't any. Nevertheless, it's a pleasant place for an evening stroll.

Casa No'j (Map p160; ☎ 7768-3139; www.casanoj.blogspot.com; 7a Calle 12-12, Zona 1; ☻ 8am-5pm Mon-Sat) This recently inaugurated place, just off the park's southwest corner, is Xela's premier cultural center. Besides staging photo and art exhibits, it also hosts film, theater and poetry festivals throughout the year. Check the blog for upcoming events.

Centro Cultural Los Chocoyos (Map p160 ☎ 7761-649/; centroculturalloschocoyos.com; /a Calle 15-20) Another happening space that regularly stages performance events, including plays and concerts.

Teatro Municipal (Map p160; ☎ 7761-2218; 14a Av & 1a Calle) Quetzaltenango's grand neoclassical theater north of the center is the main venue for plays, concerts and dance performances. Inside are three tiers of seating, the lower two with private boxes for prominent families.

Teatro Roma (Map p160; ☎ 7768-3305; 14a Av A-34) Close to the Teatro Municipal is another palace of culture, a showcase for plays and, on occasion, some interesting movies.

LIVE MUSIC

The music scene is particularly strong in Xela. Many of the town's restaurants, cafes and bars double as performance venues, including the Royal Paris, El Cuartito, Infinito Lounge, Ojalá, Arguile and El Árabe. To see what's on, pick up a copy of *XelaWho* or check www.

xelawho.com. Also check out **Bari** (Map p160; 1a Calle 14-31; ☻ 8pm-1am Wed-Sat), one of several nightspots opposite the Teatro Municipal. It regularly hosts live trova, rock and pop and sells a good selection of wine and draft beers.

CINEMA

Though there's no proper movie house in the center of town, a number of venues run weekly film series, including Ojalá, Time Coffee Shop and Royal Paris, as well as El Orejón, the lounge inside the Hostal 7 Orejas (see p164). In addition, the **Blue Angel Video Café** (Map p159; 7a Calle 15-79, Zona 1; admission Q10) shows Hollywood films nightly at 8pm, besides serving a nice range of vegetarian meals, herbal teas and hot chocolate. See *XelaWho* for the schedule.

DANCE CLUBS

La Parranda (Map p160; 14a Av 4-47, Zona 1; ☻ Wed-Sat; cover Fri & Sat Q20) This glitzy, strobe-lit disco offers free salsa classes on Wednesday night (basic and intermediate); other evenings have guest DJs and drinks giveaways.

La Rumba (Map p160; 13a Av, Zona 1; ☻ Wed-Sat) The big dance floor at this highly popular hall fills up fast, with plenty of Guate–gringo/a couples teaching each other how to salsa, merengue and cumbia.

Shopping

Manos Creativas (Map p159; ☎ 7761-6408; cnr 6a Calle & 5 Av 6-17), a shop belonging to the women's empowerment association AMA, sells quality textiles and clothing produced by Maya weavers. **Trama Textiles** (Map p160; ☎ 7765-8564; 3a Calle 10-56, Zona 1), just uphill from the park, is a similar weaving cooperative, comprised of 400 Maya women.

Xela's central market (Map p160) is three floors of reasonably priced handicrafts and souvenirs. Bargain hard. For a more intense, everyday marketing experience, hit the **Mercado La Democracia** (Map p159; 1a Calle, Zona 3), about 10 blocks north of Parque Centro América in Zona 3, with food, clothing, pirated CDs and other necessities for city dweller and villager alike.

Getting There & Away
BUS

All 2nd-class buses depart from Terminal Minerva, a dusty, crowded yard on 7a Calle, Zona 3, in the west of town, unless otherwise

THE HIGHLANDS

VOLUNTEERING IN XELA

The Quetzaltenango area has many nonprofit organizations working on social projects with the local K'iche' Maya people that need volunteers. Volunteer jobs can range from designing websites for indigenous organizations to working in orphanages for disabled children. You can volunteer part-time for a week or two while also studying Spanish, or you can live and work in a close-knit indigenous village for a year. Obviously, the more Spanish you speak the better, but in a few weeks at one of Xela's schools, you can learn enough to be effective. Indeed, many schools are connected with particular social projects – some in fact exist primarily to generate funds for them – and can help students to participate in their free time. Skills in fields such as medicine, nursing, teaching, youth work and computers are prized, but there are possibilities for anyone with the will to help. Volunteers must normally meet all their own costs and be willing to commit to a project for a specified minimum time. Three months is fairly typical for full-time posts, though the minimum can be as little as a week or as long as a year.

EntreMundos (Map p160; ☎ 7761-2179; www.entremundos.org; El Espacio, 6a Calle 7-31, Zona 1; ☯ 1-5pm Mon-Thu) is a forum for social projects in Xela. Its website has details on more than 150 nonprofit projects all over Guatemala, many of which need volunteers, and its bi-monthly magazine, *EntreMundos*, has articles and ads about volunteer opportunities. EntreMundos asks a donation of Q25 for drop-in visitors wanting to be placed.

Asociación de Mujeres del Altiplano (Map p160; ☎ 7761-6408; www.amaguate.org; 5a Av & 6a Calle 6-17, Zona 1), a group seeking to empower women in five Maya communities, needs volunteers to participate in the operation of a textile-weaving facility, as well as to support health education efforts.

Asociación Nuevos Horizontes (Map p160; ☎ 7761-6140; www.ahnh.org; 3a Calle 6-51, Zona 2) runs a shelter for abused women and children and needs volunteers to devise and supervise activities for the kids.

Hike & Help (Map p160; ☎ 7765-0883; www.fdiguate.org; 15a Av 7041, Zona 1) is a guide service that contributes its profits toward developing educational opportunities in poor rural communities. Volunteers are needed to publicize and administer the tours.

noted. First-class companies operating between Quetzaltenango and Guatemala City have their own terminals.

Leaving or entering town, some buses make a stop east of the center at the Rotonda, a traffic circle on Calz Independencia, marked by the Monumento a la Marimba. Getting off here when you're coming into Xela saves the 10 to 15 minutes it will take your bus to cross town to Terminal Minerva.

Almolonga (Q2.50, 40 minutes, 6km) Buses every 15 minutes, 5:30am to 5pm, departing from the west side of the market building. Additional stop at the corner of 9a Av and 10a Calle, southeast of Parque Centro América.

Antigua (170km) Take any bus bound for Guatemala City via the Interamericana and change at Chimaltenango.

Chichicastenango (Q40, three hours, 94km) Buses at 9am, 10:30am, 11:30am, noon, 1:30pm, 2:30pm and 3:30pm. Or take a bus heading to Guatemala City by the Interamericana and change at Los Encuentros.

Ciudad Tecún Umán (Mexican border) (Q25, three hours, 129km) Hourly buses from 5am to 6pm.

Cuatro Caminos (Q3, 15 minutes, 11km) Take any bus bound for Huehuetenango, Totonicapán, San Francisco El Alto and so on.

El Carmen/Talismán (Mexican border) Take a bus to San Marcos (Q10, two hours, every 30 minutes), then catch another to Malacatán (Q15, two hours) where you can find a collective taxi (Q5) or microbus to El Carmen (Q4).

Guatemala City (Q60, four hours, 201km) Línea Dorada (☎ 7767-5198; www.lineadorada.info; 12 Av & 5 Calle, Zona 3) Two deluxe buses (Q70), 4am and 2:30pm, door-to-door shuttle service for passengers getting the early departure (Q25 from Zona 1); Transportes Álamo (☎ 7763-5044; 14 Av 5-15, Zona 3) Seven Pullman buses, from 4:30am to 4:45pm; Transportes Galgos (☎ 7761-2248; Calle Rodolfo Robles 17-43, Zona 1) Pullmans at 4am, 8:30am and 12:30pm. Cheaper 2nd-class buses (Q35) depart Terminal Minerva every 10 minutes, 5am to 5pm, but make many stops and take longer.

Huehuetenango (Q20, two hours, 90km) Buses every 15 minutes, 5:30am to 7pm.

La Mesilla (Mexican border) (Q15, 3½ hours, 170km) Buses at 5am, 6am, 7am, 8am, 1pm and 4pm. Or take a bus to Huehuetenango and change there.

Momostenango (Q7, 1½ hours, 26km) Buses every 15 minutes, 5:45am to 7pm.

Panajachel (Q25, three hours, 100km) Buses at 10am, 11am, 1pm, 2pm and 4:30pm. Or take any bus for

Guatemala City via the Interamericana and change at Los Encuentros.

Retalhuleu (Q13, 1½ hours, 58km) 'Reu' buses every 10 minutes, 4:30am to 7:30pm.

San Andrés Xecul (Q3.50, 40 minutes) Buses every 15 minutes, from 6am to 3pm. Or take any bus to San Francisco El Alto or Totonicapán, get out at the Esso station by the Moreiria junction and flag a pickup (Q2).

San Martín Sacatepéquez (Chile Verde) (Q5, one hour, 22km) Frequent service; placards may say 'Colomba' or 'El Rincón.' Additional stop at 6a Calle, two blocks north of Parque Benito Juárez.

San Pedro La Laguna (Q35, 3½ hours, 65km) Buses at 10am, noon, 2pm, 2:30pm and 4:30pm.

Zunil (Q4.50, one hour, 10km) Buses every 10 minutes, 6:30am to 5:30pm, departing from the west side of the market building. Additional stop at the corner of 9a Av and 10a Calle, southeast of Parque Centro América.

CAR & MOTORCYCLE
Tabarini (Map p160; ☎ 7763-0418; www.tabarini.com; 9a Calle 9-21, Zona 1) Tabarini rents cars for about Q300 per day.

SHUTTLE MINIBUS
Adrenalina Tours (Map p160; ☎ 7761-4509; www.adrenalinatours.com; 13a Av, Zona 1, inside Pasaje Enríquez) runs shuttle minibuses to many destinations including Guatemala City (Q290 per person), Antigua (Q210), Chichicastenango (Q140), Panajachel (Q115) and San Cristobal de Las Casas (Mexico; Q290). **Monte Verde Tours** (Map p160; ☎ 7761-6105; www.monte-verdetours.com; 13 Av 8-34, Zona 1) offers the same runs for similar prices. See p158 for additional shuttle operators.

Getting Around
Terminal Minerva is linked to the city center by microbuses, charging Q1.50 for the 10- to 15-minute ride. From the terminal, walk south through the market to the intersection by the Templo de Minerva, where you'll see the vehicles waiting on the south side of 4a Calle. Going from the center to the terminal, you can catch the microbuses on 13a Av at the corner of 7a or 4a Calle. Taxis await fares at the north end of Parque Centro América; a ride to the Terminal Minerva costs around Q30.

The Rotonda bus stop on Calz Independencía is also served by 'Parque' microbuses running to the center.

Inguat has information on other city bus routes. Fares double after 7pm and on public holidays.

AROUND QUETZALTENANGO
The beautiful volcanic country around Xela makes for numerous exciting day trips. For many, the volcanoes themselves pose irresistible challenges (p161). You can feast your eyes and soul on the wild church at San Andrés Xecul, hike to the ceremonial shores of Laguna Chicabal, or soak in the idyllic hot springs at Fuentes Georginas. Or simply hop on a bus and explore the myriad small traditional villages that pepper this part of the highlands. Market days are great opportunities to observe locals in action, so Sunday and Wednesday in Momostenango, Monday in Zunil, Tuesday and Saturday in Totonicapán and Friday in San Francisco El Alto are good days to visit.

Los Vahos
If you're a hiker and the weather is good, you'll enjoy a trip to the rough-and-ready sauna/steam baths at **Los Vahos** (The Vapors; admission Q10; ⏱ 8am-6pm), 3.5km from the Parque Centro América in Xela. Take a bus headed for Almolonga and ask to get out at the road to Los Vahos. Walk uphill around half a kilometer and turn right onto a dusty road. Continue walking some 45 minutes to reach the sauna. Or better still, walk south straight out of the city center along 13a Av to its end, where you'll see the little yellow-and-red Monte Sinai evangelical church. Continue straight ahead, passing the right-hand side of the church. The road soon zigzags uphill, becoming a dirt track and then a good footpath. Follow the path past the dairy and school to where it joins the main track to Los Vahos. From here it's 1km or so uphill to the steam baths.

The saunas are just two dark stone rooms behind plastic curtains. Occasionally, the vents are carpeted with eucalyptus leaves, giving the steam an herbal quality. Straight in front of the steam-bath entrance is a rocky hillside, which you can climb to some caves.

Altiplanos Tours organizes hikes up to Los Vahos at 8am, taking about 1½ hours from the city center and spending two hours at the sauna (Q150 per person).

Almolonga
pop 13,800 / elev 2322m
On the way to Zunil the road passes through Almolonga, 6km from Quetzaltenango; it's an indigenous town become relatively wealthy from vegetable-growing and with a population that is more than 90% evangelical

THE HIGHLANDS

Christian. Market days are Tuesday, Thursday and Saturday, when you'll see piles and piles of cabbages, limes, chilis, *güisquil* (a squashlike vegetable), onions and other gorgeous veggies, handled by hordes of indigenous women in embroidered aprons. Don't miss the **Iglesia de San Pedro**, which has a gilded altarpiece with a backdrop of incongruous neon lights, and an inverted galleon ceiling. Almolonga celebrates its annual fair on June 27.

At the lower end of the village the road passes through **Los Baños**, an area with natural hot sulfur springs. Several little places down here have bath installations with rather tomblike enclosed concrete tubs renting for Q15 to Q20 an hour. **El Manantial** has one of the better set-ups.

Zunil
pop 13,000 / elev 2262m

As you speed downhill toward Zunil from Quetzaltenango, you'll see this pretty market town, spreading across a lush valley framed by steep hills and dominated by a towering volcano, with its white colonial church gleaming above the red-tiled roofs of the low houses. A road on the left bridges a river and, 1km further, reaches Zunil's plaza.

Founded in 1529, Zunil is a typical Guatemalan highland town, where traditional indigenous agriculture is practiced. The cultivated plots, divided by stone fences, are irrigated by canals; you'll see the farmers scooping up water with a shovel-like instrument and tossing it over their plants. Women wash their clothes near the river bridge in pools of hot water that come out of the rocks.

SIGHTS

Zunil boasts a particularly striking **church**. Its ornate facade, with eight pairs of serpentine columns, is echoed inside by a richly worked altar of silver. On Monday the plaza in front is bright with the predominantly red-and-pink traditional garb of the local K'iche' Maya people buying and selling.

Half a block downhill from the church plaza, the **Cooperativa Santa Ana** (🕐 7am-7pm) is a handicrafts cooperative made up of more than 600 local women. Finely woven vests, jackets and traditional *huipiles* (from Q400) are displayed and sold here. The amiable director of the cooperative, Candelaria Ramos Chay, is happy to discuss how they're made. Weaving lessons are offered, too.

While you're in Zunil, visit the image of **San Simón**, the name given here to the much-venerated non-Christian deity known elsewhere as Maximón. His effigy, propped up in a chair, is moved each year to a different house during the **festival of San Simón**, held on October 28. Ask any local where to find him. You'll be charged a few quetzals for each photograph taken. For more on San Simón, see boxed text, p146.

The **festival of Santa Catarina Alejandrí**, official patron saint of Zunil, is celebrated on November 25.

SLEEPING & EATING

Hotel Las Cumbres (☎ 5399-0029; www.lascumbres. com.gt; Km 210 Carretera al Pacífico; r from Q350; Ⓟ) Las Cumbres is built on top of natural steam vents, and each cozy room comes equipped with its own sauna and/or hot-spring-fed Jacuzzi. It has a good restaurant (mains Q50 to Q80) serving organic vegetables from the hotel garden, along with a squash court, gymnasium and handicrafts store. Nonguests can use the public sauna (Q25 per hour, open 7am to 7pm), a modern pine-paneled installation,

---

EXPLORE MORE OF QUETZALTENANGO

The wide-open spaces and mountainous countryside around Xela offer an almost endless array of opportunities for getting out there and doing a bit of solo exploration. Small villages dotted around the valley mean that you shouldn't ever have much trouble getting directions, and the relative safety of the area means that the biggest danger you're ever likely to face is that of a yapping dog (carry a stick). A few destinations to head towards:

Santiaguito lookout Get a close-up view of volcanic eruptions, going off like clockwork every 20 minutes.

Lava fields Over near Mt Candelaria, these extensive fields are a great place for a picnic and a spot of sunbathing.

San Cristóbal waterfall Halfway between Xela and San Francisco, the falls are much more impressive in the wet season.

Las Mojadas The walk to this pretty flower-growing village takes you from Llanos del Pinal and past the Santiago volcano. And the best part — you can catch a bus back.

THE HIGHLANDS

or spa, offering massages and facials. Located 500m south of Zunil village, Las Cumbres looks like a colonial village amid a volcanic landscape where great plumes of steam emanate from the earth.

GETTING THERE & AWAY
See p167 for details on getting to Zunil from Quetzaltenango. Returning, buses depart from the main road beside the bridge. The Fuentes Georginas shuttle (see below) makes a brief (15-minute) stop in Zunil if you'd just like a quick look at the church. Any bus bound for Retalhuleu or Mazatenango can drop you at the entrance to Hotel Las Cumbres (Q5).

Fuentes Georginas
The prettiest, most popular natural spa in Guatemala is **Fuentes Georginas** (☎ 5904-5559; www.lasfuentesgeorginas.com; adult/child Q25/15; ☷ 8am-5:30pm), an 8km drive uphill from Zunil. It's named after the wife of 'benevolent dictator' Jorge Ubico, who customarily comandeered the installations on weekends for his personal use. Four pools of varying temperatures are fed by hot sulfur springs and framed by a steep, high wall of tropical vines, ferns and flowers. Though the setting is intensely tropical, the mountain air currents keep it deliciously cool through the day. There is a little 500m walk starting from beside the pool, worth doing to check out the birds and orchids. Bring a bathing suit; towels are available (Q10 plus deposit). Lockers cost Q5.

Besides the **restaurant/bar** (meals Q60-75; ☷ 8am-7pm), which serves great grilled steaks, sausage and *papas,* there are three sheltered picnic tables with cooking grills. Big-time soakers will want to spend the night: down the valley a bit are nine rustic but cozy **cottages** (per person Q95), each with a hot tub and cold shower, barbecue and a fireplace to ward off the mountain chill at night (wood and matches provided). Included in the price of the cottages is access to the pools all day and all night, when rules are relaxed.

Trails lead to two nearby volcanoes: **Volcán Zunil** (15km, about three hours one way) and **Volcán Santo Tomás** (25km, about five hours one way). Guides (essential) are available for either trip. Ask at the restaurant.

Fuentes Georginas offers daily shuttles to the site (Q75 return, including entrance fee), leaving Xela at 9am and 2pm from their **office** (☎ 7763-0596; 5a Calle 14-14). They return at 1pm and 6pm.

Alternatively, take any bus to Zunil, where pickup trucks wait to give rides up to the springs, a half-hour away (Q100, including a 1½-hour wait while you soak).

El Palmar Viejo
The turnoff to El Palmar Viejo is signposted immediately before the Puente Samala III bridge, about 30km down the Retalhuleu road from Xela. It's 4km west from the main road to the village itself – or rather the overgrown remnants of the village, for El Palmar was destroyed by a mudslide and floods emanating from Santiaguito volcano at the time of Hurricane Mitch in the 1990s. Its inhabitants were resettled at a new village, El Palmar Nuevo, east of the main highway, but some still come here to tend plantations. A river has cut a deep ravine through the heart of the old village, slicing the **church** in two. A pair of **swing bridges** cross the ravine. Downstream, to the right of the river, you can see the top of the village cemetery **chapel** poking up through the trees – but beware, reaching the cemetery involves crossing an unstable bridge. Atop the hill behind the **cemetery** is a modern Maya **altar**.

Buses bound for Retalhuleu can drop you at the El Palmar Viejo turnoff, but it's probably best to come with a guide, as this is an isolated place. Adrenalina Tours (p158) is one agency that comes here.

Salcajá
Seven kilometers from Xela, this is an apparently unremarkable town bypassed by the highway north. But despite its aloofness, Salcajá harbors some special qualities to which it alone can lay claim.

Dating from 1524, the **Iglesia de San Jacinto**, two blocks west on 3a Calle from the main road, was the first Christian temple in Central America. The facade retains some character, with carved lions and bunches of fruit, but the real treat is inside, where you'll find original paintings and an ornate altar.

Salcajá is famed for its traditional *ikat-*style textiles, remarkable for the hand-tied and dyed threads that are laid out in the preferred pattern on a loom. Shops selling bolts of this fabric are ubiquitous here, and you can usually visit their workshops before purchasing.

Perhaps the town is best known, though, for its production of two alcoholic beverages that locals consider akin to magic elixirs. *Caldo de frutas* (literally, fruit soup) is like a high-octane sangria, made by combining *nances* (cherry-like fruits), apples, peaches, and pears and fermenting them for six months or so. You can purchase fifths of it for around Q30 after viewing the production process. *Rompopo* is an entirely different type of potent potable, made from rum, egg yolks, sugar and spices. Little liquor shops all over Salcajá peddle the stuff, but you may like to try the friendly **Rompopo Salcajá** (4a Calle 2-02), a block east of the main road along 4a Calle.

Frequent buses depart for Salcajá from Quetzaltenango's Terminal Minerva, stopping en route at the Monumento a la Marimba on the eastern side of town.

San Andrés Xecul

A few kilometers past Salcajá and less than 1km before Cuatro Caminos, the road from Quetzaltenango passes the Morería crossroads, where the road to San Andrés Xecul branches off to the west. After about 3km on this uphill spur, you'll start seeing rainbow cascades of hand-dyed thread drying on the roofs and you'll know you have arrived in San Andrés Xecul. Boxed in by fertile hills, this small town boasts the most bizarre, stunning **church** imaginable. Technicolored saints, angels, flowers and climbing vines fight for space with whimsical tigers and frolicking monkeys on the shocking yellow facade. The red, blue and yellow cones on the bell tower are straight from the circus big top.

Inside, a carpet of candles illuminate bleeding effigies of Christ. These are unabashedly raffish, with slabs of thick makeup trying to make him look alive and boyish. In one display, a supine Jesus is surrounded by gold and satin trimmings that hang thick inside his glass coffin. The pews are generally packed with praying indigenous women.

Continue walking up the hill and you'll come to a smaller, and decidedly more sedate, **yellow church**. Maya ceremonies are still held here, and the panoramic view across the valley is phenomenal. The **annual festival** is November 29 and 30.

To get here take any northbound bus from Xela, alighting at the Esso station at the Morería crossroads and hailing a pickup or walking the 3km uphill. Buses returning to Xela line up at the edge of the plaza and make the trip until about 5pm.

Totonicapán

pop 55,300 / elev 2476m

San Miguel Totonicapán is a pretty Guatemalan highland town known for its artisans. Shoemakers, weavers, tinsmiths, potters and woodworkers all make and sell their goods here. Market days are Tuesday and Saturday; it's a locals' market, not a tourist affair, and it winds down by late morning.

The ride from Cuatro Caminos is along a pine-studded valley. From Totonicapán's bus station it's a 600m walk up 4a Calle to the twin main plazas. The lower plaza has a statue of Atanasio Tzul, leader of an indigenous rebellion that started here in 1820, while the upper one – fenced off for renovations at time of research – is home to the large **colonial church** and neoclassical **municipal theater**.

ACTIVITIES

The **Casa de la Cultura Totonicapense** (☎ 5630-0554; kiche78@hotmail.com; 8a Av 2-17), 1½ blocks off the lower plaza, has displays of indigenous culture and crafts and administers a program to introduce tourists to some of the town's many craftspeople. A one-day program, requiring two weeks' advance booking, includes visits to various craft workshops (including potters, carvers of wooden masks and musical instruments, and weavers), a bit of sightseeing, a marimba concert and a traditional lunch in a private home. Rates are Q475/540/630 per person in groups of four/three/two participants, or Q655/770/900 including a stay with a local family and two meals.

An alternative program, costing Q250/288/328 per person for four/three/two participants, takes you on foot to nearby villages to visit community development projects, natural medicine projects, schools, craft workshops and Maya sacred sites. Tours in English are available on request.

Encompassing some 13 hectares of old-growth forest northeast of Totonicapán, the **Sendero Ecológico El Aprisco** (☎ 7766-2175; admission Q20; ☿ 8am-4pm) makes for some delightful hiking. Well-marked trails traverse the community-run reserve, domain of the endangered *pinabete* tree and 29 endemic bird species such as the amethyst-throated hummingbird, ocellated quail and colorfully plumed *quetzalillo* (mountain trogon). A small museum displays traditional outfits of the region, and there are adobe cabins with fireplaces, bunk beds and straw bedding. El

Aprisco is 5km up the Santa Cruz del Quiché road from Toto. Pickup trucks head this way from the east end of 7a Calle. Alternatively, the Casa de la Cultura (see opposite) can organize trips to the reserve at Q165 per person.

FESTIVALS & EVENTS

The festival of the **Apparition of the Archangel Michael** is on May 8, with fireworks and traditional dances. The **Feria Titular de San Miguel Arcángel** (Name-Day Festival of the Archangel Saint Michael) runs from September 24 to 30, peaking on September 29. Totonicapán keeps traditional masked dances very much alive with its **Festival Tradicional de Danza** – dates vary but recently it was over a weekend in late October.

SLEEPING & EATING

The Casa de la Cultura (see opposite) can arrange stays with local families, including breakfast and dinner, at Q345/410/490 per person in groups of four/three/two, including dinner and breakfast.

Hospedaje Paco Centro (☎ 7766-2810; 3a Calle 8-18, Zona 2; s/d Q35/70) Practically hidden inside a shopping center a couple of blocks from the lower plaza, this sternly managed place has big, tidy rooms of three to four beds each.

Hotel Totonicapán (☎ 7766-4458; www.hoteltotonicapan.com; 8a Av 8-15, Zona 4; s/d Q150/275) The fanciest digs in town are reasonable for the price, with big, modern rooms featuring carpeted floors, a few bits of furniture and some good views.

Restaurante Bonanza (7a Calle 7-17, Zona 4; meals Q40-60; ☉ 7am-9pm; ☎) Totonicapán's most conventional restaurant is a meat-and-tortillas sort of establishment, where bow-tied waiters deliver heaping helpings of steak, chicken and seafood.

GETTING THERE & AWAY

'Toto' buses from Quetzaltenango depart every 20 minutes or so (Q5, one hour) throughout the day from the Rotonda on Calz Independencia (passing through Cuatro Caminos). The last direct bus to Quetzaltenango leaves Toto at 6:30pm.

San Francisco El Alto

pop 41,100 / elev 2582m

High on a hilltop overlooking Quetzaltenango (17km away) stands the town of San Francisco El Alto, whose Friday **market** is regarded as the biggest and most authentic in the country.

The large plaza in front of the 18th-century church is covered in goods. Stalls are crowded into neighboring streets, and the press of traffic is so great that a special system of one-way roads is established to avoid colossal traffic jams.

The whole town is Guatemala's garment district: every inch is jammed with vendors selling sweaters, socks, blankets, jeans, scarves and more. Bolts of cloth spill from storefronts packed to the ceiling with miles of material, and this is on the quiet days!

Around mid-morning, when the clouds roll away, panoramic views can be had from throughout town, but especially from the roof of the **church**. The caretaker will let you go up for a small tip. On the way through, have a look at the church's six elaborate gilded altarpieces and remains of what must once have been very colorful frescoes.

San Francisco's big party is the **Fiesta de San Francisco de Asís**, celebrated around October 4 with traditional dances such as La Danza de Conquista and La Danza de los Monos.

Banco Reformador (2a Calle 2-64; ☉ 9am-5pm Mon-Fri, 9am-1pm Sat) changes traveler's checks and has a Visa ATM.

Hotel Vista Hermosa (☎ 7738-4010; cnr 2a Calle & 3a Av; s/d Q60/120, without bathroom Q30/60) does indeed have beautiful views, out over the valley to the Santa María volcano. Rooms are spacious, with balconies and (thankfully) hot showers. Thursday nights it's likely to fill up.

Good *chuchitos* (small tamales), *chiles rellenos* and other prepared foods are sold from stacks in the marketplace. For a sit-down meal, **El Manantial** (2a Calle 2-42; mains Q30), a couple of blocks below the plaza, is pleasant and clean, serving up steaks and a few *tipica* dishes.

Buses to San Francisco leave Quetzaltenango's Terminal Minerva (passing through Cuatro Caminos) frequently throughout the day. The trip takes about 1½ hours and costs Q9. Because of San Francisco's one-way streets, arriving from Quetzaltenango you'll want to get off on 4a Av at the top of the hill (unless you like walking uphill) and walk towards the church. To go back to Cuatro Caminos, buses run downhill along 1a Av.

Momostenango

pop 58,900 / elev 2259m

Beyond San Francisco El Alto, 26km from Quetzaltenango, this town, set in a pretty

THE HIGHLANDS

mountain valley along a road through pine woods, is famous for the making of *chamarras*, or thick woolen blankets, as well as ponchos and other woolen garments. The best days to look for these are Wednesday and Sunday, the main market days. A good basic blanket costs around Q150.

Momostenango is noted for its adherence to the ancient Maya calendar and observance of traditional rites. The town's five main altars are the scene of ceremonies enacted on important celestial dates such as the summer solstice; the spring equinox; the start of the Maya solar year, known as El Mam, observed in late February; and Wajshakib' B'atz, the start of the 260-day *tzolkin* year. Observance of these ceremonies can be particularly powerful and rewarding, but few are open to outsiders, so don't assume showing up means you'll be able to participate. Should you be allowed access, be sure to treat altars and participants with the utmost respect.

INFORMATION

Banco Reformador (1a Calle 1-3, Zona 1; ☯ 9am-5pm Mon-Fri, 9am-1pm Sun) changes traveler's checks and has a Cajero 5B.

The **Centro Cultural** (☯ 8am-6pm Mon-Fri, 8am-1pm & 2-5pm Sat), in the *municipalidad* building, is good for tourist information.

SIGHTS & ACTIVITIES

Los Riscos, geological oddities on the edge of town, are worth the brief hike it takes to see them. Technically eroded pumice, these bunches of tawny spires would make a fine location for a low-budget sci-fi flick. To get there, go one block south of the plaza and head downhill on 3a Av, Zona 2. Turn right at the bottom of the hill, go left at a fork (signed 'A Los Riscos'), then after 100m turn right along 2a Calle and walk 300m to Los Riscos.

Takiliben May Wajshakib Batz (☎ 7736-5537; wajshkibbatz13@yahoo.es; 3a Av 'A' 6-85, Zona 3) is a 'Maya Mission,' dedicated to studying and teaching Maya culture and sacred traditions. Its director, Rigoberto Itzep Chanchavac, is a *chuchkajau* (Maya priest) responsible for advising the community on when special days of the Maya calendars fall. Rigoberto also does Maya horoscopes (Q40) and leads full- or half-day workshops where groups of around eight can gain an understanding of customs that usually remain hidden from outsiders. His **chuj** (traditional Maya sauna; per person Q100; ☯ 4-6pm Tue & Thu) requires advance bookings. It's

located at the southern entrance to town – turn up a signed path just north of the Texaco station to find it.

The Takiliben May can also provide tourist guides for Q100 an hour. A tour with visits to Los Riscos, the sacred hill of Paclom and the ritual hot springs of Payashú costs Q100, including a homestay with a local family.

FESTIVALS & EVENTS

Wajshakib Batz' (eight thread), marking the start of the ritual *tzolkin* calender, is considered the holiest day in the cycle, when Maya 'daykeepers' are ordained. During the ceremony, usually enacted atop sacred Paclom hill (accessed from the end of 5a Calle), the candidates for priesthood are presented with a 'sacred bundle' of red seeds and crystals, which they'll use for divination readings based on the ritual calendar, then they dance around the ceremonial fire holding their bundle. As it falls at the end of a 260-day cycle, the date varies from year to year. Contact Takiliben May (see left) to find out when it falls in the current year.

SLEEPING & EATING

Hospedaje y Comedor Paclom (☎ 7736-5174; cnr 2a Av & 1a Calle, Zona 2; r per person Q25) This humble guesthouse, located over a store and eatery a block uphill from the main plaza, sports oddly colorful cinderblock-and-wood paneled rooms. Toilets are down a pink plank corridor, moldy showers are downstairs.

Hotel Otoño (☎ 7736-5078; gruvial.m@gmail.com; 3a Av A 1-48, Zona 2; r per person Q100; ☐) Momostenango's one luxury lodging has 14 modern rooms with glossy tile floors and huge bathrooms. Some feature balconies or picture windows taking in the surrounding hills.

Restaurante La Cascada (1a Calle 1-35, Zona 2; meals Q30; ☯ breakfast, lunch & dinner) This bright and clean upstairs eatery serves up simple and filling home-cooked fare with plenty of thick homemade tortillas. Try the *fresco de manzana*, a warm apple beverage.

GETTING THERE & AWAY

You can get buses to Momostenango from Quetzaltenango's Terminal Minerva (Q7, 1½ hours), from Cuatro Caminos (Q6, one hour), or from San Francisco El Alto (Q5, 45 minutes). Buses run about every 15 minutes, with the last one back to Quetzaltenango normally leaving Momostenango at 4:30pm.

THE HIGHLANDS

Laguna Chicabal

This magical, sublime lake is nestled in the crater of Volcán Chicabal (2712m) on the edge of a cloud forest. Laguna Chicabal is billed as the 'Center of Maya-Mam Cosmovision' on huge signs, both on the path leading out of town and at the crater itself. As such, it is a very sacred place and a hotbed of Maya ceremonial activity. There are two active Maya altars on its sandy shores, and Maya priests and worshippers come from far and wide to perform ceremonies and make offerings here, especially on and around May 3. The lake is 575m wide and 331m deep.

Adding to the atmosphere of mystery, a veil of fog dances over the water, alternately revealing and hiding the lake's placid contours. Amid the thick, pretty vegetation are picnic tables and one of Guatemala's most inviting campsites, right on the lakeshore. Because the lake and grounds have great ceremonial significance, campers and hikers are asked to treat them with the utmost respect. In addition, Laguna Chicabal is pretty much off-limits to tourists during the entire first week of May, so that ceremonial traditions can be observed without interference.

Laguna Chicabal is a two-hour hike from **San Martín Sacatepéquez** (also known as Chile Verde), a friendly, interesting village about 22km from Xela. This place is notable for the elaborate traditional dress worn by the village men, who sport a white tunic with red pinstripes that hangs to mid-shin and has densely embroidered red, pink and orange sleeves. A thick, red sash serves as a belt. The tunic is worn over pants that nearly reach the ankles and are similarly embroidered.

To get to the lake, head down from the highway towards the purple-and-blue church and look for the Laguna Chicabal sign on your right (you can't miss it). Hike 5km (about 45 minutes) uphill through fields and past houses until you crest the hill. Continue hiking, going downhill for 2km (15 minutes) until you reach the ranger station, where you pay the Q15 entrance fee. From here, it's another 3km (about 30 minutes) uphill to a *mirador* and then a whopping 615 steep steps down to the edge of the lake. Start early for best visibility. Coming back up, allow two hours.

For bus information, see p167. For the return, there are fairly frequent minibuses from San Martín. There are a few basic cookshacks on the square in San Martín, though you may prefer to hop off in **San Juan Ostuncalco** for a meal. In this interesting town, halfway between San Martín and Xela, the artisans are renowned for their wicker furniture and fine handcrafted instruments. San Juan's market day is Sunday.

HUEHUETENANGO
pop 144,900 / elev 1909m

Mostly a stopping-off point for more interesting places, Huehuetenango, or Huehue (*way*-way), offers few charms of its own, but some people do like it for its true Guatemalan character. Either way, there are enough eating and sleeping options to keep you happy, and the sight of the Cuchumatanes mountain range (highest in Central America) in the background makes for some striking scenery.

The lively *indígena* market is filled daily with traders who come down from surrounding villages. Surprisingly, it's about the only place you'll see traditional costumes in this town, as most citizens are *ladinos* in modern garb. Coffee growing, mining, sheep raising, light manufacturing and agriculture are the region's main activities.

For travelers, Huehue is usually a leg on the journey to or from Mexico – the logical place to spend your first night in Guatemala. The town is also the perfect staging area for forays deeper into the Cuchumatanes or through the highlands on back roads.

History

Huehuetenango was a Mam Maya region until the 15th century, when the K'iche', expanding from their capital K'umarcaaj, which is near present-day Santa Cruz del Quiché, pushed them out. Many fled into neighboring Chiapas, Mexico, which still has a large Mam population near its border with Guatemala. In the late 15th century, the weakness of K'iche' rule brought about civil war, which engulfed the highlands and provided a chance for Mam independence. The turmoil was still unresolved in 1525 when Gonzalo de Alvarado, the brother of Pedro, arrived to conquer Zaculeu, the Mam capital, for Spain.

Orientation & Information

The town center is 4km northeast of the Interamericana, and the bus station is off the road linking the two, about 2km from each. Almost every service of interest to tourists is in Zona 1 within a few blocks of the Parque Central.

THE HIGHLANDS

Huehue has no official tourist office, but folks in the *municipalidad* can generally answer any queries you might have. **Asistur** (☎ 5460-7042) can come to your assistance in a jam.

Banrural (3a Calle 6-16; ☺ 8:30am-4pm Mon-Fri, 9am-4pm Sat) has a whopping two Cajero 5B ATMs and they change euros. There are other ATMs at Banco Industrial, a block further north, and at the Banrural on Av Kaibal Balam, 100m east of the bus terminal.

The **post office** (2a Calle 3-54; ☺ 8:30am-5:30pm Mon-Fri, 9am-1pm Sat) is half a block east of the park.

Cyber Café Arrow (1a Calle 5-08; ☺ 8am-10pm) and **Internet Milenio** (4a Av 1-54; ☺ 8am-6pm Mon-Sat & 9am-1pm Sun) charge Q5 per hour for internet access.

Adrenalina Tours (☎ 7768-1538; www.adrenalina tours.com; 4a Calle 6-54) leads a bunch of interesting tours and hikes throughout the region, and offers shuttle service to key destinations (see p178).

Sights & Activities
PARQUE CENTRAL
Huehuetenango's main plaza is shaded by cylindrical-topped laurels and surrounded by the town's imposing buildings: the **municipalidad** (with its band shell on the upper floor) and the imposing neoclassical **church**. For a bird's-eye view of the situation, check out the little relief map of Huehuetenango department, which lists altitudes, language groups and populations of the various municipal divisions.

ZACULEU
With ravines on three sides, the late Postclassic religious center Zaculeu ('White Earth' in the Mam language) occupies a strategic defensive location that served its Mam Maya inhabitants well. It finally failed, however, in 1525, when Gonzalo de Alvarado and his conquistadors laid siege to the site for two months. It was starvation that ultimately defeated the Mam.

The parklike **Zaculeu archaeological zone** (admission Q50; ☺ 8am-6pm), about 200 sq m, is 4km west of Huehuetenango's main plaza. A small museum at the site holds, among other things, skulls and grave goods found in a tomb beneath Estructura 1, the tallest structure at the site.

HUEHUETENANGO		
INFORMATION		
Adrenalina Tours	1	B2
Banco Industrial	2	B1
Banrural	3	B2
Cyber Café Arrow	4	B1
Internet Milenio	5	C1
Post Office	6	C1
SIGHTS & ACTIVITIES		
Church	7	C2
Municipalidad (Town Hall)	8	B1
SLEEPING		
Hotel Casa Blanca	9	A2
Hotel Central	10	B1
Hotel Gobernador	11	C1
Hotel La Sexta	12	B2
Hotel Mary	13	C1
Hotel San Luis de la Sierra	14	A2
Hotel Zaculeu	15	B1
Royal Park Hotel	16	B2
EATING		
Café Bougambilias	17	B2
Cafetería Las Palmeras	18	C2
Hotel Casa Blanca	(see 9)	
La Fonda de Don Juan	19	B1
Mi Tierra Café	20	B2
Pastelería Monte Alto	21	B1
Restaurante Las Brasas	22	C1
Restaurante Lekaf	(see 24)	
Tacontento	23	B2
DRINKING		
Kaktus Disco	24	B3
La Biblioteca	25	B3
Museo del Café	26	A2
TRANSPORT		
Buses from Main Bus Station	27	C2
Buses to Main Bus Station	28	B2
Buses to Zaculeu	29	A2
Taxis	30	B2

Restoration by the United Fruit Company in the 1940s has left Zaculeu's pyramids, ball courts and ceremonial platforms covered by a thick coat of graying plaster. Their Disneyesque approach was hardly authentic, but the work goes further than others in making the site look as it might have done to the Mam priests and worshipers when it was still an active religious center. All that's missing are the colorful frescoes that must have once covered the exterior.

Buses to Zaculeu (Q2.50, 20 minutes) leave about every 30 minutes, 7:30am to 6pm, from in front of the school at the corner of 2a Calle and 7a Av. Make sure they're going to 'Las Ruinas' – Zaculeu is the name of a community, too. A taxi from the town center costs Q30 one way. One hour is plenty of time to look round the site and museum.

Courses

Xinabajul Spanish Academy (☎ 7764-6631; academia xinabajul@hotmail.com; 4a Av 14-14, Zona 5) offers one-to-one Spanish courses and homestays with local families. The school is located two blocks east of the bus station and two blocks south of the Interamericana.

Festivals & Events

Fiestas Julias This special event, held from July 13 to 20, honors La Virgen del Carmen, Huehue's patron saint.

Fiestas de Concepción Honoring the Virgen de Concepción, this festival is celebrated on December 5 and 6.

Sleeping

BUDGET

Hotel Central (☎ 7764-1202; 5a Av 1-33; r per person Q30; P) This rough-and-ready little number might be to your liking. Rooms are large and plain, with bathrooms downstairs. The pillared wooden interior balcony gives the place a sliver of charm and it sure is central.

Hotel Gobernador (☎ /fax 7764-1197; 4a Av 1-45; s/d Q52/80, without bathroom Q35/60; P) A little maze of rooms (don't get lost!), some much better than others – check your bed for sponge factor and your window for openability and you should be happy.

Hotel Mary (☎ 7764-1618; 2a Calle 3-52; s/d Q80/130; P) This large, older hotel has a cafe on the ground floor and worn sofas in the halls. Though sparely furnished, rooms do have comfy beds and large green-tiled bathrooms. At least one – No 310 – features a balcony.

Hotel La Sexta (☎ 7764-1488; 6a Av 4-29; s/d Q85/140; P) Cubicles flank either side of a barnlike

interior here, cheered up a bit by tropical birds and plants, not to mention aquamarine faux-leather chairs. There's a small, checkered tablecloth cafe near the front. Choose a room as far back as you can – La Sexta, as 6a Av is known, is relentless.

MIDRANGE

Hotel Zaculeu (☎ 7764-1086; www.hotelzacu leu.com; 5a Av 1-14; s/d Q115/225; 🖳 P) With nearly 125 years in operation, the Zaculeu has oodles of character, and despite its advanced age, recent renovations have kept things quite spiffy. The 36 big rooms are in two sections; those in the 'new section' (just 20 years old) are a bit pricier but brighter and more stylish. The sprawling patio area, overflowing with plants and chirping birds, is conducive to lounging, as is the excellent brick-walled bar.

Hotel San Luis de la Sierra (☎ 7764-9216; hsanluis@ intellnet.net.gt; 2a Calle 7-00; s/d Q159/207; P) The simple, smallish rooms here have pine furniture and homey touches, and there's a decent restaurant on the premises. The real attraction, though, is the rambling rainforest garden out back, with paths for strolling. No internet but you can use the cybercafe just outside.

Royal Park Hotel (☎ 7762-7774; hotelroyalpark1@ gmail.com; 6a Av 2-34; s/d Q160/300; P 🖳) This newish business hotel is one of Huehue's poshest, with gold filigree bedspreads, padded headboards and jumbo flatscreen TVs. Rooms ending in -08 have mountain views.

Hotel Casa Blanca (☎ 7769-0777; www.ecommhue hue.com/casablanca; 7a Av 3-41; s/d Q220/280; P) The bright attractive courtyard here leads onto spacious modern rooms with arched pine ceilings and good hot showers. The restaurant out back serves up good-value set lunches.

Eating

Pastelería Monte Alto (2a Calle 4-24; cakes & pastries Q6-10; 🕑 9am-9pm) This old-fashioned white-tablecloth establishment just off the plaza has a tempting array of cheesecake, eclairs, plum pie and other tantalizing pastries, plus all the essential espresso variations.

Tacontento (4a Calle 6-136; order of 3 tacos Q24) A bright, modern *taquería* with a popular patio. Aside from the beef and pork tacos they have veggie *'gringas,'* with grilled peppers, pineapple and melted cheese. The bar features a good selection of tequilas.

Mi Tierra Café (4a Calle 6-46; mains Q25-40; 🕑 breakfast, lunch & dinner) An informal cafe-restaurant

THE HIGHLANDS

ASK A LOCAL

'I'd say Huehuetenango has Guatemala's – and maybe the world's – best coffee, first because I'm a *huehueteco* (Huehueutenango local), but also because it's received so many awards at international auctions. But it has to be well processed, well selected and well roasted.'

Manrique López, Huehuetenango

serving good homemade soups and burgers. It also takes a good crack at some international dishes, muffins and a range of other goodies. Good, cheap and filling set lunches are available.

our pick **Cafetería Las Palmeras** (4a Calle 5-10; mains Q25; ☺ breakfast, lunch & dinner) One of three *comedores* in a line along the southern part of the Parque Central, Las Palmeras is a popular spot, with a team of busy cooks preparing food on the ground floor, while the open-air upper floor has dining with views over the park. The *caldo de pollo criollo* (Q25) is a must, brimming with chicken, *güisquil* and corn. Saturdays there are tasty tamales. The next door Café Bougambilias is under the same ownership with similar food, though a bit humbler in style.

Restaurante Lekaf (☎ 7764-3202; 6a Calle 6-40; pizzas Q35-100; ☺ 10am-11pm) This modern, airy dining hall has a varied menu, including sandwiches, pizza and seafood. There's live music (marimbas, folk) Thursday to Sunday evening.

Restaurante Las Brasas (4a Av 1-36; steaks Q40-55; ☺ breakfast, lunch & dinner) With a good combination of steaks, seafood stew and chop suey on offer, this retro diner should satisfy most appetites. The specialty is Cuchumatán lamb.

La Fonda de Don Juan (2a Calle 5-35; pizzas Q47-97; ☺ 24hr) The place for Huehue's night owls and early risers, La Fonda serves varied Guatemalan and international fare including good-value pizzas.

Hotel Casa Blanca (7a Av 3-41; salads Q20, steaks Q50; ☺ breakfast, lunch & dinner) For lovely surroundings, you can't beat the two restaurants at this classy hotel, one indoors, the other in the garden. On Sunday morning there's a popular breakfast buffet for Q30.

Drinking

Museo del Café (7a Av 3-24; ☺ Mon-Sat) This recently inaugurated 'museum' serves some of

Huehue's best coffee, and that's saying something. Started by Manrique López, son of a small-scale producer who grew up in Barrillas, it's not only a place to get a well-prepared cup but also learn something about the history of this bewitching bean that has so influenced Guatemala's history. Besides examining antique coffee-processing paraphernalia and some diagrams demonstrating coffee production techniques, you can roast your own for purchase. Manrique also organizes coffee plantation tours.

Kaktus Disco (6a Calle 6-40; cover Q20; ☺ 9pm-late Fri & Sat) There's not a whole lot going on in the center after hours, but the big dance floor here is a good bet, with a nonstop mix of bachata, merengue, reggaetón…anything with a beat.

La Biblioteca (6a Calle 6-28; ☺ 6pm-1am Tue-Sat, 11am-4pm Sun) Not much reading going on in 'the library,' unless it's the football scores on the big-screen TV over the bar. Popular with middle-class Guatemalans, the music and sports bar has various cozy nooks on two levels.

Getting There & Away

The bus terminal is in Zona 4, 2km southwest of the plaza along 6a Calle. It's a trash-ridden, chaotic place, where a number of companies ply the same routes, though information is not posted in any coherent fashion. Microbuses leave from the south end of the station.

Two lines with service to Guatemala City depart from their own private terminals.
Línea Dorada (☎ 7768-1566; www.lineadorada.info; Av Kaibil Balam 8-70)
Transportes Los Halcones (☎ 7765-7986; 10a Av 9-12, Zona 1)

Buses serving the main terminal include the following:
Antigua (230km) Take a Guatemala City bus and change at Chimaltenango.
Aguacatán (Q8, 30 minutes, 22km) Microbuses every 20 minutes.
Barrillas (Q50, seven hours, 139km) Continuous flow of San Pedro, Cifuentes, Lupita, San Rafael and Autobuses del Norte chicken buses, among others.
Cuatro Caminos (Q15, 1½ hours, 77km) Take any bus heading for Guatemala City or Quetzaltenango.
Gracias a Dios (Mexican border) (Q30, five hours) Four departures daily via Nentón by La Chiantlequita.
Guatemala City (five hours, 266km) Los Halcones Pullman buses (Q65) leave at 2am, 4:30am, 7am and 2pm;

Línea Dorada (Q90) buses at 2:30pm, 11pm and midnight. From the main terminal, various lines (Q50 to Q60) leave continuously until about 4pm, including Transportes El Condor, Díaz Álvarez and Velásquez.

La Mesilla (Mexican border) (Q20, two hours, 84km) Buses depart four times an hour, by various companies. In addition, Línea Dorada has one Pullman at 4:30am.

Nebaj (68km) Take a bus to Sacapulas from where there are frequent microbuses to Nebaj (or take a microbus to Aguacatán, then another to Sacapulas).

Panajachel (159km) Take a Guatemala City bus and change at Los Encuentros.

Quetzaltenango (Q20, 1½ hours, 90km) At least 14 buses depart between 6am and 4pm, by various companies.

Sacapulas (Q20, 1½ hours, 42km) Buses at 11:30am and 12:45pm (Transportes Rivas).

San Mateo Ixtatán (Q40, five hours, 111km) Take a Barillas bus.

Santa Cruz del Quiché (Q25, 2½ hours, 173km) Frequent microbuses from 5am to 5:30pm.

Soloma (Q25, 2½ hours, 70km) About 16 buses daily, from 2am to 10pm, by Transportes Josué, Transportes González and Autobuses del Norte, plus frequent microbuses.

Todos Santos Cuchumatán (Q25, 2½ hours, 40km) Four buses from 4am to 6am, after which there are sporadic microbuses going to Tres Caminos (the Todos Santos junction); from there onward transport is available. These microbuses depart from the El Calvario gas station at the corner of 1a Av and 1a Calle. After 11am, buses run roughly every half hour till 2pm, then hourly until 5pm by the Vargas, Flor de María, Todo Santera, Concepcionerita and Autobuses del Sur companies.

Adrenalina Tours (☎ 7768-1538; www.adrenalinatours.com; 4a Calle 6-54) offers daily shuttle services to Nebaj (Q165), Quetzaltenango (Q165), Panajachel (Q250) and elsewhere.

Getting Around

City buses circulate between the bus station and the town center from 5am to around 9pm. Arriving in Huehue, leave the east side of the station through the gap between the Díaz Álvarez and Transportes Fortaleza offices; cross this street and walk through the covered market opposite to a second street, where 'Centro' buses depart every few minutes (Q2). After dark, these depart from Av Kaibil Balam (aka La Pasarela), up the same street to the right; there's also a taxi stand here (Q20 to the center of town). To return to the bus station from the center, catch the buses outside the **Hotel La Sexta** (6a Av 4-29).

AROUND HUEHUETENANGO

Except for Todos Santos Cuchumatán, the mountainous far northwest of Guatemala is little visited by travelers. The adventurous few will often be a novelty to the local Maya folks they meet. Spanish skills, patience and tact will pave the way in these parts.

Chiantla
pop 10,100 / elev 2056m

Just before the climb into the Cuchumatanes, you'll come across this village, the former seat of the municipality, now practically a suburb of Huehuetenango. Its church holds the **Virgen del Rosario**, a silver statue donated by the owner of a local mine. The virgin is believed to have mystical healing powers and people come from all over the country to seek her assistance. The main date for the pilgrimage is February 2, when the town packs out with supplicants and the infirm.

Also in the church are some interesting **murals** painted in the 1950s, showing local Maya having miraculous experiences while working in the silver mines.

Another 4km on from Chiantla, **El Mirador Juan Diéguez Olaverri** overlooks Huehuetenango from a point up in the Cuchumatanes. On a clear day it offers a great view of the entire region and many volcanoes. Mounted on plaques here is the poem, *A Los Cuchumatanes*, penned by the lookout point's namesake. Local kids will recite it to you for a tip. And thanks to the recently installed **Café del Cielo**, you can now savor a cup of Huehuetenango's fine coffee along with the views.

Any bus from Huehue heading for Todos Santos, Soloma or Barillas goes through Chiantla and past the lookout.

Chancol

The Guatemalan- and French-run **Unicornio Azul** (☎ /fax 5205-9328; www.unicornioazul.com; s/d/tr Q295/560/780) is a horseback-riding ranch at Chancol, about 25km by road northeast of Huehuetenango. It offers riding through the Cuchumatanes along trails used only by local inhabitants, camping out or staying in rural accommodations. The 14 horses are well trained and cared for, and comfortable, quality saddles are provided. Besides the treks, they also offer horseback-riding workshops.

Unicornio Azul also functions as a *posada rural*, with 10 simple but comfortable rooms in the estate home or a separate building.

THE HIGHLANDS

Plenty of blankets are provided for the often-chilly nights at 3000m. Breakfast and an hour of riding are included in the rate.

Rides can range from one hour (Q130) to two/four/seven days (per person Q2000/4300/7040 with four riders, more with fewer riders). Among the options is a two-day journey to **Laguna Magdalena**, a turquoise lagoon nestled in the mountains, with massive boulders and ancient, gnarled trees scattered around. The seven-day option traverses the Cuchumatanes to the Mexican border through a number of different climatic zones and four distinct ethnic regions. The longer journeys are done only during the dry season (November to April). There are also one-day trips (Q620) for those who'd rather sleep at the *posada*.

To get to Chancol, take any bus heading for Todos Santos or Barillas and get off in La Capellanía; the owners will come pick you up (Q45).

Chiabal

High in the Sierra Cuchumatanes (3400m) amid a rocky plateau dotted with maguey plants and sheep, Chiabal, 17km east of Todos Santos, welcomes visitors looking to experience rural life in a tiny **Mam community** (☎ 5381-0540; www.asocuch.com.gt/turismoactividades.html). The villagers provide simple accommodations in four local houses and prepare hearty local fare (Q130 for three meals and a night's stay). A community-built 2.5km interpretive trail leads to the Piedra Cuache, an oddly shaped boulder at a 3666m lookout point. Guides can take you to various sites in the 18,000-hectare Todos Santos Forest Reserve, including the summit of La Torre. As compelling as the scenery is the chance to participate in community activities like herding llamas, weaving *huipiles* and planting potatoes while getting to know the local inhabitants.

Microbuses go directly to Chiabal (Q10) from the El Calvario gas station at the corner of 1a Av and 1a Calle in Huehuetenango. Otherwise, hop a Todos Santos bus and get off at Chiabal, 4km west of the turn off the Huehue–Barillas road.

Todos Santos Cuchumatán
pop 4000 / elev 2392m

Way up in the highlands, Todos Santos is as raw as Guatemalan village life gets – dramatic scenery, mud streets, beans and tortillas, and everything shut by 9pm. The community is nestled at the bottom of a deep valley and bordered by forested slopes, and the last 1¼ hours of the approach by bus are down a sporadically paved road that leaves the Huehuetenango–Soloma highway after a 1½-hour climb up from Huehue.

Traditional clothing is very much in use here and, unusually, it's the male costume that is the more eye-catching. Men wear red-and-white-striped trousers, little straw hats with blue ribbons, jackets with multicolored stripes and thick woven collars. Saturday is the main market day; there's a smaller market on Wednesday. The notorious postmarket inebriation ritual has faded into history since dry laws took over (the November 1 celebrations now being the only permissible time to get smashed).

Reasons to visit Todos Santos include good walking in the hills, learning Spanish or Mam, and getting to know a traditional and close-knit but friendly community. Todos Santos suffered terribly during Guatemala's civil war when, by some accounts, 2000 area inhabitants were murdered. It is still very poor. To supplement their subsistence from agriculture, families travel in the early part of the year to work for meager wages on coffee, sugar and cotton plantations on the Pacific Slope. Working in the US is, however, proving a more lucrative alternative for some *todosanteros* today, as the amount of new construction in the valley demonstrates, not to mention the incorporation of urban elements into the traditional outfit.

If you're coming to Todos Santos in the wet season (mid-May to November), bring warm clothes, as it's cold up here, especially at night.

ORIENTATION & INFORMATION

Todos Santos' main street is about 500m long. Towards its west end are the church and market, with the central plaza raised above street level on the south side. Buses stop here. A side street going uphill beside the plaza leads to most of the accommodations. No street names are in common use, but businesses and sights are either well signposted or known by everyone.

The Grupo de Mujeres weaving shop at the base of the Hotel Casa Familiar functions as a de facto information center and they can give you a town map.

To make telephone calls look for signs saying 'Llamadas Nacionales y Internacionales' in

THE HIGHLANDS

the area around the church. There's no ATM in Todos Santos.

Banrural (central plaza) Changes traveler's checks and euros.

Post office (8:30am-5pm Mon-Fri, 7am-11am Sat) On the central plaza.

Viajes Express (internet access per hr Q6; 8am-6pm Mon-Sat, noon-6pm Sun) Next door to Hotel Mam.

SIGHTS & ACTIVITIES

The ruins of **Tuj K'man Txun** are 500m up the uphill street beside the central plaza. Among trees on the left of the road, the site consists of a few grassy mounds and two crosses with indications of contemporary Maya offerings. The more recently installed cross commemorates the incidents of August 1982, when the army executed or tortured hundreds of alleged guerrilla collaborators, then torched many homes.

Todos Santos' **Museo Balam** (admission Q5) is in a two-story house, along a sidestreet one block east of the plaza. The collection of outfits and masks, traditional kitchen implements, archaeological finds and musical instruments comes to life when Fortunato, its creator and a community leader, is there to provide commentary.

Walking around Todos Santos provides superb opportunities to check out the rugged countryside. January to April are the best months for walking, with the best and warmest weather, but you can usually walk in the morning, before the weather closes in, year-round (except maybe in July). Get trail maps and info on hikes at Tienda Grupo de Mujeres, downstairs from Hotel Casa Familiar.

Román Stoop (5900-7795; romanstoop@yahoo.com), a Swiss expat who settled in Todos Santos in 1993, is a seasoned hiker and knows all the area trails. He can give you detailed directions or act as a guide. You can usually find him at the Tienda Grupo de Mujeres at the base of the Hotel Casa Familiar. Besides the hikes described here, he can accompany you on a five-day trek to Nebaj, traversing five linguistic zones and a number of landscapes with accommodation in community-run huts. You determine the rates.

English-speaking *todosantero* **Rigoberto Pablo Cruz** (5781-0145; rigoguiadeturismo@yahoo.com) also does guided walks of the area and runs his own agency, Viajes Express, next door to the Hotel Mam. He charges Q80 per person to take you to Las Letras.

One of the most spectacular destinations is **La Torre** (3828m), the highest nonvolcanic point in Central America. Take a bus east up the valley to the hamlet of La Ventosa (Q10, one hour) from where it's a trail walk of 8km (about 1½ hours) through limestone and gnarly *huite* trees to the top. At the summit (marked by a radio mast), the southern horizon is dotted with almost a dozen volcanoes from Tacaná on the Mexican border to Volcán Agua near Antigua. Don't do this walk in cloudy weather – you may get lost.

Las Letras, on a hillside above town, is a good morning hike of about 40 minutes. The 'Letters' spell out Todos Santos, but may be illegible; it depends on when the stones were last rearranged. Still, it's a hale hike and affords beautiful views, especially in the morning after the fog lifts. You can continue up beyond Las Letras to the villages of **Tuicoy** and **Tzichim** (30km, about five hours from Todos Santos). From Tuicoy you can detour to the Puerta del Cielo, an outstanding lookout. There's a daily bus up to Tzichim at 5:15am, if you'd rather hike down than up.

The walk to **Las Cuevas**, a sacred cave still used for Maya rituals, starts from 'La Maceta,' a tree growing out of rock beside a football field, 30 minutes by bus up the Huehue road from Todos Santos (Q6). Another trail leads to the little-visited traditional village of **San Juan Atitán**, where the women wear dazzling *huipiles*, over the mountains to the south of Todos Santos (20km, about five hours one way).

Todos Santos' chilly climate makes it a great place to try the traditional **Maya sauna** called a *chuj*. This is a small adobe building (traditionally with space for three small people) with wooden boards covering the entrance. A wood fire burns in a stone hearth inside, and water is sprinkled on the stones or heated in a ceramic jug to provide steam. Sometimes herbs are used to create aromatic vapors. If you're interested, check out the large *chuj* at the Hotel Casa Familiar (p182).

COURSES

Todos Santos' one language school, the **Hispanomaya** (5163-9293; academiahispanomaya.org), is a nonprofit that funds scholarships for village kids to go to high school in Huehue. The standard weekly price for 25 hours' one-on-one Spanish tuition, with lodging and meals in a village home, is Q985. Included

THE HIGHLANDS

are two guided walks, a seminar on local life and issues, and movies, including the documentary *Todos Santos*, which deals with local traditions and the devastation of the civil war. (Nonstudents pay a Q10 admission fee to see the film.) The school also offers classes in Mam and Maya weaving (per hour Q15).

The Hispanomaya is opposite the Museo Balam, down a sidestreet one block east of the plaza.

FESTIVALS & EVENTS

Todos Santos is famous for the annual **horse races** held on the morning of November 1 (El Día de Todos los Santos), which are the culmination of a week of festivities and an all-night spree of male dancing and *aguardiente* (cane liquor) drinking on the eve of the races. Traditional foods are served throughout the day, and there are mask dances.

SLEEPING & EATING

You can arrange **rooms** (r per person Q30, with 3 meals Q45) with families through the language school whether or not you're studying. You'll get your own bedroom, and share the bathroom and meals with the family.

Hotel Mam (s/d Q40/80) This quiet establishment just downhill from the Hotelito Todos Santos has cramped, minimally maintained rooms, all sharing electric showers. It's OK for a night or two, though, especially if you get one of the upper-level units with a big window.

Hotelito Todos Santos (☎ 5327-9313; r Q125, s/d without bathroom Q45/90) Along a side street that goes off to the left a few meters up the hill beside the plaza, this budget option has small and bare but well-scrubbed rooms with tile floors and firm beds. Three of the four rooms with private bathroom open onto the street, separate from the main part of the hotel upstairs. The casual cafe here is noted for its pancakes.

our pick **Hotel Casa Familiar** (☎ 5580-9579; roman stoop@yahoo.com; s/d Q150/200) Undergoing major renovations at the time of writing, this central lodging just down from the main plaza has the town's coziest rooms, with hardwood floors, window frames, traditional textile bedspreads, good hot showers and plenty of blankets. New features include a common room with fireplace and a roof deck with a traditional *chuj*. Have a breakfast bowl of *mosh* (porridge) at the hotel restaurant. Just two of a planned 12

rooms are done so far but if they're taken you can stay at the real family home (single/double Q60/95), a log cabin with shared kitchen and showers about a 10-minute walk uphill from the center.

Comedor Martita (meals Q20) This simple family-run *comedor*, opposite Hotel Mam, serves great food prepared with fresh ingredients by friendly hosts. You walk through the kitchen to get to the eating area, which has a nice view over the town and valley. A typical meal might be boiled chicken, rice, vegetables, beans, a *refresco* (soft drink or fruit juice) and coffee.

Comedor Katy (meals Q22) Women in traditional garb attend to pots of *pepián* and chicken soup bubbling over glowing embers at this similarly rustic cook shack just below the central plaza. There are tables on a terrace overlooking the market activity.

SHOPPING

Tienda Grupo de Mujeres, downstairs from the Hotel Casa Familiar, has a great selection of *típica* clothing and accessories, all produced by a women's weaving cooperative. They also prepare a fine espresso with 100 percent Huehuetenango beans.

GETTING THERE & AWAY

Buses and microbuses depart from the main street between the plaza and the church. About 10 buses leave for Huehuetenango (Q25, 2½ hours) between 5am and 7am, then run roughly hourly until 4pm. Occasional microbuses leave throughout the day, whenever they fill up. There are three buses northwest to Jacaltenango at 4:30am, 5am and 6am. The first goes all the way to the Mexican border at La Mesilla

Adrenalina Tours (p179) offers shuttle service from Huehuetenango on Saturdays (Q165). From Todos Santos, Viajes Express has shuttles to Huehuetenango (Q100 per person), Panajachel (Q250) and La Mesilla (Q150), all with a minimum of six passengers.

San Juan Ixcoy
pop 3400

North of the Todos Santos turnoff, the paved road winds up between often mist-shrouded cliffs and a precipitous gorge. Out of the mists emerge a pair of massive fingers of granite, known as the **Piedras de Captzín**.

Soon after, you arrive in San Juan Ixcoy, where the women wear traditional white *hui-*

THE HIGHLANDS

piles embroidered at the collar and hanging almost to their ankles. A rough 10km track leads to the **Pepajaú waterfalls** from the village of San Lucas Quisil, just north of San Juan. Their 250m drop is an impressive sight, particularly after the rains. Pickup trucks can get you to the trailhead at the Río Quisil, from where it's a delightful two- to three-hour walk to the falls.

Soloma

pop 16,800 / elev 2300m

Some 70km north of Huehuetenango, Soloma fills a valley and spreads up into the hills. This agricultural town is one of the biggest in the Cuchumatanes. The Maya here speak Q'anjob'al, but most of the *ladino* cowboys will greet you in English! Soloma's prosperity and its residents' language skills can be attributed to the migratory laborers who annually make the arduous trip to the US, working as cowhands, auto detailers or landscapers. On Sunday, market day, the town floods with people from surrounding villages. There's a **Banrural** (closed Sun), with Cajero 5B ATM, on Soloma's plaza.

Hotel Don Chico (7780-6087; 4a Calle 3-55; s/d Q90/180;), a pink-and-pastel palace, is the most comfortable lodging in town. Rooms are large, with good firm beds and waterfall scenes on the walls. The **Comedor Chiantlequita** (mains Q20-40; breakfast, lunch & dinner), a busy, upstairs joint just down from the main plaza, serves toothsome home-cooked fare like *pepián de chumpipe* (turkey in pumpkin-seed sauce).

See p178 for details on buses to Soloma. Microbuses serving San Juan Ixcoy and other nearby villages leave from beside the plaza.

Santa Eulalia

pop 9100 / elev 2520m

Just over the hill from Soloma, the town of Santa Eulalia feels much more remote and traditional. It can get quite chilly here. This is sheep-farming territory, and you'll see shepherds wearing *capixays* (short woolen ponchos) in the fields. The town has a reputation for producing some of the finest marimbas in the country, with locally grown hormigo trees providing the wood for the keys. Factories and workshops producing marimbas line the streets around the plaza. If you're interested in the production process, wander in and ask to be shown around.

Nearby is the **Cerro Cruz Maltín protected area**, comprised of over 7000 hectares of primary cloud forest. Contact **Luic Mateo** (5784-3686; luicmateo@hotmail.com), a resident naturalist, for information about guided tours through the reserve.

If you want to spend the night, try the **Hotel del Coronado** (4010-8524; s/d Q50/100), a pink, pyramidal tower easily spotted from the plaza. The hotel takes fine advantage of its lofty porch; room No 8 has the best views. All rooms have good, firm beds with plenty of blankets, and the attached *comedor* serves hearty chicken soup and tamales.

A couple of buses per day make the run from Soloma to Santa Eulalia (Q5, 30 minutes) and minibuses leave from the plaza whenever full.

San Mateo Ixtatán

pop 25,500 / elev 2469m

From Santa Eulalia the rough road keeps climbing through pasturelands and occasional pine forest – sit on the left and you can see all the way to Mexico – and after 30km reaches San Mateo Ixtatán. Perched on an aerie with the jagged peaks of the Cuchumatanes trailing off into the clouds, the town unfolds organically over the green slopes. (The mist can descend early here, wiping out visibility by early afternoon.) Quaint buildings with pillared verandas and painted designs on the doors line largely traffic-free paths. The women of this small Chuj town wear captivating *huipiles*, lacy white affairs with concentric floral patterns embroidered on the neckline.

San Mateo is the logical place to break the journey if you're heading for Laguna Lachuá from Huehue – it's smaller but better looking than Barillas down the road, and there are a couple of interesting sights around town.

San Mateo's **church** has a primitive charm. Beyond a rather dumpy facade is an austere interior with crude fruit motifs painted on the pillars. The real action seems to be out front in the atrium, where a smoking altar attests to the enduring Maya influence.

Just below town, the unrestored ruins of **Wajxaklajunh** feature some weathered stelae, a ball court and a few pyramid-shaped temples, with outstanding views over the valley. They're a 10-minute walk from the church. Head 200m down the main street and turn right at the Tienda San Rafael. Go downhill, bearing right past the *hospedaje*. Continue down (bearing left) and take a right at the Ferretería y Librería Gómez, then the first

THE HIGHLANDS

left between two buildings. Follow that path 100m to the ruins.

Down in the valley east of town is a **salt mine** (☉ 1-4pm) that was used by the Mam Maya during the Classic period. Bring a flashlight if you'd like to descend into the mineshaft, housed beneath an ancient stone structure, as do many local inhabitants to gather their supply of the copious black salt, believed to have medicinal qualities.

The newish **Hotel Magdalena** (☎ 5374-3390; s/d Q75/150) is easily the most comfortable option in town and the showers are scalding hot (but ask if the heater is on beforehand). From the park, go uphill and take the first street on the right; the yellow box is adjacent to the Banco Agromercantil. Right above that turnoff is **Los Picones al Chaz Chaz** (☉ breakfast, lunch & dinner), a spiffy dining hall where in the morning you can have fresh tamales with delicious salsas, as well as tacos and steaks.

Buses leave regularly for Huehue (Q5, six hours) and Barillas (Q15, 4½ hours).

East to Playa Grande

Leaving San Mateo, the road drops and weather becomes slightly kinder. After 28km, you'll reach **Barillas**, a prosperous coffee-growing town with a lowland feel. The **Hotel Arizona** (☎ 7780-2758; r per person Q74), a garish structure near the bus terminal, has sparkling rooms and comfy beds. It's your best bet if planning an early departure to Playa Grande. There are regular microbuses between the terminal and the town center, a seven-minute ride (Q1.50). In town, the efficiently run **Hotel Villa Virginia** (☎ 7780-2236; cnr 3a Calle & 3 Av; r per person Q77) is right on the plaza, with a restaurant attached. There's a Banrural, with Cajero 5B ATM, at the corner of the park. Three restaurants are along 3a Calle within a block of the park; Restaurant El Café, opposite the Villa Virginia, does a mean *caldo de gallina*.

If you're moving on for Cobán or El Petén, get an early start. Pickups head for Playa Grande (Q50, four hours) hourly from 3am to 4pm. They depart from opposite the Hotel Arizona, around the corner from the terminal, then make a stop in town by the market to pick up more people and cargo. The road goes through the remote villages and forests of the Ixcán region, alternating between packed gravel and a tortuous exposed-boulder surface, but the trip is fascinating. Bad weather can extend the travel time by two or three hours. Ask around to see what conditions are like before committing to this trip.

Nentón, Los Huistas & Gracias a Dios

In a lower-lying, more lushly vegetated zone between the Cuchumatanes and the Mexican border, Nentón and the Los Huistas area to its south suffered grievously during the civil war. The area has a few archaeological remains and a distinctive culture including the Popti' (Jakalteko) Maya language.

About 30km north of Nentón along the paved road from the Interamericana at Finca La Trinidad is the junction for the planned Transversal del Norte, the highway that will eventually traverse northern Guatemala. It's possible to cross into Mexico at remote Gracias a Dios, 10km west, but only Guatemalan immigration maintains a post there and you would have to head to Mexican immigration at Comitán or San Cristóbal de Las Casas to get your passport stamped. Microbuses travel between here and Comitán, Mexico, on a regular basis. There is basic accommodation in Gracias a Dios if you get stuck. For details on buses to Nentón and Gracias a Dios, see p178.

Approximately 5km south of the Finca La Trinidad junction is the turnoff for the **Posada Rural Finca Chaculá** (☎ 5205-9328; www.unicornioazul. com; s/d/tr Q190/300/390), a community-tourism project started by returnees from five different ethnic groups who took refuge in Mexico during the civil war. Their 37-sq-km farm features a small lagoon, some Maya archaeological sites, a waterfall and abundant forest. The old estate house has been outfitted with three comfortable rooms with hot showers, and meals are served. Inguat-trained guides lead excursions to the Laguna Brava (Yolnajab; see below) and Hoyo Cimarrón, a gigantic, almost perfectly cylindrical crater near the Mexican border. From Huehuetenango, buses bound for Yalambojoch and Gracias a Dios pass by here.

Yalambojoch & Laguna Brava

East from Gracias a Dios, along the route that is destined to become the Transversal del Norte northern highway, is the hamlet of Yalambojoch. Most of the inhabitants fled during the conflict of the 1980s, and have only recently returned to pick up the pieces of their lives. A European NGO has provided funding to resettle the community, constructing wells,

THE HIGHLANDS

houses, a school and a **cultural center** (per@cnl.nu), and ecotourism is being developed in the area.

One of the chief attractions for visitors is the Laguna Brava (also known as Laguna Yolnajab), 6.5km to the north, an extension of Mexico's Lagunas de Montebello. There's good swimming in the crystalline waters of the lagoon, reached by a two-hour descent on foot or horseback from Yalambojoch (best attempted from March to June). There's a Q25 entry fee to the lagoon, and guides charge Q75 to take you down, plus Q75 per day for horses. Adrenalina Tours in Huehuetenango (see p175) brings groups down to camp; cabins with stoves are also available.

East of Yalambojoch, a series of surprisingly intact Maya pyramids dating from the 10th century stand near the site of what used to be the village of San Francisco, which fell victim to one of the army's most atrocious massacres as part of Rios Montt's scorched earth campaign during the civil war.

Some visitors come here to experience rural life in a Chuj community, and volunteer opportunities are available teaching at the cultural center or working on reforestation projects.

Accommodations at Yalambojoch include a few comfortable cabins and a large but well-maintained dorm (Q50 per person). Guests have access to a well-equipped kitchen or can get meals at a pair of *comedores* for about Q20.

Buses by La Chiantlequita (Q30, six hours) depart for Yalambojoch from Huehuetenango at 4:45am and 1pm, returning at 4:45am and 9:30am. There is also transport from San Mateo Ixtatán.

LA MESILLA

The Guatemalan and Mexican immigration posts at La Mesilla and Ciudad Cuauhtémoc are 4km apart, and you can take a taxi (Q4) between the two. The strip in La Mesilla leading to the border post has a variety of services, including a police station, a post office and a bank. There are also moneychangers who will do the deal – at a good rate if you're changing dollars, a terrible one for pesos or quetzals.

With an early start from Huehuetenango you should have no trouble getting through this border and onward to Comitán or San Cristóbal de Las Casas, Mexico, in one day (or in reverse). During daylight hours fairly frequent buses and combis run from Ciudad Cuauhtémoc to Comitán (Q30 to Q40, 1¼ hours), where you can find onward transport to San Cristóbal (two hours). From La Mesilla buses leave for Huehuetenango (Q20, two hours) at least 20 times between 5:45am and 6pm. Línea Dorada runs Pullmans to Guatemala City (Q130, eight hours) at 12:30pm and 9pm. If you get marooned in La Mesilla, try **Hotel Mily's** (☎ 7773-8665; s/d Q120/160; 🕸), 500m up from immigration on the right, with cell-like rooms around a garden of tropical foliage. Bargaining may be in order here. Another reasonable option is **Hotel María Eugenia 2** (☎ 7722-8077; s/d Q100/200), 300m from the border and down an alley to the left.

The Pacific Slope

Divided from the highlands by a chain of volcanoes, the flatlands that run down to the Pacific are known universally as La Costa. It's a sultry region – hot and wet or hot and dry, depending on the time of year – with rich volcanic soil good for growing coffee at higher elevations and palm-oil seeds and sugarcane lower down.

Archaeologically, the big draws here are Takalik Abaj and the sculptures left by pre-Olmec civilizations around Santa Lucía Cotzumalguapa.

The culture is overwhelmingly *ladino* (of mixed European and indigenous heritage), and even the biggest towns are humble affairs, with low-rise wooden or concrete houses and the occasional palm-thatched roof.

A fast highway, the Carretera al Pacífico (Hwy 2), roughly parallels the coast all the way from Ciudad Tecún Umán on the Mexican border to Ciudad Pedro de Alvarado on the El Salvador border. The 250km from Ciudad Tecún Umán to Guatemala City can be covered in five hours by bus – much less than the 345km of the Interamericana (Hwy 1) through the highlands from La Mesilla.

Guatemalan beach tourism is seriously underdeveloped. Monterrico is the only real contender in this field, helped along by a nature reserve protecting mangroves and their inhabitants. Almost every town on the beach has places to stay, although more often than not they're very basic affairs. Sipacate gets the best waves and is slowly developing as a surf resort, although serious surfers find much more joy in Mexico or El Salvador.

HIGHLIGHTS

- Getting away from absolutely everything at the one-hotel town of **Tilapita** (p187)
- Investigating the bridge in history between the Olmec and the Maya while strolling through the grassy **Parque Arqueológico Takalik Abaj** (p192)
- Spotting wildlife among the mangrove-lined canal and lagoons of the **Biotopo Monterrico-Hawaii** (p201)
- Checking out the big mysterious heads carved by the non-Maya Pipil culture at **Santa Lucía Cotzumalguapa** (p195)
- Getting wet at **Parque Acuático Xocomil** (p192) and dizzy at **Parque de Diversiones Xetulul** (p192), two fun parks near Retalhuleu

History

Despite it being one of the first settled areas in Guatemala, relatively little is known about the Pacific region's early history. Many archaeological sites are presumed overgrown by jungle; others have been destroyed to make way for agriculture.

What *is* known is that the Olmecs were among the first to arrive, followed by the Ocós and Iztapa, whose cultures appear to have flourished around 1500 BC.

Although these cultures were much more humble than those of their northerly counterparts, they developed a level of sophistication in stone carving and ceramics. It's also thought that the coastal region acted as a conduit, passing cultural advances (like the formation of writing and the Maya calendar) from north to south.

Between AD 400 and 900, the Pipil moved in, most likely displaced by the turmoil in the Mexican highlands, and began farming cacao, which they used to make a (rather bitter) chocolate drink. They also used cacao beans as currency.

Towards the end of the Postclassic period, the K'iche', Kaqchiquel and Tz'utujil indigenous groups began moving in as population expansion in Guatemala's highlands had made food become scarce and land squabbles common.

Pedro de Alvarado, the first Spaniard to land in Guatemala, arrived here in 1524, pausing briefly to fight the K'iche' as a sort of forerunner to a much larger battle around present-day Quetzaltenango. Franciscan missionaries were dispatched to the region and began a lengthy, largely unsuccessful attempt to convert the locals.

Further agricultural projects (mostly indigo and cacao) were started around this time, but it wasn't until independence that the region became one of the country's main agricultural suppliers, with plantations of coffee, bananas, rubber and sugarcane.

In the languid tropical climate here, not much changes, particularly the social structure. The distribution of land – a few large landholders and many poorly paid, landless farm workers – can be traced back to these early post-independence days. You'll see the outcome as you travel around the region – large mansions and opulent gated communities alongside squalid, makeshift workers' huts.

CIUDAD TECÚN UMÁN

This is the preferable and busier of the two Pacific Slope border crossings, having better transport connections with other places in Guatemala. A bridge links Ciudad Tecún Umán with Ciudad Hidalgo (Mexico). The border is open 24 hours daily, and several basic hotels and restaurants are available, but you should aim to be clear of the border well before dark. The town has all the trademarks of the seedy border town. Banks here change US dollars and traveler's checks.

From Ciudad Tecún Umán frequent buses depart until about 6pm along the Carretera al Pacífico to Coatepeque, Retalhuleu, Mazatenango, Escuintla and Guatemala City. There are direct buses to Quetzaltenango (Q35, 3½ hours) up until about 2pm. If you don't find a bus to your destination, take one to Coatepeque or, better, Retalhuleu, and change buses there. On the Mexican side, buses run from Ciudad Hidalgo to the city of Tapachula (M$15, 50 minutes) every 10 minutes, 4:30am to 10pm.

EL CARMEN

A bridge across the Río Suchiate connects El Carmen with Talismán (Mexico). The border is open 24 hours daily. It's generally easier and more convenient to cross at Tecún Umán. There are few services at El Carmen, and those are very basic. Most buses between here and the rest of Guatemala go via Ciudad Tecún Umán, 39km south, and then along the Carretera al Pacífico through Coatepeque, Retalhuleu and Escuintla. On the way to Ciudad Tecún Umán, most stop at Malacatán on the road to San Marcos and Quetzaltenango, so you could try looking for a bus to Quetzaltenango there, but it's more dependable to change at Coatepeque (Q20, two hours from El Carmen) or Retalhuleu.

On the Mexican side, minibuses run every 10 minutes between Talismán and Tapachula, from 5am to 9pm (M$10).

TILAPITA

Just south of the Mexican border, this little fishing village is the place to come for some seriously laid-back beach time. There's exactly one hotel here (and it's a good one) and it's a world away from the often hectic, scruffy feel of other towns along the coast.

The village, which sits on a sandbar cut off from the mainland by the Ocós estuary,

THE PACIFIC SLOPE

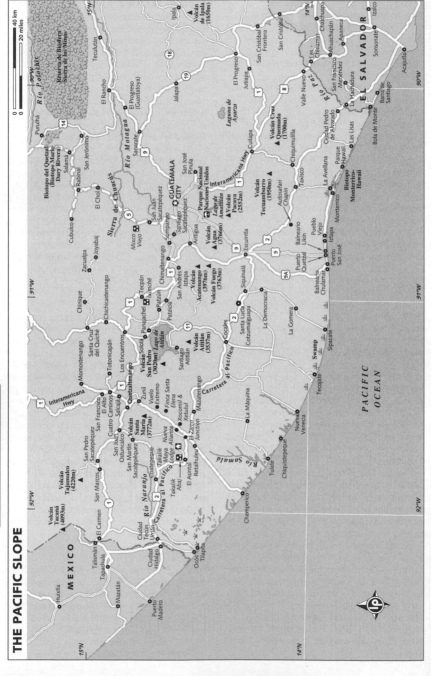

is only reachable by boat from the town of Tilapa. There's some excellent swimming to be had here, although as with all the beaches along this coast, the undertow can be quite serious and there are no lifeguards. If you're not a strong swimmer, don't go too far out.

There's not a whole lot to do (which is kind of the point), but local fishermen offer fascinating boat tours of the estuary, mangroves and adjoining **Reserva Natural El Manchón** for Q150 per boat per hour. There are no guarantees, but local wildlife includes iguanas, crocodiles, white herons, egrets and kingfishers.

Back in Tilapita, the **Tortugario Tilapita**, across the path from Hotel El Pacífico, is fighting an uphill battle to preserve the local sea turtle population, and would be quite happy for whatever help they can get if you're looking for some volunteer work.

One of the best accommodation deals along the coast, **Hotel Pacific Mar** (☎ 5914-1524; www.playatilapa.com; s/d Q60/80; ☲) is nothing fancy, but it has decent-sized, clean concrete rooms. Delicious meals (Q45) are served in an oversized thatched-roof *palapa* (thatched palm-leaf shelter), and generally consist of the catch of the day – shrimp, fish and *caldo de mariscos* (seafood stew) are always a good bet. The good-sized swimming pool is a welcome addition, as things can get slightly warm here.

Coming from Tecún Umán, you might luck onto a direct minibus (Q10, 45 minutes) to Tilapa – if not, take any bus heading out of town, get off at the Tilapa turnoff and wait for an onward bus there. A much more scenic option is to take a bus to Ocós (Q6, 30 minutes) and a *lancha* (small boat; Q15, 45 minutes) to Tilapita from there. Coming in the other direction, direct buses run from Coatepeque to Tilapa (Q10, 1½ hours). Once you get to Tilapa, turn left down the side street and follow it to the dock, where you will find *lanchas* waiting. The 10-minute ride to Tilapita costs Q10 per person in a shared *lancha,* or you can hire a private one to make the trip for Q50. Tell the *lanchero* you are going to *el hotel* (although he will probably know that already). If you get stuck, there are cheap, not-so-lovely hotels in Tilapa.

Pullman drivers doing the Guatemala City–Tecún Umán run often stop in at Tilapa. If you're headed straight for the capital or anywhere in between, ask around to find out when the next departure is.

COATEPEQUE
pop 55,700

Set on a hill and surrounded by lush coffee plantations, Coatepeque is a brash, fairly ugly and chaotic commercial center, noisy and humid at all times. If you read the papers, the name Coatepeque should be familiar. A major stopover on the Columbia–Mexico drugs 'n' guns route, this town probably has more gang-related activity than any other outside of Guatemala City. Barely a day goes by without somebody getting shot in a turf war or revenge killing. Tourists are never the target, and rarely get caught in the crossfire (although one foreign volunteer did quite literally in 2006).

It *is* another facet of Guatemala, and probably not one you want to get too acquainted with. If you're here to see the ruins at Takalik Abaj, Retalhuleu is a much better bet. If you really want to stay here or (more likely) get stuck, there are a couple of places in the relatively quiet town center that will put you up admirably.

Maya Expeditions (see p74) runs rafting expeditions on the nearby Río Naranjo for Q790 per person per day.

Hotel Baechli (☎ 7775-1483; 6a Calle 5-45, Zona 1; s/d Q95/165; ℗) has cool, simple rooms with fan.

Hotel Europa (☎ 7775-1396; 6a Calle 4-01, Zona 1; s/d Q90/180) is a cool and tranquil older-style hotel. Front rooms have balconies overlooking the plaza, but can be noisy during the day.

Good restaurants (mostly in the steakhouse and/or Chinese vein) are scattered around the park. **Itabo's** (5a Av 3-65; mains Q30-50; ☯ breakfast & lunch) is vaguely hip and completely out of place in otherwise workaday Coatepeque, and serves good breakfasts and a decent range of coffee drinks.

Coatepeque is a major transport hub for the Pacific Slope, and bus connections here are good. The bus terminal, in the center of town, has departures to El Carmen (Q20, two hours), Tecún Umán (Q20, two hours), Quetzaltenango (Q25, 2½ hours), Tilapa (Q10, 1½ hours) and Retalhuleu (Q9, one hour), among others. Several Pullman bus companies stop here on the Guatemala City–Tecún Umán run, providing much more comfort and possibly a welcome spot of air-conditioning in the tropical heat. They stop on the street one block east of the bus terminal and charge Q50 for the four-hour run to Guatemala City.

THE PACIFIC SLOPE

RETALHULEU
pop 42,350 / elev 240m

Arriving at the bus station in Retalhuleu, or Reu (*ray-oo*) as it's known to most Guatemalans, you're pretty much guaranteed to be underwhelmed. The neighborhood's a tawdry affair, packed out with dilapidated wooden cantinas and street vendors.

The town center, just five blocks away, is like another world – a majestic, palm-filled plaza, surrounded by some fine old buildings. Even the city police get in on the act, hanging plants outside their headquarters.

On the outskirts are the homes of wealthy plantation owners, impressive weekend getaways, and the gated communities that are springing up all over the country.

The real reason most people visit is for access to Takalik Abaj, but if you're up for some serious downtime, a couple of world-class fun parks are just down the road (see p192).

Tourists are something of a curiosity in Reu and are treated well. The heat is fairly stifling, and if you can splurge for digs with a pool, you'll be thankful for it; at the very least, make sure your room has a fan.

Orientation & Information

The town center is 4km southwest of the Carretera al Pacífico, along Calzada Las Palmas, a grand boulevard lined with towering palms. The main bus stop is on 10a Calle between 7a and 8a Avs, northeast of the plaza. To find the plaza, look for the twin church towers and walk toward them.

There is no official tourist office, but people in the *municipalidad* (town hall), on 6a Av facing the east side of the church, will do their best to help.

Banco Industrial (cnr 6a Calle & 5a Av) changes US dollars and traveler's checks, gives cash advances on Visa cards and has a Visa ATM.
Banco Agromercantil (5a Av), facing the plaza, changes US dollars and traveler's checks and has a MasterCard ATM.
Internet (cnr 5a Calle & 6a Av; per hr Q5) provides internet access.
ReuXtreme (☎ 5202-8180; www.reuxtreme.com; 4a Calle 4-23, Zona 1), operating out of the Hostal Casa Santa María (see opposite) is the local tour operator, offering kayaking trips, birdwatching and nature walks, tours of local archaeological sites and shuttles to Antigua,

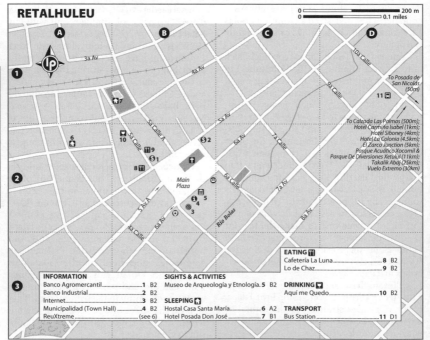

RETALHULEU

0 — 200 m
0 — 0.1 miles

To Posada de San Nicolás (50m)

To Calzada Las Palmas (500m);
Hotel Carmiña Isabel (1km);
Hotel Siboney (4km);
Hotel La Colonia (4.5km);
El Zarco Junction (5km);
Parque Acuático Xocomil &
Parque De Diversiones Xetulul (11km);
Takalik Abaj (25km);
Vuelo Extremo (30km)

Main Plaza

Río Bolas

INFORMATION		SIGHTS & ACTIVITIES		EATING 🍴	
Banco Agromercantil	1 B2	Museo de Arqueología y Etnología	5 B2	Cafetería La Luna	8 B2
Banco Industrial	2 B2			Lo de Chaz	9 B2
Internet	3 B2	SLEEPING 🛏			
Municipalidad (Town Hall)	4 B2	Hostal Casa Santa María	6 A2	DRINKING 🍷	
ReuXtreme	(see 6)	Hotel Posada Don José	7 B1	Aquí me Quedo	10 B2
				TRANSPORT	
				Bus Station	11 D1

THE PACIFIC SLOPE

Quetzaltenango and Panajachel, among others.

Sights & Activities

The **Museo de Arqueología y Etnología** (6a Av 5-68; admission Q15; 🕑 8am-12:30pm & 2-5pm Tue-Sat, 9am-12:30pm Sun) is a small museum of archaeological relics. Upstairs are historical photos and a mural showing locations of 33 archaeological sites in Retalhuleu department.

You can **swim** at the Siboney and La Colonia hotels (see below and right) even if you're not staying there. The cost is Q15 at the Siboney and Q25 at La Colonia, where there's also a poolside bar.

Sleeping

Out on the Carretera al Pacífico are several hotels. These tend to be 'tropical motels' by design, with bungalows, pools and restaurants. They are convenient if you have a car or can get a bus to drop you on the spot.

Posada de San Nicolás (☎ 7771-4386; posadasan nicolasreu@hotmail.com; 10a Calle 8-50, Zona 1; r per person with fan/air-con Q80/100; 🔀) The best budget deal in town are these simple, clean rooms a couple of blocks from the bus stop.

ourpick **Hostal Casa Santa María** (☎ 7771-6136; www.hostalcasasantamaria.com; 4a Calle 4-23, Zona 1; s/d from Q120/240; 🔀 🛜 🛒) One of the more atmospheric options in town, this small hotel offers eight cool and spacious rooms with minimal but tasteful decorations. The small swimming pool in the courtyard is a good place for a dip.

Hotel Carmiña Isabel (☎ 7771-7217; Calz Las Palmas 2-71, Zona 2; s/d Q150/250; 🔀 🛒) The Calzada Las Palmas used to be *the* place to live in Reu, and is still lined with stately mansions. This hotel is a fine example – rooms aren't huge but the grounds and pool area are lovely.

Hotel Siboney (☎ 7772-2174; www.hotelsiboney .com; Cuatro Caminos, San Sebastián; s/d Q200/300; 🅿 🔀 🖥 🛒) There's a good blend of tropical and modern themes going on here. Poolside rooms fill quickly, especially on weekends, so you might want to book ahead. You'll find it 4km northeast of town where Calzada Las Palmas meets the Carretera al Pacífico. Coming from Quetzaltenango or the south, ask the bus to drop you here to avoid backtracking.

Hotel Posada Don José (☎ 7771-0180; www.hotel posadadedonjose.com; 5a Calle 3-67, Zona 1; s/d Q260/330; 🅿 🔀 🛒) A beautiful colonial-style hotel built around a huge swimming pool. Swan dives from the top balcony are tempting, but probably unwise. Rooms are spacious and comfortable – they're slowly remodeling here, so it's worth having a look at a few before deciding.

Hotel La Colonia (☎ 7772-2048; www.hlacoloniareu. com; Carretera al Pacífico Km 178; s/d Q320/400; 🅿 🔀 🛒) A few hundred meters east of the Siboney, La Colonia has a fairly luxurious layout. The sweet little duplex bungalows seem trapped in the '70s, but they still offer a pretty good deal. The big swimming pool with poolside bar doesn't go astray in this heat.

Eating & Drinking

Reu seems to be slightly obsessed with pizza – 5a Av north of the plaza is almost wall-to-wall pizzerias.

Cafetería La Luna (5a Calle 4-97; lunch incl drink Q20, dinner Q30; 🕑 breakfast, lunch & dinner) Opposite the west corner of the plaza, this is a town favorite for simple but filling meals in a low-key environment.

Lo de Chaz (5a Calle 4-65; mains Q25-40; 🕑 breakfast, lunch & dinner) A simple place, right off the plaza, serving up good breakfasts, icy beer, soups, snacks and seafood.

Aquí me Quedo (5a Calle 4-20; 🕑 Wed-Sat 10pm-1am) Your best bet for a few drinks in a lively atmosphere without bursting your eardrums is this friendly little upstairs bar with a great balcony that catches the odd breeze.

Getting There & Away

Most buses traveling along the Carretera al Pacífico detour into Reu. Departures include the following:

Champerico (Q9, one hour, 38km) Buses every few minutes, 6am to 7pm.

Ciudad Tecún Umán (Q13, 1½ hours, 78km) Every 20 minutes, from 5am to 10pm.

Guatemala City (Q45/70 regular/Pullman, three hours, 196km) Every 15 minutes, from 2am to 8:30pm.

Quetzaltenango (Q11, one hour, 46km) Buses every 30 minutes, from 4am to 6pm.

Santa Lucía Cotzumalguapa (Q22, two hours, 97km) Some Escuintla- or Guatemala City–bound buses might drop you at Santa Lucía; otherwise get a bus to Mazatenango ('Mazate') and change there.

Shared taxis (Q5) are the best way to get to El Asintal (for Takalik Abaj). Look for station wagons with 'Asintal' painted on the windscreen around the bus stop and plaza.

AROUND RETALHULEU
Parque Acuático Xocomil & Parque de Diversiones Xetulul

If you have children along, or simply if the heat is getting to you, head out to the **Parque Acuático Xocomil** (☎ 7772-9400; www.irtra.org.gt; Carretera CITO Km 180.5; adult/child Q100/50; ☼ 9am-5pm Thu-Sun), a gigantic water park in the Disneyland vein, but with a distinct Guatemalan theme. Among the 14 water slides, two swimming pools and two wave pools are re-creations of Maya monuments from Tikal, Copán and Quiriguá. Visitors can bob along a river through canyons flanked with ancient temples and Maya masks spewing water from the nose and mouth. Three real volcanoes – Santiaguito, Zunil and Santa María – can be seen from the grounds. Xocomil is very well executed and maintained, and kids love it. It's at San Martín Zapotitlán on the Quetzaltenango road, about 12km north of Reu.

Next door to Xocomil on the same road is the even more impressive **Parque de Diversiones Xetulul** (☎ 7722-9450; www.irtra.org.gt; Carretera CITO Km 180.5; adult/child Q100/50; ☼ 10am-6pm Thu-Sun). It's a theme park with representations of a Tikal pyramid, historical Guatemalan buildings and famous buildings from many European cities, plus restaurants and many first-class rides. You need an extra Q50 bracelet for unlimited rides.

These two attractions are both run by **IRTRA** (Instituto de Recreación de los Trabajadores de la Empresa Privada de Guatemala; Guatemalan Private Enterprise Workers' Recreation Institute), which administers several fun sites around the country for workers and their families. Between them, Xocomil and Xetulul comprise the most popular tourist attraction in Guatemala, with over a million visitors a year.

If you'd like to stay close to all this action, there are a few hotels along this stretch of the highway, but none so nice as the IRTRA-run **Hostales** (☎ 7722-9100; www.irtra.org.gt; Carretera CITO Km 180.5; r with fan/air-con from Q330/360; P ⊠ �), right across the road. It's set on lush, tropical grounds that feature swimming pools, spa bath, various sports fields and probably the most impressive mini-golf course in the country. There are seven main buildings within the complex, each decorated in a different style – Colonial, Mediterranean, Asian, African, Maya – but rooms are spacious, modern and comfortable throughout. The best time to come is Sunday to Wednesday – otherwise the place packs out and prices rise considerably. There are a few restaurants (mains from Q50) on the premises, serving Guatemalan staples at reasonable prices.

Any bus heading from Retalhuleu toward Quetzaltenango will drop you at Xocomil, Xetulul or Hostales.

Vuelo Extremo

Continuing towards Quetzaltenango from Retalhuleu, right by the roadside, you'll find this **zip line park** (☎ 7764-1931; Carretera a Retalhuleu Km 198; 3/4/11 cables Q75/100/150; ☼ 6am-6pm). If you're into the whole zip line/canopy tour thing, this is one of the better-value ones in the country. It starts and ends with a terrifying 300m-long, 29m-high zip across the valley over the highway and then follows a circuit zigzagging down the hill on the other side. For the fainter of heart there are some nice walking trails (Q25), crossing swinging bridges and passing by small waterfalls.

Parque Arqueológico Takalik Abaj

About 25km west of Retalhuleu is the **Parque Arqueológico Takalik Abaj** (admission Q50; ☼ 7am-5pm), a fascinating archaeological site set on land now occupied by coffee, rubber and sugarcane plantations. Takalik Abaj was an important trading center in the late pre-Classic era, before AD 250, and forms a historical link between Mesoamerica's first civilization, the Olmecs, and the Maya. The Olmecs flourished from about 1200 to 600 BC on Mexico's southern Gulf coast, but their influence extended far and wide, and numerous Olmec-style sculptures have been found at Takalik Abaj.

The entire 6.5-sq-km site spreads over nine natural terraces, which were adapted by its ancient inhabitants. Archaeological work is continuing outside the kernel of the site, which is the Grupo Central on terrace No 2, where the most important ceremonial

ASK A LOCAL

'People come to the coast and they head straight for the beach, but there are many great places that they just drive straight past – Takalik Abaj (see right), coffee *fincas* (farms), mangroves, IRTRA (above)…for foreigners, a lot of the coast is like an unknown region.'

Daniel Vásquez, Retalhuleu

and civic buildings were located. Classic-era baths and multicolored floors were discovered here in late 2005. The largest and tallest building is Estructura 5, a pyramid 16m high and 115m square on terrace No 3, above No 2. This may have formed one side of a ball court. Estructura 7, east of Estructura 5, is thought to have been an observatory. What's most impressive as you move around the park-like grounds, with temple mounds, ball courts and flights of steps paved with rounded river stones, is the quantity of stone sculpture dotted about, including numerous representations of animals and aquatic creatures (some in a curious pot-bellied style known as *barrigón*), miniature versions of the characteristic Olmec colossal heads, and early Maya-style monuments depicting finely adorned personages carrying out religious ceremonies.

Takalik Abaj, which had strong connections with the city of Kaminaljuyú (in present-day Guatemala City), was sacked about AD 300 and its great monuments, especially those in Maya style, were decapitated. Some monuments were rebuilt after AD 600 and the site retained a ceremonial and religious importance for the Maya, which it maintains to this day. Maya from the Guatemalan highlands regularly come here to perform ceremonies.

To reach Takalik Abaj by public transportation, catch a shared taxi from Retalhuleu to El Asintal (Q5, 30 minutes), which is 12km northwest of Reu and 5km north of the Carretera al Pacífico. Less frequent buses leave from a bus station on 5a Av A, 800m southwest of Reu plaza, about every half-hour, 6am to 6pm. Pickups at El Asintal provide transportation on to Takalik Abaj (Q5), 4km further by paved road. You'll be shown round by a volunteer guide, whom you will probably want to tip. You can also visit Takalik Abaj on tours from Quetzaltenango (see tour operators on p163).

Takalik Maya Lodge (☎ 2333-7056; www.takalik.com; package/bed & breakfast per person Q620/370), set on the grounds of a working farm 2km past the entrance to the Takalik Abaj (and on top of a large, unexcavated section of it) is by far the most comfortable place to stay in the area. Accommodation options include the old farmhouse, or newly constructed 'Maya-style' houses set in the middle of the forest. Package rates include meals and tours of the coffee, macadamia and rubber plantation as well as guided horseback tours of the waterfalls on the property and the archaeological site. Any

pickup from El Asintal passing Takalik Abaj will drop you at the entrance.

Nueva Alianza

This fair-trade **coffee farm** (☎ 5348-5290, in Quetzaltenango 5047-2233; www.comunidadnuevaalianza.org; dm/s/d without bathroom Q65/85/170; ☐) was taken over by its ex-employees when the owner went bankrupt and ran off with their back wages. They now offer a range of tours (Q25 per person) around the farm and local countryside as well as workshops detailing the community's fascinating history and present. Set on a hillside overlooking the coast, the farm has gorgeous views, and the hike to the nearby waterfall comes with some very welcome swimming at the end of it. Various short- and long-term volunteer positions are available. The easiest way to get here is by contacting the office in Quetzaltenango and coming when a Spanish school comes on tour (most weekends). Otherwise it's easy enough from Retalhuleu. Buses leave at midday (but get there early) from the main terminal – look for the one that says 'Hochen' – and it's about a one-hour ride out to the farm. For more rural tourism options in the area, see boxed text, p194.

CHAMPERICO
pop 8500

Built as a shipping point for coffee during the boom of the late 19th century, Champerico, 38km southwest of Retalhuleu, is a tawdry, sweltering, dilapidated place that sees few tourists. Nevertheless, it's one of the easiest ocean beaches to reach on a day trip from Quetzaltenango, and heat-starved students still try their luck here. Beware of strong waves and an undertow if you go in the ocean, and stay in the main, central part of the beach: if you stray too far in either direction you put yourself at risk from impoverished, potentially desperate shack dwellers who live towards the ends of the beach. Tourists have been victims of violent armed robberies here.

Most beachgoers come only to spend the day, but there are several cheap hotels. **Hotel Maza** (☎ 7773-7180; r with fan/air-con Q125/250), with large clean rooms just across the road from the beach, is a good bet. All the seaside eateries offer a similar deal – fresh seafood for around Q40 to Q80 per plate. *Camarones al ajillo* (garlic shrimp) and *caldo de mariscos* (seafood stew) are the standout items. As always, the busiest place will have the freshest food. All

THE PACIFIC SLOPE

AGROTURISMO

With so many beautiful *fincas* (farms) in gorgeous rural settings, it was only a matter of time before agro-tourism started to take hold in Guatemala. This is seriously low-impact tourism – often you can stay in the original farmhouse and tours basically consist of walking around the property. Most *fincas* offering tours and accommodation still make most of their money from agriculture – they're not just sitting around waiting for you to show up. If you're planning on staying at any of the places below, get in touch a few days in advance to let them know you're coming.

Aldea Loma Linda (☎ 5724-6035; www.aldealomalinda.com; r per person without bathroom volunteers/visitors Q25/50) A beautiful little village set right on the southern foothills of the Santa María volcano. There are some great walks (Q50 for around three hours) in the surrounding countryside, where an estimated 280 bird species (including the quetzal) make this place their home throughout the year. Accommodations are basic but comfortable and meals (Q25/10 volunteers/visitors) are eaten with local families. Volunteers can work in the community's organic vegetable garden, the worm farm or in forest conservation. Buses for Loma Linda (Q8, two hours) leave from Retalhuleu at midday, 12:30pm, 1:30pm and 3pm.

Finca Santa Elena (☎ 7772-5294; www.fincasantaelena.com; Carretera a Quetzaltenango Km 187; s/d without bathroom Q125/250;) Set just off the main highway, this is one of the most easily accessible *fincas* in the region. Tours (Q55 to Q80 per person) are wonderfully informative – one takes you through the coffee production process, while the other plunges into the local forest, passing rivers, waterfalls, bamboo forest and a spot that thousands of butterflies naturally inhabit. Accommodation is in the original farmhouse, a lovely wooden building, and most rooms have great views. Home-cooked meals cost around Q50. To get here, take any bus between Quetzaltenango and Retalhuleu and ask to be let off at the Entrada a Palmarcito (Km 187). The *finca* entrance is up the concrete road, 400m on the right.

Reserva El Patrocinio (☎ 7771-4393; www.reservapatrocinio.com; r per person all-inclusive Q820) By far the fanciest option listed here, this is a working coffee, macadamia and rambutan (among other crops) farm that has been converted into a private nature reserve. Sitting on 140 hectares, there are walks galore, canopy zip lines (Q100), informative tours (Q40 to Q120) through the plantations and a decent restaurant (meals around Q100) with panoramic views. Accommodation is in a stylish, modern house set on the hillside overlooking the valley. If you're staying here, all meals and the above activities are included in the price. The reserve is 14km off the main road about 18km north of Retalhuleu – ask for transport options when making reservations.

---

other things being equal, Adolfo's has a great wooden deck out over the sand and some of the best shower/bathroom facilities along this strip. The last buses back to Quetzaltenango leave at about 6pm, a bit later for Retalhuleu.

MAZATENANGO
pop 53,100 / elev 370m

Mazatenango, 23km east of Retalhuleu, is the capital of the Suchitepéquez department. It's a center for the farmers, traders and shippers of the Pacific Slope's agricultural produce. There are a few serviceable hotels if you need to stop in an emergency. Otherwise just keep on keeping on.

TULATE

Another beach town that's yet to make it onto the radar of most travelers is Tulate. The great thing about this beach is that, unlike others along the coast, the water gets deep very gradually, making it a great place to swim and just hang around and have some fun. The waves rarely get big enough to surf, but bodysurfers should be able to get a ride any time of the year. To get to the beach you have to catch a boat (Q5) across the estuary. Once on the other side, the water's 500m in front of you, straight down the only paved street. If you're heading towards the Paraíso or Iguana, avoid the long hot walk along the beachfront by taking the riverfront path to the left as soon as you get off the *lancha*. If you don't feel like walking, the *lancha* to the Paraíso/Iguana costs Q50/100.

There are three hotels in Tulate worth mentioning. All have restaurants, but the best, most atmospheric dining is at the little shacks right on the beachfront where good fresh seafood meals start at around Q35.

Villa Victoria (☎ 4185-3605; r with fan/air-con Q150/300; ⚡ ⛵), on the main street, halfway between the boat landing and the beach, is a reasonable deal. Rooms are fresh and simple, with two double beds. It also doubles as a Turicentro, meaning that local kids come and use the pool (which has an awesome waterslide, by the way) and they crank up the music ridiculously early on weekends.

Hotel La Iguana (☎ 2478-3135; r midweek/weekend Q250/300; ⛵), 1km further along from the Paraíso, has simple, pleasing rooms with a double bed and a bunk in each. It's a fair walk from the center, but good-value meals (Q35) are available in the restaurant.

Playa Paraíso (☎ 7872-1191; bungalows Q350; ⛵) is a comfortable if slightly worn option about 1km down the beach to the left from the main street. The bungalows here have two double beds, a sitting room and laid-back little balconies out front. There are hammocks strung around the property and a good, if somewhat pricey, restaurant serves meals any time. Things can get a little hectic on weekends, but midweek you may just have the place to yourself.

Buses run direct to Tulate from Mazatenango (Q12, two hours) along a good, newly paved road. Coming from the west, it's tempting to get off at Cuyotenango and wait for a bus there to avoid backtracking. The only problem with this is that buses tend to leave Mazatenango when full, so you might miss out on a seat.

CHIQUISTEPEQUE

On a virtually untouched stretch of beach, this little fishing village is home to the **Hamaca y Pescado Project** (☎ 7858-2700; www.hamacaypescadoesp.blogspot.com; s/d Q60/120), a grassroots education and environmental awareness project.

You can come to volunteer in the literacy program that they run, or just hang out on the beach. Accommodation is in comfortable rustic beachside *cabañas* (cabins), and home-cooked meals go for Q25 each. If you've got a group together, you can rent out a house for Q500 per night that sleeps five comfortably. If you're coming from Tulate, get off at La Máquina and change buses there. Otherwise, it's best to get to Mazatenango for one of the two daily buses (10:30am and 1:30pm) to Chiquistepeque (three hours, Q15).

SANTA LUCÍA COTZUMALGUAPA
pop 95,300 / elev 356m

Another 71km eastward from Mazatenango is Santa Lucía Cotzumalguapa, an important stop for anyone interested in archaeology. In the fields and *fincas* near the town stand great stone heads carved with grotesque faces and fine relief scenes, the product of the enigmatic Pipil culture that flourished here from about AD 500 to 700. In your explorations you may get to see a Guatemalan sugarcane *finca* in full operation.

The town, though benign enough, is unexciting. The local people around here are descended from the Pipil, an ancient culture that had linguistic and cultural links with the Nahuatl-speaking peoples of central Mexico. In early Classic times, the Pipil who lived here grew cacao, the money of the age. They were obsessed with the ball game and with the rites and mysteries of death. Pipil art, unlike the flowery, almost romantic style of the Maya, is cold, grotesque and severe, but still very finely done. When these 'Mexicans' settled in this pocket of Guatemala, and where they came from, is not known, though connections with Mexico's Gulf Coast area, whose culture

---

EXPLORE MORE OF THE PACIFIC SLOPE

The coast is, logically, all about the beach. The two most popular beach spots for travelers happen to be the ones closest to Quetzaltenango and Antigua – Champerico and Monterrico respectively, and they suffer for their popularity, both with foreign and Guatemalan tourists.

There are, however, plenty of little beach towns that are worth considering, where quite often you'll have the place to yourself:

Tilapita (p187) Literally a one-hotel village, this is a great place to get away from it all and take a couple of mangrove tours while you're at it.

Tulate (p194) The coastline's gentle slope into the ocean makes this one of Guatemala's best swimming beaches.

Sipacate (p198) Guatemala's surf capital goes off year round, especially between December and April.

Chiquistepeque (p195) A mellow little beach town with an excellent community project that's always looking for volunteers.

was also obsessed with the ball game, have been suggested.

Orientation & Information

Santa Lucía is now bypassed to the south by Hwy 2, but the original highway running through the south of town is still known as the Carretera al Pacífico, and the best places

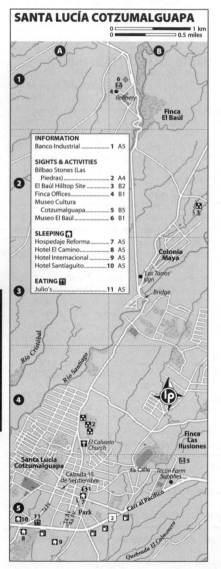

SANTA LUCÍA COTZUMALGUAPA

INFORMATION		
Banco Industrial	1	A5

SIGHTS & ACTIVITIES		
Bilbao Stones (Las		
Piedras)	2	A4
El Baúl Hilltop Site	3	B2
Finca Offices	4	B1
Museo Cultura		
Cotzumalguapa	5	B5
Museo El Baúl	6	B1

SLEEPING		
Hospedaje Reforma	7	A5
Hotel El Camino	8	A5
Hotel Internacional	9	A5
Hotel Santiaguito	10	A5

EATING		
Julio's	11	A5

to stay are on and just off it. The main plaza is 400m north from the highway, along 3a or 4a Avs.

There are three main sites to visit, all outside town: El Baúl hilltop site, about 4.5km north; the museum at Finca El Baúl, 2.75km further north; and the Museo Cultura Cotzumalguapa, off the highway 2km northeast of town.

Taxi drivers in Santa Lucía's main square will take you round all three sites for about Q200 without too much haggling. In this hot and muggy climate, riding at least part of the way is the least you can do to help yourself.

Banco Industrial (cnr 4a Av & 4a Calle), a block north of the plaza, changes US dollars cash and traveler's checks and has a Visa ATM.

Sights
EL BAÚL HILLTOP SITE

This site has the additional fascination of being an active place of pagan worship for local people. Maya people regularly, and especially on weekends, make offerings, light fires and candles and sacrifice chickens here. They will not mind if you visit as well, and may be happy to pose with the idols for photographs in exchange for a small contribution.

Of the two stones here, the great, grotesque, half-buried head is the most striking, with its elaborate headdress, beaklike nose and 'blind' eyes with big bags underneath. The head is stained with wax from candles, splashes of liquor and other drinks, and with the smoke and ashes of incense fires, all part of worship. People have been coming here to pay homage for more than 1400 years.

The other stone is a relief carving of a figure with an elaborate headdress, possibly a fire god, surrounded by circular motifs that may be date glyphs.

To get there you leave town northward on the road passing El Calvario church. From the intersection just past the church, go 2.7km to a fork in the road just beyond a bridge; the fork is marked by a sign saying 'Los Tarros.' Buses heading out to Finca El Baúl, the plantation headquarters, pass this sign. Take the right-hand fork, passing a settlement called Colonia Maya on your right. After you have gone 1.5km from the Los Tarros sign, a dirt track crosses the road: turn right here, between two concrete posts. Ahead now is a low mound topped by three large trees: this is the hilltop site. After about 250m, fork right between two more identical concrete posts, and follow this track round in front of the mound to its end after some 150m, and take the path up on to the mound, which is actually a great ruined temple platform that has not been restored.

MUSEO EL BAÚL

About 2.75km on foot, or 5km by vehicle, from the hilltop site is **Museo El Baúl** (admission free; ☻ 8am-4pm Mon-Fri, 8am-noon Sat). It comprises a very fine open-air collection of Pipil stone sculpture collected from around Finca El Baúl's sugarcane fields. A large stone jaguar faces you at the entrance. Other figures include four humans or monkeys with arms folded across their chests, a grinning, blank-eyed head reminiscent of the one at the hilltop site, carvings of skulls, and at the back a stela showing a personage wearing an animal headdress, standing over a similarly attired figure on the ground: seemingly winner and loser of a ball game.

To get there, if driving, return to the fork with the Los Tarros sign. Take the other fork this time (what would be the left fork as you come from Santa Lucía), and follow the paved road 3km to the headquarters of the Finca El Baúl sugarcane plantation. Buses trundle along this road every few hours. (If you're on foot, you can walk from the hilltop site back to the crossroads with the paved road. Cross the road and continue along the dirt track. This will eventually bring you to the asphalt road that leads to the *finca* headquarters. When you reach the road, turn right.)

Approaching the *finca* headquarters (6km from Santa Lucía's main square), you cross a bridge at a curve. Continue uphill and you will see the entrance on the left, marked by a guard post and a sign 'Ingenio El Baúl Bienvenidos.' Tell the guards that you would like to visit the *museo*, and you should be admitted. Pass the sugar refinery buildings to arrive at the museum on the right.

MUSEO CULTURA COTZUMALGUAPA

At the headquarters of another sugarcane plantation, Finca Las Ilusiones, is **Museo Cultura Cotzumalguapa** (admission Q25; ☻ 8am-4pm Mon-Fri, 8am-noon Sat). The collection here, of sculptures found around Las Ilusiones' lands, has some explanatory material and you'll probably be shown around by the caretaker. It includes a reconstruction of a sacrificial altar with the original stones, and photos of some fine stelae that were removed to the Dahlem Museum in

Berlin in 1880. The most impressive exhibit, Monumento 21, is actually a fiberglass copy of a stone that still stands in the fields of Finca Bilbao (part of Las Ilusiones' plantations), depicting what may be a shaman holding a sort of puppet on the left, a ball-game player in the middle with a knife in one hand, and a king or priest on the right holding what may be a heart. Another copy of this stone, along with one of Monumento 19, lies on the ground across the street from the museum. Along the road just before the bridge to the *finca* house are copies of some of the sculptures from the El Baúl museum.

About 1.5km east of the town center on Carretera al Pacífico (Hwy 2), shortly before the Tecún farm supplies depot, take a side track 400m to the left (north) to find the museum.

BILBAO STONES

Monumento 21, whose copy is in the Museo Cultura Cotzumalguapa, still stands with three other fine sculpted stones dotted about the Finca Bilbao cane fields to the northeast of El Calvario church, on the north edge of Santa Lucía town. In the past, tourists have regularly visited these stones, often guided through the tall cane to Las Piedras (the Bilbao Stones) by local boys. This is an isolated area and assaults on tourists are not unknown – ask around to find out what the current safety situation is.

Sleeping & Eating

The best hotels around are out on the entrance to town. You're not missing much by being out here.

Hospedaje Reforma (4a Av 4-71; s/d Q40/70) This hotel has exactly three things going for it: it's cheap, it's central, and the patio is decorated with stuffed boars' heads. And if you like sleeping in dark and airless little concrete cells, make that four.

Hotel Internacional (☎ 7882-5504; Callejón los Mormones; s/d Q90/140; P 🕸) Down a short lane (signposted) off Carretera al Pacífico is the best budget hotel in town. It has clean, good-sized rooms with a fan, cold showers and a TV. Air-con is Q70 extra.

Hotel El Camino (☎ 7882-5316; Carretera al Pacífico Km 90.5; s/d with fan Q140/220; P 🕸 ☎) About 200m east along the highway from the Santiaguito, Hotel El Camino's rooms are almost ridiculously large, with a few sticks of furniture like clothes racks and writing tables. You could organize a game of five a side with the rest of the floor space, but don't tell management it was our idea.

Hotel Santiaguito (☎ 7882-5435; Carretera al Pacífico Km 90.4; s/d Q380/420; P 🅿 🗙 🏊) On the highway on the west edge of town, the Santiaguito is fairly lavish for Guatemala's Pacific Slope, with spacious tree-shaded grounds and a nice swimming pool (open to nonguests for Q20). The large rooms have huge, firm beds and are set around a jungly patio/parking area. The spacious restaurant is cooled by ceiling fans and serves up good cheeseburgers and slightly overpriced meals (Q30 to Q80).

Julio's (Carretera al Pacífico Km 90.5; mains Q30-50; ☯ breakfast, lunch & dinner) An excellent little local diner serving up satisfying breakfasts and good-value set meals.

Getting There & Away

As Hwy 2 now bypasses Santa Lucía, a lot of buses along it do not come into town. Coming to Santa Lucía from the east, you will almost certainly need to change buses at Escuintla (Q9, 30 minutes). From the west you will probably have to change at Mazatenango (Q13, 1¼ hours). At Cocales, 23km west of Santa Lucía, a road down from Lago de Atitlán meets Hwy 2, providing a route to or from the highlands. Eight buses daily run from Cocales to Panajachel (Q22, 2½ hours, 70km, between about 6am and 2pm). Ask about the current situation, as at the time of writing there were reports of robberies along this stretch of road.

LA DEMOCRACIA
pop 6600 / elev 165m

La Democracia, a nondescript Pacific Slope town 10km south of Siquinalá, is hot day and night, rainy season and dry season. During the late Preclassic period (300 BC to AD 250), this area, like Takalik Abaj to the northwest, was home to a culture showing influence from southern Mexico. There is a 5B ATM on the main plaza.

Sights

Facing the plaza, along with the church and the modest Palacio Municipal, is the small, modern **Museo Regional de Arqueología** (☎ 7880-3650; admission Q30; ☯ 8am-4pm Tue-Sat), which houses some fascinating archaeological finds. The star of the show is an exquisite jade mask. Smaller figures, yokes used in the ball game, relief carvings and other objects make up the rest of this small but important collection.

At the archaeological site called Monte Alto, on the outskirts of La Democracia, huge basalt heads and pot-bellied sculptures have been discovered. These heads resemble crude versions of the colossal heads that were carved by the Olmecs on Mexico's southern gulf coast some centuries previously.

Today, these great **Olmecoid heads** are arranged around La Democracia's newly renovated main plaza, set in their own little roofed stands and illuminated at night. As you come into town from the highway, follow signs to the *museo*.

Sleeping & Eating

Guest House Paxil de Cayala (☎ 7880-3129; s/d without bathroom Q50/100) Half a block from the plaza, La Democracia's only place to stay is OK for the night, with big, mosquito-proofed rooms.

Burger Chops (mains Q25-45; ☯ breakfast, lunch & dinner) Also just off the square, this is as close as the town gets to a restaurant.

The flour tortillas stuffed with meat from the little roadside stands around the plaza are delicious, and a bargain at Q15.

Getting There & Away

The Chatía Gomerana company runs buses every half-hour, 6am to 4:30pm, from the Centra Sur terminal in Guatemala City to La Democracia (Q20, two hours) via Escuintla. From Santa Lucía Cotzumalguapa, catch a bus 8km east to Siquinalá (8km) and change there.

SIPACATE

An hour and a half down the road from Santa Lucía is Guatemala's surf capital. Waves here average 6ft, the best time being between December and April. The town is separated from the beach by the Canal de Chiquimulilla. Oddly unexploited, the beach here has only a couple of hotels, the budget choice being **El Paradon** (☎ 4593-2490; www.surfguatemala.net84.net; campsite/dm/r per person without bathroom Q20/45/170), a rustic little surf camp to the east of the village. It's run by a couple of Guatemalan surfers. Board and kayak hire, surf lessons and good, simple meals (Q30 to Q50) are available. Book in advance.

Straight across the canal from Sipacate is **Rancho Carillo** (☎ 5517-1069; www.marmaya.com; r from Q375, 6-person bungalow from Q800; 🗙 🏊), a short boat ride (Q30 return) from town. The only trouble you'll have sleeping is from the noise of crashing waves. Call ahead and you'll probably be able to get a better price. Surfboards are available for rent here. There are a couple of cheaper, basic *hospedajes* (budget hotels; single/double Q35/80) in town, but remember you'll be paying for the boat ride every day. Buses from Guatemala City's Centra Sur terminal (Q32, 3½ hours) pass through La Democracia en route to Sipacate every two hours.

ESCUINTLA
pop 144,700

Surrounded by rich green foliage, Escuintla should be a tropical idyll where people swing languidly in hammocks and concoct pungent meals of readily available exotic fruits and vegetables. In fact, it's a hot, shabby commercial and industrial city that's integral to the Pacific Slope's economy but not at all important to travelers, except for making bus connections. Banks are located around the plaza. There's an ATM in the **Farmacia Herdez** (cnr 13a Calle & 4a Av), one block uphill from the bus terminal. Escuintla's hotel and restaurant scene is limited. For budget digs, try the **Hotel Costa Sur** (☎ 5295-9528; 12a Calle 4-13; s/d Q80/110; ☒), which has decent, cool rooms with TV and fan. Air-con costs an extra Q20. More comfortable is the **Hotel Sarita** (☎ 7888-1959; Av Centro América 15-32; s/d Q380/480; ☒ ☜ ☒), behind the gloriously air-conditioned restaurant (mains Q40 to Q70) of the same name. It's a short walk from the bus terminal. Even closer is **Jacobo's** (4a Av 14-62; mains Q20-40; ☽ lunch & dinner), which offers reasonable Chinese food in clean and tranquil surrounds.

All buses from the terminal pass along 1a Av, but if you really want to get a seat, head to the main bus station in the southern part of town, just off 4a Av. The station entrance is marked by a Scott 77 fuel station. Buses depart for Antigua (Q7, one hour) about every half-hour, from 5:30am to 4:30pm. Buses going to Guatemala City (Q35, 1½ hours) go about every 20 minutes from the street outside, from 5am to 6pm. Buses to Puerto San José (Q6, 45 minutes), some continuing to Iztapa, have similar frequency. There are buses all the way through to Monterrico at 12:50pm, 3:30pm and 4:50pm (Q25, one hour); otherwise catch a bus to Puerto San José or Iztapa and make a connection there. Buses coming along the Carretera al Pacífico may drop you in the north of town, necessitating a sweaty walk through the hectic town center if you want to get to the main station.

AUTOSAFARI CHAPÍN

About 25km southeast of Escuintla, **Autosafari Chapín** (☎ 2363-1105; www.autosafarichapin.com; Carretera al Pacífico Km 87.5; adult/child Q60/50; ☽ 9:30am-5pm Tue-Sun) is a drive-through safari park and animal conservation project earning high marks for its sensitivity and success in breeding animals in captivity. Species native to Guatemala here include white-tailed deer, tapir and macaws. Around the grounds also roam non-native species such as lions, rhinos and leopards. There is a restaurant and pool, and it makes a good day if you're traveling with kids. It's more fun if you have your own vehicle, but if not, a 20-minute cruise through the park in a minibus is included in the admission price. Various companies run buses here (Q10, 1½ hours) from the Centra Sur terminal in Guatemala City. They leave every 10 minutes, from 4:30am to 5:30pm.

PUERTO SAN JOSÉ & BALNEARIO LIKÍN

Guatemala's most important seaside resort leaves a lot to be desired. But if you're eager to get into the Pacific surf, head 50km south from Escuintla to Puerto San José and neighboring settlements.

Puerto San José (population 19,600) was Guatemala's most important Pacific port in the latter half of the 19th century and well into the 20th. Now superseded by the more modern Puerto Quetzal to the east, Puerto San José languishes and slumbers, except at weekends and holidays when thousands of Guatemalans pour into town. The beach, inconveniently located across the Canal de Chiquimulilla, is reached by boat.

It's smarter to head west along the coast 5km (by taxi or car) to **Balneario Chulamar**, which has a nicer beach and also a suitable hotel or two.

About 5km east of Puerto San José, just past Puerto Quetzal, is Balneario Likín, one of Guatemala's only upmarket Pacific resorts. Likín is much beloved by well-to-do families from Guatemala City who have seaside houses on the tidy streets and canals of this planned development.

IZTAPA
pop 5900

About 12km east of Puerto San José is Iztapa, Guatemala's first Pacific port, used by none other than Pedro de Alvarado in the 16th century. When Puerto San José was built in

1853, Iztapa's reign as the port of the capital city came to an end, and it relaxed into a tropical torpor from which it has yet to emerge.

Iztapa has gained renown as one of the world's premier **deep-sea fishing** spots. World records have been set here, and enthusiasts can fish for marlin, sharks and yellowfin tuna, among others. November through June is typically the best time to angle for sailfish. **B&B Worldwide Fishing Adventures** (☎ in USA 888-479-2277; www.wheretofish.com) and **Fishing International** (☎ in USA 800-950-4242; www.fishinginternational.com) run all-inclusive deep-sea fishing tours to Iztapa from the USA. It is also possible to contract local boat owners for fishing trips, though equipment and comfort may be nonexistent and catch-and-release could prove a foreign concept. The boat owners hang out at the edge of the Río María Linda – bargain hard. Yellowfin tuna will likely be out of reach for the local boats, as these fish inhabit the waters some 17km from Iztapa.

There's not much to do in Iztapa. The best thing to do is get a boat across the river to the sandbar fronting the ocean, where the waves pound and a line of palm-thatched restaurants offer food and beer.

Should you want to stay, the **Sol y Playa Tropical** (☎ 7881-4365/6; 1a Calle 5-48; s/d Q200/250; 🗪) has tolerable rooms with fan and a bathroom, on two floors around a swimming pool that monopolizes the central patio. Air-con costs an extra Q50.

Getting There & Away

The bonus about Iztapa is that you can catch a bus from Guatemala City all the way here (Q25, 1½ hours). They leave about every half-hour, from 5am to 6pm, traveling via Escuintla and Puerto San José. The last bus heading back from Iztapa goes around 5pm.

Most people will be just passing through here en route to Monterrico – there are two

---

THE ONE THAT DIDN'T GET AWAY

Somewhere between five and 40 miles off the coast of Iztapa, chances are that right now a sportfisher is hauling in a billfish. This area is recognized as one of the world's top sportfishing locations – the coastline here forms an enormous, natural eddy and scientists who have studied the area have concluded this might be the largest breeding ground for Pacific sailfish in the world.

Catches of 15 to 20 billfish per day are average throughout the year. During high season (October to May) this number regularly goes over 40.

Guatemala preserves its billfish population by enforcing a catch-and-release code on all billfish caught. Other species, such as dorado and tuna, are open game, and if you snag one, its next stop could well be your frying pan.

If you'd like lessons, or you're looking for an all-inclusive accommodation-and-fishing package, check www.greatsailfishing.com. Also, see listings above for more operators offering tours and packages.

Fish here run in seasons. There's fishing all year round, but these are the best months:

- May to October – dorado
- June to September – roosterfish
- September to December – marlin
- September to January – yellowfin tuna
- October – sea bass
- October to May – sailfish

As in any part of the world, overfishing is a concern in Guatemala. The prime culprits here, though, are the commercial fishers, who use drag netting. Another concern, particularly for inland species and shrimp, is the practice of chemical-intensive agriculture. Runoff leeches into the river system, decimating fish populations and damaging fragile mangrove ecosystems.

It's estimated that Guatemala's Pacific coast has lost more than 90% of its original mangrove forests. The mangroves serve as nurseries for fish and shellfish and the trees maintain water quality and prevent erosion. They also provide food and income for local populations, but all along the Pacific coast, commercial shrimp farming is moving in. Over the past decade, commercial shrimp farms have consumed about 5% of all the remaining mangroves in the world.

options. Follow the street 1km east from Club Cervecero bar, where the buses stop, and get a boat across the river to Pueblo Viejo (Q5 per person in passenger *lanchas;* Q10 per vehicle, including passengers, on the vehicle ferry). From the far side regular buses leave for the pretty ride to Monterrico (Q8, one hour). The other option for drivers is to keep following the road east until you get to the new bridge (Q15 one way) across to Pueblo Viejo.

MONTERRICO

The coastal area around Monterrico is a totally different Guatemala. Life here is steeped with a sultry, tropical flavor – it's a place where hanging out in a hammock is both a major endeavor and a goal. Among the main cash crops here is *pachete* (loofah), which get as big as a man's leg. In season, you see them everywhere growing on trellises and drying in the sun. The architecture, too, is different, with rustic wooden slat-and-thatched roofed houses instead of the dull cinderblock, corrugated-tin models common elsewhere. When the sky is clear, keep your eyes peeled for the awesome volcanoes that shimmer in the hinterland. This part of Guatemala is also treated to sensational lightning storms from around November to April.

Monterrico is a coastal village with a few small, inexpensive hotels right on the beach, a large wildlife reserve and two centers for the hatching and release of sea turtles and caimans. The beach here is dramatic, with powerful surf crashing onto black volcanic sand at odd angles. This wave-print signals that there are rip tides; deaths have occurred at this beach, so swim with care. Strong swimmers, however, can probably handle and enjoy the waves. Behind the town is a large network of mangrove swamps and canals, part of the 190km Canal de Chiquimulilla.

Monterrico is probably the best spot for a weekend break at the beach if you're staying in Antigua or Guatemala City. It's fast becoming popular with foreigners. On weekdays it's relatively quiet, but on weekends and holidays it teems with Guatemalan families, and everything seems a bit harried.

Orientation & Information

From where you alight from the La Avellana boat, it's about 1km to the beach and the hotels. You pass through the village en route. From the *embarcadero* (jetty) walk straight ahead and then turn left. Pickups (Q3) meet scheduled boats or *lanchas.*

If you come by bus from Pueblo Viejo, from the stop walk about 300m toward the beach on Calle Principal.

Banrural, just off the main street on the road to Parque Hawaii, changes cash and may change traveler's checks. There's an ATM in the Supermercado Monterrico. The **post office** (Calle Principal) is on the main street. Internet access is available from the optimistically named **Speed Internet** (per hr Q12) on the main street near the ferry dock.

Sights & Activities

BIOTOPO MONTERRICO-HAWAII

Sometimes called the Reserva Natural Monterrico, Biotopo Monterrico-Hawaii is administered by Cecon (Centro de Estudios Conservacionistas de la Universidad de San Carlos), and is Monterrico's biggest attraction. This 20km-long nature reserve of coast and coastal mangrove swamps is bursting with avian and aquatic life. The reserve's most famous denizens are the endangered leatherback and ridley turtles, who lay their eggs on the beach in many places along the coast. The mangrove swamps are a network of 25 lagoons, all connected by mangrove canals.

Boat tours of the reserve, passing through the mangrove swamps and visiting several lagoons, take around 1½ to two hours and cost Q75 for one person, Q50 for each additional person. It's best to go just on sunrise, when you're likely to see the most wildlife. If you have binoculars, bring them along for bird-watching. January and February are the best months for bird-watching. Locals will approach you on the street (some with very impressive-looking ID cards), offering tours, but if you want to support the Tortugario (who incidentally have the most environmentally knowledgeable guides), arrange a tour directly through the Tortugario Monterrico (see below).

Some travelers have griped about the use of motorboats (as opposed to the paddled varieties), because the sound of the motor scares off the wildlife. If you're under no time pressure, ask about arranging a paddled tour of the canal.

TORTUGARIO MONTERRICO

The Cecon-run **Tortugario Monterrico** (admission Q40; ☺ 8am-noon & 2-5pm) is just a short walk east down the beach from the end of Calle Principal and then a block inland. Several endangered species of animals are raised here, including leatherback, olive ridley and green sea turtles, caimans and iguanas. There's an interesting interpretative trail and a little museum with pickled displays in bottles. The staff offer lagoon trips, and night walks (Q25) from September to February to look for turtle eggs, and will accept volunteers.

PARQUE HAWAII

This nature reserve operated by **Arcas** (Asociación de Rescate y Conservación de Vida Silvestre, Wildlife Rescue & Conservation Association; ☎ 4144-2142; www.arcasguate mala.com) comprises a sea-turtle hatchery with some caimans 8km east along the beach from Monterrico. It is separate from and rivals Cecon's work in the same field. Volunteers are welcome year round, but the sea turtle nesting season is from June to November, with August and September being the peak months. Volunteers are charged Q580 a week for a room, with meals extra and homestay options. Jobs for volunteers include hatchery checks and maintenance, local school education sessions, mangrove reforestation, basic construction and data collection. Most of the egg collection happens at night. It's a way out of town, but there are usually other volunteers to keep you company and while you're here you can use the kayaks, go on village trips and go fishing in the sea and mangroves.

A bus (Q5, 30 minutes) leaves the Monterrico jetty every couple of hours during the week and every hour on weekends for the bumpy ride to the reserve. Pickups also operate on this route, charging Q30 per person. Check out the Arcas website for more information.

WHALE WATCHING

Productos Mundiales (☎ 2366-1026; www.productos -mundiales.com; 3a Av 17-05, Zona 14, Guatemala City) offers marine wildlife-watching tours (six hours, from Q1250 per person), leaving from nearby Puerto Iztapa. Throughout the year you stand a pretty good chance of seeing pilot whales, bottlenose dolphins, spinner dolphins, olive ridley turtles, leatherback turtles, giant manta rays and whale sharks. From December to May, humpback and sperm whales can also be seen. Reservations (five days in advance via bank account deposit) are essential – see the website for details.

Courses

Proyecto Lingüístico Monterrico (☎ 5475-1265; espa-nolmonterrico@yahoo.com; Calle Principal), about 250m from the beach, is quite professional. Classes are generally held outdoors in a shady garden area. You can study in the morning or afternoon, depending on your schedule. Twenty hours of study per week costs Q750/1150/1250 tuition only/with homestay/in self-catering accommodation. Even if you're not studying here, the school is the best source of tourist information in town.

Sleeping
LEFT OF CALLE PRINCIPALE

All hotels listed here are on the beach, unless otherwise stated. To save a difficult, hot walk along the beach, take the last road to the left before you hit the beach. All these hotels either front or back onto it. Most hotels have restaurants serving whatever is fresh from the sea that day. Many places offer discounts for stays of three nights or more. Reserve for weekends if you want to avoid a long hot walk while you cruise around asking for vacancies. Weekend prices are given here. Midweek, you'll have plenty more bargaining power.

Johnny's Place (☎ 5812-0409; www.johnnysplacehotel .com; dm/r Q45/160, 4-person bungalow Q350; P 🏊) While Johnny's may not be everyone's cup of tea, it's easy enough to find – it's the first place you come to turning left on the beach, and one of the biggest operations here. It's got a decent atmosphere, though, and attracts a good mix of backpackers and family groups. Every pair of bungalows shares a barbecue and small swimming pool. There's also a larger general swimming pool. The rooms are not glamorous but have fans and screened windows. Its bar-restaurant overlooks the sea and is a popular hangout: the food is not gourmet but there are plenty of choices and imaginative *licuados* (fresh fruit drinks) and other long cool drinks.

Brisas del Mar (☎ 5517-1142; s/d Q60/120; P 🏊) Behind Johnny's, one block back from the beach, this popular newcomer offers good-sized rooms and a 2nd-floor dining hall with excellent sea views.

El Mangle (☎ 5514-6517; r with fan/air-con Q125/250; P ❄ 🏊) Eclectic decorations fill the grounds of this friendly little place 300m further along the beach. Rooms are decent sized, with hammocks strung on individual porches. There's a big open space with a very pleasant pool for hanging out, and it's quiet. The seafront

FREE AT LAST?

A local tradition in tourist season in Monterrico is the Saturday-night baby-turtle race, hosted by the Tortugario Monterrico. You buy a baby turtle, let it go and the first person's turtle to reach the finish line wins dinner in a local restaurant.

On the surface, it's a good deal. The *tortugario* (turtle sanctuary) raises funds, the turtles go free and the punters go home with a warm fuzzy feeling.

There's a problem here, though. Turtles can hatch on any day of the week. During peak season, the tortugario has daily releases, but when there aren't so many turtles (or tourists) the tortugario keeps them in holding tanks until race day on Saturday.

Now, turtles are born with their tiny metabolisms racing, biologically amped up to make it from their nests, across the sand, through the waves and out into the currents that will (hopefully) carry them to safety. In the holding tanks, they burn off a good deal of body fat and energy swimming aimlessly around, waiting to be released. By the time they finally make it down the beach and into the ocean, they're worn out, and if you pay attention, you'll notice that many can't even make it past the breaking waves and keep getting washed back up on shore.

Given that, under perfect conditions, baby turtles stand about a one in 1000 chance of making it to adulthood, giving them an extra obstacle hardly seems fair.

The *tortugario* is reluctant to stop the Saturday-night races because they're an excellent fundraiser. If you really want to save a turtle, there are a few alternatives:

■ Donate the money to the *tortugario* and explain why you aren't interested in the race.

■ Buy a turtle and release it on your own, explaining why you don't want to wait till Saturday.

■ Donate your time and/or money to the other turtle sanctuary in the area, at Parque Hawaii (see opposite), which has twice-daily releases through the year and takes a much more low-key, serious approach to conservation issues.

restaurant here pumps out some very tasty wood-fired pizza.

Dulce y Salado (☎ 5579-8477; www.dulceysalado guatemala.com; s/d Q200/400; P ☻) About 2km east of the center, these neat little thatched-roof cabins are set around a good-sized swimming pool. The place is Italian owned, so the restaurant out front does good pastas (Q45) and excellent coffee.

Hotel Pez de Oro (☎ 2368-3684; www.pezdeoro.com; s/d Q350/390; P ☻) This is the funkiest looking place in town, with comfortable little huts and bungalows scattered around a shady property. The color scheme is a cheery blue and yellow and the rooms have some tasteful decorations and big overhead fans. The excellent restaurant, with big sea views, serves up great Italian cuisine and seafood dishes. Pastas cost from Q50, whole fish from Q60.

Dos Mundos Pacific Resort (☎ 7848-1407; www.dos mundospacific.com; bungalows from Q720; P ✕ ☏ ☻) The biggest complex around is pushing resort status – manicured grounds, two swimming pools, and a gorgeous beachfront restaurant. The bungalows are spacious and simply but beautifully presented, with wide shady balconies out front.

RIGHT OF CALLE PRINCIPALE

Going in the opposite direction, heading right from Calle Principal, are more options.

Hostel El Gecko (dm with/without kitchen use Q50/35) The first place you'll come to is this very basic hostel run by a couple of young Guatemalans. There are very few frills here, but it's a backpackers' favorite, for the cheap beds and friendly atmosphere. No telephone.

Café del Sol (☎ 5810-0821; www.cafe-del-sol.com; economy s/d Q230/290, standard r Q350; P ☻) Set all under one big thatched roof, the 'economy' rooms here are a bit disappointing compared to the rest of the place. Across the road, the new annex offers 'standard' rooms that are a better deal – more spacious, with an on-site swimming pool. The restaurant's menu has some original dishes and you can eat on the terrace or in the big *palapa* (thatched) dining area.

Hotel Atelie del Mar (☎ 5752-5528; www.hotelatelie delmar.com; s/d with fan Q440/550, with air-con Q350/400; P ✕ ☻) Further along is one of the most formal hotels in town, with lovely landscaped grounds and spacious, simple and beautiful rooms. It can be found a block back from the beach.

Eating

There are many simple seafood restaurants on Calle Principal. For the best cheap eats, hit either of the two nameless *comedores* on the last road to the right before the beach, where you can pick up an excellent plate of garlic shrimp, rice tortillas, fries and salad for Q40.

All of the hotels have restaurants. See listings for details.

our pick Taberna El Pelicano (mains Q60-120; ☯ lunch & dinner Wed-Sat) By far the best place to eat in town, with the widest menu and most interesting food, like seafood risotto (Q70), beef carpaccio (Q55) and a range of jumbo shrimp dishes (Q120).

Drinking

El Animal Desconicido (☯ 8pm-2pm Fri & Sat) A very happening little bar, with happy hours, cocktails and excellent music. Comfy seating fills up early out front, and the rest of the place starts rocking around 11pm. To find it, go down the main street till you hit the beach, then walk 200m to your right.

Las Mañanitas (☯ lunch-late) On the beachfront at the end of the main street, this little bar is what Monterrico really needed – plenty of hammock chairs looking out over the beach, a good range of drinks and low-key music playing in the background. Also has meals (Q50 to Q80).

Playa Club (☎ 5812-0409) This venue, located at Johnny's Place (see p202), heats up on weekends, with plenty of reggaetón, house music and drinks specials keeping the crowd moving.

Getting There & Away

There are two ways to get to Monterrico. Coming from Guatemala City or Antigua, it's most logical to catch a bus which, with the new bridge at Pueblo Viejo, goes right through to Monterrico. The Pueblo Viejo–Monterrico stretch makes for a pretty journey, revealing local life at a sane pace.

The other option is to head to La Avellana, where *lanchas* and car ferries depart for Monterrico. The Cubanita company runs a handful of direct buses to and from Guatemala City (Q40, four hours, 124km). Alternatively, you reach La Avellana by changing buses at Taxisco on Hwy 2. Buses operate half-hourly from 5am to 4pm between Guatemala City and Taxisco (Q35, 3½ hours) and roughly hourly from 7am to 4:30pm between Taxisco and La Avellana (Q5, 40 minutes), although taxi drivers will tell you that you've missed the last bus, regardless of what time you arrive. A taxi between Taxisco and La Avellana costs around Q60.

From La Avellana catch a *lancha* or car ferry to Monterrico. The collective *lanchas* charge Q5 per passenger for the half-hour trip along the Canal de Chiquimulilla, a long mangrove canal. They start at 4:30am and run more or less every half-hour or hour until late afternoon. You can always pay more and charter your own boat. The car ferry costs Q80 per vehicle.

Shuttle buses also serve Monterrico. **Mario's Tours** (☎ 7762-6040; www.mariostours.net; Calle Principal, Panajachel) goes to Panajachel (Q370 per person). **Adrenalina Tours** (www.adrenalinatours.com) covers Antigua (Q125), Panajachel (Q415) and San Pedro la Laguna (Q330). These services may not leave every day, but there is a daily shuttle that runs from outside the Proyecto Lingüístico Monterrico at 1pm and 4pm which charges Q60/130 to Antigua/Guatemala City. Book tickets at the school.

AROUND MONTERRICO

East down the coast from Monterrico, near Las Lisas, is the Guatemalan Pacific coast's best-kept secret, **Isleta de Gaia** (☎ 7885-0044; www.isleta-de -gaia.com; 2-/4-person bungalow Q800/1600; ☐ ☎ ☎). It's a bungalow-hotel built on a long island of sand and named for the Greek earth goddess. Overlooking the Pacific on one side and a romantic and silent lagoon with mangroves on the other, this small, friendly, ecological, French-owned resort is constructed from natural materials. There are 12 bungalows, on one and two levels, with sea, lagoon or pool views. Each has good beds, fan, bathroom, balcony and hammock; decorations are Mexican and Costa Rican. The seafront restaurant (mains Q60 to Q120) offers Italian, Spanish and French cuisine, with fresh fish naturally the star. There are boogie boards and kayaks for rent and a boat for fishing trips. Reserve your stay in this little paradise by email four days in advance. The staff run a shuttle service to and from Guatemala City and Antigua. From Monterrico there is no road east along the coast beyond Parque Hawaii, so you have to backtrack to Taxisco and take Carretera al Pacífico for about 35km to reach the turnoff for Las Lisas. From the turnoff it's 20km to Las Lisas, where you take a boat (Q100) to Isleta de Gaia.

Chiquimulilla & the El Salvador Border

Surfers found in this part of Guatemala will likely be heading to or from La Libertad in El

THE PACIFIC SLOPE

Salvador. Most people shoot straight through Escuintla and Taxisco to Chiquimulilla and on to the Salvadoran border at Ciudad Pedro de Alvarado/La Hachadura, from where it is about 110km along the coast of El Salvador to La Libertad. Be sure about whether or not you need a visa to enter El Salvador. See 'Visas para Extranjeros' at www.rree.gob.sv for more information.

Buses leave Taxisco for the border every 15 minutes until 5pm. There are two serviceable *hospedajes* in La Hachadura on the El Salvador side of the border, but the *hostales* (budget hotels) in Ciudad Pedro de Alvarado on the Guatemalan side are not recommended. Should you need to stop for the night before crossing the border, you could do worse than head to the friendly cowboy town of **Chiquimulilla** (population 14,820), some 12km east of Taxisco. There isn't much going on here, but it's a decent enough place to take care of errands and regroup. The new bus terminal is way out on the outskirts of town – ask to be dropped off in *el centro*. Failing that, shared tuk-tuks take you anywhere you want to go in town for Q3.

The family-run **Hotel San Juan de Letrán** (☎ 7885-0831; cnr 2a Av & 2a Calle; s/d Q80/100; **P**) is a clean place offering fair-sized rooms with a fan and bathroom. There are also less attractive rooms with a shared bathroom. Drinking water is provided and there are nice plantings. The *cafetería* attached serves some of the iciest drinks in Guatemala, which are very welcome in this sweltering heat, and big plates of tasty, cheap food. Buses run every hour between Taxisco and Chiquimulilla, and also hourly, until 6pm, from Chiquimulilla to the border (Q7, 45 minutes).

The other option for getting to El Salvador is to turn north from Chiquimulilla and take local buses through Cuilapa to the border at Valle Nuevo/Las Chinamas, traveling inland before veering south to La Libertad.

CUILAPA
pop 22,600

Surrounded by citrus and coffee plantations, the capital of Santa Rosa department isn't much of a tourist attraction in its own right, although the area's fame for woodcarvings, pottery and leather goods may turn up a couple of decent souvenirs.

People coming this way are usually headed for the border with El Salvador, but there are a couple of volcanoes just out of town that are easily climbed and afford some excellent views. Cuilapa is connected by a good road with Guatemala City. Buses (Q25, 2½ hours) leave from the Centra Sur bus terminal in Guatemala City.

Volcán Cruz Quemada

This dormant volcano towers 1700m over the tiny village of Santa María Ixhuatán at its base. Coffee plantations reach about one third of the way up its slopes, after which you move into thick rainforest. The summit, littered with radio towers, offers excellent views of the land running down to the coast, the Cerro la Consulta mountain range and the nearby Tecuamburro volcanic complex (see below).

From Santa María it's an easy-to-moderate climb to the top that should take about three hours. The 12km hike is possible to do on your own, asking plenty of directions along the way. Alternatively, guides can be hired in Santa María – ask at the taxi stand on the main square.

To get to Santa María, catch a minibus (Q4, 25 minutes) from Cuilapa.

Tecuamburro

The Tecuamburro volcanic complex comprises various peaks, including Cerro de Miraflores (1950m), Cerro la Soledad (1850m) and Cerro Peña Blanca (1850m). This last, which has several small vents releasing steam and sulfur, provides the most interesting climb, although thick forest on its slopes means you'll have to wait till you're almost at the top for views of the surrounding fields, the coastline and nearby volcanoes.

Buses and minibuses (Q13, 1½ hours) leave regularly for the village of Tecuamburro from Cuilapa. From there it's a two- to three-hour hike (14km) to the summit.

LAGO DE AMATITLÁN

Lago de Amatitlán is a placid lake backed by a looming volcano and situated a mere 25km south of Guatemala City, making it a good day trip. After suffering years of serious neglect, the lake is slowly being rejuvenated, thanks mainly to local community groups who hope to see it once again function as a tourist attraction. On weekends, people from Guatemala City come to row boats on the lake (its waters are too polluted for swimming) or to rent a hot tub for a dip.

Many people from the capital own second homes here.

A **teleférico** (chairlift; adult/child return Q15/5; ☉ 8am-6pm Fri-Sun) heads out over the lakeshore then pretty much straight up the hillside. It's a half-hour ride with some stunning views of the surrounding countryside from the top.

Boat tours are about the only other thing to do here – rides cost Q75/20 in private/shared tours. If you're feeling energetic, rowboats rent from Q35 per hour.

A string of *comedores* along the lakefront offer fried fish, tacos and simple meals. For something a bit more refined, follow the signs up the hill to the right to **La Rocarena** (mains Q50-120; ☉ breakfast, lunch & dinner), which has lovely grounds, good views and a couple of warm-water swimming pools.

The lake is situated just off the main Escuintla–Guatemala City highway (Hwy 9). Coming from Guatemala City (one hour, Q3), just ask to be dropped at the *teleférico*. The waterfront is about half a kilometer from the signposted turnoff. Coming from Escuintla, or heading back to Guatemala City, buses stop on the main road, about 1km away. It's an easy 10- to 15-minute walk, and taxis are rare.

Central & Eastern Guatemala

Stretching from the steamy lowland forests of El Petén to the dry tropics of the Río Motagua valley, and from the edge of the western highlands to the Caribbean, this is the country's most diverse region.

The Carretera al Atlántico (Hwy 9) shoots eastward to the sea from Guatemala City. Along the way are numerous attractions – side trips to the pilgrim town of Esquipulas, and beyond to the wonderfully preserved ruins of Copán in Honduras. Further along the highway is Quiriguá, boasting impressive stelae more than 10m tall.

Another short detour brings you to Río Dulce, a favored resting spot for Caribbean sailors and gateway to the wilds of the Bocas del Polochic. While you're here, don't miss the gorgeous boat ride down the Río Dulce to the Garífuna enclave of Lívingston.

The north of the region is lush and mountainous coffee-growing country. As you climb, you enter cloud forest where rain or at least mist will become a guaranteed daily part of your travels.

The limestone crags around Cobán attract cavers the world over, but those at Lanquín, Rey Marcos and elsewhere are easily accessible for amateurs.

The two must-sees in the Cobán area are the beautiful pools and cascades of Semuc Champey and the Biotopo del Quetzal, a nature reserve where you stand a reasonable chance of seeing the elusive national bird, the quetzal.

HIGHLIGHTS

- Splashing around the turquoise waters of **Semuc Champey** (p222) and getting deep in the caves at **Grutas de Lanquín** (p221)

- Admiring the impressive carvings at **Copán** (p239) and **Quiriguá** (p236) and relaxing in the Antigua-rivaling beauty of **Copán Ruinas** (p245)

- Going bush in the jungle hideaway of **Las Conchas** (p226), where waterfalls, jungle treks and village tours await

- Getting down with the Garífuna in the unique Caribbean town of **Lívingston** (p261)

- Taking in the natural beauty of such little-visited protected areas as **Parque Nacional Laguna Lachuá** (p224) and the **Bocas del Polochic** (p256)

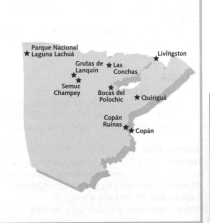

Parque Nacional
★ Laguna Lachuá
Grutas de ★ Las
Lanquín Conchas
Lívingston
Semuc
Champey
Bocas del
Polochic
★ Quiriguá
Copán
Ruinas
★ Copán

ALTA & BAJA VERAPAZ

Hwy 14 (also marked Hwy 17) leaves the Carretera al Atlántico at El Rancho, 84km from Guatemala City. It heads west through a dry, desertlike lowland area, then turns north and starts climbing up into the forested hills. After 47km, at the junction called La Cumbre Santa Elena, Hwy 17 to Salamá divides from Hwy 14 for Cobán. Descending the other side of the ridge, Hwy 17 winds down into the broad valley of the Río Salamá, and enters Salamá town, 17km from the highway.

Before the Spanish conquest, the mountainous departments of Baja Verapaz and Alta Verapaz were populated by the Rabinal Maya, noted for their warlike habits and merciless victories. They battled the powerful K'iche' Maya for a century but were never conquered.

When the conquistadors arrived, they too had trouble defeating the Rabinal Maya. It was Fray Bartolomé de Las Casas who convinced the Spanish authorities to try peace where war had failed. Armed with an edict that forbade Spanish soldiers from entering the region for five years, the friar and his brethren pursued their religious mission, and succeeded in pacifying and converting the Rabinal Maya. Their homeland thus was renamed Verapaz (True Peace) and is now divided into Baja Verapaz, with its capital at Salamá, and Alta Verapaz, which is centered on Cobán. The Rabinal Maya have remained among the most dedicated and true to ancient Maya customs, and there are many intriguing villages to visit in this part of Guatemala, including Rabinal itself (p210).

Excellent information on both Alta and Baja Verapaz can be found online at www.infocoban.com.

SALAMÁ
pop 30,100 / elev 940m

A wonderful introduction to Baja Verapaz's not-too-hot, not-too-cold climate, Salamá is a smallish town with a couple of attractions.

Information
Banrural (🕙 9am-5pm Mon-Fri, 9am-1pm Sat) On the south side of the plaza (opposite the church), changes cash and traveler's checks and has a Visa and MasterCard ATM.
Police station One block west of the plaza.
Telgua (internet access per hr Q6) East of the plaza.

Sights
Salamá has some attractive reminders of colonial rule. The main plaza, for instance, boasts an ornate **church** with gold-encrusted altars and a carved pulpit, which is located just to the left before the altar. Be sure to check out Jesus lying in a glass coffin with cotton bunting in his stigmata and droplets of blood seeping from his hairline. His thick mascara and the silver lamé pillow where he rests his head complete the scene. The Salamá **market** is impressive for its colorful, local bustle, particularly on Sunday.

Tours
EcoVerapaz (🕿 5722-9095; ecoverapaz@hotmail.com; 8a Av 7-12, Zona 1; 1-day tour per person Q350) is in the shop Imprenta Mi Terruño – a block west of the plaza on the road to La Cumbre. Its local, trained naturalists offer interesting tours throughout Baja Verapaz including caving, bird-watching, hiking, horseback riding and orchid trips. EcoVerapaz also goes to Rabinal (p210) to check out its museum and crafts and arrange trips to see the famous rodeos of Baja Verapaz. Guides speak some English. Group discounts are offered.

Sleeping
Turicentro Las Orquídeas (🕿 7940-1622; Carretera a Salamá Km 147; campsite Q30) Travelers with tents may want to check out this place, a few kilometers east of Salamá on Hwy 17. It has a grassy area for camping, plus a cafe, pool and open spaces hung with hammocks. You can use the pool (Q20 per person per day) even if you're not camping here.

Hotel San Ignacio (🕿 7940-0186; 4a Calle A 7-09; s/d Q75/130; 🅿) Not the loveliest place you're ever likely to stay, but it's a reasonable deal for the price, and super-close to the park. Look for the big palapa (open-sided palm-leaf shelter) sitting area up on the rooftop.

Hotel Rosa de Sharon (🕿 5774-8650; 5a Calle 6-39; s/d Q80/130; 🅿) The neat, bright rooms here loom over the busy market area, but they're set back from the road, so remain peaceful. They're big and clean, with wacky decorations such as wrought-iron hat stands made to look like trees.

Posada de Don Maco (🕿 7940-0083; 3a Calle 8-26; s/d Q110/140; 🅿) This clean, family-run place has simple but spacious rooms with fan and good bathrooms. The courtyard boasts a collection of caged squirrels.

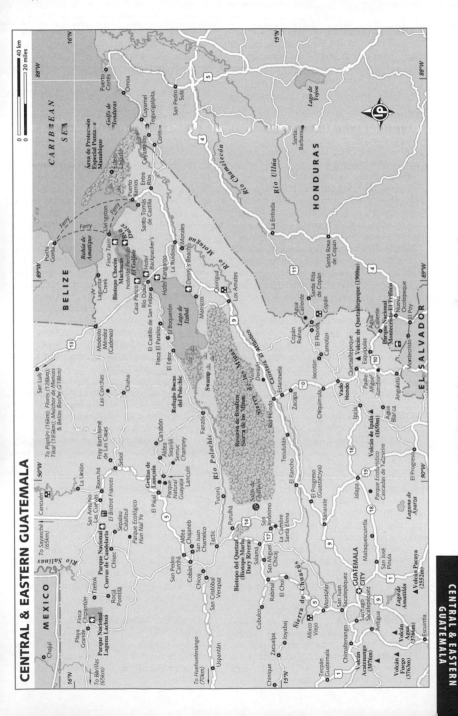

CENTRAL & EASTERN GUATEMALA

Hotel Real Legendario (☎ 5348-5189; 8a Av 3-57, Zona 1; s/d Q120/150; **P**) You'll recognize this place, three blocks east of the plaza, by the stands of bamboo in the car park. The clean, secure rooms have fan, hot-water bathroom and cable TV.

Eating

You don't have to step far from the plaza to eat well, but don't plan a late dinner – restaurants close early here, with the exception of Pollo Campero on the plaza.

Café Deli-Donas (15a Calle 6-61; cakes Q15, sandwiches Q25, licuados Q15; ⊙ 8am-6pm Mon-Sat) This exceedingly pleasant little cafe (where even the bathrooms smell good) is like an oasis in Salama's busy market zone. Excellent coffee, homemade cakes and light meals are the go here.

Antojitos Zacapanecos (cnr 6a Calle & 8a Av; mains Q20; ⊙ lunch & dinner) For something a little different in the fast-food vein, check out the huge flour tortillas filled with pork, chicken or beef from this place. Better yet, grab one to go and have a picnic in the plaza.

Cafetería Central (cnr 15a Calle & 9a Av; lunch Q30; ⊙ breakfast & lunch) Try the savory, filling lunches at this place a few doors back toward the plaza from Café Deli-Donas. The chicken broth followed by grilled chicken, rice and salad, with perhaps a mango to finish, is a worthy feast.

Getting There & Away

Buses going to Guatemala City (Q30 to Q40, three hours, 151km) depart hourly between 3am and 8pm from the northeast corner of the park. There is a scheduled Pullman at 3am, with others sometimes rolling through unannounced. Arrive early for a seat. Buses coming from Guatemala City continue west from Salamá to Rabinal (Q5, 40 minutes, 19km) and then 15km further along to Cubulco. Buses for San Jerónimo (Q4, 25 minutes), La Cumbre (Q3, 25 minutes) and Cobán (Q20, 1½ to two hours) all leave from the northwest corner of the park in front of Antojitos Zacapanecos, about every half hour from early morning to 4pm.

AROUND SALAMÁ

A few kilometers along the road to Salamá from Hwy 14, you come to the turnoff for **San Jerónimo** (population 12,200). Behind the town's beautiful church is a 16th-century sugar mill now used as a **museum** (⊙ 8am-4pm Mon-Fri, 10am-noon & 1-4pm Sat & Sun) displaying a decent collection of artifacts and photographs, though none of the former is labeled. The grounds here are immaculate and there's a playground to keep the kids out of trouble. On the plaza are some large stones that were carved in ancient times.

About a five-minute walk from the town center are **Los Arcos**, a series of 124 arches in various states of decay. These formed a sophisticated aqueduct system to power the sugar mill. To get there, take the main road heading east (away from Salamá), bear right and slightly downhill, where you'll see a 'Barrio El Calvario' sign. Keep an eye to your right along this road and you'll start to see the arches. A second set of arches can be seen by going right at the second dirt alley on this road. If you continue straight ahead for about 50m, rather than going right, you'll see more arches through gaps in the trees. Continue straight on this road to reach **Finca San Lorenzo**, a coffee farm open to the public. The last bus of the day returning to Salamá leaves San Jerónimo at 4pm.

Nine kilometers west of Salamá along Hwy 5 is the village of **San Miguel Chicaj** (population 12,800), known for its weaving and for its traditional fiesta from September 25 to 29. Continue along the same road for another 10km to reach the colonial town of **Rabinal** (population 13,900), founded in 1537 by Fray Bartolomé de Las Casas as a base for his proselytizing. Rabinal has gained fame as a pottery-making center (look especially for the hand-painted chocolate cups), and for its citrus-fruit harvest (November and December). Rabinal is also known for its adherence to pre-Columbian traditions, folklore and dance. If you can make it here for the annual fiesta of San Pedro, between January 19 and 25 (with things reaching fever pitch on January 21), or Corpus Cristi (40 days after Easter), do so. Market day here is Sunday. Rabinal also has the **Museo Communitario Rabinal Achi'** (cnr 4a Av & 2a Calle, Zona 3), which is devoted to history, culture and the Achi' Maya who live in the district.

Accommodation options are slim in Rabinal, but the **Posada Don Pablo** (☎ 7940-0211; 3a Av 1-50, Zona 4; s/d Q50/75) is simple and clean and does the job. Cheaper rooms with shared bathroom are available. If the attached restaurant doesn't grab you, try **Angello's** (1a Calle 2-50, Zona 4; mains Q25-40; ⊙ lunch & dinner) around the

---

LOOK, UP IN THE SKY

Surely one of the most spectacular pre-Hispanic rituals alive today is that of the *palo volador* (flying pole). Dating from the Postclassic era, the ritual involves the installation of a tree trunk measuring up to 30m in the town square. One man sits atop the pole, playing the flute and directing the ceremony. Four flyers, or angels (the number four symbolizing the cardinal points of the compass) then leap off the top of the trunk, attached by ropes, and spin back to earth.

If all goes according to plan, the four flyers will circle the pole 13 times – thus making the number 52, which corresponds to the number of years in a Maya Calendar Round. In some places there are only two flyers, symbolizing Hun-Hunahpú and Vucub-Hunahpú, the wizard twins from the *Popul Vuh*, who descended to the underworld to battle the lords of darkness.

The tradition has changed somewhat since the time of its origins – the tree trunk is no longer carried by hand to town for one, and the flyers' costumes have become increasingly gaudy over the years, incorporating such nontraditional items as mirrors sewn into the fabric. The *palo volador* is widely practiced in Mexico, most notably in Puebla and Veracruz, but is becoming less common in Guatemala. Your best chance of seeing it is during the fiestas of Chichicastenango (p143; December 21), Cubulco (see below; July 25) and nearby Joyabaj (August 15) in the department of Quiché.

---

corner – it's the only real restaurant in town and triples handily as a bar and pool hall.

It's possible to continue on from Rabinal another 15km to the village of **Cubulco** (population 14,000), where the *palo volador* tradition (see boxed text, above) is still observed.

From Rabinal you can also follow Hwy 5 all the way to Guatemala City, a trip of about 100km passing through several small villages. Buses ply this mostly unpaved route, albeit very slowly. Along the way you could detour 16km north from Montúfar to the ruins of **Mixco Viejo** (admission Q50), which was the active capital of the Poqomam Maya when the Spaniards came and crashed the party. The location of this ceremonial and military center is awesome, wedged between deep ravines, with just one way in and one way out. To further fortify the site, the Poqomam built impressive rock walls around the city. It took Pedro de Alvarado and his troops more than a month of concerted attacks to conquer Mixco Viejo. When they finally succeeded, they furiously laid waste to this city, which scholars believe supported close to 10,000 people at its height. There are several temples and two ball courts here. Self-sufficient campers can overnight here for free. It's difficult to reach this site by public transportation. From Guatemala City you need to get a Servicios Unidos San Juan bus from the SEGMA bus terminal in Zona 12 to San Juan Sacatepéquez (Q3, one hour, departures every few minutes from 4am to 6pm) then change to onward transportation there. It's 12km north from San Juan to Montúfar.

SALTO DE CHALISCÓ

What's claimed to be Central America's highest **waterfall** (www.chilasco.net.ms; admission Q15) lies 12km down a dirt road from a turnoff at Km 145 on the highway to Cobán. At 130m and surrounded by cloud forest, it's an impressive sight, especially if it's been raining and the fall is running at full force. Another waterfall, the Lomo de Macho, lies 8km away – an enjoyable walk, or you can hire a horse from the visitor center in town (about 5km from the falls). You can stay here as part of a **community tourism project** (☎ 5301-8928; per person Q75), in a rustic bunkhouse attached to the visitor center. Buses to Chaliscó leave every half hour from Salamá (Q15, 1½ hours), passing La Cumbre Santa Elena (Q9, 45 minutes) out on Hwy 14.

BIOTOPO DEL QUETZAL

Along the main Cobán highway (Carretera a Cobán or Hwy 14), 34km beyond the La Cumbre turnoff for Salamá, you reach the Biotopo Mario Dary Rivera nature reserve, commonly called **Biotopo del Quetzal** (admission Q35; 7am-4pm), at Km 161, just east of the village of Purulhá.

You need a fair bit of luck to see a quetzal, as they're rare and shy. For more about the quetzal, see boxed text, p212. You have the best chance of seeing them from March to June. If you're really keen to see Guatemala's national bird in the wild, contact Proyecto EcoQuetzal in Cobán (p216).

It's well worth stopping to explore and enjoy this lush high-altitude cloud-forest ecosystem that is the quetzal's natural habitat at any time – and you may happen to see one. Early morning or early evening when the quetzals feed on *aguacatillo* trees are the best times to watch out for them – try around the Parque Ecológico Gucumatz (see right).

Trail guide maps in English and Spanish (Q5) are sometimes available at the visitor center. They contain a checklist of 87 birds commonly seen here. Other animals include spider monkeys and *tigrillos*, which are similar to ocelots. Good luck spotting either of these.

Two excellent, well-maintained nature trails wind through the reserve: the 1800m Sendero los Helechos (Fern Trail) and the 3600m Sendero los Musgos (Moss Trail). As you wander through the dense growth, treading on the rich, spongy humus and leaf-mold, you'll see many varieties of epiphytes (air plants), which thrive in the *biotopo*'s humid atmosphere.

Both trails pass by waterfalls, most of which cascade into small pools where you can take a dip; innumerable streams have their headwaters here, and the Río Colorado pours through the forest along a geological fault. Deep in the forest is **Xiu Gua Li Che** (Grandfather Tree), some 450 years old, which germinated around the time the Spanish fought the Rabinal in these mountains.

The reserve has a visitor center, a little shop for drinks and snacks, and a camping and barbecue area. The ruling on camping changes from time to time. Check by contacting **Cecon** (Centro de Estudios Conservacionistas de la Universidad de San Carlos; ☎ 2331-0904; www.usac.edu.gt/cecon, in Spanish) in Guatemala City, which administers this and other *biotopos*.

Sleeping & Eating

There are three lodging places close to the reserve.

Parque Ecológico Gucumatz (☎ 5368-6397; s/d old bldg Q100/140, new bldg Q130/170; **P**) Carved out of the jungle on a hillside 200m away from the Biotopo del Quetzal entrance, this place has good-sized, simple rooms with warm (ie tepid) showers in the older wooden building and hot showers in the newer concrete one. Reasonably priced, simple meals (mains Q30) are served, and there are vegetarian options.

Posada Montaña del Quetzal (☎ 2332-4969; www.hposadaquetzal.com; Hwy 14 Km 156.5; s/d Q130/170, 2-bedroom bungalow s/d Q280/350; **P** **Ⓡ**) This hospitable place is 5km before the Biotopo del Quetzal if you're coming from Guatemala City. Accommodations are rustically styled, but extremely comfortable. It's set on a huge property that includes an orchid nursery, fishing holes, forest walks and a 30-minute mountain-bike track out to a private waterfall. The bungalows are a real steal, featuring living rooms with huge open fireplaces. The restaurant is popular with tour groups, mainly for its excellent *cack'ik* (turkey stew; Q35).

ourpick Hotel Restaurant Ram Tzul (☎ 2355-1904; www.m-y-c.com.ar/ramtzul; Hwy 14 Km 158; s/d Q245/355; **P**) Quite likely the most beautiful hotel in either of the Verapaces, this place is about halfway between the Posada Montaña del Quetzal and the *biotopo* entrance. The restaurant/sitting area is in a tall, thatched-roofed structure with fire pits and plenty of atmosphere. The rustic, upmarket theme extends to

---

COURTING THE QUETZAL

The resplendent quetzal, which gave its name to Guatemala's currency, was sacred to the Maya. Its feathers grace the plumed serpent Quetzalcoatl and killing one was a capital offence. In modern times it enjoys no such protection, and hunting (mostly for the male's long, emerald-green tail feathers) and habitat loss have made the bird a rarity in Guatemala. You'd stand a much better chance of seeing one in Costa Rica or Panama.

The best place to look for a quetzal here is in the cloud forests of the Alta Verapaz, especially in the hopefully named Biotopo del Quetzal (p211).

Avocado and fruit trees are what you're looking for here – that's the preferred food of the quetzal (along with insects, snails, frogs and lizards). But you'll have to look closely – the quetzal's green plumage is dull unless it's in direct sunlight, providing perfect camouflage, and it often remains motionless for hours.

The females lay two eggs per year, from March to June, and this is the best time to go looking, as the males' tail feathers grow up to 75cm long during this period. Keep an ear out for their distinctive call – sharp cackles and a low, burbling whistle: *keeeoo-keeeoo*.

the rooms and bungalows, which are spacious and elegantly decorated. The hotel property includes waterfalls and swimming spots.

Getting There & Away

Any bus to or from Guatemala City will set you down at the park entrance. Heading in the other direction, it's best to flag down a bus or microbus to El Rancho and change there for your next destination.

COBÁN

pop 67,000 / elev 1320m

Not so much an attraction in itself, but an excellent jumping-off point for the natural wonders of Alta Verapaz, Cobán is a prosperous city with an upbeat air. Return visitors will marvel at how much (and how tastefully) the town has developed since their last visit.

As you enter Cobán, a sign says 'Bienvenidos a Cobán, Ciudad Imperial,' referring to the city charter granted in 1538 by Emperor Carlos V.

The town was once the center of Tezulutlán (Tierra de Guerra, or 'Land of War'), a stronghold of the Rabinal Maya.

In the 19th century, when German immigrants moved in and founded vast coffee and cardamom *fincas* (plantations), Cobán took on the aspect of a German mountain town, as the *finca* owners built town residences. The era of German cultural and economic domination ended during WWII, when the USA prevailed upon the Guatemalan government to deport the powerful *finca* owners, many of whom actively supported the Nazis.

Today, Cobán is an interesting town to visit, though dreary weather can color your impression. Most of the year it is either rainy or overcast, dank and chill. You can count on sunny days in Cobán for only about three weeks, in April. In the middle of the 'dry' season (January to March) it can be misty and sometimes rainy, or bright and sunny with marvelous clear mountain air.

Guatemala's most impressive festival of Indian traditions, the national folklore festival of **Rabin Ajau** with its traditional dance of the Paabanc, takes place here in the latter part of July or in the first week of August. The **national orchid show** is hosted here every December.

There is not a lot to do in Cobán itself except enjoy the local color and mountain scenery, but the town is a base for marvelous side trips, including to the Grutas de Lanquín (p221) and the pools and cascades of Semuc Champey (p222).

Orientation

Most of the services you'll need are within a few blocks of the main plaza and the cathedral. The shopping district is around and behind the cathedral, and you'll smell the savory cardamom, which vendors come from the mountains to sell, before you see it.

Most buses will drop you at the terminal known as Campos Dos, just north of town. It's a 15-minute walk (2km) or Q10 taxi ride to the plaza from there.

The heart of Cobán is built on a rise, so unless what you're looking for is in the dead center, be prepared to walk uphill and down.

Information

INTERNET ACCESS

Plenty of places offer internet access. The going rate is Q5 per hour.

Cybercobán (3a Av 1-11, Zona 4; 8:30am-7pm Mon-Sat) East (200m) of the plaza.

Mayan Internet (6a Av 2-28; 8:30am-8pm Mon-Sat, 2:30-9pm Sun) Fast connections; 500m west of the plaza.

LAUNDRY

Lavandería Econo Express (7a Av 2-32, Zona 1) Laundry places are in short supply in Cobán – these folks wash and dry a load for Q30.

MONEY

The banks listed here change US-dollar cash and traveler's checks.

Banco G&T (1a Calle) Opposite Hotel La Posada; has a MasterCard ATM.

Banco Industrial (cnr 1a Calle & 7a Av, Zona 1) Has a Visa ATM.

POST & TELEPHONE

Post office (cnr 2a Av & 3a Calle) A block southeast from the plaza.

Telgua On the plaza; has plenty of card phones outside.

TOURIST INFORMATION

Inguat (7951-0216; 7a Av 1-17, Zona 1; 8am-4pm Mon-Fri, 9am-1pm Sat) has an office. If Inguat can't help you, try the **municipalidad** (1a Calle, Zona 1; 7952-1305, 7951-1148), where some switched-on young staff work in an office behind the police office. Casa D'Acuña (p216) can also give you loads of information.

CENTRAL & EASTERN GUATEMALA

COBÁN

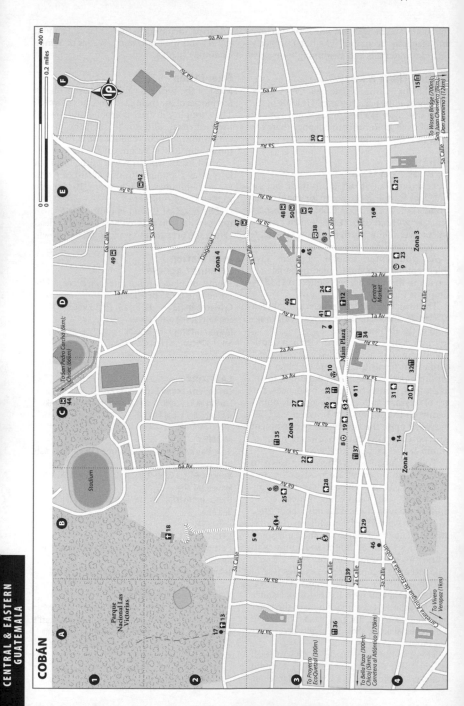

Sights

TEMPLO EL CALVARIO

You can get a fine view over the town from this church atop a long flight of stairs at the north end of 7a Av. Indigenous people leave offerings at outdoor shrines and crosses in front of the church. Don't linger here after 4pm, as muggings are not unknown in this area.

The **Ermita de Santo Domingo de Guzmán**, a chapel dedicated to Cobán's patron saint, is 150m west of the bottom of the stairs leading to El Calvario.

PARQUE NACIONAL LAS VICTORIAS

This forested 82-hectare **national park** (admission Q10; ⊗ 8am-4:30pm, walking trails 9am-3pm), right in town, has ponds, barbecue, picnic areas, children's play areas, a lookout point and kilometers of trails. The entrance is near the corner of 9a Av and 3a Calle, Zona 1. Most trails are very isolated – consider hiking in a group. You can camp here for Q20 per person.

VIVERO VERAPAZ

Orchid lovers mustn't miss the chance to see the many thousands of species at this famous **nursery** (☎ 7952-1133; Carretera Antigua de Entrada a Cobán; admission Q10; ⊗ 9am-noon & 2-4pm). The rare *monja blanca* (white nun orchid), Guatemala's national flower, can be seen here; there are also hundreds of species of miniature orchids, so small that you'll need the magnifying glass staff will loan you to see

them. Visits are by guided tour. The national orchid show is held here each December, and by all accounts it's spectacular. Otherwise, try to visit between October and February, when many flowers are in bloom.

Vivero Verapaz is about 2km from the town center – a 30-minute walk southwest from the plaza. You can hire a taxi for around Q20.

MUSEO EL PRÍNCIPE MAYA

This private **museum** (☎ 7952-1541; 6a Av 4-26, Zona 3; admission Q10; ⊗ 9am-6pm Mon-Sat) features a collection of pre-Columbian artifacts, with an emphasis on jewelry, other body adornments and pottery. The displays are well designed and maintained.

Courses

The **Oxford Language Center** (☎ 5892-7718; www.olcenglish.com; 4a Av 2-16, Zona 3) charges around Q1400 for 20 hours of Spanish lessons in groups of four or less with homestay included. Its rationale for charging more than the competition is that it pays its teachers better.

CENTRAL & EASTERN GUATEMALA

Tours

Aventuras Turísticas (☎ /fax 7951-4213; www. aventurasturisticas.com; 3a Calle 2-38, Zona 3), in the Hostal de Doña Victoria, leads tours to Laguna Lachuá, the Grutas de Lanquín, Rey Marcos and Candelaria, as well as to Semuc Champey, Tikal, Ceibal, and anywhere else you may want to go; it will customize itineraries. Guides speaking French, English and Spanish are available. Prices ranges from Q150 to Q2000 per person.

Adrenalina Tours (☎ 7951-2200; www.adrenalina tours.com; Diagonal 4, 3-36, Zona 2) offers tours to pretty much everywhere, and has the most extensive range of shuttle services in town.

Casa D'Acuña (☎ 7951-0484; casadacuna@yahoo. com; 4a Calle 3-11, Zona 2) offers tours to Semuc Champey, the Grutas de Lanquín and other places further afield. The guides have been repeatedly recommended.

Proyecto EcoQuetzal (☎ /fax 7952-1047; www.eco quetzal.org; 2a Calle 14-36, Zona 1; ☒ 8:30am-1pm & 2-5:30pm Mon-Fri) is an innovative project offering 'ethnotourism' trips to the Chicacnab cloud forests (near Cobán) and the subtropical rainforests of Rokjá Pomtilá (near the Laguna Lachua) in which participants stay in villages with a Q'eqchi' Maya family. To maximize the experience, travelers are encouraged to learn some Q'eqchi' words and stay with their host family for at least two days. For Q300 you'll get a guide for a couple of days, lodging for two nights, and four meals. Your guide will take you on hikes to interesting spots. The men of the family are the guides, providing them an alternative, sustainable way to make a living. Reservations are required at least one day in advance. The Proyecto also rents boots, sleeping bags and binoculars at reasonable prices, so you need not worry if you haven't come prepared for such a rugged experience. Participants should speak at least a little Spanish. With a month's notice, this outfit also offers quetzal-viewing platforms; contact the office for full details.

COFFEE TOURS

A working coffee farm in the middle of downtown Cobán, **Finca Santa Margarita** (☎ 7952-1586; 3a Calle 4-12, Zona 2; admission Q30; ☒ guided tours 8am-12:30pm & 1:30-5pm Mon-Fri, 8am-noon Sat) offers stellar guided tours. From propagation and planting to roasting and exporting, the 45-minute tour will tell you all you ever wanted to know about these powerful beans. At tour's end, you're treated to a cup of coffee and you can

purchase beans straight from the roaster for Q25 to Q40 a pound (0.45kg). The talented guide speaks English and Spanish.

Just 15 minutes out of town by bus, the **Chicoj cooperative** (☎ 7859-8178; tours Q50) is a community-tourism initiative, offering 2km, 45-minute tours of its coffee farm. Halfway through there's the standard stop for a canopy zip line tour and the tour winds up with a cup of coffee grown and roasted at the farm. Cobán tour operators offer this tour for Q160, but you can easily catch a bus from the stop near the police station on 1a Calle, which goes straight to the village of Chicoj.

Sleeping

When choosing a room in Cobán, you may want to ensure that the showers have hot water; it can be cold in these parts.

BUDGET

Parque Nacional Las Victorias Camping (campsite per person per night Q20) Camping is available at Parque Nacional Las Victorias, right in town. Facilities include water and toilets but no showers.

Casa Blanca Hostel (☎ 4034-9291; 1a Calle 3-25, Zona 1; dm/s/d without bathroom Q35/50/100) This backpackers' favorite is a total winner in terms of location, and offers decent shared rooms, sleeping four in two bunks. The patio has a good simple cafe and the young staff are full of info and tips.

Hotel La Paz (☎ 7952-1358; 6a Av 2-19, Zona 1; s/d Q40/75; ℗) This cheerful, clean hotel, 1½ blocks north and two blocks west of the plaza, is an excellent deal. It has many flowers, and a good cafeteria next door.

Posada de Don Pedro (☎ 7951-0562; cobnposadadon pedro@hotmail.com; 3a Calle 3-12, Zona 2; r per person with/ without bathroom Q75/40) This family-run place has spacious rooms with terracotta-tiled floors around a happy little courtyard. There are good sitting areas to while the day away in.

Casa Luna (☎ 7951-3528; www.cobantravels.com; 5a Av 2-28, Zona 1; dm/s/d without bathroom incl breakfast Q50/75/150; ☐ ☎) Modern rooms set around a pretty, grassy courtyard. Dorms have lockers and private rooms are well decorated. The shared bathrooms are spotless and breakfast is good.

Casa D'Acuña (☎ 7951-0482; casadacuna@yahoo.com; 4a Calle 3-11, Zona 2; dm/d without bathroom Q50/100; ☎) This clean, very comfortable European-style hostel has four dormitories (each with four beds) and two private doubles, all with shared bathroom with good hot-water showers. Also here is a fabulous restaurant called El Bistro (p219), a gift shop, laundry service and reasonably priced local tours.

MIDRANGE

Hotel Rabin Ajau (☎ 7951-4296; cnr 1a Calle & 6a Av, Zona 1; s/d Q100/160) With their wooden floorboards and log-trunk bedheads, rooms here have a bit more style than most in town. Those at the front have small balconies but can get noisy.

Hotel Central (☎ 7952-1442; 1a Calle 1-79, Zona 1; s/d Q120/160; P 🛜) Reasonable-sized rooms and lovely outdoor sitting areas make this a decent choice. Try for a room at the back for better ventilation and views out over the town.

Pensión Monja Blanca (☎ 7952-1712; 2a Calle 6-30, Zona 2; s/d Q170/225, without bathroom Q120/150; P) This place is peaceful despite being on busy 2a Calle. After walking through two courtyards, you come to a lush garden packed with fruit and hibiscus trees around which the spotless rooms are arranged. Each room has an old-time feel to it and is furnished with two good-quality single beds with folksy covers, and has cable TV; the light switches are on the outside. This is a good place for solo women travelers.

Hostal de Doña Victoria (☎ /fax 7951-4213; www. hotelescoban.com; 3a Calle 2-38, Zona 3; s/d Q150/215; P) This lovely hotel in a restored mansion more than 400 years old is jam-packed with eye-catching decorations varying from an old copper coffee machine to wooden masks to antique religious statues. Eight brightly painted comfortable rooms, with bathroom and TV, surround a central courtyard with lush plants and a restaurant-bar.

Hotel Los Faroles (☎ 7952-2091; 2a Calle 3-61, Zona 1; s/d Q150/300; P) A modern hotel built with plenty of faux-colonial stylings. Rooms here are small but comfortable. There are good views from the tiny balconies and the roof terrace.

Posada de Don Antonio (☎ 7951-1792; 5a Av 1-51 Zona 4; s/d Q180/330; P 🚭 🛜) This atmospheric two-story place provides some of the best value in town. Rooms are spacious with two (or even three!) double beds, high ceilings and loving attention to detail. Breakfast (Q30 to Q50) in the lush patio area is a great way to start the day.

Casa Duranta (☎ 7951-4188; www.casaduranta.com; 3a Calle 4-46, Zona 3; s/d Q280/350) Some rooms at this carefully restored, eclectically decorated place are excellent value, while others are a bit cramped for the price. Have a look around if you can.

Hotel La Posada (☎ 7952-1495; www.laposadacoban. com; 1a Calle 4-12, Zona 2; s/d Q350/390) Just off the plaza, this colonial-style hotel is Cobán's best, though rooms streetside suffer from traffic noise. Its colonnaded porches are dripping with tropical flowers and furnished with easy chairs and hammocks from which you can enjoy the mountain views. The rooms are a bit austere, with plenty of religious relics around the place, but they have nice old furniture, fireplaces and wall hangings of local weaving. La Posada has a restaurant and cafe (p218).

COFFEE: FROM THE BEAN TO THE CUP

It's a long way from the farm to the table for the humble coffee bean. First, you have to wait until they're ripe – a sunburst red color – then they're picked and put in water. Those that float are skimmed off and sold as second-grade beans. The rest soak in the water for 12 to 24 hours (depending on the altitude) until they ferment and shed their outer skin.

Then it's into the wash to remove any residues and the fleshy substance that covers the kernel, before being baked in an oven to dry.

All the above, from picking to drying, should take place in around one day to maintain flavor, but after this the bean can be stored for months without any loss in quality.

Many small-scale producers sell the beans at this point – buyers often prefer to take over from here, as the rest of the process greatly influences the flavor of the finished product.

A machine is now used to remove a fine, transparent skin that covers the inner kernel. This is done just prior to toasting. A lighter toast makes for a more aromatic, less flavorsome brew. Longer toasting means more flavor but less aroma.

The degree of acidity in a coffee bean is directly related to the altitude it's grown at – the higher the altitude, the greater the acidity.

Of Guatemala's main coffee-growing regions, Huehuetenango and Cobán produce the most acidic beans, Lago de Atitlán and Antigua produce a medium acidity, and the smoothest beans come from the Pacific Slope and El Petén.

WAKE UP & SMELL THE EXPLOITATION

Coffee is not just a drink in Guatemala. For many, it's a livelihood. It's also a neat analogy to the country's history and society.

The majority of coffee *fincas* (plantations) are large landholdings, many passed down for generations since the Spanish came and took over the land. Others, according to the Central America Report, have been 'gifted' from the government – often to political allies and ex-military types for…services rendered.

Wages and conditions on coffee farms are hard to imagine. Around harvest time, subsistence farmers from the area are brought in to live on the farm in crude dormitory-style buildings. Workers are paid by weight of beans picked, and you will often see entire families – including small children – out in the fields.

Minimum wage (around Q56 per day for rural workers) is not a relevant concept here. The unsteady world coffee market means that farm owners sometimes get rich, but workers barely scrape by.

A small group of owners and workers have come up with an alternative model. Working on a cooperative basis, they shun the exploitative model and market their produce as fair-trade coffee.

For a product to claim fair-trade status, it must be certified by the **Fair Trade Labeling Organization** (www.fairtrade.net). The main requisites for certification are that the producer:

- respects the human rights of workers
- grants equal pay and conditions to men and women
- doesn't use child labor
- assists in community development.

There are around 24 communities producing fair-trade coffee in Guatemala. The vast majority of produce is exported, and much of it is organic, using natural, plant-based herbicides and pesticides.

To find out more about fair-trade coffee, log on to www.cafeconciencia.org. You can visit, stay and even volunteer at a fair-trade coffee farm at Nueva Alianza (see p193).

Eating

Most of the hotels in Cobán come with their own restaurants. In the evening, food trucks (kitchens on wheels) park around the plaza and offer some of the cheapest dining in town. As always, the one to go for has the largest crowd of locals hanging around and chomping down.

Café Fantasia (Oficinas Profesionales Fray Bartolomé de Las Casas, 1a Calle 3-13; breakfast Q20-30; Mon-Sat) Another good central cafe, this one offers several types of hot chocolate. It's a cozy little place in which to enjoy breakfasts, pastries and coffee or light meals, with a pleasant terrace away from the traffic.

El Cafeto (2a Calle 1-36 B, Zona 2; mains Q25-40; breakfast, lunch & dinner) This cute little cafe right on the square does good, light set lunches (Q25), has a half-decent wine selection and serves delicious coffee.

Xkape Koba'n (2a Calle 5-13, Zona 2; snacks Q15, mains Q30; 10am-7pm) The perfect place to take a breather or while away a whole afternoon, this beautiful, artsy little cafe has a lush garden out back. Some interesting indigenous-inspired dishes are on the small menu. The cakes are homemade, the coffee is delectable and there are some interesting handicrafts on sale.

Café La Posada (1a Calle 4-12, Zona 2; snacks under Q35; 11am-7pm) This cafe has tables on a veranda overlooking the square, and a comfortable sitting room inside with couches, coffee tables and a fireplace. All the usual cafe fare is served. Snacks comprise nachos, tortillas, sandwiches, burgers, tacos, tostadas, fruit salad and more.

Bella Pizza (1a Calle 13-47, Zona 1; mains Q40-60; lunch & dinner) It's worth making the short trek out to this family-run pizzeria for the good range of tasty pizzas, pastas and salads.

Bokatas (4a Calle 2-34, Zona 2; mains Q40-80; dinner) This large outdoor eatery pumps out big juicy steaks and loud disco music in equal portions. Also on offer is a good range of seafood and Mediterranean options.

Restaurant Kam Mun (1a Calle 8-12, Zona 2; mains Q40-100; lunch & dinner) Standard Chinese fare, served in a nice, clean atmosphere, 500m west of the plaza. Enjoy your meal surrounded by Chinese dragons, Buddhas and floral paintings.

El Peñascal (5a Av 2-61; mains Q55-90; ☺ lunch & dinner) Probably Cobán's finest stand-alone restaurant, this one has plenty of regional specialties, Guatemalan classics, mixed meat platters, seafood and snacks in a relaxed, up-market setting.

ourpick El Bistro (4a Calle 3-11; mains Q60-120; ☺ from 7am) Casa D'Acuña's restaurant offers authentic Italian and other European style dishes served in an attractive oasis of tranquility to background classical music. In addition to protein-oriented mains, there is a range of pastas (Q40 to Q65), salads, homemade breads, cakes and outstanding desserts.

Entertainment

Cobán has several places where you can get down and boogie. **Bar Milenio** (3a Av 1-11, Zona 4) has a bar, food, a pool table and mixed music disco.

Bohemios (8a Av & 2 Calle, Zona 2; admission Q10-25; ☺ Thu-Sat) is a mega-disco with balcony seating and bowtied waiters.

Getting There & Away

BUS

The highway connecting Cobán with Guatemala City and the Carretera al Atlántico is the most traveled route between Cobán and the outside world. The road north through Chisec to Sayaxché and Flores is now paved all the way, providing much easier access than before to El Petén. The off-the-beaten-track routes west to Huehuetenango and northeast to Fray Bartolomé de Las Casas and Poptún are mostly unpaved and still provide a bit of an adventure. Always double-check bus departure times, especially for less frequently served destinations.

Buses leave from a variety of points around town. Minibuses, known as microbuses, are replacing, or are additional to, chicken buses on many routes.

The table below lists buses leaving from Cobán's Campo Dos bus terminal. Please be aware that the road to Uspantan and Nebaj is prone to landslides – get the latest before setting out.

Destinations not served by the Campo Dos terminal include the following:

Cahabón (Q40, 4½ hours, 85km) Same buses as to Lanquín (see below).

El Estor (Q45, five hours, 166km) Two minibuses daily leave from Transportes Imperial, behind the Monja Blanca terminal at 9:30am and 11:30pm. This road gets washed out in heavy rains – check at the office to see if the bus is running. There are additional departures from Transportes Brenda Mercedes (3a Av & 3a Calle, Zona 4) at 9:30am, 11:30am and 1:30pm.

Guatemala City (Q40-55, four to five hours, 213km) Transportes Monja Blanca (☎ 7951-3571; www.tmb.com.gt; 2a Calle 3-77, Zona 4) has buses leaving for Guatemala City every 30 minutes from 2am to 6am, then hourly until 4pm.

Lanquín (Q30, 2½ to three hours, 61km) Transportes Martínez (6a Calle 2-40, Zona 4) has multiple departures throughout the day. Minibuses also depart from the corner of 5a Calle and 3a Av, in Zona 4, from 7am to 4pm, some continuing to Semuc Champey. Do check these times, though, as they seem to be fluid.

San Pedro Carchá (Q3, 20 minutes, 6km) Buses every 10 minutes, from 6am to 7pm, from the lot in front of the Monja Blanca terminal.

CAR

Cobán has a couple of places that rent cars. Reserve your choice in advance. If you want to go to the Grutas de Lanquín or Semuc Champey, you'll need a 4WD vehicle. Rental companies include **Inque Renta Autos** (☎ 7952-1994;

BUSES FROM COBÁN

Destination	Cost (Q)	Duration (hr)
Biotopo del Quetzal	10	1¼
Chisec	15	2
Fray Bartolomé de Las Casas	35	4
Nebaj	55	5½-7
Playa Grande (for Laguna Lachuá)	50	4
Raxruhá	25	2½-3
Salamá	20	1½
Sayaxché	60	4
Tactic	6	40min
Uspantán	30	4½

inque83@hotmail.com; 3a Av 1-18, Zona 4) and **Tabarini Rent A Car** (☎ 7952-1504; www.tabarini.com; 7a Av 2-27, Zona 1).

AROUND COBÁN

Cobán, and indeed all of Alta Verapaz, has become a magnet for Guatemalan adventure travel, both independent and organized. Not only are there scores of villages where you can experience traditional Maya culture in some of its purest extant forms, there are also caves running throughout the department, waterfalls, pristine lagoons and many other natural wonders yet to be discovered. Go find them!

San Cristóbal Verapaz is an interesting Poqomchi' Maya village set beside Lake Chicoj, 19km west of Cobán. During Semana Santa (Easter Week), San Cristóbal artists design elaborate *alfombras* (carpets) of colored sawdust and flower petals rivaled only by those in Antigua. Check out the town's excellent community website at www.sancrisav. net. In addition, San Cristóbal is home to the **Centro Communitario Educativo Pokomchi** (Cecep; ☎ 7950-4039; www.ajchicho.50g.com), an organization dedicated to preserving traditional and modern ways of Poqomchi' life. To this end, Cecep inaugurated the **Museo Katinamit** (Calle del Calvario 0-33, Zona 3; ☺ 8am-5pm Mon-Sat, 9am-noon Sun), which re-creates a typical Poqomchi' house, with well-ordered displays of household items and everyday products. Other rooms feature art, tools and textiles still in daily use, and an introduction and orientation on the Poqomchi'. Cecep also offers volunteer and ethnotourism opportunities and houses the **Aj Chi Cho Language Center** (www.ajchicho.50g.com; courses incl homestay per week Q1160) for teaching Spanish. **El Portón Real** (☎ 7950-4604; oscar_capriel@hotmail.com; 4a Av, 1-44, Zona 1; s/d Q65/110) is a Poqomchi'-owned and -operated hostelry a few blocks away from the museum and school.

Tactic is a small town 32km south of Cobán that offers myriad opportunities to experience traditional Maya culture. On the plaza is the **Cooperativa de Tejadores**, where women demonstrate weaving techniques and sell their wares. On the outskirts of Tactic, atop the hill called Chi Ixhim, is an altar to the God of Maize; anyone in town can point you in the right direction. There are a few places to stay, including the reasonable **Hotel Villa Linda** (☎ 7953-9216; 4a Calle 6-25, Zona 1; s/d Q75/160). Back out on the highway and several steps up in comfort is the **Country Delight** (☎ 5514-0955; countrydelight@ hotmail.com; Hwy 14 Km 166.5; r from Q280), where there

are hiking trails, camping facilities (Q60 per person), cabins, rooms and a restaurant. Staff can supply information on the area and its attractions. Tactic celebrates the **Fiesta de la Virgen de la Asunción** from August 11 to 16.

Balneario Las Islas

At the town of San Pedro Carchá, 6km east of Cobán on the way to Lanquín, is the Balneario Las Islas, with a river coming down past rocks and into a natural pool that's great for swimming. It's a five- to 10-minute walk from the bus stop in Carchá; anyone can point the way. Buses operate frequently between Cobán and Carchá (Q3, 20 minutes).

San Juan Chamelco

About 8km southeast of Cobán is the village of San Juan Chamelco, where you can swim at the Balneario Chio. The **church** here sits on top of a small rise, providing awesome views of the villages below. The colonial church may have been the first in Alta Verapaz. Paintings inside depict the arrival of the conquistadors. Mass is still held here in both Spanish and Q'eqchi'.

Buses (Q3, 20 minutes) to San Juan Chamelco leave from the Wasen Bridge, Diagonal 15, Zona 7, on the eastern edge of Cobán.

Grutas Rey Marcos

Near **Aldea Chajaneb**, 12km east of Cobán, is the cave system **Grutas Rey Marcos** (☎ 7951-2756; www.grutasdelreymarcos.com; admission Q25; ☺ 9am-5pm). It's set in the **Balneario Cecilinda** (admission Q10), which is, incidentally, a great place to go for a swim or a hike on scenic mountain trails. The caves themselves go for more than 1km into the earth, although chances are you won't get taken that far. A river runs through the cave (you have to wade through it at one point) and there are some impressive stalactites and stalagmites. Headlamps, helmets and rubber boots are included in the admission price to the cave. According to local legend, any wishes made in the cave are guaranteed to come true. The Balneario Cecilinda is located 1km past Don Jerónimo's.

In Aldea Chajaneb, **Don Jerónimo's** (☎ 5301-3191; www.dearbrutus.com/donjeronimo; s/d Q210/375), owned by Jerry Makransky (Don Jerónimo), rents comfortable, simple bungalows. He dotes on his guests, and the atmosphere is friendly. The price includes three ample, delicious vegetarian meals fresh from the garden.

Jerry also offers many activities, including tours to caves and the mountains, and inner-tubing on the Río Sotzil. He can also hook you up with a local Maya priest who will perform a traditional fire ceremony.

To reach Don Jerónimo's, take a bus or pickup (Q2, 15 minutes) from San Juan Chamelco towards Chamil and ask the driver to let you off at Don Jerónimo's. Alternatively, hire a taxi from Cobán (Q80).

Lanquín

One of the best excursions to make from Cobán is to this pretty village, 61km to the east. People come for two reasons: to explore the wonderful cave system just out of town, and as a jumping-off point for the natural rock pools at Semuc Champey (p222). The Banrural on Lanquín's main square changes US dollars and traveler's checks, but at the time of writing did not have an ATM. For more on the area, check the community website www.semucchampey.com.

SIGHTS

The **Grutas de Lanquín** (admission Q30; ☼ 7am-6pm) are about 1km northwest of the town, and extend for several kilometers into the earth. There is now a ticket office here. The first cave has lights, but do take a powerful flash-light (torch) anyway. You'll also need shoes with good traction, as inside it's slippery with moisture and bat crap.

Though the first few hundred meters of the cavern have been equipped with a walk-way and are lit by diesel-powered electric lights, most of this subterranean system is untouched. If you are not an experienced spe-lunker, you shouldn't wander too far into the caves; the entire extent has yet to be explored, let alone mapped.

As well as featuring funky stalactites, mostly named for animals, these caves are crammed with bats. Try to time your visit to coincide with sunset, when hundreds of them fly out of the mouth of the cave in formations so dense they obscure the sky. For a dazzling display of navigation skills, sit at the entrance while they exit. The river here gushes from the cave in clean, cool and delicious torrents. You can swim in the river, which has some comfortably hot pockets close to shore.

Just downhill from the entrance to the caves, you'll see the entry to **Parque Natural Guayaja** (☎ 4154-4010; www.guayaja.com; admission Q10, campsite Q50), the area's latest attraction. Here you'll find the near-obligatory canopy tour (Q100), plus rappelling (Q75) and hiking trails (Q10). If you don't have a tent, you can rent one for Q75 per night.

ACTIVITIES

Maya Expeditions (see p74), based in Guatemala City, offers exciting one- to five-day rafting expeditions on the Río Cahabón.

Guatemala Rafting (☎ 7983-3056; www.guatemalarafting.com), operating out of El Retiro lodge (see below), has a variety of trips on offer, including kayaking on the river beneath Semuc Champey. Travelers heading for Río Dulce or Flores may be interested in the Adventure Route trip (two days, from Q850 per person), which takes you down the Río Cahabón and out to Hwy 13. Guests at El Retiro get a 20% discount on rafting trips.

ADETES (☎ 5063-6001; www.guaterafting.com) is an excellent new community-tourism initiative based in Aldea Saquijá, 12km out of Lanquín. It offers rafting trips led by well-trained community members on the Río Cahabón. Prices are Q290/375 per person for a 2½-/five-hour trip. To get to the headquarters catch any bus leaving Lanquín headed towards Cahabón.

SLEEPING & EATING

El Retiro (☎ 4513-6396; www.elretirolanquin.com; hammock/dm Q20/35, r with/without bathroom Q190/70, cabin without bathroom Q120; ▯ ☎) This sublimely located hotel is about 500m along the road beyond Rabin Itzam. *Palapa* buildings look down over the greenest of green fields to a beautiful wide river – the same river that flows out from the Lanquín caves. It's safe to swim, and to inner-tube if you're a confident swimmer. Attention to detail in every respect makes this a back-packers' paradise. Dorm rooms have only four beds. Individual decor includes some clever use of tiles, shells, strings of beads and local fabrics. Excellent vegetarian food (three-course dinner Q35) is available in the bar/restaurant. Plenty of info is provided for onward journeys and there are organized activities such as jungle walks.

Hotel El Centro (☎ 7983-0012; r per person with/without bathroom Q40/30) Just downhill from the central park, this budget option offers clean, decent-sized rooms. Those with shared bathroom are much more spacious.

El Recreo (☎ 7983-0057; hotel_el_recreo@hotmail.com; s/d Q255/320, without bathroom Q35/70; ▯ ▣) Between the town and the caves, this place has that 'made for tour groups' feel to it, but the bungalows set around forested grounds are a good deal – spacious and well decorated. The rooms set in the basement with shared bathrooms might be a bit grim for some.

Rabin Itzam (☎ 7983-0076; s/d Q80/120, without bathroom Q60/80) The most comfortable option in the center, although the beds sag a bit. Rooms upstairs at the front (with shared bathroom) have good valley views.

Restaurante Champey (mains Q20-50; ☼ breakfast, lunch & dinner) This large outdoor eatery halfway between town and El Retiro serves up good-sized plates of steak, eggs and rice and gets rowdy and beerish at night.

GETTING THERE & AWAY

Overnight tours to the Grutas de Lanquín and Semuc Champey, offered in Cobán for Q270 per person (see p213), are the easiest way to visit these places, but it's really not that complicated to organize yourself. Tours take about two hours to reach Lanquín from Cobán; the price includes a packed lunch.

Buses operate several times daily between Cobán and Lanquín, continuing to Cahabón. At least one bus per day passes through en route to El Estor. There are eight buses to Cobán (Q30, three hours) between 6am and 5:30pm. There are scheduled departures for Semuc Champey at 1pm and 3pm (Q10, 30 minutes), tourist shuttles (Q15) at 9:30am (book at your hotel) and pickups (Q10) leaving whenever they are full half a block from the main square.

If it's been raining heavily and you're driving, you'll need a 4WD vehicle. The road from San Pedro Charca to El Pajal, where you turn off for Lanquín, is paved. The 11km from El Pajal to Lanquín is not. You can head on from Lanquín to Flores in 14 to 15 hours via El Pajal, Sebol, Raxrujá and Sayaxché. The road from El Pajal to Sebol is not paved. Or you can head from Lanquín to Sebol and Fray Bartolomé de Las Casas and on to Poptún.

If you're heading towards Río Dulce, a back road exists, although it's unpaved for most of the way and gets washed out in heavy rains. Transportation schedules along here are flexible at best. Ask around to see what the current situation is. Five minibuses daily leave Lanquín for Cahabón (Q12, one hour). The last of these leaves at 4pm, although you'll want to leave earlier to avoid getting stuck here. From Cahabón, there are various departures for El Estor, the last one being at 4:30pm

(Q45, four hours), although if you miss it you should be able to get a ride in a pickup without too much trouble.

Road to Semuc Champey

If you're into walking, this 2½-hour trip from Lanquín is a fairly pleasant one, passing through lush countryside and simple rural scenes. If not, there are plenty of transportation options (see below left). About 3km before Semuc Champey on your right you'll see **Posada El Zapote** (☎ 5568-8600; dm Q25, s/d Q75/125, without bathroom Q40/70), which has good, simple rooms set on ample grounds. There's a reasonable Italian restaurant on the premises and it has its own cave system on the property, which you're welcome to swim through by candlelight.

A couple of kilometers on, you'll see a turnoff to the right for the **K'anba Caves** (admission Q50), which many find to be much more interesting than the Lanquín ones. Bring a flashlight for the two-hour tour, or you'll be stumbling around by candlelight. A half hour of river tubing is generally included in the price.

Across the bridge and up the hill is **El Portal** (☎ 7983-0016; dm Q35, r with/without bathroom Q150/80), about 100m short of the entrance to Semuc Champey. There's no electricity, but the well-spaced wooden huts built on the bank sloping down to the river are by far the best accommodation deal in the area. Meals and tours are available, but make sure you book in advance – despite being new this place is already extremely popular.

Semuc Champey

Eleven kilometers south of Lanquín, along a rough, bumpy, slow road, is **Semuc Champey** (admission Q50), famed for its great 300m-long natural limestone bridge, on top of which is a stepped series of pools with cool, flowing river water good for swimming. The water is from the Río Cahabón, and much more of it passes underground, beneath the bridge. Though this bit of paradise is difficult to reach, the beauty of its setting and the perfection of the pools, ranging from turquoise to emerald-green, make it worth it. Many people consider this the most beautiful spot in all Guatemala.

If you're visiting on a tour, some guides will take you down a rope ladder from the lowest pool to the river, which gushes out from the rocks below. Plenty of people do this and love it, though it is a bit risky.

It's possible to **camp** (per tent Q50) at Semuc Champey, but be sure to pitch a tent only in the upper areas, as flash floods are common down below. It's risky to leave anything unattended, as it might get stolen. The place now has 24-hour security, which may reassure potential campers, but you should keep your valuables with you. A simple restaurant at the parking area serves OK meals (including *cack'ik*; Q40), but is a long way from the pools. It's a better idea to bring a picnic.

Pickups run from the plaza in Lanquín to Semuc Champey – your chances of catching one are better in the early morning and on market days: Sunday, Monday and Thursday. If there are a lot of local people traveling, expect to pay Q6; otherwise, it's Q10. Minibuses also serve this route – see opposite for details.

PARQUE ECOLÓGICO HUN NAL YE

At Km 259, 41km north of Cobán, you'll see the turnoff for this wonderful **private reserve** (☎ 7951-5921; www.parquehunnalye.com; admission Q85; ☺ 8am-6pm Wed-Sun), set on 135 hectares of lush, tropical grounds. There's an abundance of wildlife here – the park claims to be home to over 200 species of birds and around 23 types of reptiles. The admission price includes guided walks, river tubing, use of the swimming pools and entry to a small museum showcasing archaeological items found on the site. Activities such as canopy tours, scuba diving in the cenote, kayaking, horseback riding and ATV hire cost extra. If you want to stay here, very comfortable, colonial-styled **rooms** (per person incl park entrance & breakfast Q330) are available or you can pitch your own tent for Q40 per person. To get here from Cobán, catch any bus from Campo Dos bus station heading towards San Vincente Chicatal and tell the driver to let you off at the park entrance.

CHISEC

pop 28,800

The town of Chisec, 66km north of Cobán, is becoming a center for reaching several exciting destinations. This is thanks to the paving of the road from Cobán to Sayaxché and Flores, which runs through here, and some admirable community tourism programs aiming to help develop this long-ignored region, the population of which is almost entirely Q'eqchi' Maya.

Chisec has a few places to stay. **Hotel Nopales** (☎ 5514-0624; central plaza; s/d Q60/90) has surprisingly large rooms (with smell) set around a courtyard dominated by a permanently empty (unless it's been raining) swimming pool. The best hotel, **Hotel La Estancia de la Virgen** (☎ 5514-7444; s/d Q120/170; P ❷), on the main road at the northern exit from town, has neat and sensible rooms with fan and cable TV. It has a restaurant and the swimming pool has some excellent waterslides in the shape of fallen tree trunks. The **Restaurante Bonapak** (central plaza; mains Q30; ☺ breakfast, lunch & dinner) is one of the few places you'd want to eat in town.

Buses leave Chisec for Cobán (Q15, two hours) eight times daily, from 3am to 2pm. Buses or minibuses to San Antonio and Raxrujá (one hour) go hourly, from 6am to 4pm. Some of these continue to Fray Bartolomé de Las Casas. There are also two services daily, morning and afternoon, to Playa Grande (two hours), for the Parque Nacional Laguna Lachuá. Some Cobán–Sayaxché minibuses and buses pass through Chisec.

AROUND CHISEC

Lagunas de Sepalau

Surrounded by pristine forest, these turquoise **lagoons** (admission Q60; ☺ 8am-3pm) are 8km west of Chisec. Recently developed as a community ecotourism project by local villagers, tours of the area include a fair bit of walking and some rowboat paddling. The area is rich in wildlife: jaguars, tapir, iguanas, toucans and howler monkeys are all in residence.

There are three lagoons, the most spectacular of which is the third on the tour, Q'ekija, which is ringed by steep walls of thick jungle. This is a water source for the local community and swimming is prohibited at certain times of the year.

Pickups leave Chisec's plaza for the village of Sepalau Cataltzul throughout the day and there's usually a bus (Q9, 45 minutes) at 10:30am. On arrival at the village, you pay the entrance fee and a guide will take you on the 3km walk to the first lagoon.

Cuevas de B'ombi'l Pek

A mere 3km north of Chisec, these **painted caves** (admission Q75; ☺ 8am-3pm) remained undiscovered until 2001. They haven't been fully mapped yet, but some claim that they connect to the Candelaria caves. The community-run guide office is by the roadside. Pay the entrance fee and the guide will take you on the 3km walk through cornfields to the entrance. The entire tour takes about four hours. The first, main cavern is the most impressive for its size (reaching 50m in height; you have the choice of rapelling or descending via a slippery 'jungle ladder' to enter), but a secondary cave – just 1m wide – features paintings of monkeys and jaguars.

Any bus running north from Chisec can drop you at the guide office.

PARQUE NACIONAL LAGUNA LACHUÁ

This **national park** (☎ 4084-1706; www.lachua.org; park admission Q40, campsite Q25, bunk with mosquito net Q50) is renowned for the perfectly round, pristine turquoise lake (220m deep) for which it was named. Until recently, this Guatemalan gem was rarely visited by travelers because it was an active, violent area during the civil war and the road was in pathetic disrepair. Now it fills up quickly on weekends and public holidays, and if you're thinking about coming at these times, it's a good idea to call and reserve a space. Overnight visitors can use the cooking facilities, so come prepared with food and drink. There is only one shower. You can no longer rent canoes for exploring the lake, but there are about 4km of interpretative trails to explore. The Cobán tour outfits (p216) offer two-day and one-night trips for Q600 per person.

A new road (unpaved from the main highway) means you can get to the park entrance from Cobán in four hours by bus. Take a Playa Grande (Cantabal) bus from Cobán via Chisec and ask the driver to leave you at the park entrance, from which it's about a 2km walk to the lake. There are two roads to Playa Grande – if you're going to Finca Chipantún, make sure you ask the driver if they go that way.

AROUND LAGUNA LACHUÁ

Outside Parque Nacional Laguna Lachuá, about 7km southwest of the park entrance, is **Finca Chipantún** (http://webspace.webring.com/people/kc/chipantun; campsite per person Q15, hammock/dm Q20/40), 4 sq km of private land bordering the Río Chixoy (Negro). It has teak and cardamom plantations plus virgin tropical rainforest, and some uncovered Maya ruins. In addition to accommodation, there are horseback-riding opportunities, forest trails, river trips, kayaking, and bird- and wildlife-watching. The owners can take you by boat on the Río Negro to El Peyan, a magical gorge. Meals cost Q25 to Q50.

In the community of Rocjá Pomtilá, 20km before the park entrance, a small **community tourism project** (☎ 5381-1970; rocapon@yahoo.com) offers homestays, river trips (Q225 per boat), bird-watching and cave tours. The village has a wonderful location on the banks of the Río Icbolay and accommodation (Q25 per person) is with Q'eqchi' families who also provide meals (Q25 to Q35). This is very basic stuff – bathing is done in the river, you'll be using pit toilets and it's quite likely that only the men in the family will speak Spanish. But still – if you're itching to get off the beaten track, this is one of the places you can really do it. Buses leave Cobán via Chisec at 11am for Tzetok (Q40, five hours), the nearest village to the community. From there it's an hour's walk to the village. Sometimes these buses continue on to Rocjá Pomtilá – be sure to ask. Call to let them know you're coming at least two days in advance. If that all sounds too complicated, get in touch with Proyecto EcoQuetzal (p216) in Cobán – they have contact with the community and can make arrangements for you.

PLAYA GRANDE

pop 13,000 / elev 85m

Also known as Cantabal or Ixcán, the closest town of any size to the Laguna Lachuá park is an extremely humble affair, comprising dirt roads, a sprawling market and a large army base. The (largely unpatrolled) Mexican border is a mere 30km away, and you're likely to see plenty of cross-border commerce going on. There are a couple of decent hotels in town (and plenty of indecent ones) and reasonable transport connections west to the highlands and east to the Verapaces. Banrural, opposite the Reina Vasty hotel, has an ATM and changes US dollars.

If you're staying the night, the **Hotel España** (☎ 7755-7645; s/d Q120/160, without bathroom Q60/80; P ⊠) does the job, and charges an extra Q40 for air-con. The best hotel in town is the **Reina Vasty** (☎ 5514-6693; s/d Q140/180; P ⊠). The Hotel España has a reasonable **restaurant** (mains Q30-50; ⊠ breakfast, lunch & dinner) with some very odd breakfast options (beef pancakes, anyone?). There are more humble *comedores* (cheap eateries) up and down the main street and around the market.

Getting There & Away

Minibuses for Cobán (Q50, four hours) passing Laguna Lachuá leave from beside the central park.

Buses (more likely pickups) west for Barrillas (five hours, Q45) leave from the new bus terminal downhill from the market.

Departures are much more frequent before noon.

Barillas is the first stop on the backdoor route to Huehuetenango in the western Highlands. The road here is unsealed and liable to get washed out in the wet season, but it's a spectacular, fascinating journey well off the beaten track. Check with locals for current road conditions. For details on the onward journey from Barillas, see p184.

RAXRUHÁ

pop 15,000 / elev 195m

A sleepy little crossroads town, Raxruhá provides a good base for exploring the nearby attractions of Cancuén and the Cuevas de Candelaria. Services are few – Banrural at the main intersection changes cash but not traveler's checks and the nearest ATMs are in Chisec or Fray Bartolomé. Reasonably fast internet access is available in the Hotel Cancuén.

The best hotel in town is the **Hotel Cancuén** (☎ 7983-0720; www.cuevaslosnacimientos.com; s/d from Q70/100, without bathroom Q35/70; P), a family-run affair just on the outskirts of town (a two-minute walk from the center). Rooms are clean and well decorated, and there's a good little *comedor* onsite. It has good information about visiting Cancuén and can arrange walking/tubing tours of the nearby Cueva los Nacimientos, the northernmost point in the Candelaria complex (Q125 per person, four to six hours). Otherwise, **Hotel El Amigo** (☎ 5872-4136; r per person Q60; P) has large, vaguely clean rooms and a swimming pool that may have water in it. The place has great potential but is terribly rundown – it may have been fixed up by the time you get there.

Both of the hotels listed serve basic meals and there are good-value *comedores* around the market/bus terminal area. Surprisingly good pizza and calzones are on offer at the **pizzeria** (mains Q40-60; lunch & dinner) attached to Hotel El Amigo. The best eating for miles around is at **El Bistrot Frances** (Km 318; mains Q50-60; breakfast & lunch), oddly located a few kilometers west of town on the road to the Candelaria caves. The small, French-inspired menu offers decent variety and the daily special is always worth investigating. Any bus heading south from Raxruhá can drop you here.

Most buses leave from the T intersection at the center of town. Pickups and the occasional bus for La Union (to access Cancuén; Q7, one hour) leave from the stop one block uphill.

There are at least five scheduled departures daily to both Sayaxché (Q25, 2½ hours) and Cobán (Q25, two hours) from Raxruhá.

AROUND RAXRUHÁ
Parque Nacional Cuevas de Candelaria

Just west of Raxruhá, this 22km-long cave system, dug out by the subterranean Río Candelaria, boasts some monumental proportions – the main chamber is 30m high, 200m wide and has stalagmites measuring up to 30m in length. Natural apertures in the roof allow sunlight in, creating magical, eerie reflections.

The caves were used by the Q'eqchi' Maya and you'll see some platforms and ladders carved into the stone. Community-run operations offer tours into the various entrances to the cave complex. You can walk, tube and spelunk the entire underground passage in about two days, but must do so with a guide. Prices depend on group size, but will probably average around Q2000 per person, not including food. Contact any of the organizations listed here or **Maya Expeditions** (www.mayaexpeditions.com) for details. The following are listed from north to south.

El Mico (Km 316.5; www.cuevasdecandelaria.com; tubing/walking tour Q30/40; 9am-5pm). Located behind – and forming part of – the Complejo Cultural de Candelaria, this is probably the most easily accessible and spectacular of the various cave tours. It was here that Frenchman Daniel Dreux, the cave system's modern-day discoverer, chose to locate the Complejo Cultural, both as a way to provide income to local communities and to help protect the natural wonders of the caves. From the highway, look for the sign for the **Complejo Cultural de Candelaria** (☎ 4035-0566; www.cuevasdecandelaria.com; s/d from Q300/400), which offers supremely comfortable accommodation in stylishly decorated cabins. Excellent, French-influenced meals are included in the rates. Some slightly cheaper cabins with shared bathrooms may be available.

A couple of kilometers west on the same highway is the turnoff to **Comunidad Mucbilha'** (Km 315; tubing/walking tour Q60/40; 9am-5pm). From the highway it's 2km along a dirt road to the parking lot, then another 1km to the visitor center, where you can walk or tube through the Venado Seco cave. The small **ecolodge** (dm Q30) here has bunk beds and shower facilities.

Another couple of caves can be visited nearby at the **Comunidad Candelaria** (Km 309.5; tubing/walking tours Q60/40; 9am-5pm). Guides can be organized at the roadside *tienda* (store) for the short walk to the caves.

For more inforamtion about these last two options, you can contact the **office** (☎ 5978-1465) in Chisec.

Any bus running between Chisec and Raxruhá can drop you at any of these three places.

Cancuén

This large **Maya site** (admission Q40) hit the papers when it was 'discovered' in 2000, even though it had already been 'discovered' back in 1907. Excavations are still under way, but estimates say that Cancuén may rival Tikal (see p287) for size.

It's thought that Cancuén was a trading, rather than religious, center, and the usual temples and pyramids are absent. In their place is a grand palace boasting more than 150 rooms set around 11 courtyards. Carvings here are impressive, particularly on the grand palace, but also along the ball courts and the two altars that have been excavated to date.

Cancuén's importance seems to stem from its geographical/tactical position. Hieroglyphics attest to alliances with Calakmul (Mexico) and Tikal, and its relative proximity to the southern Highlands would have given it access to pyrite and obsidian, prized minerals of the Maya.

Artisans certainly worked here – their bodies have been discovered dressed, unusually, in royal finery. Several workshops have also been uncovered, one containing a 17kg piece of jade.

Casual visitors will need about an hour to see the main, partially excavated sections of the site and another hour or two to see the rest.

You can camp, sleep in the 'ecolodge' and eat in the *comedor* at Cancuén, but if you're planning on doing any of those things, contact the local **community tourism office** (☎ 5978-1465) in Chisec a few days beforehand to let them know your plans.

Cobán tour companies (see p216) make day trips to Cancuén. To get here independently, catch a pickup (leaving hourly) from Raxruhá to La Unión (Q7, 40 minutes), from where you can hire a boat (Q200 to Q350 for one to 16 people, round trip) to the site. You can also hire a guide (Q75) to take you on the 4km walk to the site from La Unión, but in rainy season this will be a very muddy affair. Walking or going by *lancha*, pay at the small store where the bus stops – the boat dock is an easy 1km walk from there. Pay your entrance fee at the site when you arrive. The last pickup leaves La Unión for Raxruhá at 3pm.

Fray Bartolomé de Las Casas
pop 8600 / elev 180m

This town, often referred to simply as Fray, is a way station on the backdoor route between the Cobán/Lanquín area and Poptún on the Río Dulce–Flores highway. This route is nearly all along unpaved roads and is dotted with traditional Maya villages where only the patriarchs speak Spanish, and then only a little. This is a great opportunity for getting off the 'gringo trail' and into the heart of Guatemala.

Fray is pretty substantial for being in the middle of nowhere, but don't let its size fool you. This is a place where the weekly soccer game is the biggest deal in town, chickens languish in the streets and siesta is taken seriously.

The town itself is fairly spread out, with the plaza and most tourist facilities at one end and the market and bus terminus at the other. Walking between the two takes about 10 minutes. Coming from Cobán, you'll want to hop off at the central plaza.

The post office and police station are just off the plaza. Nearby, Banrural changes US dollars and travelers checks and has an ATM. The *municipalidad* (town hall) is on the plaza.

The friendly **Hotel La Cabaña** (☎ 7952-0352; 2a Calle 1-92 Zona 3; s/d Q70/140, without bathroom Q35/75) is the best accommodation in town. Eating options are limited here – try Comedor Jireh and Restaurante Doris on the main street. Otherwise, grab a steak (with tortillas and beans; Q15) at the informal barbecue shacks that open up along the main street at night.

At least one daily bus departs from the plaza at 4am for Poptún (Q80, seven hours, 100km). Buses for Cobán leave hourly between 4am and 4pm. Some go via Chisec (Q35, 3½ hours). Others take the slower route via San Pedro Carchá.

Las Conchas

From Fray you can visit Las Conchas, a series of limestone pools and waterfalls (admission Q20) on the Río Chiyú, which some say are better than those at Semuc Champey. The pools are up to 8m deep and 20m wide and connected by a series of spectacular waterfalls. The pools are not turquoise like those at Semuc.

Oasis Chiyú (☎ 5839-4473; www.naturetoursguatemala.com; dm/s/d Q60/100/120), a few kilometers from the pools, has a wonderful tropical feel to it. Accommodation is in big, new rustic thatched-roof huts. Reservations are absolutely essential. The whole place has an atmosphere of serenity and seclusion. There's plenty to do here: kayaking (free for guests), 10m-high waterfalls to jump from, caves to explore, jungle trekking and visits to nearby Q'eqchi' communities. Volunteer work on community projects is also available. Contact them for shuttle service from Río Dulce or Flores. Local tour prices start at Q60 per person.

Regular minibuses (Q12, one hour) leave Fray for Chahal when full. From there you must change buses for Las Conchas (Q8, one hour). If you're in your own vehicle, look for the marked sign to Las Conchas, a few kilometers east of Chahal. If you're coming south from El Petén, get off in Modesto Mendez (known locally as Cadenas), catch a Chahal-bound minibus to Sejux (*Say*-whoosh) and wait for another minibus to take you the remaining 3km to Las Conchas. Whichever direction you're coming from, travel connections are always easiest in the morning and drop off severely in the late afternoon.

EL ORIENTE

Heading east from Guatemala City brings you into the long, flat valleys of the region Guatemalans call El Oriente (the East). It's a dry and unforgiving landscape of stunted hillsides covered in scraggly brush. They breed them tough out here and the cowboy hats, boots, buckles and sidearms sported by a lot of men in the region fit well against this rugged backdrop.

Most travelers pass through on their way to Copán in Honduras, or to visit the pilgrimage town of Esquipulas. Further east, the landscape becomes a lot more tropical and you'll see plenty of fruit for sale at roadside stalls. If you've got some time in this area, a quick sidetrip to the ruins at Quiriguá is well worth your while.

RÍO HONDO

pop 9100 / elev 210

Río Hondo (Deep River), 50km east of El Rancho junction and 130km from Guatemala City, is where Hwy 10 to Chiquimula heads south off the Carretera al Atlántico (Hwy 9). Beyond Chiquimula are turnoffs to Copán, just across the Honduras border; to Esquipulas and on to Nueva Ocotepeque (Honduras); and a remote border crossing between Guatemala and El Salvador at Anguiatú, 12km north of Metapán (El Salvador).

An attraction near Río Hondo is **Valle Dorado** (☎ 7943-6666; www.hotelvalledorado.com; Hwy 9 Km 149; r from Q200 per person), an aquatic park and tourist center. This large complex 14km past the Hwy 10 junction and 23km from the other Río Hondo hotels includes an **aquatic park** (adult/child Q60/50; 9am-5pm Tue-Sun) with giant pools, waterslides, toboggans and other entertainment. Check the website for promotional deals and make reservations on weekends.

The actual town of Río Hondo is northeast of the junction. Lodging places hereabouts may list their address as Río Hondo, Santa Cruz Río Hondo or Santa Cruz Teculután. Nine kilometers west of the junction are several attractive motels right on Hwy 9, which provide a good base for explorations of this region if you have your own vehicle. By car, it's an hour from here to Quiriguá, half an hour to Chiquimula and 1½ hours to Esquipulas. These motels are treated as weekend resorts by locals and residents of Guatemala City, so they are heavily booked on weekends. They're all modern, pleasant places, with well-equipped bungalows (all have cable TV and bathroom), spacious grounds with large or giant swimming pools, and good restaurants, open from 6am to 10pm daily. You can find other eateries along the highway.

The town is home to the **Parque Acuatico Longarone** (adult/child Q50/35; 9am-5pm Mon-Fri) with giant waterslides, an artificial river and other water-based fun. Attached is the **Hotel Longarone** (☎ 7933-0488; www.hotel-longarone.com; s Q410-600, d Q520-640; P), with good-looking grounds, playgrounds for kids and an OK Italian restaurant. Rooms are comfortable if somewhat dated.

Budget watchers can crash at the **Hotel Buen Gusto** (s/d Q75/120), just off the highway next to the gas station. It's not a bad deal for the price, with small, clean and modern rooms. There's no telephone.

The motels are near each other at Km 126 on Hwy 9. Nonguests can use their pools for around Q25 per person. On the north side of the highway, **Hotel Nuevo Pasabién** (☎ 7933-0606; www.hotelpasabien.com; s/d with fan Q100/200, r with air-con Q400; P) has large rooms with big windows. This hotel is a good choice for people traveling with children who can enjoy the three pools with all manner of fancy slides.

Hotel El Atlántico (☎ 7933-0598; s/d Q250/350; P ⊠ ⌨ ⌐ ⊠), the best-looking place in town, has plenty of dark-wood fittings and well-spaced bungalows. The pool area is tranquil, with some shady sitting areas.

ESTANZUELA
pop 10,500 / elev 195

Traveling south from Río Hondo along Hwy 10, you are in the midst of the Río Motagua valley, a hot expanse of what is known as 'dry tropic,' which once supported a great number and variety of dinosaurs. Three kilometers south of Hwy 9 you'll see a small monument on the right-hand (west) side of the road commemorating the earthquake disaster of February 4, 1976.

Less than 2km south of the earthquake monument is the small town of Estanzuela, with its **Museo de Paleontología, Arqueología y Geología Ingeniero Roberto Woolfolk Sarvia** (admission free; ⏱ 8am-5pm Mon-Fri), a startling museum filled with prehistoric skeletons – some reconstructed and rather menacing-looking. Most of the bones of three giant creatures are here, including those of a huge ground sloth some 30,000 years old and a prehistoric whale. Other exhibits include early Maya ar-

tifacts. To find the museum, go west from the highway directly through the town for 1km, following the small blue signs pointing to the *museo*.

ZACAPA
pop 51,300 / elev 230m

Capital of the department of the same name, Zacapa is just east of Hwy 10 a few kilometers south of Estanzuela. This town offers little to travelers, though the locals do make cheese, cigars and superb rum. The few hotels in town are basic and will do in an emergency, but better accommodation is available in Río Hondo, Esquipulas and Chiquimula. The bus station is on the road into town from Hwy 10.

CHIQUIMULA
pop 50,700 / elev 370m

Another departmental capital, this one set in a mining and tobacco-growing region, Chiquimula is on Hwy 10, 32km south of the Carretera al Atlántico. It is a major market town for all of eastern Guatemala, with lots of daily buying and selling activity. For travelers it's not a destination but a transit point. Your goal is probably the fabulous Maya ruins at Copán in Honduras, just across the border from El Florido. There are also some interesting journeys between Chiquimula and Jalapa, 78km to the west (p231). Among other things,

---

DEM BONES

Most of the people you hear about who are digging stuff up in Guatemala these days are archaeologists. Or mining companies. But there's another group out there, sifting patiently through the soil in search of treasure – paleontologists.

While it's unclear whether dinosaurs ever inhabited what is now Guatemala, evidence shows that large prehistoric mammals – such as giant armadillos, 3m-tall sloths, mammoths and saber-toothed tigers certainly did. As they migrated southwards from North America they found they could go not much further than present-day Guatemala – back then the landmass stopped at northern Nicaragua, and 10 million years would pass before South and Central America joined, creating the American continents more or less as they are today.

Various theories seek to explain the disappearance of the dinosaurs and other large prehistoric mammals – the most widely accepted one being that a massive meteorite slammed into the Yucatán Peninsula 66 million years ago, causing global climate change.

The great bulk of the fossil and bone evidence uncovered in Guatemala has been in the country's southeast corner, but giant sloth and mastodon remains have been found in what is now Guatemala City. Paleontologist Roberto Woolfolk Sarvia (founder of the Estanzuela museum; see above) alone claims to have collected more than 5000 fragments and skeletons, and he says there's a lot more out there, just that (you guessed it) the funding isn't available to dig it up.

If you have even a passing interest in prehistoric life, the museum in Estanzuela makes for a worthy detour – it's been remodeled recently, and on display are remains of mastodons, giant sloths and armadillos, a prehistoric horse measuring 50cm, and two molar teeth from a mammoth.

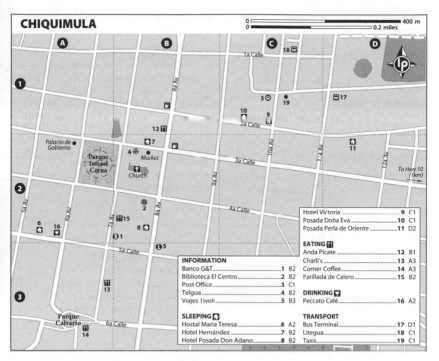

Chiquimula is famous for its sweltering climate and its decent budget hotels (a couple have swimming pools).

Orientation & Information

Though it's very hot, Chiquimula is easy to get around on foot.

Banco G&T (7a Av 4-75, Zona 1; ☺ 9am-8pm Mon-Fri, 10am-2pm Sat) Half a block south of the plaza. Changes US dollars and traveler's checks, and gives cash advances on Visa and MasterCard.

Biblioteca El Centro (cnr 4a Calle & 8a Av; per hr Q5; ☺ 8am-7pm Mon-Fri, 8am-6pm Sat & Sun) For email and internet access.

Post office (10a Av) Between 1a and 2a Calles.

Telgua (3a Calle) Plenty of card phones; a few doors downhill from Parque Ismael Cerna.

Viajes Tivoli (☎ 7942-4933; 8a Av 4-71, Zona 1) Can help you with travel arrangements.

Sleeping

Hotel Hernández (☎ 7942-0708; 3a Calle 7-41, Zona 1; s/d with fan Q80/120, with air-con Q120/180, without bathroom Q40/80; P ☒ ☎ ☒) It's hard to beat the Hernández – it's been a favorite for years, and keeps going strong, with its central position, spacious, simple rooms and good-sized swimming pool.

Posada Doña Eva (☎ 7942-4956; 2a Calle 9-61, Zona 1; s/d Q50/60) Set way back from the busy streets, the cool clean rooms here offer a minimalist approach to comfort, with TV and fans.

Hotel Victoria (☎ 7942-2732; cnr 2a Calle & 10a Av, Zona 1; s/d Q50/70) If you're just looking for somewhere to crash close to the bus terminal, these rooms are a pretty good bet. Clean and not too cramped, with TV and a decent *comedor* downstairs. Get one at the back – the street noise can be insane.

Posada Perla de Oriente (☎ 7942-0014; 2a Calle 11-50, Zona 1; r per person with fan/air-con Q80/125; P ☒ ☒) Surprisingly tranquil for its location just around the corner from the bus terminal, with some of the best-value rooms in town. They're large and unadorned, but the grounds are quiet and leafy and the big swimming pool is a bonus.

Hotel Posada Don Adano (☎ 7942-3924; 8a Av 4-30, Zona 1; s/d Q100/150; P ☒) The Don offers the best deal in this price range – neat, complete rooms with TV, fan, air-con, a couple of sticks of furniture and good, firm beds.

Hostal Maria Teresa (☎ 7942-0177; 5a Calle 6-21, Zona 1; s/d Q190/350; ⚡ 🛜) Set around a gorgeous colonial courtyard with wide shady passageways. The single rooms are a bit poky, but the doubles are generous and all the comforts are here: cable TV, hot showers and air-con.

Eating & Drinking

There's a string of cheap *comedores* on 8a Av behind the market. At night, snack vendors and taco carts set up along 7a Av opposite the plaza, selling the cheapest eats in town.

Anda Picate (8a Av 2-34, Zona 1; mains Q25-40; 🕑 lunch & dinner) For that late-night (until 11pm) Tex-Mex munchout, this is the place to be – big burritos, tacos three for Q10 and cheap beer in a relaxed, clean environment.

Corner Coffee (6a Calle 6-70, Zona 1; bagels Q30, breakfast Q25-30; 🕑 7am-10pm) You could argue with the syntax of the name, but this air-con haven right on the lovely Parque Calvario serves up the best range of sandwiches, burgers and bagels in town.

Peccato Café (cnr 5a Calle & 6a Av; mains Q30-60; 🕑 7pm-1am) About the only place you'd want to go drinking in town, this is a friendly and stylish little bar/restaurant. Drinks are well priced, TVs are huge and the food is OK if nothing mindblowing.

Charli's (7a Av 5-55; mains Q40-90; 🕑 8am-9pm) Chiquimula's 'fine dining' option (tablecloths!) has a wide menu, featuring pasta, pizza, seafood and steaks, all served up amid chilly air-con, with relaxed and friendly service.

Parillada de Calero (7a Av 4-83; mains Q45-90; 🕑 breakfast, lunch & dinner) An open-air steakhouse, serving the juiciest flame-grilled cuts in town. This is also the breakfast hot spot – the Tropical Breakfast (pancakes with a mound of fresh fruit; Q40) goes down well in this climate.

Getting There & Away

Several companies operate buses and microbuses, arriving and depart from the bus station area on 11a Av, between 1a and 2a Calles. **Litegua** (☎ 7942-2064; 1a Calle btwn 10a & 11a Avs), which operates buses to El Florido (the border crossing on the way to Copán) has its own bus station a half block north. For the Honduran border crossing at Agua Caliente take a minibus to Esquipulas and change there. If you're headed to Jalapa, you'll need to go to Ipala to make the connection. For Río Dulce, take a Flores bus, or a Puerto Barrios bus to La Ruidosa junction and change there. If you're going to Esquipulas, sit on the left for the best views of the basilica.

AROUND CHIQUIMULA
Volcán de Ipala

Volcán de Ipala is a 1650m volcano, notable for its especially beautiful clear crater lake measuring nearly 1km around and nestled below the summit at 1493m. The dramatic hike to the top takes you from 800m to 1650m in about two hours, though you can drive halfway up in a car. There are trails, a visitor center and a campsite on the shores of the lake. To get there, take a bus from Chiquimula (1½ hours) or Jalapa (two hours) to Ipala and transfer to a microbus to Agua Blanca (Q6, every 15 minutes). The trailhead is at El Sauce just before Agua Blanca; look for the blue Inguat sign. Of the very limited accommodation options in Ipala, the **Hotel Peña** (☎ 7942-8064; 2a Calle 2-26; s/d Q50/80; Ⓟ) is about the best. Enter through the unmarked garage door next to the G&T bank. There are banks with ATM and *comedores*

BUSES FROM CHIQUIMULA

Destination	Cost (Q)	Duration (hr)	Departures
Anguiatú (Salvador border)	25	1	5am-5:30pm
El Florido (Honduras border)	25	1½	5:30am-4:30pm
Esquipulas	10	45min	5am-9pm
Flores	100	7-8	10am & 3pm
Guatemala City	50	3	3am-3.30pm
Ipala	6	1½	5am-7pm
Puerto Barrios	40	4½	3:30am-4pm
Quiriguá	25	2	3:30am-4pm
Río Hondo	15	35min	5am-6pm

around the plaza. The **Restaurante Galactico** (3a Av 1-58, Zona 1; mains Q30-60; ☾ lunch & dinner) has the widest menu in town. Buses pull up a block away from Ipala's plaza, from where everything listed here is an easy walk.

Jalapa

pop 61,700 / elev 1360m

Jalapa is a small, friendly town 78km west of Chiquimula, and the route between the two is a stunning one: verdant gorges choked with banana trees alternate with fog-enveloped valleys. Crossing the winding mountain passes you'll see waterfalls, rivers and creeks flowing through the undergrowth. Though there isn't much going on in Jalapa proper, it's a good stopover before or after Volcán de Ipala. There are plenty of services for travelers. Banks that change US dollars and traveler's checks are clustered around the bus terminal.

SLEEPING & EATING

Jalapa has probably the best-value accommodation in the country – it's a pity there isn't more to do around here.

Hotel Recinos (☎ 9722-2580; s/d Q55/92) If you're just passing through, this pink palace on the west side of the terminal is your best bet. The clean rooms with fan are a good deal, although it can get cramped when they squeeze two beds in.

Hotel Casa Real (☎ 7922-2804; 1a Calle 0-74, Zona 2; s/d Q110/160; ⊠) If the Posada de Don José around the corner is full, this is a good fallback option, with large, modern rooms. Air-con costs an extra Q30 and the attached restaurant is probably the best in town.

our pick **Posada de Don José Antonio** (☎ 7922-5751; Av Chipilapa A 0-64, Zona 2; s/d Q120/160; P ⌨ ☎) Beautifully decorated with colonial flourishes, the rooms here are huge and the bathrooms massive. There are some lovely sitting areas, a shady patio and an onsite restaurant.

Hotel Puente Viejo (☎ 7922-3782; www.hotelpuenteviejo.com; 4a Calle 0-41, Zona 5; s/d Q140/240; P ☎ ☒) By far the best-looking hotel in town, with huge, cool rooms set around a grassy patio which features a bubbling fountain and small swimming pool. There's a bar/cafe/restaurant out front.

Restaurante Casa Real (1a Calle 0-74, Zona 2; mains Q40-80; ☾ breakfast, lunch & dinner) Japala's main street has plenty of fast food and *comedor* options, but this restaurant attached to the hotel of the same name has a good range of steaks, seafood and salads.

GETTING THERE & AROUND

At the time of writing, buses were still arriving at the classic bus terminal/market chaos in the center of town, a couple of blocks behind the Hotel Casa Real. This all looks set to change with the construction of a new terminal, about 1km away on the other side of town. All the hotels listed here (with the exception of the Puente Viejo) are on or near the main street, 2a Calle. Unless you're really pinching pennies, don't bother trying to navigate on foot with your luggage – tuk-tuks are everywhere and charge Q5 per person to go pretty much anywhere you'd want to.

There are no longer direct buses to Chiquimula, but microbuses head to Ipala (Q14, 30 minutes) every half hour from 5am to 4:30pm. From Ipala there are multiple departures for Chiquimula. For Esquipulas, change in Chiquimula. Buses to Guatemala City leave half-hourly between 2am and 5pm. Transportes Melva travels via Jutiapa and Cuilapa (Q30, 3½ hours, 167km). Other buses take the quicker route via Sanarate and the Carretera al Atlántico.

Parque Ecoturístico Cascadas de Tatasirire

Set on 15 hectares of heavily forested valley overlooking Jalapa, this private **reserve** (☎ 5202-4150; www.cascadasdetatasirire.com; entry Q60, campsite per person Q70, s/d without bathroom Q150/200) features 6km of well-signposted walking trails, taking in the small Cascada Altar and the more impressive, 15m Catarata Tatasirire waterfalls. Some adventure activities – the obligatory five-line canopy tour (Q120), rappelling down the Cascada Altar (Q120) and giant swings set in the forest (free) – are on offer, but the real charm of the place is to be found wandering the pine-needle-strewn mountain pathways with bubbling creeks and birdsong the only sounds you can hear. There are a couple of spots where you could swim (or at least take a dip), but the water's cold and the air is cooler than Jalapa below.

Campgrounds are basic (pit toilets, no showers), but they do provide camping equipment and rooms are available in the 'ecolodge' – a very rustic log-cabin affair with kitchen facilities and running water. If that doesn't appeal, the park makes an easy day trip from Jalapa – any bus headed towards Mataquescuintla can drop you here. They leave frequently from Jalapa (Q5, 30 minutes), from 5am to 4pm. The last one back from the park leaves at 6pm.

GETTING TO EL SALVADOR

Between Chiquimula and Esquipulas (35km from Chiquimula and 14km from Esquipulas), Padre Miguel junction is the turnoff for Anguiatú, at the border with El Salvador, which is 19km (30 minutes) away. Minibuses pass by frequently, coming from Chiquimula, Quetzaltepeque and Esquipulas.

The border at Anguiatú is open 24 hours, but you're best crossing during daylight. Plenty of trucks cross here. Across the border there are hourly buses to San Salvador, passing through Metapán and Santa Ana.

VOLCÁN DE QUETZALTEPEQUE

About 10km east of the village of Quetzaltepeque, this volcano tops out at 1900m. The walk to the top is tough going, through thick subtropical pine forest, and the trail disappears in sections, but if you have a car you can drive almost all the away to the top. From the summit are excellent views of the nearby Ipala and Suchitán volcanoes and the surrounding countryside. Due to the condition of the trail, you really need a guide to undertake this trek. Ask in the Quetzaltepeque **municipalidad** (town hall; ☎ 7944-0258) on the main plaza to be put in touch with a volunteer guide. He'll accompany you for free (although you may want to tip him).

In Quetzaltepeque, you can stay at the very friendly, very basic **Hotel El Gringo** (☎ 7944-0186; 3a Av 2-25, Zona 2; r per person Q50), which has bright, spacious rooms and very suspect beds. All things considered, you're probably better off staying in either Chiquimula or Esquipulas.

Buses running between Chiquimula and Esquipulas pass through Quetzaltepeque.

ESQUIPULAS

pop 26,000 / elev 950m

From Chiquimula, Hwy 10 goes south into the mountains, where it's a bit cooler. After an hour's ride through pretty country, the highway descends into a valley ringed by mountains, where Esquipulas stands. Halfway down the slope, about 1km from the center of town, there is a *mirador* (lookout) from which to get a good view. The reason for a trip to Esquipulas is evident as soon as you catch sight of the place, dominated by the great Basílica de Esquipulas towering above the town, its whiteness shimmering in the sun.

The view has changed little in over 150 years since explorer John L Stephens saw it and described it in his book *Incidents of Travel in Central America, Chiapas and Yucatan* (1841):

> Descending, the clouds were lifted, and I looked down upon an almost boundless plain, running from the foot of the Sierra, and afar off saw, standing alone in the wilderness, the great church of Esquipulas, like the Church of the Holy Sepulchre in Jerusalem, and the Caaba in Mecca, the holiest of temples…I had a long and magnificent descent to the foot of the Sierra.

History

This town may have been a place of pilgrimage before the Spanish conquest. Legend has it that the town takes its name from a noble Maya lord who ruled this region when the Spanish arrived, and who received them in peace.

With the arrival of the friars a church was built here, and in 1595 an image that came to be known as the Cristo Negro (Black Christ; see boxed text, p234) was installed behind the altar. In response to the steady increase in pilgrims to Esquipulas, a huge new church was inaugurated in 1758, and the pilgrimage trade has been the town's livelihood ever since.

Esquipulas has assured its place in modern history as well: in 1986, president Vinicio Cerezo Arévalo spearheaded a series of meetings here with the other Central American heads of state to negotiate regional agreements on economic cooperation and peaceful conflict resolution. The resulting pact, known as the Esquipulas II Accord, became the seed of the Guatemalan Peace Accords, which were finally signed in 1996.

Orientation & Information

The basilica is the center of everything. Most of the good hotels are within a block or two of it, as are numerous small restaurants. The town's biggest hotel, El Gran Chortí, is on the outskirts, along the road to Chiquimula. The highway does not enter town; 11a Calle, also sometimes called Doble Vía Quirio Cataño, comes in from the highway and is the town's main drag.

Banco Internacional (3a Av 8-87, Zona 1) Changes cash and traveler's checks, gives cash advances on Visa and

MasterCard, is the town's American Express agent and has a Visa ATM.

Global.com (3a Av; per hr Q5) Opposite Banco Internacional; check your email here.

Post office (6a Av 2-15) About 10 blocks north of the center.

Telgua (cnr 5a Av & 9a Calle) Plenty of card phones.

Sights

BASILICA

A massive pile of stone that has resisted the power of earthquakes for almost 250 years, the basilica is approached through a pretty park and up a wide flight of steps. The impressive facade and towers are floodlit at night.

Inside, the devout approach the surprisingly small (with all the fuss, you'd think it was life-sized) El Cristo Negro with extreme reverence, many on their knees. Incense, murmured prayers and the scuffle of sandaled feet fill the air. When there are throngs of pilgrims, you must enter the church from the side to get a close view of the famous Black Christ. Shuffling along quickly, you may get a good glimpse or two before being shoved onward by the crowd behind you. On Sundays, religious holidays and (especially) during the festival around January 15, the press of devotees is intense. On weekdays, you may have the place to yourself, which can be very powerful and rewarding. On weekends, you may feel very removed from the intensity of emotion shown by the majority of pilgrims, whose faith is very deep.

The annual **Cristo de Esquipulas festival** (January 15) sees mobs of devout pilgrims coming from all over the region to worship at the altar of the Black Christ.

When you leave the church and descend the steps through the park and exit right to the market, notice the vendors selling straw hats that are decorated with artificial flowers and stitched with the name 'Esquipulas,' perfect for pilgrims who want everyone to know they've made the trip. These are very popular rearview mirror accessories for chicken-bus drivers countrywide. Cruising the religious kitsch sold by the throngs of vendors around the basilica is an entertaining diversion.

OTHER SIGHTS

The **Centro Turístico Cueva de las Minas** (admission Q15; 6:30am-4pm) has a 50m-deep cave (bring your

---

ESQUIPULAS

0 — 200 m
0 — 0.1 miles

To Post Office (500m)

Monument

Market Area

Park

Cemetery

To Hotel El Gran Chortí & Mirador (800m); Chiquimula (49km)

To Parque Chatún (2.5km); Honduras (10km)

EL CRISTO NEGRO

Attracting more than a million pilgrims from Mexico, Central America, the US and further afield every year, the Black Christ of Esquipulas is one of Guatemala's top tourist draws.

Myths surround the sculpture's color. It was long believed that the Spaniards who commissioned it in 1594 requested a Christ with a skin tone resembling Esquipulas' Chortí natives, so that they would be easier to convert. Studies have shown, though, that it was made from a light wood, possibly cedar. Some believers say it turned black mysteriously overnight – others say that it happened as a result of human contact and the amount of incense burnt in the church over the centuries.

The Black Christ first gained widespread attention when the Archbishop of Guatemala recovered miraculously from a chronic illness after visiting Esquipulas in 1737, and the town got a healthy publicity kick when Pope John Paul II visited in 1996.

But the statue's popularity has also been explained by the syncretism of pre-Christian and Christian beliefs. All throughout the Americas, when the Spanish arrived, indigenous peoples soon discovered it was less painful to appear to accept the new religion, basically retaining their traditional beliefs and renaming the old gods accordingly. In Maya culture, black was the color of warriors, and associated with magic, death, violence and sacrifice. Accordingly, the Cristo Negro can be seen as a warrior Christ, defeater of death.

There are two authorized copies of Esquipulas' Cristo Negro in the United States. One in New York has come to represent the sufferings and hardships experienced by the Latino community there, while the one in Los Angeles (which was smuggled into the country, allegedly aided by bribed officials) has taken on a special significance for undocumented immigrants there.

own light), grassy picnic areas and the Río El Milagro, where people come for a dip and say it's miraculous. The cave and river are half a kilometer from their entrance gate, which is behind the basilica's cemetery, 300m south of the turnoff into town on the road heading towards Honduras. Refreshments are available.

If you've got kids along (or even if you don't), **Parque Chatún** (☎ 7873-0909; www.parquechatun.com; adult/child Q65/55; 9am-6pm Tue-Sat), a fun park 3km out of town, should provide some light relief from all the religious business. There are swimming pools, a climbing wall, campgrounds, a petting zoo, a canopy tour and a mini bungee jump. Entry includes the use of all these, except the canopy tour. If you don't have a vehicle, look for the minibus doing rounds of the town, or get your hotel to call it – it will take you out there for Q3.

Sleeping

Esquipulas has an abundance of places to stay. On holidays and during the annual festival, every hotel in town is filled, whatever the price; weekends are super-busy as well, with prices substantially higher. These higher prices are the ones given here. On weekdays when there is no festival, there are *descuentos* (discounts). For cheap rooms, look in the streets immediately north of the towering basilica.

BUDGET

Hotel La Favorita (☎ 7943-1175; 2a Av 10-15, Zona 1; s/d Q150/200, without bathroom Q40/70; P) The real budget-watcher's choice, the rooms with shared bathroom here are a bit grim, but those with bathrooms are good enough.

Hospedaje Esquipulas (☎ 7943-2298; cnr 1a Av & 11 Calle 'A', Zona 1; s/d Q80/130) A reasonable little no-nonsense budget hotel. Rooms are clean enough and on the small side, but bathrooms are spacious.

Hotel Monte Cristo (☎ 7943-1453; 3a Av 9-12, Zona 1; s/d Q180/250, without bathroom Q80/100; P) Good-sized rooms with a bit of furniture and super-hot showers. A policy of not letting the upstairs rooms until the downstairs ones are full might see you on the ground floor.

MIDRANGE

Hotel El Peregrino (☎ 7943-1054; www.elperegrinoesquipulas.com; 2a Av 11-94, Zona 1; s/d Q200/360, without bathroom Q140/240) Motel-style rooms looking out onto plant-filled balconies. The rooftop pool is what makes this place.

Hotel Vistana al Señor (☎ 7943-4294; hotelvistana@gmail.com; 1a Av 'B' 1-42; s/d Q200/300) By far the best deal in this price range are these sweet little rooms just south of the market. There's a pretty common balcony area with good views upstairs.

Hotel Real Santa María (☎ 7943-0214; www.hotelrealsantamaria.com; 2a Av 9-83, Zona 1; s/d from Q200/350;

P X 🛜 🛁) Well-appointed if slightly cramped rooms in a good central location. The decor is modern-colonial. Check for street noise in the front rooms.

Hotel Mahanaim (☎ 7943-1131; www.mahanaim hotelinternacional.com; 10a Calle 1-85, Zona 1; s/d Q200/250, with air-con Q350/400; P X 🖳 🛜 🛁) This establishment is on three levels around a covered courtyard. Rooms are comfortable but plain. It wouldn't be such a good deal if it weren't for the big covered swimming pool out back.

Hotel Payaquí (☎ 7943-1143; www.hotelpayaqui.com; 2a Av 11-56; s/d from Q200/350; P X 🖳 🛜 🛁) Once the fanciest hotel in town, this one's showing a bit of wear. It *is* trying, though, with a decent restaurant, a couple of swimming pools and a day spa offering massages, facials and so on.

TOP END

Hotel Posada Santiago (☎ 7943-2023; 2a Av; s/d Q250/450; P) With some interesting (but don't get excited) architecture, these rustic-chic rooms are some of the most attractive in town. They're spacious and clean, with good showers and cable TV.

Hotel Portal de la Fe (☎ 7943-4261; www.portaldelafe.com; 11 Calle 1-70, Zona 1; s/d Q250/450; P X 🖳 🛜 🛁) One of the few hotels with any real style in town. Subterranean rooms are predictably gloomy, but upstairs the situation improves considerably.

Hotel El Gran Chortí (☎ 7943-1201; www.realgran chorti.com; Carretera a Honduras Km 222; s/d Q400/550; P X 🛜 🛁) One kilometer west of the church on the road to Chiquimula, this hotel has a lobby floor that's composed of a hectare of black marble; behind it a serpentine swimming pool is set amid lawns, gardens and umbrella-shaded cafe tables. It has a games room and, of course, a good restaurant, bar and cafeteria. The rooms have all comforts.

Hotel Legendario (☎ 7943-1824; www.hotel legendario.com; cnr 3a Av & 9a Calle, Zona 1; s/d Q500/700; P X 🖳 🛜 🛁) The fanciest hotel in town goes all out on the services, right down to a separate kids' swimming pool. Rooms are reasonable – big enough, with new beds, large windows opening onto a grassy courtyard and all the comforts you'd expect for the price.

Eating

Restaurants are slightly more expensive here than in other parts of Guatemala. Budget restaurants are clustered at the north end of the park, where hungry pilgrims can find them

readily. Most eateries open from 6:30am until 9pm or 10pm daily.

The street running north opposite the church – 3a Av – has several eateries. All of the midrange and top-end hotels have their own dining rooms.

Restaurant El Angel (☎ 7943-1372; cnr 11a Calle & 2a Av; mains Q30-50; 🕙 lunch & dinner) This main-street Chinese eatery does all the standard dishes, plus steaks and a good range of *licuados* (milkshakes). Home delivery is available.

Restaurante Calle Real (3a Av; breakfast Q20-30, mains Q30-60; 🕙 breakfast, lunch & dinner) Typical of many restaurants here, this big eating barn turns out cheap meals for the pilgrims. It has a wide menu, strip lighting and loud TV.

Restaurant Payaquí (Hotel Payaquí; breakfast Q30, mains Q50-90; 🕙 breakfast, lunch & dinner) On the west side of the park in the hotel of the same name, this is a bright and clean cafeteria with big windows looking out onto the park. Prices are reasonable, and there's a good selection.

Restaurante La Frontera (breakfast Q30-50, mains Q50-120; 🕙 breakfast, lunch & dinner) Opposite the park and attached to the Hotel Las Cúpulas, this is a spacious, clean place serving up a good variety of rice, chicken, meat, fish and seafood dishes for good prices.

ourpick La Hacienda (cnr 2a Av & 10a Calle, Zona 1; mains Q70-130; 🕙 breakfast, lunch & dinner) The best steakhouse in town also serves up some decent seafood and pasta dishes. There's a cafe-bakery attached and the breakfasts (Q45) are a good (but slightly pricey) bet.

La Rotonda (11a Calle; breakfast from Q25, large pizzas Q100; 🕙 breakfast, lunch & dinner) Opposite Rutas Orientales bus station, this is a round building with chairs arranged around a circular open-air counter under a big awning. It's a welcoming place, clean and fresh. There are plenty of selections to choose from, including pizza, pasta and burgers.

Getting There & Away

Buses to Guatemala City (Q50, four hours) arrive and depart hourly from 2am to 5pm from the **Rutas Orientales bus station** (☎ 7943-1366; cnr 11a Calle & 1a Av), near the entrance to town.

Minibuses to Agua Caliente (Honduran border; Q20, 30 minutes) arrive and depart across the street, leaving every half hour from 5am to 5pm; taxis also wait here, charging the same as the minibuses, once they have five passengers.

Minibuses to Chiquimula (Q10, 45 minutes, every 15 minutes 5am to 6pm) and to

Anguiatú (Salvador border; Q15, one hour, every 30 minutes 6am to 6pm) depart from the east end of 11a Calle; you'll probably see them hawking for passengers along the main street.

For Flores/Santa Elena (Q110, eight hours), **Transportes María Elena** (☎ 7943-0448; 11 Calle 0-54, Zona 1) buses depart at 6am, 10am and 2pm from its office, passing Quiriguá (Q45, two hours), Río Dulce (Q60, four hours) and Poptún (Q90, six hours).

QUIRIGUÁ
pop 4600 / elev 97m

From Copán it is only some 50km to Quiriguá as the crow flies, but the lay of the land, the international border and the condition of the roads make it a journey of 175km. Quiriguá is famed for its intricately carved stelae – the gigantic brown sandstone monoliths that rise as high as 10.5m, like ancient sentinels, in a quiet, well-kept tropical park.

From Río Hondo junction it's 67km along the Carretera al Atlántico to the village of Los Amates, where there are a couple of hotels, a restaurant, food stalls, a bank and a little bus station. The village of Quiriguá is 1.5km east of Los Amates, and the turnoff to the ruins is another 1.5km to the east. The 3.4km access road leads south through banana groves.

History

Quiriguá's history parallels that of Copán, of which it was a dependency during much of the Classic period. Of the three sites in this area, only the present archaeological park is of interest.

Quiriguá's location lent itself to the carving of giant stelae. Beds of brown sandstone in the nearby Río Motagua had cleavage planes suitable for cutting large pieces. Though soft when first cut, the sandstone dried hard in the air. With Copán's expert artisans nearby for guidance, Quiriguá's stone carvers were ready for greatness. All they needed was a great leader to inspire them – and to pay for the carving of the huge stelae.

That leader was K'ak' Tiliw Chan Yo'at (Cauac Sky; r 725–84), who decided that Quiriguá should no longer be under the control of Copán. In a war with his former suzerain, Cauac Sky took King 18 Rabbit of Copán prisoner in 737 and later had him beheaded. Independent at last, Cauac Sky commissioned his stonecutters to go to work, and for the next 38 years they turned out giant stelae and zoomorphs dedicated to the glory of King Cauac Sky.

Cauac Sky's son Sky Xul (r 784–800) lost his throne to a usurper, Jade Sky. This last great king of Quiriguá continued the building boom initiated by Cauac Sky, reconstructing Quiriguá's Acrópolis on a grander scale.

Quiriguá remained unknown to Europeans until John L Stephens arrived in 1840. Impressed by its great monuments, Stephens lamented the world's lack of interest in them in his book *Incidents of Travel in Central America, Chiapas and Yucatan* (1841):

> Of one thing there is no doubt: a large city once stood there; its name is lost, its history unknown; and...no account

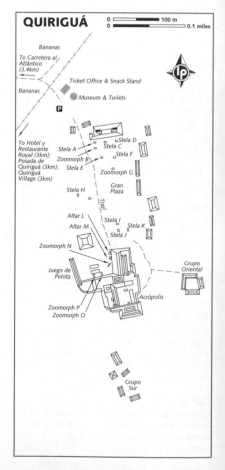

BANANA REPUBLIC

Bananas were first imported to the US in 1870. Few Americans had ever seen a banana, let alone tasted one. By 1898 they were eating 16 million bunches annually.

In 1899 the Boston Fruit Company and Brooklyn-born Central American railroad baron Minor C Keith joined forces, forming the United Fruit Company (UFC). The aim was to cultivate large areas of Central America, growing bananas that Keith would transport by rail to the coast for shipment to the USA.

Central American governments sold UFC large tracts of undeveloped jungle. The company created road and/or rail access to the land, cleared and cultivated it and built extensive port facilities.

By 1930, UFC – the largest employer in Central America – was capitalized at US$215 million and owned one of the largest private navies in the world. By controlling Puerto Barrios and the railroads, UFC effectively controlled Guatemala's international commerce, banana or otherwise.

Local journalists began referring to UFC as El Pulpo, 'the Octopus,' accusing it of corrupting government officials, exploiting workers and exercising influence far beyond its role as a foreign company in Guatemala.

On October 20, 1944, a liberal military coup paved the way for Guatemala's first-ever free elections. The new president was Dr Juan José Arévalo, who sought to remake Guatemala into a democratic, liberal nation. His successor, Jacobo Arbenz, was an even more vigorous reformer. Labor unions began clamoring for better conditions, with almost constant actions against UFC. The government demanded more equitable tax payments from the company and divestiture of large tracts of unused land.

The US government supported UFC. Powerful members of Congress and the Eisenhower administration were convinced that Arbenz was intent on turning Guatemala communist. Several high-ranking US officials had ties to UFC, and others were persuaded that Arbenz was a threat.

In 1954 a CIA-orchestrated invasion by 'anti-communist' Guatemalan exiles led to Arbenz' resignation and exile. His replacement was Carlos Castillo Armas, an old-school military man, who returned Guatemala to rightist military dictatorship.

A few years later, the US Department of Justice brought suit against UFC for operating monopolistically. UFC was ordered to reduce its size by two-thirds within 12 years. It began by selling off its Guatemalan holdings and yielding its monopoly on the railroads.

UFC later became part of United Brands, which later sold its remaining land in Guatemala to the Del Monte Corporation, which is still active in Guatemala.

---

of its existence has ever before been published. For centuries it has lain as completely buried as if covered with the lava of Vesuvius. Every traveler from Yzabal to Guatemala has passed within three hours of it; we ourselves had done the same; and yet there it lay, like the rock-built city of Edom, unvisited, unsought, and utterly unknown.

Stephens tried to buy the ruined city in order to have its stelae shipped to New York, but the owner, Señor Payes, naturally assumed that Stephens (being a diplomat), was negotiating on behalf of the US government and that the government would pay. Payes quoted an extravagant price, and the deal was never made.

Between 1881 and 1894, excavations were carried out by Alfred P Maudslay. In the early 1900s all the land around Quiriguá was sold to the United Fruit Company and turned into banana groves (see boxed text, above). The company is gone, but the bananas and Quiriguá remain. Restoration of the site was carried out by the University of Pennsylvania in the 1930s. In 1981, Unesco declared the ruins a World Heritage Site, one of only three in Guatemala (the others are Tikal and Antigua).

Sights

The beautiful parklike **archaeological site** (admission Q80; ☻ 8am-4:30pm) has a small *tienda* near the entrance selling cold drinks and snacks, but you'll be better off bringing your own picnic. A small **museum** just past the entrance has a few information displays and a model of how the site (much of it unexcavated) would have looked in its heyday.

Despite the sticky heat and (sometimes) bothersome mosquitoes, Quiriguá is a wonderful place. The giant stelae on the **Gran Plaza** (Great Plaza) are all much more worn than those at Copán. To impede further deterioration, each has been covered by a thatched roof.

The roofs cast shadows that make it difficult to examine the carving closely and almost impossible to get a good photograph, but somehow this does little to inhibit one's sense of awe.

Seven of the stelae, designated A, C, D, E, F, H and J, were built during the reign of Cauac Sky and carved with his image. **Stela E** is the largest Maya stela known, standing some 8m above ground, with another 3m or so buried in the earth. It weighs almost 60,000kg. Note the exuberant, elaborate headdresses; the beards on some of the figures (an oddity in Maya art and life); the staffs of office held in the kings' hands; and the glyphs on the sides of the stela.

At the far end of the plaza is the **Acrópolis**, far less impressive than the one at Copán. At its base are several **zoomorphs**, blocks of stone carved to resemble real and mythic creatures. Frogs, tortoises, jaguars and serpents were favorite subjects. The low zoomorphs can't compete with the towering stelae in impressiveness, but as works of art, imagination and mythic significance, the zoomorphs are superb.

Sleeping & Eating

Both of the hotels listed here have restaurants. To get to the Royal, walk down the main street, veering right at the first fork and then follow the road around to the left at the bend. The Posada de Quiriguá is further around, past the football field and very badly signposted – you'll need to ask plenty of directions, or hire a tuk-tuk (Q5 per person) from the highway.

Hotel y Restaurante Royal (☎ 7947-3639; s/d Q60/85; ℗) Of the budget options in town, this is by far the better choice, with spacious clean rooms and a restaurant serving simple, filling meals. Room prices are heavily negotiable.

Posada de Quiriguá (☎ 7934-2448; www.posadade quirigua.com; s/d from Q130/300) By far the finest place to stay in town is this Japanese-run inn, enjoying a lovely hilltop location set in a lush tropical garden. Rooms are simple but comfortable and the posada's menu (mains Q40 to Q70) features a couple of Japanese dishes alongside your Guatemalan standards.

Getting There & Around

The turnoff to Quiriguá village is 205km (four hours) northeast of Guatemala City, 70km northeast of the Río Hondo junction, 41km southwest of La Ruidosa junction (for Río Dulce and Flores) and 90km southwest of Puerto Barrios.

Buses running from Guatemala City to Puerto Barrios, Guatemala City to Flores, Esquipulas to Flores or Chiquimula to Flores will drop you off or pick you up here. If you're heading for the hotels, make sure you get dropped at the *pasarela de Quiriguá* (the pedestrian overpass). They'll also drop you at the turnoff to the archaeological site if you ask.

From the highway it's 3.4km to the archaeological site – Q5 by bus or pickup, but if one doesn't come, don't fret: it's a pleasant walk (without luggage) on a new road (complete with dedicated bicycle/tuk-tuk lane) running through banana plantations to get there. You may have to wait to get from the ruins back to the main highway, but eventually some transportation will turn up.

If you're staying in the village of Quiriguá or Los Amates and walking to the archaeological site, you can take a shortcut along the railway branch line that goes from the village through the banana fields, crossing the access road very near the entrance to the archaeological site. There have been no reports of safety issues here. A tuk-tuk from Quiriguá village to the site should cost around Q15.

To head on to Río Dulce (Q25, two hours) if you don't want to wait for a bus to Flores (around 20 daily coming from Guatemala City), you can take any bus or minibus to Morales (the transportation hub for the area) and a bus on from there to Río Dulce. This is a bit of a detour off the main road, but at least you'll get a seat from Morales. Alternatively, take a Puerto Barrios bus and get off at La Ruidosa, where you can wait for a minivan or bus for the 34km to Río Dulce. For Chiquimula, take any bus the 3km from the turnoff to the ruins to Los Amates and wait for the next bus through to Chiquimula (Q25, two hours).

COPÁN (HONDURAS)

Just over the border in Honduras is the ancient city of Copán, one of the most outstanding Maya achievements, ranking in splendor with Tikal, Chichén Itzá and Uxmal. To fully appreciate Maya art and culture, you must visit Copán. This can be done on a long day trip by private car, public bus or organized tour, but it's better to take at least two days, staying the night in the town of Copán Ruinas. This is a sweet town, with good facilities, so unless you're in a huge rush, try to stay overnight here.

Crossing the Border

The Guatemalan village of El Florido, which has no services beyond a few soft drink stands, is 1.2km west of the border. At the border crossing is a branch of **Banrural** (☺ 7am-6pm), the Litegua bus office and one or two snack stands. The border crossing is open 24 hours, but (as always) it's best to cross in daylight hours.

Moneychangers will approach you on both sides of the border anxious to change quetzals for Honduran lempiras, or either for US dollars. Usually they're offering a decent rate because there's a Guatemalan bank right there and the current exchange rate is posted in the Honduran immigration office – look for it. There's no bank on the Honduran side of the border.

Still, if the moneychangers give you a hard time, change enough at the border to get you into Copán Ruinas and then hit one of the banks there. Though quetzals and US dollars may be accepted at some establishments in Copán Ruinas, it's best to change some money into lempiras.

All border formalities are handled on the Guatemalan side – you must first present your passport to the Guatemalan immigration and customs authorities, pay fees (although there is no official fee for leaving Guatemala) of somewhere up to Q10, then move over to the Honduran window where you should get a stamp and will have to pay around L60. Guatemala and Honduras (along with Nicaragua and El Salvador) are members of the CA-4, a trade agreement much like the EU but with more infighting and chaos.

Supposedly, the CA-4 is designed to facilitate the movement of people through the region. Having entered the CA-4, you should be authorized to move throughout the region freely for 90 days (or as long as your visa stipulates). In practice, the reality is somewhat more Central American. Basically, border officials are bored, unsupervised and underpaid. Most likely you'll end up paying a few dollars to get across. Travelers have tried playing the waiting game here and lost – all you do is end up standing around for a few hours, then paying the fee anyway. The Hondurans, at least, issue a nice, official-looking receipt. For more on the CA-4, see p322.

When you return through this border point, you must again pass through both sets of immigration and customs. Whether you pay fees again is at the whim of the officials,

but you could point out that you've already done so and see where that gets you. For information on transportation to and from Copán Ruinas, see p250.

COPÁN SITE

Get to the site around opening time to avoid the heat and the crowds. There are two Copáns: the town (p245) and the **ruins** (admission L280; ☺ 8am-4pm). The town is about 12km east of the Guatemala–Honduras border. Confusingly, the town is named Copán Ruinas, though the actual ruins are just over 1km further east. Minivans coming from the border may take you on to the ruins after a stop in the town. If not, the *sendero peatonal* (footpath) alongside the road makes for a pretty 20-minute walk, passing several stelae and unexcavated mounds along the way to the Copán ruins and Las Sepulturas archaeological site, a couple of kilometers further.

History
PRE-COLUMBIAN

People have been living in the Copán valley since at least 1200 BC; ceramic evidence has been found from around that date. Copán must have had significant commercial activity since early times, as graves showing marked Olmec influence have been dated to around 900 to 600 BC.

In the 5th century AD one royal family came to rule Copán, led by a mysterious king named Mah K'ina Yax K'uk' Mo' (Great Sun Lord Quetzal Macaw), who ruled from AD 426 to 435. Archaeological evidence indicates that he was a great shaman, and later kings revered him as the semidivine founder of the city. The dynasty ruled throughout Copán's florescence during the classic period (AD 250–900).

Of the subsequent kings who ruled before AD 628 we know little. Only some of their names have been deciphered: Mat Head, the second king (no relation to Bed Head); Cu Ix, the fourth king; Waterlily Jaguar, the seventh; Moon Jaguar, the 10th; and Butz' Chan, the 11th.

Among the greatest of Copán's kings was Smoke Imix (Smoke Jaguar), the 12th king, who ruled from 628 to 695. Smoke Imix built Copán into a major military and commercial power in the region. He may have taken over the nearby princedom of Quiriguá, as one of the famous stelae at that site bears his

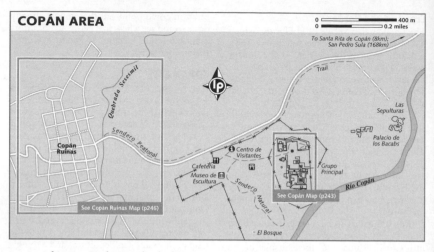

COPÁN AREA

To Santa Rita de Copán (8km);
San Pedro Sula (168km)

Quebrada Sexemil

Trail

Las
Sepulturas

Palacio de
los Bacabs

Copán
Ruinas

Sendero Peatonal

Centro de
Visitantes

Cafetería

Grupo
Principal

Museo de
Escultura

Sendero
Natural

See Copán Map (p243)

Río Copán

See Copán Ruinas Map (p246)

El Bosque

name and image. By the time he died in 695, Copán's population had grown substantially.

Smoke Imix was succeeded by Uaxaclahun Ubak K'awil (18 Rabbit; r 695–738), the 13th king, who willingly took the reins of power and pursued further military conquest. In a war with his neighbor from Quiriguá, King Cauac Sky, 18 Rabbit was captured and be-headed. He was succeeded by K'ak' Joplaj Chan K'awiil (Smoke Monkey; r 738–49), the 14th king, whose short reign left little mark on Copán. Smoke Monkey's son, K'ak' Yipyaj Chan K'awiil (Smoke Shell; r 749–63), was, however, one of Copán's greatest builders. He commissioned the city's most famous and im-portant monument, the great Escalinata de los Jeroglíficos (Hieroglyphic Stairway), which immortalizes the achievements of the dynasty from its establishment until 755, when the stairway was dedicated. It is the longest in-scription ever discovered in the Maya lands.

Yax Pac (Sunrise or First Dawn; r 763–820), Smoke Shell's successor and the 16th king, con-tinued the beautification of Copán. The final occupant of the throne, U Cit Tok', became ruler in 822, but it is not known when he died.

Until recently, the collapse of the civiliza-tion at Copán had been a mystery. Now, ar-chaeologists have begun to surmise that near the end of Copán's heyday the population grew at an unprecedented rate, straining ag-ricultural resources. In the end, Copán was no longer agriculturally self-sufficient and had to import food from other areas. The urban core expanded into the fertile lowlands in the center

of the valley, forcing both agricultural and residential areas to spread onto the steep slopes surrounding the valley. Wide areas were de-forested, resulting in massive erosion that fur-ther decimated food production and brought flooding during rainy seasons. Interestingly, this environmental damage of old is not too different from what is happening today – a disturbing trend, but one that meshes with the Maya belief that life is cyclical and history repeats itself. Skeletal remains of people who died during Copán's final years show marked evidence of malnutrition and infectious dis-eases, as well as decreased life spans.

The Copán valley was not abandoned over-night – agriculturists probably continued to live in the ecologically devastated valley for maybe another one or two hundred years. But by the year 1200 or thereabouts even the farmers had departed, and the royal city of Copán was reclaimed by the jungle.

EUROPEAN DISCOVERY

The first known European to see the ruins was a representative of Spanish King Felipe II, Diego García de Palacios, who lived in Guatemala and traveled through the region. On March 8, 1576, he wrote to the king about the ruins he found here. Only about five fam-ilies were living here at the time, and they knew nothing of the history of the ruins. The discovery was not pursued, and almost three centuries went by until another Spaniard, Colonel Juan Galindo, visited the ruins and made the first map of them.

It was Galindo's report that stimulated John L Stephens and Frederick Catherwood to come to Copán on their Central American journey in 1839. When Stephens published the book *Incidents of Travel in Central America, Chiapas and Yucatán* in 1841, illustrated by Catherwood, the ruins first became known to the world at large.

COPÁN TODAY

The history of Copán continues to unfold today. The remains of 3450 structures have been found in the 27 sq km surrounding the Grupo Principal (Principal Group), most of them within about half a kilometer of it. In a wider zone, 4509 structures have been detected in 1420 sites within 135 sq km of the ruins. These discoveries indicate that at the peak of civilization here, around the end of the 8th century AD, the valley of Copán had more than 27,500 inhabitants, a population figure not reached again until the 1980s.

In addition to examining the area surrounding the Grupo Principal, archaeologists continue to make new discoveries in the Grupo Principal itself. Five separate phases of building on this site have been identified; the final phase, dating from AD 650 to 820, is what we see today. But buried underneath the visible ruins are layers of other ruins, which archaeologists are exploring by means of underground tunnels. This is how they found the Templo Rosalila (Rosalila Temple), a replica of which is now in the Museo de Escultura (see above right). Below Rosalila is yet another, earlier temple, Margarita, and below that, Hunal, which contains the tomb of the founder of the dynasty, Yax K'uk' Mo' (Great Sun Lord Quetzal Macaw). Two of the excavation tunnels, including Rosalila, are open to the public.

Occasionally the ruins are a stage for more controversial, political actions. In September 2005, 1500 indigenous Maya Chortí, descendants of the original builders of Copán, occupied the ruins and barred visitors. Their five-day occupation of the site was in protest at stalled government land reforms, aimed at giving indigenous communities a way of lifting themselves out of poverty. At least one Maya Chortí leader has been killed in the past decade. While the protests have subsided recently, the difficult social conditions for many of the 8000 Maya Chortí in the area remains a major, unresolved issue.

Information

Admission to Copán includes entry to Las Sepulturas archaeological site but not to the two **excavation tunnels** (🕒 8am-3:30pm), for which admission is L280.

Also at the site is the **Museo de Escultura** (admission L130), where many of the original stelae are housed, as well as an awesome replica of the impressive and colorful Rosalila Temple.

The Centro de Visitantes (visitor center) at the entrance to the ruins houses the ticket office and a small exhibition about the site and its excavation. Nearby are a cafeteria, and souvenir and handicrafts shops. There's a picnic area along the path to the Principal Group of ruins. A **Sendero Natural** (Nature Trail) entering the forest several hundred meters from the visitor center passes by a small ball court.

Pick up a copy of the booklet *History Carved in Stone: A Guide to the Archaeological Park of the Ruins of Copán* by noted archaeologists William L Fash and Ricardo Agurcia Fasquelle; it's available at the visitors center for L110. It will help you to understand and appreciate the ruins. It's also a good idea to go with a guide, who can help to explain the ruins and bring them to life. Guides are L470 for groups of up to nine and L740 for groups of 10 to 19. These prices are just for the main site – guides for the tunnels, Las Sepulturas or the sculpture museum cost an additional L180 per site.

The quality of guides has improved remarkably over the last few years, thanks mostly to the formation of the **Asociación de Guías Copán** (☎ 651-4018), a cooperative of trained and qualified guides who manage to keep the amount of wild stories to a minimum and have all but abolished the days of mad jostling for tourists when they arrived at the site. You can find them at the entrance to the parking lot. Guides are available in English, French, Italian, German and of course Spanish.

As with any archaeological site, visitors should not touch any of the stelae or sit on the altars at Copán.

Grupo Principal

The Principal Group of ruins is about 400m beyond the visitor center across well-kept lawns, through a gate in a fence and down shady avenues of trees. A group of resident macaws loiters along here. The ruins themselves have been numbered for easy identification and a well-worn path circumscribes the site. It's suggested that you take a right as soon as you enter the gate, but there's a fairly obvious circuit around the site – you can't really go wrong.

Stelae of the Gran Plaza

The path leads to the **Gran Plaza** (Great Plaza; Plaza de las Estelas) and the huge, intricately carved stelae portraying the rulers of Copán. Most of Copán's best stelae date from AD 613 to 738. All seem to have originally been painted; a few traces of red paint survive on Stela C. Many stelae had vaults beneath or beside them in which sacrifices and offerings could be placed.

Many of the stelae on the Gran Plaza portray King 18 Rabbit, including stelae A, B, C, D, F, H and 4. Perhaps the most beautiful stela in the Gran Plaza is Stela A (AD 731); the original has been moved inside the Museo de Escultura, and the one outdoors is a reproduction. Nearby and almost equal in beauty are Stela 4 (731); Stela B (731), depicting 18 Rabbit upon his accession to the throne; and Stela C (782), with a turtle-shaped altar in front. This last stela has figures on both sides. Stela E (614), erected on top of Estructura 1 (Structure 1) on the west side of the Great Plaza, is among the oldest.

At the northern end of the Gran Plaza at the base of Estructura 2, Stela D (736) also portrays King 18 Rabbit. On its back are two columns of hieroglyphs; at its base is an altar with fearsome representations of Chac, the rain god. In front of the altar is the burial place of Dr John Owen, an archaeologist with an expedition from Harvard's Peabody Museum who died during excavation work in 1893.

On the east side of the plaza is Stela F (721), which has a more lyrical design than other stelae here, with the robes of the main figure flowing around to the other side of the stone, where there are glyphs. Altar G (800), showing twin serpent heads, is among the last monuments carved at Copán. Stela H (730) may depict a queen or princess rather than a king. Stela I (692), on the structure that runs along the east side of the plaza, is of a person wearing a mask. Stela J, further off to the east, resembles the stelae of Quiriguá in that it is covered in glyphs, not human figures.

Juego de Pelota

South of the Great Plaza, across what is known as the Plaza Central, is the Juego de Pelota (Ball Court; 731), the second largest in Central America. The one you see is the third one on this site; the two smaller courts were buried by this construction. Note the macaw heads carved atop the sloping walls. The central marker in the court is the work of King 18 Rabbit.

Escalinata de los Jeroglíficos

South of the ball court is Copán's most famous monument, the Escalinata de los Jeroglíficos (Hieroglyphic Stairway; 743), the work of King Smoke Shell. Today it's protected from the elements by a canvas roof. The flight of 63 steps bears a history (in several thousand glyphs) of the royal house of Copán; the steps are bordered by ramps inscribed with more reliefs and glyphs. The story told on the inscribed steps is still not completely understood because the stairway was partially ruined and the stones jumbled, but archaeologists are using 3D scanning technology to make a digital version of the original, with the hope of one day reading it in its entirety.

At the base of the Hieroglyphic Stairway is Stela M (756), bearing a figure (probably King Smoke Shell) dressed in a feathered cloak; glyphs tell of the solar eclipse in that year. The altar in front shows a plumed serpent with a human head emerging from its jaws.

Beside the stairway, a tunnel leads to the tomb of a nobleman, a royal scribe who may have been the son of King Smoke Imix. The tomb, discovered in June 1989, held a treasure-trove of painted pottery and beautiful carved jade objects that are now in Honduran museums.

Acrópolis

The lofty flight of steps to the south of the Hieroglyphic Stairway mounts the **Templo de las Inscripciones** (Temple of the Inscriptions). On top of the stairway, the walls are carved with groups of hieroglyphs. On the south side of the Temple of the Inscriptions is the **Patio Occidental** (West Court), with the **Patio Oriental** (East Court), also called the Patio de los Jaguares (Court of the Jaguars) to its east. In the West Court, check out Altar Q (776), among the most famous sculptures here; the original is inside the Museo de Escultura. Around its sides, carved in superb relief, are the 16 great kings of Copán, ending with its creator, Yax Pac. Behind the altar is a sacrificial vault in which archaeologists discovered the bones of 15 jaguars and several macaws that were probably sacrificed to the glory of Yax Pac and his ancestors.

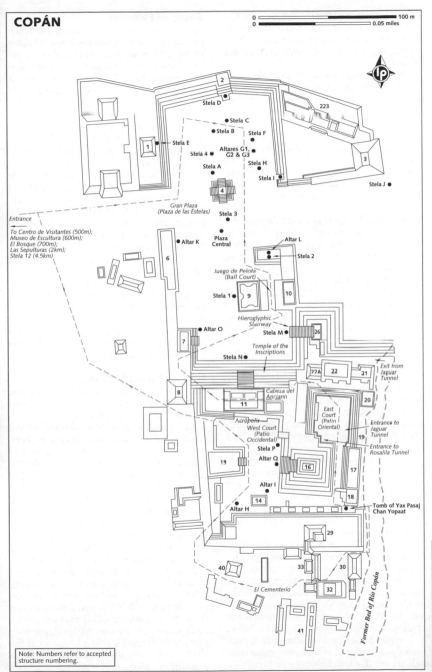

COPÁN

Gran Plaza (Plaza de las Estelas)

Plaza Central

Juego de Pelota (Ball Court)

Hieroglyphic Stairway

Temple of the Inscriptions

Cabeza del Anciano

Acrópolis

West Court (Patio Occidental)

East Court (Patio Oriental)

Entrance to Jaguar Tunnel

Entrance to Rosalila Tunnel

Exit from Jaguar Tunnel

Tomb of Yax Pasaj Chan Yopaat

El Cementerio

Former Bed of Río Copán

Entrance
To Centro de Visitantes (500m);
Museo de Escultura (600m);
El Bosque (700m);
Las Sepulturas (2km);
Stela 12 (4.5km)

Stela D · · Stela C · Stela B · Stela F · Altares G1, G2 & G3 · Stela 4 · Stela H · Stela A · Stela I · Stela E · Stela J · Stela 3 · Altar K · Altar L · Stela 2 · Stela 1 · Altar O · Stela M · Stela N · Stela P · Altar Q · Altar I · Altar H

2 · 223 · 1 · 3 · 4 · 6 · 9 · 10 · 7 · 26 · 22 · 21 · 20 · 11 · 19 · 13 · 16 · 17 · 14 · 18 · 29 · 40 · 33 · 30 · 32 · 41

??A

0 — 100 m
0 — 0.05 miles

Note: Numbers refer to accepted structure numbering.

This group of temples, known as the Acrópolis, was the spiritual and political core of the site – reserved for royalty and nobles, a place where ceremonies were enacted and kings buried.

The East Court also contains evidence of Yax Pac – his **tomb**, beneath Estructura 18. Unfortunately, the tomb was discovered and looted long before archaeologists arrived. Both the East and West Courts hold a variety of fascinating stelae and sculptured heads of humans and animals. To see the most elaborate relief carving, climb Estructura 22 on the northern side of the East Court. This was the **Templo de Meditación** (Temple of Meditation) and has been heavily restored over recent years.

Túnel Rosalila & Túnel de los Jaguares

In 1999 exciting new additions were made to the wonders at Copán when two excavation tunnels were opened to the public. The Túnel Rosalila (Rosalila Tunnel) exposes the Rosalila Temple below Estructura 16 (although only a small section of it, behind thick glass), and the Túnel de los Jaguares (Jaguar Tunnel) shows visitors the Tumba Galindo (Galindo Tomb), below Estructura 17 in the southern part of the East Court.

Descending into these tunnels is interesting, but not so exciting as when they were opened in 1999; at the time of writing you could only visit 25m of the Rosalila Tunnel and 80m of the longer Jaguar Tunnel. The Rosalila Tunnel reveals a little of the actual temple over which Estructura 16 was built; the carvings are remarkably crisp and vivid, especially the Sun God mask looming over the doorway. This is considered by some scholars to be the best-preserved stucco edifice in the Maya world. Everything is behind Plexiglas to protect it from natural and human elements. Under the Rosalila Temple is the Margarita Temple, built 150 years earlier. Beneath that, there are other even earlier platforms and tombs.

The Jaguar Tunnel is less dramatic, with its burial tombs and niches for offerings. The Galindo Tomb was one of the first tombs discovered at Copán, in 1834. Bones, obsidian knives and beads were found here, and archaeologists date the tomb's antebase mask to AD 540. The decorative macaw mask here is incredible. The full extent of this tunnel is 700m.

Though the L280 price of admission is dear for a short-lived pair of highlights, these tunnels are worth a look if you're into history.

Museo de Escultura

Copán is unique in the Maya world for its sculpture, and the **Museo de Escultura** (Museum of Sculpture; admission L130; ☺ 8am-3:40pm) is fittingly magnificent. Just entering the museum is an impressive experience in itself. Walking through the mouth of a serpent, you wind through the entrails of the beast, then suddenly emerge into a fantastic world of sculpture and light.

The highlight of the museum is a true-scale replica (in full color) of the Rosalila Temple, discovered in nearly perfect condition by archaeologists in 1989 by means of a tunnel dug into Estructura 16, the central building of the Acrópolis (p242). Rosalila, dedicated in AD 571 by Copán's 10th ruler, Moon Jaguar, was apparently so sacred that when Estructura 16 was built over it, the temple was not destroyed but was left completely intact. The original Rosalila Temple is still in the core of Estructura 16.

The other displays in the museum are stone carvings, brought here for protection from the elements. All the important stelae may eventually be housed here, with detailed reproductions placed outdoors to show where the stelae originally stood. So far, at least Altar Q and Stelae A, P, G1 and Fachada 22A have been brought into the museum, and the ones you see outdoors are reproductions.

El Bosque & Las Sepulturas

Excavations at El Bosque and Las Sepulturas have shed light on the daily life of the Maya in Copán during its golden age.

Las Sepulturas, once connected to the Gran Plaza by a causeway, may have been the residential area where rich and powerful nobles lived. One huge, luxurious residential compound seems to have housed some 250 people in 40 or 50 buildings arranged around 11 courtyards. The principal structure, called the **Palacio de los Bacabs** (Palace of the Officials), had outer walls carved with the full-sized figures of 10 males in fancy feathered headdresses; inside was a huge hieroglyphic bench.

To get to Las Sepulturas you have to go back to the main road, turn right, then right again at the sign (2km from the Gran Plaza).

The walk to get to El Bosque is the real reason for visiting it, as it is removed from the main ruins. It's a one-hour (5km) walk on a well-maintained path through foliage dense with birds, though there isn't much of note at the site itself save for a small ball court. Still, it's a powerful experience to have an hour-long walk on the thoroughfares of an ancient Maya city all to yourself. To get to El Bosque, go right at the hut where your ticket is stamped. There have been no reports of crimes against tourists here.

COPÁN RUINAS
pop 8000 / elev 548m

The town of Copán Ruinas, often simply called Copán, is just over 1km from the famous Maya ruins of the same name. It's a beautiful place paved with cobblestones and lined with white adobe buildings with red-tiled roofs. There's even a lovely colonial church on the recently remodeled plaza. The Maya have inhabited this valley, which has an aura of timeless harmony, for about 2000 years. Copán has become a primary tourist destination, but this hasn't disrupted the town's integrity to the extent one might fear.

Orientation & Information

The Parque Central, with the church on one side, is the heart of town. Copán is very small, and everything is within a few blocks of the plaza. The town only introduced street names a couple of years ago, but few people use them; most people know what street their own house or business is on, but everything else works by landmarks. There are no street numbers. The ruins are on the road to La Entrada. Las Sepulturas archaeological site is a few kilometers further along.

IMMIGRATION
Honduran immigration office (Palacio Municipal, Av Centroamericana; ☺ 7am-4:30pm Mon-Fri) On the plaza; come here for visa matters.

INTERNET ACCESS
Internet services cost around L15 per hour.
Cibernet (cnr Calle Independencia & Av Mirador) One block south and one block west of the plaza.
Maya Connections (cnr Calle 18 Conejo & Av Sesesmil) Inside La Casa de Todo, one block east of the plaza.

CALLING COPÁN

The telephone country code for Honduras is ☎ 504. Like Guatemala, Honduras has no area or city codes. So when dialing a number in Copán Ruinas from Guatemala, or any other country, you dial the international access code (usually 00), then 504, then the local number.

International phone and fax services are also available; also offers laundry service, plus book exchange and can refill water bottles (L4 per liter).

MONEY
For US dollars, the banks give a better rate than the moneychangers at the border, but slightly less than banks elsewhere in Honduras. The following banks have ATMs that accept foreign cards.
Banco Atlántida (Calle de la Plaza) On the plaza, changes US dollars and traveler's checks and gives cash advances on Visa cards.
Banco Credomatic (Calle de la Plaza) Also on the plaza.
Banco de Occidente (cnr Calle 18 Conejo & Av Copán) On the plaza, changes US dollars and traveler's checks, and quetzals, and gives cash advances on Visa and MasterCard.

POST
Post office (Calle de la Plaza) A few doors from the plaza.

TELEPHONE
Hondutel (Av Centroamericana) Telephone office around the corner from the post office.

TOURIST INFORMATION
Tourist office (☎ 651-3829; Calle Independencia; www.copanhonduras.org; ☺ 8am-5pm Mon-Fri, 8am-noon Sat) Run by the chamber of commerce; one block south of the plaza.

Sights & Activities

Though the main attraction of the Copán region is the archaeological site, there are other fine places to visit in the area. The **Museo de Arqueología Maya** (Av Centroamericana; admission L57; ☺ 9am-5pm), on the town plaza, is well worth a visit. It contains various stelae as well as exhibits of painted pottery, carved jade, Maya glyphs and a calendar round. Also here is the Tumba del Brujo, the tomb of a shaman or priest who died around AD 700 and was buried with many items under the east corner of the Plaza de los Jaguares.

Also on the plaza, inside the Palacio Municipal, is **Memorias Fragiles** (☎ 651-3900; Av Centroamericana; ☺ 8am-5pm Mon-Fri), a permanent photo exhibition that was a gift from Harvard University's Peabody Museum. It features a worthwhile collection of rare photos detailing the first archaeological expeditions to Copán at the turn of the 20th century.

About four blocks north of the plaza is the **Mirador El Cuartel** (Av Centroamericana), the old jail, with a magnificent view over town. Inside is the **Casa K'inich** (☎ 651-4105; admission L20; ☯ 8am-noon & 1-5pm Mon-Sat), an interactive museum for kids all about the Maya.

A pleasant, easy walk on the road on the south side of town provides a fine view over the corn and tobacco fields surrounding Copán. On this same side of town is an agreeable walk to the river.

The **Macaw Mountain Bird Park** (☎ 651-4245; www.macawmountain.com; admission L180; ☯ 9am-5pm), 2.5km out of town, is an extensive private reserve aimed at saving Central American macaws. There's plenty of them in evidence, along with toucans, motmots, parrots, kingfishers and orioles, all flying around in spacious, humanely constructed cages. A favorite

for many is the 'Encounter Center' where uncaged birds fly onto your shoulders or hands and are happy to pose for photos. If caged birds give you the willies, bear in mind that nearly all of these birds have been donated to the park by owners who didn't want them anymore. Even if you're not a bird freak, it's a lovely place to wander around, with plenty of walking trails weaving through the lush forest and over boardwalks to lookout points and swimming holes. The entrance ticket – which includes a guided tour in English – is valid for three days and there's a cafe-restaurant on the property. To get here, catch a mototaxi (tuk-tuk) for L20 per person. If you buy your ticket in advance at Café ViaVia (see p247), they'll throw in the mototaxi for free.

COPÁN RUINAS

INFORMATION			SLEEPING 🏠	
Banco Atlántida...............1 B3	Post Office...............7 B3		Café ViaVia...............14 A4	
Banco Credomatic...............2 B3	Tourist Office...............8 B4		Don Udo's...............15 B4	
Banco de Occidente...............3 B3			Hostel Iguana Azul...............(see 26)	
Cibernet...............4 B4	SIGHTS & ACTIVITIES		Hotel Camino Maya...............16 B3	
Finca El Cisne Office...............(see 14)	Base Camp Tours...............(see 14)		Hotel Clásico Copán...............17 C3	
Hacienda San Lucas Office...............(see 8)	Casa K'inich...............(see 12)		Hotel La Posada...............18 B3	
Honduran Immigration Office...............(see 6)	Church...............9 B3		Hotel Los Jaguares...............19 B3	
Hondutel...............5 B4	Guacamaya Spanish Academy...10 B2		Hotel Madrugada...............20 C3	
Maya Connections...............(see 34)	Ixbalanque Spanish School...11 A3		Hotel Marina Copán...............21 B3	
Palacio Municipal (City Hall)...............6 B3	Memorias Fragiles...............(see 6)		Hotel Patty...............22 B3	
	Mirador El Cuartel...............12 B2		Hotel Posada Honduras...............23 B3	
	Museo de Arqueología Maya...13 B3		Hotel Yaragua...............24 B3	
	Yaragua Tours...............(see 24)		Hotel Yat B'alam...............25 B4	
			La Casa de Café B&B...............26 A4	
			Manzana Verde...............27 B3	
			Posada de Belssy...............28 B3	
			EATING 🍴	
			Asados Copán...............29 B3	
			Café San Rafael...............30 B3	
			Café ViaVia...............(see 14)	
			Café Viva Honduras...............31 B3	
			Café Welchez...............32 B3	
			Carnitas Nia Lola...............33 B4	
			Hacienda San Lucas Office...............(see 8)	
			La Casa de Todo...............34 C3	
			Llama del Bosque...............35 A3	
			Picame...............36 B3	
			Twisted Tanya...............37 B4	
			ENTERTAINMENT 🎭	
			Barcito...............38 B4	
			Centro de Recreación...............39 C4	
			Papa Chango's...............40 C4	
			SHOPPING 🛍	
			Artisan Market...............41 B4	
			Supermarket...............42 B3	
			TRANSPORT	
			Buses to Agua Caliente...............43 C3	
			Casasola...............44 C3	
			Hedman Alas Bus Terminal...............45 C4	
			Minibuses & Pickup Trucks to the Border...............46 B3	

Map references on map:
To Macaw Mountain Bird Park (2.5km); Luna Jaguar Spa Resort (23km); Agua Caliente Hot Springs (24km); Finca El Cisne (24km)
To Ruins (1.5km); Las Sepulturas (3km); Santa Rita de Copán (9km); Hacienda El Jaral (11.5km); La Entrada (61km)
To Enchanted Wings Butterfly House (300m); Guatemala Border (10km); Quiriguá (by road; 175km)
To River (100m); Copán Canopy Tour (1.5km); Hacienda San Lucas (2km); Los Sapos (4km)

The **Enchanted Wings Butterfly House** (☎ 651-4133; www.copannaturecenter.com; adult/child L115/40; ⏱ 8am-5pm) is a nature center about a 10-minute walk west of the plaza on the road back to Guatemala. It has beautiful live and preserved butterflies, and numerous tropical flowers including around 200 species of orchids. With such a pretty name, how could you miss it?

Horseback rides can be arranged by any of the town's tour companies and most hotels. You can ride to the ruins or make other, lengthier excursions. You will most likely be approached on the street by somebody wanting to rent you a horse. Unfortunately, there have been a number of incidents of payment without delivery, and it's recommended that you go through an agency. Hacienda El Jaral (p251) also offers horseback riding. Three- to five-hour rides (L280 to L850) out of Café ViaVia visit the hot springs, Hacienda San Lucas, Los Sapos and the small Chortí village of La Pintada.

It's also possible to walk to **Los Sapos** (admission L30), 5km from town. The *sapos* (toads) are old Maya stone carvings in a spot with a beautiful view over the town. This place is connected with Maya fertility rites. You can get there by horseback in about half an hour or walk in about an hour, all uphill. From Los Sapos you can walk to a Stela 10 – if you're planning on doing that, stop by the Café ViaVia for a free map, as the trail is not well marked. Los Sapos is on the grounds of Hacienda San Lucas, a century-old farmhouse that has been converted into a B&B and restaurant (p251). There are walking trails here too.

At the entrance to the hacienda, you'll see Copán's latest attraction, the **Copán Canopy Tour** (☎ 9856-3758; L660). They'll take you up to the top of the hill where you can zig-zag your way down via 14 zip lines. At one point you get a nice little view of the ruins, and at another station you can take a break to check out Los Sapos.

Courses

Ixbalanque Spanish School (☎ 651-4432; www.ixbalanque.com; Av los Jaguares), around the corner from Café ViaVia, offers 20 hours of one-on-one instruction in Spanish for L4440 per week, including homestay with a local family that provides three meals a day. Instruction only costs L2550 per week. **Guacamaya Spanish Academy** (☎ 651-4360; www.guacamaya.com; cnr Av Copán & Calle de las Gradas), near the Manzana Verde hostel, offers much the same deal for slightly less.

Tours

A huge number of tours can be organized from Copán Ruinas. Local companies promote these widely. You can cave, tube a river, visit a Maya village and make tortillas or manufacture ceramics, plunge into hot springs, visit a coffee plantation or head off into the wilds of Honduras.

Yaragua Tours (☎ 651-4147; www.yaragua.com; cnr Av Copán & Calle de la Plaza) is set inside the Hotel Yaragua. Samuel from Yaragua leads local tours, horseback-riding trips and excursions to Lago de Yojoa. Caving trips are another option.

Base Camp Tours (☎ 651-4695; www.basecamphonduras.com; Calle de la Plaza), located inside Café ViaVia, offers a range of original and adventurous tours around the local area on foot (L380 to L760, four to six hours), motorcycle (L760 to L1040, three to five hours) and horseback (L280 to L850, three to five hours). Its highly recommended two-hour Alternative Copán walking tour (L180) delves beneath the glossy surface of the town and investigates the reality of life for many Hondurans.

Bird-watching tours are very popular in the area around Copán – it's said that there are more quetzals in the surrounding cloudforest than there are in the whole of Guatemala, where it is the national bird. Two recommended, English-speaking bird-watching guides are **Alexander Chacón** (☎ 9751-1680; alexander2084@hotmail.com), who can also be contacted through the Macaw Mountain Bird Park (see opposite) and **Robert Gallardo** (☎ 651-4133; www.copannaturecenter.com), who can be contacted through the Enchanted Wings Butterfly House (above left).

Sleeping
BUDGET

Hostel Iguana Azul (☎ 651-4620; www.iguanaazulcopan.com; dm/s/d L95/210/250; 🛜) This funky place three blocks west and two blocks south of the plaza is next door to La Casa de Café B&B (p248) and operated by the same friendly people. It has eight comfy bunk beds in two rooms with wonderful shared bathrooms in a colonial-style ranch home. Three private rooms sleep two. There's also a pretty garden. The common area has books, magazines, travel guides, a great bulletin board and lots of travel information. This is backpacking elegance at its finest.

Manzana Verde (☎ 651-4652; www.lamanzanaverde.com; Av Copán; dm L100) A beautifully decked-out hostel, run by the same people as the Café ViaVia, with six beds in bunks per dorm.

Common areas are comfortably set up, there's heaps of free, reliable tourist advice, and there's kitchen access for guests.

Hotel Posada Honduras (☎ 651-4082; Av Sesesmil; s/d L140/200, without bathroom L100/140; **P**) It's kind of refreshing to see a back-to-basics, cold-water, no-TV budget hotel that's not a complete shambles. The courtyard at least is pretty: full of mango, mamey and lemon trees and rooms are basic but clean – a penny-pincher's delight.

our pick **Café ViaVia** (☎ 651-4652; www.viaviacafe. com; Calle de la Plaza; s/d L225/300; ☎) This small Belgian-run European-style hotel is part of the Joker group, a Belgian-led organization of cafes with a travel theme around the world including at Louvain, Zanzibar, Kathmandu and Yogyakarta. Café ViaVia Copán has five spotless rooms with private hot-water bathroom, tiled floors and great beds (2m long for the tall folks reading this!). There are hammocks, a small garden and enough space to chill out. It's a great place to come for tourist information, and has an art gallery and lively bar attached. English, French, German and Dutch are spoken here.

Posada de Belssy (☎ 651-4680; Calle Acrópolis; s/d L250/400) Run by a charming local family, this place has great rooms with balconies overlooking the mountains on the outskirts of town. Rooms are big for the price and very comfortable.

Hotel Patty (☎ 651-4021; cnr Av Acrópolis & Av Sesesmil; s/d L300/400; **P**) The large, spacious rooms here come with a few colonial flourishes and are set upstairs, around a central parking lot/patio. There are good breezes on the communal balcony and it's run by a friendly family.

Hotel Clásico Copán (☎ 651-4040; Av Sesesmil; r L400; **P**) Good-sized standard rooms set upstairs around a lush courtyard. If you don't want TV, they'll take a couple of bucks off the price.

Hotel Yaragua (☎ 651-4147; www.yaragua.com; cnr Av Copán & Calle de la Plaza; r L400) The bright-yellow paint job and jungly patio area give this place a cheery feel. Rooms are smallish but comfortable and you can't beat the central location.

MIDRANGE & TOP END

Hotel Los Jaguares (☎ 651-4451; jaguares@copanhonduras .org; cnr Calle 18 Conejo & Av Centroamericana; s/d L380/760; **P** ⊠) A surprisingly good deal right on the plaza. The rooms don't have views, but are clean and cheery enough, without being overly stylish.

Hotel Madrugada (☎ 651-4092; Av Sesesmil; L470/570; **P**) Possibly the most atmospheric hotel in town, this beautiful little place is tucked away in a corner, in a great location, overlooking a babbling creek. Rooms are generously sized and fitted out with period touches such as four-poster beds. There are plenty of armchairs and hammocks on the wide wooden balcony.

Hotel La Posada (☎ 651-4059; www.laposadacopan .com; Av Centroamericana; s/d L570/760; ☎) Good value, tranquil and comfortable, La Posada is only half a block from the plaza. Its 19 rooms with hot-water bathroom, fan and TV are set around two leafy patios. There's very tasty, free black coffee first thing in the morning.

Don Udo's (☎ 651-4533; www.donudos.com; Av Mirador; s L760-1500, d L1150-1900; ⊠ ☎) A lovely little B&B run by a Dutch-Honduran couple (and guess which one decided that all the tap water – even in the showers – should be purified?). Rooms are decently sized and well decorated, and set around a cheery courtyard patio.

La Casa de Café B&B (☎ 651-4620; www.casadecafe copan.com; s/d incl breakfast L850/1040) This classy B&B four blocks from the plaza has loads of character in a beautiful setting – the garden area with tables and hammocks has a wide view over cornfields to the mountains of Guatemala. The 10 rooms with hot-water bathroom have wooden ceilings and antique ceiling fans, and all prices include a hearty breakfast. This place has a good library pertaining to Honduras. It also rents comfortable, fully equipped two-bedroom houses, starting from L1100 per night, with discounts for longer stays. Check them online at www.casadecafecopan.com and www.casadedonsantiagocopan.com.

Hotel Plaza Copán (☎ 651-4039; www.plazacopan hotel.com; cnr Calle de la Plaza & Av Copán; s/d L1100/1200; **P** ⊠ ▯ ☎ ▣) This classically styled hotel right on the plaza has a range of good-smelling, atmospheric but modern rooms. The darkwood furniture and Spanish tiling give it that extra boost of class. Some rooms have private balconies and views of the church. Each room differs, so look at a few before choosing. The hotel has a restaurant and a terrace with views.

Hotel Camino Maya (☎ 651-4646; www.caminomaya hotel.com; cnr Calle de la Plaza & Av Centroamericana; s/d L1200/1350; **P** ⊠ ▯ ☎) Shades of old British colonial rule run through this place – the decor's all very stiff upper lip, with a bit of exotic native carving thrown in. The restaurant downstairs lays on a big fry-up breakfast (L150), just to drive the point home. Rooms downstairs can be a bit dark, and overall they're small for the prices, but the location's hard to beat.

Hotel Yat B'alam (☎ 651-4338; www.yatbalam.com; Calle Independencia; r L1380; P ✗ 🖜) A beautiful little boutique hotel with just four rooms. Each is spacious and comes with all the usual comforts as well as minibar and DVD player (the hotel has a selection of movies you can borrow). The whole place is pleasantly decorated with a mix of colonial and indigenous furnishings.

Hotel Marina Copán (☎ 651-4070; www.hotel marinacopan.com; Av Centroamericana; s/d L1750/2000; P ✗ 🖥 🖜 🖳) This business-class hotel is large and actually quite lovely, with a cobblestoned courtyard featuring a decent-sized swimming pool. The onsite restaurant gets props from readers and there's a cozy little bar/cafe here, too. Rooms are spacious and cool, with pleasing touches like exposed wooden ceiling beams.

Eating

The town's little food market is right by the Parque Central.

Café San Rafael (Av Centroamericana; snacks L40; 🕑 9am-7:30pm) This cafe serves organic coffee grown at the *finca* of the same name, just out of town. There's also a yummy range of teas and homemade snacks on offer.

Café ViaVia (Calle de la Plaza; breakfast L40-60, mains L60-100; 🕑 7am-10pm; 🖜) This terrific restaurant serves breakfast, lunch and dinner in a convivial atmosphere, with tables overlooking the street and a replica of Altar Q behind the bar. The organically grown coffee it prepares is excellent, bread is homemade and there's always a good selection of vegetarian and meat-based dishes on offer.

Café Welchez (cnr Calle 18 Conejo & Av Centroamericana; breakfast L50-100, cakes per slice L60; 🕑 8am-8pm) This pleasant, wood-paneled cafe has good views out over the plaza from the upper floor. The menu doesn't go much beyond coffee, cakes, juice and breakfast, but it does them all well.

Picame (Calle Acrópolis; mains L60-100; 🕑 breakfast, lunch & dinner Wed-Mon) This cute little cafe-restaurant does a seriously full breakfast, yummy roast chicken and an assortment of burgers and sandwiches.

Asados Copán (cnr Calle Acrópolis & Av Copán; mains L80-140; 🕑 lunch & dinner) With one of the best settings in town, this big open-air steakhouse is popular with tourists and locals alike. The menu's simple but effective – a variety of beef and chicken dishes, flame grilled to perfection.

Café Viva Honduras (cnr Calle Acrópolis & Av Centroamericana; breakfast L95, burgers L90-110; 🕑 6:30am-9:30pm; 🖜) Some of the best views in town are from the rooftop terrace of this cute little cafe. The menu is small, but reasonably priced, with plenty of breakfast options (available all day) and there's a tempting range of juices and smoothies on offer.

La Casa de Todo (cnr Av Sesesmil & Calle 18 Conejo; mains L100-130; 🕑 breakfast, lunch & dinner; 🖜) This restaurant/cafe/gift shop/stationery store has a lush backyard, perfect for sipping a cold *licuado* or sampling the healthy, innovative breakfasts and salads on offer.

Carnitas Nia Lola (Av Centroamericana; mains L150-300; 🕑 breakfast, lunch & dinner) Two blocks south of the plaza, this open-air restaurant has a beautiful view toward the mountains over corn and tobacco fields. It's a relaxing place with simple and economical food; the specialties are charcoal-grilled chicken and beef. Happy hour starts at 6:30pm.

Twisted Tanya (cnr Calle Independencia & Av Mirador; mains L320; 🕑 10am-10pm) Set upstairs, with a lovely balcony sporting views out to the mountains, Tanya's serves up some good versions of Italian- and Asian-influenced dishes. Cardboard Moroccan-style lampshades add an artistic flourish. The 'backpacker special' of a three-course set meal for L120 is available between 4pm and 6pm and is a good deal.

our pick Hacienda San Lucas (☎ 651-4106; www. haciendasanlucas.com; 5-course meal L470) Set on farmland overlooking the town and archaeological site, this is the town's date-night favorite. The romance of dining by candlelight in the restored farmhouse can't really be exaggerated. Cuisine draws heavily on traditional ingredients and techniques and comes accompanied by fine South American wines. Reservations should be made two days in advance, either by phoning or dropping into the hacienda's downtown office (Calle de la Plaza; open 8am-5pm). A mototaxi here from town should cost L60 one way.

Entertainment

Café ViaVia and the bar in Carnitas Nia Lola are happening spots in the evening. Café ViaVia also shows movies on Sunday, Monday and Tuesday. **Barcito** (cnr Calle Independencia & Av Centroamericana; 🕑 7pm-midnight Thu-Sat), Copán's newest bar, is a friendly and happening little spot. It's open-walled and set upstairs, so you can catch some good views and the occasional breeze. Salads, snacks and sandwiches are on offer and it has cool music and a good selection of wines and cocktails.

The Hotel Camino Maya's **Centro de Recreación** (admission L40; ☺ disco 6pm-2am Fri & Sat) has a disco that's popular with locals and a few tourists. It's beside the Quebrada Sesesmil, two blocks south and one block east of the plaza. Also down here is **Papa Chango's** (☺ from midnight Thu-Sat), a popular, laid-back reggae bar. It heats up around midnight, when all the bars in the center are required by a town council ordnance to close. This area's a bit suspect – lone travelers (particularly women) are probably better off avoiding these places, and if they decide to go, are advised to take a mototaxi, both to and from.

Getting There & Away
If you need a Honduran visa in advance, you can obtain it at the Honduran consulate in Esquipulas or Guatemala City (p317).

Several Antigua travel agencies offer weekend trips to Copán, which may include stops at other places, including Quiriguá. All-inclusive day trips from Antigua to Copán are very rushed. For more information, check with the agencies in Antigua (p99).

BUS
It's 227km (five hours) from Guatemala City to El Florido, the Guatemalan village on the Honduras border. **Hedman Alas** (☎ in Copán 651-4037, in Guatemala City 502-2362-5072; www.hedmanalas.com) runs direct 1st-class services daily in both directions between Copán Ruinas and Guatemala City (L660, five hours), leaving its office in Copán Ruinas at 1pm and 6pm and Guatemala City at 5am and 9pm. Coming from other places, you have to take a bus to Chiquimula, and change there for a connecting service to the border.

If you're coming from Esquipulas, you can get off the bus at Vado Hondo, the junction of Hwy 10 and the road to El Florido, and wait for a bus there. As the buses to El Florido usually fill up before departing from Chiquimula, it may be just as well to go the extra 8km into Chiquimula and secure your seat before the bus pulls out. Traveling from the border to Esquipulas, there's no need to go into Chiquimula; minibuses ply the route to Esquipulas frequently.

Minivans and some pickups depart for Copán Ruinas from the Honduras side of the border regularly throughout the day. They should charge around L20, payable before you depart, for the 20-minute ride. Drivers may hassle you about the fare but late in the day they have the trump card.

Minibuses and pickups from Copán Ruinas to Guatemala depart from the intersection one block west of the plaza. They leave every 40 minutes (or when full), from 6am to 6pm, and charge around L20 – check the price beforehand. On the Guatemala side, buses to Chiquimula (Q25, 1½ hours, 58km) leave the border hourly from 5:30am to 11:30am then hourly from noon to 4pm and at 4:30pm.

Buses serving points further afield in Honduras depart from a few different places in Copán Ruinas. **Hedman Alas** (☎ 651-4037; www.hedmanalas.com) goes to San Pedro Sula (L320, three hours) and on to Tegucigalpa (L470, seven hours) at 5:30am, 10:30am and 2:30pm daily.

Casasola (☎ 651-4078; Av Sesesmil) offers semi-direct service to San Pedro Sula (L100) and La Ceiba (L230) at 6am, 7am and 2pm.

If you're hoping to make it to the Bay Islands in one day, you really have to be on either the 5:15am Hedman Alas or the 7am Casasola bus to La Ceiba.

CAR
You could conceivably visit the ruins as a day trip from Guatemala City by car, but it would be exhausting and far too harried. From Río Hondo, Chiquimula or Esquipulas, it still takes a full day to get to Copán, tour the ruins and return, but it's easier. It's better to spend at least one night in Copán Ruinas if you can – the town itself is much prettier and livelier than any of those three, anyway.

Drive 10km south from Chiquimula (or 48km north from Esquipulas) and turn eastward at Vado Hondo (Km 178.5 on Hwy 10). Just opposite the turnoff there is a small motel, which will do if you need a bed. A sign reading 'Vado Hondo Ruinas de Copán' marks the way on the one-hour, 50km drive along the paved road that runs from this junction to El Florido.

Twenty kilometers northeast of Vado Hondo are the Chortí Maya villages of Jocotán and Camotán, set in mountainous tropical countryside dotted with thatched huts in lush green valleys. Jocotán has a small *centro de salud* (medical clinic) and the **Hotel Katú**

Sukuchuje (☎ 7946-5205; s/d Q45/90; P), which also has a restaurant.

Since the formation of the CA-4, vehicle inspections have become token to nonexistent at the Guatemala–Honduras border. If you're driving a rented car, check with the company that you have permission to take it over the border (you should) – it's better getting some ~~piece of paper signed beforehand than getting~~ shaken down by bored immigration officials on the spot.

SHUTTLE MINIBUS
Base Camp Tours (p247) in Copán Ruinas and nearly every Antigua travel agency (p99) run shuttles between those two towns. Scheduled shuttles leave Copán for Antigua (L245, minimum four passengers, six hours) at noon daily and can drop you in Guatemala City (five hours) en route. You can also get off at Río Hondo (L225), or it can organize shuttle/Pullman combinations to Río Dulce (L415) or Flores (605).

AROUND COPÁN RUINAS
Hacienda San Lucas (☎ 651-4106; www.haciendasan lucas.com; L2380/2830; 🛜) is a magical place 3km south of town. Beautifully restored, utterly unique and with fabulous views of the valley, taking in the town and archaeological site, the place has to be seen to be believed. Phone beforehand or drop in to its **office** (Calle de la Plaza; 🕑 8am-5pm) in Copán Ruinas. The recently restored and expanded adobe hacienda is solar-powered, but the rooms are candlelit at night, adding to the serene atmosphere. The food here is highly praised, and many people come just for dinner (see p249). Los Sapos archaeological site (p247) is on the property.

Visiting **Finca El Cisne** (☎ 651-4695; www.fincael cisne.com; overnight package per person L1455), 24km from Copán Ruinas, is more like an agro-eco experience than a tour. Founded in the 1920s and still operating, the *finca* mainly raises cattle and grows coffee and cardamom, but it also produces corn, avocados, beans, breadfruit and star fruit, among other things. Day-long (L1115 per person) and overnight packages include guided horseback riding through the forests and pastures (with a stop to swim in the Río Blanco) and tours of the coffee and cardamom fields and processing plants. If you come between February and October you can help with the harvest. Lodging is five simple, rustic rooms in the old workers' quarters,

with meals and a visit to nearby hot springs included. You can book tours in the office inside Café ViaVia in Copán Ruinas.

Hacienda El Jaral (☎ 552-4457; www.haciendaeljaral. com; campsite per person L100, s/d L1150/1250; P 🛜 🏊), a lush ecotourism resort offering many activities, is 11km from town on the way to La Entrada. The luxurious rooms with air-con, hot-water bathroom, cable TV and fridge are all in duplex cabins with outdoor terraces. The resort has a shopping mall, water park, children's play area and a couple of restaurants. The activities offered to guests and nonguests alike include bird-watching in a bird-sanctuary lagoon (thousands of herons reside here from November to May), horseback riding, cycling, hiking, river swimming, inner-tubing, canoeing and 'soft rafting' on the Río Copán.

Santa Rita de Copán
Nine kilometers from town (20 minutes by bus) on the road towards La Entrada, Santa Rita de Copán is a lovely village at the confluence of two rivers. Just outside Santa Rita is **El Rubí** waterfall, with an inviting swimming hole. This was the scene of some nasty tourist robberies in the past, but things seem to have quietened down now. It's about a half-hour uphill walk (3km) on a trail departing from opposite where the bus stops across the bridge on the entrance to town on the highway. The waterfall is on private land – if you've got doubts, Yaragua Tours (p247) in Copán Ruinas comes out here with armed guards.

Agua Caliente
The attractively situated **Agua Caliente** (hot springs; admission L20; 🕑 8am-8pm), not to be confused with Agua Caliente in Honduras, not far from Esquipulas, are 23km north of Copán Ruinas via the road running north out of town. Here hot water flows and mingles with a cold river. There are facilities for changing, a basketball court and bathrooms plus a *tienda* (small shop) for soft drinks and snacks. Frequent minibuses leave from in front of the football field in Copán Ruinas, passing right in front of the hot springs (L35). Coming back, wait for one of the same buses, or you can hitch a ride in any passing pickup – most will happily give you a ride back into town.

LUNA JAGUAR SPA RESORT
Directly across the river from the hot springs, this is a high-concept Maya **day spa**

CENTRAL & EASTERN GUATEMALA

(www.lunajaguar.com; admission L100; ☺ 8am-5pm). The idea is that this is what the Maya kings would have done to relax if they had the chance.

Thirteen 'treatment stations' (offering hot tub, herbal steam baths and so on) are scattered around the hillside, connected by a series of stone pathways. The jungle here has been left as undisturbed as possible, and reproduction Maya sculptures dot the landscape. The water used in the hot tub and steam baths comes directly from the volcanic spring. It's an amazing and beautiful spot, and worth checking out even if you're not a spa junkie.

CARIBBEAN COAST

This is a very different Guatemala – a lush and sultry landscape dotted with palm trees and inhabited by sailors (around the yachtie haven of Río Dulce and the working port of Puerto Barrios) and one of the country's lesser-known ethnic groups, the Garífuna (around Lívingston).

A boat ride down the Río Dulce is pretty much mandatory for any visit to this region, and many visitors find a few days in Lívingston to be a worthy detour. Nature buffs will want to check out the huge wetlands reserves at Bocas del Polochic and Punta de Manabique.

LAGO DE IZABAL

Guatemala's largest lake, to the north of the Carretera al Atlántico, is starting to earn its place on the travelers' map. Most visitors checking out the lake stay at Río Dulce town, by the long, tall bridge where Hwy 13, heading north to Flores and Tikal, crosses the Río Dulce emptying out of the east end of the lake. Downstream, the beautiful river broadens into a lake called El Golfete before meeting the Caribbean at Lívingston. River trips are a highlight of a visit to eastern Guatemala. If you're looking for lakeside ambience minus the Río Dulce congestion and pace, head to Denny's Beach at Mariscos (p257) or El Castillo de San Felipe (p254), about 3km west of the bridge. The neat town of El Estor near the west end of the lake gives access to the Bocas del Polochic river delta, where there is lots of wildlife (see p256). There are many undiscovered spots in this area waiting to be explored, so don't limit yourself.

Río Dulce
pop 3000
At the east end of the Lago de Izabal where it empties into the Río Dulce, this town still gets referred to as Fronteras. It's a hangover from the days when the only way across the river was by ferry, and this was the last piece of civilization before embarking on the long, difficult journey into El Petén.

Times have changed. A huge bridge now spans the water and El Petén roads are some of the best in the country. The town sees most tourist traffic from yachties – the US coast guard says this is the safest place on the western Caribbean for boats during hurricane season. The rest of the foreigners here are either coming or going on the spectacular river trip down to Lívingston (see p261).

ORIENTATION & INFORMATION
Unless you're staying at Hotel Backpacker's (see opposite) or volunteering at its Casa Guatemala, get off the bus on the north side of the bridge. The Fuente del Norte and Litegua bus offices are both here, opposite each other. Otherwise you'll find yourself trudging over what is believed to be the longest bridge in Central America – it's a very hot 30-minute walk (3.5km).

The main dock is now under the bridge on the opposite side of the main road from Bruno's (see opposite) – you'll see a side road leading down to it.

The websites www.mayaparadise.com and www.riodulcechisme.com have loads of information about Río Dulce. Bruno's has an excellent notice board, advertising everything from boats for sale to captains looking for crew.

If you need to change cash or traveler's checks, hit one of the banks in town, all on the main road.

Banco Agromercantil Will give cash advances on credit cards if there is a problem with the ATMs.

Banco Industrial (☺ 9am-5pm) Has a Visa ATM.

Banrural Has Visa and MasterCard ATMs.

Captain Nemo's Communications (☎ 7930-5174; www.mayaparadise.com; internet access per hr Q8; ☺ 7am-8pm Mon-Sat, 9am-2pm Sun) Beside Bruno's on the river, Nemo's offers email and international phone and fax services. Other, cheaper internet cafes can be found on the main street.

Otitrans (☎ 7930-5223; otitours@hotmail.com) The town's most complete tour operator is located under the bridge, on the road to the dock. You can book lanchas, tours, sailing trips and shuttles here.

TOURS

Check the noticeboard at Bruno's or ask around at any of the marinas for the latest on which sailboats are offering charter tours.

Aventuras Vacacionales (☎ 7873-9221; www.sailing -diving-guatemala.com) runs fun sailing trips on the sailboat *Las Sirenas* from Río Dulce to the Belize reefs and islands (from Q3200, seven days) and Lago Izabal (from Q1450, four days). The office is in Antigua but you can also hook up with this outfit in Río Dulce. It makes the Belize and lake trips in alternate weeks.

SLEEPING

Many places in Río Dulce communicate by radio. Captain Nemo's, the bar at Bruno's, and Restaurant Río Bravo will radio your choice of place to stay if necessary.

On the Water

The places listed here are out of town on the water, which is the best place to be. You can call or radio them and they'll come and pick you up. **Mansión del Río** (www.mansiondelrio.com.gt) and **Banana Palms Resort** (www.bananapalms.com.gt), both just out of town, provide all-inclusive resort-style accommodation on the lakefront.

Hotel Backpacker's (☎ 7930-55480; www.hotel backpackers.com; dm Q40, s/d Q80/150, without bathroom Q60/120) Across the bridge, this is a business run by Casa Guatemala and the orphans it serves. It's an old (with the emphasis on old) backpacker favorite, set in a rickety building with very basic rooms. The bar kicks on here at night. If you're coming by *lancha* or bus, ask the driver to let you off here to spare yourself the walk across the bridge.

Casa Perico (☎ 7930-5666; dm Q45, bungalow Q200, s/d without bathroom Q60/120) One of the more low-key options in the area, this is set on a little inlet about 200m from the main river. Cabins are well built and connected by boardwalks. The Swiss guys who run it offer tours all up and down the river and put on an excellent buffet dinner, or you can choose from the menu. The place has a good book exchange and a young, fun atmosphere. If you want the one bungalow with private bathroom make sure you book ahead.

ourpick Hotel Kangaroo (☎ 4513-9602, in English 5363-6716; www.hotelkangaroo.com; dm Q70, r Q150-180, cabin with/without bathroom Q220/180; 💻 🛜) On the Río La Colocha, just across the water from the Castillo San Felipe, this beautiful, simple Australian-run place is built up on stilts in the mangroves. The whole place is constructed from wood, with thatched roofs, and windows are mosquito-netted – there's not a pane of glass to be seen. Wildlife is particularly abundant around here, with blue warblers, pelicans, a 7ft iguana and turtles making the surrounds their home. Drinks on the deck overlooking the river are a great way to start, finish or while away the day. There's a small but well-prepared menu on offer (mains Q40 to Q80). Call from Río Dulce or San Felipe and they'll come and pick you up for free, even if you're just dropping in for lunch.

El Tortugal (☎ 7742-8847; www.tortugal.com; dm Q75, r without bathroom Q250, bungalow from Q350; 🛜) The best-looking bungalows on the river are located here, a five-minute *lancha* ride east from town. There are plenty of hammocks, the showers are seriously hot and kayaks are free for guest use.

Hacienda Tijax (☎ 7930-5505/7; www.tijax.com; s Q160-560, d Q240-610; 🅿 🛁) This 500-acre hacienda, a two-minute boat ride across the cove from Bruno's, is a special place to stay. Activities include horseback riding, hiking, bird-watching, sailboat trips and walking and canopy tours around the rubber plantation. Accommodation is in lovely little cabins connected by a boardwalk. Most cabins face the water and there's a very relaxing pool/bar area. Access is by boat or by a road that turns off the highway about 1km north of the village. The folks here speak Spanish, English, Dutch, French and Italian, and they'll pick you up from across the river.

Isla Xalaja (☎ 7930-5767; www.xalaja.com; bungalow Q350, house with fan/air-con Q1100/1500; 🍽 💻 🛜 🛁) Set on the Isla Xalaja, a five-minute *lancha* ride upstream from town, this place with beautiful, fully furnished houses (sleeping eight comfortably) and bungalows (capacity six) is one of the finest accommodation options in the area. Attention to detail is wonderful, and the place has a great rustic feel despite offering all the conveniences. There's a good, authentic Mexican (not Tex-Mex) restaurant onsite.

Hotel Catamaran (☎ 7930-5494; www.catamaranisland .com; s/d from Q490/630; 🍽 💻 🛜 🛁) Built on its own little island, this is one of the most up-market options around. Bungalows are surprisingly plain, but comfortable enough, and the grounds strike a neat balance between lush and manicured.

In Town

Bruno's (☎ 7930-5721; www.mayaparadise.com/brunoe. htm; dm Q35, s Q170-220, d Q250-300; 🅿 🍽 🛜 🛁) A path leads down from the northeast end of the bridge to this riverside hang-out for yachties needing to get some land under their feet. The dorms are clean and spacious and the new building offers some of the most comfortable rooms in town, with air-con and balconies overlooking the river. They're well set up for families and sleep up to six.

Las Brisas Hotel (☎ 7930-5124; s/d Q70/130; ⊠) This hotel is opposite the Fuentes del Norte office. All rooms are clean enough and have three beds and fans. Three rooms upstairs have private bathroom and air-con (Q200). It's central and good enough for a night, but there are much better places around.

Hotel Vista al Río (☎ 7930-5665; www.hotelvistario. com; r with fan/air-con Q150/180; ⊠ ⊚) Under the bridge just south of Bruno's, this little hotel/marina offers spacious, spotless rooms, some with river views. There's a good restaurant here, serving juicy steaks and big breakfasts.

EATING
All of the hotels listed above have restaurants. Bruno's and the Vista al Río serve good breakfasts and gringo comfort food and have full bars. The Hacienda Tijax is a popular lunch spot – give them a call and they'll come pick you up.

our pick **Sundog Café** (sandwiches Q25, meals from Q35; ⊠ breakfast, lunch & dinner) Down the hill a bit from Tijax express, this open-air bar-restaurant makes great sandwiches on homemade bread, a good selection of vegetarian dishes and fresh juices. It's also the place to come for unbiased information about the area.

Ricky's Pizza (pizzas from Q50; ⊠ lunch & dinner) Upstairs in the main part of town, offering surprisingly good pizzas. The set lunches (Q20) are excellent value.

Restaurant Río Bravo (breakfasts Q30, mains Q60-100; ⊠ breakfast, lunch & dinner) With an open-air deck over the lake, this place has some good eats and a very local flavor. It doesn't get too fancy, but there is a good range of steaks, pasta and seafood on offer in a relaxed environment.

GETTING THERE & AWAY
Beginning at 7am, 14 Fuente del Norte buses a day head north along a paved road to Poptún (Q30, two hours) and Flores (Q60, four hours). The 12:30pm bus continues all the way to Melchor de Mencos (Q90) on the Belize border. With good connections you can get to Tikal in a snappy six hours. There

are also services to San Salvador (El Salvador; Q125) and San Pedro Sula (Honduras; Q135), both leaving at 10am.

At least 17 buses daily go to Guatemala City (Q55, six hours) with Fuente del Norte and Litegua. Línea Dorada has 1st-class buses departing at 1:30pm for Guatemala City (Q120) and at 3:30pm for Flores (Q100). This shaves up to an hour off the journey times.

Minibuses leave for Puerto Barrios (Q20, two hours) when full, from the roadside in front of Hotel Las Brisas.

Otitrans (see p252) has shuttles to Antigua (Q330), Cobán (Q330), Copán (Q290) and Flores (Q290).

Dilapidated Fuente del Norte buses and better-looking minibuses leave for El Estor (Q20, 1½ hours) from the San Felipe and El Estor turnoff in the middle of town, hourly from 7am to 6pm. The road is paved about half way, and smooth dirt for the remainder.

Colectivo lanchas go down the Río Dulce (from the new dock) to Lívingston, usually requiring eight to 10 people, charging Q125/200 per person one-way/round-trip. The trip is a beautiful one and the morning departure makes a 'tour' of it, with several halts along the way (see p264). Boats usually leave from 9am to about 2pm. There are regular, scheduled departures at 9:30am and 1:30pm. Pretty much everyone in town can organize *lancha* service to Lívingston and most other places you'd care to go, but they charge more.

El Castillo de San Felipe
The fortress and castle of San Felipe de Lara, **El Castillo de San Felipe** (admission Q20; ⊠ 8am-5pm), about 3km west of the bridge, was built in 1652 to keep pirates from looting the villages and commercial caravans of Izabal. Though the fortress deterred the buccaneers a bit, a pirate force captured and burned it in 1686. By the end of the next century, pirates had disappeared from the Caribbean, and the fort's sturdy walls served as a prison. Eventually, though, the fortress was abandoned and became a ruin. The present fort was reconstructed in 1956.

Today the castle is protected as a park and is one of the Lago de Izabal's principal tourist attractions. In addition to the fort itself, there are grassy grounds, barbecue and picnic areas, and the opportunity to swim in the lake. The place rocks from April 30 to May 4 during the **Feria de San Felipe**.

SLEEPING & EATING

Hotel Don Humberto (☎ 7930-5051; s/d Q50/85; P) Near the Castillo, offering basic rooms with big beds and good mosquito netting. It's nothing fancy, but more than adequate for a cheap sleep.

Viñas del Lago (☎ 7930-5053; www.vinasdelago.com; s/d Q280/330; P ⊠ ☐ ☎) The much fancier del Lago, near the Hotel Don Humberto, has 18 spacious, plain rooms, all with hot-water bathroom, air-con and TV. Rooms out the back have good views. The grounds are large and there's a restaurant (mains Q50 to Q100) with views of Lago de Izabal.

Between the turnoff from the El Estor–Río Dulce road and the castle are a few good-value places:

La Cabaña del Viajero (☎ 7930-5062; s/d Q100/130; P ⊠ ☎) The smallish rooms in these two-story cabins are an excellent deal. They're clean and colorfully decorated and there's a shady pool area to splash around in. Air-conditioning costs an extra Q70.

Hotel Monte Verde (☎ 5036-8469; hotelmonte verde@hotmail.com; r with fan/air-con Q200/250; P ⊠ ☎) Under renovation at the time of research, this promises to be an excellent deal once work is completed – rooms are generously sized and there's a huge pool set in a lush garden.

GETTING THERE & AWAY

San Felipe is on the lakeshore, 3km west of Río Dulce. It's a beautiful 45-minute walk between the two towns, or take a minivan (Q8, every 30 minutes). In Río Dulce it stops on the corner of the highway and road to El Estor; in San Felipe it stops in front of the Hotel Don Humberto, at the entrance to El Castillo.

Boats coming from Livingston will drop you in San Felipe if you ask. The Río Dulce river tours usually come to El Castillo, allowing you to get out and visit the castle if you like, or you can come over from Río Dulce by private *lancha* for Q80.

Finca El Paraíso

On the north side of the lake, between Río Dulce and El Estor, **Finca El Paraíso** (☎ 7949-7122; cabin Q350) makes a great day trip from either place. This working ranch's territory includes an incredibly beautiful spot in the jungle where a wide, hot waterfall (admission Q10) drops about 12m into a clear, deep pool. You can bathe in the hot water, swim in the cool pool or duck under an overhanging promontory and enjoy a jungle-style sauna.

Also on the *finca* are a number of interesting caves, a restaurant and cabins scattered along a sandy lake beach.

If you're just coming for the waterfall, head north (away from the lake) where the bus drops you off – you pay the admission fee there, from where it's about a 2km walk to the falls. To get to the restaurant and hotel, head south (toward the lake) for about 3km.

A slightly humbler, but completely adequate option can be found by turning right just before the *finca* house – follow the signs for *cabañas* **Brisas del Lago** (cabin per person Q75). There is a good restaurant here and plenty of hammocks strung around, catching the lake breezes.

The *finca* is on the Río Dulce–El Estor bus route, about one hour (Q9) from Río Dulce and 30 minutes (Q6) from El Estor. The last bus in either direction passes at around 4:30pm to 5pm.

El Boquerón

This beautiful, lushly vegetated canyon abutting the tiny Maya settlement of the same name is about 6km east of El Estor. For around Q5 per person, villagers will paddle you 15 minutes up the Río Sauce through the canyon, drop you at a small beach, where you can swim and if you like scramble up the rocks, and return for you at an agreed time. Río Dulce–bound buses from El Estor will drop you at El Boquerón (Q5, 15 minutes), as will El Estor–bound buses from Río Dulce.

El Estor

pop 20,000

The major settlement on the northern shore of Lago de Izabal is El Estor. The nickel mines a few kilometers to the northwest (for which the town grew up) were closed for decades but were recently reopened by Canadian companies as world nickel stocks run low. A friendly, somnolent little town with a lovely setting, El Estor is the jumping-off point for the Bocas del Polochic, a highly biodiverse wildlife reserve at the west end of the lake. The town is also a staging post on a possible route between Río Dulce and Lanquín.

ORIENTATION & INFORMATION

The main street, running parallel to the lakeshore two blocks back from the water, is 3a Calle. Buses from Río Dulce terminate at the corner of 3a Calle and 4a Av. Walk one block

CENTRAL & EASTERN
GUATEMALA

west from here along 3a Calle to find the Parque Central.

Asociación Feminina Q'eqchi' sells clothes, blankets and accessories that are made from traditional cloth woven by the association's members. To find it, go two blocks north along 5a Av from the Parque Central, then two blocks west. All profits benefit the women involved in the program.

Banrural (cnr 3a Calle & 6a Av; 🕑 8:30am-5pm Mon-Fri, 9am-1pm Sat) Changes US dollars and Amex traveler's checks and has an ATM.

Café Portal (5a Av 2-65; 🕑 6:30am-10pm) On the east side of Parque Central, this place provides information, tours and transportation.

Municipal police (cnr 1a Calle & 5a Av) Near the lakeshore.

SLEEPING & EATING

Hotel Villela (☎ 7949-7214; 6a Av 2-06; s/d Q70/110) The rooms are less attractive than the neat lawn and trees they're set around, but some are airier and brighter than others. All have fan and bathroom.

Restaurante Típico Chaabil (☎ 7949-7272; 3a Calle; r per person Q75; P) Although they go a bit heavy on the log-cabin feel, the rooms at this place, at the west end of 3a Calle, are the best deal in town. Get one upstairs for plenty of light and good views. The restaurant here, on a lovely lakeside terrace, cooks up delicious food, such as *tapado* (Garífuna seafood and coconut stew; Q60). The water here is crystal clear and you can swim right off the hotel's dock.

Hotel Vista al Lago (☎ 7949-7205; 6a Av 1-13; s/d Q90/150) Set in a classic, historic building down on the waterfront, this place has plenty of style, although the rooms themselves are fairly ordinary. Views from the upstairs balcony are superb.

Hotel Marisabela (☎ 7949-7206; 6a Av; r Q180; ⊠) Reasonable value, spacious rooms with fan. If you can get one at the front upstairs you'll have great lake views. There's a reasonable little restaurant out front. Air-con costs Q50 extra.

Hotel Ecológico (☎ 7949-7245; www.ecohotelcaba nasdellago.blogspot.com; s/d Q125/175) Carved into a lush jungly setting a couple of kilometers east of El Estor, the cabins here are pleasing, rustic affairs, but the lakefront setting is the real winner. The good-value, open-air restaurant has great views.

The Chaabil apart, the best place to look for food is around the Parque Central, where **Café Portal** (mains Q25-45; 🕑 breakfast, lunch & dinner) serves a broad range of fare with some vegetarian options. On the other side of the park, **Restaurante del Lago** (mains Q40-80; 🕑 breakfast, lunch & dinner), on the 2nd floor, catches some good breezes and a bit of a lake view – it has the widest menu in town.

GETTING THERE & AWAY

See Río Dulce (p254) for information on buses from there. The schedule from El Estor to Río Dulce is hourly, from 6am to 4pm.

The road west from El Estor via Panzós and Tucurú to Tactic, south of Cobán, has had a bad reputation for highway holdups and robberies in the past, especially around Tucurú – ask around for current conditions. It's also prone to getting flooded out during the wet season – another reason to enquire. You can get to Lanquín by taking the truck that leaves El Estor's Parque Central at 9am for Cahabón (Q30, four to five hours), and then a bus or pickup straight on from Cahabón to Lanquín the same day. Four buses go direct to Cobán (Q45, six hours) on this route, leaving at the very unfriendly times of 1am, 2am, 4am and 6am from El Estor's Parque Central.

Refugio Bocas del Polochic & Reserva de Biosfera Sierra de las Minas

The Refugio Bocas del Polochic (Bocas del Polochic Wildlife Reserve) covers the delta of the Río Polochic, which provides most of Lago de Izabal's water. A visit here provides great bird-watching and howler-monkey observation. The reserve supports more than 300 species of birds – the migration seasons, September to October and April to May, are reportedly fantastic – and many varieties of butterflies and fish. You may well see alligators and, if you're very lucky, glimpse a manatee. Café Portal (see above left) can set up early-morning trips costing Q600 for two people plus Q100 for each extra person for 3½ hours. The reserve is managed by the **Fundación Defensores de la Naturaleza** (☎ 7949-7130; www.defensores.org.gt; cnr 5a Av & 2a Calle, El Estor), whose research station, the **Estación Científica Selempim**, just south of the Bocas del Polochic reserve, in the Reserva de Biosfera Sierra de las Minas, is open for ecotouristic visits. Contact Defensores' El Estor office for bookings and further information. You can get to the station on a local *lancha* service leaving El Estor at noon on Monday and Saturday (Q30 round trip, 1¼ hours each way) or by special hire (Q350 for a boatload of up to 12 people), and stay in attractive wood-and-thatch *cabañas* (per person Q125) or camp (Q40 per person). Meals are available for Q35 each or you can use the Estación Científica's kitchen. To explore the reserves you can use canoes free of charge, take boat trips (Q200 to Q300) or walk any of the three well-established trails. At the time of writing, the foundation was developing another community tourism site at Chapín Abajo, on the other side of the lake. If you're interested, get in touch and see if it's up and running by now.

Mariscos

Mariscos is the principal town on the lake's south side. Ferries from here used to be the main access to El Estor and the north side of the lake, but since a road was built from Río Dulce to El Estor, Mariscos has taken a back seat. As a result, **Denny's Beach** (☎ 4636-6516; www. dennysbeach.com; dm Q75, s/d from Q240/375; ✷ ▣), 20 minutes by boat from Mariscos, is a good place to get away from it all. Dennis Gulck and his wife, Lupe, offer tours, hiking, swimming and wakeboarding. Accommodation is in 15 lovely cabins, villas and chalets set on the hillside, most with great views out over the lake. Delicious meals ((Q40 to Q100) are available. There's free boat transportation from Mariscos between noon and 1pm and 3:30pm, and 4:30pm, but try to call the day before to let them know you're coming. Denny's dock is behind the Tienda Rosita, in the middle of Mariscos. To get to Mariscos, take any bus heading along the Carretera al Atlántico and get off at Trincheras junction (Km 218) – the turnoff for Mariscos, where minibuses (Q8) make the run into town. Coming from Los Amates or Quiriguá, there are direct minibuses to Mariscos. From Río Dulce, you can radio from Captain Nemo's Communications (p252) and they'll send someone to pick you up (Q50 per person, minimum six people).

PUERTO BARRIOS
pop 76,500

The country becomes even more lush, tropical and humid heading east from La Ruidosa junction toward Puerto Barrios. Port towns have always had a reputation for being slightly dodgy, and those acting as international borders doubly so. Perhaps the town council wants to pay homage to that here. Or perhaps the edgy, slightly sleazy feel is authentic. Either way, for foreign visitors, Puerto Barrios is mainly a jumping-off point for boats to Punta Gorda (Belize) or Lívingston, and you probably won't be hanging around.

The powerful United Fruit Company once owned vast plantations in the Motagua valley and many other parts of Guatemala. The company built railways to ship its produce to the coast, and it built Puerto Barrios early in the 20th century to put that produce onto ships sailing for New Orleans and New York (see boxed text, p237). Laid out as a company town, Puerto Barrios has long, wide streets arranged neatly on a grid plan, and lots of Caribbean-style wood-frame houses, many of which have seen better days.

MANATEES

In the days of New World exploration, reports of mermaid sightings were commonplace. Columbus' ship's log from January 1493 recorded: 'On the previous day when the Admiral went to the Rio del Oro he saw three mermaids which rose well out of the sea…' It's pretty much accepted now that what sailors were seeing were in fact manatees – who, along with the dugong, belong to the biological order Sirenia, a name taken from the Greek word for mermaid.

Distantly related to elephants, these huge (the largest recorded manatee weighed 1775kg while newborns weigh around 30kg) vegetarian mammals seem destined to become an endangered species. They were hunted as far back as Maya times – their bones were used for jewelry and their meat (called *bucan*) was prized for its restorative properties. It's believed that the buccaneers (the original pirates of the Caribbean) were so named because they lived almost exclusively on *bucan* meat.

Some scientists claim that manatees were once sociable creatures who swam in packs and readily approached humans, but have adapted in response to human hunters, becoming the shy, furtive creatures they are today. You have to be extremely fortunate to see one in the wild – they scare easily, can swim in short bursts at up to 30km per hour, and can stay underwater for 20 minutes. In Guatemala, your best chance of seeing one is in the Bocas del Polochic (p256) or the Punta de Manabique (p260). Good luck.

When United Fruit's power and influence declined in the 1960s, the Del Monte company became successor to its interests. But the heyday of the imperial foreign firms was past, as was that of Puerto Barrios. A more modern and efficient port was built a few kilometers to the southwest at Santo Tomás de Castilla, and Puerto Barrios sank into tropical torpor. In the last few years, however, things have started to look up again with the construction of a huge new truck container depot where the old railway yards were.

El Muñecón (intersection 8a Av, 14a Calle & Calz Justo Rufino Barrios) is a statue of a dock worker; this is a favorite landmark and monument in the town.

Orientation & Information

Because of its spacious layout, you must walk or ride further in Puerto Barrios to get from place to place. For instance, it's 800m from the bus terminals by the market in the town center to the Muelle Municipal (Municipal Boat Dock) at the end of 12a Calle, from which passenger boats depart. Very few businesses use street numbers – most just tell you which street it's on, and the cross streets it's in between.

Banco Industrial (7a Av; 9am-5pm Mon-Fri, 9am-1pm Sat) Changes US dollars and traveler's checks, and has Visa ATMs.

Banrural (8a Av; 8:30am-5pm Mon-Fri, 9am-1pm Sat) Changes cash (dollars only) and has a MasterCard ATM.

Immigration office (cnr 12a Calle & 3a Av; 24hr) A block from the Muelle Municipal. Come here for your entry or exit stamp if you're arriving from or leaving for Belize. If you're leaving, there is a Q85 departure tax to pay. If you are heading to Honduras, you can get your exit stamp at another immigration office on the road to the border.

Police station (9a Calle)

Post office (cnr 6a Calle & 6a Av)

Red Virtu@l (cnr 17a Calle & Calz Justo Rufino Barrios; per hr Q6; 8am-9:30pm) Internet access.

Sleeping

Hotel Miami (7948-0537; 3a Av; s/d Q50/80, with air-con Q150/180; P X) Not bad if you want to save your pennies to spend elsewhere…otherwise a bit grim.

Hotel Lee (7948-0685; 5a Av; s/d Q60/90) This is a friendly, family-owned place, between 9a and 10a Calles, close to the bus terminals. Typical of Puerto Barrios' budget hotels, it offers straightforward, vaguely clean rooms. The little balcony out front catches the odd breeze.

Hotel La Caribeña (7948-0384; 4a Av; s/d Q70/100) Good little budget rooms in a quiet location.

Its restaurant has been repeatedly recommended for its seafood dishes, particularly the 'super sopa' seafood stew.

Hotel Henry Berrisford (7948-7289; cnr 9a Av & 17a Calle; s/d Q80/160) A big four-story modern concrete construction offering decent-sized, slightly shabby rooms with cable TV. The lobby is an impressive sight and there are plenty of sitting areas scattered around.

Hotel Europa 2 (7948-1292; 3a Av; s/d Q100/150, with air-con Q150/200; P X) The best of the budget options in the port area, this hotel, between 11a and 12a Calles, just 1½ blocks from the Muelle Municipal, is run by a friendly family and has clean rooms with TV, arranged around a parking courtyard.

ourpick **Hotel El Reformador** (7948-0533; refor mador@intelnet.net.gt; cnr 7a Av & 16a Calle; s/d with fan Q100/160, with air-con Q150/200; P X ☎) Like a little haven away from the hot busy streets outside, the Reformador offers big, cool rooms set around leafy patios. Air-con rooms lead onto wide interior balconies. There is a restaurant (meals Q50 to Q80) here.

Hotel del Norte (7948-2116; 7a Calle; s/d Q120/165, with air-con Q170/250; P X X) A large, classically tropical wooden construction with mosquito-screened corridors wide enough to run a banana train through, the century-old Hotel del Norte is in a class by itself. Its weathered and warped frame is redolent of history and most of the floorboards go off at crazy angles. In the airy dining room overlooking the Bahía de Amatique you can almost hear the echoing conversation of bygone banana moguls and smell their pungent cigars. Spare, simple and agreeably dilapidated, this is a real museum piece. Meals are served with old-fashioned refinement by white-jacketed waiters, though the food isn't always up to the same standard. Pick a room carefully – some are little more than a wooden box, others have great ocean views and catch good breezes. Rooms with airconditioning are in the newer, less atmospheric building, but are still an excellent deal. There's a swimming pool beside the sea.

Hotel Santa Fe (7948-8799; hotel_santafe56@hot mail.com; 8a Av; s/d Q150/280; P X X ▢) A small step up from the budget options, the Santa Fe has clean, modern rooms in a tranquil environment. There's a pleasant little cafe attached. It's located between 8a and 9a Calles.

Hotel Valle Tropical (7948-7084; 12 Calle; s/d Q275/300; P X X) The medium-sized, un-renovated rooms here are nothing special, but

PUERTO BARRIOS

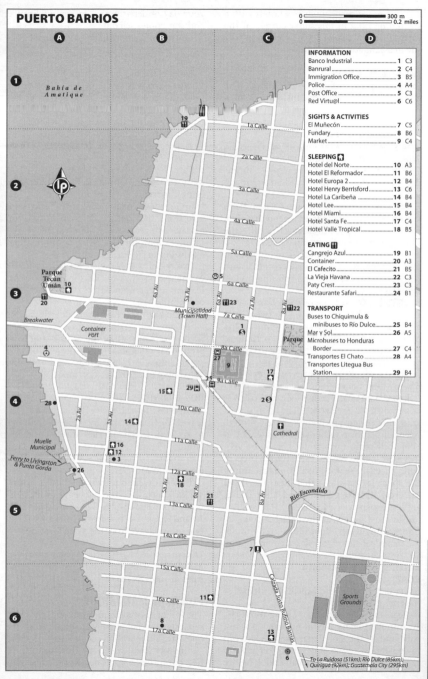

INFORMATION	
Banco Industrial	1 C3
Banrural	2 C4
Immigration Office	3 B5
Police	4 A4
Post Office	5 C3
Red Virtu@l	6 C6

SIGHTS & ACTIVITIES	
El Muñecón	7 C5
Fundary	8 B6
Market	9 C4

SLEEPING	
Hotel del Norte	10 A3
Hotel El Reformador	11 B6
Hotel Europa 2	12 B4
Hotel Henry Berrisford	13 C6
Hotel La Caribeña	14 B4
Hotel Lee	15 B4
Hotel Miami	16 B4
Hotel Santa Fe	17 C4
Hotel Valle Tropical	18 B5

EATING	
Cangrejo Azul	19 B1
Container	20 A3
El Cafecito	21 B5
La Vieja Havana	22 C3
Paty Crest	23 C3
Restaurante Safari	24 B1

TRANSPORT	
Buses to Chiquimula & minibuses to Río Dulce	25 B4
Mar y Sol	26 A5
Microbuses to Honduras Border	27 C4
Transportes El Chato	28 A4
Transportes Litegua Bus Station	29 B4

Bahía de Amatique

Parque Tecún Umán

Breakwater

Container Port

Municipalidad (Town Hall)

Parque

Muelle Municipal

Ferry to Livingston & Punta Gorda

Cathedral

Río Escondido

Sports Grounds

Calzada Justo Rufino Barrios

To La Ruidosa (51km); Río Dulce (85km); Quirigua (92km); Guatemala City (295km)

0   300 m
0   0.2 miles

it is one of the surprisingly few hotels with a swimming pool in this sultry corner of the earth. Prices are very negotiable – don't be shy in asking for a discount.

Eating & Drinking

Container (7a Calle; snacks Q20; ☺ lunch & dinner) The oddest cafe in town – made from two shipping containers, at the west end of 7a Calle. It has fine bay views, thatched huts out over the water and plenty of cold, cold beer.

La Vieja Havana (8a Av; mains Q30-60; ☺ lunch & dinner) This laid-back little place does good Cuban dishes (including *ropa vieja* – a shredded beef stew) and has excellent-value set lunches for Q20.

Paty Crest (cnr 6a Av & 7a Calle; mains Q40-60; ☺ lunch & dinner) With one of the widest menus in town, stretching from pizza to lasagna to steaks (the T-bone comes heartily recommended at Q65). Also features one of the best-looking bars in town, a long, wooden affair, decorated with nautical paraphernalia and offering a very complete selection of drinks.

ourpick El Cafecito (13a Calle 6-22; mains Q40-90; ☺ breakfast, lunch & dinner Mon-Sat) This sweet little air-conditioned spot whips up some of the most interesting food in town. Portuguese dishes such as *feijoada* (stewed beans, pork, beef, chicken and other stuff; Q55) and a good range of seafood, sandwiches and breakfasts. There's draft beer on tap, too.

Restaurante Safari (☎ 7948-0563; cnr 1a Calle & 5a Av; seafood Q60-100; ☺ 10am-9pm) The town's most enjoyable restaurant is on a thatch-roofed, open-air platform right over the water about 1km north of the town center. Locals and visitors alike love to eat and catch the sea breezes here. Excellent seafood of all kinds including the specialty *tapado* – that great Garífuna casserole (Q100). Chicken and meat dishes are less expensive (Q40 to Q80). There's live music most nights. If the Safari is full, the Cangrejo Azul next door offers pretty much the same deal, in a more relaxed environment.

Getting There & Around

BOAT

Boats depart from the Muelle Municipal at the end of 12a Calle.

Regular *lanchas* depart for Lívingston (Q30, 30 minutes) every day at 6:30am, 7:30am, 9am and 11am. For departure times from Lívingston, see p266. Buy your ticket as early as you can on the day (you can't book before

your day of departure) – spaces are limited and sometimes sell out.

Outside of these regular times, *lanchas* depart whenever they have five people ready to go and cost Q50.

Most of the movement from Lívingston to Puerto Barrios is in the morning, returning in the afternoon. From Lívingston, your last chance of the day may be the 5pm *lancha*, especially during the low season when fewer travelers are shuttling back and forth.

A *lancha* service of **Transportes El Chato** (☎ 7948-5525; www.transporteselchato.com.gt; 1a Av) departs from the Muelle Municipal at 10am daily for Punta Gorda, Belize (Q200, one hour), arriving in time for the noon bus from Punta Gorda to Belize City. Tickets are sold at El Chato's office. Before boarding you also need to get your exit stamp at the nearby immigration office (p258). The return boat leaves Punta Gorda at 2pm.

Mar y Sol (☎ 7942-9156) at the Muelle Municipal also has *lanchas* for Punta Gorda, leaving at 10am and 1pm (Q175 to Q200, one hour).

If you want to leave a car in Puerto Barrios while you visit Lívingston for a day or two, there are plenty of *parqueos* (parking lots) around the dock area that charge around Q30 per 24 hours. Any of the hotels with parking listed here offer this service, too.

BUS & MINIBUS

Transportes Litegua (☎ 7948-1172; cnr 6a Av & 9a Calle) leaves for Guatemala City (Q60 to Q90, five to six hours, 295km), via Quiriguá and Río Hondo, 19 times between 1am and noon, and also at 4pm. *Directo* services avoid a half-hour detour into Morales.

Buses for Chiquimula (Q40, 4½ hours, 192km), also via Quiriguá, leave every half-hour, from 3am to 4pm, from the corner of 6a Av and 9a Calle. Minibuses to Río Dulce (Q20, two hours) leave from the same location.

TAXI

Most cabs charge around Q20 for longish rides around town.

PUNTA DE MANABIQUE

The Punta de Manabique promontory, which separates the Bahía de Manabique from the open sea, along with the coast and hinterland all the way southeast to the Honduran frontier, comprises a large, ecologically fascinating, sparsely populated wetland area. Access to the area, which is under environmental protection as the **Área de Protección Especial Punta de Manabique**, is not cheap, but the attractions for those who make it there include pristine Caribbean beaches, boat trips through the mangrove forests, lagoons and waterways, bird-watching, fishing with locals, and crocodile and possible manatee sightings. To visit, get in touch – a week in advance, if possible – with the NGO (nongovernment organization) involved in the reserve's management, **Fundary** (Fundación Mario Dary; ☎ 7948-0944; www.fundary.org; 17a Calle) in Puerto Barrios.

Fundary is helping to develop several ecotouristic possibilities in the reserve. It offers accommodation in an **ecolodge** (☎ 4433-4930; per person Q50) in the community of Estero Lagarto, on the south side of the promontory, where you can take mangrove and laguna tours in wooden canoes (Q350 per canoe) to nearby Santa Isabel, on the Canal de los Ingleses – a waterway connecting the Bahía de Manabique with the open sea – where you may see manatees and you can rent snorkeling gear (Q30) and try your hand at fishing using traditional techniques on fishing tours (Q50 per person). If you have a tent, you can camp at Estero Lagarto for Q25. Meals are available for Q20 to Q50. Transport to Estero Lagarto is in a canoe (Q900 per canoe, round trip). Contact Fundary to organize a ride.

Fundary is constantly working on new community tourism initiatives – if you're at all interested, get in touch with them to see what's currently on offer.

LÍVINGSTON
pop 25,380

Quite unlike anywhere else in Guatemala, this largely Garífuna town is fascinating in itself, but also an attraction for a couple of good beaches, and its location at the end of the river journey from Río Dulce.

Unconnected (for the moment) by road from the rest of the country (the town is called 'Buga' – mouth – in Garífuna, for its position at the river mouth), boat transportation is logically quite good here, and you can get to Belize, the Cayes, Honduras and Puerto Barrios with a minimum of fuss.

The Garífuna (Garinagu, or Black Carib) people of Caribbean Guatemala, Honduras, Nicaragua and southern Belize trace their roots to the Caribbean island of St Vincent,

where shipwrecked African slaves mixed with the indigenous Carib in the 17th century. It took the British a long time, and a lot of fighting, to establish colonial control over St Vincent, and when they finally succeeded in 1796, they decided to deport its surviving Garífuna inhabitants. Most of the survivors wound up, after many had starved on Roatán island off Honduras, in the Honduran coastal town of Trujillo. From there, they have spread along the Caribbean coast. Their main concentration in Guatemala is in Lívingston but there are also a few thousand in Puerto Barrios and elsewhere. The Garífuna language is a unique mélange of Caribbean and African languages with a bit of French. Other people in Lívingston include the indigenous Q'eqchi' Maya (who have their own community a kilometer or so upriver from the main dock), *ladinos* and a smattering of international travelers.

Orientation & Information

Lívingston stands where the Río Dulce opens out into the Bahía de Amatique. After being here half an hour, you'll know where everything is. The main street, Calle Principal, heads straight ahead, uphill, from the main dock, curving round to the right at Hotel Río Dulce. The other important streets head to the left off this: Calle Marcos Sánchez Díaz heads southwest, parallel to the river, to the Q'eqchi' Maya community, and another street leads northwest from the town center to several places to stay, eat and drink. Though we use street names here for ease of orientation, in reality no-one uses them.

For more on Lívingston, check out its community website, www.livingston.com.gt.
Banrural (Calle Principal; ☼ 9am-5pm Mon-Fri, 9am-1pm Sat) Changes US dollars and traveler's checks and has an ATM.
Happy Fish (Calle Principal; per hr Q10) Internet access.
Immigration office (Calle Principal; ☼ 6am-7pm) Issues entry and exit stamps for travelers arriving direct from or going direct to Belize or Honduras, charging Q85 for exit stamps. Outside business hours, you can knock for attention at any time.
Laundry (Hotel Casa Rosada; per load Q40) It can be difficult to get laundry properly dry in the rainy season.

Dangers & Annoyances

Lívingston has its edgy aspects and a few hustlers operate here, trying to sweet-talk tourists into 'lending' money, paying up front for tours that don't happen and the like. Take care with anyone who strikes up conversation for no obvious reason on the street or elsewhere.

Like many coastal locations in Guatemala, Lívingston is used as a *puente* (bridge) for northbound drug traffic. There's very little in the way of turf wars, and so on – the industry is fairly stable – but there are some big-time players around, and a lot of money at stake. Keep your wits about you.

The beachfront between Lívingston and the Río Quehueche and Siete Altares had a bad reputation for some years, but locals 'took care' of the troublemakers (we don't really want to know details). It now makes a fine walk, with some great swimming at the end of it. You can go independently or as part of a tour.

Use mosquito repellent and other sensible precautions here, especially if you go out into the jungle; mosquitoes here on the coast carry both malaria and dengue fever.

Sights & Activities

The **Museo Multicultural de Lívingston** (admission Q20; 9am-6pm), upstairs on the municipal park in front of the public dock, has some excellent displays on the history and culture of the area, focusing on the ethnic diversity, with Garífuna, Q'eqchi', Hindu and *ladino* cultures represented. While you're down here, check out the open-air alligator enclosure in the middle of the park.

Beaches in Lívingston itself are disappointing, as buildings or vegetation come

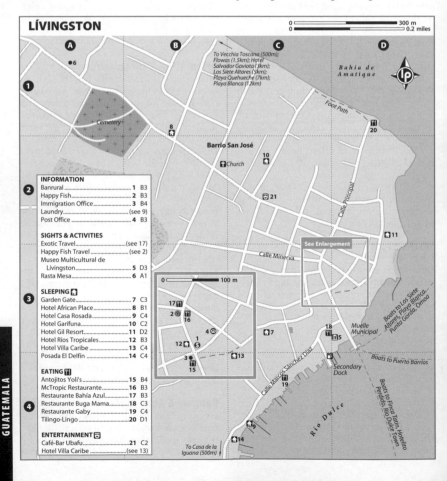

LÍVINGSTON

To Vecchia Toscana (500m); Flowas (1.5km); Hotel Salvador Gaviota (3km); Los Siete Altares (5km); Playa Quehueche (7km); Playa Blanca (12km)

Bahía de Amatique

Foot Path

Cemetery

Barrio San José

Church

Calle Minerva

Calle Principal

See Enlargement

Muelle Municipal

Boats to Los Siete Altares, Playa Blanca, Punta Gorda, Omoa

Boats to Puerto Barrios

Secondary Dock

Boats to Finca Tatin, Hotelito Perdido, Río Dulce Town

Río Dulce

Calle Marcos Sánchez Díaz

To Casa de la Iguana (500m)

INFORMATION	
Banrural	1 B3
Happy Fish	2 B3
Immigration Office	3 B4
Laundry	(see 9)
Post Office	4 B3

SIGHTS & ACTIVITIES	
Exotic Travel	(see 17)
Happy Fish Travel	(see 2)
Museo Multicultural de Lívingston	5 D3
Rasta Mesa	6 A1

SLEEPING	
Garden Gate	7 C3
Hotel African Place	8 B1
Hotel Casa Rosada	9 C4
Hotel Garífuna	10 C2
Hotel Gil Resort	11 D2
Hotel Ríos Tropicales	12 B3
Hotel Villa Caribe	13 C4
Posada El Delfin	14 C4

EATING	
Antojitos Yoli's	15 B4
McTropic Restaurante	16 B3
Restaurante Bahía Azul	17 B3
Restaurante Buga Mama	18 C3
Restaurante Gaby	19 C4
Tilingo-Lingo	20 D1

ENTERTAINMENT	
Café-Bar Ubafu	21 C2
Hotel Villa Caribe	(see 13)

GETTING TO HONDURAS

Minibuses leave for the Honduran frontier (Q15, 1¼ hours) every 20 minutes, from 5am to 5pm, from 6a Av outside the market in Puerto Barrios. The paved road to the border turns off Hwy 9 at Entre Ríos, 13km south of Puerto Barrios. Buses and minibuses going in all directions wait for passengers at Entre Ríos, meaning that you can get to or from the border fairly easily, whichever direction you are traveling in. The minibuses from Puerto Barrios stop en route to the border at Guatemalan immigration, where you may be required to pay Q10 for an exit stamp. Honduran ~~entry formalities will leave you around L50 lighter.~~

Buses wait on the other side leaving for Puerto Cortés (L50, two hours) every 20 minutes and passing Omoa (L40, one hour) along the way. You can continue by bus from Puerto Cortés to San Pedro Sula and from there to La Ceiba, and you *might* make the 4:30pm ferry from La Ceiba to Roatán island in one day from Puerto Barrios, if you took the first vehicle out in the morning, but more likely you'll end up spending the night in La Ceiba.

---

right down to the water's edge in most places. Those beaches that do exist are often contaminated. However, there are better beaches within a few kilometers to the northwest. You can reach **Playa Quehueche** by taxi (Q15) in about 10 minutes: this beach near the mouth of the Río Quehueche has been cleaned up by Exotic Travel (see right). The best beach in the area is **Playa Blanca** (admission Q10), around 12km from Lívingston. This is privately owned and you need a boat to get there (see right).

Rasta Mesa (☎ 4200-4371; www.site.rastamesa.com; Barrio Nevago; ☼ 10am-2pm & 7-10pm) is a friendly, informal little cultural center where you can drop in for classes in Garífuna cooking (Q50 per person) and drumming (Q100 per person) or just get a massage (Q150). You can volunteer here as well.

LOS SIETE ALTARES

About 5km (1½-hours' walk) northwest of Lívingston along the shore of Bahía de Amatique, Los Siete Altares (The Seven Altars) is a series of freshwater falls and pools. It's a pleasant goal for a beach walk and is a good place for a picnic and swim. Follow the shore northward to the river mouth and walk along the beach until it meets the path into the woods (about 30 minutes). Follow this path all the way to the falls.

Boat trips go to the Seven Altars, but locals say it's better to walk there to experience the natural beauty and the Garífuna people along the way. About halfway along, just past the rope bridge is **Hotel Salvador Gaviota** (mains Q40-80; ☼ breakfast, lunch & dinner), serving decent food and ice-cold beers and soft drinks. You can stay out here, too – see p264.

Tours

A few outfits in Lívingston offer tours that let you get out and experience the natural wonders of the area. **Exotic Travel** (☎ 7947-0133; www.bluecaribbeanbay.com; Restaurante Bahía Azul, Calle Principal) and **Happy Fish Travel** (☎ 7947-0661; www.happyfishtravel.com; Restaurante Happy Fish, Calle Principal) are both well-organized operations offering basically the same range of trips. The popular Ecological Tour/Jungle Trip takes you for a walk through town, out west up to a lookout spot and on to the Río Quehueche, where you take a half-hour canoe trip down the river to Playa Quehueche (see left). Then you walk through the jungle to Los Siete Altares (see left), hang out there for a while, then you walk down to the beach and back along it to Lívingston. The trip leaves the Restaurant Bahía Azul on Calle Principal every day at 9am and arrives back around 4:30pm; it costs Q75 including a box lunch. This is a great way to see the area, and the friendly local guides can also give you a good introduction to the Garífuna people who live here.

The Playa Blanca tour goes by boat first to Los Siete Altares, then on to the Río Cocolí, where you can swim, and then on to Playa Blanca for two or three hours at the best beach in the area. This trip goes with a minimum of six people and costs Q100 per person.

Also on offer are day trips to the Cayos Sapodillas (or Zapotillas), well off the coast of southern Belize, where there is great snorkeling (Q400). A minimum of six people is required.

For sailing tours, contact **Capitán Eric** (☎ 4275-5278; capiteric@yahoo.fr), who offers day tours for Q200 per person (food and drinks included) and trips to Placencia or the Cayos Zapotillos (Belize) or Utila and Omoa (Honduras) in the Kia, a 35ft monohull sleeping five people. Three-day tours cost Q1700, with a minimum of four people.

RÍO DULCE TOURS

Tour agencies in town offer day trips up the Río Dulce to Río Dulce town, as do most local boatmen at the Lívingston dock. Many travelers use these tours as one-way transportation to Río Dulce, paying Q125/180 one way/round trip. It's a beautiful ride through tropical jungle scenery, with several places to stop on the way. Be aware that of the two departures per day, only the 9:30am one does the following tour; the 2:30pm boat goes direct to Río Dulce.

Shortly after you leave Lívingston, you pass the tributary Río Tatin on the right, then will probably stop at an indigenous arts museum set up by Asociación Ak' Tenamit, an NGO working to improve conditions for the Q'eqchi' Maya population of the area. The river enters a gorge called **La Cueva de la Vaca**, its walls hung with great tangles of jungle foliage and the humid air noisy with the cries of tropical birds. Just beyond that is **La Pintada**, a rock escarpment covered with graffiti. Local legend says people have been tagging this spot since the 1700s, though the oldest in evidence is from the 1950s. If you're lucky, you might spot a freshwater dolphin in these parts. Further on, a **thermal spring** forces sulfurous water out of the base of the cliff, providing a chance for a warm swim. The river widens into **El Golfete**, a lake-like body of water that presages the even vaster expanse of Lago de Izabal further upstream.

On the northern shore of El Golfete is the **Biotopo Chocón Machacas**, a 72-sq-km reserve established within the Parque Nacional Río Dulce to protect the beautiful river landscape, the valuable forests and mangrove swamps and their wildlife, which includes such rare creatures as the tapir and above all the manatee. The huge, walrus-like manatees are aquatic mammals weighing up to a ton, yet they glide effortlessly beneath the calm surface of the river. They are elusive, however, and the chances of seeing one are very slim. A network of 'water trails' (boat routes around several jungle lagoons) provide ways to see other bird, animal and plant life of the reserve. A nature trail begins at the visitor center and winds its way through forests of mahogany, palms and rich tropical foliage.

Boats will probably visit the **Islas de Pájaros**, a pair of islands where thousands of water-birds live, in the middle of El Golfete. From El Golfete you continue upriver, passing increasing numbers of expensive villas and boathouses, to the town of Río Dulce, where the soaring Hwy 13 road bridge crosses the river, and on to El Castillo de San Felipe on Lago de Izabal (p254).

You can also do this trip starting from Río Dulce (see p254).

Festivals & Events

Lívingston is packed with merrymakers during **Semana Santa**. **Garífuna National Day** is celebrated on November 26 with a variety of cultural events.

Sleeping

BUDGET

Prices in Lívingston hit their peak from July to December – outside of these months many midrange and top-end places listed here halve their rates.

Casa de la Iguana (☎ 7947-0064; Calle Marcos Sánchez Díaz; dm Q40, cabin with/without bathroom Q150/110; ☜) Five minutes' walk from the main dock, this party hostel offers good-value cabins. They're clean, wooden affairs, with simple but elegant decoration. Happy hour here rocks on and you can camp or crash in a hammock for Q20 per person. Spanish classes are available for Q570 for 20 hours.

Hotel African Place (☎ 7947-0435; Calle al Cementario; s/d Q50/80, without bathroom Q40/70) One of the more original hotels in Guatemala, built by a Spaniard to resemble a series of Moroccan castles. They're set on lush grounds and turtles swim in the 'moat.' The whole place is looking very much the worse for wear, but rooms with private bathroom are as good as any in this price range.

Hotel Garífuna (☎ 7947-0183; Barrio San José; s/d Q50/75) About a five-minute walk from the main street, these big breezy rooms are a solid budget choice. Beds are good, bathrooms are spotless and the folks are friendly.

Hotel Ríos Tropicales (☎ 7947-0158; www.mctropic.com; Calle Principal; s/d Q100/150, without bathroom Q50/100; ☜) The Ríos Tropicales has a variety of big, well-screened rooms facing a central patio with plenty of hammocks and chill-out space. Rooms with shared bathroom are bigger, but others are better decorated.

Hotel Salvador Gaviota (☎ 7947-0874; www.hotel salvadorgaviota.es.tl; Playa Quehueche; s/d Q125/250, without bathroom Q50/100) Beautiful, simple wood and bamboo rooms set back a couple of hundred meters from a reasonably clean beach. Day-trippers going to and from the Seven Altars drop in for meals (Q40 to Q80) and drinks here – otherwise you may have the place to yourself. It's 500m from the swing bridge where the road ends – a taxi will charge about Q15 to get you there.

Garden Gate (☎ 7947-9272; www.gardengate-guest house.com; s/d without bathroom Q120/150; ☎) Just putting on the finishing touches at time of research, this lush hilltop property offers three spotless rooms with a simple, pleasing decor. Maria, the founder of Tilingo Lingo (see below right) runs the place, so you know the food is good. There's a big garden, plenty of hammocks and bicycle rental for guests.

MIDRANGE & TOP END

Flowas (☎ 7947-0376; infoflowas@gmail.com; dm/s/d Q75/150/200) A rightly popular little backpacker getaway, this place offers rustic wood and bamboo cabins set up on the 2nd floor (catching the odd breeze) right on the beachfront. The atmosphere is relaxed and there's good, cheap food available. A taxi (Q10 from the dock) will drop you within 150m of the front gate.

Posada El Delfín (☎ 7947-0694; www.posadaeldelfin.com; s/d Q125/250; ☎ ☎) Down by the waterfront, this is a big modern construction with reasonably sized, spotless rooms and a great swimming pool overlooking the river. Don't expect views from your room – the highly recommended 2nd floor restaurant steals them all.

Hotel Casa Rosada (☎ 7947-0303; www.hotelcasarosada .com; Calle Marcos Sánchez Díaz; r Q160; ☎) The Casa Rosada (Pink House) is an attractive place to stay right on the river, 500m upstream from the main dock; it has its own pier where boats will drop you if you ask. The charming little wooden cabins are jammed up against each other, so you may get a bit of noise from your neighbors. And they might get a bit from you. But the garden area is pretty and the restaurant (mains from Q60) has great views out over the water. The shared bathrooms are very clean. Also available are a laundry service and tours.

Hotel Gil Resort (☎ 7947-0990; www.gilresorthotel. com; s/d Q300/480; ☎) Built on a hillside sloping down to the water, the rooms here are comfortable and modern if somewhat bland affairs. Views from the various decks and balconies really make the place.

Vecchia Toscana (☎ 7947-0884; www.vecchiatoscana -livingston.com; Barrio Paris; r with fan/air-con Q420/670; ☎ ☎) This beautiful new Italian-run place

down on the beach has some of the best rooms in town. Fan-cooled ones are a bit squishy, but the more expensive numbers are spacious enough and the grounds and common areas are immaculate. There's a good Italian restaurant with sea views out the front.

Hotel Villa Caribe (☎ 7947-0072; www.hotelvilla caribeguatemala.com; Calle Principal; s/d Q750/920, bungalow s/d Q920/1100; ☎ ☎ ☎ ☎) The 45-room Villa Caribe is a luxurious anomaly among Lívingston's laid-back, low-priced Caribbean lodgings. Modern but still Caribbean in style, it has many conveniences and comforts, including extensive tropical gardens, a big swimming pool and a large poolside bar. Rooms are fairly large, with modern bathrooms, ceiling fans and little balconies overlooking the gardens and river mouth. Rooms are fan-cooled, bungalows have air-con. Rates include breakfast and dinner.

Eating

Food in Lívingston is relatively expensive because most of it (except fish and coconuts) must be brought in by boat. There's fine seafood here and some unusual flavors for Guatemala, including coconut and curry. *Tapado*, a rich stew made from fish, shrimp, shellfish and coconut milk, spiced with coriander, is the delicious local specialty. A potent potable is made by slicing off the top of a green coconut and mixing in a healthy dose of rum. These *coco locos* hit the spot

Calle Principal is dotted with many open-air eateries.

Antojitos Yoli's (Calle Principal; items Q10-30; ☎ 8am-5pm) This is the place to come for baked goods. Especially recommended are the coconut bread and pineapple pie.

Restaurante Gaby (Calle Marcos Sánchez Díaz; mains Q30-50; ☎ breakfast, lunch & dinner) For a good honest feed in humble surrounds, you can't go past Gaby's. She serves up the good stuff: lobster, *tapado*, rice and beans and good breakfasts at good prices. The *telenovelas* (soap operas) come free.

our pick Tilingo-Lingo (Calle Principal; mains Q40-80; ☎ breakfast, lunch & dinner) An intimate little place down near the beach. It advertises food from 10 countries, and makes a pretty good job of it, with the Italian and East Indian dishes being the standouts.

McTropic Restaurante (Calle Principal; mains Q40-100; ☎ breakfast, lunch & dinner) Some of the best-value seafood dishes in town are on offer at this laid-back little place. Grab a table streetside for people-watching and sample some of the good Thai cooking.

Restaurante Bahía Azul (Calle Principal; mains Q60-100; ☺ breakfast, lunch & dinner) The Bahía's central location, happy decor and good fresh food keep it popular. The menu's wide, with a good mix of Caribbean, Guatemalan and Asian influences. It opens early for breakfast.

Restaurante Buga Mama (Calle Marcos Sánchez Díaz; mains Q40-100; ☺ breakfast, lunch & dinner; ☎) This place enjoys the best location of any restaurant in town, and profits go to the Asociación Ak Tenemit (www.aktenamit.org), an NGO with several projects in the area. There's a wide range of seafood, homemade pasta, curries and other dishes on the menu, including a very good *tapado* (Q100). Most of the waiters here are trainees in a community sustainable tourism development scheme, so service can be sketchy, but forgivable.

Drinking

Adventurous drinkers should try *guifiti*, a local concoction made from coconut rum, often infused with herbs. It's said to have medicinal as well as recreational properties.

A handful of bars down on the beach to the left of the end of Calle Principal pull in travelers and locals at night (after about 10pm or 11pm). It's very dark down here, so take care. The bars are within five minutes' walk of each other, so you should go for a wander and see what's happening. Music ranges from punta to salsa, merengue and electronica. Things warm up on Friday but Saturday is the party night – often going until 5am or 6am.

Happy hour is pretty much an institution along the main street, with every restaurant getting in on the act. One of the best is at Casa de la Iguana (p264).

Entertainment

See the boxed text, opposite, for details about traditional Garífuna music and dance.

Quite often a roaming band will play a few songs for diners along the Calle Principal around dinnertime. If you like the music, make sure to sling them a few bucks. Several places around town have live Garífuna music, although schedules are unpredictable.

Café-Bar Ubafu Probably the most dependable. Supposedly has music and dancing nightly, but liveliest on weekends.

Hotel Villa Caribe At this hotel (see p265) diners can enjoy a Garífuna show each evening at 7pm.

Getting There & Away

Frequent boats come downriver from Río Dulce and across the bay from Puerto Barrios (p260). There are also international boats from Honduras and Belize.

Exotic Travel (p263) operates combined boat and bus shuttles to La Ceiba (the cheapest gateway to Honduras' Bay Islands) for Q400 per person, with a minimum of six people. Leaving Lívingston at 7:30am or earlier will get you to La Ceiba in time for the boat to the islands, making it a one-day trip, which is nearly impossible to do independently.

There's also a boat that goes direct to Punta Gorda on Tuesday and Friday at 7am (Q200, 1½ hours), leaving from the public dock. In Punta Gorda, the boat connects with a bus to Placencia and Belize City. The boat waits for this bus to arrive from Placencia before it sets off back for Lívingston from Punta Gorda at about 10:30am.

If you are taking one of these early international departures, get your exit stamp from immigration in Lívingston (see p261) the day before.

AROUND LÍVINGSTON

Hotelito Perdido (☎ 5725-1576; www.hotelitoperdido. com; dm Q45, bungalow with/without bathroom Q180/130), a beautiful new place a five-minute boat ride from Finca Tatin, is run by a couple of young travelers. The ambience is superb – relaxed and friendly. The whole place is solar powered and constructed in such a way as to cause minimal impact on the environment. The two-story bungalows are gorgeous – simple yet well decorated, with a sleeping area upstairs and a small sitting area downstairs. It's a small, intimate place, so it's a good idea to book ahead. You can organize many of the activities available at Finca Tatin from here as well. Call to get picked up from Lívingston (Q40) or get dropped off by any boat going between there and Río Dulce.

Finca Tatin (☎ 5902-0831; www.fincatatin.com; dm Q45, s/d Q125/160, without bathroom Q65/110), a wonderful, rustic B&B at the confluence of Ríos Dulce and Tatin, about 10km from Lívingston, is a great place for experiencing the forest. Four-hour guided walks and kayak trips, some visiting local Q'eqchi' villages, are offered. Accommodation is in funky wood-and-thatched cabins scattered through the jungle. There are trails, waterfalls and endless river tributaries that you can explore with one of

---

CATCH THE RHYTHM OF THE GARÍFUNA

Lívingston is the heartland of Guatemala's Garífuna community, and it won't take too long before you hear some of their distinctive music. A Garífuna band generally consists of three drums (the *primera* takes the bass part, the other two play more melodic functions), a shaker or maraca, a turtle shell (hit like a cowbell) and a conch shell (blown like a flute).

The lyrics are often call and response – most often sung in Garífuna (a language with influences from Arawak, French and West African languages) but sometimes composed in Spanish. Most songs deal with themes from village life – planting time, harvests, things that happen in the village, honoring the dead and folktales of bad sons made good. Sometimes they simply sing about the beauty of the village.

Traditional Garífuna music has given birth to an almost bewildering array of musical styles, among them Punta Rock, Jugujugu, Calachumba, Jajankanu, Chumba, Saranda, Sambé and Parranda.

There are many local groups who play in Lívingston, the best known of which are Ubafu, Gayuza, Ibimeni and Zugara. While wandering bands play for diners on Lívingston's main street, your best chance of catching a concert is at Café-Bar Ubafu (see opposite) on weekends. Unlike some of Belize's Garífuna musicians, no musician from Lívingston has ever become famous in the 'outside world.'

Punta Rock is by far the most widely known adaptation of traditional Garífuna rhythms, and you can hear 'Punta' in most discos throughout Central America. The dance that accompanies it (also called *punta*) is a frenzied sort of affair, following the nature of the percussion. The left foot swivels back and forth while the right foot taps out the rhythm. Perhaps coincidentally, this movement causes the hips to shake wildly, leading some observers to comment on the sexual nature of the dance.

If you're interested in learning more about Garífuna culture or want drumming lessons, drop in to Rasta Mesa (p263).

---

the *cayucos* available for guest use (Q80 per day). Guided night walks through the jungle offer views of elusive nightlife, and cave tours are good for swimming and soaking in a natural sauna. You can walk to Lívingston from here in about four hours, or take a kayak and staff from Finca Tatín will come pick you up.

Lanchas traveling between Río Dulce and Lívingston (or vice versa) will drop you here. The *finca* can send its own *lancha* to pick you up at Lívingston (Q30 per person, minimum two people), Río Dulce (Q100 per person, minimum six) or Puerto Barrios (Q150 per person, minimum eight).

Heading in the other direction, northwest from Lívingston, brings you to the Río Sarstun, which forms the border between Belize and Guatemala. Ten kilometers upstream is the small community of **Lagunita Creek** (☎ 7753-4991, 5241-9342), where a community-tourism project offers lodging in a simple **ecolodge** (per person Q80). Simple meals (Q50 to Q65) are available here, or you can bring your own food to cook. Included in the price is use of kayaks to explore the beautiful, turquoise waters of the river and guided nature walks/bird-watching tours. Transport isn't complicated but it can be expensive – the only way to get here is by boat, and *lanchas* from Lívingston charge Q1200 per boatload (up to eight people), with a small discount for smaller groups.

El Petén

Vast, sparsely populated and jungle-covered, Guatemala's largest department is ripe for further exploration.

Two things really stand out about El Petén – the well-preserved (and often unrestored) archaeological sites and the abundance of wildlife that inhabits the jungle surrounding them.

There are so many Maya ruins here that you can take your pick depending on ease of access. The towering temples of Tikal can be reached by tour from just about anywhere in the country, minimizing your time outside of air-conditioned comfort. Other, more remote sites like El Mirador and Piedras Negras require days of planning, and further days of jungle trekking.

Wherever you go, you'll be accompanied by a jungle symphony – the forests are alive with parrots, monkeys and larger, more elusive animals.

The 21,000-sq-km Reserva de Biosfera Maya (Maya Biosphere Reserve) occupies approximately the whole northern third of El Petén. This Guatemalan reserve adjoins the vast Calakmul Biosphere Reserve in Mexico and the Río Bravo Conservation Area in Belize, forming a multinational wildlife haven that spans more than 30,000 sq km. The great variety of animal, bird and plant life is as exciting as the mysteries of the ancient Maya cities – and sites in El Petén combine both.

HIGHLIGHTS

- Taking in the majesty of the jungle-shrouded ruins at **Tikal** (p287)
- Exploring little-excavated ruins like **El Mirador** (p308) and **Piedras Negras** (p306)
- Spotting rare birds, monkeys and other rainforest wildlife at **Tikal** (see boxed text, p294) and other sites
- Taking a break at the picturesque island town of **Flores** (p272) or marvelously mellow **El Remate** (p284)
- Boating, horseback riding and trekking your way to ancient Maya ruins around **Sayaxché** (p301)

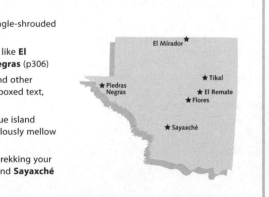

History

Often referred to as the cradle of Maya civilization, El Petén has historically been isolated from the rest of present-day Guatemala, a situation that continued until quite recently.

The major Maya population centers here – Tikal and El Mirador – almost certainly had more contact with neighboring settlements in Belize and Mexico than with those down south.

The arrival of the Spanish changed little in this regard. The Itzá, who lived on the island now known as Flores, earned a reputation for cruelty and ferocity which, along with El Petén's impenetrable jungles and fierce wildlife, kept the Spanish at a distance until 1697, about 150 years after the rest of the country had been conquered.

Even after conquest, the Spanish had no great love for El Petén. The island of Flores was a penal colony before a small city was founded, mostly to facilitate the trade in chicle, hardwood, sugarcane and rubber that had been planted in the region.

The big change came in 1970, when the Guatemalan government saw the opportunity to market Tikal as a tourist destination and work began on a decent road network.

El Petén's population boom – largely a result of government incentives for farmers to relocate – has seen the population increase from 15,000 to a staggering 500,000 in the last 50 years.

Some of the new neighbors are not entirely welcome, however – large tracts of land, particularly in the northwest corner and in the

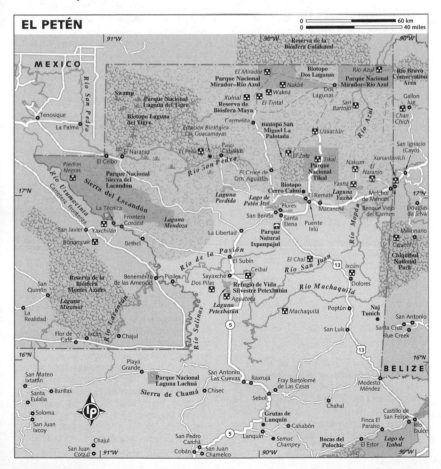

Parque Nacional Laguna del Tigre, have been taken over by drug traffickers and people smugglers, capitalizing on the unpatroled border with Mexico.

Climate

If you visit from December to February, expect cool nights and mornings. Weather-wise this can be the best time to visit El Petén. March and April are the hottest and driest months. The rains begin in May or June, and with them come the mosquitoes – bring rain gear, repellent and, if you plan on slinging a hammock, a mosquito net. July to September is muggy and buggy. October and November see the end of the rains and a return to cooler temperatures.

Getting There & Around

El Petén's main tourism node is at the twin towns of Flores and Santa Elena, about 60km southwest of Tikal. The main roads to Flores (from Río Dulce to the southeast, from Cobán and Chisec to the southwest, from the Belize border to the east and from the Mexican border to the northwest) are now all paved and in good condition, except for a few short stretches. Frequent buses and minibuses carry travelers along these routes. Flores also has the only functioning civil airport in the country aside from Guatemala City.

POPTÚN

pop 24,600 / elev 537m

Unfolding along the verdant foothills of the Maya Mountains, the terrain of south Petén makes a hilly and scenically varied gateway to what is otherwise a lowland area. About halfway between Río Dulce and Flores, the town of Poptún is the region's bustling commercial center. It's also the base for interesting excursions around southern Petén, including the Maya cave paintings at Naj Tunich, and the archaeological site of Ixcún, notable for its huge stele. Most travelers come here, though, to visit Finca Ixobel (see opposite), a jungly retreat south of town.

There are a couple of banks on the main drag: **Banco Industrial** (Av 15 de Septiembre 7-27; 🕑 9am-5pm Mon-Fri, 9am-1pm Sat) and **Banrural** (Av 15 de Septiembre & Calle del Parque; 🕑 8am-5pm Mon-Fri, 8:30am-1pm Sat). Both have Visa/MasterCard ATMs and change American Express traveler's checks. Get online at Café Internet Jungle, next door to the Tropical Inn.

Sleeping

Hotel Izalco (☎ 7927-7372; 4a Calle 7-11; s/d Q92/153, without bathroom Q60/75; [P]) This cordially managed budget option is smack in the center of town over a bank of stores, though behind the pink facade it's relatively tranquil around the courtyard/parking lot. Clean, simple rooms have comfortable beds and big ceiling fans; there are plenty of shared facilities for units without bathrooms.

Hotel Ecológico Villa de los Castellanos (☎ 7867-4773; ecovilla@intelnet.net.gt; s/d/tr Q85/150/180; [P]) Seven kilometers north of Poptún along the road to Flores, this hotel is right by the Río Machaquilá, which is good for swimming. Its sprawling grounds – through which you can take a 3km walk – are dedicated to the cultivation of medicinal plants. Accommodations are in wooden, thatch-roofed bungalows, each with two four-poster beds, mosquito nets, hot-water bathroom and TV, and there's a mid-priced restaurant. Any bus or microbus en route to Poptún can drop you here.

Tropical Inn (☎ 7927-7533; Av 15 de Septiembre 5-54; s/d with fan Q158/219, with air-con Q183/244; [P] [💺] [💺]) The designers of this lodging on Poptún's main drag had the good sense to place rooms well away from the entrance, facing a tropical patio, with a small pool.

Getting There & Away

Most buses and minibuses stop by the Las Flores gas station at the north end of Av 15 de Septiembre, the main road through town. Pullman buses leave from the **Línea Dorada office** (☎ 7821-4890) at the south end of the same avenue.

Bus departures from Poptún include the following:

Flores/Santa Elena Línea Dorada offers 1st-class service at 4:30am, 5am and 5pm among the sleepy passengers coming from Guatemala City. Less comfortable and reportedly less secure, Fuente del Norte buses (Q25, two hours, 113km) go every hour or two almost around the clock. The best option is to take a minibus (Q30, about every 10 minutes, 6am to 6pm).

Fray Bartolomé de Las Casas (Q65, five hours, 100km) A bus departs at 10:30am daily from opposite the Banrural branch a block south of Av 15 de Septiembre; the journey takes up to seven hours in the rainy season. If you want to push on from Fray to Lanquín the same day, try getting a Guatemala City–bound bus as far as Modesto Méndez (also called Cadenas; Q20, 45 minutes), 60km south on Hwy 13. Change for a westbound bus or minibus to Fray, then get onward transport to Lanquín.

Guatemala City (seven hours, 387km) First-class buses by Línea Dorada (Q115 to Q160) depart at 11:30am, 11pm and 11:30pm. Fuente del Norte buses (Q80) pass through approximately every hour from 5:30am to midnight.
Río Dulce (Q50, two hours, 99km) All Guatemala City–bound buses make a stop in Río Dulce.

AROUND POPTÚN
Finca Ixobel

Just 5km south of Poptún but a world apart, the **Finca Ixobel** (☎ 5892-3188; www.fincaixobel.com; campsite per person Q25, dm Q35, treehouse s/d Q60/90, s/d without bathroom Q75/110, s/d Q125/250, bungalow s/d Q150/275; P 🖥 📶) is an ecological resort/bohemian hideaway amid pine forests and patches of jungle. Its friendly, relaxed atmosphere makes a great place to meet other travelers from around the globe, with a wide range of activities, accommodation options and lip-smacking homemade meals. American Carole DeVine founded this hideaway in the 1970s with her husband Michael, who was tragically murdered in 1990 during the civil war, when Poptún was a training ground for the antiguerrilla forces called Kaibiles.

There's plenty to do around here. The grounds contain a natural pool for swimming, and horseback riding (from two hours to four days), treks, cave trips, and inner-tubing on the Río Machaquilá (in the rainy season) are all organized on a daily basis. One of the most popular outings is the guided two-hour hike to Cueva del Río, an underground river with rapids and waterfalls (Q75 per person). Other excursions visit the ruins at Ixcún and caves of Naj Tunich with their galleries of Maya painting (see right); the cost of Q275 per person (minimum of four) includes admission, guide and lunch.

Among the numerous options for bedding down here are *palapas* (thatched palm-leaf shelters) for hanging hammocks, bungalows and 'treehouses' – most of which are actually cabins on stilts. The large, grassy camping area has good bathrooms and plenty of shade. Assorted other accommodations include a couple of dormitories and rooms with shared and private bathroom, all with fan, mosquito nets and screened windows. Meals are excellent, including the eat-all-you-like buffet dinner for Q60. Finca Ixobel has its own bakery, grows its own salad ingredients and produces its own eggs. You can cook in the campground if you bring your own supplies. After dinner, many people move to the poolside bar for reasonably priced cocktails and other drinks. Everything at Finca Ixobel works on the honor system: guests keep an account of what they eat and drink and the services they use.

There are often volunteer opportunities for fluent English and Spanish speakers in exchange for room and board. If the *finca* (and its) suits your style and you want to help/ hang out for six weeks minimum, ask about volunteering.

The turnoff for the *finca* is marked on Hwy 13. In the daytime ask the bus or minibus driver to let you off there; it's a 15-minute walk to the *finca*. After hours, or to skip the hike in, get off the bus in Poptún and take a taxi (Q30) or tuk-tuk (Q20). When leaving Finca Ixobel, most buses will stop on the highway to pick you up, but not after dark. The *finca* also offers shuttles to/from Flores for Q50.

Naj Tunich

When they were discovered in 1979, these caves created a stir in the archaeological world. Measuring 3km long, they're packed with hieroglyphic texts and Maya murals, depicting religious ceremonies, art education, ball games and even sex scenes – though whether they're of a gay nature is a question still being disputed by anthropologists. In all, there are 94 images, completed during the Maya Classic period. Scribes and artists traveled from as far away as Calakmul in Mexico to contribute to the murals.

The caves were closed in 1984, due to vandalism, reopened briefly, then closed permanently a decade later for conservation purposes. Fortunately, a superb replica has been created in a nearby cave. Reproductions of the murals were painted by local artists under the supervision of archaeological and cultural authorities.

Independent access to the site is difficult – it's best to go with one of the reasonably priced tours from Finca Ixobel (see left), proceeds of which go to development projects in local communities.

Dolores

Displaying some of the most significant finds from southern Petén sites, the **Museo Regional del Sureste de Petén** (admission free; ⊗ 8am-5pm) is the main draw of Dolores (pop 17,800), a town 25km north of Poptún along the CA13. The collection features pottery, arrowheads and stelae. El Petén's oldest church is also found in Dolores.

The second-largest stele in the Maya world can be viewed amid a protected jungle zone at **Ixcún** (admission Q30), the remains of a late-Classic Maya kingdom, an hour's walk north of Dolores. Depicting a ruler wearing a headdress of quetzal feathers, it stands at one end of a large ceremonial center of three plazas, an unrestored temple and an acropolis. Archaeologists speculate that the complex of structures on the Plaza Principal may have been used as an astronomical observatory. Ixcún's sister city, Ixtontón, a major trading center until the 11th century AD, is another 6km along the Río Mopán.

All microbuses traveling between Flores and Poptún stop in Dolores. Taxis in front of the museum can take you to Ixcún for Q125, including a two-hour wait at the site.

FLORES & SANTA ELENA
pop Flores 30,600, Santa Elena 29,000 / elev 117m

With its cubist houses cascading down from a central plaza to the emerald waters of Lago de Petén Itzá, the island town of Flores evokes a Mediterranean ambience. A 500m causeway connects Flores to its humbler sister town of Santa Elena on the lakeshore, which then merges into the even homelier community of San Benito to the west. The three towns actually form one large settlement, often referred to simply as Flores.

Flores proper is by far the more attractive place to base yourself. Small hotels and restaurants line the streets, many featuring rooftop terraces with lake views. Residents take great pride in their island-town's gorgeousness, and recently a lakeside promenade was being installed around its perimeter. Flores does have a twee, built-up edge to it, though, and some Tikal-bound shoestringers opt for the natural surrounds and tranquility of El Remate (p284), just down the road.

Santa Elena is where you'll find banks, supermarkets and buses. Adjoining Santa Elena is San Benito (population 46,250). There's not really much for the average traveler here, unless you're up for a night of slumming it in one of the numerous *cantinas*.

History

Flores was founded on an island (*petén*) by a people called the Itzáes, who came here after being expelled from Chichén Itzá on Mexico's Yucatán Peninsula, maybe in the 13th century AD, maybe in the 15th. Flores was originally named Tayasal. Hernán Cortés dropped in on King Canek of Tayasal in 1525 on his way to Honduras, but the meeting was, amazingly, peaceable. Cortés left behind a lame horse, which the Itzáes fed on flowers and turkey stew. When it died, the Itzáes made a statue of it which, by the time a couple of Spanish friars visited in 1618, was being worshiped as a manifestation of the rain god Chac. It was not until 1697 that the Spaniards brought the Itzáes of Tayasal – by some distance the last surviving independent Maya kingdom – forcibly under their control. The God-fearing

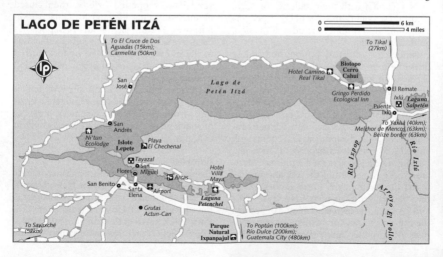

LAGO DE PETÉN ITZÁ

Spanish soldiers destroyed its many pyramids, temples and statues, and today you won't see a trace of them, although the modern town is doubtless built on the ruins and foundations of Maya Tayasal. Confusingly, the overgrown ruins named Tayazal, on the mainland peninsula just north of the island, date mostly from the Classic period, well before the Itzáes came to Flores.

Orientation

The airport is on the eastern outskirts of Santa Elena, 2km from the causeway connecting Santa Elena and Flores. Long-distance buses drop passengers at the terminal in Santa Elena, located 1km south of the causeway along 6a Av.

Information

EMERGENCY

Asistur (Tourist Police; ☎ 5414-3594)
Hospital San Benito (Calz de San Benito)

INTERNET ACCESS

Petén Net (Map p276; Calle Centro América; per hr Q10; 8am-10pm Mon-Sat, 9am-9pm Sun)
Tayasal Net (Map p276; per hr Q8; 8am-10pm Mon-Sat, 1-10pm Sun) Inside Hotel Posada Tayasal.

LAUNDRY

Lavandería San Miguel (Map p276; Calle Fraternidad; 8:30am-6pm Mon-Sat) Q35 to wash and dry a load.

MONEY

Banrural (Map p276; Avenida Flores), just off the Parque Central in Flores, changes traveler's checks, as does its airport branch. If you just need an ATM and aren't going to Santa Elena,

there is a Cajero 5B (on the Cirrus and Plus networks) in front of the Hotel Petén on Calle 30 de Junio (Map p276).

Other banks are on 4a Calle in Santa Elena. The following all change at least American Express US-dollar traveler's checks and have ATMs on the Cirrus and Plus networks:
Banco Agromercantil (Map p274; 9am-6pm Mon-Fri, 9am-1pm Sat) Also changes euros.
Banco Continental (Map p274; 9am-5pm Mon-Fri, 9am-1pm Sat)
Banrural (Map p274; 8:30am-7pm Mon-Fri, 8:30am-1pm Sat) On the west end of the street, toward San Benito. Also changes euros.

The bus terminal in Santa Elena also has a Cajero 5B ATM.

Many travel agencies and places to stay will change cash US dollars, and sometimes traveler's checks, though at poorer rates. **San Juan Travel** (see p274) will also change euros, Belize dollars and Mexican pesos, and give Visa, MasterCard, Diner's Club and American Express cash advances.

POST

Post office Flores (Map p276; Av Barrios); Santa Elena (Map p274; inside Centro Comercial Karossi, 4a Calle & 4a Av)

TOURIST INFORMATION

Inguat (Map p276; ☎ 7867-5334; ciudadfloresinfo center@gmail.com; Av Santa Ana; 8am-4pm Mon-Fri) The official tourist office has town maps and brochures, though reliable information may be harder to obtain.
Inguat Info Kiosk (Map p276; Playa Sur; 7-11am & 2-6pm) There's another info kiosk at the Aeropuerto Internacional Mundo Maya.

TRAVEL AGENCIES

Several travel agencies in Flores and Santa Elena offer trips to archaeological sites, shuttle minibuses and other services. In addition, most hotels can book tours, shuttles, buses and flights. Full-service agencies include the following:
Aventuras Turísticas (Map p276; ☎ 4034-9550; www.aventurasturisticas.com; Av Barrios) Shuttles to Cobán, tours to Tikal, bicycle rentals.
Martsam Travel (Map p276; ☎ 7867-5093; www.martsam.com; Calle 30 de Junio) At the entrance to Capitán Tortuga restaurant, this is a well-organized agency with a wide range of services.
Mayan Princess (Map p276; ☎ 7867-5045; bbbetore mate@hotmail.com; Calle Centro América)

San Juan Travel (☎ 5461-6010; sanjuant@hotmail. com) Flores (Map p276; Playa Sur); Santa Elena (Map p274; 2a Calle) Shuttles to Tikal; has two offices on Playa Sur.

Sights

On an island to the west of Flores, **Museo Santa Bárbara** (Map p274; ☎ 7926-2813; admission Q10; ☻ 9am-5pm) holds a grab bag of Maya artifacts from nearby archaeological sites, yellowing articles from National Geographic, and radio broadcasting equipment, all crammed into a small room. There are over 9000 pieces, according to the caretaker who has a story about every one of them. The old radios and phonographs were contributed by his father, who was an announcer for 40 years at Radio Petén, which still broadcasts from an adjacent building. After

browsing the museum, enjoy chilled coconuts at the cafe by the dock. It's a stone's throw from San Benito dock: phone or whistle for the boatman, who'll take you across for Q10.

Activities
VOLUNTEER WORK

The **Estación Biológica Las Guacamayas** (p306), in the Parque Nacional Laguna del Tigre, and the rehabilitation center at **Arcas** (p282) both offer the chance to work with wildlife. At Las Guacamayas, volunteers can observe and monitor species for research projects. There's a minimum two-week commitment, and volunteers pay Q170 a day for accommodation, kitchen use and transport to site; the fee is slightly lower for longer-term volunteers. If you're interested,

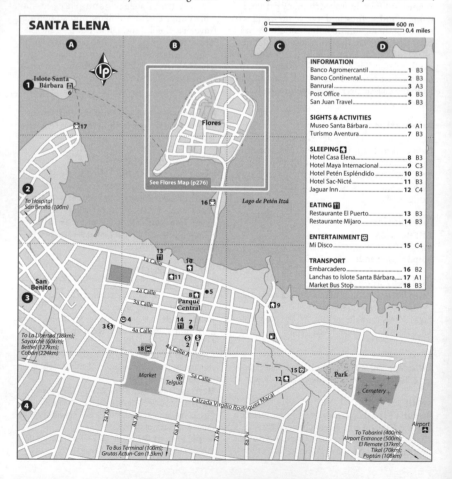

SANTA ELENA

0 ——————— 600 m
0 ——————— 0.4 miles

INFORMATION
Banco Agromercantil **1** B3
Banco Continental **2** B3
Banrural **3** A3
Post Office **4** B3
San Juan Travel **5** B3

SIGHTS & ACTIVITIES
Museo Santa Bárbara **6** A1
Turismo Aventura **7** B3

SLEEPING 🛏
Hotel Casa Elena **8** B3
Hotel Maya Internacional **9** C3
Hotel Petén Espléndido **10** B3
Hotel Sac-Nicté **11** B3
Jaguar Inn **12** C4

EATING 🍴
Restaurante El Puerto **13** B3
Restaurante Mijaro **14** B3

ENTERTAINMENT 🎭
Mi Disco **15** C4

TRANSPORT
Embarcadero **16** B2
Lanchas to Islote Santa Bárbara **17** A1
Market Bus Stop **18** B3

Islote Santa Bárbara 🏛 6

Flores

See Flores Map (p276)

Lago de Petén Itzá

To Hospital San Benito (100m)

San Benito

1a Calle

2a Calle

3a Calle

Parque Central

4a Calle

4a Calle A

To La Libertad (28km); Sayaxché (60km); Bethel (127km); Cobán (224km)

Market

Telgua

5a Calle

Calzada Virgilio Rodríguez Macal

3a Av

4a Av

6a Av

1a Av

8a Av

Park

Cemetery

Airport 🛫

To Tabarini (400m); Airport Entrance (500m); El Remate (37km); Tikal (70km); Poptún (106km)

To Bus Terminal (100m); Grutas Actun-Can (1.5km)

contact **Asociación Balám** (Map p276; ☎ 7867-5098; www.asociacionbalam.org), a Guatemalan NGO that develops and manages sustainable development projects in the Maya Biosphere Reserve. At Arcas, a reserve for the protection of endangered species, volunteers 'adopt' and feed animals. The fee of Q1000 a week covers food and accommodation. Language schools in San Andrés (p282) and San José (p282) provide the chance to get involved in community and environmental projects.

Tours

Various travel agencies in Flores (see p273) offer day tours to archaeological sites such as Tikal, Uaxactún, Yaxhá and Ceibal. Prices, with a guide and lunch, range from Q110 for a basic Tikal tour to Q1120 for a Ceibal excursion.

More demanding hiking-and-camping experiences to remote archaeological sites such as Nakum, El Perú, El Zotz, El Mirador, Nakbé and Wakná are offered by the outfits listed here. The three ecotourism committees, in the villages of El Cruce de Dos Aguadas (about 45km north of Flores by dirt road), Carmelita (some 35km beyond El Cruce de Dos Aguadas) and Paso Caballos (west of El Cruce de Dos Aguadas), were set up with the help of Conservation International and ProPetén, with the aim of fostering low-impact tourism benefiting local jungle communities. Comité guides are usually *xateros* (collectors of *xate*, a palm used in flower bouquets) or *chicleros* (collectors of chicle, used to make chewing gum) who know the forest very well, but may be light on the archaeological significance of the sites. There's no luxury on these trips: participants should be in good shape mentally and physically, as they'll sleep in hammocks, hike for long stretches through thick jungle, eat what's fed them and be munched by whatever ants, mosquitoes and ticks they're sharing the forest with.

Hostel Los Amigos (Map p276; ☎ 7867-5075; www.amigoshostel.com; Calle Central) Offers some of the lowest-cost tours to El Mirador and El Zotz.

Martsam Travel (Map p276; ☎ 7867-5093; www.martsam.com; Calle 30 de Junio) Works with Comités Comunitarios de Ecoturismo (Community Ecotourism Committees), which employ local guides from jungle communities, in the villages of El Cruce de Dos Aguadas and Carmelita.

Mayan Adventure (Map p276; ☎ 5830-2060; www.the-mayan-adventure.com; Av 15 de Septiembre) Coordinated by a German Mayanologist, it offers 'scientific' tours to sites currently under excavation, with commentary by archaeologists working at the sites.

Turismo Aventura (www.tours.guatemala.com) Flores (Map p276; ☎ 5510-2965; Calle Unión); Santa Elena (Map p274; ☎ 7926-0398; 6a Av 3-44) Guatemalan owned and operated agency offering quality excursions to such remote sites as Piedras Negras and El Mirador.

Maya Expeditions (see p74), based in Guatemala City, offers mild (ie good for families or inexperienced rafters) one- to three-day rafting expeditions on the Río Chiquibul, with options to visit lesser-known sites like Yaxhá, Nakum and Topoxte for Q700 to Q3750 per person.

LAKE TOURS

Boats at the *embarcaderos* (docks) opposite Hotel Petenchel and beside the Hotel Santana in Flores, and in the middle of the Flores–Santa Elena causeway, can be hired for lake tours. Prices are negotiable. An hour-long jaunt runs around Q150. A three-hour tour, which might include the Arcas animal conservation preserve

---

TOURS TO LOCAL ARCHAEOLOGICAL SITES

The sample prices are per person for two/four/five-plus people, normally including food, water, sleeping gear and Spanish-speaking guide.

Location	Duration	Cost
El Zotz and Tikal	3 days	Q2285/1620/1579
El Perú	3 days	Q2495/1540/1290
	2 days	Q2120/1250/1125
El Mirador-Nakbé-Wakná	7 days	Q4865/4200/3745
Yaxhá-Nakum-Tikal	3 days	Q2620/1830/1665
Yaxhá & Nakum	2 days	Q1625/1165/1040
Dos Pilas, Aguateca & Ceibal	3 days	Q3620/3080/3035

(p282), the Petencito Zoo, the isle of Santa Bárbara and its museum (p274) and the ruins of Tayazal should cost Q400 for three passengers, with stops and waiting time included.

Courses

Dos Mundos Spanish School (Map p276; ☎ 5830-2060; www.cafeyaxha.com; Calle Fraternidad) offers both one-on-one and group courses (Q835 and Q665 per week, respectively, for four hours of study daily). Accommodation and meals with a local family costs Q625 a week. Volunteer opportunities include working in a local orphanage.

Sleeping

Except for a few upscale properties along Santa Elena's waterfront, Flores makes a far

more desirable place to stay, unless you have a thing for traffic and dust.

FLORES
Budget

Hostel los Amigos (Map p276; ☎ 7867-5075; www.amigos hostel.com; Calle Central; dm Q30, r per person Q80; ☐) Flores' one true hostel, with a 10-bed dorm, hammocks and even a tree house, has grown quite organically in its six years of existence. All the global traveler's perks are here in abundance: nightly bonfires, happy hours, heaping helpings of organic food, yoga and cut-rate jungle tours.

Hospedaje Doña Goya (Map p276; ☎ 7867-5513; hospedajedonagoya@yahoo.com; Calle Unión; dm Q30, s/d Q70/110, without bathroom Q60/80) This family-run

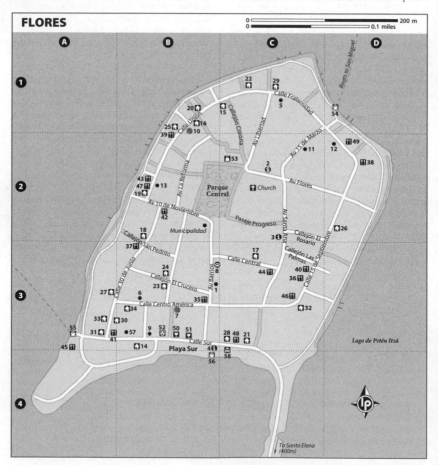

guesthouse is one of the best budget choices in town and, therefore, often full. The beds are comfortable, the water's hot and there's a roof terrace with a palm-thatched shelter and hammocks for enjoying lake views. The dorms are spacious and spotless. Breakfast is served with a smile in the cafe downstairs.

Hotel Mirador del Lago (Map p276; Calle 15 de Septiembre; s/d Q50/80, r with view Q100; 💻) Though minimally maintained, this holds a good position just up from the causeway, with a terrace facing the lake. Upstairs units catch good afternoon breezes. No telephone.

Hotel La Unión (Map p276; ☎ 5908-1037; Calle Unión; s/d Q50/90, r with view Q110; 💻) Considering the location beside the waterfront promenade, this well-maintained property is quite a deal, with relatively stylish decor in fan-cooled rooms. Check email at the downstairs cybercafe or enjoy cocktails on the lakeside terrace.

Hotel Santa Rita (Map p276; Calle 30 de Junio; s/d/tr Q60/80/120) It's never going to be beautiful, but at least the Santa Rita is cheap and central, with smallish, institutional green rooms along shared balconies. The upper-level units are a bit nicer than the lower ones, with tiled floors. No telephone.

Hotel Casa del Lacandón (Map p276; ☎ 7867-5594; Calle Unión; s/d/tr Q60/100/140) This one makes the most of its lakeside setting, with a lookout terrace and cafe. Though basic, the rooms

get a dash of style, and the ones at the back feature dandy views.

Hospedaje Doña Goya the 2nd (Map p276; ☎ 7867-5516; hospedajedonagoya@yahoo.com; Calle Unión; s/d Q70/140, r with balcony Q140; 🔀 💻) Doña Goya's second effort is even spiffier than her first – this one's got a jungle theme, with banisters made to look like climbing vines. Rooms are plain, airy and well scrubbed, with screened windows, and most give some kind of view. And like its predecessor, DG2 features a hammock-slung terrace.

Hotel Casablanca (Map p276; ☎ 5699-1371; Playa Sur; s/d Q70/100) The first hotel you reach coming off the causeway is family-run with simple, spacious rooms and a terrace for lake-gazing. The steady flow of traffic from Santa Elena means you'll probably be up early.

Hotel La Mesa de los Mayas (Map p276; ☎ /fax 7867-5268; mesamayas@hotmail.com; Callejón El Crucero; s/d Q75/150, with air-con Q125/200; 🔀) Alongside a narrow alley, the Mesa's one of the stalwarts on the Flores hotel scene. Rooms are very neat and decked out with pretty, checkered bedspreads and reading lamps; some feature plant-laden balconies.

Hotel Petenchel (Map p276; ☎ 7867-5450; Playa Sur; s/d Q100/120, with air-con Q150/170; 🔀) Eight spacious rooms, with firm beds and high arched ceilings, are set around a lush courtyard just off the causeway. In the event that El Petén ever experiences a chilly night, have no fear – showers here are superhot.

Hotel El Peregrino (Map p276; ☎ 7867-5115; peregrino@itelgua.com; Calle La Reforma; s/d Q100/150, with air-con Q175/300) El Peregrino is an older, family-run place with home cooking in the front *comedor*. Large rooms feature tile floors, powerful overhead fans and window screens.

Posada de la Jungla (Map p276; ☎ 7867-5185; Calle Centro América; s/d Q100/150, with air-con Q190/250) Also worth considering is this slender, three-story building with front balconies. Though a bit cramped, rooms are comfortably arranged, with quality beds.

Mayab Hotel (Map p276; ☎ 7867-5469; mayabhotel@gmail.com; Calle 30 de Junio; s/d Q125/175; 🖳) Despite the homely green facade, this shoreline property features an interior patio and an upstairs terrace overlooking the lake. Decent-sized, low-lit rooms have safes and good hot showers – No 8, with its rear balcony, is by far the nicest.

Midrange

our pick **Hotel Casa Amelia** (Map p276; ☎ 7867-5430; www.hotelcasamelia.com; Calle Unión; s/d Q180/280; 🅇 🖳 🛜) A newcomer on the Flores scene, the boutique-ish Casa Amelia offers bright, stylish chambers with excellent lake views. One of the taller structures along Flores' western shore, it features a balustraded roof terrace with views to San Miguel. Amelia and family also run the adjacent restaurant/bar, where a complimentary breakfast is served

Hotel Sabana (Map p276; ☎ /fax 7867-5270; www.hotelsabana.com; Calle Fraternidad; s/d Q190/250; 🅇 🛍) On the north side of the island, this larger, 28-room, less personal place has a rhomboidal pool in the middle (featuring family-sized Jacuzzi) and a super chilled terrace overlooking the lake.

Hotel Villa del Lago (Map p276; ☎ /fax 7867-5131; www.hotelvilladelago.com.gt; Calle 15 de Septiembre; s/d Q250/290; 🅇 🖳 🛜) Behind the old-fashioned facade, there's a cool, breezy interior that's long on potted plants and Grecian column work. Comfortable rooms have good furnishings and big ceiling fans; lake-view units are pricier. Breakfast is available, there's a delightful terrace upstairs, and the staff can do your laundry, exchange books and book flights.

Hotel Casazul (Map p276; ☎ 7867-5451; www.hotelesdepeten.com; Calle Fraternidad; s/d Q315/385; 🅇 🖳) They're not kidding when they call this the blue house – there's shades of it everywhere, from the plantation-style balconies to the nine individually decorated, spacious and

comfortable rooms. A couple have their own balconies and everyone can enjoy the 3rd-floor terrace.

Hotel Santana (Map p276; ☎ /fax 7867-5123; www.santanapeten.com; Calle 30 de Junio; s/d Q332/374; 🅇 🖳 🛍) 'Eclectic' best describes the melange of concrete, wood, thatch and wickerwork here, but it all hangs together somehow. Rooms are generously sized with ceiling fans and aquamarine walls, and if you get one out the back, you'll have a little balcony looking over the lake onto Isla Santa Bárbara.

Hotel Petén (Map p276; ☎ 7867-5203; www.hotelesdepeten.com; Calle 30 de Junio; s/d Q375/435; 🅇 🖳 🛍) Rooms are cheerily decorated here with a dash of chintz. Definitely choose the lake balcony units as they cost no more than interior ones. A good-sized indoor/outdoor swimming pool is inside the courtyard, and a restaurant/bar opens on a lakeside terrace.

Top End

Hotel La Casona de la Isla (Map p276; ☎ 7867-5200; www.hotelesdepeten.com; Calle 30 de Junio; s/d from Q410/475; 🅇 🖳 🛍) Popular with groups, this has a definite Caribbean flavor, augmented by cheery blue-and-yellow paint. Decorated with restraint, the smallish rooms line a long veranda facing a pool with a rock garden and an adjacent lake-view deck. The most appealing units, 31, 303 and 304, have windows facing the lake and gorgeous sunsets.

Gran Hotel de La Isla (Map p276; ☎ /fax 7867-5549; www.granhoteldeflorespeten.com; Playa Sur; s/d Q542/620; 🅿 🅇 🖳 🛍) This glossy business-class lodging holds a commanding presence at the west end of the Playa Sur. Along arched corridors with images of Maya royalty, the 45 rooms are luxuriously appointed, though the lake-view balconies are skimpier than you might expect. Leisure moments can be spent soaking in the outdoor and indoor pools or downing daiquiris in the Fisherman's Bar.

SANTA ELENA
Budget

Hotel Sac-Nicté (Map p274; ☎ 7926-2356; 1a Calle; s/d/tr from Q50/80/100; 🅿) About the best budget option on this side of the causeway, it's just a block up from the waterfront, though the glitzy Espléndido hotel eclipses any views. Standing behind a giant hedge, the place has an enticing air of abandonment. Rooms have ceiling fans and cold showers. Quality varies, and some downstairs units feel rather musty;

get one of the triples on the south side, with dusty balconies facing the interior gardens.

Jaguar Inn (Map p274; ☎ 7926-0002; Calz Rodríguez Macal 8-79; s/d Q125/180, with air-con Q170/225; P 🖳) Comfortable without being fancy, the Jaguar Inn is inside a secure compound by the river, with wood-paneled, faded rooms along a leafy patio. It's a decent deal, though its out-of-the-way location, 150m off the main road near the airport, may only appeal to travelers with vehicles.

Midrange

Hotel Casa Elena (Map p274; ☎ 7926-2223; www.hotel casaelenadelasflores.com; cnr 6a Av & 2a Calle; s/d Q358/400; P 🖳 🛒) Just south of the causeway, Casa Elena has bright, attractive rooms with photo art on soothing pastel walls. Some overlook Santa Elena's diminutive plaza, though *tuk-tuks* may get on your nerves. The interior units are the best, facing the big pool with waterslide. It has a bar, restaurant, roof terrace and spa for facials and pedicures.

Top End

Hotel Maya Internacional (Map p274; ☎ 7926-2083; www.villasdeguatemala.com; Av del Periférico, Calle 0, Zona 1; s/d Q705/830; P 🖳 🖵 🛒 🛒) One of the best reasons to stay in Santa Elena is this tropical-chic resort spreading over a landscaped marsh by the waterfront. The thatched big-top dining room is the center of activity; an adjacent wooden deck with a small infinity pool is great for sunset daiquiris. A boardwalk snakes through tropical gardens to reach the 26 rooms, thatch-and-teak affairs combining a jungly ambience with modern comforts. Rooms 49 to 54 give the best lake views.

Hotel Petén Espléndido (Map p274; ☎ 7926-0880; www.petenesplendido.com; 1a Calle 5-01; s/d Q1370/1520; P 🖳 🛒 🛒 🖴) Standing alongside the causeway with its own marina, the most formal hotel in the region pulls out all the stops, featuring room safes, bathroom telephones, great balcony views and possibly the only elevator in all of El Petén. Rooms could be bigger, but they're definitely comfortable and a couple of good restaurants and a poolside bar can keep you happy. If you're flying in, hook up a free shuttle from the airport.

Eating

FLORES

Antojitos Mamelina (Map p276; cnr Calle Centro América & Av Barrios; tostadas Q3; 🕙 5-9pm Thu-Sun) Mamelina opens her kitchen to the public on weekend evenings, attracting crowds of locals for her tostadas (topped with ground beef, beets or avocado), chicken sandwiches and flan.

Cool Beans (Map p276; Calle 15 de Septiembre; sandwiches Q18-30; 🕙 breakfast, lunch & dinner Wed-Mon; 🛒) Also known as Café Chilero, this laid-back place is more clubhouse with snacks than proper restaurant, featuring salons for chatting, watching videos or laptop browsing. The lush garden with glimpses of the lake makes a *tranquilo* spot for breakfast or veggie burgers. Be warned – the kitchen closes at 9:01pm sharp.

Restaurante Los Peches (Map p276; Playa Sur; mains Q25; 🕙 7am-10pm) Down by the causeway, family-run Peches serves inexpensive platters of chicken, steak or veggies, along with rice, tortillas and salad, in humble surroundings – and it's open early for breakfast.

Restaurante Casa Amelia (Map p276; ☎ 7867-5430; Calle Unión; mains Q25-70; 🕙 breakfast, lunch & dinner; 🛒) With to-die-for lake views from a rear terrace, comfy sofas and a pool table, Amelia's restaurant has a friendly, casual vibe. It's a place to kick back, watch the sun go down over a Cuba libre, and nosh on shrimp *ceviches*, fajitas and chicken wings.

Café Arqueológico Yax ha (Map p276; ☎ 5830 2060; Calle 15 de Septiembre; mains Q30-60; 🕙 breakfast, lunch & dinner Wed-Mon) Wallpapered with photos and articles relating to Maya sites, this cafe-restaurant is home base for an archaeological tour outfit. Apart from the usual egg-and-bean breakfasts, what's special here is the pre-Hispanic and Itzá items – pancakes with ramón seeds, yucca scrambled with mora herbs, chicken in chaya sauce.

La Galería del Zotz (Map p276; Calle 15 de Septiembre; mains Q40-60; 🕙 breakfast, lunch & dinner) An exhaustive survey of Flores' eateries concluded that this unassuming gallery-cum-natural foods cafe serves the town's finest cappuccinos and lattes, along with healthful breakfasts, pizzas, pastas and curries.

Restaurante & Pizzería Picasso (Map p276; Calle 15 de Septiembre; pizza Q35-120; 🕙 10:30am-10:30pm Tue-Sun) This long-standing, Italian-owned joint does primo wood-fired pizzas, with artwork on the walls courtesy of you-know-who and a cool little courtyard area.

Las Puertas (Map p276; ☎ 7867-5242; cnr Calle Central & Av Santa Ana; pastas & salads Q40-50; 🕙 8am-midnight Mon-Sat) An airy, atmospheric salon where overhead fans whir from wood beams and sweet-natured Q'eqchi' women work the bar, Las Puertas prepares an eclectic choice of dishes highlighted by pasta variations and abundant salads. There's live jazz or reggae most nights.

Suica Café (Map p276; ☎ 5353-5357; Calle Fraternidad; mains Q40-60; ☺ lunch & dinner Mon-Sat) Sushi in El Petén? Well, why not. The Japanese owners take a fair stab at all your faves (miso soup, tempura, sashimi) and only come up short when ingredients are lacking. Definitely worth a look.

our pick Il Terrazo (Map p276; Calle Unión; pasta Q48-72; ☺ breakfast, lunch & dinner Mon-Sat) Started by a Guatemalan couple who worked under a chef from Bologna, this Italian gourmet restaurant takes up a rooftop terrace underneath a thatched canopy. The fettuccine, tortellini and taglioni are all produced inhouse, and they'll prepare panini to go. The fruit smoothies are also unbelievable.

Restaurante El Peregrino (Map p276; ☎ 7867-5115; Av La Reforma; mains Q50; ☺ 7am-10pm) This refreshingly non-touristy *comedor* serves heaping helpings of homecooked fare such as porkbelly stew and breaded tongue. Ask for the daily lunch specials (Q20).

Capitán Tortuga (Map p276; Calle 30 de Junio; mains Q55-105; ☺ breakfast, lunch & dinner) A barnlike venue with a pair of lakeside terraces, this Carlos & Charlie's clone serves heapings of comfort food – especially pizzas – at medium prices. Beer-quaffing groups should opt for the *cubetazos* – five bottles in a bucket for Q75.

La Villa del Chef (Map p276; Calle Unión; salads Q34, mains Q59-95; ☺ lunch & dinner) Go out back to reach the rustic little deck built over the water at this casual, German-run restaurant emphasizing natural ingredients. Choose from a good selection of Middle Eastern salads and Guatemalan favorites. Don't miss the happy hour(s), from 5pm to 8pm.

La Luna (Map p276; cnr Calles 30 de Junio & 10 de Noviembre; mains Q63-115; ☺ noon-midnight Mon-Sat) In a class by itself, this popular restaurant cultivates a classic tropical ambience, with innovative chicken, fish and beef dishes surpassing similar dishes anywhere else in Guatemala. There are also good pasta and vegetarian options.

Raíces (Map p276; Playa Sur; mains Q80-100; ☺ 4-10pm Sun-Thu, 4pm-1am Fri & Sat) A broad deck and a flaming grill are the main ingredients at Raíces, a trendy, lakefront restaurant/bar. Chargrilled meats and seafood are the specialty, and you can choose your grills by the

pound or half-pound. Start things off with a Muppet (tequila plus 7-Up), one of many posh cocktails on the menu.

La Hacienda del Rey (Map p276; Calle 30 de Junio; steaks Q100; ☺ breakfast, lunch & dinner) This open-air affair at the west end of Playa Sur has an inviting tropical feeling, where you can catch an evening breeze and quaff a cold Gallo before tearing into a juicy steak. A 'Pyrex,' consisting of a pound and a half of Argentine cuts, feeds two or three (Q165). If it's just a snack you're after, order a couple of tacos de *arrachera* (skirt steak, Q15).

SANTA ELENA

Restaurante Mijaro (Map p274; 4a Calle; mains Q35-45; ☺ breakfast, lunch & dinner) You'll find good home cooking at both branches of this friendly, locally popular *comedor*, one on the main street and the other round the corner on 6a Av. The latter features a thatch-roofed garden area. Besides the grub, they do good long *limonadas* (lime-juice drink).

Restaurante El Puerto (Map p274; 1a Calle 2-15; main dishes Q100; ☺ 11am-11pm) Seafood is the star attraction at this breezy, open-air hall by the lakefront with a well-stocked bar at the front. It's an ideal setting to enjoy shellfish stews, *ceviches* or the famous *pescado blanco* – whitefish from the lake.

For a splurge with style, try the waterfront restaurant at the Hotel Maya Internacional (see p279).

Drinking

Flores doesn't exactly jive at night but there are a couple of places to hang out. Flores' little Zona Viva is a strip of bars along Playa Sur, and nearly all the lakeside restaurants in Santa Elena have afternoon happy hours, a great way to unwind and watch the sunset.

El Trópico (Map p276; Playa Sur; ☺ 5:30pm-1am Mon-Sat) This is a nice spot to start the night: the candlelit terrace is good for gazing at the lights of Santa Elena reflected across the lake while enjoying an icy *cerveza*.

La Playita (Map p276; Playa Sur) A mostly male gathering place (though they'll let girls in their playhouse), this waterfront drinking barn has been a Flores fixture for decades. Don Rafael, who spent his career building Johnson outboard motors, still works the bar. Sol by the liter for Q20, Gallos are Q10.

Entertainment

Locals gather in the cool of the evening for long drinks, snacks and relaxation in the

Parque Central, where a marimba ensemble plays some nights.

For cinematic options, Cool Beans (p279) has a video lounge and Hostel Los Amigos (p276) shows documentaries on Guatemala.

Aadictos (Map p276; Playa Sur) If you're up for dancing, join the raucous throngs on the raised floor of Aadictos, where DJs pump out merengue, rock and reggaetón each weekend

Mi Disco (Map p274; cnr 4a Calle & Calz Rodríguez Macal; cover Fri & Sat Q25) 'El Mi' is Santa Elena's major disco, a cavernous hall with a big stage for salsa combos. If you'd rather croon than dance, Monday to Wednesday evenings are reserved for karaoke.

Shopping

The **Castillo de Arizmendi** (Map p276; Parque Central; ☽ 8am-9pm) houses a series of shops with local handicrafts, particularly wood carvings by artists from El Remate working in mahogany, cedar and chicozapote.

Getting There & Away

AIR

Mundo Maya International Airport, sometimes called Petén International Airport, is just east of Santa Elena. **Taca** (☎ 2470-8222) has three flights daily between here and the capital (Q1177/1989 one way/return); it also flies to Cancún, Mexico. The Belizean airline **Tropic Air** (☎ 7926-0348) flies twice a day from and to Belize City, charging Q945 each way for the one-hour trip.

BUS & MICROBUS

The Terminal Nuevo de Autobuses is on 6a Av, about 1km south of the causeway to Flores. The following lines use the terminal:
Autobuses del Norte (☎ 7924-8131; www.adnauto busesdelnorte.com)
Fuente del Norte (☎ 7926-2999)
Línea Dorada (☎ 7924-8535)
Transportes María Elena (☎ 5850-4190)

Santa Elena's terminal is also used by a slew of microbuses, with frequent services to numerous destinations. The cooperative **ACTEP** (☎ 7924-8215), with an office on the left side of the terminal, runs micros to Poptún, Melchor de Mencos, San Andrés, Bethel-La Técnica, Paso Caballos and elsewhere, while others offer services to Sayaxché, El Remate and Tikal. Another cooperative, **AMSAP** (☎ 4250-9584), goes to San Andrés and San José on the north side of Lago de Petén Ixta; their micros depart from the left side of the terminal entrance. Second-class buses and some micros make an additional stop at 5a Calle, in the market area (the 'old' terminal) before heading out.

Departures include the following (as always, schedules are highly changeable and should be confirmed before heading out):
Belize City (four to five hours, 330km) Línea Dorada (Q160) leaves at 7am, returning from Belize City at 9:30am. This bus connects with boats to Caye Caulker and Ambergris Caye. It's cheaper but slower to take microbuses to the border and on from there (see Melchor de Mencos, p300).
Bethel/La Técnica (Mexican border) (Q35/40, 4½ hours, 127km) ACTEP runs microbuses to Bethel at 11am, 11:45am, 2:30pm, 3:45pm and 4pm, continuing on to La Técnica. For onward connections to Palenque, see p301.
Carmelita (Q25, five hours, 82km) Two Pinitas buses at 5:30am and noon, returning from Carmelita at 5am and 9am.
Chetumal (Mexico) (eight hours, 350km) Via Belize City, Línea Dorada (Q225) leaves at 7am, returning from Chetumal at 6am. Check Belizean visa regulations before you set off.
Cobán (six hours, 245km) Transportes Luna offers shuttle service from 9am (Q125), picking up passengers from their hotels; purchase tickets at Aventuras Turísticas (see p273). Or take a bus or minibus to Sayaxché, from where connecting microbuses leave for Cobán at 11am and 3pm. (See also p282.)
El Ceibo/La Palma (Mexico border) (Q30, four hours, 151km) Eleven El Naranjo–bound microbuses nearly every hour, from 4:40am to 6pm, stop at the El Ceibo junction, from where there are shuttles to the border (Q10, 15 minutes). At La Palma, on the Mexican side, you can find transport to Tenosique, Tabasco (one hour).
El Remate (Q20, 40 minutes, 29km) Microbuses leave every half hour from 5am to 6pm. Buses and minibuses to and from Melchor de Mencos will drop you at Puente Ixlú junction, 2km south of El Remate.
Esquipulas (Q110, eight hours, 440km) Transportes María Elena goes at 6am, 10am and 2pm via Río Dulce (Q60) and Chiquimula (Q100).
Guatemala City (eight to nine hours, 500km) Línea Dorada runs first-class buses at 10am and 10pm (Q150), plus a deluxe bus (Q190) at 9pm. Autobuses del Norte has 1st-class (Q150) and deluxe (Q200) buses at 9pm and 11pm, respectively. All Línea Dorada and Autobuses del Norte buses pick up passengers in front of the Gran Hotel de la Isla (p278) an hour prior to the Santa Elena terminal departure. Fuente del Norte runs 16 buses between 3:30am and 10:30pm (Q110), plus deluxe buses at 10am, 2pm, 9pm and 10pm (Q160), although security problems have been reported by passengers using this line.

Melchor de Mencos (Belizean border) (two hours, 100km) Microbuses (Q25) go about every hour, 5:45am to 6pm. Línea Dorada Pullmans en route to Belize City depart at 7am (Q35). See boxed text, p301, for more information on crossing the border here.

Poptún (1¾ hours, 113km) Take a Guatemala City–bound Línea Dorada bus (Q40) or a microbus (Q25), going every 10 minutes, via Dolores, from 5am to 6:30pm.

Puerto Barrios Take a Guatemala City–bound Fuente del Norte bus and change at La Ruidosa junction, south of Río Dulce.

Río Dulce (four hours, 212km) Take a Guatemala City–bound bus with Fuente del Norte (Q60) or Línea Dorada (Q100/125 *económico*/deluxe).

San Andrés/San José (Q7/10, 35/50 minutes, 22/25km) Microbuses depart around every 15 minutes, from 5am to 6:30pm, from the left side of the terminal entrance.

Sayaxché (Q20, 1½ hours, 60km) Microbuses depart about every 15 minutes, 5:45am to 6pm.

Tikal (Q50, 1¼ hours, 62km) Microbuses by Agencia Exploradores de la Cultura Maya depart at 5am, 7am, 9am and 1pm, returning at noon, 1:30pm, 3pm and 6pm. You could also take the Uaxactún-bound bus (Q35) at 2pm, which goes a bit slower.

CAR & MOTORCYCLE

Several car-rental companies have desks at the airport, including the following:

Hertz (☎ 7926-0415; peten@rentautos.com.gt)
Tabarini (☎ 7926-0253; www.tabarini.com)

SHUTTLE MINIBUS

Aventuras Turísticas (Map p276; ☎ 4034-9550; www.aventurasturisticas.com; Av Barrios) offers daily shuttles to Cobán (Q125, four hours), Lanquín, Semuc Champey and Antigua. **San Juan Travel** (see p274) operates shuttle minibuses to Tikal (Q60, 1¼ hours each way). They leave hourly from 5am to 10am. Most hotels and travel agencies can book these shuttles and they will pick you up where you're staying. Returns leave Tikal at 12:30pm, 2pm, 3pm, 4pm and 5pm. If you know which round-trip you plan to be on, ask your driver to hold a seat for you or arrange one in another minibus. If you stay overnight in Tikal and want to return to Flores by minibus, it's a good idea to reserve a seat with a driver when they arrive in the morning.

Getting Around

A taxi from the airport to Santa Elena or Flores costs Q20. Tuk-tuks will take you anywhere between or within Flores and Santa Elena for Q5. Aventuras Turísticas (p273) rents mountain bikes for Q30 per day.

AROUND FLORES
San Miguel & Tayazal

Covering the western end of the San Miguel peninsula, reached by frequent ferries from Flores, are the remains of **Tayazal** (admission Q5; ☉ 6am-6pm), among the last of the Maya capitals. It was settled by the Itzáes, refugees from the destroyed city of Chichén Itzá in Yucatán, who held out against the Spanish until 1697. Scholars concur that Tayazal was actually centered on the island of Flores, but remnants of the Itzáes' reign are scattered around the peninsula. The chiefly Classic-era mounds are overgrown by vegetation, and a few pockmarked stelae have been recovered. The real draw, though, is the chance to wander the forested spine of the peninsula, taking in panoramic views of the lake.

Colectivos (Q5 per person) make the five-minute crossing to San Miguel village from the northeast side of Flores whenever they have a boatload. San Miguel itself is a quiet, slow-moving place. To reach the ruins, walk 250m to the left along the shore from where the boat drops you, then turn up the paved street to the right. After 300m, turn left at the 'Playa' sign, passing a football field on your right. About another 600m on, a trail on the right leads to **Playa El Chechenal**, a swimming beach with a dock extending over turquoise waters and a picnic tables. Continue west another 300m to reach the main entrance to the site. From here it's a precipitous climb up the hillside – actually one of the pyramids of ancient Tayazal – to reach **El Mirador del Rey Canek**, an observation point with 360-degree views around Lago de Petén Itzá. The walk is best done in the morning, to avoid afternoon heat.

Arcas

The **Asociación de Rescate y Conservación de Vida Silvestre** (Wildlife Rescue & Conservation Association; ☎ 5476-6001; www.arcasguatemala.com; ☉ 8am-4pm), a Guatemalan NGO, has a rescue and rehabilitation center on the mainland northeast of Flores for wildlife such as macaws, parrots, jaguars, monkeys, kinkajous and coatis that have been rescued from smugglers and the illegal pet trade. Visitors can learn about Arcas' activities at its environmental education center (admission Q50), with a 1.5km interpretative trail featuring medicinal plants and animal tracks, an area for viewing animals that cannot be returned to the wild, and a bird observation deck. Phone ahead for a tour. Boatmen from Flores charge Q100, including an hour's wait while you tour the facility. It's also possible to walk the 5km (about 45 minutes) east from San Miguel.

Grutas Actun-Can

Try a bit of spelunking at the nearby limestone caverns of **Actun-Can** (admission Q20; 8am-5pm), which translates from Q'eqchi' Maya as 'Cave of the Serpent.' The caretaker will turn on the lights and provide the authorized interpretation of the weirdly shaped stalagmite and stalactite formations, including the Frozen Falls, the Marimba, and the Elephant's Foot. Bring a flashlight and adequate shoes – it can be slippery. Explorations take about 30 to 45 minutes.

A taxi from Flores should cost you Q30 to Q40, or Q100 to Q150 return with waiting time.

Laguna Petenchel

Hotel Villa Maya (7931-8350; www.villasdeguatemala. com; s/d Q635/705; P), on Laguna Petenchel, a small lake east of Santa Elena, is among the finest hotels in the area. Bungalows feature ceiling fans, views of the lake and blissful quiet. It has a patio restaurant, a tennis court, two swimming pools, two lagoons and a wildlife refuge. It's 4km north of the crossroads where the Guatemala City road diverges from the Tikal road, 8km east of Flores.

San Andrés

pop 11,100 / elev 112m

This small town on the northwest side of the lake hosts two Spanish-language schools: **Eco-Escuela de Español** (5940-1235; www. ecoescuelaespanol.org) This community-owned school emphasizes ecological and cultural issues and organizes environmental trips and volunteer opportunities; Q1230 a week includes room and board with a local family. **Nueva Juventud Spanish School** (5711-0040; www.volunteerpeten.com; Restaurant La Troja) Also environmentally oriented, this school is tied to a volunteer program that cares for the ecological park where the school is sited, and encourages volunteers to develop community projects. Classes cost Q25 per hour, homestays Q985 per week.

A few kilometers west of San Andrés, **Ni'tun Ecolodge** (5201-0759; www.nitun.com; s Q1045-1410, d Q1690-2010; P) is a beautiful property, set on 35 hestares of grounds where six species of hummingbird nest year-round. Bernie and Lore, who built and operate the lodge, are adventurers and conservationists. There are four spacious huts, with accommodation in

the rustic vein. Room rates include airport transfers and breakfast. They also offer adventure trips with transport in Land Cruisers to such destinations as Ceibal, Yaxhá and Tikal, with prices ranging from Q1000 to Q1200 per person per day.

For information on microbuses and buses to San Andrés, see p281.

San José

pop 1350 / elev 202m

San José, a few kilometers east along the lake from San Andrés, is peopled by Itzá Maya, descendants of the Flores area's pre-Hispanic inhabitants. The extraordinarily neat and orderly village climbs a hillside, with a little blue church at the top and a waterslide park at the lakefront. There's a Cajero 5B ATM.

The community-owned **Escuela Bio-Itzá** (7928-8056; escuelabioitza@hotmail.com) is part of an association working to keep Itzá traditions and language alive. It also manages a 35-sq-km nature reserve bordering the southern section of the Biotopo El Zotz, which is being outfitted for ecotourism. Cost for the usual 20 hours of one-on-one Spanish classes is Q1250 per week to live with a local family, or Q1670 to stay on the reserve. Students can help with community projects such as producing cosmetics and remedies from the medicinal plant garden, or helping the reserve rangers to monitor wildlife.

Hotel Bahía Taitzá (7928-8125; www.taitza.com; s/d Q300/400), west of the village, is an elaborate spread where you can truly unwind. Eight well-designed rooms, with high wood ceilings, soothing colors and lovely porches, are in two buildings, facing the lake across a lawn dotted with ficus trees. Wood-fired pizzas, paellas and other Euro-influenced fare are served under a beachfront *palapa*. The owners are a French-Guatemalan couple who run tours to Tikal, Yaxhá and further afield.

San José is a special place to be on the night of October 31, when perfectly preserved human skulls, normally housed in the church, are paraded around town on a velvet pillow followed by devotees in traditional dress, carrying candles. Throughout the night, the skulls make visits to predetermined houses, where blessings are sought, offerings made and a feast eaten.

For information on microbuses and buses to San José, see p281. There is no regular boat service.

Parque Natural Ixpanpajul

At **Parque Natural Ixpanpajul** (☎ 4146-7557; www.ixpanpajul.com; zip-line tour or Skyway adult/child Q205/124; ☑ 7:30am-6:30pm) you can ride horses, mountain bikes or tractors, or zip line your way through the jungle canopy. The big attraction is the Skyway, a 3km circuit of stone paths and six linked suspension bridges through the upper levels of the forest. Early morning and late afternoon are best for wildlife viewing. Camping and cabins are available for overnight stays. It's 2.5km south down the Guatemala City road from its junction with the Tikal road, 8km east of Flores. Get here by catching any Guatemala City-bound bus from Santa Elena, or call the park's **shuttle service** (☎ 5897-6766; Q75) to arrange transportation.

EL REMATE

The closest decent accommodation to Tikal lies in this idyllic spot on the shores of Lago de Petén Itzá. Just two roads, really, it's more relaxed and less built up than Flores, though there's plenty to do. Like Flores, it's accustomed to seeing foreigners but El Remate has its own ramshackle vibe. Most hotels are set up for swimming in – and watching the sun set over – the lake.

El Remate begins 1km north of Puente Ixlú (also called El Cruce), where the road to the Belize border diverges from the Tikal road. The village strings along the Tikal road for 1km to another junction, where an unpaved road branches west along the north shore of the Lago de Petén Itzá to the Biotopo Cerro Cahuí and beyond, to the villages of San José and San Andrés near the west end of the lake.

El Remate is known for its wood carving. Several shops on the lakeshore opposite La Mansión del Pájaro Serpiente sell local handicrafts.

If you're stuck for cash, you can change US dollars and traveler's checks and Belize dollars, at low rates, at La Casa de Don David (p286) or Sak Luk Hostel (see opposite). Hotel Las Gardenias offers ATM trips to Flores (Q200 for groups of up to five), as well as internet access (per hour Q12).

Sights & Activities

BIOTOPO CERRO CAHUÍ

The entrance to the 6.5-sq-km subtropical forest reserve, **Biotopo Cerro Cahuí** (admission Q40; ☑ 7am-4pm), is 1.75km west along the north-shore road from El Remate. The vegetation here ranges from *guamil* (regenerating slash-and-burn land) to rainforest. Trees include mahogany, cedar, ramón, broom, sapodilla (the extremely hard wood used in Maya temple-door lintels) and cohune palm, along with many types of bromeliads, ferns and orchids.

More than 20 mammal species roam the reserve, including spider and howler monkeys, ocelots, white-tailed deer, raccoons and armadillos. Bird life, too, is rich and varied. Depending on the season and migration patterns, you might see kingfishers, ducks, herons, hawks, parrots, toucans, woodpeckers and the famous ocellated (or Petén) turkey, a big bird resembling a peacock.

A network of loop trails starts at the road and goes up the hill, affording a view of the whole lake and of Laguna Salpetén to the east. The trail called Los Escobos (4km long – it takes about 2¼ hours), through secondary growth forest, is good for spotting monkeys. The guards at the entrance can give you directions.

The admission fee includes the right to camp or sling your hammock under small thatch shelters inside the entrance. There are toilets and showers.

The dock opposite the entrance is the best place to swim along the generally muddy shore of the lake.

VOLUNTEERING

Project Ix-Canaan (www.ixcanaan.com) supports improvement of health, education and opportunities for rainforest inhabitants. Operating here since 1996, the group runs a community clinic, women's center, library and research center. Volunteers work in the clinic, build and maintain infrastructure and lead workshops or teach classes to local children.

OTHER ACTIVITIES

Most El Remate accommodations can book five-hour **horseback rides** to Laguna Salpetén and a small archaeological site there (Q150 per person) or two-hour boat trips for **birdwatching** or nocturnal **crocodile spotting** (each Q100 per person). Try Casa de Ernesto or Hotel Mon Ami (see p286; the latter also offers sunset lake tours with detours up the Ixlu and Ixpop rivers (Q150 per person).

Ascunción, next door to the Sak-Luk Hostel, rents kayaks (Q35 per hour), bicycles (per hour/day Q10/60) and horses (Q150 for 2½ hours).

BIG DAY COMING

With the turn-of-the-millennium hysteria well behind us, here comes the next apocalyptic date: December 20, 2012 – though it may be December 23 or it may not even be in this century, depending on whose interpretation you believe. According to certain new age prophets – and at least Hollywood appears to believe them – this date will mark the end of the world as we know it. It's all foretold by Maya prophets, they say, since the Maya calendar comes to a grinding halt on that date. Although there is no evidence that the ancient Maya linked the date to any doomsday scenarios, apocalyptic forecasts have a way of gaining their own momentum, and gazes will be fixed on the Mundo Maya as this big day approaches.

The winter solstice of 2012 corresponds to the Maya long count calendar date of 13.0.0.0.0. This number represents the end of the 13th *baktun* – each of which equals about 394 years on the Gregorian calendar. Thirteen being a magic number in Maya numerology, the calendar of historical time was set at 13 *baktuns* (or about 5125 years) from the beginning of the current world, after which the calendar is reset and the whole cycle starts again. However, nothing in the *Popul Vuh* or any other Maya annals suggests the freeway-crashing, asteroid-colliding spectacle played out in the 2009 movie, *2012*. The only existing reference within the catalogue of Maya glyphs has been found on a monument at Tortuguero, a small site in Tabasco, Mexico, but it is so oblique that few archaeologists agree on how to interpret it. More likely the date will simply entail a bit of chronological housekeeping, something like setting the clock forward in springtime.

Still, Maya ceremonial activity is sure to be on the upswing for this putatively momentous occasion. And among the shamanistic-minded, there'll be plenty to do in Guatemala, especially for those with a more upbeat interpretation of the calendar transition (the ones predicting catastrophe probably shouldn't be making travel plans anyway). The country is gearing up for throngs of seekers who are already planning to descend on Maya turf to herald the dawning of a new 'age of Brotherhood … the coming together of the Eagle and the Condor,' according to Anne Lossing, director of Project Ix-Canaan, the El Remate–based group that is organizing **Unificación Maya** (www.unificationmaya.com), an event that has since 2005 attracted visitors on a long count of their own. This annual jamboree unfolds at various energy centers around El Petén for a week before the solstice, drawing shamans and spiritual guides from throughout Guatemala and beyond its borders. It's all leading up to the mother of all dates, 13.0.0.0.0, when the culminating ceremony will be held on Tikal's Gran Plaza. It's all free, though accommodation certainly won't be: 2012 looks to be the highest of high seasons in Guatemala.

Tours

The Hotel Mon Ami (p286) and Sak-Luk Hostel (see right) offer reasonably priced jungle treks to El Mirador, Yaxhá and Nakum. **La Casa de Don David** (p286) offers tours to Yaxhá (Q370/410/490 per person with four/three/two people), Uaxactún (Q535 per person) and Tikal (Q200 per person for collective tour, departing at 5:30am daily). Prices include English-speaking guide and lunch but not admission to site. **Hotel Gardenias** (p286) has slightly cheaper tours and runs a collective excursion to Yaxhá at 7:30am and 1:30pm (Q100 per person, minimum four people).

Lou Simonich (☎ 5883-2905; lou_simonich@yahoo.com) offers a four-day cycling/camping tour to Xultun and Uaxactún, with a visit to the recently discovered Maya murals at San Bartolo. He also offers three- to four-day canoe trips to El Perú with camping at the Estación Biológica Las Guacamayas (p306; Q2200 to 3000 per person), as well as local bird-watching expeditions along the two rivers that enter Lago Petén-Itzá (Q150 per person). Lou provides all camping gear and bakes pastries and whole-wheat bread for the group.

Sleeping

ALONG THE MAIN ROAD

Sak-Luk Hostel (☎ 5494-5925; www.sakluk.com; dm/hammock/bungalow per person Q33/35/60) Run by sculptor Erwin, this slice of hippie heaven offers fancifully designed huts in adobe constructions scattered around a hillside. Though the facilities could use an upgrade – or even a proper dusting – you may appreciate the artistic contributions made by former guests. The dorm, with mosquito-netted beds, has a good lake vantage. The restaurant offers toothsome Italian and vegetarian dishes.

Hotel Sun Breeze (☎ 7928-8044; sunbrezzehotel@ gmail.com; s/d Q75/100, without bathroom Q40/60) Down the lane toward the lake, nearly at the junction, is this excellent-value homey guesthouse. Rear units are best, with lake views through well-screened windows. It's a short stroll to El Remate's public beach.

Hostal Hermano Pedro (☎ 2261-4419; www.hhpedro. com; s/d Q75/150) Set in a two-story wood-and-stone house, 20m off to the right from the main road, the spacious rooms are refreshingly simple and comfortable, with a few frills like lacy curtains, big fans and balcony porches. Guests can use the kitchen or grab a hammock in the common room.

Posada Ixchel (☎ 7928-8475; hotelixchel@yahoo.com; s/d Q80/120, without bathroom Q50/60) This family-owned place nearer the village's main junction is a superior deal, with spotless, airy rooms around a cobbled courtyard. The little private sitting areas out front of the rooms are a nice touch.

Hotel Las Gardenias (☎ 5992-3380; hotellasgarde nias@yahoo.com; s/d from Q85/125; 🍴 🖥) Right at the junction with the north shore road, this cordial hotel/restaurant/shuttle operator has two sections: the wood-paneled rooms at the front are bigger, those in the rear are appealingly removed from the road. All feature comfortable beds with woven spreads, attractively tiled showers and porches with hammocks.

our pick Hotel La Mansión del Pájaro Serpiente (☎ 7928-8498; s/d Q270/390, with air-con Q370/450; 🍴 🖥) Dotted along a steep hillside, these cottage-like cabins all make the most of their perch, with wraparound windows and front lounges overlooking the lake. Peacocks strut around the landscaped grounds, which feature a pool with hammocks under nearby *palapa* shelters, and a reasonably priced restaurant-bar.

ALONG THE NORTH-SHORE ROAD

Casa de Doña Tonita (☎ 5767-4065; dm/s/d Q25/40/60) Managed by an adorable family, Doña Tonita's has four basic rooms with two single beds each in a two-story wood-and-thatch *rancho*, plus a dorm over the restaurant, which serves tasty, reasonably priced meals. There's just one shower. Across the road is a fine perch for sunset gazing.

Casa de Ernesto (☎ 5750-8375; casadeernesto@ymail. com; s/d Q100/200, without bathroom Q40/70; 🍴) Ernesto and his clan offer cool and comfortable adobe huts in the woods with thatched roofs, tile floors, and good rustic-style beds. Add Q50 for air-con. Canoe rentals, horseback riding to Laguna Salpetén and expeditions for the great white fish are among the activities offered.

Hotel Mon Ami (☎ 7928-8413; www.hotelmonami. com; dm Q57, s/d Q125/205, without bathroom Q85/165; 🛜) A 15-minute walk from the Tikal road and a stone's throw from the Biotopo Cerro Cahui, this maintains a good balance between jungle wildness and Euro sophistication. Quirkily furnished cabins and dorms with hammocks are reached along candlelit paths through gardens bursting with local plant life, though the bathhouse needs a feng-shui overhaul. Fans of French cuisine will appreciate the open-air restaurant (see opposite).

La Casa de Don David (☎ 7928-8469; www.lacasade dondavid.com; s/d incl breakfast Q225/425; 🍴 🖥) Just west of the junction, this full-service outfit has spotless, modern rooms with Maya textiles for decor. All feature verandas and hammocks facing the broad lakefront lawn, dotted with wacky topiary. Owner David Kuhn – the original Gringo Perdido – is a botanist from Florida, who'd love to show you his garden, including a young ceiba tree and the night-blooming *pitaya petenera*.

Gringo Perdido Ecological Inn (☎ 5804-8639; www. hotelgringoperdido.com; campsite per person Q40, r per person Q290, incl breakfast & dinner Q370; 🅿) Waking up here is like waking up in paradise, with no sound but the lake lapping at the shore a few steps from your door. Eight rooms have one double and one single bed or bunk bed, mosquito nets and full-wall canvas roll-up blinds to give you the sensation of sleeping in the open air. A few lakeside bungalows offer a bit more seclusion. There's also a grassy campground with thatched-roof shelters for slinging hammocks and a Maya sauna. The inn will be a center of Maya ceremonial activity during the 2012 calendar change (see boxed text, p285). By the time you read this, the inn will have opened an 'eco-luxury resort' next door, the Hotel Pirámide Paraíso. The Gringo Perdido is 3km along the north-shore road from the main Tikal road.

Hotel Camino Real Tikal (☎ 7926-0204; www. caminorealtikal.com.gt; r Q1212; 🅿 🍴 🖥) Two kilometers further along the lake is the luxury Camino Real, the fanciest hotel in El Petén, with 72 air-con rooms featuring lake-view balconies and all the comforts. Two restaurants, a bar and a coffee shop keep guests happy, as do the Tikal and Cerro Cahuí tours, pool, kayaking, sailing, windsurfing and beach sports. See the website for package deals.

Eating

Most hotels have their own restaurants and there are simple *comedores* scattered along the main road.

Nakun's (pizza Q35; ☺ breakfast, lunch & dinner) Out on the main drag, this cheery shack features a lakeside balcony. Pizzas are the main attraction, made with real mozzarella cheese.

La Casa de Don David (mains Q15; ☺ breakfast, lunch & dinner) Staffed by waitresses in fetching mini-*cortes* (wraparound skirts), this splendid open-air dining hall serves a good breakfast, including banana pancakes (Q30), fruit and granola, and a collection of *National Geographic* articles on Maya sites to browse over coffee. Nightly specials include vegetarian fare.

Mon Ami (mains Q50-80; ☺ breakfast, lunch & dinner) Further along the north-shore road, here's the French jungle bistro you've dreamt of, a peaceful palm-thatched affair. Try the fresh whitefish or the big *ensalada francesa*.

Las Orquideas (pasta Q55, mains Q65; ☺ lunch & dinner Mon-Sat) Almost next door to Doña Tonita, Las Orquideas has a genial Italian owner-chef cooking up genuine Mediterranean fare, with tempting desserts too.

Getting There & Around

El Remate is linked to Flores by a frequent microbus service (see p281).

For Tikal, collective shuttles leave El Remate at 5:30am, 6:45am, 7:45am and 8:45am, starting back at 2pm, 3pm, 4pm and 6pm (Q50 round trip). Any El Remate accommodations can make reservations. Or catch one of the hourly shuttles (Q30) or regular microbuses (Q15) passing through from Santa Elena to Tikal.

For taxis, ask at Hotel Sun Breeze. A one-way ride to Flores costs about Q200; round trip to Tikal costs Q350.

For Melchor de Mencos on the Belizean border, get a minibus or bus from Puente Ixlú, 2km south of El Remate. Alternatively, Casa de Ernesto offers daily departures to Belize City at 5:45am and 8:15am (Q160), as well as to Palenque, Mexico, at 4:30pm (Q340).

MACANCHÉ

Situated along the banks of the lagoon of the same name, this little village is home to one of the finer accommodations options in the region, **El Retiro** (☎ 5751-1876; www.retiro-guatemala. com; campsite per person Q25, cabin per person incl breakfast & dinner Q200). The three, soon to be four, comfortable cabins, down by the water's edge, are reached along pebbly trails through plantings of cedar, allspice and bird of paradise. Camping is also possible, with the option of renting a tent for Q50 per person. You'll find an excellent dock for swimming and a good restaurant offering a different buffet dinner daily (Q50).

El Retiro sits on a private nature reserve, with walking trails through the ruin-dotted rainforest to several lagoons populated by crocodiles. Boat tours of these lagoons and jungle walks are offered (Q100 per person). Also on the grounds is a herpetarium, holding specimens of the venomous fer-de-lance and Morelet's crocodile.

Scattered around the property is a series of *chultunes* – holes carved into the ground rock with a circular capping stone. Their purpose remains a mystery, but educated guesses suggest they were used either for food storage or religious rituals.

Any bus heading for Belize can drop you at Macanché village, from where it's a 2km walk to the hotel, or you can call and get picked up.

TIKAL

Towering pyramids poke above the jungle's canopy to catch the sun. Howler monkeys swing noisily through the branches of ancient trees as brightly colored parrots and toucans dart to a cacophony of squawks. When the complex warbling of some mysterious jungle bird tapers off, the buzz of tree frogs fills the background and it will dawn on you that this is indeed hallowed ground.

Certainly the most striking feature of **Tikal** (☎ 2367-2837; www.parque-tikal.com; admission Q150; ☺ 6am-6pm) is its steep-sided temples, rising to heights of more than 44m. But Tikal is different from Copán, Chichén Itzá, Uxmal, and most other great Maya sites, because it is fairly deep in the jungle. Its many plazas have been cleared of trees and vines, its temples uncovered and partially restored, but as you walk from one building to another you pass beneath the dense canopy of rainforest. Rich, loamy aromas of earth and vegetation, a peaceful air, and animal noises contribute to an experience not offered by other Maya sites.

You can visit Tikal on a day trip from Flores or El Remate. You can even make a literal flying visit from Guatemala City in one day, using the daily flights between there and

MUNDO MORMON

You've no doubt seen their young troops in white shirts and ties, proselytizing in pairs around the globe. But members of The Church of Jesus Christ of Latter Day Saints have a special interest in the Mundo Maya, and Mormon tourism to El Petén is consistently strong. According to Mormon scripture, the sect's forebears migrated here around the time of the Maya golden age. Cities that resemble Tikal and Aguateca are described, and the Preclassic El Mirador flourished around the same time the lost tribe is supposed to have shown up in this part of the world. Coincidence? They don't think so. Though their link to the Maya race may seem tenuous, contemporary Mormons, curious about the location where the story of their ancestors unfolded, travel to the Maya world to learn about the history of the Mesoamerican civilizations and to glean some connection to their seminal tract, *The Book of Mormon*. As the story goes, a group of Israelites crossed the sea to arrive somewhere in the Americas around 600 BC, a journey which they recorded in their annals. Jesus Christ himself is believed to have visited this hemisphere after being crucified and resurrected. The records of this refugee sect were subsequently interred, turning up some 1500 years later when they were miraculously delivered to the American Joseph Smith, who translated them as *The Book of Mormon*, 'a record of God's dealings with the ancient inhabitants of the Americas.' Though the church has not authorized any Maya sites as specifically referred to in the book, various Mormon researchers have devoted themselves to combing the archaeological record throughout El Petén and Yucatán, citing for example the appearance of white-skinned figures with Semitic features in Maya murals and pottery at Ceibal (see p302) as evidence for the presence of the Nephites, as the early Christian tribe was known, among the Maya.

Flores airport. But you'll get more out of Tikal by spending a night here, enabling you to visit the ruins twice and to be here in the late afternoon and early morning, when there are fewer other tourists and the wildlife is more active.

History

Tikal is set on a low hill, which becomes evident as you ascend to the Gran Plaza from the entry road. The hill, affording relief from the surrounding low-lying swampy ground, may be why the Maya settled here around 700 BC. Another reason was the abundance of flint, used by the ancients to make clubs, spear points, arrowheads and knives. The wealth of this valuable stone meant good tools could be made, and flint could be traded for other goods. Within 200 years the Maya of Tikal had begun to build stone ceremonial structures, and by 200 BC there was a complex of buildings on the site of the Acrópolis del Norte.

CLASSIC PERIOD

The Gran Plaza was beginning to assume its present shape and extent by the time of Christ. By the dawn of the early Classic period, around AD 250, Tikal had become an important religious, cultural and commercial city with a large population. King Yax Ehb' Xooc, in power about AD 230, is looked upon as the founder of the dynasty that ruled Tikal thereafter.

Under Chak Tok Ich'aak I (King Great Jaguar Paw), who ruled in the mid-4th century, Tikal adopted a brutal method of warfare, used by the rulers of Teotihuacán in central Mexico. Rather than meeting their adversaries on the plain of battle in hand-to-hand combat, the army of Tikal used auxiliary units to encircle the enemy and throw spears to kill them from a distance. This first use of 'air power' among the Maya of Tikal enabled Siyah K'ak' (Smoking Frog), the Tikal general, to conquer the army of Uaxactún; thus Tikal became the dominant kingdom in El Petén.

By the middle of the Classic period, in the mid-6th century, Tikal's military prowess and its association with Teotihuacán allowed it to grow until it sprawled over 30 sq km and had a population of perhaps 100,000. But in 553, Yajaw Te' K'inich II (Lord Water) came to the throne of Caracol (in southwestern Belize), and by 562, using warfare methods learned from Tikal, he had conquered Tikal and sacrificed its king. Tikal and other Petén kingdoms suffered under Caracol's rule until the late 7th century.

TIKAL'S RENAISSANCE

A powerful king named Jasaw Chan K'awiil I (682–734, also called Ah Cacao or Ruler A), 26th successor of Yax Ehb' Xooc, restored not only Tikal's military strength but also its primacy in the Maya world. He conquered the greatest rival Maya state, Calakmul in Mexico, in 695, and his successors were responsible for building most of the great temples around the Gran Plaza that survive today. King Ah Cacao was buried beneath the staggering height of Templo I.

Tikal's greatness waned around 900, but it was not alone in its downfall, which was part of the mysterious general collapse of lowland Maya civilization.

REDISCOVERY

No doubt the Itzáes, who occupied Tayazal (now Flores), knew of Tikal in the late Postclassic period (1200–1530). Perhaps they even came here to worship at the shrines of old gods. Spanish missionary friars who moved through El Petén after the conquest left brief references to these jungle-bound structures, but their writings moldered in libraries for centuries.

It wasn't until 1848 that the Guatemalan government sent out an expedition, under the leadership of Modesto Méndez and Ambrosio Tut, to visit the site. This may have been inspired by John L Stephens' bestselling accounts of fabulous Maya ruins, published in 1841 and 1843 (though Stephens never visited Tikal). Like Stephens, Méndez and Tut took an artist, Eusebio Lara, to record their archaeological discoveries. An account of their findings was published by the Berlin Academy of Science.

In 1877 the Swiss Dr Gustav Bernoulli visited Tikal. His explorations resulted in the removal of carved wooden lintels from Templos I and IV and their shipment to Basel, where they are still on view in the Museum für Völkerkunde.

Scientific exploration of Tikal began with the arrival of English archaeologist Alfred P Maudslay in 1881. Others continued his work, Teobert Maler, Alfred M Tozzer and RE Merwin among them. Tozzer worked at Tikal on and off from the beginning of the 20th century until his death in 1954. The inscriptions at Tikal were studied and deciphered by Sylvanus G Morley.

Since 1956 archaeological research and restoration have been carried out by the University Museum of the University of Pennsylvania (until 1969) and the Guatemalan Instituto de Antropología e Historia. Since 1991, a joint Guatemalan-Spanish project has worked on conserving and restoring Templos I and V.

In the mid-1950s an airstrip was built at Tikal. In the early 1980s the road between Tikal and Flores was improved and paved, and direct flights to Tikal were abandoned. The Parque Nacional Tikal (Tikal National Park) was declared a Unesco World Heritage Site in 1979.

Orientation & Information

The 550-sq-km Parque Nacional Tikal contains thousands of separate ruined structures. The central area of the city occupied about 16 sq km, with more than 4000 structures.

The road from Flores enters the national park 17km south of the ruins. The gate opens at 6am. From the parking lot, it's a short walk to the information kiosk; the ticket booth is to the left, along the path to the site entrance. Tickets are Q150 per person and are valid only for the day of purchase. Multilingual guides are available at the information kiosk. These authorized guides always display their accreditation carnet, listing the languages they speak. Before 7am, the charge for a half-day tour is Q100 per person. After that you pay Q450 for a group of up to eight people; or ask if you can join a private group.

The visitor center sells books, maps, souvenirs, hats, insect repellent, sun block and other necessities; it also houses a restaurant and museum. Near the visitor center are Tikal's three hotels, a camping area, a few small comedores, another museum and a disused airstrip. The Jaguar Inn will exchange US dollars cash and traveler's checks at a poor rate. You can check your email at the Jaguar Inn (p294); it's a hefty Q50 per hour, but you are out in the jungle after all.

It's a five-minute walk from the ticket booth to the entry gate where tickets are checked. Just beyond, there's a large map posted. From here, it's a 1.5km walk (20 to 30 minutes) southwest to the Gran Plaza. The walk from the Gran Plaza southeast to the Templo de las Inscripciones is over 1km; from the Gran Plaza north to Complejo P, it's 800m; from the Gran Plaza west to Templo IV it's over 600m. Seeing the sunrise from Templo IV at the west end of the main site is possible from about October to March: although the site officially opens at 6am, those staying at park hotels may enter at 5am.

To visit all the major building complexes, you must walk at least 10km, probably more, so wear comfortable shoes with good rubber

TIKAL

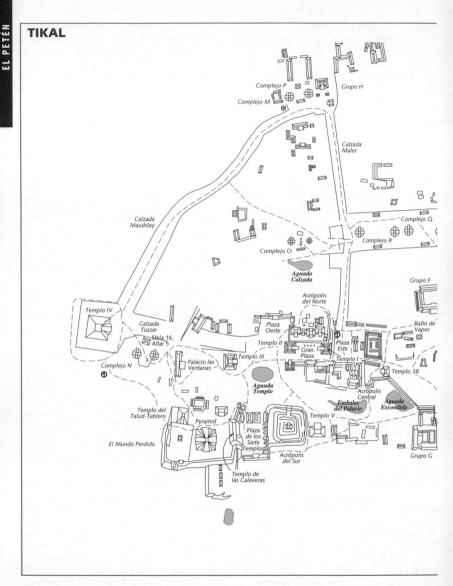

treads that grip well. The ruins here can be very slick from rain and organic material, especially during the wet season. Bring plenty of water, as dehydration is a real danger if you're walking around all day in this heat. Please don't feed the coatis (pisotes) that wander about the site.

For more complete information on the monuments at Tikal, pick up a copy of Tikal –

A Handbook of the Ancient Maya Ruins, by William R Coe, which is available in Flores and at Tikal for Q150. A book you're best off finding before you come is The Lords of Tikal, by Peter D Harrison, a vivid, cogent summary of the city's history. Guards at the ticket booth will try to sell you an 'official' site map but it's fairly useless. A better map, available at the

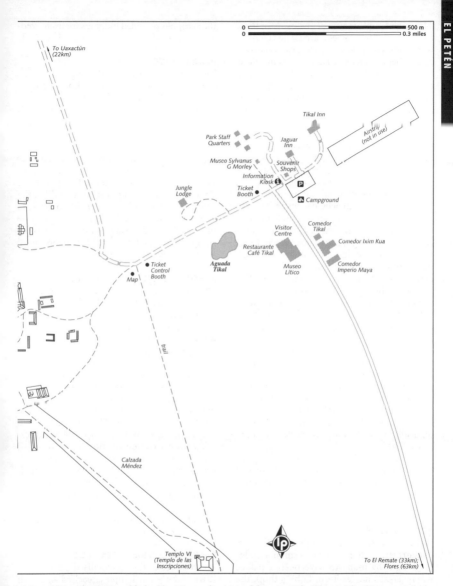

0 — 500 m
0 — 0.3 miles

To Uaxactún
(22km)

Tikal Inn

Park Staff
Quarters

Jaguar
Inn

Airstrip
(not in use)

Museo Sylvanus
G Morley

Souvenir
Shops

Information
Kiosk

Jungle
Lodge

Ticket
Booth

P

Campground

Comedor
Tikal

Comedor Ixim Kua

Visitor
Centre

Restaurante
Café Tikal

Museo
Lítico

Comedor
Imperio Maya

Aguada
Tikal

Ticket
Control
Booth

Map

trail

Calzada
Méndez

Templo VI
(Templo de las
Inscripciones)

To El Remate (33km);
Flores (63km)

visitor center shops, is published by Mapas de Guatemala (Q20).

Sights & Activities
GRAN PLAZA

The path comes into the Gran Plaza around the **Templo I**, the Templo del Gran Jaguar (Temple of the Grand Jaguar). This was built to honor –

and bury – Ah Cacao. The king may have worked out the plans for the building himself, but it was actually erected above his tomb by his son, who succeeded to the throne in 734. The king's rich burial goods included stingray spines, which were used for ritual bloodletting, 180 jade objects, pearls and 90 pieces of bone carved with hieroglyphs. At the top of the

44m-high temple is a small enclosure of three rooms covered by a corbeled arch. The sapodilla-wood lintels over the doors were richly carved; one of them was removed and is now in a Basel museum. The lofty roofcomb that crowned the temple was originally adorned with reliefs and bright paint. When it's illuminated by the afternoon sun, it is still possible to make out the figure of a seated dignitary.

Although climbing to the top of Templo I is prohibited, the views from **Templo II** just across the way are nearly as awe-inspiring. Templo II, also known as the Temple of the Masks, was at one time almost as high as Templo I, but it now measures 38m without its roofcomb.

Nearby, the **Acrópolis del Norte** (North Acropolis), while not as immediately impressive as the twin temples, is of great significance. Archaeologists have uncovered about 100 different structures, the oldest of which dates from before the time of Christ, with evidence of occupation as far back as 600 BC. The Maya built and rebuilt on top of older structures, and the many layers, combined with the elaborate burials of Tikal's early rulers, added sanctity and power to their temples. Look especially for the two huge, powerful wall masks, uncovered from an earlier structure and now protected by roofs. The final version of the acropolis, as it stood around AD 800, had more than 12 temples atop a vast platform, many of them the work of King Ah Cacao. Several objects unearthed from the burial tombs within the North Acropolis are on display in the Sylvanus G Morley Museum (see p294).

On the plaza side of the North Acropolis are two rows of stelae. These served to record the great deeds of the kings, to sanctify their memory and to add power to the temples and plazas that surrounded them.

ACRÓPOLIS CENTRAL
South and east of the Gran Plaza, this maze of courtyards, little rooms and small temples is thought by many to have been a palace where Tikal's nobles lived. Others think the tiny rooms may have been used for sacred rites and ceremonies, as graffiti found within them suggest. Over the centuries the configuration of the rooms was repeatedly changed, suggesting that perhaps this 'palace' was in fact a noble or royal family's residence and alterations were made to accommodate groups of relatives. A hundred years ago, one part of the acropolis provided lodgings for archaeologist Teobert Maler when he worked at Tikal.

PLAZA OESTE
The West Plaza is north of Templo II. On its north side (obscured by vegetation) is a large late-Classic temple. To the southwest, across the Calzada Tozzer (Tozzer Causeway), is **Templo III**, 55m high. Only its tippy top has been excavated, allowing you to see a temple the way the last Tikal Maya and first white explorers saw them. A scene carved into the lintel at its summit depicts a figure in an elaborate jaguar suit, believed to be the ruler Dark Sun. From this point, you could strike south toward the Mundo Perdido or west to Templo IV along the Tozzer Causeway, one of several sacred byways built in the temple complexes of Tikal, no doubt for astronomical as well as aesthetic purposes.

ACRÓPOLIS DEL SUR & TEMPLO V
Due south of the Gran Plaza is the South Acropolis. Excavation has hardly even begun on this mass of masonry. The palaces on top are from late-Classic times (the time of King Moon Double Comb), but earlier constructions probably go back 1000 years.

Templo V, the remarkably steep structure just east of the South Acropolis, is 58m high and was built sometime between the 7th and 8th centuries AD. Unlike the other great temples, this one has slightly rounded corners, and one tiny room at the top. The room is less than 1m deep, but its walls are up to 4.5m thick. A recent excavation of the temple revealed a group of embedded structures, some with geometric designs and Maya calendars on their walls. Rather than using the broad front stairs to scale the structure, you ascend via a steep wooden staircase on its left side. The view from the top is wonderful, giving you a 'profile' of the temples on the Gran Plaza.

PLAZA DE LOS SIETE TEMPLOS
To the west of the Acrópolis del Sur is the Plaza of the Seven Temples, reached via a path that enters the plaza at its south end. The little temples with their stout roof combs, all in a line along the east side of the plaza, were built in late-Classic times. Three additional temples stand at the south end. On the north side of the plaza is an unusual triple ballcourt; another, larger version in the same design stands just south of Templo I. The seven temples are

currently the subject of an ongoing excavation project to restore them to their early splendor, and a model of the complex's layout can be viewed amid the maintenance buildings by the north entry to the plaza.

EL MUNDO PERDIDO
About 400m southwest of the Gran Plaza is El Mundo Perdido (Lost World), a large complex of 38 structures with a huge pyramid in its midst. Unlike the rest of Tikal, where late-Classic construction overlays work of earlier periods, El Mundo Perdido exhibits buildings of many different periods: the large pyramid is thought to be essentially Preclassic (with some later repairs and renovations); the Templo del Talud-Tablero, early Classic; and the Templo de las Calaveras (Temple of the Skulls), late Classic.

The pyramid, 32m high and 80m along the base, has a stairway on each side and had huge masks flanking each stairway, but no temple structure at its top. Each side of the pyramid displays a slightly different architectural style. Tunnels dug into the pyramid by archaeologists reveal four similar pyramids beneath the outer face; the earliest (Structure 5C-54 Sub 2B) dates from 700 BC, making this pyramid the oldest Maya structure at Tikal.

TEMPLO IV & COMPLEJO N
Complex N, near Templo IV, is an example of the 'twin-temple' complexes popular with Tikal's rulers during the late-Classic period (though it will take some imagination to discern the partially excavated mounds). These complexes are thought to have commemorated the completion of a *katun,* or 20-year cycle in the Maya calendar. This one was built in 711 by Ah Cacao to mark the 14th *katun* of *baktun* 9. (A *baktun* equals about four centuries.) The king himself is portrayed on Stele 16, one of the finest stelae at Tikal, in an enclosure just across the path. Beside the stele is the remarkably preserved Altar 5, a circular stone depicting the same king accompanied by a priestly figure in the process of exhuming the skeleton of a female ruler.

Templo IV, at 65m, is the highest building at Tikal and the second-highest pre-Columbian building known in the western hemisphere, after La Danta at El Mirador. It was completed about 741, probably by order of Ah Cacao's son, Yax Kin, who was depicted on the carved lintel over the middle doorway (now in a museum in Basel, Switzerland), as the western boundary of the ceremonial precinct. From the base it looks like a precipitous little hill. Steep wooden steps lead to the top. The view east is almost as good as from a helicopter – a panorama across the jungle canopy, with the temples of the Gran Plaza and Temple V (to the right) poking through.

TEMPLO DE LAS INSCRIPCIONES (TEMPLO VI)
Compared to Copán or Quiriguá, there are relatively few inscriptions on buildings at Tikal. The exception is this temple, 1.2km southeast of the Gran Plaza. On the rear of the 12m-high roofcomb is a long inscription; the sides and cornice of the roofcomb bear glyphs as well. The inscriptions give us the date AD 766. Stele 21 and Altar 9, standing before the temple, date from 736. The stele had been badly damaged (part of it was converted into a *metate* for grinding corn!) but has now been repaired.

NORTHERN COMPLEXES
About 1km north of the Gran Plaza is **Complejo P**. Like Complejo N, it's a late-Classic twin-temple complex that probably commemorated the end of a *katun*. **Complejo M**, next to it, was partially torn down by the late-Classic Maya to provide building materials for a causeway, now named after Alfred Maudslay, which runs southwest to Templo IV. **Grupo H**, northeast of Complexes P and M, with one tall, cleared temple, had some interesting graffiti within its temples (we're not talking about the moronic modern scrawls now disfiguring them).

Complejo Q and **Complejo R**, about 300m due north of the Gran Plaza, are very late-Classic twin-pyramid complexes with stelae and altars standing before the temples. Complex Q is perhaps the best example of the twin-temple type, as it has been partly restored. Stele 22 and Altar 10 are excellent examples of late-Classic Tikal relief carving, dated 771.

MUSEUMS
Tikal has two museums. The **Museo Lítico** (Stone Museum; admission Q10; ⏱ 8am-4:30pm Mon-Fri, 8am-4pm Sat & Sun), the larger of the two, is in the visitor center. It houses a number of stelae and carved stones from the ruins. Outside is a large model showing how Tikal would have looked around AD 800. The photographs taken by Alfred P Maudslay and Teobert Maler of the jungle-covered temples in various stages of discovery, in the late 19th century, are particularly striking.

BIRD-WATCHING AT TIKAL

As well as howler and spider monkeys romping through the trees of Tikal, the plethora of birds flitting through the canopy and across the green expanses of the plazas is impressive. The ruined temple complexes present ideal viewing platforms for this activity, often providing the ability to look down upon the treetops to observe examples of the 300 or so bird species (migratory and resident) that have been recorded here. Bring binoculars and a copy of *The Birds of Tikal: An Annotated Checklist*, by Randell A Beavers, or *The Birds of Tikal*, by Frank B Smythe, both available at the visitor-center shop. Early morning is the best time to go bird-watching, and even amateur bird-watchers will have their share of sightings here. Tread quietly and be patient, and you'll probably see some of the following birds in the areas specified:

- Tody motmots, four trogon species and royal flycatchers around the Templo de las Inscripciones.

- Two oriole species, keel-billed toucans and collared aracaris in El Mundo Perdido.

- Great curassows, three species of woodpecker, crested guans, plain chachalacas and three tanager species around Complejo P.

- Three kingfisher species, jacanas, blue herons, two species of sandpiper, and great kiskadees at the Aguada Tikal (Tikal Reservoir) near the entrance. Tiger herons sometimes nest in the huge ceiba tree along the entrance path.

- Red-capped and white-collared manakins near Complejo Q; emerald toucanets near Complejo R.

Also, look for several hawk species near the reservoirs, hummingbirds and ocellated turkeys (resembling a cross between a turkey and peacock) throughout the park, and several parrot species and Aztec parakeets while exploring the ruins.

The **Museo Sylvanus G Morley** (Museo Cerámico, Museum of Ceramics; admission Q10, free with Tikal site ticket; 9am-5pm Mon-Fri, 9am-4pm Sat & Sun) is near the Jaguar Inn. It has some fascinating exhibits, including the burial goods of King Moon Double Comb, carved jade, inscribed bones, shells, stelae, ceramics and other items recovered from the excavations.

TIKAL CANOPY TOUR

At the national park entrance, you can take a fairly expensive one-hour treetop tour through the forest by harness attached to a series of cables linking trees up to 300m apart, with **Tikal Canopy Tour** (☎ 5819-7766; www.canopy tikal.com; admission Q248; 7am-5pm).

Sleeping & Eating

The days when intrepid visitors could convince park guards (with a Q50 'tip') to let them sleep atop Templo IV are over. If you are caught in the ruins after hours, you're likely to be escorted out for your own safety. Your best bet to catch some solitude at the ruins and get an early glimpse of the wildlife is to stay overnight and be at the ticket control booth at opening time.

Other than camping, there are only three places to stay at Tikal, and tour groups often have many of the rooms reserved. But staying here does enable you to relax and savor the dawn and dusk, when most of the jungle birds and animals can be seen and heard (especially the howler monkeys). The chances of getting a room depend a lot on the season. In the low season (from after Easter to late June, and from early September to Christmas), you will probably secure a room without reservation. At other times it's advisable to book. Arrive by early afternoon to sort out any difficulties – if everything fails, you'll still have time to get back to El Remate. One way of ensuring a room is to become a group tourist yourself. Almost any travel agency in Guatemala offers Tikal tours, including lodging, a meal or two, a guided tour and transportation, and they needn't be prohibitively expensive.

Jaguar Inn (☎ 7926-0002; www.jaguartikal.com; campsite per person Q25, with tent Q75, s/d Q346/504; P ⊠ ⌨) Although the little duplex bungalows here are kinda jammed together and the walls are thin, it still makes a decent, relatively cheap sleep in the park. Hammocks on the little porches are a bonus. An attractive little restaurant serves pastas and salads.

our pick Jungle Lodge (☎ 7861-0446, 2476-8775; www.junglelodgetikal.com; s/d Q562/710, without bathroom Q290/314; P ⌨ ⌨) The largest and loveliest of the hotels was originally built to house archae ologists working at Tikal. Self-contained bungalows are well spaced throughout rambling, jungly grounds where ocellated turkeys and agoutis roam. The restaurant-bar is the classiest around these parts, serving veggie pastas, crepes, pepper steak and other international dishes in a tropical ambience (main dishes Q80 to Q100).

Tikal Inn (☎ 7861-7444· www.tikalinn.com· s/d from Q530/620, s/d bungalow Q677/843; P ☐ ☎) Built in the late '60s, this resort-style lodging offers rooms in the main building and thatched bungalows alongside the pool and rear lawn, with little porches out front. All are simple, spacious and quite comfortable. The most secluded accommodations are the least expensive, in a handful of cabins at the end of a sawdust trail through the forest. Rates drop substantially when the hotel decides it isn't high season. You can pay an extra Q150 for the breakfast and dinner package.

There's no need to make reservations if you want to stay at Tikal's **campground** (campsite per person Q30), opposite the visitor center. This is a large, grassy area with a clean bathroom block, plenty of space for tents, and *palapa* shelters for hanging hammocks.

As you arrive in Tikal, look on the right-hand side of the road to find the little *comedores:* Comedor Imperio Maya, Comedor Ixim Kua (the most appealing), and Comedor Tikal. These comedores offer dining in rustic surroundings with generally unimaginative fare like grilled chicken or grilled steak (Q40 to Q50); some serve veggie plates consisting of boiled *güisquil* (squash), carrots, beans and plantains. All are open from 5am to 9pm daily.

In the visitor center, Restaurant Café Tikal has a more upmarket attitude, though prices are only slightly higher than at the *comedores*, with pastas and hamburgers among the offerings. Among the hotel restaurants the Jungle Lodge is best.

Picnic tables beneath shelters are located just off Tikal's Gran Plaza, with soft-drink and water vendors standing by, but no food is sold. If you want to spend all day at the ruins without having to make the 20- to 30-minute walk back to the *comedores*, carry food and water with you.

Getting There & Away
For details of transport to and from Flores and Santa Elena, see p281. From Belize, you could hire one of the red microbuses run by Asetur,

which charge Q575/660 one way/return for up to four persons from Melchor de Mencos to Tikal; additional passengers are Q60 each. To go to Tikal and continue onward to Flores, they charge Q905, plus Q85 for additional passengers. Otherwise, get a bus to Puente Ixlú, sometimes called El Cruce, and switch there to a northbound minibus or bus for the remaining 36km to Tikal. Note that there is little northbound traffic after lunch. Heading from Tikal to Belize, start early and get off at Puente Ixlú to catch a bus or minibus eastward. Be wary of shuttles to Belize advertised at Tikal: these have been known to detour to Flores to pick up passengers!

UAXACTÚN
pop 700 / elev 175m
Uaxactún (wah-shahk-*toon*), 23km north of Tikal along an unpaved road through the jungle, was Tikal's political and military rival in late Preclassic times. It was conquered by Tikal's Chak Tok Ich'ak I (King Great Jaguar Paw) in the 4th century, and was subservient to its great sister to the south for centuries thereafter, though it experienced an apparent resurgence during the Terminal Classic, after Tikal went into decline.

Uaxactún village lies either side of a disused airstrip, a remnant of the age when planes were the only way to reach this inaccessible spot and a flight from Santa Elena cost Q5.

EXPLORE MORE OF EL PETÉN

The Petén region is literally brimming with smaller, largely unexcavated archaeological sites. Some are hard to get to, some are right by the highway. Here are a few of the more intriguing ones that you might want to check out:

El Chal Right by the Poptún–Flores highway, this site with a ballcourt and some carvings is built on a ridge, with some good views.

Ixlú Two kilometres south of El Remate on the shore of Laguna de Salpetén.

Machaquilá Some finely preserved stelae are left from this mysterious city, located on the banks of the Río Machaquilá, some 55km west of Poptún.

San Bartolo Discovered in 2003, this features one of the best-preserved Maya murals with a depiction of the creation myth from the *Popul Vuh*. It's approximately 40km northeast of Uaxactún, near the Río Azul.

The strip now serves as pasture and a football field. Villagers make an income from collecting chicle, *pimienta* (allspice) and *xate* (exported to Holland for floral arrangements) in the surrounding forest. A new timber extraction operation is supposedly employing sustainable methods but critics have their doubts about this. Most of the wood is exported to the US for building materials; a sawmill operates on the east end of the village.

About halfway along the airstrip, roads go both left and right to the ruins. Village boys will want to guide you: you don't need a guide to find the ruins, but you might want to let one or two of them earn a small tip.

At the time of writing there was still just one phone for public use, in an office on the south side of the airstrip, open till around 6pm. To reach anyone in Uaxactún call ☎ 7783-3931, then wait a few minutes for them to fetch your party. There is currently no cellphone coverage, though that may well have changed by the time you read this.

Sights

Research performed by the Carnegie Institute in the 1920s and '30s laid the groundwork for much of the archaeological study that followed in the region, including the excavations at Tikal. Back then, excavators simply cut into the sides of the temples indiscriminately, looking for graves. Instead of leaving things in situ, they'd cart off their finds to display in faraway museums. Sometimes they used dynamite, destroying many of the temples. The pyramids at Uaxactún were uncovered and stabilized so that no further deterioration would result, but they were not restored.

The buildings are grouped on five low hills. Head south from the airstrip to reach Grupo E, a 10- to 15-minute walk. The most significant temple here is **Templo E-VII-Sub**, among the earliest intact temples excavated, with foundations going back perhaps to 2000 BC. It lay beneath much larger structures, which have been stripped away. Holes discovered on its flat top could have been used for poles that would have supported a wood-and-thatch temple. The pyramid is part of a group with astronomical significance: seen from it, the sun rises behind **Templo E-I** on the longest day of the year and behind **Templo E-III** on the shortest day. Also look for the somewhat deteriorated jaguar and serpent masks on this pyramid's sides.

About a 20-minute walk to the northwest of the runway are Grupo B and Grupo A, the latter featuring the more formidable structures around the city's main square. In 1916 the American archaeologist Sylvanus Morley uncovered a stele dating from the 8th *baktun* at Grupo A. Thus the site was called Uaxactún, meaning 'eight stone.' Stele 5, at Grupo B, displays Tikal's signature glyph, from which archaeologists deduced that Uaxactún was under that city's sway by the date inscribed, 358.

Although officially there's an admission fee to enter the site, there's seldom anyone around to collect it.

Much of the attraction here is the absolute stillness and isolation. Few visitors make it up this way. Cedar, *ramón* (breadnut) and *escobo* are among the giant trees around the park grounds.

Though many of the objects unearthed at the site ended up in museums around the world, the **Colección Dr Juan Antonio Valdez** at the Hotel El Chiclero (see opposite) holds a remarkable wealth of Maya pottery from Uaxactún, Yaxhá and as far away as Oaxaca, Mexico. Almost everything remains perfectly intact, and many objects feature clearly visible embellishments. There are vases, cups, plates, bowls, incense burners and tall vessels for drinking chocolate. Some of the objects were brought to caretaker Neria by villagers who knew of the collection, and she can tell you the history, origin, meaning and use of each one. A case contains some of the most precious finds: stone earrings, arrowheads and three plates showing the dance of the corn god. The plates were the only items ever purchased for the collection, from looters.

Tours

Tours to Uaxactún can be arranged in Flores or at the hotels in El Remate and Tikal. The Jungle Lodge in Tikal (p294) has a trip departing daily at 8am and returning at 3pm, costing Q625 per person, including guide and lunch.

Hector Aldana Nuñez, from Aldana's Lodge (see opposite), is an English-speaking guide specializing in nature-oriented tours of the region. He leads three-day treks to El Zotz and Tikal for around Q1500 per person. He also offers survival training (Q620 per day), in which participants learn to find sustenance and shelter in the jungle; machetes are provided.

Neria from El Chiclero can organize trips to more remote sites such as El Mirador (p308),

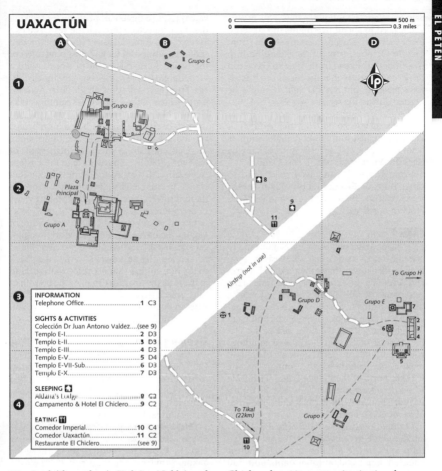

UAXACTÚN

Río Azul (three days), Xultún, Nakbé and San Bartolo.

Sleeping & Eating

See p295 for information about phoning Uaxactún.

Aldana's Lodge (posadaaldana@gmail.com; campsite per person Q15, s/d Q25/40) To the right off the street leading to Grupos B and A, the Aldana family offers half a dozen clapboard cabins, with thin mattresses on pallets. Father and son Alfido and Hector Aldaña lead tours to jungle sites, and Amparo prepares good meals. Camping using Aldana's equipment costs Q20 per person.

Campamento, Hotel & Restaurante El Chiclero (campamentoelchiclero@gmail.com; campsites per person Q25, r Q100) On the north side of the airstrip, El Chiclero has 10 spartan, institutional green rooms underneath a thatched roof, with decent mattresses and mosquito-netted ceilings and windows. Clean showers and toilets are in an adjacent out-building; lights out at 10pm. Perky owner Neria does the best food in town (Q50 for soup and a main course with rice). Accommodation prices are very negotiable.

A few basic *comedores* also provide food, including Comedor Uaxactún and Comedor Imperial Okan Arin.

Getting There & Away

A Pinita bus leaves Santa Elena for Uaxactún (Q35) at 2pm, passing through El Remate around 3pm and Tikal by 4pm, and starting back for Santa Elena from Uaxactún between

6am and 7am the following day. This means you'll need to spend two nights in Uaxactún to see the ruins. During the rainy season (from May to October, sometimes extending into November), the road from Tikal to Uaxactún can become pretty muddy: locals say it is always passable but a 4WD vehicle might be needed during the wet.

If you're driving, the last chance to fill your fuel tank as you come from the south is at Puente Ixlú, just south of El Remate. Shuttles from El Remate to Uaxactún and back, by La Casa de Don David (p285), cost Q580.

From Uaxactún, unpaved roads lead to other ruins at El Zotz (about 30km southwest), Xultún (35km northeast) and Río Azul (100km northeast).

YAXHÁ

The Classic Maya sites of Yaxhá, Nakum and El Naranjo form a triangle that's the basis for a national park covering more than 37,000 hectares and bordering the Parque Nacional Tikal to the west. Yaxhá (☎ 5204-1851; admission Q80; ⏱ 6am-5pm), the most visited of the trio, stands on a hill between two sizable lakes, Lago Yaxhá and Lago Sacnab. The setting, the sheer size of the site, the number of excellently restored buildings and the abundant jungle flora and fauna all make it particularly worth visiting. The site is 11km north of the Puente Ixlú–Melchor de Mencos road, accessed via unpaved road from a turnoff 32km from Puente Ixlú and 33km from Melchor de Mencos.

Occupied as early as 600 BC, Yaxhá (translated as 'blue-green water') achieved its cultural apex in the 8th century AD, when it counted some 20,000 inhabitants and 500 buildings, including temples, palaces and residential complexes.

It takes about two hours to wander round the main groups of ruins, which have been extensively excavated and reconstructed. Cover the site in a clockwise fashion, traversing the original road network. The first group of buildings you come to, Plaza C, is one of a pair of astronomical observatories. Take the Calzada de las Canteras to the Southern Acropolis, a complex of palatial structures from which Yaxhá's aristocracy could watch the games going on in the ball court below. To the northwest stands one of Yaxhá's most ancient constructions, the Greater Astronomical Complex (Plaza F). The arrangement is similar to the one at Uaxactún's Grupo E, with an observation tower (unexca-

vated) facing a three-part platform for tracking the sun's trajectory through the year. You can ascend the pyramidal tower (there's a wooden staircase alongside) for jaw-dropping views of the North Acropolis to the northeast, with a formidable temple rising above the jungle foliage. From here, take the Calzada de las Aguadas north to reach the Plaza de las Sombras (aka Grupo Maler), where, archaeologists say, throngs of citizens once gathered for religious ceremonies. Return toward the entrance along the Calzada Este to reach the high point of the tour (literally), **Structure 216** in the Eastern Acropolis. Also called the Temple of the Red Hands, because red handprints were discovered there, it towers over 30m high, affording views in every direction.

On an island near the far (south) shore of Laguna Yaxhá is a late Postclassic archaeological site, **Topoxté**, where the dense covering of ruined temples and dwellings may date back to the Itzá culture that occupied Flores island at the time the Spanish came. At the bottom of the Calzada del Lago is the boat landing, from where a boatman might be willing to take you to Topoxté for around Q250.

Sleeping & Eating

On the lake shore below the Yaxhá ruins is Campamento Yaxhá, where you can camp for free on raised platforms with thatched roofs. Outbuildings have showers and toilets. Drinking water can be purchased at a store, but you must bring food.

Campamento Ecológico El Sombrero (☎ 4147-6830; www.ecosombrero.com; s/d Q420/560, without bathroom Q180/345; ℗), on the southern shore of Laguna Yaxhá, 2km from the ruins and 250m off the approach road, is an excellent place to stay. It has good-sized, neat and clean rooms in solar-powered, mosquito-netted bungalows amid gardens overlooking the lake. You could also camp here or sling a hammock for Q40. The kitchen, overseen by the Italian owner, is of a high standard, and there's a small library on local archaeology. *Lancha* tours to Topoxté are offered (Q250) as well as night crocodile observation tours, horseback riding and overnight trips to Nakum, El Naranjo and Holmul and other lesser-known Maya sites in the vicinity. There's a 2km trail on the grounds, where monkeys, armadillos and pumas have been spotted. Call here in advance and the friendly owners will pick you up from the bus stop.

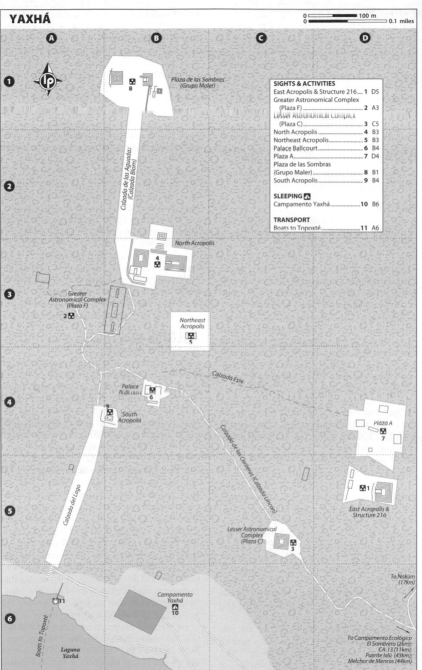

YAXHÁ

0 — 100 m
0 — 0.1 miles

SIGHTS & ACTIVITIES

East Acrópolis & Structure 216 .... **1**	D5
Greater Astronomical Complex (Plaza F).................................. **2**	A3
Lesser Astronomical Complex (Plaza C).................................. **3**	C5
North Acrópolis **4**	B3
Northeast Acrópolis **5**	B3
Palace Ballcourt............................. **6**	B4
Plaza A... **7**	D4
Plaza de las Sombras (Grupo Maler)............................ **8**	B1
South Acrópolis............................. **9**	B4

SLEEPING
Campamento Yaxhá......................**10**	B6

TRANSPORT
Boats to Topoxté..........................**11**	A6

Plaza de las Sombras (Grupo Maler)

Calzada de las Aguadas (Calzada Blom)

North Acrópolis

Greater Astronomical Complex (Plaza F)

Northeast Acrópolis

Calzada Este

Palace Ballcourt

South Acrópolis

Plaza A

Calzada de los Canteras (Calzada Lincón)

Calzada del Lago

East Acrópolis & Structure 216

Lesser Astronomical Complex (Plaza C)

To Nakúm (17km)

Campamento Yaxhá

Boats to Topoxté

Laguna Yaxhá

To Campamento Ecológico El Sombrero (2km); CA-13 (11km); Puente Ixlú (43km); Melchor de Mencos (44km)

Getting There & Away

Agencies in Flores (p275) and El Remate (p285) offer organized trips to Yaxhá, some combined with Nakum and/or Tikal. To get there independently, take the daily 1pm bus from Santa Elena's terminal (Q25); in the reverse direction buses go at 7am and 3pm. Red Asetur microbuses can be hired from Melchor de Mencos for around Q550 return for up to four passengers; or Q820 with onward transport to Flores. Alternatively, catch any Melchor–Flores microbus to the Yaxhá turnoff (also called 'La Maquina'), from which there is a 6am bus to Yaxhá; otherwise, be prepared to walk the 11km to the site.

NAKUM

A contemporary of Tikal, Nakum was a significant port on the Holmul river during the late-Classic period, when that waterway linked Tikal with the Caribbean coast. It's 17km north of Yaxhá, a 1½ hour drive over a rough road that's impassable from August to January (though it was improved by the crew of *Survivor Guatemala,* which was shot here).

Remote as this spot is, it's particularly exciting to find such a formidable group of structures here. The excavated section is not huge but it packs a lot in. Excavation is ongoing here and you're likely to see the archaeology crews at work. Archaeological research focuses on the predominance of *talud-tablero* (stepped building style, with alternating vertical and sloping sections) type structures in the south section, suggesting a connection with Teotihuacán in Mexico, and seeks to understand why Nakum flourished during the Terminal Classic at a time when its contemporaries were collapsing all around it.

The site features two major architectural groups, the North and South Sectors, connected by a causeway; most of the excavated structures are in the latter. The most interesting of these, in the part dubbed the **Plaza Central**, features an unusually well preserved roofcomb with a clearly visible mask. In tandem with the pyramidal structure opposite (under excavation), it presumably served as some kind of astronomical observatory like similar ones found in Tikal, Uaxactún and Yaxhá.

Moving south from the Plaza Central, you enter the **South Acropolis**, a walled compound on a raised platform covering a 170m-by-150m area, comprising 12 courtyards surrounded by 33 buildings, which housed palatial residences. This arrangement was in place around 900 AD, though there is evidence that the site had been occupied for the previous 14 centuries. What's unique about some of the courtyards here, like Patio 1, is that they were completely enclosed by buildings, a layout not found elsewhere in the Maya world. To the south, Patio 6 contained the Palacio Real, where Nakúm's ruling class dwelled. To study some examples of pre-Hispanic graffiti, enter **Edificio N**, a striking oblong structure below the plaza's southwest corner. To the northeast, Patio 9 features a squat rectangular building with an arched entryway that may have served as a *temascal,* or ceremonial sauna. Outside the South Acropolis to the east are stelae bearing dates from the 9th century, among the latest recorded dates in the Maya lowlands.

Campamento Ecológico El Sombrero (p298) in Yaxhá can arrange horseback rides with a night spent sleeping in hammocks (Q150 per person). To get here independently, you'll need a 4WD. Should you wish to spend the night, Nakum has a handful of tent platforms, free of charge, but bring food and water.

MELCHOR DE MENCOS

pop 13,900 / elev 137m

Most travelers pass through Melchor, right on the Belize–Guatemala border, only getting a glimpse of border officials and moneychangers. There is an actual town across the Río Mopán, with hotels, banks and businesses, but not much to beautify it. There is a Cajero 5B ATM at the Texaco station 500m west of the bridge.

There's little reason to linger but if you're done traveling for the day, Melchor has one fine place to stay, the **Río Mopan Lodge** (☎ 7926-5196; www.tikaltravel.com; s/d from Q150/200). Set back from the road in lush, jungly grounds, it's so tranquil that you'll find it hard to comprehend you're just 50m from the immigration booth. The rooms are big, cool and well decorated, with balconies overlooking the Río Mopan, and the kitchen prepares good Mediterranean fare. The Swiss-Spanish couple who run the place offer trips to Tikal and other, lesser-known sites in the area, and they've got a library of archaeology books you can browse. It's between the bridge and Guatemalan immigration.

In Melchor proper are various budget hotels, the best of the batch being the family-run **Hotel Zaculeu** (☎ 7926-5163; hzaculeu@gmail.com; s/d Q30/50), two blocks north of the Parque Central.

Travelers bound for Flores or Tikal, after clearing immigration, should cross the bridge, where there's a microbus stop on the right side with departures to Santa Elena every half hour until 6pm. Red Asetur vans provide shuttle service to Yaxhá, Tikal and Flores with highly negotiable rates. See those sections for details.

MEXICAN BORDER (CHIAPAS & TABASCO)
Via Bethel/La Técnica & Frontera Corozal
Regular transportation service reaches the Mexican border at Bethel or La Técnica, on the eastern bank of the Río Usumacinta, from where there is regular ferry service to Frontera Corozal on the Mexican bank. Guatemalan immigration is in Bethel, but the crossing is quicker and much cheaper from La Técnica (Q10 per person). Microbus drivers will normally stop and wait for you to do the formalities in Bethel before proceeding to La Técnica. For details of microbus service to and from Bethel and La Técnica, see p281.

Autotransporte Chamoán vans run hourly from Frontera Corozal *embarcadero* to Palenque (M$70, 2½ to three hours), with the last departure at 5pm.

To visit the Maya ruins at Yaxchilán on the Mexican side of the river, boats from Frontera Corozal to Yaxchilán cost from M$680 to M$1300 per person for two to 10 people, round trip, with a 2½-hour wait at the ruins.

Via El Ceibo/La Palma
A new border crossing further north enters the Mexican state of Tabasco from El Ceibo, a village on the Río San Pedro. See p281 for details on microbus service from Flores. Immigration posts operate on both sides of the border from 9am to 5pm. From the Mexican side, vans and buses proceed to Tenosique, Tabasco (M$35, one hour, hourly 6am to 5pm), from where minibuses leave for Palenque up to 7pm (M$50, two hours).

Via Benemérito de las Américas
You can also cross into Mexico by boat down the Río de la Pasión from Sayaxché to Benemérito de las Américas, but there are no regular passenger services. See p302 for details on arranging private transport. Benemérito has good bus and minibus connections with Palenque and a few basic accommodations. Note that neither Mexico nor Guatemala has immigration facilities at this crossing.

SAYAXCHÉ
pop 13,700 / elev 133m
Sayaxché, on the south bank of the Río de la Pasión, 61km southwest of Flores, is the closest town to around 10 scattered Maya archaeological sites, including Ceibal, Aguateca, Dos Pilas, Tamarindito and Altar de Sacrificios. Otherwise, for travelers it's little more than a transportation halt between Flores and the Cobán area. A helpful map of the region is posted on the wall of the Restaurant Yaxkín, just up from the riverbank on the right.

Minibuses and buses from Santa Elena drop you on the north bank of the Río de la Pasión. Frequent ferries (pedestrian/car Q2/25) cross the river to the town.

Banrural (⏱ 7:30am-4:30pm Mon-Fri, 7:30am-1pm Sat), two blocks up from Hotel Guayacán, then

---

GETTING TO THE BELIZEAN BORDER

It's 100km from Flores to Melchor de Mencos, the Guatemalan town on the border with Belize. From the Tikal junction at Puente Ixlú, 27km from Flores, the road continues paved until 13km short of the border. For information on bus services to the border and onward, to Belize City and Chetumal, Mexico, see p281.

Officially there are no fees at the border for entering or leaving Guatemala, but in reality, immigration officials on the Guatemalan side charge a Q10 fee to enter or leave the country. Technically you don't have to pay it but most travelers fork over this de facto tip and move on. No fee is charged to enter Belize, but travelers leaving that country have to pay a B$30 departure tax and a B$7.50 protected areas conservation fee, in Belizean or US dollars.

There are moneychangers at the border with whom you can change sufficient funds for immediate needs. For changing quetzals to Belize dollars, rates are better on the Guatemalan side. Taxis run between the border and the nearest town in Belize, Benque Viejo del Carmen, 3km away, for B$10. Authorized rates are posted for other destinations, including Belize International Airport (B$200). Buses run from Benque to Belize City (B$10, three hours) about every hour from 3:30am to 6pm.

one block left, has a Cajero 5B and changes euros and American Express traveler's checks. Get online at **Internet El Tecnológico** (per hr Q10), across the street from the church.

Sleeping

Hospedaje Yaxkín Chen (☎ 4053-3484; bungalow per person Q50). A bit east of the center are these 10 cheery bungalows amid an impressive variety of plants and trees. A big, open-air restaurant serves tacos, river fish and chicken cacciatore. It's four blocks east and a block south of the church. The hospitable owners will pick you up at the dock if you phone ahead.

Hotel Petexbatún (☎ 7928-6166; r Q100, with bathroom Q175) Overlooking the Río Petexbatún, this establishment features few frills but has a peaceful setting. Bare but clean rooms have simple beds, lacy curtains and powerful fans. From the dock, go up to the first intersection, then three blocks to the right; the blue building has no sign.

Hotel Del Río (☎ 7928-6138; hoteldelriosayaxche@ hotmail.com; r with fan/air-con Q150/225; P ⚡) A few steps to the right of the Hotel Guayacán (with your back to the river), this newer hotel is the cushy choice, with modern, sparkling rooms alongside an airy lobby.

Hotel Guayacán (☎ 7928-6111; d with fan/air-con Q170/200; P ⚡) Just up from the riverbank at a chaotic intersection, the Guayacán offers decent rooms with solid wooden beds and tile floors. Upstairs units are best, opening on a river-view terrace.

Eating

Restaurante Yaxkín (mains Q25-35; ☺ breakfast, lunch & dinner) The upstairs river-view dining room is a good spot to enjoy the home-cooked fare whipped up by Cecilia and family. They also do picnic boxes in case you're going somewhere. From the riverbank, it's the fourth place to the right – the one with the thatched awning.

Café del Río (mains Q40; ☺ breakfast, lunch & dinner) The town's most atmospheric eatery is across the river on the big wooden dock, where you can enjoy wholesome food, sweet breezes and icy beer. It's got its own boat to shuttle people over from the south bank.

Getting There & Away

Southbound from Sayaxché, buses and microbuses leave at 5am, 11am and 3pm for Cobán (Q60, three hours). More frequent micros go as far as Raxrujá (Q25, two hours), about

hourly from 5:30am to 4pm, from where there are frequent departures for Cobán. For Chisec, you can change in Raxrujá or at San Antonio Las Cuevas. Vehicles depart from a lot behind the Hotel Guayacán. From the north side, micros leave for Santa Elena every 15 minutes, from 5:45am to 6pm (Q20, 1½ hours).

For river transportation, enquire at **Viajes Don Pedro** (☎ 4580-9389; servlanchasdonpedro@hot mail.com), next door to Restaurante Yaxkín. A trip all the way down the Río de la Pasión to Benemérito de las Américas (Mexico), with stops at the ruins of Altar de Sacrificios, should not cost more than Q3000 (3½ hours to ruins, up to four passengers). Alternatively, you could ride on one of the freight ferries passing through a few times a week for around Q150. Another reliable operator is **Viajes Acuáticos Glendy** (☎ 5801-8791), on the northern side of the river, 500m up from the northern bank.

AROUND SAYAXCHÉ

Of the archaeological sites reached from Sayaxché, Ceibal and Aguateca are the most interesting to the amateur visitor. Both are impressively restored and can be reached by boat trips along jungle-fringed waterways followed by forest walks. Most people arrive in the context of a tour but it is possible to make arrangements independently.

Ceibal

Unimportant during most of the Classic period, Ceibal (sometimes spelt Seibal) grew rapidly in the 9th century AD under the rule of the Putun Maya merchant-warrior culture from the Tabasco area of Mexico. With its strategic position along the west bank of the Río de la Pasión, the independent kingdom amassed considerable power controlling commerce along this key stretch of the waterway. It attained a population of around 10,000 by AD 900, then was abandoned shortly afterwards. Its low, ruined temples were quickly covered by a thick carpet of jungle.

Excavation of the site is ongoing under the supervision of University of Arizona archaeologist Takeshi Inomata. People of Cobán still journey to Ceibal to perform rituals that include animal sacrifices.

Though the inventory of buildings may be less amazing than at some other sites, the river journey to it is among the most memorable.

A one-hour ride up the Río de la Pasión from Sayaxché brings you to a primitive dock. After landing, you clamber up a narrow, rocky path beneath gigantic ceiba trees and jumbles of jungle vines to reach the archaeological zone, perched about 100m above the river. Spider monkeys, tapir, wild boars and deer customarily roam the forest here.

There's a large scale model of the site by the entrance. The ceremonial core of the city covers three hills, connected over steep ravines by the original causeways. Smallish temples, many of them covered with jungle, surround two principal groups, A and D. In front of some temples, and standing seemingly alone on paths deeply shaded by the jungle canopy, are magnificent stelae, their intricate carvings

still in excellent condition. It takes about two hours to explore the site.

Most of the stelae appear at Grupo A. Numbers 5 and 7 depict ball players, who might have performed in the ball court west of its central plaza. Some have distinctly non-Maya features and dress, which has led to wild speculation that foreigners once inhabited the area. This is particularly evident in the looks of the character on stele 10, which stands on the north side of Structure A-3, a platform with a staircase on each side at the center of the Plaza Sur. Another stele shows a finely dressed king holding his war club upside down in a classic gesture of submission – believed to be a reference to the site's surrender to neighboring Dos Pilas.

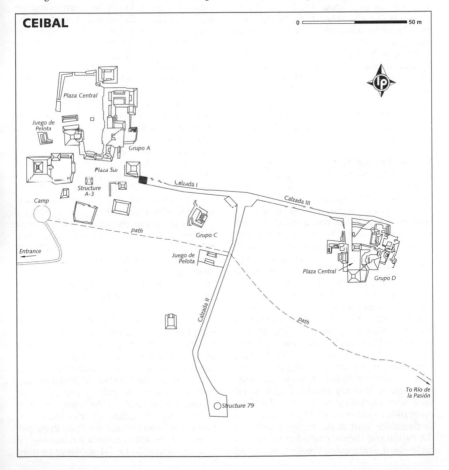

Following Calzada I east, you reach Grupo D, a more compact series of temples that backs up on a precipitous gorge. One of Ceibal's more interesting structures is a bit removed from the rest: the recently restored Structure 79 is reached by taking Calzada II to the south. Three stone steps surround the unusual ring-shaped structure, which stands alone in a clearing with a small altar in the shape of a jaguar's head. It is believed to have served as an astronomical observatory, from which the inhabitants studied planetary movements.

For information on tours to Ceibal, see p275. Otherwise, Café del Río (p302) in Sayaxché, on the north side of the river, runs *lanchas* here (Q450 for up to three persons) and Viajes Don Pedro (p302) charges Q500 for up to five passengers. The fee should include a guide, who may actually be the boatman. In high season, ask the *lancheros* about joining a tour group.

If you wish, you can get to Ceibal cheaper by land: get any bus, minibus or pickup heading south from Sayaxché on Hwy 5 (toward Raxrujá and Chisec) and get off after 9km at Paraíso, from where a dirt track leads 8km east to Ceibal. You may have to walk this last 8km. In the rainy season check first that this stretch is passable.

Laguna Petexbatún

Laguna Petexbatún is a 6km-long lake southwest of Sayaxché, approached by an hour's *lancha* ride up the Río Petexbatún, a tributary of the Río de la Pasión, from Sayaxché. The lake, river and surrounding forests harbor many birds, including kingfishers, egrets, vultures, eagles, cormorants and herons. Within reach of the waterways are five archaeological sites (Dos Pilas, Tamarindito, Arroyo de Piedra, Punta de Chiminos and Aguateca), and three jungle-hideaway accommodations close to the water's edge. What we know of the history of these archaeological sites has mostly been unraveled by archaeologists since the late 1980s. Dos Pilas was founded about AD 640 by a prince who left Tikal and later defeated it in two wars, capturing its ruler Nuun Ujol Chaak (Shield Skull) in 679, according to inscriptions at Dos Pilas. Dos Pilas' second and third rulers carried out monumental building programs, waged wars of conquest and came to dominate most of the territory between the Pasión and Chixoy rivers, but in AD 761 their vassal Tamarindito rebelled and killed

the fourth ruler, causing the Dos Pilas nobility to relocate to the naturally fortified site of Aguateca, which was already functioning as a twin capital. Aguateca in turn was abandoned in the early 9th century, around the same time as three defensive moats were cut across the neck of the Chiminos peninsula on the edge of Laguna Petexbatún. Archaeologists surmise that Punta de Chiminos was the last refuge of the Petexbatún dynasty founded at Dos Pilas.

AGUATECA

If you have limited time and funds, this **site** (☼ 8am-4:30pm), at the far south end of the lake, is both the easiest reached and the most immediately impressive. It's a 1¼-hour *lancha* trip direct from Sayaxché, via mangrove canals full of egrets, kingfishers, turtles and the odd crocodile. A five-minute walk from the dock is the visitor center. The rangers can guide you round the site in about 1½ hours (a small tip is in order). Howler monkeys are much in evidence early and late in the day.

The ruins are on a hilltop, defended by cliffs facing the lake and split by a ravine. Carved stelae suggest that the city enjoyed military successes (including one over nearby Ceibal) up until about AD 735. It's fairly certain that rulers from Dos Pilas abandoned that city for the better-fortified Aguateca around AD 761, and that the city was finally overrun by unknown attackers around 790 – a wealth of arrowheads and skeletons have been found dating back to that time. The city was abandoned shortly afterwards.

Two main groups feature well-restored structures: the Grupo del Palacio where the ruler lived, and the Plaza Mayor (Main Plaza) to its south, where fiberglass copies of stelae showing finely attired rulers stand beside the fallen originals. The two groups are connected by a causeway over the ravine.

From the visitor center, you can skirt the cliff wall north to reach a *mirador* (lookout) with views over the rivers and swamplands toward the east. The trail then turns left and descends into the ravine, continuing 100m between two sheer limestone walls, then climbs back up to emerge onto the Grupo del Palacio. Proceed through the palatial complex back toward the entrance. At the lower end, turn right to take the causeway over the ravine (70m deep here) to reach the Plaza Principal.

Since 1996, the Aguateca Archaeological Project, directed by Dr Takeshi Inomata from the University of Arizona, has extensively excavated and mapped the site. To learn more about their findings, visit www.ic.arizona.edu/ic/anth453/web.

DOS PILAS

This fascinating site is a mere 16km from Sayaxché, but getting here is a serious undertaking. If you have the time, it's well worth considering for the fine carvings on display, particularly the hieroglyphic staircase, with five 6m-wide steps, each with two rows of superbly preserved glyphs, climbing to the base of the royal palace near the main plaza.

The city began life as a breakaway from the Tikal group when that city was taken by Calakmul. Dos Pilas appears to have been governed by a set of aggressive rulers – it clashed with Tikal, Ceibal, Yaxchilán and Motul all within 150 years, often ignoring the traditional 'war season,' which finished in time for the harvest.

Dos Pilas was virtually abandoned in 760 AD, but some farmers hung on into the 9th century when the city was overrun and subsequently evacuated.

A few caves nearby are thought to have been used for human sacrifices, having contained skeletons, altars and ceremonial bloodletting objects.

Many stelae at this site have been relocated to museums and replaced by crushed-rock and fiberglass replicas, in a pilot program designed to deter looters.

The best way to reach Dos Pilas is by tour from Sayaxché (p301) or by staying at the Posada Caribe (see below) and organizing a tour there. Either way, you'll be up for about 3½ hours of jungle trekking on foot or horseback from the Posada, passing the sites of Tamarandito (which also features a hieroglyphic stairway) and the smaller site of Arroyo de Piedra, which has a plaza and some well-preserved stelae.

SLEEPING & EATING

All three lodging options are stellar in their way but vary in style and setting. The first one you reach, about 40 minutes from Sayaxché at a lazy stretch of the river, is **Posada Caribe** (☎ 5304-1745; ecologico.posadacaribe@hotmail.com; s/d Q410/490), managed by the ebullient don Julián Mariona and family. The least flashy option, it has seven homey, thatched bungalows on a grassy field set back from the riverbank.

Breakfast, lunch and dinner are served for around Q85 each. From here you can walk to the Dos Pilas ruins in about 3½ hours, including stops at the lesser ruins of Tamarindito and Arroyo de Piedra en route. You can organize horses for this trip at Posada Caribe for Q100 each, plus Q100 for the guide.

Just up from the western shore of the lake in the **Petexbatún Lodge** (☎ 7926-0501; dm Q85, bungalow per person Q180), the economy version of a jungle retreat. Spacious cabins feature wood floors, mosquito-netted beds and huge bathrooms with circular tiled tub and garden, plus porches with hammocks overlooking the lake. Meals are prepared atop a pile of embers in a thatched-roofed dining hall with lakefront seating. It is possible to arrive here more economically by taking a bus from Sayaxché to Tamarindo, on the lake bank, where the lodge boatman can pick you up.

Two minutes further south by *lancha* is the choicest place to stay, **Chiminos Island Lodge** (☎ 5865-8183; www.chiminosisland.com; s/d incl 3 meals Q1030/1855), which shares its promontory with a largely unexcavated Maya citadel. Five spare but elegantly furnished bungalows, with private bathroom, fan and porch, are spaced well apart from one another and reached along trails through the forest. Built of natural hard woods and equipped with wraparound screened windows, they give the feeling of sleeping in the jungle without all those nasty bugs and bats. Naturally prepared food is served in an open-air restaurant/clubhouse, and folders full of absorbing archaeological information and articles about the area are available to peruse as you chill out here.

GETTING AROUND

Getting to all these places involves making arrangements with boatmen at Sayaxché, or taking a tour. Viajes Don Pedro (see p302) offers a straightforward half-day return trip from Sayaxché to Aguateca, charging Q600 for up to five people. You could, for example, arrange to be dropped at one of the lodges afterwards and to be picked up the next afternoon after making a trip to Dos Pilas. Turismo Aventura and other outfits in Flores (see p275) offer one-day tours to Aguateca, including lunch and guide.

REMOTE MAYA SITES

Several Maya sites buried in the Petén forest, of interest to archaeology buffs and adventurous travelers, are open for limited tourism. They're exciting not just because of the ruins but because of the jungle and its wildlife that you encounter en route. Few of these sites can be visited without a guide because of their remote location, the difficult jungle terrain you must brave to get there and the lack of water (potable or otherwise), but tour operators and hotels in Flores and El Remate offer trips to these sites. Be prepared for buggy, basic conditions.

Outfits like Martsam Travel and Turismo Aventura (p275) work with the local Comités Comunitarios de Ecoturismo (Community Ecotourism Committees) in the remote villages that serve as starting points for these treks. By choosing them, you'll be participating in a considered program of low-impact, sustainable tourism and you will have a guide who is highly knowledgeable about local conditions.

El Perú (Waká)

Trips to this site 62km northwest of Flores in the Parque Nacional Laguna del Tigre are termed La Ruta Guacamaya (the Scarlet Macaw Trail), because the chances of seeing these magnificent birds are high, chiefly during their February-to-June nesting season. You normally journey by road to Paso Caballos (2½ hours from Flores), then travel an hour by boat down the Río San Pedro and its northern tributary, the Río San Juan, to reach El Perú. From the riverbank, it's a 20-minute walk to the site entrance, then a half-hour climb through primary-growth forest to the ruins. If you arrive independently, the resident rangers will set you up with a guide.

Several important Classic-period structures and stelae at El Perú have led archaeologists to believe it may have allied with Calakmul, Tikal's great rival to the north (in what is now the Mexican state of Campeche). A number of stelae, in various states of deterioration, occupy four plazas. Stele number 16 in plaza 3 (the original lies under a thatched roof next to a fiberglass replica) portrays Siyaj K'ak', aka Smoking Frog, a warrior from Teotihuacán who arrived here in 378 and apparently allied with El Perú in a campaign to overthrow Tikal. The highlight of any trip here is the rather strenuous climb up the Mirador de los Monos, a 16m tower that's been erected atop a 35m pyramid. With jaw-dropping views over the jungle canopy, it's a good perch for *zopilote* (turkey vulture) observation.

To get here independently, take the bus to Paso Caballos, which leaves Santa Elena terminal at approximately 1pm. From Paso Caballos, *lanchas* charge Q350 to Q400. There are tent platforms at the ranger station if you'd like to camp out.

Estación Biológica Las Guacamayas

Twenty minutes south of El Perú down the Río San Juan, the **Scarlet Macaw Biological Station** (☎ 7882-4427; www.lasguacamayasbiologicalstation.com) is a scientific station surrounded by rainforest, where not just macaws, but jaguars and Mesoamerican river turtles (*tortuga blanca*) are observed, among other creatures.

The station offers one- to three-day tours, consisting of a visit to El Perú, nighttime observation of the endemic Morelet's crocodile, and the chance to tag along with researchers as they monitor macaws and butterflies. See the Flores section, p274, for information about working as a volunteer here.

Perched on a hillside overlooking the broad lazy river, it's a splendidly isolated spot to spend a few days, and there is comfortable accommodation in several thatched-roof houses with wraparound screened windows and front porches. A separate building contains clean toilets and good showers; another has a *comedor*, where healthy meals are prepared. Rates for one/two/three persons on a two-day stay are Q1115/1830/2505, including meals and accommodation but not transport, plus Q400 per person for each additional day.

Piedras Negras

On the banks of the Río Usumacinta, which forms the border with Mexico, these little-visited ruins boast an impressive size and a wealth of carvings. The original name of the city, Yokib' (the entrance), is believed to be a reference to a large cenote found in its center, believed to be an opening to the underworld.

The entrance to the site is probably its most impressive aspect – black cliffs (from which it gets its modern name) loom over the riverbanks. A large rock protrudes, carved with a kneeling man making an offering of incense to a female figure beneath him, perhaps entombed. A (now crumbling) stairway leads up the riverbank to the building complex 100m above.

The best-preserved buildings are the sweat baths and acropolis complex, which incorporates rooms, courtyards and passageways. Other buildings show a mix of styles, often with Classic structures built on top of Preclassic ones. Several of the finest pieces found here – including a carved throne – are now in the Museo Nacional de Arqueología y Etnología in Guatemala City (see p72).

It was here in the 1930s that part-time archaeologist Tatiana Proskouriakoff deciphered the Maya hieroglyphic system, recognizing patterns between the glyphs and certain dates, events and people. Although her theory played out when she tested it at nearby Yaxchilán, it was not accepted by the wider archaeological community until the 1960s.

It is possible to reach Piedras Negras in a day's travel from Flores, but it's an expensive undertaking. First you have to get to Bethel (4½ hours over an unpaved road), from which a cooperative runs boats downriver to Piedras Negras (four to five hours, Q2500 to Q3000), a journey that can only be made in the rainy season when the river is high enough for navigation. Turismo Aventura (p275) is one of several tour operators that offers a three-day excursion to the site.

El Zotz

Completely unrestored and barely excavated, the large site of El Zotz ('bat' in many Maya languages) occupies its own *biotopo* abutting the Tikal National Park. The three major temples here are all covered in soil and moss, but you can scramble to the top of the tallest, the Pirámide del Diablo, for views of Tikal's temples, 24km to the west. If you're here around dusk, you'll see where the place gets its name, as thousands of bats come pouring out of nearby caves.

Tour operators in Flores (p275) and El Remate (p285) offer jeep/horse/trekking tours here, often incorporating Tikal – see those sections for details. Coming independently, it's a 30km (five-hour) trek (with the possibility of a ride in a *xate* truck) from Cruce Dos Aguadas, which is connected to Santa Elena by bus. You

---

THE RESERVA DE BIOSFERA MAYA

The Maya Biosphere Reserve, occupying 18,449 sq km stretched right across the north of El Petén, is part of the Unesco world biosphere reserve network, which recognizes that the many human demands on this planet's land require innovative strategies if nature is to be conserved. In this vein, the Maya reserve is split into three spheres. Along its southern fringe is a buffer zone where economic activities are permitted, supposedly within a framework of environmental protection. The main part of the reserve is divided into a multiple-use zone, composed of tropical forest and supposedly dedicated to the sustainable harvest of xate ferns, chicle gum and timber, and eight core areas (the Sierra del Lacandón, Tikal, Laguna del Tigre and Mirador–Río Azul national parks, and the Cerro Cahuí, San Miguel La Palotada, Laguna del Tigre and Dos Lagunas biotopes) for scientific research, conservation of the natural environment and/or archaeological sites, and tightly controlled ecological and cultural tourism.

Unfortunately, the theory is prettier than the reality: the forest is still being ravaged by people illegally harvesting timber on a massive scale, looters desecrating Maya tombs, and tourists (no matter how conscientious) negatively impacting on the fragile ecosystem. The buffer zone is rapidly changing from a forested landscape with scattered agricultural patches to an agricultural landscape with scattered forest patches. New roads meant to provide access to the core zones for researchers and tourists become a lifeline for land-hungry peasants from further south.

In fact, the most successful of the three zones, according to conservationists, has been the one designated for multiple uses. This is because it is in the interest of the forest concessions to deter illegal activities, since the supposedly sustainable harvesting they engage in provides employment for their communities. These groups determinedly patrol their turf to ward off poachers, whom they see as competition, whereas violators in the core zones are less likely to face punitive action from the governmental agencies that are charged with managing them. And in the case of the oil firms operating in the northwest corner of the Biotopo Laguna del Tigre, one of the biosphere's designated core areas, authorities stand to gain from such violations, as oil revenues inject capital into the economy. Despite the widespread pollution caused by oil drilling – by some estimates, over 300,000 barrels a day are being pumped out of the reserve – the oil producers claim not to be subject to the biosphere restrictions, having set up operations in the 1980s before the establishment of the reserve, a claim the Guatemalan government accepts.

can also take the longer route from Uaxactún, where Aldana's Lodge provides guides (p296). Camping is permitted near the site.

Río Azul

This medium-sized site (its population is believed to have peaked at around 5000) is located in the Parque Nacional Mirador–Río Azul, up near the corner where the Belize, Guatemala and Mexico borders meet. Once an independent city, it fell under the domain of Tikal in the early Classic period and became a key trading post for cacao from the Caribbean on its way to Tikal and Central Mexico. The city was overrun in 530 AD by forces from Calakmul, then regained by Tikal during its resurgence in the late-Classic era before being finally destroyed by the Puuc Maya from the Yucatán.

There are over 350 structures here, but most notable are the tombs, with vibrant red glyphs painted inside, as well as three round altars, with carvings depicting ritual executions.

Looting reached a frenzy point here during the 1960s and '70s. International treaties banning the trafficking in Maya artifacts were precipitated, in part, by the volume of ceramics and other objects stolen from Río Azul – one archaeological team returned to the site after the rainy season to find 150 trenches dug in their absence. We can only guess at the full extent of the treasures carted away, but some of the documented losses include jade masks, murals, pendants and other carved objects.

The tallest temple, AIII, a smaller replica of those found at Tikal, stands 47m high, high enough to give a panoramic view out over the jungle canopy.

There's no public transportation anywhere near Río Azul. Hotel El Chiclero (p297) leads a recommended excursion from Uaxactún. It's a four- or five-hour drive north when the road is passable, with visits to La Honradez and a bunch of other small sites along the way, camping out at a lovely site called El Cedro where dinner is prepared by acclaimed chef Neria Herrera. The second day is for exploring the site, and the third you return to Uaxactún. Tours here also leave from Flores and Melchor de Mencos.

El Mirador

Buried within the furthest reaches of the Petén jungle, just 7km south of the Mexican border, the late-Preclassic metropolis at El Mirador contains the largest cluster of buildings in any single Maya site. Among them is the biggest pyramid ever built in the Maya world: La Danta (the Tapir), with three pyramidal structures atop two massive platforms. From atop this mammoth structure, some 70m above the forest floor, virgin canopy stretches into the distance as far as your eye can see. The green bumps hovering on the horizon are other pyramids still buried under dense jungle.

Though not as big as La Danta, another pyramid, El Tigre, measures 55m high and its base covers 18,000 sq meters – six times the area of Tikal's biggest structure, Templo IV. La Danta, El Tigre and the other temples erected here display the unusual 'triadic' style, in which three pyramids crown a large platform, with the one in the middle dominating the other two, which face each other at a lower level. The facades of these buildings were once embellished with carved masks.

There are hundreds of buildings at El Mirador, but ongoing excavations have only scratched the surface, so many are still hidden beneath the jungle. You'll have to use your imagination to picture this city that at its height spread over 16 sq km and supported tens of thousands of citizens. It was certainly the greatest Maya city of the Preclassic era, far exceeding in size anything built subsequently in the Maya world. Within the complex, more than a dozen internal causeways link the main architectural complexes.

Scholars are still figuring out why and how El Mirador thrived (there are few natural resources and no water sources save for the reservoirs built by ingenious, ancient engineers) and what led to its abandonment in 150 AD. Some five centuries after that date, El Mirador appears to have been resettled, as suggested by the existence of Classic architecture amongst the older structures. Pottery unearthed from this era displays the highly refined codex-style of decoration, in which calligraphic lines are painted on a cream-colored surface, with designs believed to resemble Maya codices.

Richard Hansen, a professor from Idaho State University, is leading the effort to map the Mirador basin, a vast swathe of northern El Petén comprising dozens of interconnected cities, with funding from an assortment of international and Guatemalan foundations and private sources. In March 2009, Dr Hansen and his crew made a significant discovery when they excavated a frieze at the base of La Danta, dating from 300 BC, which they surmise decorated a royal pool. The carved images upon it depict the twin heroes Hunahpú and Ixbalnqué swimming away from the underworld domain of Xibalbá, a tale that is related in the *Popul Vuh*. The finding underlines the importance of El Mirador in establishing the belief systems of Classic-era civilizations. To find out more about their efforts, see www.miradorbasin.com.

GETTING TO EL MIRADOR

Recognizing the importance of El Mirador, President Álvaro Colóm in his inauguration speech pledged to seek funding and invest in infrastructure to make it more accessible to visitors. Until that actually happens, though, a visit here involves an arduous jungle trek of at least five days and four nights (it's about 60km each way), with no facilities or amenities aside from what you carry in and what can be rustled from the forest. During the rainy season, especially September to December, the mud can make it extremely difficult; February to July is the best period to attempt a trek.

The trip usually departs from a cluster of houses called Carmelita, 82km up the road from Flores, though it is also possible to approach from the east, departing from Uaxactún. Certain outfits in Flores and El Remate work with the community tourism committees in Carmelita (see p275), or you can contact them directly. The **Comisión de Turismo Cooperativa Carmelita** (☎ /861-2641; tono.centeno@gmail.com), a group of 16 Inguat-authorized guides, can make all arrangements for a trek to El Mirador, with optional visits to the Preclassic sites of Nakbé, El Tintal, Wakná and Xulnal. Travelers who participate in these treks should be in good physical shape, able to withstand high temperatures (average of nearly 100 degrees) and humidity (average 85 percent) and be prepared to hike or ride long distances (up to 30km per day).

On the first day of a typical six-day itinerary, you'll hike six hours through mostly agricultural country to El Tintal, where you'd camp for the night. On the second day, you'll have a look around El Tintal, then proceed through denser forests to El Mirador and set up camp there. The third day is reserved for exploring El Mirador. On Day 4, you hike four hours southeast to arrive at Nakbé and camp there. The next day the expedition begins the return south via an eastern trail, stopping for the night at the site of La Florida. On Day 6, you head back to Carmelita.

For a five-day trip, the cooperative charges Q2760/2800/3680 per person in groups of four/three/two persons; six-day trips cost Q3280/3376/4520 and seven-day trips are Q3712/4016/5384. The fee includes tents, hammocks and mosquito netting; all meals and drinking water; Spanish-speaking guide; mules and muleskinners; and first-aid supplies.

Two buses daily travel from Flores to Carmelita (see p281). In Carmelita, **Comedor Pepe Toño** (☎ 7783-3812) is about it for accommodation, with two very basic thatched huts containing five lumpy, mosquito-netted beds

---

THE MIRADOR BASIN

The 2169 sq km of tropical forest surrounding El Mirador harbors dozens of other substantial cities that flourished during the middle- and late-Preclassic eras as well. At least six major causeways connected El Mirador to these satellites, an engineering feat that enabled it to become what was possibly the New World's first political state. The four largest cities in the vicinity are all within a day's walk of El Mirador.

El Tintal (23km southwest of El Mirador) One of the largest and most important Preclassic cities, with a large moat surrounding the civic center and one of the largest ball courts in El Petén.

Wakná (15km south) Built around what is possibly the largest astronomical observatory in the Maya world, with Preclassic murals and a series of internal causeways. Unlike other Preclassic sites in the Mirador zone, it has a north–south orientation.

Nakbé (13km southeast) Established around 1200 BC, it grew to be one of the most important Preclassic sites. El Mirador was probably modeled upon this predecessor. All the characteristic features of Maya civilization – monumental architecture, palaces, causeways and ball courts – had appeared here by 600 BC.

Xulnal (7km west of El Tintal) Discovered in 2001. Pottery found here is evidence of some of the earliest occupation in the Mirador Basin.

each, and primitive bathroom facilities. Some local families may also provide lodging; ask around. Pepe Toño will also whip up some eggs and beans or chicken soup for dinner.

It's also possible to get here from Uaxactún, a longer but in some ways gentler approach, since there are fewer *bajos* (seasonal swamps) and it's less affected by agricultural clearing so you're underneath the jungle canopy from the outset. Hotel El Chiclero (p297) offers a six-day tour at Q1000 per person per day. The first leg of the journey you're driven in a monster truck to a campground at the former *chiclero* camp of Yucatán, a five-hour journey. The next morning the group is outfitted with mules and proceeds to another camp, La Leontina, a 3½-hour tramp through the jungle. The following day it's a 2½-hour walk to Nakbé. After visiting that site, the expedition continues to El Mirador. The journey back follows the same route in reverse.

If expense is not a concern, you can go the easy way: by helicopter. **Tikal Park** (www.tikalpark. com) offers one- and two-day 'heli-tours' to El Mirador from Flores, arriving in just half an hour at the site.

Directory

CONTENTS

BOOK YOUR STAY ONLINE

For more accommodations reviews and recommendations by Lonely Planet authors, check out the online booking service at www.lonelyplanet.com/hotels. You'll find the true, insider low-down on the best places to stay. Reviews are thorough and independent. Best of all, you can book online.

ACCOMMODATIONS

Guatemalan accommodations range from luxury hotels to budget hotels to ultrabudget guesthouses called *hospedajes, casas de huéspedes* or *pensiones.*

This book lists accommodation options in order of price – from cheapest to most expensive. The budget category covers places where a typical double costs Q150 or less. Doubles less than Q80 are generally small, dark and not particularly clean. Security may not be the best in such places. A Q150 double should be clean, sizable and airy, with a bathroom, TV and, in hot parts of the country, a fan.

Midrange covers establishments with doubles between Q150 and Q400. These rooms are always comfortable: private hot-water bathroom, TV, decent beds, fan and/or air-con are standard. Good midrange hotels have attractive public areas such as dining rooms, bars and swimming pools. In hot regions, the rooms may be attractive wooden bungalows, with thatch roofs, verandas and hammocks; in cooler areas they may be in beautiful old colonial-style houses with antique furnishings and lovely patios.

Anything more expensive than Q400 is top end. Guatemala City's international-class business-oriented hotels, Antigua's very finest hostelries, and a few resort hotels elsewhere constitute nearly the whole of the top end options.

Room rates often go up in places popular with tourists during Semana Santa (the week leading up to Easter Sunday), Christmas–New Year and July and August. Semana Santa is the major Guatemalan holiday period, and prices can rise by anything from 30% to 100% on the coast and in the countryside – anywhere Guatemalans go to relax. At this time advance reservations are a very good idea.

Regardless of your budget, if you're planning on staying for longer than a few days, it's worth asking for a discount.

Be aware that room rates are subject to two large taxes – 12% IVA (value-added tax) and 10% to pay for the activities of the Guatemalan Tourism Institute (Inguat), although there is discussion about eliminating this second tax. All prices in this book include both taxes. Some of the more expensive hotels forget to include them when they quote their prices.

DIRECTORY

Camping

In Guatemala, camping can be a hit-or-miss affair, as there are few designated campgrounds and safety is rarely guaranteed. Where campsites are available, expect to pay from Q20 to Q50 per person per night.

Homestays

Travelers attending Spanish school have the option of living with a Guatemalan family. This is usually a pretty good bargain – expect to pay between Q250 and Q500 a week on top of your tuition for your own room, shared bathrooms, and three meals a day except Sunday. It's important to find a homestay that gels with your goals – some families host several students at a time, creating more of an international hostel atmosphere than a family environment.

ACTIVITIES
Climbing, Trekking & Hiking

The many volcanoes are irresistible challenges, and many of them can be done in one day from Antigua (p96) or Quetzaltenango (p157). There's further great hill country in the Ixil Triangle and the Cuchumatanes mountains to the north of Huehuetenango, especially around Todos Santos Cuchumatán (p180) and Nebaj (p153). The Lago de Atitlán (p116) is surrounded by spectacular trails, though robberies here have made some routes inadvisable.

Treks of several days are perfectly feasible, and agencies in Antigua, Quetzaltenango and Nebaj can guide you. In the Petén jungles, treks to remote archaeological sites (p305) such as El Mirador and El Perú offer an exciting challenge.

Coffee Tours

With so much great farmland set in lush surroundings, it was only a matter of time before Guatemalan coffee farms started getting some serious tourist attention. Coffee tours are a great way to learn about the history and present-day reality of Guatemalan farm life. See the boxed text on p194 for some farm tours, and also check out the individual listings for Finca los Nietos (p111), Nueva Alianza (p193), Cobán (p216), Finca San Lorenzo (p210) and Finca El Cisne (p251) in Honduras.

Cycling

There's probably no better way to experience the Guatemalan highlands than by bicycle. Panajachel (p118), San Pedro La Laguna (p133), Quetzaltenango (p157) and Antigua (p97) in particular are the best launch points, with agencies offering trips and equipment.

Horseback Riding

Opportunities for a gallop, a trot or even a horse trek are on the increase in Guatemala. There are stables in Antigua (p97), Santiago Atitlán (p130), Quetzaltenango (p157), El Remate (p284), Laguna Brava (p184) and San Pedro La Laguna (p133). Unicornio Azul (p179), north of Huehuetenango, offers treks of up to nine days in the Cuchumatanes.

PRACTICALITIES

- Guatemalans use the metric system for weights and measures, except that they pump gasoline by the *galón* (US gallon) and occasionally weigh things such as laundry and coffee in pounds.

- Videos and DVDs on sale use the NTSC image registration system.

- Electrical current is 115V to 125V, 60Hz, and plugs are two flat prongs, all the same as in the US and Canada.

- The most respected of Guatemala's many newspapers are *La Prensa Libre* (www.prensalibre.com), *Siglo Veintiuno* (www.sigloxxi.com), *La Hora* (www.lahora.com.gt) and *El Periódico* (www.elperiodico.com.gt). Some of the best investigative journalism in the country can be found in the magazine *Revista …Y Qué?* (www.revistayque.com).

- For Guatemala-related articles from around the world and Guatemala in English, check the *Guatemala Times* (www.guatemala-times.com). *The Revue* (www.revuemag.com) is Guatemala's free, widely distributed, monthly English-language magazine – a lot of ads, a few interesting articles.

- Almost every TV is cable, which ensures reception and brings a number of US stations to hotel TVs.

Paragliding

Paragliding is a relatively new sport in Guatemala, but it's bound to catch on – the mountains and volcanoes make excellent launch points and the views are superb. There are reliable, experienced operators in Panajachel (p122) and San Marcos La Laguna (p139).

Spelunking

Guatemala attracts cavers from all around the world. The limestone area around Cobán is particularly riddled with cave systems whose full extents are unknown. The caves of Lanquín (p221), B'omb'il Pek (p223), Candelaria (p225) and Rey Marcos (p220) are all open for tourist visits. There are also exciting caves to visit from Finca Ixobel (p271), near Poptún, and some near Flores (p283).

Water Sports

You can dive inside a volcanic caldera at Lago de Atitlán (p116), raft the white waters of the Río Cahabón near Lanquín (p221), or sail from the yachtie haven of Río Dulce (p252). You can also canoe or kayak the waterways of Monterrico (p201), Lago de Atitlán (p116) and Lago de Petén Itzá (p284), Lívingston (p261), the Bocas del Polochic (p256) or Punta de Manabique (p260).

Wildlife-Watching & Bird-Watching

National parks and nature reserves generally have few tourist facilities, but they do offer lots of wildlife- and bird-watching opportunities. Fine locations in the Petén jungles for bird-watching include Tikal (p287), El Mirador (p308), Cerro Cahuí (p284), Laguna Petexbatún (p304) and (for scarlet macaws) the Estación Biológica Las Guacamayas (p306) and the Macaw Mountain Bird Park (p246). Elsewhere, the wetlands of Bocas del Polochic (p256), Punta de Manabique (p260) and Monterrico (p201), and the Río Dulce (p252) and Laguna Lachuá (p224) national parks provide lots of avian variety, as does the Biotopo del Quetzal (p211). Mammals tend to prove more elusive but you should see several species at Tikal. Monkey fans will also be happy at the Reserva Natural Atitlán (p121), the Bocas del Polochic (p256) and Cerro Cahuí (p284).

Zip Lining/Canopy Tours

Zip lining has taken off in a big way in Guatemala, and pretty much anywhere that

has an open space and a couple of trees between which to string a cable, you'll see people zipping between them. New courses spring up all the time, but here are some that were happening at the time of writing: Reserva Natural Atitlán outside of Panajachel (p121), Vuelo Extremo (p192), the Chicoj cooperative (p216), Parque Natural Guayaja (p221), Parque Ecológico Hun Nal Ye (p223), Parque Ecoturístico Cascadas de Tatasirire (p231), Parque Chatún (p234), Parque Natural Ixpanpajul (p284), Parque Nacional Tikal (p294) and the Copán Canopy Tour (p247).

BUSINESS HOURS

Guatemalan shops and businesses are generally open from 8am to noon and 2pm to 6pm, Monday to Saturday, but there are many variations. Banks typically open 9am to 5pm Monday to Friday (again with variations), and 9am to 1pm Saturday. Government offices usually open 8am to 4pm, Monday to Friday. Official business is always better conducted in the morning.

Restaurant hours are typically 7am to 9pm, but can vary by up to two hours either way. Most bars open from 11am to midnight. The *Ley Seca* (dry law) stipulates that bars and *discotecas* must close by 1am, except on nights before public holidays. It is rigidly adhered to in large cities and universally laughed at in smaller towns and villages. Antigua has a municipal law on the books that is yet to be enforced, stating that no alcohol is to be served after 10pm – you can imagine how the majority of the tourist industry feels about it.

If restaurants or bars have a closing day, it's usually Sunday. Typical shopping hours are 8am to noon and 2pm to 6pm Monday to Saturday.

Businesses listed in this guide adhere (roughly) to the hours noted above, unless otherwise stated.

CHILDREN
Practicalities

Facilities such as safety seats in hired cars are rare but nearly every restaurant can rustle up something resembling a high chair. If you are particular about brands of diapers and creams, bring what you can with you and stock up in supermarkets in Guatemala City, Antigua or Quetzaltenango. Fresh milk is rare and may not be pasteurized. Packet UHT milk and, even more so, milk powder to which you must add purified water are much more common. If your child has to have some particular tinned or packaged food, bring supplies with you. Public breastfeeding is not common among urban, non-indigenous women and, when done, is done discreetly.

Sights & Activities

Guatemala is so culturally dense, with such an emphasis on history and archaeology, that children can get easily bored. To keep kids entertained, parents will need to make a point of visiting some of the more kid-friendly sights such as Guatemala City's Museo de los Niños (p72) and La Aurora Zoo (p72), Autosafari Chapín (p199) south of the capital, and Retalhuleu's Xocomil water park (p192) and Xetulul theme park (p192). Most kids enjoy a trip to the beach, but beware that the Pacific coast is notorious for its riptides – many adults drown here each year.

Most Spanish courses are open to kids, too. Many older kids will enjoy activities such as kayaking, cave exploration and horseback riding.

For a wealth of good ideas, get hold of Lonely Planet's *Travel with Children*.

CLIMATE CHARTS

For climatic considerations concerning your trip, see the charts and When to Go (p12).

COURSES
Dance

Dancing is *everything* in Guatemala (a party is thought to be a flop unless people are dancing). The most popular formal style is merengue, with salsa coming more or less second. You'll see locals and gringos grinding it to reggaetón pretty much anywhere where there's a dancefloor. Dance schools in Quetzaltenango (p163), Panajachel (p127) and Antigua (p108) can help you get your groove on at a fraction of the price you'd pay back home.

Language

Guatemala is celebrated for its many language schools. A spot of study here is a great way not only to learn Spanish but also to meet locals and get an inside angle on the culture. Many travelers heading south through Central America to South America make Guatemala an early stop so they can pick up the Spanish skills they need for their trip.

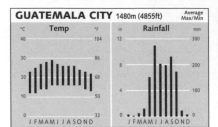

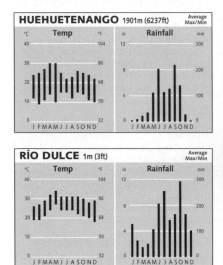

Guatemalan language schools are some of the cheapest in the world, but few people go away disappointed. There are so many schools to choose from that it's essential to check out a few before deciding.

Antigua is the most popular place to study, with close to 100 schools (see p98). Courses in Quetzaltenango (p162) are the second most popular, perhaps attracting a more serious type of student; Antigua has a livelier students' and travelers' social scene. San Pedro La Laguna (p135) and Panajachel (p122) both have a handful of language schools, and if you'd like to learn Spanish while hanging out in a remote mountain town, there are schools in Todos Santos Cuchumatán (p181) and Nebaj (p162). You'll also find schools in San Juan (p138), Huehuetenango (p177), Cobán (p215), Copán in Honduras (p247), and San Andrés (p283) and San José (p283) in El Petén. On average, schools charge Q900 to Q1200 for four hours of one-on-one classes five days a week and accommodation with a local family.

Studying in a small town has its pros and cons. On the upside, you may be the only foreigner around, so you won't be speaking any English. On the downside, Spanish may be the second language of the inhabitants of the village (including your teacher), meaning that you could pick up all sorts of bad habits.

You can start any day at most schools, and study for as long as you like. If you're coming in peak season and hoping to get into one of the more popular schools, it's a good idea to book ahead, although many schools charge around Q300 for phone or internet reservations. All decent schools offer a variety of elective activities from salsa classes to movies

to volcano hikes. Many schools offer classes in Maya languages as well as Spanish.

Weaving

Guatemalan fabrics are famed worldwide, mostly because they are produced by a traditional method known as backstrap weaving. If you'd like to learn this craft, lessons are available in San Pedro La Laguna (p135), Panajachel (p122), Zunil (p170), Todos Santos Cuchumatán (p180) and Quetzaltenango (p163).

Other Courses

If you're still looking for something to learn, you can try enrolling in cooking classes in Antigua (p99), learning traditional painting techniques in San Pedro La Laguna (p133),

---

GOING BACK TO SCHOOL? BETTER DO YOUR HOMEWORK

Choosing between the mass of Spanish schools in Guatemala can be tough. Many schools don't have in-house teacher training programs, so there aren't so many 'good schools' as there are 'good teachers.' It's best to pay for as little time as possible (a week, usually) so you can change if you're really unhappy. You should be completely up-front about what your goals (conversation, grammar, vocabulary etc) are when starting, as well as any specialized interests that you have (politics, medical, legal etc) so the school can design a curriculum and assign you a teacher to best suit your needs. If you end up liking like the school, but not the teacher, ask for a new teacher as soon as possible – personality conflicts occur, and four or five hours of one-on-one with someone you don't like can soon turn into hard work.

Here are some questions to think about when you're looking at schools. Some you can find out just by turning up, some you should ask the school, others you'll have to talk to current and ex-students to get a feel for.

■ Where do the classes take place – on a quiet, shaded patio or in hot classrooms with buses roaring along the street outside?

■ What experience and qualifications do the teachers have in teaching as a second language?

■ Is Spanish your teacher's first language?

■ What afternoon and evening activities are available (many schools offer activities like salsa classes, movies and excursions – some of them free)?

■ Many schools offer gimmicks to get you in, like a half hour of free internet per day, which ends up saving you around Q2.50 per day – should these little perks really sway your judgment?

■ What is the general atmosphere of the school? Serious students probably won't fit in at a school whose activities include all-night bar crawls, and party animals may feel out of place at schools with names like the Christian Spanish Academy.

■ Does the school offer opportunities for voluntary work – for example, assisting in local schools, visiting hospitals or playing with children at orphanages?

■ If the school claims to be involved in social/community projects, is it a serious commitment, or just a marketing ploy?

For (completely unverified) reviews of *some* of Guatemala's Spanish schools by ex-students, check out www.guatemala365.com.

or getting to the heart of Garífuna culture, with drumming classes in Lívingston (p263).

CUSTOMS REGULATIONS

Customs officers only get angry and excited about a few things: weapons, drugs and paraphernalia, large amounts of currency, and automobiles and other expensive items that might be sold while you're in the country. It is also illegal to bring fruit, vegetables or plants through the international airports at Guatemala City and Flores.

Normally customs officers won't look seriously in your luggage and may not look at all. At some border points the amount of search is inversely proportional to the amount of 'tip' you have provided: big tip no search, no tip big search.

Whatever you do, keep it formal. Anger, hostility or impoliteness can get you thrown out of the country or into jail, or worse.

DANGERS & ANNOYANCES

No one could pretend that Guatemala is a very safe country. There are just too many stories of robbery, often armed robbery, for that. Rapes and murders of tourists have also happened. These days, the most frequently reported type of nasty incident involves robbery on walking trails. For a scary litany of recent incidents, visit the website of Guatemala City's **US embassy** (http://guatemala.usembassy.gov) and click on 'Recent Crime Incidents Involving Foreigners.' Be aware that when they talk about crime statistics involving US citizens, they include Guatemalans who have gone to the States, gotten citizenship and returned home, not just tourists. This bloats the figures quite substantially.

Some further, marginally less alarming, information is on the website of the **US Department of State** (http://travel.state.gov) and the website of the **UK Foreign and Commonwealth Office** (www.fco.gov.uk).

The days of robbers targeting buses and tourist shuttles out on the open highway seem to be thankfully in the past – recent statistics indicate that the biggest danger that tourists face on the roads is in rental cars on isolated stretches. At the time of writing, the Carretera al Pacífico (Hwy 2) near the Salvadoran border and around Santa Lucía Cotzumalguapa was a red spot, as were the back roads from Cocales to San Lucas Tolimán and Antigua to Escuintla, and the road from San Pedro La Laguna to Santiago de Atitlán. This informa-

tion is incredibly fluid – if you're planning on driving yourself around, check with **Asistur** (☎ 1500 in English) for the latest.

Robberies against tourists on walking trails tend to occur in isolated spots on well-known walks. Some trails around the Lago de Atitlán (see p116) and on the volcanoes outside Antigua are particularly notorious.

Other potential dangers are pickpocketing, bag-snatching, bag-slitting and the like in crowded bus stations, buses, streets and markets, but also in empty, dark city streets.

It's best to travel and arrive in daylight hours. If that's not possible, travel at night using 1st-class buses and catch a taxi to your hotel once you arrive. For a warning on solo female travelers traveling on intercity buses, see p329.

It is impossible to remove the element of risk from traveling in Guatemala, but it's possible to reduce the risk by always staying alert to the behavior of people around you (watch out for people who get unwarrantedly close to you in any situation) and by following a few simple precautions:

- Only carry the money, cards, checks and valuables that you need. Leave the rest in a sealed, signed envelope in your hotel's safe, and obtain a receipt for the envelope. If your hotel doesn't have a safe, it is usually safer to secrete your money and valuables in three or four different stashes among your locked luggage in your room than to carry them with you.
- Be aware that any purse or bag in plain sight may be slashed or grabbed. At ticket counters in bus stations, keep your bag between your feet.
- Don't flaunt jewelry, cameras or valuable-looking watches. Keep your wallet or purse out of view.
- On buses keep your important valuables with you, and keep a tight hold on them.
- Don't wander alone in empty city streets or isolated areas, particularly at night.
- Use normal precautions when using ATMs. See Scams, opposite, for more on ATM usage.
- Keep informed by talking to travelers, hotel staff and others, and consulting official information sources such as the US and UK government websites (see left), your country's embassy in Guatemala City, and Inguat (see p65).
- Hiking in large groups and/or with a police escort reduces the risk of robbery.

■ Resisting or trying to flee from robbers usually makes the situation worse.

Hiking on active volcanoes obviously has an element of risk. Get the latest story before you head out. In the wet season, hike in the morning before rain and possible thunderstorms set in.

There have been a few bizarre incidents in which foreign visitors have been unjustly suspected of malicious designs, mostly from the (largely imagined) ideas that foreigners kidnap Guatemalan babies. Be careful, especially in rural areas, when talking to small children, always ask permission to take photographs and generally try not to put yourself in any situation that might be misinterpreted.

Any crowd can be volatile, especially when drunk or at times of political tension.

Scams

One common scenario is for someone to spray ketchup or some other sticky liquid on your clothes. An accomplice then appears to help you clean up the mess and robs you in the process. Other methods of distraction, such as dropping a purse or coins, or someone appearing to faint, are also used by pickpockets and bag snatchers.

Regrettably, ATM card cloners have moved into Guatemala, targeting Guatemalans and foreigners alike. They operate by attaching a card reading device to the ATM (often inside the slot where you insert your card) and once they have your data, proceed to drain your account. There have been reports of card cloning in all the major tourist destinations. The only way to avoid it is to use ATMs that cannot be tampered with easily (inside supermarkets or shopping malls) or by going into the bank and getting a cash advance there. The ATMs most prone to tampering are the ones in the little unlocked room at the front of a bank.

You should *never* have to enter your PIN number to gain access to an ATM room.

EMBASSIES & CONSULATES

New Zealand and Australia do not have embassies in Guatemala, although New Zealand has an Honorary Consulate. The Canadian embassy can be of some assistance, but otherwise you'll have to go to Mexico City. The following are all in Guatemala City:

Belize (☎ 2367-3883; embelguate@yahoo.com; Europlaza 2, Office 1502, 5a Av 5-55, Zona 14)

Canada (☎ 2363-4348; www.guatemala.gc.ca; 8th fl, Edificio Edyma Plaza, 13a Calle 8-44, Zona 10)

Cuba (☎ 2332-4066; http://embacu.cubaminrex.cu; Av Las Américas 20-72, Zona 13)

El Salvador (☎ 2360-7660; emsalva@intel.net.gt; Av Las Américas 16-46, Zona 13)

France (☎ 2421-7370; www.ambafrance.org.gt; 5a Av 8-59, Zona 14)

Germany (☎ 2364-6700; www.guatemala.diplo.de; Edificio Plaza Marítima, 20a Calle 6-20, Zona 10)

Holland (☎ 2381-4300; www.embajadadeholanda-gua.org; 13th fl, Torre Internacional, 16a Calle 0-55, Zona 10)

Honduras (☎ 2366-5640; embhond@intelnet.net.gt; 19a Av 'A' 20-19, Zona 10)

Ireland (☎ 2384-9446; irelandgua@gmail.com; Edificio La Galería, Office 15A, 7a Av 14-44, Zona 9)

Israel (☎ 2333-4624; 13 Av 14-07, Zona 10)

Japan (☎ 2382-7300; Av La Reforma 16-85, Zona 10)

Mexico (☎ 2420-3400; embamexguat@itelgua.com; 2a Av 7-57, Zona 10)

New Zealand (☎ 2363-1848; 13 Calle 7-71, Zona 10)

Nicaragua (☎ 2368-2284; embaguat@terra.com.gt; 13 Av 14-54, Zona 10)

Spain (☎ 2379-3530; 6a Calle 6-48, Zona 9)

UK (☎ 2380-7300; www.ukinguatemala.fco.gov.uk; 11th fl, Torre Internacional, 16a Calle 0-55, Zona 10)

REPORTING A CRIME

Reporting a crime is always a toss-up in Guatemala. If you're the victim of something really serious, of course you should take it to the police – the phrase you're looking for here is *'Yo quisiera denunciar un crimen'* ('I'd like to report a crime'). If you've been robbed, get a statement filed so you can show your insurance company.

If it's a minor thing, on the other hand, you might want to toss up whether or not it's really worth your while reporting it to the police.

Specially trained tourist police (often English speaking) operate in some major tourist areas – you can call them in **Antigua** (☎ 5978-3586) and **Guatemala City** (☎ 2251-4897).

Outside of those areas (and normal office hours) your best bet is to call **Asistur** (☎ 1500), which operates a 24-hour nationwide toll-free hotline in English and Spanish. It can give you information and assistance, help deal with the police and even arrange a lawyer if need be.

USA (☎ 2326-4000; http://guatemala.usembassy.gov; Av La Reforma 7-01, Zona 10)

FESTIVALS & EVENTS
The following events are of national significance in Guatemala.

January
El Cristo de Esquipulas On January 15 this festival in Esquipulas brings pilgrims from all over Central America for a glimpse of the Black Jesus housed in the basilica.

March/April
Semana Santa Easter week – the week leading up to Easter Sunday – sees statues of Jesus and Mary carried around the streets of towns all around the country, followed by devout, sometimes fervent crowds, to mark Christ's crucifixion. The processions walk over and destroy *alfombras,* elaborate carpets of colored sawdust and flower petals. The celebrations climax on Good Friday.

August
Fiesta de la Virgen de la Asunción Peaking on August 15, this fiesta is celebrated with folk dances and parades in Tactic, Sololá, Guatemala City and Jocotenango.

November
Día de Todos los Santos All Saints' Day, November 1, sees giant kite festivals in Santiago Sacatepéquez and Sumpango, near Antigua, and the renowned drunken horse races in Todos Santos Cuchumatán.

December
Quema del Diablo On December 7 the Burning of the Devil starts at around 6pm throughout the country when everyone takes to the streets with their old garbage, physical and psychic, to stoke huge bonfires of trash. This is followed by impressive fireworks displays.

FOOD
See the Food & Drink chapter (p49) for what you can eat where and when and what it will cost. Where we have divided city eating sections into different price ranges, you can expect a main dish to cost under Q40 in a budget eatery, Q40 to Q70 at a midrange place and more than Q70 at a top-end venue.

GAY & LESBIAN TRAVELERS
Few places in Latin America are outwardly gay-friendly, and Guatemala is no different. Technically, homosexuality is legal for persons over 18 years, but the reality can be another story, with harassment and violence against gays too often poisoning the plot. Don't even consider testing the tolerance for homosexual public displays of affection here.

Though Antigua has a palatable – if subdued – scene, affection and action are still kept behind closed doors; the chief exception is the gay-friendly club La Casbah (p108). In Guatemala City, Genetic and the Black & White Lounge are the current faves (see p80). Mostly, though, gays traveling in Guatemala will find themselves keeping it low-key and pushing the twin beds together.

Gay.com (www.gay.com) has a personals section for Guatemala and **The Gully** (www.thegully.com) usually has some articles and information relevant to Guatemala. The best site, **Gay Guatemala** (www.gayguatemala.com), is in Spanish.

HOLIDAYS
The main Guatemalan holiday periods are Semana Santa, Christmas–New Year and July and August. During Semana Santa room prices rise in many places and it's advisable to book all accommodation and transport in advance.

Guatemalan public holidays include the following:

New Year's Day (Año Nuevo) January 1
Easter (Semana Santa; Holy Thursday to Easter Sunday inclusive) March/April
Labor Day (Día del Trabajo) May 1
Army Day (Día del Ejército) June 30
Assumption Day (Día de la Asunción) August 15
Independence Day (Día de la Independencia) September 15
Revolution Day (Día de la Revolución) October 20
All Saints' Day (Día de Todos los Santos) November 1
Christmas Eve afternoon (Víspera Navidad) December 24
Christmas Day (Navidad) December 25
New Year's Eve afternoon (Víspera de Año Nuevo) December 31

INSURANCE
Getting travel insurance to cover theft, loss and medical problems is recommended. Some policies specifically exclude dangerous activities, which can include scuba diving, motorcycling, even trekking.

You may prefer a policy that pays doctors or hospitals directly, rather than your having to pay on the spot and claim later. If you have to claim later, ensure you keep all documentation.

Check that the policy covers ambulances or an emergency flight home.

For more information on insurance, see p327 and p332.

INTERNET ACCESS

Most travelers make constant use of internet cafes and free web-based email such as **Yahoo** (www.yahoo.com) or **Gmail** (www.gmail.com). Most medium-size towns have cybercafes with fairly reliable connections. Internet cafes typically charge between Q5 and Q10 an hour.

Wi-fi is becoming readily available across the country, but can only really be counted on in large and/or tourist towns. Most (but not all) hostels offer wi-fi, as do many hotels in the midrange and up category. The best reliable source of wi-fi around the country is at Pollo Campero restaurants – they're in pretty much every town of any size and all offer free, unsecured access.

See p15 for a few Guatemala-related websites to start with.

LEGAL MATTERS

You may find that police officers in Guatemala might, at times, be somewhat unhelpful. Generally speaking, the less you have to do with the law, the better.

Whatever you do, don't get involved in any way with illegal drugs – even if the locals seem to do so freely. As a foreigner, you are at a distinct disadvantage, and you may be set up by others. Drug laws in Guatemala are strict, and though enforcement may be uneven, penalties are severe. If you do get caught doing something you shouldn't, your best line of defense is to apologise, stay calm and proceed from there.

MAPS

International Travel Maps' *Guatemala* (1:500,000) is overall the best country map for travelers, costing around Q100 in Guatemala. The cheaper *Mapa Turístico Guatemala*, produced locally by Intelimapas, tends to be the most up to date on the state of Guatemala's roads, many of which have been newly paved in recent years. It also includes plans of many cities. Inguat's *Mapa Vial Turístico* is another worthwhile map. Bookstores that sell these maps can be found in Guatemala City (p64), Antigua (p87), Panajachel (p119) and Quetzaltenango (p157). For 1:50,000 and 1:250,000 topographical sheets of all parts of Guatemala, head to the Instituto Geográfico Nacional (p64).

MONEY

Guatemala's currency, the quetzal (ket-*sahl*, abbreviated to Q), was fairly stable at around Q7.5 = US$1 for years, but currency manipulation by the Guatemalan central bank has seen it hovering around Q8. The quetzal is divided into 100 centavos. For exchange rates at the time of research, see the inside front cover; for information on costs in Guatemala, see p12.

You'll find ATMs (cash machines, *cajeros automáticos*) for Visa/Plus System cards in all but the smallest towns, and there are MasterCard/Cirrus ATMs in many places too, so one of these cards is the best basis for your supply of cash in Guatemala. The 5B network is widespread and particularly useful, as it works with both Visa and MasterCard cards. For a warning about ATM use, see Scams, p317.

In addition, many banks give cash advances on Visa cards, and some on MasterCard. You can pay for many purchases with these cards or with American Express (Amex) cards, but always ask if there is a *recargo* (transaction fee).

If you're not packing plastic, a combination of Amex US-dollar traveler's checks and some cash US dollars is the way to go. Take some of these as a backup even if you do have a card. Banks everywhere cash US dollars, and many also change US-dollar traveler's checks too. Amex is easily the most recognized traveler's check brand.

In many places you can make payments with cash dollars, but few places will accept traveler's checks. Currencies other than the US dollar are virtually useless, although a small handful of places now change cash euros.

Banks generally give the best exchange rates on both cash and traveler's checks. If you can't find an open bank, travel agencies, hotels or shops often change cash (and occasionally checks).

Some towns suffer from change shortages: always try to carry a stash of small bills.

See p316 for security tips about your money.

Tipping

A 10% tip is expected at restaurants and automatically added to your bill in places such as Antigua – a practice that is spreading to other tourist towns as well. In small *comedores* (basic, cheap eateries) tipping is optional, but follow local practice and leave some spare change. Tour guides are generally tipped, around 10%, especially on longer trips.

PHOTOGRAPHY & VIDEO

Ubiquitous film stores and pharmacies sell film, though you may not find the brand you like without a hunt. A 36-exposure, 100-ASA print film normally costs around Q40. There are quick processing labs in the main cities. Most internet cafes have card readers (*lectores de tarjeta*), so you can upload your digital photos or burn them onto CD.

Photographing People

Photography is a sensitive subject in Guatemala. Always ask permission before taking portraits, especially of Maya women and children. Don't be surprised if your request is denied. Children often request payment (usually Q1) in return for posing. In certain places such as the church of Santo Tomás in Chichicastenango, photography is forbidden. Maya ceremonies (should you be so lucky to witness one) are off-limits for photography unless you are given explicit permission to take pictures. If local people make any sign of being offended, put your camera away and apologize immediately, both out of decency and for your own safety. Never take photos of army installations, men with guns or other sensitive military subjects.

POST

The Guatemalan postal service was privatized in 1999. Generally, letters take eight to 10 days to travel to the US and Canada and 10 to 12 days to reach Europe. Almost all cities and towns (but not villages) have a post office where you can buy stamps and send mail. A letter sent to North America costs around Q15 and to anywhere else around Q20.

The Guatemalan mail system no longer holds poste restante or general delivery mail. The easiest and most reliable way to receive mail is through a private address. Language schools and some hotels will be happy to do this. If you want to get a package couriered to you, make sure the courier company has an office in the town where you are staying; otherwise you will be charged some hefty 'handling fees.'

SHOPPING
Bargaining

Be aware that bargaining is essential in some situations and not done in others. Supermarkets, restaurants and large chain stores are examples of places where bargaining is a no-no, but it's standard practice when buying handicrafts: the first price you're told may be double or triple what the seller really expects. Remember that bargaining is not a fight to the death. The object is to arrive at a price agreeable to both you and the seller, thereby creating a win-win situation.

Coffee

Although most of Guatemala's finest beans are exported, some are (thankfully) held back for the tourist trade. To get the finest, freshest beans available, visit a coffee farm and/or roaster and buy from them directly. Cobán, Quetzaltenango, Huehuetenango and Antigua produce some of the world's greatest coffee and support growers and roasters. For more on coffee and fair trade, see p217 and p218. For farms offering coffee tours, see p312.

Jade

Beloved of the ancient Maya, jade is mined in Guatemala today and you'll find it both as jewelry and as miniature sculpture. For more on jade, see p109.

Leather Goods

Guatemala has some terrific leather goods. Fine briefcases, duffel bags, backpacks and belts are sold in most handicrafts markets. Cowboy boots and hats are a specialty in some areas, and custom work is welcome – the best place to head for is the village of Pastores just outside Antigua. The prices and craftsmanship of these items are usually phenomenal.

Shipping

It's best to use an international shipping service if you want to ensure the relatively safe, timely arrival of your goods. You'll find information on such courier services in this book's city sections, under Post. A 1kg package sent from Antigua to California by UPS, for example, will cost you around Q466 for express (two-day) service. See www.ups.com for more information.

Textiles

Guatemala's intricate and brilliantly colored textiles are world famous. Weaving is a traditional and thriving art of the Maya here. Clothing – especially the beautiful embroidered *huipiles* (tunics), *cortes* (skirts) and *fajas* (sashes) of the Maya women – as well as purses, tablecloths, blankets, hacky-sacks and many other woven items, are ubiquitous and good value, some for practical use, some more for souvenirs.

The largest craft markets are in Chichicastenango, the Mercado Central and Mercado de Artesanías in Guatemala City, and the Mercado de Artesanías in Antigua. Fine textiles of an infinite variety are also available in Antigua's shops. Elsewhere, in places such as Nebaj, Sololá, Santa Catarina Palopó, Santiago Atitlán and Todos Santos Cuchumatán, you can obtain local textiles at weekly markets or a few permanent stalls.

Wooden Masks

Ceremonial masks are fascinating, eye-catching and still in regular use. In Chichicastenango you can visit the artists in their *morerías* (workshops).

SOLO TRAVELERS

On your own, you need to be even more alert to what's going on around you than other travelers, and you need to be more cautious about where you go.

Guatemala is a pretty good place for meeting both locals and other travelers. Attending a language school, joining a group tour, doing volunteer work and bedding down in dormitory accommodations are just some of the situations where travelers are thrown together with other people.

Since single rooms cost more per person than doubles and triples, solo travelers face higher accommodation costs than others unless they sleep in dormitories or find others to share with.

TELEPHONE

Guatemala has no area or city codes. Calling from other countries, you just dial the international access code (☎ 00 in most countries), then the Guatemala country code (☎ 502), then the eight-digit local number. Calling within Guatemala, just dial the eight-digit local number. The international access code from Guatemala is ☎ 00.

Many towns and cities frequented by tourists have privately run call offices where you can make international calls for reasonable rates. If the telephone connection is by internet, the rates can be very cheap (Q1 a minute to the USA, Europe and Australia), but line quality is unpredictable.

Many travelers use an account with a VOIP service such as Skype (www.skype.com). If an

internet cafe does not have Skype installed, it can usually be downloaded in a matter of minutes. Headphone and microphone equipment in Guatemala is of varying quality, if it exists at all – if you're planning on using internet cafe computers to make calls, buy earbuds with a microphone attached before you leave – they take up very little room in your pack and you can plug them into the front of most computers in the country.

The most common street phones are those of Telgua, for which you need to buy a Telgua phone card (*tarjeta telefónica de Telgua*) from shops, kiosks and the like. Card sales points may advertise the fact with red signs saying *'Ladatel de Venta Aquí.'* The cards come in denominations of Q20, Q30 and Q50: you slot them into a Telgua phone, dial your number, and the display will tell you how much time you have left.

Unless it's an emergency, don't use the black phones placed strategically in tourist towns that say 'Press 2 to call the United States free!' This is a bait and switch scam; you put the call on your credit card and return home to find you have paid between US$8 and US$20 per minute.

Telgua street phones bear instructions to dial ☎ 147110 for domestic collect calls and ☎ 147120 for international collect calls.

Cell Phones

Cell phones are widely used. It's possible to bring your cell phone from home, have it 'unlocked' for use in Guatemala (this costs around Q50 in Guatemala), then substitute your SIM card for a local one. This works on some phones and not others and there doesn't appear to be a logic behind it. Guatemalan phone companies work on either 850, 900 or 1900 MHz frequencies – if you have a tri- or quad-band phone you should be OK. Compatibility issues, and the possibility of theft (cell phones are a pickpocket's delight) makes buying a cheap prepaid phone on arrival the most popular option.

Prepaid phones are available pretty much everywhere and cost around Q100 to Q150, often coming with Q100 or so in free calls. Cards to restock the credit on your phone are sold in nearly every corner store. Calls cost Q1.50 per minute anywhere in the country, the same for the US (depending on the company you're with) and up to five times that for the rest of the world.

At the time of writing, Movistar had the cheapest rates (with coverage limited to major cities) and Tigo and Claro had the best coverage.

TIME

Guatemala runs on North American Central Standard Time (GMT/UTC minus six hours). Daylight saving time has been trialed in Guatemala, meeting with fairly heavy opposition, particularly in rural areas, where villagers worked on a dual time system – the *hora oficial* (official time) and the *hora de Dios* (God's time). At the time of writing, it appeared that daylight saving had been scrapped permanently.

The 24-hour clock is often used, so 1pm may be written as 13 or 1300. When it's noon in Guatemala, it's 1pm in New York, 6pm in London, 10am in San Francisco and 4am next day in Sydney. For more time conversions, see www. timeanddate.com/worldclock.

TOILETS

You cannot throw *anything* into Guatemalan toilets, including toilet paper. Bathrooms are equipped with some sort of receptacle (usually a small wastebasket) for soiled paper. Toilet paper is not always provided, so always carry some. If you don't have any and need some, asking a restaurant worker for *un rollo de papel* (a roll of paper), accompanied by a panicked facial expression, usually produces fast results.

Public toilets are rare. Use the ones at cafes, restaurants, your hotel and archaeological sites. Buses rarely have toilets on board and if they do, don't count on them working.

TOURIST INFORMATION

Guatemala's national tourism institute, **Inguat** (www.visitguatemala.com), has information offices in Guatemala City, Antigua, Panajachel, Quetzaltenango, Cobán and Santa Elena airport; a few other towns have departmental, municipal or private-enterprise tourist information offices. See city sections for details. **Asistur** (www. asisturcard.com), a joint private-government initiative, operates a 24-hour toll-free advice and assistance hotline on ☎ 1500.

TRAVELERS WITH DISABILITIES

Guatemala is not the easiest country to negotiate with a disability. Although many sidewalks in Antigua have ramps and cute little inlaid tiles depicting a wheelchair, the streets are cobblestone, so the ramps are anything but smooth and the streets worse!

Many hotels in Guatemala are old converted houses with rooms around a courtyard; such rooms are wheelchair accessible. The most expensive hotels have facilities such as ramps, elevators and accessible toilets. Transportation is the biggest hurdle for travelers with limited mobility: travelers in a wheelchair may consider renting a car and driver as the buses will prove especially challenging due to lack of space.

Mobility International USA (www.miusa.org) advises disabled travelers on mobility issues, runs exchange programs (including in Guatemala) and publishes some useful books. Also worth consulting are **Access-Able Travel Source** (www.access-able.com) and **Accessible Journeys** (www.disabilitytravel.com).

Antigua-based **Transitions** (transitionsguatemala yahoo.com) is an organization aiming to increase awareness and access for disabled persons in Guatemala.

VISAS

Citizens of the US, Canada, EU countries, Norway, Switzerland, Australia, New Zealand, Israel and Japan are among those who do not need a visa for tourist visits to Guatemala. On entry into Guatemala you will normally be given a 90-day stay. (The number 90 will be written in the stamp in your passport.)

In August of 2006 Guatemala joined the Centro America 4 (CA-4), a trading agreement with Nicaragua, Honduras and El Salvador. Designed to facilitate the movement of people and goods around the region, it has one major effect on foreign visitors – upon entry to the CA-4 region, travelers are given a 90-day stay *for the entire region*. You can get this extended once, for an additional 90 days, for around Q120. The exact requirements change with each government, but just for kicks, here's how it was working at the time of writing: you needed to go to the **Departamento de Extranjería** (Foreigners' Office; Map p66; ☎ 2411-2411; 6a Av 3-11, Zona 4, Guatemala City; ⏰ 8am-2:30pm Mon-Fri), with *all* of the following:

■ A credit card with a photocopy of both of its sides.
■ Two photocopies of the first page of your passport and one of the page where your entry visa was stamped.
■ A recent, passport-sized color photograph.

VOLUNTEERING: SOME OPTIONS

There's a wealth of volunteering opportunities in Guatemala. A lot of them center on education and environmental issues. Here are a few offbeat ones that may appeal:

Arcas (www.arcasguatemala.com) Works to protect the endangered sea turtle population on the southern coast. Also has projects in El Petén.

Entre Mundos (www.entremundos.org) Produces a bi-monthly newspaper and acts as a bridge between volunteers and NGOs.

Estación Biológica Las Guacamayas (www.laguacamayasbiologicalstation.com) A combined research/ conservation center in El Petén.

La Calambacha (www.lacambalacha.org) Based in San Marcos La Laguna, fosters confidence-building, social integration and artistic formation through arts workshops for kids.

Proyecto Payaso (www.proyectopayaso.org) A traveling clown troupe specializing in community AIDS awareness and education.

Safe Passage (www.safepassage.org) Provides education, health care and opportunities for kids working scavenging in Guatemala City garbage dumps.

If you got in before noon, extensions were being issued on the afternoon of the day that you applied. If not, they were issued the next morning

Citizens of some Eastern European countries are among those who do need visas to visit Guatemala. Enquire at a Guatemalan embassy well in advance of travel.

Visa regulations are subject to change – it's always worth checking with a Guatemalan embassy before you go.

If you have been in the CA-4 for your original 90 days and a 90-day extension, you must leave the region for 72 hours (Belize and Mexico are the most obvious, easiest options), after which you can return to the region to start all over again. Some foreigners have been repeating this cycle for years.

VOLUNTEERING

If you really want to get to the heart of Guatemalan matters and you've altruistic leanings, consider volunteer work. It's rewarding and exposes foreigners to the local culture typically out of reach for the average traveler. Opportunities abound, from caring for abandoned animals and kids to writing grant applications to tending fields. Travelers with specific skills such as nurses, doctors, teachers and website designers are particularly encouraged to investigate volunteering in Guatemala.

Most volunteer posts require basic or better Spanish skills and a minimum time commitment. Depending on the organization, you may have to pay for room and board for the duration of your stay. Before making a commitment, you may want to talk to past

volunteers and read the fine print associated with the position.

Three excellent sources of information on volunteer opportunities are Proyecto Mosaico Guatemala and AmeriSpan Guatemala, both in Antigua (see p96), and EntreMundos in Quetzaltenango (see p168). You only have to visit the websites of Entremundos or Proyecto Mosaico to see the huge range of volunteer opportunities that exists. Many language schools have close links to volunteer projects and can introduce you to the world of volunteering. The best worldwide site for volunteer positions (with many Guatemala listings) is www.idealist.org.

WOMEN TRAVELERS

Women should encounter no special problems traveling in Guatemala. In fact, solo women will be pleasantly surprised by how gracious and helpful most locals are. The primary thing you can do to make it easy for yourself while traveling here is to dress modestly. Modesty in dress is highly regarded, and if you practice it, you will usually be treated with respect.

Specifically, shorts should be worn only at the beach, not in town, and especially not in the highlands. Skirts should be at or below the knee. Wear a bra, as going braless is considered provocative. Many local women swim with T-shirts over their swimsuits – you may want to follow suit to avoid stares.

Women traveling alone can expect plenty of attention from talkative men. Often they're just curious and not out for a foreign conquest. It is, of course, up to you how to respond, but there's no need to be intimidated.

Consider the situation and circumstances (on a bus is one thing, on a barstool another) and stay confident. Try to sit next to women or children on the bus. Local women rarely initiate conversations, but usually have lots of interesting things to say once the ball is rolling.

Nasty rumors about Western women kidnapping Guatemalan children for a variety of sordid ends have all but died down. Still, women travelers should be cautious around children, especially indigenous kids, lest misunderstandings occur.

While there's no need to be paranoid, the possibility of rape and assault does exist. Use your normal traveler's caution – avoid walking alone in isolated places or through city streets late at night, and skip hitchhiking. For a warning on women traveling alone on buses, see p329.

WORK

Some travelers find work in bars, restaurants and places to stay in Antigua, Panajachel or Quetzaltenango, but the wages are just survival pay. If you're looking to crew a yacht, there's always work being offered around the Río Dulce area, sometimes for short trips, sometimes to the States and further afield. Check noticeboards (Bruno's, p253, has the best one) for details.

Transportation

CONTENTS

GETTING THERE & AWAY

ENTERING THE COUNTRY

When you enter Guatemala, by land, air, sea or river, you should simply have to fill out straightforward immigration and customs forms. In the normal course of things you should not have to pay a cent.

However, immigration officials sometimes request unofficial fees from travelers. To determine whether these are legitimate, you can ask for *un recibo* (a receipt). You may find that the fee is dropped. When in doubt, try to observe what, if anything, other travelers are paying before it's your turn.

To enter Guatemala, you need a valid passport. For information on visas, see p322.

Flights and tours can be booked online at www.lonelyplanet.com/travel_services.

AIR
Airports & Airlines

Guatemala City's Aeropuerto La Aurora (GUA) is the country's major international airport. The only other airport with international flights (from Cancún, Mexico, and Belize City) is Flores (FRS). The Guatemalan national airline, Aviateca, is part of the regional Grupo Taca, along with El Salvador's Taca and Costa Rica's Lacsa. The US Federal Aviation Administration recently upgraded Guatemala's and El Salvador's civil aviation authorities to Category 1, meaning they comply with international aviation safety standards.

AIRLINES FLYING TO/FROM GUATEMALA
The following airlines fly to and from Guatemala. See p81 for office locations.

American Airlines (AA; ☎ 2422-0000; www.aa.com)
Aviateca See Grupo Taca.
Continental Airlines (CO; ☎ 2385-9610; www.continental.com)
Copa Airlines (CM; ☎ 2353-6555; www.copaair.com)
Cubana (CU; ☎ 2367-2288/89/90; www.cubana.cu)
Delta Air Lines (DL; ☎ 2263-0600; www.delta.com)
Grupo Taca (TA; ☎ 2470-8222; www.taca.com)
Iberia (IB; ☎ 2332-0911; www.iberia.com)
Lacsa See Grupo Taca.
Maya Island Air (MW; ☎ 501-223-1140; www.mayaairways.com)
Mexicana (MX; ☎ 2333-6001; www.mexicana.com)
Spirit Airlines (NK; www.spiritair.com) No telephone number.
Taca See Grupo Taca.

Guatemala
The best place to buy flight tickets out of Guatemala is Antigua, which has many agencies offering good fares (see p92). Some agencies also issue the student, youth and teacher cards needed to obtain the best fares.

Australia & New Zealand
The cheapest routes usually go via the USA (often Los Angeles). Many Australasians visiting Guatemala are doing so as part of a longer trip through Latin America, so the most suitable ticket might be an open-jaw (into one city, out of another) or even a round-the-world

---

THINGS CHANGE...

The information in this chapter is particularly vulnerable to change. Check directly with the airline or a travel agent to make sure you understand how a fare (and ticket you may buy) works and be aware of the security requirements for international travel. Shop carefully. The details given in this chapter should be regarded as pointers and are not a substitute for your own careful, up-to-date research.

TRANSPORTATION

ticket. From Sydney, you'll pay approximately A$2800 round-trip to Guatemala City via LA or San Francisco.

The following are well-known agents for cheap fares, with branches throughout Australia and New Zealand:

Flight Centre Australia (☎ 133-133; www.flightcentre.com. au); New Zealand (☎ 0800-243-544; www.flight centre.co.nz)

STA Travel Australia (☎ 134-782; www.statravel.com.au); New Zealand (☎ 0800-474-400; www.statravel.co.nz)

Canada

There are no direct flights. Routes are usually via the USA. Montréal to Guatemala City costs in the region of C$700 return. **Travel Cuts** (☎ 1866-246-9762; www.travelcuts.com) is Canada's national student travel agency. For online bookings try www.expedia.ca and www.travelocity.ca.

Central America & Cuba

Grupo Taca flies from San Salvador (economy round-trip fare from US$330); Tegucigalpa, Honduras (US$384); Managua, Nicaragua (US$415); and San José, Costa Rica (from US$220). Copa flies direct from Panama City (US$390), and from San José (US$300).

Continental Europe

Iberia is the only airline flying direct from Europe to Guatemala at the time of writing (with a stop in Miami), and the cheapest fares from many European cities are usually with Iberia via Madrid. Depending on the season, you can expect to pay from £680 (round-trip) from London, from €685 from Frankfurt and €665 from Madrid.

Recommended UK ticket agencies include the following:

Journey Latin America (☎ 020-8747-3108; www. journeylatinamerica.co.uk)

STA Travel (☎ 0870-160-0599; www.statravel.co.uk) For travelers under the age of 26.

For online bookings try www.dialaflight.com or www.lastminute.com.

Mexico

Airlines Grupo Taca and Mexicana both fly daily direct between Mexico City and Guatemala City, with round-trip fares starting from around US$625. Grupo Taca flies most days from Guatemala City to Flores to Cancún and back. Round-trip fares from Cancún to Flores/Guatemala City are US$410/522.

South America

Lacsa (with transfers in San José, Costa Rica) and Copa (with transfers in Panama City, Panama) both fly to Guatemala City from Bogotá (Colombia), Caracas (Venezuela), Quito (Ecuador) and Lima (Peru).

CLIMATE CHANGE & TRAVEL

Climate change is a serious threat to the ecosystems that humans rely upon, and air travel is the fastest-growing contributor to the problem. Lonely Planet regards travel, overall, as a global benefit, but believes we all have a responsibility to limit our personal impact on global warming.

Flying & Climate Change

Pretty much every form of motor travel generates CO_2 (the main cause of human-induced climate change) but planes are far and away the worst offenders, not just because of the sheer distances they allow us to travel, but because they release greenhouse gases high into the atmosphere. The statistics are frightening: two people taking a return flight between Europe and the US will contribute as much to climate change as an average household's gas and electricity consumption over a whole year.

Carbon Offset Schemes

Climatecare.org and other websites use 'carbon calculators' that allow jetsetters to offset the greenhouse gases they are responsible for with contributions to energy-saving projects and other climate-friendly initiatives in the developing world – including projects in India, Honduras, Kazakhstan and Uganda.

Lonely Planet, together with Rough Guides and other concerned partners in the travel industry, supports the carbon offset scheme run by climatecare.org. Lonely Planet offsets all of its staff and author travel.

For more information check out our website: lonelyplanet.com.

DEPARTURE TAX

Guatemala levies a departure tax of US$30 on outbound air passengers, which is mostly (but not always) included in your ticket price. If it's not, it has to be paid in cash US dollars or quetzals at the airline check-in desk. There's a separate US$3/Q25 airport security tax which must be paid before departure

USA

Nonstop flights to Guatemala City arrive from Atlanta (US$605) with Delta; from Dallas with American (US$540); from Houston (US$520) with Continental; from Los Angeles (US$560) with Grupo Taca; from Miami (US$245) with American and Grupo Taca; and from New York (from US$440) with American and Grupo Taca.

The following websites are recommended for online bookings:

www.cheaptickets.com
www.expedia.com
www.lowestfare.com
www.orbitz.com
www.sta.com

LAND

Bus is the most common way to enter Guatemala, though you can also do so by car, river or sea. It's advisable to get through all borders as early in the day as possible. Onward transportation tends to wind down in the afternoon and border areas are not always the safest places to hang around late. You'll find more detail on the services mentioned here in the destination sections of this book. There is no departure tax when you leave Guatemala by land, although many border officials will ask for Q10. If you're willing to argue and wait around, this may be dropped, but most travelers take the path of least resistance and simply pay up.

Car & Motorcycle

The mountain of paperwork and liability involved with driving into Guatemala deters most travelers. You will need the following documents, all clear and consistent, to enter Guatemala with a car:

- current and valid registration
- proof of ownership (if you don't own the car, you'll need a notarized letter of authorization from the owner that you are allowed to take it)
- your current and valid driver's license or an International Driving Permit (IDP), issued by the automobile association in your home country
- temporary import permit available free at the border and good for a maximum 30 days.

Insurance from foreign countries is not recognized by Guatemala, forcing you to purchase a policy locally. Most border posts and nearby towns have offices selling liability policies. To deter foreigners from selling cars in Guatemala, the authorities make you exit the country with the vehicle you used to enter it. Do not be the designated driver when crossing borders if you don't own the car, because you and it will not be allowed to leave Guatemala without each other.

Border Crossings

BELIZE

The border is at Benque Viejo del Carmen/Melchor Mencos. **Línea Dorada/Mundo Maya** (☎ 7924-8535; www.tikalmayanworld.com) runs one direct bus daily from Belize City to Flores (Q160, four to five hours) and back. Otherwise, buses run between Belize City and Benque (B$10, three hours) about every hour from 3:30am to 6pm. Microbuses (Q25, two hours) leave hourly between Benque and Flores from 5:45am to 6pm. There are also a few buses daily between Melchor Mencos and Guatemala City via Poptún and Río Dulce.

EL SALVADOR

There are road borders at La Hachadura/Ciudad Pedro de Alvarado on the Carretera al Pacífico (Hwy 2), Las Chinamas/Valle Nuevo (Hwy 8), San Cristóbal/San Cristóbal (Interamericana Hwy, or Hwy 1) and Anguiatú/Anguiatú (Hwy 10). Several companies run buses between San Salvador and Guatemala City, taking five to six hours and costing from Q80 to Q290 depending on the service. One of them, Tica Bus, has buses between San Salvador and all other Central American capitals except Belize City. Crossing at the other border points is usually a matter of taking one bus to the border and another onward from it.

HONDURAS

The main road crossings are at Agua Caliente (between Nueva Ocotepeque, Honduras, and Esquipulas, Guatemala), El Florido (between Copán Ruinas, Honduras; and Chiquimula,

TRANSPORTATION

Guatemala) and Corinto (between Omoa, Honduras; and Puerto Barrios, Guatemala). **Hedman Alas** (www.hedmanalas.com; Copán Ruinas ☎ 504-651-4037; La Ceiba ☎ 504-441-5348; San Pedro Sula ☎ 504-516-2273; Tegucigalpa ☎ 504-237-7143) runs daily 1st-class buses via El Florido to Guatemala City from Tegucigalpa (Q433 one way, 11½ hours), La Ceiba (Q433, 12 hours), San Pedro Sula (Q374, eight hours) and Copán Ruinas (Q291, 4½ hours). Cheaper local transportation serves all three border points. Shuttle minibus services run between Copán Ruinas, Guatemala City and Antigua.

MEXICO

The main border points are at Ciudad Hidalgo/Ciudad Tecún Umán and Talismán/El Carmen, both near Tapachula, Mexico, and Ciudad Cuauhtémoc/La Mesilla, on the Interamericana between Comitán, Mexico, and Huehuetenango, Guatemala. All these borders are linked by plentiful buses to nearby cities within Guatemala and Mexico, and a few buses run all the way between Tapachula and Guatemala City by the Pacific Slope route through Mazatenango and Escuintla. There are also direct buses between Guatemala City and all three border points. **Línea Dorada/Mundo Maya** (☎ 7924-8535; www.tikalmayanworld.com) departs Chetumal at 6am for Flores (Q225, seven to eight hours) via Belize City, returning at 7am.

See p281 and p301 for information on routes between Mexico and Guatemala's El Petén department.

BOAT

RIVER

Autotransporte Chamoán vans run hourly until 5pm from Palenque, Mexico, to Frontera Corozal (M$70, 2½ to three hours) on the Río Usumacinta, which divides Mexico from Guatemala. Boats cross the river to La Técnica (per person Q10, five minutes) and Bethel (Q50, 40 minutes) in Guatemala.

From La Técnica buses leave for Flores between 4am and 11am (Q40, five to six hours), passing Bethel (Q35). Travel agencies in Palenque and Flores offer bus-boat-bus packages between the two places for Q380 to Q450. If you're making this trip, it's well worth the time and expense of detouring to the outstanding Maya ruins at Yaxchilán, near Frontera Corozal; packages incorporating this are available too.

The other river route from Mexico into Guatemala's Petén department is up the Río de la Pasión from Benemérito de las Américas, south of Frontera Corozal, to Sayaxché, but there are no immigration facilities or reliable passenger services along this route.

SEA

Exotic Travel (Map p262; ☎ 7947-0133; www.bluecaribbeanbay.com) in Lívingston operates boat and minibus packages to and from La Ceiba in Honduras (Q400) with a minimum of six people. Public boats connect Punta Gorda in Belize with Lívingston (Q200) and Puerto Barrios (Q175 to Q200). The Punta Gorda services connect with bus services to/from Belize City.

There is a Q80 departure tax when leaving Guatemala by sea.

GETTING AROUND

AIR

At the time of writing the only scheduled internal flights were between Guatemala City and Flores, a route operated daily by Taca and TAG, with one-way/round-trip fares costing from Q1150/1980. For further details, see p81.

BICYCLE

Bike rentals are available in a few places; most professional outfits include Old Town Outfitters and Guatemala Ventures/Mayan Bike Tours in Antigua (p97), and Vrisa Books in Quetzaltenango (p162). For more on pedaling your way around, see p312.

BOAT

The Caribbean town of Lívingston is only reachable by boat, across the Bahía de Amatique from Puerto Barrios or down the Río Dulce from the town of Río Dulce – both great trips. In Lago de Atitlán fast fiberglass launches zip across the waters between villages.

BUS, MINIBUS & PICKUP

Buses go almost everywhere in Guatemala. Guatemala's buses will leave you with some of your most vivid memories of the country. Most of them are ancient school buses from the US and Canada (see boxed text, p330). It is not unusual for a local family of five to squeeze into seats that were originally designed for two child-sized bottoms. Many travelers know these vehicles as chicken buses, after the live cargo accompanying many passengers. They are frequent, crowded and cheap. Expect to pay Q10 (or less!) for an hour of travel.

Chicken buses will stop anywhere, for anyone. Helpers will yell '*hay lugares!*' (eye loo-*gar*-ays), which literally means 'there are places.' Never mind that the space they refer to may be no more than a sliver of air between hundreds of locals mashed against one another. These same helpers will also yell their bus's destination in voices of varying hilarity and cadence; just listen for the song of your town. Tall travelers will be especially challenged on these buses. To catch a chicken bus, simply stand beside the road with your arm out parallel to the ground.

Some routes, especially between big cities, are served by more comfortable buses with the luxury of one seat per person. The best buses are labeled 'Pullman,' 'especial' or 'primera clase.' Occasionally, these may have bathrooms, televisions and even food service.

In general, more buses leave in the morning (some leave as early as 3am) than the afternoon. Bus traffic drops off precipitously after about 4pm; night buses are rare and not generally recommended. An exception are the overnight buses from Guatemala City to Flores, which have not experienced (to our knowledge) any trouble of note in several years (we hope we're not tempting fate here).

Distances in Guatemala are not huge and, apart from the aforementioned Guate–Flores run, you won't often ride for more than four hours at a time. On a typical four-hour bus trip you'll cover 175km to 200km for Q40 to Q50.

For a few of the better services you can buy tickets in advance, and this is generally worth doing as it ensures that you get a place.

On some shorter routes minibuses, usually called 'microbuses,' are replacing chicken buses. These are operated by the same cram-'em-all-in principle and can be even more uncomfortable because they have less leg room. Where neither buses nor minibuses roam, pickup (*picop*) trucks serve as de facto buses; you hail them and pay for them as if they were the genuine article.

At least a couple of times a month, a bus plunges over a cliff or rounds a blind bend into a head-on collision. Newspapers are full of gory details and diagrams of the latest wreck, which doesn't foster affectionate feelings toward Guatemalan public transportation.

CAR & MOTORCYCLE

You can drive in Guatemala with your home-country driver's license or with an International Driving Permit (IDP). Gasoline (petrol) and diesel are widely available. Motor parts may be hard to find, especially for modern vehicles with sophisticated electronics and emissions-control systems. Old Toyota pickups are ubiquitous, though, so parts and mechanics will be more widely available.

Guatemalan driving etiquette will probably be very different from what you're used to back home: passing on blind curves, ceding the right of way to vehicles coming uphill on narrow passes and deafening honking for no apparent reason are just the start. Expect few road signs and no indication from other drivers of what they are about to do. A vehicle coming uphill always has the right of way. *Túmulos* are speed bumps that are generously (sometimes oddly) placed throughout the country, usually on the main drag through a town. Use of seat belts is obligatory, but generally not practiced.

In Guatemala driving at night is a bad idea for many reasons, not the least of which are armed bandits, drunk drivers and decreased visibility.

Every driver involved in an accident that results in injury or death is taken into custody until a judge determines responsibility.

If someone's car breaks down on the highway (particularly on curvy mountain roads), they'll warn other drivers by putting shrubs or small branches on the road for a few hundred meters beforehand. Annoyingly, they rarely pick them up afterwards, but if you're driving and you see these, it's best to be cautious and slow down.

WARNING

While bus travel at night in Guatemala is rarely a good idea for anybody, it is strongly advised that solo female travelers not catch buses – Pullman or 'chicken' – at night time, the exception being the overnight buses traveling between Guatemala City and Flores. There have been no incident reports regarding those services.

Basically, what you want to avoid is being the last person on the bus when it arrives, if it's going to arrive at night.

Rental

You can rent cars in Guatemala City (see p84), Antigua (see p110), Quetzaltenango (see p169), Cobán (see p219) and Flores (see p282). A four-door, five-seat, five-gear vehicle with air-con, such as a Chevrolet Optra, will normally cost around Q550 a day including insurance and unlimited kilometers. Discounts may apply if you rent for three days or more. The cheapest, reliable small cars we found cost a minuscule Q145 a day.

To rent a car or motorcycle you need to show your passport, driver's license and a major credit card. Usually, the person renting the vehicle must be 25 years or older. Insurance policies accompanying rental cars may not protect you from loss or theft, in which case you could be liable for hundreds or even thousands of dollars in damages. Be careful where you park, especially in Guatemala City and at night. Even if your hotel does not have parking, they will know of a secure garage somewhere nearby.

Motorcycles are available for rent in Antigua (see p110). Bringing safety gear is highly recommended.

HITCHHIKING

Hitchhiking in the strict sense of the word is generally not practiced in Guatemala because it is not safe. However, where the bus service is sporadic or nonexistent, pickup trucks and other vehicles may serve as public transport. If you stand beside the road with your arm out, someone will stop. You are expected to pay the driver as if you were traveling on a bus and the fare will be similar. This is a safe and reliable system used by locals and travelers, and the only inconvenience you're likely to encounter is full to overflowing vehicles – get used to it.

LOCAL TRANSPORTATION
Bus

Public transportation within towns and cities and to nearby villages is chiefly provided by aged, polluting, crowded and loud buses. They're useful to travelers chiefly in the more spread-out cities such as Guatemala City, Quetzaltenango and Huehuetenango. See p65 for a warning on using public transport in the capital.

Taxi

Taxis are fairly plentiful in most significant towns. A 10-minute ride can cost about Q50, which is relatively expensive – expect to hear plenty of woeful tales from taxi drivers about the price of gasoline. Except for some taxis in Guatemala City, they don't use meters: you must agree upon the fare before you set off – best before you get in, in fact. Taxis will also often take you to out-of-town archaeological sites and other places for reasonable round-

---

A CHICKEN BUS IS HATCHED

If you rode the bus to school 10 years ago or more in the US, you might just end up meeting an old friend in Guatemala, resurrected and given new life as a 'chicken bus.' Love 'em or hate 'em, chicken buses (*camionetas* or *parrillas* to Guatemalans) are a fact of life in traveling around Guatemala. A lot of times there is no alternative.

As you can probably tell by the signs that sometimes remain in these buses ('anyone breaking the rules will lose their bus riding privileges'), these buses really did once carry school kids. In the US, once school buses reach the ripe old age of 10 years, or they do 150,000 miles, they're auctioned off. This is just the first step in the long process that results in the buses hitting the Guatemalan road. They then get towed through the States and Mexico, taken to a workshop here where they are refitted (bigger engine, six-speed gearbox, roof rack, destination board, luggage rack, longer seats) and fancied up with a paint job, CD player and chrome detailing.

Drivers then add their individual touches – anything from religious paraphernalia to stuffed toys and Christmas lights dangling around the dashboard area.

Thus, the chicken bus is ready to roll, and roll they do. The average bus works 14 hours a day, seven days a week – more miles in one day than it covered in a week back on the school run.

If you've got a choice of buses to go with, looks *are* important – chances are that if the paint is fresh and the chrome gleaming, the owner also has the cash to spend on new brakes and regular maintenance. And, with a conservative estimate of an average of one chicken-bus accident per week in Guatemala, this is something you may want to keep in mind.

trip fares, including waiting time while you look around.

Shuttle Minibus

Shuttle minibuses run by travel agencies provide comfortable and quick transport along the main routes plied by tourists. You'll find these heavily advertised wherever they are offered. With a few notable exceptions (Lanquín to Antigua for Q100, anyone?) they're much more expensive than buses (anywhere between five and 15 times as expensive), but more convenient: they usually offer a door-to-door service. The most popular shuttle routes include Guatemala City airport–Antigua, Antigua–Panajachel, Panajachel–Chichicastenango and Lanquín–Antigua.

TRANSPORTATION

Health Dr David Goldberg

CONTENTS

Travelers to Central America need to be concerned about food- and water-borne, as well as mosquito-borne, infections. Most of these illnesses are not life-threatening, but they can certainly ruin your trip. Besides getting the proper vaccinations, it's important that you bring along a good insect repellent and exercise great care in what you eat and drink.

BEFORE YOU GO

Since most vaccines don't produce immunity until at least two weeks after they're given, visit a physician four to eight weeks before departure. Ask your doctor for an international certificate of vaccination (otherwise known as the yellow booklet), which will list all the vaccinations you've received. This is mandatory for countries that require proof of yellow fever vaccination upon entry, but it's a good idea to carry it wherever you travel.

INSURANCE

If your health insurance does not cover you for medical expenses abroad, strongly consider getting supplemental insurance. Check the Bookings & Services section of www.lonely planet.com for more information. See also the **US State Department website** (www.travel.state.gov) for a list of medical evacuation and travel insurance companies. Find out in advance if your insurance plan will make payments directly to providers or reimburse you later for overseas health expenditures.

MEDICAL CHECKLIST

- antibiotics
- antidiarrheal drugs (eg loperamide)
- acetaminophen/paracetamol (Tylenol) or aspirin
- anti-inflammatory drugs (eg ibuprofen)
- antihistamines (for hay fever and allergic reactions)
- antibacterial ointment (eg Bactroban) for cuts and abrasions
- steroid cream or cortisone (for poison ivy and other allergic rashes)
- bandages, gauze, gauze rolls
- adhesive or paper tape
- scissors, safety pins, tweezers
- thermometer
- pocket knife
- DEET-containing insect repellent for the skin
- permethrin-containing insect spray for clothing, tents and bed nets
- sunblock
- oral-rehydration salts
- iodine tablets (for water purification)
- syringes and sterile needles

INTERNET RESOURCES

There is a wealth of travel health advice available on the internet. For further information, the **Lonely Planet website** (www.lonelyplanet.com) is a good place to start. A superb book called *International Travel and Health,* which is revised annually and is available online at no cost, is published by the **World Health Organization** (www.who.int/ith/). Another website of general interest is **MD Travel Health** (www.mdtravelhealth.com), which provides complete travel health recommendations for every country, updated daily, also at no cost.

It's usually a good idea to consult your government's travel health website before departure, if one is available.

Australia (www.smartraveller.gov.au)
Canada (www.hc-sc.gc.ca)
UK (www.doh.gov.uk)
United States (www.cdc.gov/travel/)

FURTHER READING

For further information, see *Healthy Travel Central & South America,* also from Lonely Planet. If traveling with children, Lonely Planet's *Travel with Children* may be useful. The *ABC of Healthy Travel,* by E Walker et al, and *Medicine for the Outdoors,* by Paul S Auerbach, are other valuable resources.

IN TRANSIT

DEEP VEIN THROMBOSIS (DVT)

Blood clots may form in the legs during plane flights, chiefly because of prolonged immobility. The longer the flight, the greater the risk. Though most blood clots are reabsorbed uneventfully, some may break off and travel through the blood vessels to the lungs, where they could cause life-threatening complications.

The chief symptom of deep vein thrombosis is swelling or pain of the foot, ankle or calf, usually but not always on just one side. When a blood clot travels to the lungs, it may cause chest pain and difficulty breathing. Travelers with any of these symptoms should immediately seek medical attention.

To prevent the development of deep vein thrombosis on long flights, you should walk about the cabin, perform isometric compressions of the leg muscles (ie contract the leg muscles while sitting), drink plenty of fluids, and avoid alcohol and tobacco.

JET LAG & MOTION SICKNESS

Jet lag is common when crossing more than five time zones, and can result in insomnia, fatigue, malaise or nausea. To avoid jet lag try drinking plenty of fluids (nonalcoholic) and eating light meals. Upon arrival, get exposure to natural sunlight and readjust

---

RECOMMENDED VACCINATIONS

The only required vaccine is yellow fever, and that's only if you're arriving in Guatemala from a yellow fever-infected country in Africa or South America. However, a number of vaccines are recommended. Note that some of these are not approved for use by children and pregnant women – check with your physician.

Vaccine	Recommended for	Dosage	Side effects
hepatitis A	all travelers	1 dose before trip; booster 6-12 months later	soreness at injection site; headaches; body aches
typhoid	all travelers	4 capsules, 1 taken every other day	abdominal pain; nausea; rash
yellow fever	required for travelers arriving from a yellow fever-infected area in Africa or the Americas	1 dose lasts 10 years	headaches; body aches; severe reactions are rare
hepatitis B	long-term travelers in close contact with the local population	3 doses over 6 months	soreness at injection site; low-grade fever
rabies	travelers who may have contact with animals and may not have access to medical care	3 doses over 3-4 weeks	soreness at injection site; headaches; body aches
tetanus-diphtheria	all travelers who haven't had a booster within 10 years	1 dose lasts 10 years	soreness at injection site
measles	travelers born after 1956 who've had only 1 measles vaccination	1 dose	fever; rash; joint pains; allergic reactions
chickenpox	travelers who've never had chickenpox	2 doses 1 month apart	fever; mild case of chickenpox

Bring medications in their original containers, clearly labeled. A signed, dated letter from your physician describing all medical conditions and medications, including generic names, is also a good idea. If carrying syringes or needles, be sure to have a physician's letter documenting their medical necessity.

HEALTH

your schedule (for meals, sleep etc) as soon as possible.

Antihistamines such as dimenhydrinate (Dramamine) and meclizine (Antivert or Bonine) are usually the first choice for treating motion sickness. Their main side-effect is drowsiness. A herbal alternative is ginger, which works like a charm for some people.

IN GUATEMALA

AVAILABILITY & COST OF HEALTH CARE

Good medical care is available in Guatemala City, but options are limited elsewhere. In general, private hospitals are more reliable than public facilities, which may experience significant shortages of equipment and supplies. Many travelers use **Hospital Herrera Llerandi** (☎ 2384 5959; www.herrerallerandi.com; 6a Av 8-71, Zona 10). For an online list of hospitals and physicians in Guatemala, go to the **US embassy website** (http://guatemala.usembassy.gov/medical_infor mation.html).

Many doctors and hospitals expect payment in cash, regardless of whether you have travel health insurance. If you develop a life-threatening medical problem, you'll probably want to be evacuated to a country with state-of-the-art medical care. Since this may cost tens of thousands of dollars, be sure you have insurance to cover this before you depart.

Many pharmacies are well-supplied, but important medications may not be consistently available. Be sure to bring along adequate supplies of all prescription drugs.

INFECTIOUS DISEASES
Cholera

Cholera is an intestinal infection acquired through ingestion of contaminated food or water. The main symptom is profuse, watery diarrhea, which may be so severe that it causes life-threatening dehydration. The key treatment is drinking oral rehydration solution. Antibiotics are also given, usually tetracycline or doxycycline, though quinolone antibiotics such as ciprofloxacin and levofloxacin are also effective.

Cholera outbreaks occur periodically in Guatemala, but the disease is rare among travelers. Cholera vaccine is no longer required, and is in fact no longer available in some countries, including the US, because the old vaccine was relatively ineffective and

caused side effects. There are new vaccines that are safer and more effective, but they're not available in many countries and are only recommended for those at particularly high risk.

Dengue Fever (Breakbone Fever)

Dengue fever is a viral infection found throughout Central America. Thousands of cases occur each year in Guatemala. Dengue is transmitted by aedes mosquitoes, which bite predominantly during the daytime and are usually found close to human habitations, often indoors. They breed primarily in artificial water containers, such as jars, barrels, cans, cisterns, metal drums, plastic containers and discarded tires. As a result, dengue is especially common in densely populated, urban environments.

Dengue usually causes flu-like symptoms, including fever, muscle aches, joint pains, headaches, nausea and vomiting, often followed by a rash. The body aches may be quite uncomfortable, but most cases resolve uneventfully in a few days. Severe cases usually occur in children under the age of 15 who are experiencing their second dengue infection.

There is no treatment for dengue fever except to take analgesics such as acetaminophen/paracetamol (Tylenol) and drink plenty of fluids. Severe cases may require hospitalization for intravenous fluids and supportive care. There is no vaccine. The cornerstone of prevention is protecting against insect bites; see p337.

Hepatitis A

Hepatitis A occurs throughout Central America. It's a viral infection of the liver that is usually acquired by ingestion of contaminated water, food or ice, though it may also be acquired by direct contact with infected persons. The illness occurs all over the world, but the incidence is higher in developing nations. Symptoms may include fever, malaise, jaundice, nausea, vomiting and abdominal pain. Most cases resolve uneventfully, though hepatitis A occasionally causes severe liver damage. There is no treatment.

The vaccine for hepatitis A is extremely safe and highly effective. If you get a booster six to 12 months after the initial vaccination, it lasts for at least 10 years. You really should get it before you go to Guatemala or any other developing nation. Because the safety of hepatitis A vaccine has not been established for pregnant women or children under the age of two, they should instead be given a gammaglobulin injection.

Hepatitis B

Like hepatitis A, hepatitis B is a liver infection that occurs worldwide but is more common in developing nations. Unlike hepatitis A, the disease is usually acquired by sexual contact or by exposure to infected blood, generally through blood transfusions or contaminated needles. The vaccine is recommended only for long-term travelers (on the road more than six months) who expect to live in rural areas or have close physical contact with the local population. Additionally, the vaccine is recommended for anyone who anticipates sexual contact with the local inhabitants or a possible need for medical, dental or other treatments while abroad, especially if a need for transfusions or injections is expected.

Hepatitis B vaccine is safe and highly effective. However, a total of three injections are necessary to establish full immunity. Several countries added hepatitis B vaccine to the list of routine childhood immunizations in the 1980s, so many young adults are already protected.

Malaria

Malaria occurs in every country in Central America. It's transmitted by mosquito bites, usually between dusk and dawn. The main symptom is high spiking fevers, which may be accompanied by chills, sweats, headache, body aches, weakness, vomiting or diarrhea. Severe cases may involve the central nervous system and lead to seizures, confusion, coma and death.

Taking malaria pills is strongly recommended for all rural areas in Guatemala except at altitudes greater than 1500m. The risk is high in the departments of Alta Verapaz, Baja Verapaz, El Petén and San Marcos, and moderate in the departments of Escuintla, Huehuetenango, Izabal, Quiché, Retalhuleu, Suchitepéquez and Zacapa. Transmission is greatest during the rainy season (June through November). There is no risk in Antigua or Lago de Atitlán.

For Guatemala, the first-choice malaria pill is chloroquine, taken once weekly in a dosage of 500mg, starting one to two weeks before arrival and continuing through the trip and for four weeks after departure. Chloroquine is safe, inexpensive and highly effective. Side effects are typically mild and may include

nausea, abdominal discomfort, headache, dizziness, blurred vision and itching. Severe reactions are uncommon.

Protecting yourself against mosquito bites is just as important as taking malaria pills (see the recommendations on p337), since no pills are 100% effective.

If you may not have access to medical care while traveling, you should bring along additional pills for emergency self-treatment, which you should undergo if you can't reach a doctor and you develop symptoms that suggest malaria, such as high spiking fevers. One option is to take four tablets of Malarone once daily for three days. If you start self-medication, you should try to see a doctor at the earliest possible opportunity.

If you develop a fever after returning home, see a physician, as malaria symptoms may not occur for months.

Rabies

Rabies is a viral infection of the brain and spinal cord that is almost always fatal if not treated. The rabies virus is carried in the saliva of infected animals and is typically transmitted through an animal bite, though contamination of any break in the skin with infected saliva may result in rabies. Rabies occurs in all Central American countries. In Guatemala the risk is greatest in the northern provinces along the Mexican border. Most cases are related to dog bites.

Rabies vaccine is safe, but a full series requires three injections and is quite expensive. Those at high risk for rabies, such as animal handlers and spelunkers (cave explorers), should certainly get the vaccine. In addition, you should consider asking for the vaccine if you might be traveling to remote areas and might not have access to appropriate medical care if needed. The treatment for a possibly rabid bite consists of rabies vaccine with rabies immune globulin. It's effective, but must be given promptly. Most travelers don't need rabies vaccine.

All animal bites and scratches must be promptly and thoroughly cleansed with large amounts of soap and water and local health authorities must be contacted to determine whether or not further treatment is necessary (see p337).

Typhoid

This fever is caused by ingestion of food or water contaminated by a species of salmonella known as *Salmonella typhi*. Fever occurs in virtually all cases. Other symptoms may include headache, malaise, muscle aches, dizziness, loss of appetite, nausea and abdominal pain. Either diarrhea or constipation may occur. Possible complications include intestinal perforation, intestinal bleeding, confusion, delirium or (rarely) coma.

Unless you expect to take all your meals in major hotels and restaurants, typhoid vaccine is a good idea. It's usually given orally, but is also available as an injection. Neither vaccine is approved for use in children under the age of two.

The drug of choice for typhoid fever is usually a quinolone antibiotic such as ciprofloxacin (Cipro) or levofloxacin (Levaquin), which many travelers carry for treatment of travelers' diarrhea. However, if you self-treat for typhoid fever, you may also need to self-treat for malaria, since the symptoms of the two diseases may be indistinguishable.

Yellow Fever

Yellow fever no longer occurs in Central America, but many countries in this region, including Guatemala, require yellow fever vaccine before entry if you're arriving from a country in Africa or South America where yellow fever is known to occur. If you're not arriving from a country with yellow fever, the vaccine is neither required nor recommended. Yellow fever vaccine is given only in approved yellow fever vaccination centers, which provide validated international certificates of vaccination (also known as yellow booklets). The vaccine should be given at least 10 days before departure and remains effective for approximately 10 years. Reactions to the vaccine are generally mild and may include headaches, muscle aches, low-grade fevers, or discomfort at the injection site. Severe, life-threatening reactions have been described but are extremely rare.

Other Infections

CHAGAS DISEASE

This is a parasitic infection that is transmitted by triatomine insects (reduviid bugs), which inhabit crevices in the walls and roofs of substandard housing in South and Central America. The triatomine insect lays its feces on human skin as it bites, usually at night. A person becomes infected when he or she unknowingly rubs the feces into the bite wound or any other open sore. Chagas disease is extremely rare in travelers. However, if you sleep in a poorly constructed house, especially one made of mud, adobe or thatch, you should be sure to protect yourself with a bed net and a good insecticide.

HISTOPLASMOSIS

Caused by a soil-based fungus, histoplasmosis is acquired by inhalation, often when the soil has been disrupted. Initial symptoms may include fever, chills, dry cough, chest pain and headache, sometimes leading to pneumonia. Histoplasmosis has been reported in European travelers returning from Mazatenango.

HIV/AIDS

This has been reported in all Central American countries. Be sure to use condoms for all sexual encounters.

LEISHMANIASIS

This occurs in the mountains and jungles of all Central American countries. The infection is transmitted by sandflies, which are about one third the size of mosquitoes. Leishmaniasis may be limited to the skin, causing slowly growing ulcers over exposed parts of the body, or (less commonly) disseminate to the bone marrow, liver and spleen. The disease may be particularly severe in those with HIV. In Guatemala, most cases of cutaneous leishmaniasis are reported from the northern parts of the country at elevations less than 1000m. The greatest risk occurs in the forested areas of El Petén. The disseminated form may occur in the semiarid valleys and foothills in the east central part of the country. There is no vaccine for leishmaniasis. To protect yourself from sandflies, follow the same precautions as for mosquitoes (see opposite), except that netting must be of finer mesh (at least 18 holes to the linear inch).

LEPTOSPIROSIS

This is acquired by exposure to water contaminated by the urine of infected animals. Outbreaks often occur at times of flooding, when sewage overflow may contaminate the water sources. The initial symptoms, which resemble a mild flu, usually subside uneventfully in a few days, with or without treatment, but a minority of cases are complicated by jaundice or meningitis. There is no vaccine.

You can minimize your risk by staying out of bodies of fresh water that may be contaminated by animal urine. If you're visiting an area where an outbreak is in progress, as occurred in Guatemala after flooding in 1998, you can take 200mg of doxycycline once weekly as a preventative measure. If you actually develop leptospirosis, the treatment is 100mg of doxycycline twice daily.

ONCHOCERCIASIS (RIVER BLINDNESS)
Onchocerciasis is caused by a roundworm that may invade the eye, leading to blindness. The infection is transmitted by black flies, which breed along the banks of rapidly flowing rivers and streams. In Guatemala, the disease occurs in heavily forested areas between 500m and 1500m, chiefly the Pacific slope of the Sierra Madre and in Escuintla along the Verde and Guachipilín rivers.

TYPHUS
This may be transmitted by lice in scattered pockets of the country.

TRAVELERS' DIARRHEA
To prevent diarrhea, avoid tap water unless it has been boiled, filtered or chemically disinfected (see p338); only eat fresh fruits or vegetables if cooked or peeled; be wary of dairy products that might contain unpasteurized milk; and be highly selective when eating food from street vendors.

If you develop diarrhea, be sure to drink plenty of fluids, preferably an oral rehydration solution containing lots of salt and sugar. A few loose stools don't require treatment, but if you start having more than four or five stools a day, you should start taking an antibiotic (usually a quinolone drug) and an antidiarrheal agent (such as loperamide). If diarrhea is bloody or persists for more than 72 hours or is accompanied by fever, shaking chills or severe abdominal pain, you should seek medical attention.

ENVIRONMENTAL HAZARDS
Animal Bites
Do not attempt to pet, handle or feed any animal, with the exception of domestic animals known to be free of any infectious disease. Most animal injuries are directly related to a person's attempt to touch or feed the animal.

Any bite or scratch by a mammal, including bats, should be promptly and thoroughly cleansed with large amounts of soap and water, followed by application of an antiseptic such as iodine or alcohol. The local health authorities should be contacted immediately for possible postexposure rabies treatment, whether or not you've been immunized against rabies. It may also be advisable to start an antibiotic, since wounds caused by animal bites and scratches frequently become infected. One of the newer quinolones, such as levofloxacin (Levaquin), which many travelers carry in case of diarrhea, would be an appropriate choice.

Mosquito Bites
To prevent mosquito bites, wear long sleeves, long pants, hats and shoes (rather than sandals). Make sure you bring along a good insect repellent, preferably one that contains DEET, which should be applied to exposed skin and clothing, but not to eyes, mouth, cuts, wounds or irritated skin. Products containing lower concentrations of DEET are as effective, but for shorter periods of time. In general, adults and children over 12 should use preparations containing 25% to 35% DEET, which usually lasts about six hours. Children between two and 12 years of age should use preparations containing no more than 10% DEET, applied sparingly, which will usually last about three hours. Neurologic toxicity has been reported from DEET, especially in children, but appears to be extremely uncommon and generally related to overuse. Compounds containing DEET should not be used on children under the age of two.

Insect repellents containing certain botanical products, including oil of eucalyptus and soybean oil, are effective but last only 1½ to two hours. Repellents containing DEET are preferable for areas where there is a high risk of malaria or yellow fever. Products based on citronella are not effective.

For additional protection, you can apply permethrin to clothing, shoes, tents and bed nets. Permethrin treatments are safe and remain effective for at least two weeks, even when items are laundered. Permethrin should not be applied directly to skin.

Don't sleep with the window open unless there is a screen. If sleeping outdoors or in an accommodation that allows entry of mosquitoes, use a bed net, preferably treated with permethrin, with edges tucked in under the mattress. The mesh size should be less than

HEALTH

1.5mm. If the sleeping area is not otherwise protected, use a mosquito coil, which will fill the room with insecticide through the night. Repellent-impregnated wristbands are not effective.

Snake Bites

Snakes are a hazard in some areas of Central America. In Guatemala the chief concern is *Bothrops asper,* the Central American or common lancehead, also called the fer-de-lance and known locally as *barba amarilla* (yellow beard) or *terciopelo* (velvet skin). This heavy-bodied snake reaches up to 2m in length and is commonly found along fallen logs and other small animal runs, especially in the northern provinces.

In the event of a venomous snake bite, place the victim at rest, keep the bitten area immobilized and move the victim immediately to the nearest medical facility. Avoid tourniquets, which are no longer recommended.

Sun

To protect yourself from excessive sun exposure, you should stay out of the midday sun, wear sunglasses and a wide-brimmed sun hat, and apply sunscreen with SPF 15 or higher, with both UVA and UVB protection. Sunscreen should be generously applied to all exposed parts of the body approximately 30 minutes before sun exposure and should be reapplied after swimming or vigorous activity. Travelers should also drink plenty of fluids and avoid strenuous exercise when the temperature is high.

Water

Tap water in Guatemala is not safe to drink. Vigorous boiling for one minute is the most effective means of water purification. At altitudes greater than 2000m, boil for three minutes.

Another option is to disinfect water with iodine pills. Instructions are usually enclosed and should be carefully followed. Or you can add 2% tincture of iodine to 1 quart or liter of water (five drops to clear water, 10 drops to cloudy water) and let stand for 30 minutes. If the water is cold, longer times may be required. The taste of iodinated water may be improved by adding vitamin C (ascorbic acid). Iodinated water should not be consumed for more than a few weeks. Pregnant

---

> **TRADITIONAL MEDICINE**
>
> The following are some traditional remedies for common travel-related conditions.
>
> - Jet lag – melatonin
> - Mosquito-bite prevention – oil of eucalyptus or soybean oil
> - Motion sickness – ginger

---

women, those with a history of thyroid disease and those allergic to iodine should not drink iodinated water.

A number of water filters are on the market. Those with smaller pores (reverse osmosis filters) provide the broadest protection, but they are relatively large and are readily plugged by debris. Those with somewhat larger pores (microstrainer filters) are ineffective against viruses, although they remove other organisms. Manufacturers' instructions must be carefully followed.

Safe-to-drink, inexpensive purified water *(agua pura)* is widely available in hotels, shops and restaurants. Salvavida is a universally trusted brand.

CHILDREN & PREGNANT WOMEN

In general, it's safe for children and pregnant women to go to Guatemala. However, because some of the vaccines listed on p333 are not approved for use in children and pregnant women, these travelers should be particularly careful not to drink tap water or consume any questionable food or beverage. Also, when traveling with children, make sure they're up-to-date on all routine immunizations. It's sometimes appropriate to give children some of their vaccines a little early before visiting a developing nation. You should discuss this with your pediatrician. Lastly, if pregnant, you should bear in mind that should a complication such as premature labor develop while abroad, the quality of medical care may not be comparable to that in your home country.

Since yellow fever vaccine is not recommended for pregnant women or children less than nine months old, these travelers, if arriving from a country with yellow fever, should obtain a waiver letter, preferably written on letterhead stationery and bearing the stamp used by official immunization centers to validate the international certificate of vaccination.

Language

CONTENTS

There are around 20 Maya indigenous languages used in and around Guatemala, but Spanish is still the most commonly spoken language.

SPANISH

The Spanish of Latin America – referred to as *castellano* more often than *español* – comes in many varieties. Slang and regional vocabulary, much of it derived from indigenous languages, add to the linguistic richness. Despite this diversity, Latin American Spanish has retained a remarkable unity over time and across a vast area. With the Spanish words and phrases in this chapter, you'll be understood across Guatemala.

It's worth noting that, unlike in Spain, the plural of the familiar *tú* (you) form is *ustedes* rather than *vosotros* and that the letters c and z are never pronounced as lisped in Latin America. It's easy enough to pick up some basic Spanish, but for those who want to delve a little deeper, courses are available in many places around the country (see p314).

For a more in-depth language guide, get a copy of Lonely Planet's *Latin American Spanish* phrasebook.

PRONUNCIATION

The pronunciation of Spanish is easy to master, as most Spanish sounds are found in English – only the throaty 'kh' might require a bit of practise. If you read our pronunciation guides below as if they were English, you'll be understood just fine.

Vowels

a	as the 'a' in 'father'
ai	as in 'aisle'
ay	as in 'say'
e	as the 'e' in 'met'
ee	as the 'ee' in 'meet'
o	as the 'o' in 'more' (without the 'r')
oo	as the 'oo' in 'zoo'
ow	as in 'how'
oy	as in 'boy'

Consonants

Spanish consonants sound similar to their English counterparts. The exceptions are given in the following list.

b/v	as a very soft 'v' (somewhere between 'b' and 'v')
h	never pronounced
kh	as the throaty 'ch' in the Scottish *loch*
ll	in Guatemala this is pronounced as 'y' in 'yes'
ny	as the 'ny' in 'canyon'
r	as in 'run' but stronger and rolled, especially at the beginning of a word and in all words with *rr*
s	not lisped

Word Stress

In general, words ending in n, s or a vowel have stress on the second-last syllable, while those with other endings have stress on the last syllable. If you see an accent mark over a syllable, it cancels out these rules and you just stress that syllable instead. In our pronunciation guides, the stressed syllables are in italics, so you don't even have to worry about these rules.

LANGUAGE

GENDER & PLURALS

Spanish nouns are either masculine or feminine. Dictionaries will tell you what gender a noun is, but there are a few rules to help determine gender. Words ending with -**a**, -**ción**, -**sión** or -**dad** are generally feminine. Other endings typically indicate a masculine noun. Adjectives change to agree with the gender of the noun they modify (masculine/feminine -**o**/-**a**). Where both forms are included in this chapter, they are separated by a slash, with the masculine form given first, eg *perdido/a*.

If a noun or adjective ends in a vowel, the plural is formed by adding -**s** to the end. If it ends in a consonant, the plural is formed by adding -**es** to the end.

ACCOMMODATIONS

I'm looking for a ...	*Estoy buscando ...*	e·*stoy* boos·*kan*·do ...
Where's a ...?	*¿Dónde hay ...?*	don·de ai ...
cabin	*una cabana*	oo·na ka·*ba*·nya
camping ground	*un terreno de camping*	oon te·*re*·no de kam·peen
guesthouse	*una pensión/ una casa de huéspedes*	oo·na pen·*syon*/ oo·na ka·sa de we·spe·des
hotel	*un hotel*	oon o·*tel*
youth hostel	*un albergue juvenil*	oon al·*ber*·ge khoo·ve·*neel*

I'd like a ... room.	*Quisiera una habitación ...*	kee·*sye*·ra oo·na a·bee·ta·*syon* ...
double	*doble*	do·ble
single	*individual*	een·dee·vee·*dwal*
twin	*con dos camas*	kon dos ka·mas

How much is it per ...?	*¿Cuánto cuesta por ...?*	kwan·to kwes·ta por ...
night	*noche*	no·che
person	*persona*	per·so·na
week	*semana*	se·ma·na

Does it include breakfast?
¿Incluye el desayuno? een·*kloo*·ye el de·sa·*yoo*·no
Can I see the room?
¿Puedo ver la habitación? pwe·do ver la a·bee·ta·*syon*
I don't like it.
No me gusta. no me *goos*·ta
It's fine, I'll take it.
OK, la alquilo. o·*kay* la al·*kee*·lo
I'm leaving now.
Me voy ahora. me voy a·o·ra

cheaper	*más económico*	mas e·ko·*no*·mee·ko
discount	*descuento*	des·*kwen*·to
private/shared bathroom	*baño privado/ compartido*	*ba*·nyo pree·*va*·do/ kom·par·*tee*·do
too expensive	*demasiado caro*	de·ma·*sya*·do ka·ro

CONVERSATION & ESSENTIALS

Central America is generally more formal than many of the South American countries. The polite form *usted* (you) is used in all cases in this chapter; where options are given, the form is indicated by the abbreviations 'pol' and 'inf.'

When approaching a stranger for information, always extend a greeting, such as *buenos días* or *buenas tardes*, and use the polite form of address, especially with the police and public officials. Note that the three most common greetings are often abbreviated to simply *buenos/buenas*.

Hello.	*Hola.*	o·la
Good morning.	*Buenos días.*	bwe·nos dee·as
Good afternoon.	*Buenas tardes.*	bwe·nas tar·des
Good evening/ night.	*Buenas noches.*	bwe·nas no·ches
Goodbye.	*Adiós.*	a·*dyos*
See you later.	*Hasta luego.*	as·ta lwe·go
Yes./No.	*Sí./No.*	see/no
Please.	*Por favor.*	por fa·*vor*
Thank you.	*Gracias.*	gra·syas
Many thanks.	*Muchas gracias.*	moo·chas gra·syas
You're welcome.	*Con mucho gusto.*	kon moo·cho goos·to
Pardon.	*Perdón.*	per·don
Excuse me. (to ask permission)	*Con permiso.*	kon per·*mee*·so
Sorry. (when apologizing)	*Disculpe.*	dees·*kool*·pe

How are you?
¿Cómo está/estás? ko·mo es·*ta*/es·*tas* (pol/inf)
Fine, thanks. And you?
Bien, gracias. byen gra·syas
¿Y usted/tú? ee oos·*te*/too (pol/inf)
What's your name?
¿Cómo se llama? ko·mo se ya·ma (pol)
¿Cómo te llamas? ko·mo te ya·mas (inf)
My name is ...
Me llamo ... me ya·mo ...
It's a pleasure to meet you.
Mucho gusto. moo·cho goos·to
Where are you from?
¿De dónde es/eres? de don·de es/e·res (pol/inf)

I'm from ...
Soy de ...   soy de ...
Can I take a photo?
¿Puedo sacar una foto?   pwe·do sa·kar oo·na fo·to

DIRECTIONS
How do I get to ...?
¿Cómo puedo llegar a ...? ko·mo pwe·do ye·gar a ...
What's the address?
¿Cuál es la dirección?   kwal es la dee·rek·syon
Can you show me (on the map)?
¿Me lo podría indicar   me lo po·dree·a een·dee·kar
(en el mapa)?   (en el ma·pa)
Is it far?
¿Está lejos?   es·ta le·khos

here/there	aquí/allí	a·kee/a·yee
left	a la izquierda	a la ees·kyer·da
on the corner	en la esquina	en la es·kee·na
right	a la derecha	a la de·re·cha
straight ahead	todo derecho	to·do de·re·cho

north	norte	nor·te
south	sur	soor
east	este	es·te
west	oeste	o·es·te

avenue	avenida	a·ve·nee·da
block	cuadra	kwa·dra
highway	carretera	ka·re·te·ra
street	calle	ka·ye

EATING OUT
For a food and drink glossary, see p54.

Can you recommend a bar/restaurant?
¿Puede recomendar un   pwe·de re·ko·men·dar oon
bar/restaurante?   bar/res·tow·ran·te
Do you have an English menu?
¿Hay un menú en inglés? ai oon me·noo en een·gles
What would you recommend?
¿Qué me recomienda?   ke me re·ko·myen·da
What's the local specialty?
¿Cuál es la especialidad kwal es la es·pe·sya·lee·dad
local?   lo·kal
I'll have (that).
Yo quiero (eso).   yo kye·ro (e·so)
I'd like it with/without ...
Lo quisiera con/sin ... lo kee·sye·ra kon/seen ...
I'm a vegetarian.
Soy vegetariano/a.   soy ve·khe·ta·rya·no/a
That was delicious.
Estaba buenísimo.   es·ta·ba bwe·nee·see·mo

EMERGENCIES

Help!	¡Socorro!	so·ko·ro
Stop!	¡Pare!	pa·re
Fire!	¡Fuego!	fwe·go
Go away!	¡Váyase!	va·ya·se
Watch out!	¡Cuidado!	kwee·da·do
I was robbed.	Me robaron.	me ro·ba·ron

Call ...!	¡Llame a ...!	ya·me a ...
an ambulance	una	oo·na
	ambulancia	am·boo·lan·sya
a doctor	un médico	oon me·dee·ko
the police	la policía	la po·lee·see·a

It's an emergency.
Es una emergencia.   es oo·na e·mer·khen·sya
Can you help me, please?
¿Me puede ayudar,   me pwe·de a·yoo·dar
por favor?   por fa·vor
I'm lost.
Estoy perdido/a.   es·toy per·dee·do/a
Where are the toilets?
¿Dónde están los baños? don·de es·tan los ba·nyos

I'll buy you a drink.
Te invito a una copa.   te een·vee·to a oo·na ko·pa
Please bring the drink list.
Por favor nos trae la   por fa·vor nos tra·e la
lista de bebidas.   lees·ta de be·bee·das
Cheers!
¡Salud!   sa·lood
The bill, please.
La cuenta, por favor.   la kwen·ta por fa·vor

HEALTH
I'm sick.
Estoy enfermo/a.   es·toy en·fer·mo/a
I need a doctor.
Necesito un médico.   ne·se·see·to oon me·dee·ko
Where's the hospital?
¿Dónde está el hospital? don·de es·ta el os·pee·tal
I'm pregnant.
Estoy embarazada.   es·toy em·ba·ra·sa·da
I'm allergic to penicillin.
Soy alérgico/a   soy a·ler·khee·ko/a
a la penicilina.   a la pe·nee·see·lee·na

cough	tos	tos
diarrhea	diarrea	dya·re·a
fever	fiebre	fye·bre
headache	dolor de cabeza	do·lor de ka·be·sa
nausea	náuseas	now·se·as
sore throat	dolor de garganta	do·lor de gar·gan·ta

LANGUAGE

LANGUAGE DIFFICULTIES

Do you speak English?
¿Habla/Hablas inglés?   a·bla/a·blas een·*gles* (pol/inf)

Does anyone here speak English?
¿Hay alguien que   ai al·gyen ke
hable inglés?   a·ble een·*gles*

I (don't) understand.
Yo (no) entiendo.   yo (no) en·*tyen*·do

How do you say ...?
¿Cómo se dice ...?   ko·mo se *dee*·se ...

What does ... mean?
¿Qué significa ...?   ke seeg·*nee*·fee·ka ...

Could you please ...?	*¿Puede ...,* *por favor?*	pwe·de ... por fa·*vor*
repeat that	*repetirlo*	re·pe·*teer*·lo
speak more slowly	*hablar más* *despacio*	a·*blar* mas des·*pa*·syo
write it down	*escribirlo*	es·kree·*beer*·lo

NUMBERS

0	cero	se·ro
1	uno	oo·no
2	dos	dos
3	tres	tres
4	cuatro	kwa·tro
5	cinco	seen·ko
6	seis	says
7	siete	sye·te
8	ocho	o·cho
9	nueve	nwe·ve
10	diez	dyes
11	once	on·se
12	doce	do·se
13	trece	tre·se
14	catorce	ka·tor·se
15	quince	keen·se
16	dieciséis	dye·see·says
17	diecisiete	dye·see·sye·te
18	dieciocho	dye·see·o·cho
19	diecinueve	dye·see·nwe·ve
20	veinte	vayn·te
30	treinta	trayn·ta
40	cuarenta	kwa·ren·ta
50	cincuenta	seen·kwen·ta
60	sesenta	se·sen·ta
70	setenta	se·ten·ta
80	ochenta	o·chen·ta
90	noventa	no·ven·ta
100	cien	syen
1000	mil	meel
10,000	diez mil	dyes meel
1,000,000	un millón	oon mee·yon

SHOPPING & SERVICES

I'd like to buy ...
Quisiera comprar ...   kee·*sye*·ra kom·*prar* ...

I'm just looking.
Sólo estoy mirando.   so·lo es·*toy* mee·*ran*·do

May I look at it?
¿Puedo verlo?   pwe·do ver·lo

How much is it?
¿Cuánto cuesta?   kwan·to kwes·ta

That's too expensive.
Es demasiado caro.   es de·ma·*sya*·do ka·ro

Could you lower the price?
¿Podría bajar un poco   po·dree·a ba·khar oon po·ko
el precio?   el pre·syo

Do you accept ...?	*¿Aceptan ...?*	a·*sep*·tan ...
American dollars	*dólares* *americanos*	do·la·res a·me·ree·*ka*·nos
credit cards	*tarjetas de* *crédito*	tar·*khe*·tas de kre·dee·to
traveler's checks	*cheques de* *viajero*	che·kes de vya·*khe*·ro

Where's the ...?	*¿Dónde está ...?*	don·de es·*ta* ...
ATM	*el cajero* *automático*	el ka·*khe*·ro ow·to·*ma*·tee·ko
bank	*el banco*	el ban·ko
chemist	*la farmacia*	la far·*ma*·sya
exchange office	*la oficina de* *cambio*	la o·fee·*see*·na de kam·byo
general store	*la tienda*	la tyen·da
laundry	*la lavandería*	la la·van·de·*ree*·a
market	*el mercado*	el mer·*ka*·do
post office	*los correos*	los ko·re·os
supermarket	*el super-* *mercado*	el soo·per- mer·*ka*·do
tourist office	*la oficina de* *turismo*	la o·fee·*see*·na de too·*rees*·mo

---

SIGNS

Abierto	Open
Cerrado	Closed
Comisaría de Policía	Police Station
Entrada	Entrance
Información	Information
Prohibido	Prohibited
Salida	Exit
Servicios/Baños	Toilets
Hombres/Varones	Men
Mujeres/Damas	Women

LANGUAGE

TIME & DATES

What time is it?	*¿Qué hora es?*	ke *o*·ra es
At what time?	*¿A qué hora?*	a ke *o*·ra
It's one o'clock.	*Es la una.*	es la *oo*·na
It's (10) o'clock.	*Son las (diez).*	son las (dyes)
Quarter past ...	*... y cuarto*	... ee *kwar*·to
Half past ...	*... y media*	... ee *me*·dya
Quarter to ...	*... menos cuarto*	... me·nos *kwar*·to

at night	*por la noche*	por la *no*·che
in the afternoon	*de la tarde*	de la *tar*·de
in the morning	*de la mañana*	de la ma·*nya*·na
midnight	*medianoche*	me·dya·*no*·che
noon	*mediodía*	me·dyo·*dee*·a
now	*ahora*	a·*o*·ra
today	*hoy*	oy
tomorrow	*mañana*	ma·*nya*·na
tonight	*esta noche*	es·ta *no*·che
yesterday	*ayer*	a·*yer*

Monday	*lunes*	*loo*·nes
Tuesday	*martes*	*mar*·tes
Wednesday	*miércoles*	*myer*·ko·les
Thursday	*jueves*	*khwe*·ves
Friday	*viernes*	*vyer*·nes
Saturday	*sábado*	*sa*·ba·do
Sunday	*domingo*	do·*meen*·go

January	*enero*	e·*ne*·ro
February	*febrero*	fe·*bre*·ro
March	*marzo*	*mar*·so
April	*abril*	a·*breel*
May	*mayo*	*ma*·yo
June	*junio*	*khoo*·nyo
July	*julio*	*khoo*·lyo
August	*agosto*	a·*gos*·to
September	*septiembre*	se·*tyem*·bre
October	*octubre*	ok·*too*·bre
November	*noviembre*	no·*vyem*·bre
December	*diciembre*	dee·*syem*·bre

TRANSPORTATION
Public Transportation

At what time does the ... leave/arrive?	*¿A qué hora sale/llega el ...?*	a ke *o*·ra *sa*·le/*ye*·ga el ...
bus	*autobús*	ow·to·*boos*
plane	*avión*	a·*vyon*
ship	*barco*	*bar*·ko
train	*tren*	tren

I'd like a ticket to ...
Quisiera un boleto a ...   kee·*sye*·ra oon bo·*le*·to a ...
What's the fare to ...?
¿Cuánto cuesta a ...?   *kwan*·to *kwes*·ta a ...

airport	*aeropuerto*	a·e·ro·*pwer*·to
bus station	*estación de autobuses*	es·ta·*syon* de ow·to·*boo*·ses
bus stop	*parada de autobuses*	pa·*ra*·da de ow·to·*boo*·ses
left-luggage office	*consigna para equipaje*	kon·*seeg*·na *pa*·ra e·kee·*pa*·khe
ticket office	*boletería*	bo·le·te·*ree*·a
timetable	*horario*	o·*ra*·ryo
train station	*estación de tren*	es·ta·*syon* de tren

1st class	*primera clase*	pree·*me*·ra *kla*·se
2nd class	*segunda clase*	se·*goon*·da *kla*·se
child's	*infantil*	een·fan·*teel*
one-way	*de ida*	de *ee*·da
round-trip	*de ida y vuelta*	de *ee*·da ee *vwel*·ta
student's	*de estudiante*	de es·too·*dyan*·te

ROAD SIGNS

Acceso	Entrance
Aparcamiento	Parking
Ceda el Paso	Give Way
Despacio	Slow
Dirección Única	One Way
Mantenga Su Derecha	Keep to the Right
No Adelantar/No Rebase	No Passing
No Estacionar	No Parking
Pare	Stop
Peligro	Danger
Prohibido Aparcar	No Parking

Private Transportation

I'd like to hire a ...	*Quisiera alquilar ...*	kee·*sye*·ra al·kee·*lar* ...
4WD	*un todo terreno*	oon *to*·do te·*re*·no
bicycle	*una bicicleta*	*oo*·na bee·see·*kle*·ta
car	*un carro*	oon *ka*·ro
motorbike	*una moto*	*oo*·na *mo*·to

accident	*accidente*	ak·see·*den*·te
diesel	*diesel*	*dee*·sel
flat tire	*pinchazo*	peen·*cha*·so
gas	*gasolina*	ga·so·*lee*·na
gas station	*gasolinera*	ga·so·lee·*ne*·ra
hitchhike	*hacer dedo*	a·*ser* de·do
leaded/unleaded	*con/sin plomo*	kon/seen *plo*·mo
out of gas	*sin gasolina*	seen ga·so·*lee*·na
truck	*camión*	ka·*myon*

Is this the road to ...?
¿Se va a ... por esta carretera?   se va a ... por *es*·ta ka·re·*te*·ra

I'd like (20) liters.
Quiero (veinte) litros.   kye·ro (vayn·te) lee·tros
(How long) Can I park here?
¿(Por cuánto tiempo)   (por kwan·to tyem·po)
Puedo aparcar aquí?   pwe·do a·par·kar a·kee
The car has broken down.
El carro se ha averiado.   el ka·ro se a a·ve·rya·do

TRAVEL WITH CHILDREN

I need (a) ...	Necesito ...	ne·se·see·to ...
baby seat	un asiento	oon a·syen·to
	para bebé	pa·ra be·be
babysitter	una niñera	oo·na nee·nye·ra
(who speaks	(de habla	(de a·bla
English)	inglesa)	een·gle·sa)
child-minding	un servicio	oon ser·vee·syo
service	de cuidado	de kwee·da·do
	de niños	de nee·nyos
children's	un menú	oon me·noo
menu	infantil	een·fan·teel
(disposable)	pañales (de	pa·nya·les (de
diapers	usar y tirar)	oo·sar ee tee·rar)
milk formula	leche en polvo	le·che en pol·vo
potty	una bacinica	oo·na ba·see·nee·ka
stroller	un cochecito	oon ko·che·see·to

MODERN MAYA

Since the pre-Columbian period, the two ancient Maya languages, Yucatec and Cholan, have subdivided into about 30 separate Maya languages (such as Yucatec, Chol, Ch'orti', Tzeltal, Tzotzil, Lacandón, Mam, K'iche' and Kakchiquel). Indigenous languages are seldom written, but when they are, the Roman alphabet is used. Most Maya speakers will only be able to read and write Spanish, the language of government, schools, the church and the media – they may not be literate in Maya.

Pronunciation

Maya pronunciation is pretty straightforward. There are just a few pronunciation rules to keep in mind for the consonants:

c	always hard 'k' sound, as in 'cat'
j	similar to the 'h' in 'half'
u	as in 'prune', but at the beginning or end of a word, it's like English 'w'
x	as the 'sh' in 'shoes'

Maya consonants followed by an apostrophe (b', ch', k', p', t') should be pronounced more forcefully and 'explosively.' Vowels followed by an apostrophe indicate a glottal stop (similar to the sound between the two syllables in 'uh-oh'). Stress usually falls on the last syllable – this is often indicated by accent marks.

The following place names are useful guides to pronunciation:

Acanceh	a·kan·keh
Ahau	a·haw
Kaminaljuyú	ka·mee·nal·hoo·yoo
Pop	pope
Takalik Abaj	ta·ka·leek a·bah
Tikal	tee·kal
Uaxactún	wah·shahk·toon

K'ICHE'

K'iche' is widely spoken throughout the Guatemalan highlands, from around Santa Cruz del Quiché to the area adjacent to Lago de Atitlán and around Quetzaltenango. Around two million K'iche' Maya are estimated to be living in Guatemala.

Greetings & Civilities

These are great icebreakers, and even if you're not completely understood, there'll be goodwill and smiles all around just for making the effort.

Good morning.	Saqarik.
Good afternoon.	Xb'eqij.
Good evening/night.	Xokaq'ab'.
Goodbye.	Chab'ej.
See you soon.	Kimpetik ri.
Thank you.	Uts awech.
Excuse me.	Kyunala.
What's your name?	Su ra'b'i?
My name is ...	Nu b'i ...
Where are you from?	Ja kat pewi?
I'm from ...	Ch'qap ja'kin pewi ...

Useful Phrases

Where is a/the ...?	Ja k'uichi' ri ...?
bathroom	b'anb'al chulu
bus stop	tek'lib'al
doctor	ajkun
hotel	jun worib'al

Do you have (a) ...?	K'olik ...?
boiled water	saq'li
coffee	kab'e
copal	kach'
rooms	k'plib'al

bad	*itzel*
closed	*tzapilik*
cold	*joron*
good	*utz*
hard	*ko*
hot	*miq'in*
open	*teb'am*
sick	*yiwab'*
soft	*ch'uch'uj*
blanket	*k'ul*
vegetables	*ichaj*

north (white)	*saq*
south (yellow)	*k'an*
east (red)	*kaq*
west (black)	*k'eq*

Numbers

1	*jun*	6	*waq'ib'*
2	*keb'*	7	*wuqub'*
3	*oxib'*	8	*wajxakib'*
4	*kijeb'*	9	*b'elejeb'*
5	*job'*	10	*lajuj*

MAM

Mam is spoken in the department of Huehuetenango. This is the language you'll hear in Todos Santos Cuchumatán.

Greetings & Civilities

In Mam you only need two greetings, no matter what time of day it is.

Note that many words in Mam have been in disuse for so long that the Spanish equivalent is now used almost exclusively.

Good morning/	*Chin q'olb'el teya.* (sg inf)
afternoon/evening.	*Chin q'olb'el kyeeya.* (pl inf)
Goodbye.	*Chi nej.*
See you soon.	*Ak qli qib'.*
Thank you.	*Chonte teya.*
Excuse me.	*Naq samy.*
How are you?	*Tzen ta'ya?*

What's your name?	*Tit biya?*
My name is ...	*Luan bi ...*
Where are you from?	*Jaa'tzajnia?*
I'm from ...	*Ac tzajni ...*

Useful Phrases

Where is a/the ...?	*Ja at ...?*
bathroom	*bano*
doctor	*medico/doctor*
hotel	*hospedaje*

Where is the bus stop?	
Ja nue camioneta?	
How much is the fruit and vegetables?	
Je te ti lobj?	
Is there somewhere we can sleep?	
Ja tun kqta'n?	

Do you have ...?	*At ...?*
boiled water	*kqa'*
coffee	*café*
rooms	*cuartos*

| I'm cold. | *At xb'a'j/choj.* |
| I'm sick. | *At yab'.* |

bad	*k'ab'ex/nia g'lan*
closed	*jpu'n*
good	*banex/g'lan*
hard	*kuj*
hot	*kyaq*
open	*jqo'n*
soft	*xb'une*

north (white)	*okan*
south (yellow)	*eln*
east (red)	*jawl*
west (black)	*kub'el*

Numbers

The numbers from one to 10 are the same as in K'iche' (see above left). For numbers higher than 10, Mam speakers use the Spanish equivalents (see p342).

LANGUAGE

Glossary

alux, aluxes – Maya for gremlin, leprechaun, benevolent 'little people'
Ayuntamiento – often seen as H Ayuntamiento (Honorable Ayuntamiento) on the front of town hall buildings; translates as 'Municipal Government'

balneario – spa, health resort
barrio – district, neighborhood

cabañas – cabins
cacique – Maya chief; also used to describe provincial warlord or strongman
cafetería – literally 'coffee-shop,' but refers to any informal restaurant with waiter service; not usually a cafeteria in the North American sense of a self-service restaurant
cajero automático – automated teller machine (ATM)
callejón – alley or narrow or very short street
camión – truck or bus
camioneta – bus or pickup truck
casa de cambio – currency exchange office; offers exchange rates comparable to those of banks and is much faster to use (uncommon in Guatemala)
cenote – large, natural limestone cave used for water storage (or ceremonial purposes)
cerveza – beer
Chac – Maya god of rain
chapín – slang term for citizen of Guatemala
chicle – sap of the sapodilla tree; used to manufacture chewing gum
chicleros – men who collect *chicle*
Chinka' – small, non-Maya indigenous group living on the Pacific Slope
chuchkajau – Maya prayer leader
chuj – traditional Maya sauna; also known as *tuj*
chultún – artificial Maya cistern
cigarro – cigarette
cocina – kitchen; also used for a small, basic one-woman place to eat, often located in or near a municipal market, and in the phrases *cocina económica* (economical kitchen) or a *cocina familiar* (family kitchen)
cofradía – religious brotherhood, most often found in the highlands
colectivo – jitney taxi or minibus (usually a Kombi or minibus) that picks up and drops off passengers along its route
comal – hot griddle or surface used to cook tortillas
comedor – basic and cheap eatery, usually with a limited menu
completo – full; a sign you may see on hotel desks in crowded cities

conquistador – explorer-conqueror of Latin America from Spain
copal – tree resin used as incense in Maya ceremonies
correos – post office
corte – Maya wraparound skirt
costumbre – traditional Maya rite
criollos – people born in Guatemala of Spanish blood
cruce – crossroads, usually where you make bus connections; also known as *entronque*
cuadra – a city block
curandero – traditional indigenous healer

damas – ladies; the usual sign on toilet doors

faja – Maya waist sash or belt
ferrocarril – railroad
finca – plantation, farm

galón, galones – US gallons; fluid measure of 3.79L
glyph – symbolic character or figure; usually engraved or carved in relief
gringo/a – a mildly pejorative term applied to a male/female North American visitor; sometimes applied to any visitor of European heritage
gruta – cave

hacienda – estate; also 'treasury,' as in Departamento de Hacienda, Treasury Department
hay – pronounced like 'eye,' meaning 'there is' or 'there are'; you're equally likely to hear *no hay*, meaning 'there isn't' or 'there aren't'
hombre/s – man/men
huipil – Maya woman's woven tunic; often very colorful and elaborately embroidered

IVA – *impuesto al valor agregado* or value-added tax; on hotel rooms it is 12%

juego de pelota – ball game

kaperraj – Maya woman's all-purpose cloth; used as a head covering, baby sling, produce sack, shawl and more

ladino – person of mixed indigenous and European race; a more common term in Guatemala than *mestizo*
lancha – motorboat used to transport passengers; driven by a lanchero
larga distancia – long-distance telephone
lavandería – laundry; a *lavandería automática* is a coin-operated laundry

libra – pound; weight measurement of 0.45kg
lleno – full (fuel tank)

machismo – maleness, masculine virility
malecón – waterfront boulevard
manglar – mangrove
manzana – apple
mariachi – small group of street musicians featuring stringed instruments, trumpets and often an accordion, sometimes plays in restaurants
marimba – Guatemala's xylophone-like national instrument
mestizo – person of mixed indigenous and European blood; the word *ladino* is more common in Guatemala
metate – flattish stone on which corn is ground with a cylindrical stone roller
milla – mile; distance of 1.6km
milpa – maize field
mirador – lookout, vista point
mordida – 'bite'; small bribe paid to keep the wheels of bureaucracy turning
mudéjar – Moorish architectural style
mujer/es – woman/women
municipalidad – town hall, city hall

na – thatched Maya hut

onza – ounce; weight of 28g

pachete – a squash-type vegetable; can be eaten or used as a loofah
palacio de gobierno – building housing the executive offices of a state or regional government
palacio municipal – city hall; seat of the corporation or municipal government
palapa – thatched shelter with a palm-leaf roof and open sides
parada – bus stop; usually for city buses
picop – pickup truck
pie – foot; measure of 0.30m
posada – guesthouse
propino, propina – a tip, different from a *mordida*, which is really a bribe
punta – sexually suggestive dance enjoyed by the Garífuna of the Caribbean coast
puro – cigar

rebozo – long woolen or linen scarf covering the head or shoulders
refago – Maya wraparound skirt
retablo – ornate, often gilded altarpiece
retorno – 'return'; used on traffic signs to signify a U-turn or turnaround
roofcomb – a decorative stonework lattice atop a Maya pyramid or temple
rutelero – jitney

sacbé, sacbeob – ceremonial limestone avenue or path between great Maya cities
sacerdote – priest
Semana Santa – Holy Week preceding Easter
stela, stelae – standing stone monument(s); usually carved
supermercado – supermarket; anything from a corner store to a large, US-style supermarket

taller – shop or workshop
taller mecánico – mechanic's shop, usually for cars
teléfono comunitario – community telephone; found in the smallest towns
tepezcuintle – edible jungle rodent the size of a rabbit
tequila – clear, distilled liquor produced, like pulque and mescal, from the maguey cactus
tienda – small store that may sell anything from candles and chickens to aspirin and bread
típico – typical or characteristic of a region; particularly used to describe food
tocoyal – Maya head covering
traje – traditional clothing worn by the Maya
tuj – see *chuj*
túmulos – speed bumps found in many towns; sometimes indicated by a highway sign bearing a row of little bumps
tzut – Maya man's equivalent of a *kaperraj*

viajero – traveler

xate – low-growing fern native to the Petén region and exported for use in floral arrangements, particularly in the US
xateros – men who collect *xate*

zonas – zones
zotz – bat (the mammal) in many Maya languages

The Authors

LUCAS VIDGEN
Coordinating Author, Guatemala City, The Pacific Slope, Central & Eastern Guatemala

Lucas has been traveling and working in Latin America for 15 years. He currently lives in Quetzaltenango, Guatemala, where he sits on the board of directors of NGO Entre Mundos and publishes the city's leading culture and nightlife magazine, *XelaWho*. He obviously doesn't get out enough – even after living here for seven years, the beauty of this country and the quiet graciousness of its people still amaze him. Having contributed to various books for Lonely Planet, Lucas now mostly divides his time between Central and South America. He is a regular contributor to the LP guidebooks *Nicaragua*, *Argentina*, *South America on a Shoestring* and *Central America on a Shoestring*. His Spanish is OK, but he misses potato cakes and his mum.

DANIEL S SCHECTER
Antigua, The Highlands, El Petén

Daniel has been poking around Latin America for so long, it sometimes makes more sense to him than his native USA. Since his first foray to Bogotá in 1984 (toting *South America on a Shoestring*), he's lived and worked in Colombia, Puerto Rico and Mexico and covered six Latin American countries for Lonely Planet guides, which include *Central America on a Shoestring*, *Mexico City* and *Yucatán*. In Mexico, his home base for a decade, he worked as an editor at *The News*, Mexico City's English-language daily, and *Business Mexico*, the American Chamber magazine, and translated texts for numerous Mexican publications plus one major museum exhibit. Daniel had his first mesmerized glimpse of Guatemala in 2005, arriving in El Petén by overland journey from Mexico City.

LONELY PLANET AUTHORS

Why is our travel information the best in the world? It's simple: our authors are passionate, dedicated travelers. They don't take freebies in exchange for positive coverage so you can be sure the advice you're given is impartial. They travel widely to all the popular spots, and off the beaten track. They don't research using just the internet or phone. They discover new places not included in any other guidebook. They personally visit thousands of hotels, restaurants, palaces, trails, galleries, temples and more. They speak with dozens of locals every day to make sure you get the kind of insider knowledge only a local could tell you. They take pride in getting all the details right, and in telling it how it is. Think you can do it? Find out how at **lonelyplanet.com**.

Behind the Scenes

THIS BOOK

This 4th edition of Guatemala was written by Lucas Vidgen (coordinating author) and Daniel C Schechter. The 3rd edition was written by Lucas Vidgen, the 2nd by John Noble and Susan Forsyth and the 1st by Conner Gorry. This guidebook was commissioned in Lonely Planet's Oakland office, and produced by the following:

Commissioning Editor Catherine Craddock
Coordinating Editors Martine Power, Brana Vladisavljevic
Coordinating Cartographers Mark Griffiths, Valentina Kremenchutskaya
Coordinating Layout Designer Jacqui Saunders
Managing Editor Annelies Mertens
Managing Cartographers Alison Lyall, Herman So
Managing Layout Designers Indra Kilfoyle, Celia Wood
Assisting Editors Kate James, Simon Williamson
Assisting Cartographer Andras Bogdanovits
Cover Research Naomi Parker, lonelyplanetimages.com
Internal Image Research Sabrina Dalbesio, lonelyplanet images.com
Project Manager Rachel Imeson

Thanks to Lucy Birchley, Daniel Corbett, Melanie Dankel, Bruce Evans, Mark Germanchis, Michelle Glynn, Craig Kilburn, Yvonne Kirk, Lisa Knights, Rebecca Lalor, Katie Lynch, John, Mazzocchi, Dan Moore, Kirsten Rawlings, Averil Robertson, Fiona Siseman, John Taufa, Nick Thorpe, Juan Winata

THANKS
LUCAS VIDGEN

Firstly, I'd really like to thank all the Guatemalans for making such a great country to live, travel and work in. Sure, we've got our problems, but we're getting there, *poco a poco*. Out on the road, Virgilio Molina, Encarnación Morán, Daniel Vásquez and Daantje for standing still long enough to let me quote them. To the guy who ran into my car in Esquipulas and drove off without leaving a note: Thanks very much. To Geert in Copán, Glenn in Guatemala City and Dennis in Mariscos: Awesome work, guys. See you next time. My co-author Danny, for going way out there and finding some good stuff to report back on. And the home fire crew: James and Alma for taking care of business and of course to Sofía and América – the best traveling companions a guy could ask for.

DANIEL C SCHECHTER

First shout-outs go to Glenn A Germaine and José Fernández Ramos, my part-time travel companions. Inguat backed me every step of the way: in particular, I'd like to acknowledge Eduardo Orozco, Ángel Quiñonez, Jorge Mendoza, Eddy Cano, Francisco Cano and Ángel Gabriel Rodas. Mario Martínez accompanied me to the more remote corners of Huehue, while Julián Mariona,

---

THE LONELY PLANET STORY

Fresh from an epic journey across Europe, Asia and Australia in 1972, Tony and Maureen Wheeler sat at their kitchen table stapling together notes. The first Lonely Planet guidebook, *Across Asia on the Cheap*, was born.

Travelers snapped up the guides. Inspired by their success, the Wheelers began publishing books to Southeast Asia, India and beyond. Demand was prodigious, and the Wheelers expanded the business rapidly to keep up. Over the years, Lonely Planet extended its coverage to every country and into the virtual world via lonelyplanet.com and the Thorn Tree message board.

As Lonely Planet became a globally loved brand, Tony and Maureen received several offers for the company. But it wasn't until 2007 that they found a partner whom they trusted to remain true to the company's principles of traveling widely, treading lightly and giving sustainably. In October of that year, BBC Worldwide acquired a 75% share in the company, pledging to uphold Lonely Planet's commitment to independent travel, trustworthy advice and editorial independence.

Today, Lonely Planet has offices in Melbourne, London and Oakland, with over 500 staff members and 300 authors. Tony and Maureen are still actively involved with Lonely Planet. They're traveling more often than ever, and they're devoting their spare time to charitable projects. And the company is still driven by the philosophy of *Across Asia on the Cheap*: 'All you've got to do is decide to go and the hardest part is over. So go!'

Billy Cruz and Giovanny Tut Rodríguez steered my course in El Petén. Others who pitched in include Christian Behrenz and Stefanie Zecha, Dr Richard Hansen, Richard Morgan, Louise Rothwell, Ana Dresen, Allison Hawks, Elena Rodríguez and Estuardo Lira. My coauthor, Lucas, provided loads of leads before I hit the ground, and Myra Ingmanson once again offered her savvy editing skills. ¡Gracias a todos!

CONTRIBUTING AUTHOR

Dr David Goldberg MD wrote the Health chapter. David completed his training in internal medicine and infectious diseases at Columbia-Presbyterian Medical Center in New York City, where he has also served as voluntary faculty. At present he is an infectious-diseases specialist in Scarsdale, New York state, and the editor-in-chief of the website MDTravelHealth.com.

OUR READERS

Many thanks to the travelers who used the last edition and wrote to us with helpful hints, useful advice and interesting anecdotes:

Mariem Aameyri, Deb Adams, Sara Allen, José Amate, Ana Andrade, Eric Arons, Mieke Arts, Sue Attwood, Catherine Bach, Gabriele Baldwin, Morgan Barense, Wendy Barreno, Anaïs Begemann, Steffi Behrens, Liat Ben Rafael, Evan Bendelstein, Brent Benoit, Judy Bergen, Zoe Berman, Piet Bess, Amy Beugeling, Antoine Beurskens, Dewi Blom, Paul Boehlen, Alina Bohli, Vera Borsboom, Claire Bourgin, Anthony Brindisi, Kesse Buchanan, Lesley Buckeridge, Rachel Busch, Elena Busto, Ana Lucía Cáceres, Laura Camner, Harim Chaclàn, Emily Chandler, Susan Chavez, Jordana Chavin, Judi Cheng, Jacqueline Combs, Leslie Cruz, Susan Czigany, Anthea Dare, Julie Davies, Susan De Nies, Alva Devoy, Arndt Dobroschke, Jake Donaldson, Erin Dooley, Jonas Eelen, Irene Ernst, Dominik Eugster, Dawn Exley, Mike Ferriss, Kristen Fix, Klein Francis, Angela Funk, Guillaume Furminger, Gregorio Garcia Coj, Leah Gitter, Lisa E Goldman, Sara Golyar, Linda Goodman, Ella Gray, Paul Greenhouse, Kathryn Griffin, Laurie Guggenheim, Thilo Hackenberg, Charles Hafter, Annika Hansen, Becky Harris, Paul Helbert, Darryl Hicks, Eliza Hiscox, Robyn Hively, Louise Hof, Cristina Hofer, Wilson Hu, John Humble, Julie Hunter, Jadrino Huot, Michael Hurley, Douglas Hutchings, Iaminantigua, Michael Insel, Ian Isherwood, Sandra Jensen, Quetzal Johnson, Doug Johnston, Anne Karbe, Bernadette Kelly, Jan Krueger, Cara Kruse, Matthias Kümin, Joseph Lance, Deirdre Leask, Johane Leblanc, Eunjung Lee, John Leininger, Daisy Levine, Nancy Lin, Sarah Lloyd-Davies, Omer Malchi, Richard Malengreau, Libby Martin, Christian Martin, Monica Martinez, Julia Matonti, Ralph Mccuen, Greg Mccullough, Ruth Mcdonald, Patricia Mcdonough, Viveka Melki, Norma Meneguzzi, Trudy Mercadal, David Michiels, Virginia Miller, Pat Milne, Dennis Mogerman, Sara Monteiro, Dan Morrice, Marilyn Moss, Junko Nakai, Meira Neggaz, Lori Nevin, Dennis Nicoll, Keith Nymark, Matt O'Mansky, Catherine O'Rourke, Sally O'Sullivan, Carmen Ochoa, Julia Ossena, Aristea Parissi, Bob Parkinson, Nancy Payne, Jess Penetar, Sarah Pfoser, Markus Pletscher, David Pope, Alejandro Ravanales, Karen Rawlings, Ron and Joan Raymond, Laura Read, Javier Rebollar, Viktor Reddersen, Barbara Reisner, Elise Remling, Neil Sammonds, Kate Sanders-Fleming, Ellie Sauerzopf, Heather Schirduan, Anne Seidenberg, Dyanne Sheldon, Rog Si, Brittany Sickler, Silvan Sidler, Tara Sieling, Natalie Smart, Kelly Spencer, Jyoti Srivastava, Stephen Stiles, Stephanie Tang, Alice Thompson, Evelin Tortorici, Caitlin Trimble, Kay Unger, Jorge Urrutia, Aventuras Vacacionales, Marieke Van Der Beek, Koos Van Der Valk, Joris Van Driel, Kim Van Luijk, Alan Veys, Greta Von Bernuth, Bettina Voussen, Anna Warner, Carly Wilkinson, Paula Willars, Andrea Williams, Gerry Willms, Lisa Wilmsmeier, Henry Wilson, Ola Winkler, Steve Witney, Natasha Woollcombe, Kimberly Wright, Simon Wright, Dan Yack, Veronica Zamora, Tony Zheng, Rodolfo Zosel

ACKNOWLEDGMENTS

Many thanks to the following for the use of their content:

Globe on title page ©Mountain High Maps 1993 Digital Wisdom, Inc.

Index

INDEX

INDEX

000 Map pages
000 Photograph pages

INDEX

GREENDEX

It seems like everyone's going green and eco these days, but how can you know which businesses are really ecofriendly and which are simply jumping on the sustainable bandwagon?

The following listings have all been selected by this book's authors because they demonstrate an active sustainable-tourism policy. Some are involved in conservation or environmental education, and many are owned and operated by local and indigenous operators, thereby helping to support regional identity and culture.

We define sustainable tourism in three ways:

Environmental – minimizes negative environmental impacts and, where possible, makes positive contributions.

Socio-cultural – respects culture and traditions and fosters authentic interaction and greater understanding between travelers and hosts.

Economic – has financial benefits for the host community and operates on the principles of fair trade.

We want to keep developing our sustainable-tourism content. If you think we've omitted someone who should be listed here, or if you disagree with our choices, contact us at www.lonelyplanet .com/feedback. For more information about sustainable tourism and Lonely Planet, see www .lonelyplanet.com/responsibletravel.

INDEX

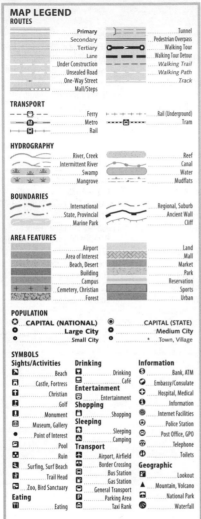

MAP LEGEND

ROUTES

Primary	Tunnel
Secondary	Pedestrian Overpass
Tertiary	Walking Tour
Lane	Walking Tour Detour
Under Construction	Walking Trail
Unsealed Road	Walking Path
One-Way Street	Track
Mall/Steps	

TRANSPORT

Ferry	Rail (Underground)
Metro	Tram
Rail	

HYDROGRAPHY

River, Creek	Reef
Intermittent River	Canal
Swamp	Water
Mangrove	Mudflats

BOUNDARIES

International	Regional, Suburb
State, Provincial	Ancient Wall
Marine Park	Cliff

AREA FEATURES

Airport	Land
Area of Interest	Mall
Beach, Desert	Market
Building	Park
Campus	Reservation
Cemetery, Christian	Sports
Forest	Urban

POPULATION

◎ CAPITAL (NATIONAL)	◉ CAPITAL (STATE)
● Large City	● Medium City
● Small City	• Town, Village

SYMBOLS

Sights/Activities
- Beach
- Castle, Fortress
- Christian
- Golf
- Monument
- Museum, Gallery
- Point of Interest
- Pool
- Ruin
- Surfing, Surf Beach
- Trail Head
- Zoo, Bird Sanctuary

Eating
- Eating

Drinking
- Drinking
- Café

Entertainment
- Entertainment

Shopping
- Shopping

Sleeping
- Sleeping
- Camping

Transport
- Airport, Airfield
- Border Crossing
- Bus Station
- Gas Station
- General Transport
- Parking Area
- Taxi Rank

Information
- Bank, ATM
- Embassy/Consulate
- Hospital, Medical
- Information
- Internet Facilities
- Police Station
- Post Office, GPO
- Telephone
- Toilets

Geographic
- Lookout
- Mountain, Volcano
- National Park
- Waterfall

LONELY PLANET OFFICES

Australia (Head Office)
Locked Bag 1, Footscray, Victoria 3011
☎ 03 8379 8000, fax 03 8379 8111
talk2us@lonelyplanet.com.au

USA
150 Linden St, Oakland, CA 94607
☎ 510 250 6400, toll free 800 275 8555
fax 510 893 8572
info@lonelyplanet.com

UK
2nd fl, 186 City Rd,
London EC1V 2NT
☎ 020 7106 2100, fax 020 7106 2101
go@lonelyplanet.co.uk

Published by Lonely Planet
ABN 36 005 607 983

© Lonely Planet 2010

© photographers as indicated 2010

Cover photograph: Church of San Andrés Xecul, near Totonicapán, Guatemala, Jeffrey Becom/Lonely Planet Images. Many of the images in this guide are available for licensing from Lonely Planet Images: lonelyplanetimages.com.

Printed by Toppan Security Printing Pte. Ltd.
Printed in Singapore

Mixed Sources
Product group from well-managed forests and other controlled sources
www.fsc.org Cert no. SGS-COC-005002
© 1996 Forest Stewardship Council